Encyclopedia of Modern Greek Literature

∽

Bruce Merry

Greenwood Press
Westport, Connecticut • London

Library of Congress Cataloging-in-Publication Data

Merry, Bruce.
   Encyclopedia of modern Greek literature / Bruce Merry.
     p. cm.
   Includes bibliographical references and index.
   ISBN 0–313–30813–6 (alk. paper)
   1. Greek literature, Modern—Encyclopedias.   I. Title.
   PA5210.M44 2004
   889′.09′0003—dc22   2003027500

British Library Cataloguing in Publication Data is available.

Library of Congress Catalog Card Number: 2003027500
ISBN: 0–313–30813–6

First published in 2004

Greenwood Press, 88 Post Road West, Westport, CT 06881
An imprint of Greenwood Publishing Group, Inc.
www.greenwood.com

Printed in the United States of America

The paper used in this book complies with the
Permanent Paper Standard issued by the National
Information Standards Organization (Z39.48–1984).

10 9 8 7 6 5 4 3 2 1

To my mother, Diana Constance Merry, *amore ineguagible*

Contents

Preface

The *Encyclopedia of Modern Greek Literature,* covering persons, topics, and themes in Greek literature from the Byzantine period to the present, provides readers with basic information on a magnificent literature written in a great language. The tradition of Hellenism, the world's richest national legacy, poses a great challenge to the bibliographer or the encyclopedist. Before the professionalization of writing and publishing in the 1980s, many Greeks published their books privately. Hundreds of reference works examine Greek culture, but many are lost, miscatalogued, or inaccessible to all but the most patient reader of Hellenistic and Byzantine Greek. Despite the significant contribution of many authors and a growing body of international scholarship, no one reference book in English provides a sympathetic, systematic coverage of modern Greek literature. This volume remedies that situation for a wide audience, including general readers, school pupils, university undergraduates, and professional academics.

The *Encyclopedia* includes 900 alphabetically arranged entries on topics related to modern Greek literature. Although some of the entries may be of interest mainly to specialists, most provide some information of value for anyone with a fondness for literature. Topics include significant themes, authors, movements, novels, battles, events, or poems. The entries provide the basic information required to answer questions of fact as well as to launch readers and students on more detailed study of larger themes. Although some of the simpler entries are brief (50–200 words), most entries are longer (1,000 words), covering more complex issues that require more examples or greater elaboration (e.g., Rangavís, Phanariot, Muses, Politicians).

The entries cover important individuals and titles in modern Greek literature, as well as any item related to modern Greek literature that the compiler found arresting or worth a reader's attention. In each entry, the term or person is described, followed by a discussion of the subject's relevance to the field of modern Greek literature. Some entries close with suggestions for further reading. For further information on a variety of topics related to modern Greek literature, readers may consult the general bibliography at the end of the *Enyclopedia.* A few titles or key terms are given in Greek as well as English. Where available, birth and death dates have been provided for biographical entries. In this context, the abbreviation "c." means "about" and the abbreviation "fl." stands for "flourished about this time." A bold phrase or word, for example, **Zei**, refers the reader to a separate article on that topic elsewhere in the text. Other related items are cross-referenced in "See also" lines at the ends of entries. A timeline of important dates and events in medieval and modern Greek history appears at the end of the volume, and a detailed subject index provides additional access to information in the book.

Breathings and Polytonic Accents In the present work, breathings and multiple accents are *retained* for quotations from any book that uses them or was published before the single accent became norma-

tive (1982). Before 1982, the progressive paper *Macedonia* (Μακεδονία) had simplified accentuation on certain pages. The editors also adopted a uniform mark for breathings over initial vowels, that is, for both the classical "smooth breathing" and "rough breathing."

Transliteration The transliteration into English of Greek names and words follows a principle outlined by L. Politis in *A History of Modern Greek Literature* (1975) and adhered to by Dia Philippides in her *Census of Modern Greek Literature* (1990). This practice uses an accent in the English version of a Greek name only when the stress falls on its last syllable.

Introduction

Modern Greek literature, in its generally accepted definition, includes work from **Athens, Crete, Cyprus,** Rhodes, the smaller Mediterranean islands, the Greek mainland (for example, Epirus, Peloponnese), **Istanbul,** Thrace, and **Asia Minor.** This territory was not always part of Greece over the last 1,000 years. In this book, the millennium is taken as the chronological starting date of "modern" Greek literature, and some readers may wonder why the epithet "modern" for a literature can be pushed so far back in time.

The reason why scholars date modern Greek writing from the ninth and tenth century A.D. is that a series of Byzantine vernacular texts and poems, speeches, and **epigrams** began to emerge within this time frame. These texts use a recognizable form of early **Demotic language.** Another group of scholars puts the watershed in the early eleventh century, when the first text in vernacular Greek, *Diyenís Akritas,* emerged, with its canvas of border warriors, battle against Saracens, castles, gardens, the abduction of women, and the duel with **Death.** These themes recur later in the Greek **demotic song** and in **Klephtic, Akritic,** and **brigand** writing. All these headings are considered in the *Encyclopedia.* They confirm the impression of a *paradosis,* a handed-down **tradition** that governs modern Greek from classical times until now. One school of **critical** thought holds that 1453, the end of Byzantine culture at the **fall of Constantinople,** began the new literature, which is at first a literature of resentment and oppression under Turkish rule.

Other scholars date modern Greek culture, because of the sheer quality of its literary product, from the so-called Cretan "Renaissance" of the seventeenth century. A 1999 Greek high school syllabus (Emmanouilidis, 1999) offers a uniform course that arranges Greek literature under the following six headings:

1. Ninth Century–1453
2. 1453–1669 (fall of Crete)
3. 1669–1821 (start of the Greek **War of Independence)**
4. 1821–1880 (emergence of the **New School of Athens)**
5. 1880–1930 (**Generation of 1930 and 1931,** publication of first poems by **Yorgos Seferis)**
6. 1930–the present

Other arguments are made for a general division of the whole of Greek literature into three historical periods: Antiquity, Byzantium, and Modern. This arrangement covers the concept of the "tradition," and also satisfies the **nationalist** aspirations of **Orthodox** Christianity (a vital ingredient in Greek writing) and of **neo-Hellenism.** One influential critic and literary historian, Ilias Voutieridis (1874–1941), divides Greek literature into "ancient" (ἀρχαία) and "modern" (νέα), placing the division before 1453. On the other hand, the critic M. Katsinis held (1975) that neo-Hellenic literature is found "in the space of the last 200 years" and that it offers "an abundance of worthwhile texts."

B. Knös argued that the notion of "medieval" was adopted by Greeks under the influence of the West. Thus, another possible date to determine the start of our modern literature is the Fourth **Crusade,** when Constantinople fell to Latin invaders in 1204. Nevertheless, Emmanuel Kriarás (b. 1906) extended the definition of medieval Greek literature to around 1700, calling 1200 to 1700 "the last medieval period," or "the pre-modern Greek period."

Many histories of modern Greek literature commence, like this book, at 1000 A.D. The *form, rhetoric,* and *content* of 1,000 years of Greek literature is therefore set out in the pages that follow. In 1821, Shelley called the contemporary Greek a "descendant of those glorious beings whom the imagination almost refuses to figure to itself as belonging to our kind." Robert Liddell expressed this devotion in its pristine form: "To some of us who most love the Aegean, it is like a type or foretaste of Paradise." And Dr. Johnson said: "Greek is like fine lace. A man gets as much of it as he can."

REFERENCES

Emmanouilidis, P., & E. Petridou-Emmanouilidou. Νεοελληνική Λογοτεχνία· Τα 14 Κείμενα της Εξεταστέας Υλης [*Modern Greek Literature: The Fourteen Set Books for School Examination*]. Athens: Metaichmio, 1999.

Knös, Börje. *L'Histoire de la Littérature Néogrecque: La période jusqu'en 1821.* Stockholm: Almqvist & Wiksell, 1962.

Kriarás, Emmanuel, ed. Βυζαντινὰ ἱπποτικὰ μυθιστορήματα [*The Byzantine Courtly Romances*]. The Basic Library, no. 2. Athens: Aetós, 1955.

Voutieridis, Ilias P. Σύντομη ἱστορία τῆς νεοελληνικῆς λογοτεχνίας (1000–1930). Τρίτη ἔκδοση. Μὲ συμπλήρωμα τοῦ Δημήτρη Γιάκου (1931–1976) [*A Short History of Modern Greek Literature from 1000 to 1930: 3rd ed., with a Supplement Covering 1931 to 1976 by Dimitris Yiakos*]. Athens: D. N. Papadimas, 1976.

Abbreviations Used in the Entries

BMGS Byzantine and Modern Greek Studies

FD Speake, G., ed. *Encyclopedia of Greece and the Hellenic Tradition.* 2 vols. London: Fitzroy Dearborn, 2000

GMT Constantinidis, S., ed. *Greece in Modern Times: An Annotated Bibliography of Works Published in English in Twenty-Two Academic Disciplines During the Twentieth Century.* Vol. 1. Lanham, MD: Scarecrow, 2000

JHD *Journal of the Hellenic Diaspora*

JHS *Journal of Hellenic Studies*

JMGS *Journal of Modern Greek Studies*

JMH *Journal of Modern Hellenism*

MEE Drandakis, P., ed. *Great Encyclopedia of Greece* [Μεγάλη Ἑλληνικὴ Ἐγκυκλοπαίδεια]. 24 vols., 1926–1934 and Supplement, 4 vols., 1957

MENL Zoras, Y. Th. and I. M. Chatzifotis, eds. *Great Encyclopedia of Modern Greek Literature* [Μεγάλη Ἐγκυκλοπαίδεια τῆς Νεοελληνικῆς Λογοτεχνίας]. 12 vols., 1969–1971

MLA Modern Language Association International Bibliography of Books and Articles on the Modern Languages and Literatures

TLS *Times Literary Supplement*

WLT *World Literature Today*

Chronology

323 B.C.	Death of Alexander the Great
306–337 A.D.	Reign of Roman Emperor Constantine, who officially recognizes Christianity
325	First Christian council at Nicaea
381	Edicts issued against the Christian heresies of Manicheism and Arianism
381	Second Ecumenical Council; ecclesiastics included in civil offices
380	Roman Emperor Theodosius retains imperial capital at Constantinople
394	Emperor Theodosius bans the Olympic Games
395	Emperor Theodosius dies, leaving Christianity the dominant force in the Roman world; division of the old Roman empire; Eastern Empire assigned to Arcadius, Western Empire assigned to Honorius
476	Rome falls to German tribal leader Odoacer; Western Empire ends; increasingly Greek Eastern (or Byzantine) Empire survives
527–565	Reign, legislation, scholarship, and military advances of Byzantine Emperor Justinian
571–632	Life of Muhammed, the Prophet and founder of Islam
622	The Hegyra, Prophet Muhammed's withdrawal from Mecca and tactical march on the Arab city of Medina
610–641	Victories of Emperor Herakleios in Persia, and north of Byzantium (Constantinople)
644–656	The *Koran,* the holy book of Islam, issued under 3rd Caliphate (Caliph Osman)
810–843	"Dark ages" of Byzantium: Antioch in Asia Minor and Alexandria in Egypt are cut adrift as forces of Islam advance from Arabia
843	First settlement of the Iconoclast controversy
863	Victory of Poson opens the Balkans to Byzantine control
867–886	Reign in Byzantium of Basil I of Macedon, known as "The Bulgar-Slayer"
867–1025	Rule of Macedonian dynasty in Byzantium; Akritic Songs written
c. 800–c. 1280	Rise of a Byzantine vernacular tradition
c. early eleventh century	*Diyenís Akritas* saga composed
1071	Byzantine defeat at battle of Manzikert allows Seljuk Turks to gain control of Asia Minor and southern Italy

1081–1180	Rule of Comnenus dynasty in Byzantium; *Spaneas* and *Prodromos* poems composed
1096–1099	First Crusade
1159	poet Glykás is active
1204	After Fourth Crusade; Byzantium dismembered into a "Latin" Empire of Greece ruled from Constantinople and comprising the "Latin" states of Salonika, Achaea, Athens, Archipelagus, Cefalonia, and Rhodes; and the "Greek" states of Trebisond, Nicaea, and Epirus
1261	Michael Palaeologus, emperor of Nicaea, recaptures Constantinople
c. 1300	*Chronicle of Morea* composed
1354	Turks capture Gallipoli
1362	Turks capture Adrianopolis
1300–1400	Romances of chivalry composed; *Assizes of Cyprus* written
1430	Turks capture Thessaloniki and Ioannina
1439	Council of Florence; union of Orthodox and Catholic churches fostered by Emperor John VIII is vetoed by Orthodox Patriarchate
1452	Death of philosopher Y. Plethon
1453	Black Tuesday: the Fall of Constantinople to the Turks and the eclipse of Byzantium
1472	Death of Cardinal Ioannis Bessarion in Italy
1489	Venice takes control of Cyprus from the Lusignan dynasty
1490–early sixteenth century	*Chronicles* of Choumnos (Crete) and Georgillás (Rhodes) composed
1513–1521	Greek high school at Rome
1519	Poem *Apokopos* composed
1522	Turks capture Rhodes
1540	Nafplion and Monemvasia taken from Venice by Turks
1566	Turks garrison Chios
1570	Turks besiege and occupy Cyprus
1571	*Siege of Malta* written by Achelis of Rethymno
1577	Greek college at Rome: St. Athanasius
1585–1600	Cretan theater flourishes under Venetian administration with works of playwright Y. Chortatsis
1593	Greek community in Venice is allowed to open a school
1595–1601	Michael of Moldavia rebels against Turkish control
1627	First edition of the *Voskopoula* ("Pretty Shepherdess") is published
1635	*The Sacrifice of Abraham* by V. Kornaros is published
1645–1669	Turks invade and capture Crete
1716	Turks besiege Kerkyra (Heptanese)
1768–1774	Russia at war with Turkey
1769–1770	Count Orloff, favorite of the Russian Empress Catherine the Great, foments pro-Russian uprisings in the Peloponnese in Greece
1783	Greek shipping protected under a Russian flag
1790–1791	Rigas Velestinlís publishes *School for Delicate Lovers* in Vienna
1797	Napoleonic troops occupy Heptanese
1799	Heptanese occupied by Turkey and Russia
1809	British mandated to govern isle of Zakynthos

1814	Secret anti-Turkish conspiracy launched at Odessa by the "Friendly Society"
1821–1827	Greek War of Independence; Greeks fight to expel Turks
1823	D. Solomós publishes *Hymn to Freedom*
1824	George Gordon, Lord Byron, the English poet who joined the Greek fight for independence, dies at Missolonghi
1827	Allied fleet destroys Turkish ships at Navarino; Count Kapodistrias elected president of Greece
1830	European powers declare Greece independent
1831–1862	Reign and abdication of King Otho I of Greece
1863–1913	Reign of King George I of the Hellenes, who is murdered in 1913
1866; 1897	Anti-Turkish revolutions on Crete
1897	Greece mourns its defeat in war with Turkey over the Balkan question
1901	Riots erupt over A. Pallis's demotic translation of the *Gospel*
1903	Further public riots over a demotic translation of Aeschylus for the Royal Theater
1908	Eleftherios Venizelos seizes control of Crete in a nationalist coup
1909	Failed military coup at Goudí (Athens)
1912–1913	Greece takes part in the Balkan Wars
1913	Greece gains territory by Treaty of Bucharest: Crete, Aegean islands, Macedonia, Epirus
1916	E. Venizelos, defying King Constantine, sets up Nationalist government at Thessaloniki
1919	King Constantine abdicates and is succeeded by King Alexander
1920	Greece gains western Thrace by treaty
1922	Greek army routed in "Asia Minor Disaster"
1923	Greek population in Anatolia and eastern Thrace exchanged for Turks in Greece
1931	Publication of first poems of Yorgos Seferis
1930–c. 1945	"Generation of 1930" writers: Y. Theotokás; I. Venezis; K. Politis; S. Myrivilis; F. Politis; A. Terzakis
1936–1941	Dictatorship of General Ioannis Metaxás (1871–1941), anti-Communist, and head of "Free Thinkers"
1941, April 6	Adolf Hitler intervenes in Greece to reinforce armies of his ally, Italian dictator Benito Mussolini
1941, April 27	German flag raised on the Acropolis in Athens
1943 March	Deportation of Jews from Greece commences
1944	Liberation of Greece from German occupation
1944, December	Attempt by KKE (Greek Communist Party) and ELAS (Greek Partisan Resistance Army) to set up a transitional Soviet party in Greece is put down by Greek royalist forces and allied British troops
1946	Greek plebiscite restores the monarchy
1946–1949	Greek civil war between Communists and Royalists is waged in rural and mountain areas of Greece
1948–1950	Novels of Nikos Kazantzakis win international reputation

1960	British declare Cyprus an independent republic within the Commonwealth
1963	Yorgos Seferis wins Nobel Prize for Literature
1967–1974	Rule of military junta of the Greek Colonels
1974, July	Turkish troops land on north coast of Cyprus and take 37 percent of the island's territory
1979	Odysseas Elytis wins Nobel Prize for Literature
1981	Greece, under Prime Minister Constantine Karamanlis, enters European Economic Community; $800 million from EEC funds assigned to Greek rural areas
1985, December	Greek Socialist Prime Minister, Andreas Papandreou, supports amendment to Rome Treaty and gains benefits from EEC for Greece
1991, November	Greece objects to name and flag of self-declared independent republic of Macedonia
1994	Greece imposes an economic blockade on FYROM (Former Yugoslav Republic of Macedonia)
1995–1996	Under ailing Prime Minister Papandreou, relations with Albania and FYROM improve
1996, January	Constantine Simitis, also of Panhellenic Socialist Movement (PASOK), replaces Papandreou as Prime Minister
1996, September	Simitis wins parliamentary selections

List of Entries

A

ACCENT REFORM The official adoption of a single accent, the "monotone" reform, came in 1982. Up to that date, many texts followed the practice of using acute, grave, or circumflex accents, whereas a few used the iota subscript and other diacritics. After 1982, a single accent was to be used over a vowel or, if the vowel was in uppercase, beside it. No accent was to be used on a word of one syllable, such as ποιος ("which?"). This reform led to a uniform, vertical mark in handwriting. The accent shows which syllable is to be uttered, or read, with a slight stress. Greek words in capital letters, designed for headlines, ads, or comics, are not printed with accents. The same newspaper may use different accent systems (atonic, monotonic, or polytonic) to go with different typefaces.

ACHELIS OF RETHYMNO. See SIEGE OF MALTA

ACHILLEID; or STORY OF ACHILLES The *Story of Achilles,* or *Achilleid,* is a fifteenth-century narrative by an unknown author. Relating the story of Achilles, the central character of the *Iliad,* the narrative is preserved in three different manuscripts (Naples, London, and Oxford) and is also known as the *Achilleid.*

The Naples version, running to 1,820 unrhyming **political verse** lines, offers a complete remake of the Trojan War hero. As a boy, Achilles is a pugnacious champion and a reader of Greek legends. As a grown warrior, he fights with 12 companions against his father's enemy, the king of a rival territory, and falls for the princess Polyxena. With a touch from medieval romance, Achilles sends her written messages (πιττάκια). She is wounded by Eros, who appears in the form of a little bird. After six years of matrimonial bliss, during which Achilles also hunts lion and wild boar, like the Byzantine champion Diyenís Akritas, the hero's wife dies.

In one version of the *Achilleid,* the hero dies of grief at the loss of such a beauty ("She was a statue of the moon, an icon of Aphrodite"). In another version, Achilles goes to the Trojan War, where Paris offers him one of his sisters in marriage. Achilles accepts, but just before the wedding, Paris kills him. The *Story of Achilles* shares other elements with *Diyenís Akritas*; in both, the hero abducts a woman and is chased by her brothers.

Further Reading

Clota, José Alsaina and C. M. Solá. *La literatura griega medieval y moderna.* Barcelona: Credsa, 1969.

Hesseling, D. D., ed. *L'Achilléide byzantine. Publiée avec une introduction, des observations et un index.* Amsterdam: Verhandelingen der Koninklijke Akademie van Wettenschappen te Amsterdam, 1919.

Lavagnini, Renata. "Note sull'*Achilleide*." *Rivista di Studi Bizantini e Neoellenici* 6–7 (1969–1970): 165–179.

ACROSTIC Poets display virtuoso skill in the Greek acrostic. The key lies in a word spelled out by the first letters of each line, or **strophe.** In "Hope" (Ἐλπίς), by **Yeoryios Paraschos** (1821–1886), the writer calls on a soulmate to "come to him" (ἔλα), says that youth is a "daybreak" (λυκαυγές), that he is a "wanderer" (πλάνης), that she was the "Rainbow" (Ἴρις), but that her vision stays "rarely" (σπάνια). The initial letters of these words make up *Elpis,* the poem's title. Paraschos underlined his effects by the subtitle "Acrostic" and by asking for *Elpis* to be carved on his tomb.
See also HYMN

ADAMANTIOU,   ADAMANTIOS (1875–1937) At the early age of 25, the writer Adamantiou was awarded a state scholarship to further his studies in France. He specialized in **Byzantinology.** Returning to Athens, he became a curator at the National Library. In 1908, he was made inspector of Byzantine and Christian antiquities. From 1912 till his death, he held the chair of Byzantine Art and Civilization at the university. As a student, he published articles on classical Greek **dance** and the battle of Salamis. As a headmaster, he published a **grammar** and *Folktales of Tinos* (1897). Fascinated by all he saw as a wandering scholar, Adamantiou published *The Chronicles of Morea* (1901), which won a French Academy prize, *The Experience of Chastity* (Munich Academy prize), *Byzantine Thessaloniki* (1914, 2 vols.), *Constantine the Great* (1933), *Julian the Apostate* (1933), and essays on **romance,** including *Imperios and Margarona.*

ADDRESS An address (προσφώνημα) was a speech commissioned for delivery before an invited audience. Myriad such addresses were produced during the **Enlightenment** and later, at academic commencements, funerals, marriages, library openings, inaugurals, and prize givings. **Yeoryios Tertsetis** (1800–1874) regularly commemorated the 25th of March with a speech on the anniversary of the declaration of the **War of Independence.** The poet **Ioulios Typaldos** (1814–1883) composed an *Oration on Dionysios Solomós,* published at Zakynthos, 1857.

ADJECTIVE The adjective is important among the 10 Greek parts of speech because its use or abuse by writers has a major effect on the literary product. The adjective changes its endings (by declension) and thus matches the noun that it describes in gender, number, and case. In Greek, it has three, two, or one sets of endings, though in **Demotic** language all adjectives have three. In classical Greek and the learned language, certain adjectives have one ending for masculine and feminine, a second for the neuter. **Ka-**

vafis once said: "Art should provide the whole image by the sole use of nouns, and if an adjective is needed, it should only be the one that fits." An apparently ornamental adjective can have a valid function, as in a line from **Kostas Varnalis,** "O *crocused* gauze of dawn." The ornamental adjective has equal validity in a **demotic song** about **Death**: "I am the son of the *black* earth and of the *cobwebbed* stone." Here the two nouns do not just have two arbitrary adjectives, but there is a pathetic fallacy that merges Death with darkness and the tomb with spiders' webs, because *few visit the dead.*

See also COMPOUND ADJECTIVE; DIMINUTIVE; STYLE

ADMONITION The admonitory pamphlet (προτρεπτικόν) employs **rhetoric** and suppliant language to persuade the audience of a desirable end (liberation of Greece, victory in battle, or devotion to study). It may incite a king, pope, minister, soldier, or student to virtuous action. Perhaps a grandson of **Plethon** is John Gemistus (secretary to the administration of Ancona in the early sixteenth century), who addresses an exhortation in Latin to the Pope, urging him to convoke a crusade on Greece, "To our Holiest Lord Leo Tenth, Supreme Pontiff, an Admonition and an Augury" (Ancona, 1516). **Neophytos Vamvas** (1770–1886), as deputy head of Greece's first university, used the opportunity of his inaugural "On True Fame" (Athens, 1837) to urge the King to the common endeavor of making Greece. The legendary preaching of the martyred monk **Kosmás the Aetolian** (1714–1779) is admonition in the form of sermon: he castigates Greek traders for their indifference, demands community solidarity, deplores conversion to Islam of Turkey's Greek subjects, regrets the loss of the Greek language, and stirs up dormant patriotism. He uses collegial, inclusive formulae, such as "What are we to do?" or "What am I to do, brothers?" His listeners must understand that letters are a lighting from God, and that school is a church.

ADYNATON (Lat. IMPOSSIBILE) The trope of *adynaton* represents an unsatisfiable condition. The word comes from the classical adjective in the neuter, "impossible thing." It states that certain terms can never be met for the breaking of an oath, or the end of love. It can also be a confession that words fail the writer. The medieval poet **Stefanos Sachlikis,** in his *Verses and Interpretations,* complains that none of his advice to his friend's son was accepted: "You derived nothing at all from my words, / So apparently I sow words in the sand. / I see birds fly and pluck them from the air. / [. . .] I tell a wolf not to bite sheep, / Or twist a tree with a spell, / Or climb the attic without a ladder; / *Since I don't think I can accomplish these things, / I don't see how I'll ever train you.*"

An anonymous sixteenth-century **Cretan** composition, *Ballad of a Young Girl and a Young Man* (usually called *Enticement of the Maiden*) survives in two versions. The longer one consists of 191 rhymed **political verse** lines, which relate how the youth asked for a kiss and the girl requested a ring, as a guarantee that he would marry her. Though he promises to get the ring, the young man utters an impossible series, in asides: "When the sun changes its route through the skies, / When you see broom transformed to myrtle, / When apple trees become mastic of the valley, / When you see the ocean dry out, / Then, mistress mine, we'll marry." This figure spread to all literature, if an Australian musterers' song says, "Till the sands of the desert grow cold / And its infinite numbers are told."

AESCHYLUS. See MYTH

AESOP, LIFE OF A popular Byzantine text, the *Life of Aesop* purports to describe the supposed classical moralist and author of *Aesop's Fables,* which drew on ancient compilations that featured talking animals to exemplify human virtue and folly. Aesop (?620–560 B.C.), according to legend, was a deaf, stuttering freed slave, a wanderer who visited King Croesus, was sent to consult the oracle (Delphi), and was hanged for sacrilege. He did not compose the tales, which were written down by Dimitrios Phalereus (c. 300 B.C.). *Life of Aesop,* prefaced by a compilation from Aesop's fables, is ascribed to **Planoudis,** who makes it an educational text for unsophisticated readers. Its prototype is a tale that accreted round the myth of Solomon, based on a Hebrew story in the second- or third-century romance *Tobit* (from the *Apokrypha*), concerning the wise man Akir, Anadam (his nephew), and the sultan Sinagrip.

In 1542, Andronikos Noukios, a learned traveler and calligrapher from Kerkyra (friend of N. Sofianós, the translator of Plutarch) rendered the *Fables* in **plain Greek** prose: "A donkey put on the skin of a lion, and scared all the people and the animals fled, for they thought the donkey was a lion. And when the wind blew and pulled his skin aside and the donkey was uncovered, then they caught him and beat him with clubs and sticks." There is only one copy of the Byzantine manuscript, in the Bavarian Library (Mu-

nich). It was described by Legrand in *Bibliographie hellénique,* Vol. 1, Paris, 1885: p. 241. The Noukios translation marks the beginning of Aesop's diffusion in printed vernacular texts. Next comes a version by **George the Aetolian,** published as "Recueil de fables ésopiques mises en verse par Georges l'Etolien," in Legrand's *Bibliothèque grecque vulgaire,* no. 8, Paris, 1896. There are several editions from the seventeenth century, but they abounded in the eighteenth, when the study of folk narrative became fashionable.

AGAPIOS. See LANDOS, AGAPIOS

AGATHANGELOS, HIERONYMOS. See VISION OF AGATHANGELOS

AGATHOPOULOU-KENTROU, MARIA. See KENTROU-AGATHOPOULOU, MARIA

AGRAS, TELLOS (1899–1944; pseudonym of Evangelos Y. Ioannou) The influential poet and critic Tellos Agras was born in Thessaly and died at Athens, killed by a random bullet toward the close of World War II. Adamantios Papadimas recalls that Agras suffered all his life from insomnia, sometimes going three or four nights before managing to sleep. He studied law and later worked as a civil servant and at the National Library. After **Xenopoulos,** Tellos Agras was one of the first intellectuals to discuss **Kavafis** (in a lecture of 1921). In "Aesthetic Shots," an early contribution to the journal *Altar,* he imitated the aphorisms devised by Oscar Wilde as a preface to *The Picture of Dorian Gray.* He produced essays on **Palamás, Gryparis, Karyotakis,** and an analysis of Paul Valéry's poem, "La fileuse," submitting Valéry's vocabulary to a close reading, in advance of his time. He belongs to the group of so-called twilight poets active in the period 1915 to 1925: **Romos Filyras** (1888–1942; pseudonym of Ioannis Oikonomopoulos), **Kostas Ouranis,** and **Napoleon Lapathiotis** (1888–1944). Their work is characterized by skilled versification, a melancholy affectation of French symbolism, and a leavening of sarcasm from Karyotakis.

Tellos Agras published an important anthology, *The Younger Poets* (1922), in the period 1910–1920. He published his own youthful poems under the neoclassical title *Bucolics and Eulogies* (1934), including translations from Theocritus and Catullus, with versions of Jules Laforgue (1860–1887) and the Greek-born French writer Jean Moréas (1865–1910; pseudonym of **I. Papadiamantopoulos**). A second collection of poems, *Everyday,* gained him the Ministry of Education prize (1940). It has bland, washed-out, pessimistic sketches of downtown Athens life. M. Lugizos called him "poet of the silent world." His third volume, *Roses from a Single Day* (1965), is more modern in tone, but appeared posthumously. He contributed most of the articles on modern Greek literature in *Great Encyclopedia of Greece* (1926–1934) and says there (vol. 13: 295) that Karyotakis's work is characterized by "a manifest idiosyncratic pathology." A special issue of the literary journal *Néa Estía* (no. 657: 1954) is devoted to Agras.

AKRITAS, LOUKÍS (1909–1965) The

themes of Loukís Akritas, a versatile novelist, war correspondent, critic, playwright, and short story writer from Cyprus, derive from the classic repertoire of this period, a happy childhood followed by social conflict, and then war. His novel

Men-at-Arms (1947) is considered by some critics the best Greek book inspired by the war on the Albanian front (1940–1941). His first novel, *Young Man with Excellent References* (1935), dealt with the bored, shiftless youth of the interwar period in Greece, a story of deprivation that the critic I. M. Panayiotopoulos compared to the Norwegian writer Knut Hamsun's *Hunger* (1888). Next came *The Plain* (1936), the play *A Person in Love Must Suffer* (1947), and other works for the stage, such as *Hostages* and *Theodora*. He was assistant minister for education (1964) in the Papandreou government.

AKRITIC SONGS; AKRITIC CYCLE

Research and editing by **Nikolaos Politis** finally saw the poems of the Akritic cycle as folk songs telling a story of legendary prowess. They are derived from material dealing with the exploits and culture of frontier guards (in Latin: *limitanei milites*) along the Eastern edge of the Byzantine empire from the eighth to eleventh centuries. They had a hierarchy of ranks like "single-mounted," "double-mounted," or "great-horsemen." The noun *Akritai* derives from the word *edge* in Byzantine Greek (ἄκρα). We first meet the term in a passage from Konstantinos Porphyrogennetos (905–959) mentioning the need for an emperor to have a military escort when visiting areas near the border because he is venturing "into the wilds," and these patrols require an officer and 500 armed troops.

In the Akritic songs, the warriors appear as paragons of elegance and nobility (λεβεντιά). Their houses are described as aristocratic, with tapestries, wall paintings, and extended gardens. Their doors are open to guests, and their hospitality is unfailing. Their education is religion.

Bards sing stories at their feasts, as in **Homer.** The fine locations in the Akritic cycle have generic names like Amori, Cappadocia, Babylon, and Araby. Some of the Akritic heroes' names carry an aura of the throne: Alexis, Doukas, Phocas, and Nikiforos. The soldiers differ from imperial cavalry dispatched to other *themes* (provincial administrative areas) because they themselves belong to just one *theme,* lying on the border. Their romantic haunts are "mountain passes," and these fighters are known as Andronikos, Armouris, Phocas, Bardas, Petrotrachilos, Xanthinos, Porphyris, and the evergreen Diyenís. The narration abandons all veracity in favor of poetic license, especially concerning the odds that the Akritai face in combat: "My enemy were not five or eighteen in number, / They were seven thousand, and I opposed them alone." Songs about the great Vlachopoulos are closely related to those depicting the sons of Andronikos. They push the military exploits of the Akritai to exaggerated proportions.

The hero Konstantinos, in one poem, is Andronikos's son. Young Vlachopoulos is his child prisoner; and the character Alexis may correspond to the Alexander of other Akritic songs. The hero gets drunk on all the blood spilled in battle and screams to his companions to take care lest, in his fury, he fail to distinguish friend from foe: "He led Vlachopoulos to the sentry-post, to guard. / He glanced at Turkey, the massed Saracens and negro pirates. / The meadows were green, the slopes ran red: / He began to count them, but there was no measuring them. / He was ashamed to retreat and afraid to advance. / He stopped, kissed his black attendant, stood firm and spoke." N.G. Politis calculated that there were around 1,350 different Akritic songs. The figure is now put closer to 2,000. In 1909, Politis collected 70 different redactions dealing with the death of Diyenís. The saga draws on four bodies of Greek myth: Herakles, the Argonauts, Thebes, and Troy. Herakles was, from the cradle, depicted as a serpent-slayer. **Diyenís Akritas** is a beast slayer, in the manner of Herakles: "Seizing hold of the deer by its hind legs, / With a quick thrust he tore it in two." A deathbed song about Diyenís employs the **trope** of hypotyposis (vivid narration) and hyperbole: "I chased, pursued and wounded an enchanted deer; / My prey had a cross on his horns; on his forehead a star; / Between his antlers a bear; between their forks, the Virgin. / These misdeeds are too great, so now I wait on death." Typical here is the fusion of Christianity and **folklore,** between Mother of God (Θεοτόκος) and the huntress Artemis.

Many Akritic songs feature the battle between **death** and Diyenís. Politis interpreted this conflict as a symbol of the struggle between the Greek people and their Muslim masters during the **Turkocracy**: "They held their ground and did not move. / Our books tell a truthful tale. / After three whole days, Charon was hit. / 'Hold me gently, and I will hold you so, Diyenís. / Give me a few minutes to take my breath.'" Diyenís was born on a Tuesday, and on a Tuesday he must die. He summons his champions and rehearses his past exploits. He rises from his deathbed because he intends to die as gloriously as he lived: "He calls his warriors and friends. / He tells Minias and Maurailis to come, and Drakos's son, / And Tremantacheilos, terror of the world and humanity." Mountains murmur and fields tremble, for he once leapt over them or tossed them like quoits. He reminds his champions how he has traversed the passes of Arabia and the glens of Syria, which others cross in groups of 150, but he went alone, on foot, with his sword four spans long, and a pike measuring three fathoms. He beat mountains, meadows, and cataracts on starless, moonless nights and feared no enemy stalwart. Now he has seen a shoeless man, in shining robes, challenging him to wrestle on the marble threshing-floor. Whoever wins will take the soul of the other: "So they went and wrestled on the marble threshing-floors: / And wherever Diyenís strikes, he makes a furrow of blood, / And wherever Charon strikes, he draws a trench of gore."

Other Akritic motifs are the speaking bird, or the exploits of specially endowed people, as in the abduction of Diyenís's bride: "When Akritas was ploughing by the river, / He went back and forth, covering five furrows in an hour. / He went back and forth, sowing nine measures of wheat. / A bird perched on the edge of his yoke. [. . .] / 'Akritas, why do you sit without action, and wait? / Your family is in trouble, and they have kidnapped your beauty, / They have saddled your choicest steed, / While the lesser horses stand and neigh.'" In **demotic songs** from the Akritic cycle, Diyenís's mother (Eirini) wears a man's armor to fight the Saracens. Her true sex is revealed in battle, and she flees to the Church of St. George. The saint hands her over to her infidel pursuer, who promises to be baptized and to baptize the child of their union.

The antecedents of these ballads are not considered sources for the long poem *Diyenís Akritas.* R. B. (in Thorlby 1969: 191) considers the Akritic songs "probably quite unlike the lays from which it [the Διγενής Ἀκρίτας] may have been composed 1,000 years ago." Fine examples of Akritic song are those with resonant Anatolian elements, *The Son of Armouris, The Son of Andronikos, Porphyris, Castle of the Beautiful Maiden, The Dead Brother* (see **Folklore**), and *The Bridge of Arta* (see **Paralogés**). The miniature **epic** *Son of Armouris* (200 **decapentasyllables**, such as nonrhyming lines of 15 syllables, preserved in a fifteenth-century manuscript) presents an Akritic story from the last years of the Byzantine era, the capture and imprisonment of Armouris. Armouris's son organizes a military expedition to rescue him. The Emir orders Armouris guarded to obstruct the boy's mission. After a conflict between father and son, Armouris is reconciled with the Saracens.

The Bridge of Arta, with its hard, simple narrative, fascinated **Kazantzakis** and other Greek intellectuals. It is the story of a bridge that cannot be completed by its master builder until a speaking bird summons his beautiful wife, at the wrong hour of the working day. She is lowered into an incomplete buttress to retrieve some trivial object and then bricked in by the masons. The song is based on the primitive notion that a building requires the sacrifice of one soul to protect it. Folk songs about Anatolian causeways at Spercheios, at Saros (in Cilicia), and the Maiden's Bridge on Chios manifest this sepulchral motif.

Further Reading

Christides, V. "Arabic Influence on the Akritic Cycle." *Byzantion* 49 (1979): 94–109.

Notopoulos, James A. *Modern Greek Heroic Oral Poetry.* New York: Folkways, 1959.

AKROPOLITIS, YEORYIOS (1217–1282)

In 1233, the great historian Akropolitis went from Constantinople to the Imperial court at Nicaea and was trained in rhetoric and philosophy. In 1244, he took the rank of Chancellor Logothete. The new emperor of 1254, Theodoros Laskaris, who also studied with Blemmydis, became Akropolitis's pupil. In 1257, Laskaris made him chief of staff in a campaign against Mikhail, despot of Epirus. Akropolitis, an inferior general, was taken prisoner. He was freed by Michael VIII Palaeologus (1259), and in 1261 this new emperor chose him to head the university at **Hagia Sophia.** Akropolitis worked for union with Rome and composed a history of the Nicaea period. He relates events from the Latin attack on Constantinople (1203) to the Byzantine reinstatement (1261), creating a continuation of Niketas Akominatos's work. Akropolitis saw history as "the passing on of deeds carried out by various people, be they fine or depraved."

ALBUM An album (λεύκωμα) was a book with white, blank pages on which to paste **epigrams,** poems, cuttings, souvenirs, and photographs about the hostess, or the book's owner. The album (in **demotic language** άλμπουμ) quickly became more than a scrapbook. By the twentieth century, it denoted a collection of memorabilia, or a journal, often edited by a woman. **A. Vlachos** (1838–1920) has a sketch, "My Lady's Reception," which includes a reference to an album being read aloud at a Thursday afternoon party or two verses from a gilt edition of the fashionable French poet François Coppée. Euterpe Skordou, who wrote stories and poems in Egypt during the 1940s, issued *Women's Album* (Cairo, 1940–1941). The writer and folklorist Athena Tarsouli (1884–1975) published an album, *Greek Costumes* (1941), with 65 illustrations of local costumes painted by herself.

ALEXANDER ROMANCE, THE The *Alexander Romance* is an accretion of stories about Alexander the Great (356–323 B.C.), the young general who founded 70 cities, 20 of which carried his own name. In spring 334, he had marched against Asia at the head of 30,000 infantry and 5,000 horses. The historian Arrian says that Darius III's army, which he defeated in late 333 by the Issus, consisted of 600,000 soldiers. Alexander's swift victories, his policy of killing or enslaving, and his premature death at Babylon feed the romance. He named a city after his horse Bucephalas, wounded at the river Hydaspes in 326 B.C. Erasmus (in 1516) warned Christian rulers against his paganism: "You allied yourself with Christ; and yet slip back into the ways of Julius Caesar and Alexander the Great?"

In medieval Greek tales, Alexander became a long-distance traveler, even a chivalrous knight. The Greek *Alexander Romance* survives in 18 manuscripts, which range in date from the eleventh to the sixteenth centuries. It was called "pseudo-Callisthenes" because it was associated with an actual historian, Callisthenes of Olynthos, who accompanied Alexander on his campaigns. The *Life of Alexander,* a fourteenth-century verse version of the romance by an unknown Greek author, runs to 6,117 unrhyming decapentasyllables. It is also known by the title *Alexander the King.* Another, rhyming, version, called *Birth, Exploits and Death of Alexander the Great, in Verse,* is written in paired rhyme couplets and is also known as *Story of Alexander,* or the *Rhymed Story.* A popular prose version is known as *Chap-book of Alexander the Great: The Story of Alexander the Macedonian.*

Although the oldest extant version,

"pseudo-Callisthenes" (c. 300 A.D.), was fancifully attributed to Callisthenes, papyrus fragments suggest that some material from a putative secretary of Alexander goes back to just after his death in 323 B.C. The medieval romance culls incidents from Cleitarchus, Diodorus Siculus, Curtius, and Justin. We read of flutes playing while the walls of Thebes are razed. Alexander is crowned king of Egypt by the Ptah-priests of Memphis. He visits the **Olympic Games,** enters a chariot race, and defeats kings who compete in the same event. He writes letters to his mother, Olympias, or his tutor, **Aristotle,** about his campaign in India. He goes to Sicily and Rome, to subjugate the Latins. He travels in disguise as an envoy to the court of Darius, or visits Candace, the Ethiopian queen, as a spy. French eleventh- and twelfth-century poetic versions of the Latin romance were composed in a characteristic 12-syllable line, which was therefore called an Alexandrine.

The Alexander Romance fascinated Byzantine readers and was later translated into Latin, Armenian, Syriac, Coptic, Ethiopic, Serbian, English, French, German, and Hebrew. The tales reached Romania in the sixteenth century (via Serbia) and inspired **icon** painters. Alexander appeared in Christmas carols, and his horse carried the bridegroom to weddings. We also find him as the villain in **Karaghiozis** puppet theater. The best copy of the Greek *Alexander Romance* is Codex Gr 5, in the Hellenic Institute in Venice; it consists of 193 folios and 200 medieval illuminated illustrations. Each picture is accompanied by a caption, as in folio 105 verso (of N. Trahoulias's edition), where the army says to Alexander: "King, we will go no further; we are unable to overcome these men, and it is possible our luck has come to an end."

Further Reading

Holton, David, ed. Διήγησις του Ἀλεξάνδρου. "The Tale of Alexander: The Rhymed Version." In *Byzantine and Modern Greek Library Series*, vol. 1, Thessaloniki, 1974.

Pritchard, R. Telfryn, ed. *The History of Alexander's Battles: Historia de preliis—the J1 Version.* Toronto: Pontifical Institute of Mediaeval Studies, 1992.

ALEXANDER THE GREAT. See *ALEXANDER ROMANCE, THE*

ALEXANDROU, ARIS (1922–1978; pseudonym of A. Vasiliadis) Alexandrou was born in Leningrad to a Greek father and Russian mother. From 1928 he lived in Athens. He fought in **the resistance,** was exiled after the **Civil War** (1947–1951), and held in **prison** from 1953 to 1957. He translated academic books from Russian and English into Greek and published verse collections: *Still This Spring* (1946), in which a tone of political defeatism modulates sharp confrontation, and *Bankrupt Line* (1952). Later (1972) came his *Collected Poems: 1941 to 1971,* which glorify the hammer-and-sickle, or pro-Communist ELAS from the resistance years, and the Socialist Party. He posed the problem of allegiance in the ideological war with these lines (1948): "Petros, who lay on the cement / Without lining in his jacket, / Each morning gave me a fake 'Good Morning' on the sly, / Because they held him to be a traitor." Alexandrou's antiauthoritarianism is expressed in an allegorical novel, *Mission Box* (1974), a troubling synopsis of the Civil War, written mostly in Paris, where he lived from 1967 to his death. Some guerrillas are charged with carrying a mysterious box across enemy lines to a rebel-held town. The band is massacred, and a single survivor completes the mission. He is gaoled because his box turns out to contain nothing, a void that he must now explain to a party court. Alexandrou warns the shade of **Kavafis,** in his poem "Meditations of Flavius Marcus" (1959), that imitating **Homer** in a modern context is not the same as entering the real city of Troy with its smoke and ash.

Further Reading

Christ, R. L. "Translating to Kivotio: At Work with Aris Alexandrou." *Translation Review,* no. 11 (1983): 37–44.

Raftopoulos, Dimitris. Άρης Αλεξάνδρου, ο εξόριστος [Aris Alexandrou: An Exile]. Athens: Sokoli, 1996.

Ricks, David. "Aris Alexandrou." *Grand Street* 8, no. 2 (winter 1989): 120–128.

Stathatos, John, ed. and trans. *Six Modern Greek Poets.* London: Oasis Books, 1975.

ALEXIOU, ELLI (1894–1986) The prose writer, playwright, and journalist Elli Alexiou was the sister of **Galateia Alexiou** Kazantzaki, first wife of **Nikos Kazantzakis.** Her father, Stylianos Alexiou, ran the biggest printery in Iraklion (Crete), held poetry discussions with his social circle, and produced a *Holy Breviary* (Ιερά Σύνοψη), considered the best available in Greek. Elli became a schoolteacher in a low-income district of Iraklion, joined the Communist Party (1928), and worked with the National Liberation Front (see **Resistance**) in the Second World War. In 1945 she won a French government scholarship to study in Paris. In 1950, the Greek government removed her citizenship. It was restored in 1965. She encountered problems with the **Colonels' Junta** over a planned production of one of her plays. Alexiou wrote novels and short stories about her

experience as a teacher and about her life as a political exile between Hungary and Romania. Her book *Lumpen* (Λουμβεν, 1940) deals, especially in its title, with values of **Marxism** (the idea of a *Lumpenproletariat*). This title was defiantly retained when the German occupation was in progress. She published *Tributaries* (1956) and *The Dominant* (1972), which uses an experimental framework to present a chorus of youthful, disaffected Athenian voices. In 1966, she published a study on Kazantzakis, *Bent on Greatness.* She divorced early, had no children, accepted the last rites (though a Marxist), spoke in a Cretan singsong voice, enjoyed wine, loved red carnations, and was a sought-after adviser to aspiring writers (Freri, 1988).

Further Reading

Alexiou, E. Γ΄ Ξριστιανικὸν Παρθεναγωγεῖον [Number 3 Christian Girls' College]. Athens, 1934.

Alexiou, E. Καὶ οὕτω καθεξῆς [And So On and So Forth]. Athens: privately printed, 1965.

Alexiou, E. Σπονδή [The Libation]. Athens: privately printed, 1965.

ALEXIOU, GALATEIA (1881–1962) Born in Iraklion, sister of the writer **Elli Alexiou,** Galateia became the first wife of the writer **N. Kazantzakis.** She won prizes in a competition to improve school readers (1911–1912), though Eleni Kazantzakis (his second wife) later hinted that Nikos Kazantzakis let Galateia sign work that was chiefly by himself. Galateia published her first poetry under the pseudonyms Lalo de Kastro or Petroula Psiloriti, and it came out in a variety of periodicals. She and her husband published articles in early volumes (from 1909) of the journal *Modern Life* (Νέα

Ζωή). It was this journal, prominent in sponsoring fiction by **A. Papadiamantis,** that printed two of Galateia's books: *The Diseased State* (1914) and the three-act play *With Every Sacrifice.* In her first novel, *Women* (1933), she created an innovative choral narration by the device of exchanged letters between a group of female acquaintances. Her play, *While the Ship Sails,* was produced by the National Theater (1933). It is based on the symbol of a city disintegrating, while transport leaves by sea. In the sonnet, "Suitors," Penelope unpicks her weaving, and we hear the howl of Ithaca's dogs as they recognize the stranger who has completed his return, pacing over their island (see C. Robinson, in Mackridge 1996: 110). By contrast, her poem "Sinner" presents the rootless individual as a modern female with different names in every city, who speaks from a topical hell, "from the rotten planking of my drowned boat."

Further Reading

Alexiou, G. Αὐλαία [Stage Curtain]. Athens: privately printed, 1952.

Alexiou, G. Ἄνθρωποι καὶ ὑπεράνθρωποι [Men and Supermen]. Athens: privately printed, 1958.

ALI PASHA (1741–1820) Ruling over a brilliant and corrupt court, Ali Pasha, the despot of Ioannina, made his name a synonym for cruelty. His deeds became the inspiration for numerous later Greek poems and plays. The wealth and military alliances that he built up for 50 years made him master of most of the Greek mainland. He stole his subjects' property, dishonored their women, and tortured their sons. He invited a whole clan to a meeting in a stockade, then had them mowed down by musket fire. He impaled his opponents or cut bits off their face. He had some allegedly adulterous Greek wives tied in sacks and drowned in the lake. This episode is related in a famous poem by **Valaoritis.** "The Drowning of Frosyne" is also the title of a long poem by Nikolaos Mavrommatis (1770–1817) about the fate met by the alleged paramour of Moukhtar Pasha, Ali's philandering son. This author was physician to Moukhtar (see **Medicine**). The play *Eufrosyne* (1876) was composed about the victim of this episode by a woman intrigued, perhaps, at having the same name, Eufrosyne Vikela (1820–1906).

The women of Ioannina, though refined, affected a way of waddling. So there is a love song from Epirus: "Let the mountains fall flat / So that I may see Athens, / So that I may see my love / Who strolls like a goose." Ali Pasha's favorite wife, Vassiliki, eluded his attempts to kill her when, at the end of his life, he was surrounded on his lake by invading troops under Hoursit. Vassiliki lived on after him, took to drink, and died in 1834. The mystery of Ali Pasha's supposed treasure (the equivalent of £300,000 sterling) was never solved. A poem tells of Ali's scorched earth policy, how he laid waste to Ioannina so that his masters at Constantinople should gain nothing by suppressing his autonomy: "So spake Ali, and ordered them to burn Jannina. / To cast flame and light fires in all four corners. / To burn Maroutsi and Metropolis, and the beautiful market-place, / And the Serayi neighborhood, the pride of Jannina, / Its three churches, two schools, houses and shining colonnades." The manuscripts, volumes and epigraphs housed in the Balanaia Library (so-called in honor of its founder Balanos Basilopoulos) were destroyed in this vast act of arson by Ali (13 August 1820). The legend of Ali Pasha is crystallized in a long

epic poem bearing his name, the *Ali Pashiad.* This text stretches to 15,000 15-syllable lines and may have been written in installments over the first 10 or 15 years of the nineteenth century. A manuscript copy was unearthed by the English traveler Leake, who met Ali at the zenith of his power, around 1817, when he controlled Epirus, Macedonia, Thessaly, the Peloponnese, parts of Euboiea, and all the mainland. Leake published the 4,500 lines that he had collected in a travel memoir (London, 1835). K. Sathas published a section of the *Ali Pashiad* in his study *Greece under Turk Rule* (1869), which dealt with the rebellion at Olympus (1808) of Euthymios Vlachavas, member of a noted family of *armatolí* from Trikkala, who was executed at Ali's orders (1809) by dismemberment. A year later, apparently following Leake's indications, Sathas found the rest of the manuscripts and published them virtually word for word in his volume *Historical Disquisitions* (1870). The poem provides evidence about a period when **Byron, Christopoulos, Vilarás,** Kolettis, **Sakellarios,** and Psalidas were among the writers, doctors, scientists, travelers, intellectuals, and painters who found Ioannina a congenial port of call. In a modern, **demotic language,** with dialectal interference and foreign expressions, the *Ali Pashiad* has the unusual feature of being written from the Muslim point of view. It describes a Pasha warlord and brings before the reader's eye the complex fiefdom of Ioannina as well as the individualist ethos of mercenary militias (ἀρματολισμός), animated by **Klephts** and the *armatolí.*

Further Reading

Plomer, William. *The Diamond of Jannina: Ali Pasha 1741–1822.* New York: Taplinger, 1970.

ALLATIOS, LEON (1588–1669) The humanist and polymath Leon Allatios was born at Chios, 20 years after the island was captured from Genova (Italy) by the Turks. The Jesuits had a continuing presence at Chios, and Allatios started his studies with them. He exerted a dual influence (Latin; Hellenic) on the coming Greek **Enlightenment.** He collected a fine library (see **Efyena**), which he later bequeathed to the **Greek College at Rome.** He was learned, prolific, and scientifically curious. He traveled, made maps, and wrote a long poem, *Greece,* aspiring to the liberation of the Greek-speaking peoples. He leaned toward Jesuit intellectuality and later **Catholicism.** Appreciated by more than one pope, he performed delicate missions, including transferring the entire Palatine library, in perhaps 90 boxes, over the Alps and across Italy to Rome. He was accused by a pope, whose poetry he had criticized, of losing one or two of those boxes. For a while, he was held in **prison.** On his release, he returned to a career as teacher, antiquarian, librarian, and **cataloguer.**

In 1661, Allatios mentioned the text of the play *King Rhodolinos,* by **I. M. Troilos.** Bounialís (1681), at the end of his *Relation in Verses of the Dreadful War Which Took Place on the Island of Crete,* wrote a further couplet on *King Rhodolinos.* Legrand (1894) looked for the play in vain. Voutieridis tells how **Yennadios** bought a copy from a Frankfurt bookseller (1910) and donated it to the new **Yennadios** Library in Athens (1930). Thus, from a hint in L. Allatios, a seventeenth-century play was tracked down to its rediscovery. The same is true of the play *David* by an unknown Chiot writer, also found among Allatios's manuscripts. The first catalogue of his works was printed in 1659. Fabricius published another in 1808, and it runs to 11 pages. In 1962, the Greek literature department at Palermo University (Sicily) sponsored a new catalogue of Allatios's writings, which includes 59 works. Among these are a commentary on the myth of Pope Joan (1630; see also **Roidis**), a list of all known writings on the **Orthodox church** (1645), a dissertation on the possibility of union between the Western and Eastern church (Cologne, 1648), a comparison of Latin and Orthodox doctrines on Purgatory (Rome, 1653), an essay on the works of **Psellus** (1634), and a book on John Damascenus.

Further Reading

Lavagnini, B., ed. *Il Carme "Hellas" di Leone Allaci*. Palermo: Quaderni dell'Istituto di Filologia Greca dell'Università di Palermo, 1966.

ALLEGORY The extended **figure of speech** known as allegory (αλληγορία) consists of the representation of an abstract meaning by a simple narrative, more practical or concrete, but not necessarily shorter. The Kostís **Palamás** poem "Fathers" is all allegorical. Although the writer uses the text to depict a garden and a child who will one day inherit that garden, he means the homeland, the nation, and the attitude of people who belong to it. Allegory provides a difficult concept with a "plain, specific shape" (Kalodikis, 1984). The **proverbs,** riddles (αινίγματα), and parables (παραβολές) of the Byzantine period are all, in a sense, an extension of allegory, which is also widely used in the Greek plastic arts.

ALLITERATION The word *alliteration* (παρήχηση) originally meant "the imitation of an echo." The term now refers to a significant repetition of some letter, or sound, in verse. Poets create an alliteration by the recurrence of specific consonants, like the letter sigma (σ, ς) in a line from **S. Skipis** about the Isle of Salamis: κι ἐσὺ τάφος ὑγρὸς τῆς Ἀσίας ("You, the watery grave of Asia"), or the letter nu (ν) in a line from **Rigas** about the Nation's rebellion: νὰ κάμωμεν τὸν ὅρκον ἐπάνω στὸν Σταυρόν ("that we make our oath upon the Cross").

ALMANAC Varying material used to come out (1850–1940) in the almanac (ημεροδείκτης) or the calendar (ημερολόγιον). These were a publishing phenomenon, with hundreds of local and national titles. The almanac had as many sheets as days of the year, stuck to each other along the top edge and down the two sides. The front of each sheet carried information about the day, its sunrise and sunset, the name of its saint (for instance, Gregory of Nazianzus for January 25), with feasts, celebrations, astronomy, and historical events. Erasmia Zafiraki, who started the journal *Greater Greece* as a schoolchild at Alexandria (1914), issued an almanac in 1920 called *Radiance,* and in 1922 and 1926 a *Modern Greek Calendar.* **Rangavís, Vamvas,** and **A. Vlachos** contributed to the bibliographer Vretos Papadopoulos's *National Almanac* (1861–1871).
See also LITURGICAL BOOKS

ALPHABETARIO. See **NOMENCLATURE; READERS**

ALPHABET OF LOVE (mid-fifteenth century) From Rhodes (or another Aegean island) comes the collection *Songs: Verses about Passion and Love.* The hypothesis that this late Byzantine set of love poems originates from Rhodes is based on internal evidence, such as "That maiden, I kissed her; at Rhodes I left her." The collection cannot be viewed as a medley of **demotic songs** because (for example) they use the word ἔρωτας, and its plural ἔρωτες, instead of the vernacular word for "love" (ἀγάπη). The noun καταλόγι denotes a commoner's song with an amorous theme. These texts were first edited by W. Wagner (1879) under the title *The ABC of Love* (*Das ABC der Liebe*). They were edited later (1913) by Hesseling and Pernot under the title *Love Games* (see **Katalógia**). There are 112 poems, making a total of 714 unrhyming 15-syllable lines. Some of them were sorted into four **alphabets**.

An interesting sequence is "Song of the Hundred Words" (at lines 140–330). Here a maiden poses consecutive questions to a "handsome, immature youth" who wishes to court her. He will have to "distinguish safely one by one" the hundred words she intends to recite and improvise 100 answers. The maiden counts as far as ten. Next she proceeds by decades. The youth wins his wager, so she concedes an embrace. Then she yields completely, with the result that he spurns her. The tone is uneven, but the poems show a naïve charm and wonderment at nature: "Dolefully, the nightingale calls at the dawning day, and hides its lovely voice, / So whoever hears that bird will say for sure it grieves." Popular copies of *The Alphabet* provide five or more distichs to cover each letter, but Stephanides points out that this is not so challenging in Greek, where plenty of words begin with z- or x-.

See also HEKATÓLOGA

Further Reading

Stephanides, Theodore. "The Alphabet of Love." *The Charioteer* 2, no. 1 (1963): 69–72.

ALPHABETS Alphabet poems have 24 lines, each beginning with a letter of the Greek alphabet, in succession. Or the poem may have successive stanzas, each beginning with the required letter in sequence. Such a poem may run to more than one alphabetical series. The significance of the opening letters is that they create an alphabet (not the vertical key word, as in an **acrostic**). There is a late Byzantine alphabet on **Xenitiá**, which may be a source for the fifteenth-century poem in 548 **political verses**, *On Expatriation* (Περὶ ξενιτειάς). Another is the *Devout and Edifying Alphabet on the Vanity of Our World.* In this text, the alphabet sequence occurs at every fifth line. The text as a whole runs to 120 lines in order to accommodate 5 × 24 spaces, enough for one occurrence of each letter of the Greek alphabet.

This (probably) mid-fifteenth-century text shows the occasional couplet linked by **rhyme,** a feature considered typical of the period: "See how your appetite defeats you, and makes you lose your soul! / Behold, repent, and cool that appetite. / Submit to fasting, and hardship, stay away from women." In Byzantium, on New Year's Day by tradition children took to the streets and sang carols in alphabet form. One such carol is recorded in a twelfth-century manuscript: "Alpha = Master of all the world / Beta = The lord reigns / Gamma = Christ is born / Delta = By divine word / Epsilon = He is coming to earth / Zeta = He brings life to the world / Eta = Sun and moon / Theta = Worshipping God." A curious *Alphabetalphabetos,* possibly composed by Meletios Galasiotis the Homologete ("Confessor"), is a thirteenth-century devotional alphabet, written in 13,000 unrhymed **political verses,** to expound theological and educational matters.

AMANÉS The *amanés* (ἀμανές) was originally a Turkish song type and consisted of a long, heartfelt, often passionately drawn-out poem in the form of a monody. Its name is due to the sorrowful cry "pity!" (ἀμάν), which is heard repeatedly in the sung performance, either as an introduction to lines or as a closing refrain. The Greeks adapted this Turkish type to their own song repertoire, fitting *amanés* to Greek rural themes. **Papadiamantis** strengthens the rural atmosphere of his short story "Country Easter" (1890) by introducing a character, Uncle Milios, who is fond of his flask and joins in the singing of "Christ is risen" at an improvised picnic: "now and again he shifted the psalm to an *amané,* or to a bandit ballad."

Further Reading

Charis, Manos. Άντες αμάν· πρωτότυπες κρητικές μαντινάδες [Let Go Alas! Original Mantinades from Crete]. Athens: Dorikos: 1996.

AMBELÁS, TIMOLEON (1850–1926) The gifted playwright Timoleon Ambelás worked as a lawyer, then a magistrate, in Greek provincial centers. As a school student he wrote two plays, which were put on by fellow pupils (1865). In 1866, his five-act play, *The Martyrs of Arkadios,* was played by the Alexiados company teaming up with amateur actors. He later submitted a series of plays for the **Voutsynas,** Pantelideios, and **Lassaneios** prizes, often successfully. In 1900 the Veronis company premiered his four-act play, *Artemisia,* at Athens. He favored Byzantine and neoclassical themes, as in *Men of Crete and Venice, Nero, Cleopatra,* and *Virginia of Rome,* and also wrote a *Prince of Morea,* based on the struggle for power in the medieval Peloponnese between Franks and Greeks, centering on the death of the last lord of Mistra, Leon Hamaretos. Ambelás drafted a series of comedies entitled "The Reformers" in three acts, successfully produced at Zakynthos by Pantopoulos's troupe on his twenty-fifth anniversary. He also produced comic one-act pieces, such as "A Mercantile Marriage," "The Dance of Michalis," "Scandalous Visits," and "The Field of Honor."

ANACOLUTHON The figure of speech known as anacoluthon (from the adjective "inconsistent," ανακόλουθος) starts a sentence with one grammatical structure, then ends it with another. Often the sentence has a clear subject, but the verb that corresponds to it does not agree syntactically. Constructions in anacoluthon may mimic colloquial speech or suggest vivid, animated narrative. **Kalvos** makes a **simile** more potent by using anacoluthon in "their souls, / Like a silvery mist, / *Rises* to the heights" (τὰ πνεύματα / ὡς ἀργυρέα ὁμίχλη / τὰ ὑψηλὰ ἀναβαίνει).

ANADIPLOSIS In **rhetoric,** anadiplosis is the repetition of the same syllable, or sound, at the start of successive words. In grammar, anadiplosis is the way Greek verbs are formed in the perfect, future perfect, or past perfect tenses. The respective terms are "doubling" (αναδίπλωση) and "reduplication" (αναδιπλασιασμός). In literature, it is the reiteration of the same words at the start of successive segments in a text. It occurs in line after line of the **demotic songs.** In "The Armatolí of the Night" we read, "Pour wine for us, slave girl, pour wine in our glasses," "They dance, the bandit lads, they dance for joy, poor wretches," "the one said to the other, the one told the other." Anadiplosis dominates whole narrative stereotypes from the demotic song, as in "the road he takes, the road he leaves," or "they go, they go on, and still they go more."

ANAGNORISI Chance recognition, or *anagnorisi* (ἀναγνωρισῃ), is a frequent device in Greek verse romance. It was a favorite resource of the classical tragedians, as in Euripides' *Iphigeneia in Tauris* (414 B.C.), where the recognition comes about by signs and proofs (τεκμήρια), such as a physical mark or a shared memory. These are familiar from the plays *Comedy of Errors, Twelfth Night,* and *Pericles* by **Shakespeare,** who may have copied the device indirectly from **Byzantine romance.** So *anagnorisi* brings hero and heroine together after separation. It was used by Greek writers to contrive a **happy ending** for their story after the alternating fortunes of the romance. In *Imperios and Margarona,* the protagonist fetches up, exhausted and penniless, at his wife's monastery, where his mother has also gone to worship. The two women recognize their lost one from coincidental details in the account of his travels and loss at sea.

ANAGNOSTAKI, LOULA (1940–) The powerful twentieth-century dramatist Loula Anagnostaki (born in **Thessaloniki,** sister of **Manolis Anagnostakis**) developed socialist and feminist themes in an alienated way. In *The City,* a man and a woman lure lonely men to an apartment for dinner. They throw them out after she has aroused their interest. In this one-act piece, the temporary guest is a photographer who refuses to snap his naked hostess in a dying pose on the floor. When the photographer leaves, the woman believes their whole city is going up in flames. *The Overnight Visitor* is a one-act play in which a teenage girl returns from a fruitless search for her father, who has vanished as an emigrant worker, a predicament typical of the 1960s. A man who has been similarly displaced (by the 1940s war) invites her to stay in his tiny apartment, but she discovers he has staged his own disappearance, leaving both his work and wife. In *The Parade,* a teenage boy, looking down from his window, tells his sister of a police atrocity being committed before his eyes. Both are seen at the window by the commanding officer. As this one-act tableau closes, they fear he may hunt them down as eyewitnesses of his squad of thugs. In 1987 came her play *The Sounds of Arms.*

Further Reading

Sakellaridou, Elizabeth. "Levels of Victimization in the Plays of Loula Anagnostaki." *JMGS* 14, no. 1 (May 1996): 85–102.

ANAGNOSTAKIS, MANOLIS (1925–) Poet and political activist Manolis Anagnostakis joined a youth branch of the pro-Communist EAM (see **Resistance**) during the **German occupation** of Greece. He was sentenced to death by a military tribunal (1948) for illegal acts committed while he fought in the Communist ranks during the **Civil War.** His sentence was commuted to three years of **prison.** He saw fellow partisans shot in the executions that he survived. From 1951, he sympathized with the international Communist cause, while opposing Soviet practice. In 1974 and 1977, he ran for election to parliament as a candidate of the Greek Communist Party of the Interior. He was a medical doctor and traveled abroad extensively. His first three collections of poetry, *Epochs I–III,* appeared in his red-hot political years (1945–1951). Later came *Continuations I–III* and *The Target,* followed in 1979 by *The Margin '68–'69.* Later in his career, Anagnostakis edited an anthology of Greek postsymbolist poets (1990).

Further Reading

Kokolis, X. A. "The Poetic 'Christology' of Manolis Anagnostakis." *JMGS* 17, no. 1 (May 1999): 125–150.

Ricks, David. "'The Best Wall to Hide Our Face Behind': An Introduction to the Poetry of Manolis Anagnostakis." *JMH,* 12–13 (1995–1996): 1–26.

ANAPHONESIS The device of "vocative address" (*anaphonesis,* αναφώνηση) occurs in many **demotic songs.** The narrative turns into an appeal to a horse, person, little bird, physical object, or nature itself, as in "O my proud rifle, my glorious sword" or "Hail to you, mountains with cliffs, hail, o ravines with frost."

ANAPHORA A report (*anaphora,* αναφορά) may consist of grievances, written or recited, by an individual to an authority or by the authority to a superior. A complainant often repeats his woes. In poetry, the term comes to mean the repetition of the same word or phrase at the start of successive lines.

ANASTROPHE The device of "reversion" (*anastrophe,* αναστροφή) is a turning toward the opposite. It also refers to the literary device of beginning one sentence with the same word as the closing word of the preceding sentence.

ANCEPS The Latin adjective *anceps* is used as a technical term in prosody. It denotes an "unfixed" syllable in a meter, that is, one that may be taken as "heavy" or "light." As a metrical element, it may also be deemed the choice between a "long" or "short" syllable. The *anceps* often sits at the end of a meter. Where there is metrical continuity (*synaphea*) between lines, or parts of a line, the *anceps* is conventionally read as "heavy."

ANCESTOR OBSESSION. See PROGONOPLIXÍA

ANDARTIS The word *andartis* (αντάρτης) refers to a partisan in **resistance** groups that continued to fight after the **Occupation** against a Greek regime backed by the U.S. Sixth Fleet. In *The Heroic Age* (1984) by **Haviaras,** government forces mop up these partisans by using napalm.

ANGHELAKI-ROOKE, KATERINA (1939–) Anghelaki-Rooke was the only child of open-minded, cultured parents and a godchild of **Kazantzakis,** with whom she exchanged letters as she grew up. She has a similarity with Sylvia Plath, who wrote as a teenager: "If I didn't have sex organs, I wouldn't waver on the brink of nervous emotion and tears all the time" (1950). **Seferis** says "a poet has one sole theme, his living body," and Rae Dalven suggests that Anghelaki-Rooke made this into "the theme of all her work." Her first collection, *Wolves and Clouds* (1963), offers a challenging, almost polemical insistence on the erotic identity of the poet's own body. Any proposal of a literature "of children and flowers" is sterile. Her collection *The Vast Mammal Magdalene* (1974) threw down the gauntlet, suggesting that the second sex could live a thrilling and redemptive adventure inside its own body. As her poetry gained in polemical energy, so did her reputation. Anghelaki-

Rooke has lectured in America and held scholarships and foundations outside Greece. She has a background in language studies (Russian, French, English) and has translated Samuel Beckett (from the French), Edward Albee, Dylan Thomas, **Shakespeare's** *The Taming of the Shrew,* Mayakovksy, Andrei Voznesensky, and letters of Kazantzakis. Among her other volumes are *Counter Love* (1982) and *Suitors* (1984). In some of her poems, she alters the stale myths of **Hellenism** by erasing the sacrifice of Iphigeneia and giving the Achaean women different roles. *Wind Epilogue* (1990) consists of short speculations in verse on the problems of existence. She writes scholarly criticism, such as, "Sex Roles in Modern Greek Poetry" (*JMGS* 1, no. 1, May 1983: 141–156) and "The Greek Poetic Landscape: Recent Trends in Greek Poetry," in *St. John's University Review of National Literatures* 5, no. 2 (fall 1974): 13–25.

Further Reading

Kazantzakis, Nikos. *The Suffering God: Selected Letters to Galatea and to Papastephanou,* trans. by Philip Ramp and Katerina Anghelaki-Rooke, introduction by K. Anghelaki-Rooke. New Rochelle, NY: Caratzas Bros., 1979.

Kolias, Helen. "Greek Women Poets and the Language of Silence." In *Translation Perspectives IV: Selected Papers, 1986–87,* edited by M. G. Rose, 99–112. Binghamton: State University of New York Press, 1988.

ANIMAL STORIES Greece's animals all pass into Christian tales or pagan **folklore.** They include the nightingale, lammergeier, hawk, pelican, hoopoe, turtledove, shrike, partridge, stork, egret, pheasant, lynx, jackal, black bear, boar, kri-kri, fox, chamois, deer, badger, wea-

sel, and marlin. The sophist Aelian (c. 165–c. 220 A.D.) wrote an essay on *Animal Peculiarities.* Later there was a vogue (c. fourteenth century) for pseudoscientific *Stories Concerning Animals.* The author, or compiler, of these works is unknown. The attribution of all the main animal stories to a single author (a theory promulgated by Y. Th. Zoras) is improbable. Scholars do not accept the attribution, in some manuscripts, of animal stories to the supposed twelfth-century author of the **Prodromic Poems**. A typical work is the *Physiologist,* which lists colorful details about animals and their fantastic disputes. Probably adapted from an earlier work (Alexandria, ?second century A.D.), the *Physiologist* was written down in the fourteenth century and survives in a fifteenth-century manuscript. The text runs to 1,131 unrhyming **decapentasyllables** and includes two short, interrupting, sections in prose. Here we are instructed on the animals of the earth: elephant, deer, basilisk, snake, or ape. Then we meet creatures that have a dual nature: satyr and centaur. The final classification is creatures of the air: peacock, Egyptian eagle, dove, phoenix, pelican.

Fanciful explanation of the names of animals, based on false etymology, is a popular ingredient. Allegorical zoology flourished in the West: Leonardo da Vinci (1452–1519), in his *Bestiary,* tells of the ermine, a creature who would rather die than get dirty and eats only once a day. The *Physiologist* (150 years earlier) reports erroneous ideas about animals, feeding popular fantasy with a semblance of wisdom. An interesting work (dated 1364) is the *Tale of the Four-Footed Animals.* Its title, Διήγησις παιδιόφραστος [or πεζόφραστος] τῶν τετραπόδων ζώων, contains either the epithet

Plain (as in σὲ φράση ἀπλή) or *Popular* (πεζή). It describes, in 1,082 lines, a lunch invitation by the lion, which turns into a council meeting of quadrupeds. In the debate, the lion decides (against the cat and rat), that one animal is entitled, in natural justice, to eat another. A general slaughter results, in which the strongest devour the weakest. The author inserts an attack on Jews and on the Latin church. He says his work can be read by "kids, students and youths, for it has been written to unite learning with pleasure." The text shows that nothing can alter the laws of nature. Less noteworthy is Ὀψαρολόγος, a fourteenth-century tale about fish.

See also BIRD STORIES; DONKEY; WINE

ANNINOS, BABIS (1852–1934) The much-loved humorous writer Babis Anninos (see **Pun**), was also a poet, historian, playwright, and journalist (see **Asmodaeos**). He was born in Cephalonia, worked in public service (Argostoli, Athens, Naples, Rome), and collaborated on the newspaper *The Daily* (published by the dramatist **Koromilás**). In 1885 he issued his satirical broadsheet, *Town*. Anninos became chief editor, in 1889, of the paper *Quotidian,* which was put out by Mikhail Lampros. Lampros was himself a translator of Italian and French plays (like Anninos) and for 32 years acted as secretary to the literary circle **Parnassós.** From 1891 to 1895, Anninos directed their journal *Parnassus.* Later he ran an encyclopedic and literary review of his own, *The Rainbow.*

ANONYMOUS GREEK (refers to a work of 1806) "Anonymous Greek" is the tantalizingly unknown author of the *Greek Rule of Law, or A Discourse on Freedom,* published "in Italy," 1806. This is a pamphlet aspiring to abolish the subservience of Greece, harnessing the energy of the **Enlightenment.** The unnamed agitator, perhaps a merchant from Livorno or Venice, dedicates his book to the Greek liberator **Rigas Velestinlís.** Scholars have speculated that he might be Spachos, Ioannis Kolettis, **Koraís,** or **Paschalis Donás.** Debate on the author's identity has gone on since the 1940s (for example, in Tomadakis, Valetas, Mandouvalos). The text presents an assault against the invention of money and the equation between wealth and power. The ultimate disgrace is to hear an **Ottoman** or a Briton say: "Today I sold ten people." The author sketches a program for freeing Greece, loosening the power of the **Phanariot** class, strengthening education, and devising laws that steer between anarchy and monarchy. His ideology suggests a germ of **Marxism** before its time: "Why should the rich man eat, drink, sleep, whoop it up, be exempt from manual labor and yet give orders, while the poor man is subordinated, provides labor, works the whole time, sleeps on the ground, and feels hunger and thirst? What causes all this evil but the discovery of gold? So what forces us to guard it? Do humans perhaps need gold to exist? Is gold perhaps what ploughs fields?"

See also RHETORICAL QUESTION

ANTHIAS, TEFKROS (1904–1968; pseudonym of Andreas Triantafyllos-Pavlos) Anthias, a poet and playwright from **Cyprus,** had strong humanitarian and socialist views. He took part in the struggle for Cypriot independence. Later he went to live in London and had some success with journalism. Anthias first appeared (1925–1930) with poems in the journal *The Pioneers.* He published several collections of verse. Among them was the successful *Whistles of the Vagabond* (Athens, 1928), which led critics to speculate about the existence of a Greek poetics of vagrancy (ἀλητισμός).

ANTHOLOGY An anthology (ἀνθολογία) is a selection of epigrams or poems. The word, as first used, meant a plucking of flowers. Literature was seen as a whole garden from which a sample garland could be gathered. By metaphor, the word came to mean any selection from an author, a genre, or a period. The first anthology is the *Garland* by Meleager of Gadara (Syria), in 80 B.C. An edition of many preceding anthologies was made around 917 A.D. by an imperial official at Constantinople, Konstantinos Kefalás. This is the *Palatine Anthology,* so called because the single tenth-century manuscript that preserves it was discovered in Count Palatine's library (at Heidelberg). It is filled with 6,000 short poems and epigrams, gathered (c. 1300) by **Maximos Planoudis** (see **Aesop**). One charming poem concerns a girl who gives up her dolls and toys before marriage. Since the early nineteenth century, many hundreds of verse anthologies have been made. Prominent is a collection (Athens, 1837) by Konstantinos Chanterís, *The New Greek Parnassus.* Distinguished anthologists who followed Chanterís include D. Tangopoulos, K. Sinokos, Sideris, **Polemis, Tellos Agras,** Kleon Paraschos, Renos Apostolidis, Y. Valetas, and L. Politis. In 1978, Maria D. Chalkiopoulou published a *Bibliography of Modern Greek Poetry Anthologies Produced between 1834 and 1978.* Many modern anthologies offer Greek writing in translation, some specially commissioned. Artemis Leontis's *Greece: A*

Traveler's Literary Companion (San Francisco: Whereabouts Press, 1997) is not so much a travel book as an anthologized Greece, a mode that involves its "literary topography" (Maria Kakavoulia). L. Politis offers a scholar's choice from the modern Greek corpus, in the seven volumes of his *Anthology of Greek Poetry* (Athens: Galaxy, 1964–1967).

ANTIPHRASIS Antiphrasis (ἀντίφρασις) is the reversal of a word's sense. The 435,000 kilometer expanse of the Black Sea, famed for its sudden, fatal storms, was called "the friendly sea." The word for "bribery" (δωροδοκία) meant "taking of a gift," but has acquired the opposite meaning, "supply of a gift." In literary writing, antiphrasis is akin to **euphemism, irony,** and **litotes,** all forms where a word is used, but the context makes it signify more or less the opposite.

ANTIQUITY WORSHIP. See AR-KHAIOLATRÍA

ANTISTROPHE The noun antistrophe (ἀντιστροφή) means "turning the dance in the opposite direction." Antistrophe refers to any answering sequence, uttered by one-half of a chorus of singers. It corresponds to a symmetrical strophe uttered by a first group of singers or dancers. It is present in classical Greek tragedy, imitated in the **epode** and in modern poems. Antistrophe comes to mean any alteration to the natural word order in a sentence or a modification of prescriptive syntax. It can refer, stylistically, to the device of ending several clauses of a period with the same word.

ANTITHESIS The **figure** of contrast known as antithesis (ἀντίθεσις) was inherited from ancient **oratory** and then used in poetry to link opposed words and contrasting ideas. The **trope** is deliberate and stylized in the **P. Soutsos** ode "To God": "Immeasurable, You measure all; unrecognized, You recognize all things: / Light is Your body, the sun is Your eye."

ANTONIADIS, ANTONIOS (1836–1905) Son of Cretan parents, Antoniadis was one of the first citizens inscribed on the list of Athens' harbor town, Piraeus. He graduated young from high school and university, later losing his headmaster position at Patras (1861) after speaking out against the dictatorial policies of King Otho (see **Monarchy**). While on Crete, he composed his first play, *Philip of Macedon,* which won a prize in the **Voutsynas** competition (1865). He then turned to research in medieval history to produce his **epic** poem *The Creteid,* dealing with events on Crete during Venetian suzerainty. Antoniadis returned from Crete to Piraeus, where he lived the rest of his life in a headmastership, which he held for decades, producing plays and epic poems year after year, gaining prizes or special mentions from the Voutsynas adjudicators. His epics extended in length to several thousand lines. Many of his plays were large-scale productions on tragic topics, slavishly following the precise historical episodes, popular with contemporary audiences, and keenly acted by the main Athenian troupes. Antoniadis compiled 50 plays, dozens of occasional poems, epic compositions, and a number of school textbooks, a resource which in nineteenth-century Greece was slow to evolve. Thus Antoniadis's four-volume *Universal History,* as well as a geography and grammar by him, formed the educational base of a generation of Greek school pupils. Some of his dramatic compositions dealt with heroes from the **War of Independence,** such as *Botsaris* and *Commander Kolokotronis,* and with the era of banditry (see **Brigand**) and gendarmes before the Uprising, characterized by the **Klephts** and *armatolí,* among them *Katsantonis.* His epic *Of Missolonghi,* which maps events across the hours, days, and weeks of the siege of **Missolonghi,** brought alive actions or persons that some authors had overlooked. Antoniadis's works are composed in pure **Katharevousa,** with conservative attention to unity of plot and action.

See also POETICS

ANTONOMASIA The **figure of speech** called antonomasia (αντονομασία) occurs when a person or object is called not by its actual name, but by a more generic or preeminent title, such as when in verse a strong man becomes a "Hercules," or Poseidon (lord of the sea) is "the blue-maned."

AODO A.O.D.O. are the initials of the Greek words "From Everything for Everyone" (Ἀπ ᾽ ὅλα δι᾽ ὅλους). *AODO* was one of many **newspapers** started by Vlasis Gavrilidis (1848–1920). The utilitarian nature of his patriotic, late nineteenth-century journalism, which broadly supported the liberal **nationalism** of E. Venizelos, is proclaimed in this acronymic masthead.

See also DON'T GET LOST; RA-BAGÁS

APOKOPOS From **Crete**, in the last quarter of the fifteenth century, comes *Apokopos,* the first book in everyday spoken Greek. It was printed at Venice (1519), in an edition by Nicholas Kalliergis that has not survived. By convention, the work carries as its title the single word *Apokopos* (Ἀπόκοπος), drawn from a phrase in the opening line: "Once upon a time, *after work,* I became drowsy." It is a sophisticated composition in 490 lines, consisting of rhyming **distichs** in **decapentasyllable meter** on the Byzantine model, with a strong flavor of **demotic song,** avoiding anapestic rhythm (⌣ −). It was apparently written by one Bergadis, of whom nothing sure is known, though he may be from Rethymno. The single name, which we meet in the codex, resembles the Hellenized form of a well-known Venetian surname on Crete, "Bragadin." Lines 301–302, with their anti-Papist flavor, led H. Pernot to surmise that the author was a Greek **Catholic**: "Opposite was the seat of the kingdom of Rome, / Which is a vessel of all arrogance and deceitful opinion." Similar attitudes to the Friars in medieval Crete make it equally likely the author was **Orthodox.** The work became a favorite of the lay public and went through several editions: 1534, 1543, 1553, 1627, 1648, 1668, 1683, and 1721.

Bergadis relates what he saw in a dream, after he climbed up onto the Tree of Life to taste honey. The branches snapped, and he was pitched into an abyss, dropping into the mouth of a dragon. He finds the dead in the Underworld sorrowing over whether they are lost to the living, wondering if the world above remembers them at all. The corpses ask the traveler for information on this, and he responds malevolently that it is rare for the living to remember the dead. Perhaps their mothers still think of them, but their widows have quite forgotten. The dead yearn to regain the world above. They give Bergadis messages to take back to their families (a motif from *Hell,* in **Dante**'s *Divine Comedy,* c. 1307). Bergadis feels a pang of terror

and gladly departs to the world of the living, but he fails to convey these messages from the Underworld. The work suggests an aristocratic environment. Nobility and fortune gained in life ought to be conserved within the family. The text mentions two princesses with a father who is "first in the state." There is also an aura of Mediterranean adventure, hinting at Eastern elements, when two young brothers in the Underworld give the narrator a lively account of a shipwreck. The narrative, with these inserted segments, may suggest a Western literary source. Like much literature from Crete before its fall to the Turks, *Apokopos* displays grace of style combined with popular realism.

APOLLONIUS OF TYRE (c. late fourteenth century) The *Tale of the Sorely Tried Apollonius of Tyre* is a Greek translation in 857 unrhyming **political** lines of a version of the Latin *Historia Apollonii regis Tyrii* (?6th century A.D.). The latter is probably drawn from a **Hellenistic** source (third–fourth century A.D.). The Latin version acquired a Christian slant, eventually influencing Chaucer and **Shakespeare.** It provides the basic plot of John Gower's poem, *Confessio Amantis* (1390), and Shakespeare's tragedy, *Pericles, Prince of Tyre* (1608/9).

What is the basic plot of this **romance**? Apollonius, his wife, and newborn daughter are separated during a sea journey. Each thinks the others have died: "Thasia had this habit of going to the cemetery, / Where she mourned for her nanny, before turning back: / Theophilos was lying there in hiding; / Suddenly he leapt out and grabbed the woman, / And drew his sword to slay her. / She wept and said to him 'Why, what evil have I done?' / The man answered her as follows: 'You did no ill. / It is your lord who committed this affront, / And delivered you into hands where you find no pity'" (lines 498–504). Various vicissitudes ensue, taking the main characters round Greek communities at Antioch, Tyre, Ephesus, Tarsus, Mytiline, and Cyrenaica. The story reunites them by chance, giving rise to the familiar topos of **Anagnorisi** and **happy ending.**

There is a later version of the romance that runs to 1,894 rhyming political verses: *Poem on Apollonius of Tyre* (Venice, 1534), by Gabriel Akontianos. It is transmitted by fifteenth-century manuscripts. According to some of these, the poet is Konstantinos Temenes. The text claims to be "translated from a Western original," probably a *Cantare* by the Italian poet Antonio Pucci (1310–c. 1388), the *Istoria d'Apollonio,* itself adapted from the Latin version mentioned previously.

Further Reading

Smyth, H. A. *Shakespeare's Pericles and Apollonius of Tyre. A Study in Comparative Literature.* Philadelphia: MacCalla & Co., 1898: 1–112.

APOSIOPESIS The **trope** of suppression, or aposiopesis (αποσιώπηση), is rare in epic verse and common in oratory and **satire.** The writer stops in midphrase, just before printing some mysterious phrase, so the reader must guess his intention. After a case of aposiopesis, there may be a series of dots, called "silencers" (αποσιωπητικά). The first verse collection by **A. Melachrinós** (1883–1952) had as its title *The Way Leads . . .* (1905). The figure of aposiopesis is actually foregrounded here. The title then became a butt of humor, as other writers vied to complete Melachrinós's cutoff title in parodistic ways, for example, " . . . to the madhouse." The Vizyinós poem "Judge of the Contest" (c. 1882) has a couplet that ends with a vulgar word truncated: "This fellow fell and was choked/Like a pig in the sh——." The full missing word must be "shit" (σκατά). Indeed, the corresponding word in **rhyme,** two lines earlier, is πετᾶ ("he flies").

APOSTOLAKIS, YANNIS (1886–1947) Yannis Apostolakis was appointed to the foundation Chair of Modern Greek Literature at the new University of **Thessaloniki** (1926–1940). He became an influential, aggravating literary scholar, an expert on **Klephtic** poems as well as a debunker of **Palamás.** He studied philosophy in **Germany** and published, on his return to Greece, *Criticism and Poetry* (1915), a study of the life of Thomas Carlyle. He tended to rarefied philosophical formulations on poetry and nationhood, but published the practical *Poetry in Our Life* (1923). He devoted himself with decisive energy to the study of **demotic songs.** His analysis of **Solomós** enjoyed considerable prestige among contemporary readers and critics. Apostolakis abandoned the **folklore** approach, assessing demotic songs solely from a critical standpoint. For those who produced editions or anthologies of demotic poems, he had many hard words.

APOSTROPHE Apostrophe, a term in **rhetoric** or literary analysis, defines an appeal in the vocative (αποστροφή). It may interrupt a narrative passage or a speech and be directed unexpectedly at some person, deity, **Muse,** animal, or object, in the singular or the plural.

APOTHEOSIS The word apotheosis (αποθέωσις) denotes any representation of the human with divine attributes, as in Callimachus's "The Lock of Hair." This poem (source of Alexander Pope's *The Rape of the Lock,* 1714) has an apotheosis of Queen Berenice, who cut off some hair and dedicated it to the Gods as a pledge for the King's safety in war. The lock disappeared, so the court astronomer suggested that it had been elevated as a faint row of seven stars in the northern hemisphere between Leo and Boötes.

ARIAN; ARIANISM The Arian heresy arose from a fourth-century controversy about whether Christ was "of the same substance or "of similar substance" with God. That Jesus was *of same* substance was taught by Athanasios the Great and sanctioned by the First Ecumenical Synod (Nicaea, 325). Arios (280–336), who may have been born in Libya, trained in Antioch and became a presbyter in Alexandria. He taught that the Word is a creature of God and consequently "of different substance" from the Father and so inferior to Him, and not Divine. According to Arius, the second person of the Trinity (Father, Son, and Holy Ghost) is not God, but God's first and perfect Creation. Christ does not co-exist from the beginning of time with God. The Divine Creator is antecedent to Christ. This overturned the trinitarian doctrine "Father and Son are co-eternal" (Ἄμα Πατὴρ, ἄμα Υἱός) and led to dispute for centuries. The West clung to Orthodox views, that is, the absolute unity of the Divine essence. For 100 years or so, the East was largely Arian, and the difference reverberated throughout Byzantium.

ARISTOCRACY Greece had no titled aristocracy. **Phanariots,** who ruled Christian provinces on behalf of the **Ot-** toman court, took the hereditary rank of Prince, but not for use in Greece. The monarchy ran from 1833 to 1974, with abdications, restoration, extralegal acts, one death to the bite of a pet monkey (1920), and one by assassination (1913). Venice's rule of the Heptanese led to titles in many Greek families, and much fuss surrounded the "Golden Book" in which their names were registered. They hoped the monarchy would confirm their aristocracy, but the titles were valid only on the islands. Nowadays, nobility amounts to having the same surname as a hero of the **War of Independence,** such as Alexandros Zaïmis (d. 15 Sept. 1936), ten times Prime Minister, ex-President of the Republic, ex-High Commissioner of Crete, and Governor of the National Bank. When Tsar Alexander of Russia met **Yennadios** on a visit to Odessa, he was so impressed by the patriot and scholar that he offered to bestow an aristocratic title on him. Yennadios turned it down with a quip: "If we Greeks start to become barons [βαρῶνοι], there's a danger that some may discard the 'bar' [βαρ] and remain 'asses' [ὄνοι]."

Further Reading

Forster, Edward S. *A Short History of Modern Greece: 1821–1940.* London: Methuen, 1941.

ARISTOTLE (384–322 B.C.) Manuscripts of Aristotle are the fourth most plentiful in Byzantine culture, after the New Testament, John Chrysostom, and John Damascenus. After 1165, the philosophy professor at the imperial school in Constantinople was required only to lecture on Aristotle. Averroës (1126–1198) wrote a commentary on a mangled version of the *Poetics.* Later, Hermannus translated it into Latin (thirteenth century). This version was published at **Venice** (in 1481 and 1515). Hierotheos the Hybirite (b. 1686), an **Enlightenment** figure who taught at Skopelos after 1723, wrote an analysis of the *Poetics*.

See also BESSARION; SEVENTEENTH-CENTURY ERUDITION; TRAPEZUNTIOS

ARKHAIOFILIA The noun αρχαιοφιλία means "love of the ancient," with a stubborn and prejudiced preference for the classical and Hellenic. It is very close to the term "antiquity worship" (αρχαιολατρία, see following). A pronounced "lover of the ancient" was the Danubian Chief Minister, Iakovos Rizos Neroulos (1778–1849). In his lectures on Greek literary history he found the masterpieces of recent **Cretan** literature "misguided in their vulgar morals, their slavish imitation of Italian literature, and their tedious chatter." Neroulos also considered dialects to be shameful and decadent because the older, learned language was the only form that should be understood right across Greece. Yet this "lover of the ancient" served in several post-Independence ministries, was a State Councillor, and wrote a history of the Uprising. Ancestor obsession (προγονοπληξία) goes in hand with love of what is ancient. Only the classical inheritance is of any value. **Pachomios Rousanos** criticized Kartanos, author of *Flower and Essence of the Old and New Testament* (1536), saying: "It is possible only to write in the ancient tradition. Otherwise, it would be futile that the Ancients composed this admirable work for their descendants: grammar." The obsession also lurks in lyric poetry. Nikos Karouzos (1926–1990), in "Triplets for Beautiful Mistra," evokes the ruined palace of the town where once upon a time

Plethon walked, now a weedy hillock gazing over past Byzantine glory: "Mistra like some innocent passion / Rests its illustrious dead in the sun."

Further Reading

Vryonis, Speros, ed. *The "Past" in Medieval and Modern Greek Culture*. Malibu, CA: Undena Publications, 1978.

ARKHAIOLATRIA The term "antiquity worship" (αρχαιολατρία) refers to an obstinate stance in favor of the archaic. Literary men fall victim to a nostalgia for ancient Athenian institutions. The Cretan Nikolaos Sofianós (early sixteenth century) declares: "Our race has fallen into decadence, and it has no memory of the degree of perfection to which our ancestors had climbed." They harp on "praise of time past," promote ancient orthography, or prize motifs from the tragedians, historians, philosophers, and poets of classical Athens. **Gatsos** (1911–1992) evokes the mood in his plaintive song "Gloria Aeterna": "Wherever we may go, / We bear memories, / Athens and Rome, / We still search you out. / White columns, / And black centuries, / Burdensome years / In this world where we've landed on our own."

Arkhaiolatria shares the conservative values of linguistic **purism.** Asa Briggs warns against the nineteenth-century antiquarians who thought modern Greeks unfit to be the custodians of their ancient treasures: "Byron, who knew his Greek literature, ancient as well as modern, was caustic in dismissing what he called 'antiquarian twaddle.'" Briggs quotes **Seferis** on the splendor and misery of *arkhaiolatría:* "I woke with this marble head in my hands." **Palamás** wrote (in *Life Immovable*) of the "people of relics" that live among the temples and olives of the

Attic landscape. He contrasts their presence with that of the modern crowd, which is like a caterpillar crawling on a white flower. The poet **Sikelianós** talks of the strain to recover classicism in modern archaeology, with its "scattered drums of a Doric column" (in *The Conscience of Personal Creativeness*). He cries out that the end of Plato's journey may be his beginning. In an enthusiastic review (1910) of *Samothrace* (1908) by **Dragoumis, Kazantzakis** remarked that Greece was threatened by an "ancestor-worshipping marasmus." He and his friend Dragoumis considered that the glory of Greece lay in the future, but others still saw it only in the past. Nicolas Calas (1907–1988) expressed the striving for the past from the perspective of a Helleno-American intellectual: "the coherence of history has vanished, cannot be found" (from "Columns of the Temple of Olympian Zeus," trans. Kimon Friar). P. D. Mastrodimitris, in *Reference to the Ancients* (Athens: Goulandrí-Horn Foundation, 1994) analyzes this magnetism in writers who admired classical Hellenism (**Vilarás, Christopoulos, Kalvos, Solomós, Palamás, Kavafis, Sykoutris,** and Kakridis), noting antiquity worship even in translations of classical Greek done in the Demotic.

Further Reading

Briggs, Asa. "The Image of Greece in Modern English Literature." In *Greek Connections: Essays on Culture and Diplomacy,* edited by John Koumoulides, 58–74. Indiana: University of Notre Dame Press, 1987.

ARMATOLÍ The word *armatolí* means "bearers of arms" and refers to Greeks who became guerrilla fighters before the Uprising (1821). They were originally enrolled by their Turkish masters as special guards because Greeks were forbidden to carry weapons during **Ottoman** rule. An area under their control was called a gendarmerie (ἀρματολίκι), as in the mainland of Thessaly, Macedonia, and Epirus. The system began in the fifteenth century, and the first such man-at-arms (ἀρματολός) was Korkodeilos Kladás of Mani, who worked for the Turks around 1490. A later such warlord was Nikolos Varnakiotis, castigated by **Kalvos** in the ninth ode of *Lyric Poems,* "To the Traitor." A decree placed his son, Yeoryios (1780–1842), in the same position, and he served as a man-at-arms under **Ali Pasha.** Before the Uprising, groups of *armatolí* had become mercenaries, hired by their Ottoman rulers to fight, chiefly in mountain areas north of the Isthmus, against Greek nationalist **brigands,** the **Klephts.** Fact and fiction become blurred in these matters. *Armatolí* and Klephts are historical figures and also popular legend. Renowned *armatolí* and their exploits are mentioned in **demotic songs**: Christos Milionis, Bovas Grivas, Malamos, Euthumios Vlachavas, Soumilas, Boukouvalas, Zidros, Stathas, and Andritsos.

Further Reading

Diamanduros, Nikiforos P., ed. *Hellenism and the First Greek War of Liberation, 1821–1830.* Thessalonica: Institute for Balkan Studies, 1976.

ARODAFNOUSA (fourteenth century). See also PARALOGÉS The *Lay of the Queen and Arodafnousa* is from Cyprus. This historical ballad dramatizes, in rhymed **decapentasyllables,** the love of the Lusignan king, Peter I (1350–1369), for a Cypriot girl called Arodafnousa and her murder at the hands of the

Queen (Eleanora). There is real foreboding in the fast tempo of the *Arodrafnousa* narrative. The queen sends her slaves to fetch the girl: "Up and away, Rodafnousa, the queen wants you." The jealous queen tells her victim it is useless to scream for help: "You can shout out once, or shout twice, as often as you like, / The king is too far away to come and save you."

The king, at his table, detects a distant cry and calls for his "black stone-devouring steed." The horse tells him to tighten the bridle and apply his spurs. In the time it takes to say one good-bye, they ride a thousand miles. The king orders his wife to open her tower. He seizes her sixty-inch-long hair and gold-palmed hands and forces her to her own burning. A funeral is then held for Arodafnousa. This poem is a typical **ballad** (παραλογή), which freely alters facts. The adulterous girl was Giovanna Dalema. She did not boast the name redolent of wild plants ("oleander") chosen by the anonymous poet. Her punishment (1369) was kidnapping and torture (according to the fifteenth-century *Chronicle* by L. Machairás).

ARSIS The noun *arsis* (ἄρσις) refers to the metrical rise of a beat and is the opposite of *thesis* (θέσις), or fall of the beat. In classical verse, these were strong (or marked) divisions of rhythm (θέσεις). Weak syllables were "raised" or "lifted" (ἄρσεις). Medieval Latin grammarians inverted these meanings. They began to use *arsis* to refer to the strong (or "marked") element in enunciation and *thesis* for its weak aspect. Modern Greek metrics has retained the Latin modification of the original Greek terms. Music has reverted to the old etymology, so the rise and fall of the conductor's ba-ton corresponds again to *arsis* and *thesis,* respectively.

ART El Greco (Dominikos Theotokopoulos, c. 1541–1614), Greece's greatest painter, worked outside **Hellenism.** He was born in **Crete,** left around 1568, had some contact in **Venice** with Titian, went to Rome (1570) where he changed his name from "Sunday's Child" to a more Catholic Dominikos, and later moved (1577) to Spain. His canvases are famous for their elongated bodies and somber background. His *Landscape of the Gods-Trodden Mount Sinai* (c. 1570) is at the Historical Museum of Iraklion (Crete). The National Gallery (Athens) has his *Resurrection, St. Francis of Assisi, Crucifixion,* and *Covenant of the Angels;* Benaki Museum has his *Adoration of the Magi.*

Mikhail Damaskinós (c. 1530–c.1592) also went to Venice from Crete and so did Yeoryios Klontzas (c. 1535–1608), a religious, miniature, **icon,** and manuscript painter. Klontzas made two paintings based on the Christian victory at the battle of Lepanto (1571). Theodoros Poulakis (Crete, seventeenth century) painted in the strictest Byzantine tradition, whereas Dionysios of Phourna (Agrafa, c. 1670–c. 1744) urged, in the *Painter's Manual,* Greek artists to pursue only Byzantine subjects and style. The studio of Stratis Plakotos (1680–1728) was burned down by order of the Zakynthos administration. Nikolaos Koutouzis (1741–1819) was apprenticed as a child to Doxarás and beside him painted the Church of the Manifestation at Zakynthos (1757). In 1776, he completed the *Litany of St. Dionysios,* which includes 400 faces, some recognizable as local dignitaries. His verse touched on family scandals. An assailant, in 1770, attacked him and wounded his face. So Koutouzis (allegedly) became a priest to hide his scars with a beard. Distressed on the subject of conjugal fidelity (see **Satire**), he improvised a couplet "When the snail wants to come out of his shell, / He puts out his horns, not his head." Still life was a common type in twentieth-century painters such as Theofrastos Triantafyllidis. Still life pictures often illustrate stories in periodicals like *Néa Estía.* Art works collected since 1923 by the Athenian Municipal Art Gallery show the **love of nature** familiar from contemporary Greek fiction.

Meditation on landscape fills the painting of Konstantinos Parthenis (1882–1964), with his studies of the cypress and olive tree, or of Dimos Braesas (1878–1967), with his landscapes from the **Cyclades.** Aimilios Prosalentis (1859–1926), son of the painter Spyridon Prosalentis (1830–1895), executed portraits of Uprising figures, painted a "Merchant of Venice," a "Traviata," and decorated the chapel of the Royal Palace for King George. Nikolaos Kartsonakis's "Street Market" (1939) conveys the folk element that underpins Greek culture. Other such painters are Nikiforos Lytras (1832–1901), who painted the "Hanging of Patriarch Gregory V" or "Burning of the Turkish Flagship by Kanaris," Epameinondas Thomopoulos (b. 1878, professor at the Athens School of Fine Arts 1915–1948), and Yeoryios Gounaropoulos (b. 1889). The latter was a refugee from East Roumeli. He acquired the patronage of **Koromilás** and studied at the Institute of Technology. He won the Averoff **Competition**, gaining a scholarship to Paris. His work was characterized by patches of light and shade, seeming to render his objects diaphanous. Apostolos Yeralís (b. Mytiline, 1886)

won an Averoff scholarship to Paris held exhibitions in the **Parnassós** hall (1926, 1928), and is known for the canvases "Eve of the Feast-Day," "Sleeping Bacchante," "Photographer in the Village," "Forgiveness," and "The Young Fish-Spearer." His brother, Loukas Yeralís (b. 1875), gained a mention at the Rome International Exhibition (1911). He painted "Girl at Embroidery," "Spring-Time with Snow," and "Watering the Flowers," subjects related to the recording of manners genre, **Ithografía.**

L. Yeralís also made sketches to accompany the publication of the story "Village Love Affair" (1910) by Chatzopoulos (1868–1920), the poet, critic, and editor of *Techni*. In one painting, we see the greasy seducer, Yoryis, hat tilted back, hands covering the eyes of a robust woman, who is lacing her boots by a well in a yard under a stumpy tree. She is the wronged heroine, Foni, scarved, wearing a coarse dress, sitting next to a pot of lilies, whose stems seem to point at both her and the man. Some writers illustrate their own books: for example, **Tarsouli** and Nikos Chouliarás (b. 1940) in his short stories *The Other Half* (1987) and his poems *Details of Black* (1993). Highbrow magazines that examine the connection between modern Greek art and literature include *Balance* (Ζυγός), published since 1973, six issues per year.

Further Reading

Christou, Chrysanthos. *The National Gallery: 19th and 20th Century Greek Painting.* Athens: National Gallery and the Ministry of Culture, 1992.

Demos, Otto. *Byzantine Art and the West.* New York: New York University Press, 1970.

Ioannou, Andreas S. *Greek Painting: The 19th Century.* Athens: Melissa, 1974.

Scarce, Jennifer. "Greek Architecture and the Decorative Arts from the 15th to the 20th Centuries: A Select Bibliography." *Mandatophoros,* no. 13 (June 1979): 48–60 and no. 14 (November 1979): 5–15.

Xingopoulos, A. Σχεδίασμα ἱστορίας τῆς θρησκευτικῆς ζωγραφικης μετὰ τὴν ἅλωσιν [Sketch for a History of Religious Painting after the Fall of Constantinople]. Athens: Library of the Archaeological Society of Athens, 1957.

ASIA MINOR DISASTER (September 1922) The Asia Minor Disaster is a watershed in the history of **Hellenism** (see **Venizelos**). On 2 May 1919, a Greek army garrisoned at Smyrna, on the coast of Asia Minor, a city with one of the largest Greek populations in the world. In September 1922, it was sacked by Turkish forces pursuing Greek troops that had pushed far inland. These two defining moments are set to verse by S. Ronás (1893–1969), in his poem "Smyrna and Smyrna": "With the fire and the slaughter / The world and the heavens turned red. / The afflicted saint turns / To bury the dead eagle / In a black mound." The disaster uprooted the Greek inhabitants of Anatolia, making them refugees in a redefined Greece. With Venizelos's mandate from the Allied Powers, the Greeks had advanced into Asia Minor in 1921, but were defeated in 1922 by Turkish nationalist forces under Mustapha Kemal (later Atatürk). In his novel *Fugitive from Death* (1939), Yeoryios Tsakalos (b. 1898), who was wounded in the retreat, describes the suffering of Greek soldiers at the hands of their Turkish victors. Several Greek generals were chosen to take the blame and put on trial under General Othonaios at a court-martial: Gounaris, Stratos, Protopapadakis, Baltazzis, Hatzianestis, Goudas, and Stratigos. The first five, plus Theotokis, were sentenced to be executed. Goudas and Stratigos got life imprisonment.

The treaty of Lausanne (1923) restored the Maritsa River as the frontier between Greece and Turkey in Europe. A separate treaty provided for the compulsory exchange of their two populations. This was supervised by a League of Nations commission. It led to 1½ million Greeks from Asia Minor being settled in Greece. It was the end of 3,000 years of Greek life in Anatolia and a human misfortune that dragged on in shantytowns. Many of those who arrived in Greece spoke Turkish, taught their children Turkish, and lived for decades in poverty. About 800,000 Turks and 80,000 Bulgarians left Greece to be settled in their respective countries. The Greek side of this exodus is told by **Ilias Venezis** in his novel *Calm* (1939). It gains a tinge of Utopian optimism in *The Mermaid Madonna,* by **Myrivilis.** The disaster spawns the title "Untold" in poems by M. Argyropoulos (1862–1949), who imagines events so appalling that they cannot be verbalized: "Nobody will ever tell of / Those unspeakable miseries, / Except by combining fullest intellect, / With the hidden rhythms of Art." The pre-1922 intoxication of Anatolian life is conveyed by Katramopoulos in his novel *How Can I Ever Forget You, Beloved Smyrna?* (Athens: Okeanida, 1994).

Further Reading

Harvey, Julietta. "Memories of Peace and War." *TLS,* 27 Dec. 1991: 17.

Hirschon, Renée. *Heirs of the Greek Catastrophe: The Social Life of Asia Minor Refugees in Piraeus.* Oxford: Berghahn, 1999.

Llewellyn-Smith, Michael. *Ionian Vision: Greece in Asia Minor, 1919–1922.* London: Allen Lane, 1973.

ASMODAEOS The humorous magazine *Asmodaeos* ran weekly from 5 January

1875 to 25 August 1885. It was started by the artist Themos Anninos and directed by **Emmanuel Roidis,** ridiculing the reactionary political party that backed Voulgaris. It relied on the famous light Attic wit, eschewing personal attack or violence of expression. Roidis wrote under the rubrics "Gnats" or "Gusts of Wind." He used pseudonyms such as "Hornet," "Theotoumpis," or "Mr. Mosquito." He produced his columns for each Sunday edition, aiming his word play at contemporary political vices or satirizing social issues. The magazine suspended publication on 11 July 1876 and appeared later with a change of staff, bright young sparks of contemporary Athenian journalism, such as **Yeoryios Sourís, Dimitrios Kokkos, Mikhail Mitsakis,** Aristidis Roukis, Evangelos Kousoulakos, and **Babis Anninos.** The magazine teased and chastised the political leader Charilaos Trikoupis, right up to its final number (25 August 1885). Sourís announced the close of the journal with light verse, in this last issue. *Asmodaeos* was a vehicle for the genius of Themos Anninos, as cartoonist. His light touch in sketching social and political figures gave the emerging Athenian bourgeoisie a pleasant, illusory contact with the corridors of power. His cartoons helped transform Greek society, in Roidis's words, "from a caterpillar to a chrysalis."

ASOPIOS, KONSTANTINOS (1785–1872) The date of birth of the great teacher Asopios is put by some scholars at 1790. A peripatetic scholar in the Heptanese when young, Asopios was another intellectual much influenced by the work of **Koraís**. While professor of classical Greek (from 1842) at Athens, he produced the controversial volume *Critique*

of Soutsos (1853), which contained a detailed investigation of the **purist** poetry of **Panayotis Soutsos** and a response to his conservative manifesto *New School of The Written Language.* Asopios's volume ranges from analysis of Soutsos's texts to prescriptions for modern Greek writing, with comments on Cretan poetry and the validity of the modern Demotic. He evaluates Soutsos's use of lines such as "Power that closes the rising and setting of the sun." A Greek reader of this line would visualize "a door closing." He would interpret the **image** to mean that Napoleon *prevents* the sun from rising or setting, rather than *enclosing* East and West in his power. Asopios admits that formal versification is not the be-all and end-all of poetry. Versification is an adornment of poetry, gives color to its youthful countenance, and may often mask its imperfections, as a horse once masked the lameness of **Byron.** Soutsos should not have composed so many non-rhythmic lines such as "Wild shapes encircling me and many weapons I see." Here Asopios suggests a way Soutsos could have corrected the line. Like his protégé **Roidis,** Asopios praised the forerunners of modern linguistic ideas, namely **A. Christopoulos, I. Vilarás,** and **D. Solomós.** *Critique of Soutsos* amounts to a major work of Greek **literary criticism** and contains an arresting analysis of **alliteration** and **onomatopoeia.**

ASSIZES OF THE KINGS OF JERUSALEM AND CYPRUS The fourteenth-century text known as *The Assizes of the Kings of Jerusalem and Cyprus* is a code of rules setting out public and private rights in the Frankish territories of the East and the crusader kingdom of Jerusalem and **Cyprus.** It defines feudal obligations between the crusaders and their Anatolian subjects. The translation of these French legal systems was first designed for use in Cyprus, but its composition may be later than the reign of King Hugh I (1205–1218).

ASTERISK The asterisk, or "star-shaped sign" (ἀστερίσκος), has five different functions in Greek writing: (1) it was placed by grammarians next to words that they judged to be "excellent"; (2) it could be placed to denote a gap in a manuscript; (3) it might be placed over a suspected scribe or copyist's error (see **Palaeography**); (4) it could be placed before the title of a book to indicate that it was not extant; and (5) in modern texts, the asterisk is placed at the above right of a word. This modern usage draws attention to a footnote concerning the marked word.

ASTROLOGY Certain popular Byzantine books contained beliefs based on the signs of the Zodiac: "If Cancer makes thunder in June, there will be warm spells and sudden pestilence." In a medical tract we read: "Understand that it is not good to draw blood on every date, because there are certain days which are good, and if it chance that someone be bled on a day that is bad, there is a danger they may die." So 10 January is good, but the 2nd, 9th, and 16th are bad. Byzantine manuals of health note the relationship between the different parts of the body and the various astrological signs. Astrology also affects diet: "In August, eat things but make sure you don't have white beet and larvae, as they generate black bile, and this causes overheating, and heavy fever, so eat sage and do not draw blood in any maner."

ATHANASIADIS, TASOS (1913–)
The prolific writer Athanasiadis, born in Asia Minor, worked for several years (1948 to 1961) on a narrative **trilogy,** *The Panthei,* revolving round a fictional family of this name. The saga presents events in three successive generations (1897–1940). It begins with *Days of Beauty* (1948). The second book in the trilogy, *Marmo Pantheu* (1954), traces the heroine's love affair with a cousin of her husband, a painter called Kitsos Galatis. The husband tolerates the relationship because he cannot face an existence without her. The cousin goes to war and is killed, after attaining the rank of second lieutenant, just when Marmo was preparing to elope with him. The saga is completed by a third volume, *The Kerkóporta* (1961), named after the gate of Constantinople that the Turkish conquerors passed through in 1453.

Athanasiadis published an essay on Fotos Politis (1936), that extraordinary intellectual who wrote more than 1,100 articles in his lifetime. Athanasiadis brought out a volume of stories, *Pilgrims of the Sea* (1943), and *Journey into Solitude* (1944), a romanticized biography of **Kapodistrias,** Greece's first President. He wrote a fictional biography, *Dostoyevski: From Labor Camp to Passion* (1955), as well as biographical sketches of V. Hugo, Tolstoy, and Dostoyevski, collected in *Three Sons of Their Century* (1957), *A Life of Albert Schweitzer* (1963), and the essays of *Reconnoiterings* (1965). He was elected to the Academy in 1986, and several of his works were successful on **television**. Some of his books, *The Throne Room* (2 vols., 1969) about 1960s youth, *The Custodians of Achaea* (2 vols., 1975) about the **Colonels' Junta,** *The Last Grandchildren* (2 vols., 1984), about the social reality of Greece after the political change-over, and *The Children of Niobe* (2 vols., 1988), about Salichli on the eve of the **Asia Minor disaster,** have attracted the less-highbrow label of *roman-fleuve* (μυθιστόρημα-ποταμός).

ATHANASIOS OF CONSTANTIA

The writer Athanasios of Constantia, born in Cyprus, studied at the Jesuit college in Constantinople and later at the **Greek College at Rome**. In 1620, he met Cardinal Mazarin and other Catholic dignitaries in Paris. After his conversion from **Orthodox** to **Catholic,** he worked to associate Patriarch Parthenios and the King of France in projects for church union. Athanasios published *Aristotle as Theorist of the Soul's Immortality* (Paris, 1641) and an essay on the primacy of the Pope (Paris, 1662).

ATHENS In the fourth and fifth centuries, the tiny city of Athens attracted figures like Libanius, St. Basil, Gregory of Nazianzus, and Julian the Apostate. Archbishop Akominatos, in a sermon written after 1175, complained that a gang of misers plundered Athens, hunting minute tax profits, and says: "I was made barbarian by a long stay at Athens." In the medieval period, Athens ceased to be a center of civilization. When the fourth **crusade** overwhelmed Constantinople (1204), its Frankish leaders established a Latin Empire, of which the prize was the Duchy of Athens. After Constantinople was reclaimed from the Franks (1261) by Michael VIII Palaeologus, Athens came under nearly 200 years of French, Spanish, or Italian control. An anonymous *On the Reduction and Enslavement of Athens in Attica Caused by the Turks* is a short poem in 69 unrhymed **decapentasyllables,** lamenting the tram-

pling of Athens by marauding Persians (Turks). It was composed a year or so after 1456, when the attack took place. An assault by **Venice** (1687) blew up munitions stored in the Parthenon. Between 1803 and 1812, Lord Elgin dispatched to England the marble friezes of the Parthenon. In the twentieth century, a Greek actress turned Minister, M. Mercouri, lobbied to get the Elgin Marbles returned. Athens prospered through shipping and being selected as Greece's capital (1832). On its image after 1880, the writer Kazantsis (1991) talks of a village growing into a garish hotchpotch, "an ugly hydrocephalous entity stuffed with hideous populism."

See also CHRONICLE OF ANTHIMOS

Further Reading

Bastéa, Eleni. *The Creation of Modern Athens: Planning the Myth.* Cambridge: Cambridge University Press, 2000.

ATTICISM The term "Atticism" refers to a trend in Greek culture that, from the end of the first century B.C., sought a return to the style and vocabulary of Athenian (that is, "Attic") books of the period 450–330 B.C. Atticism is associated with the Second Sophistic period, when orators of the second century A.D. envisaged a return to the technique of the first sophist, Gorgias (fifth century B.C.). Atticism stands for the criterion of antiquity in the **language question.** It contributes to a purist, neoclassical stance, which later motivated the more reactionary partisans of **Katharevousa.** It looks back to fifth- and fourth-century B.C. writing as the standard for all that is balanced and stylish. Atticism rejects **hiatus,** phrases in **meter,** neologisms, slang words, and imports from any other language. No word or construction is admitted by Atticists unless they find it in the forensic writing of Lysias (c. 459–380 B.C.), Demosthenes (384–322 B.C.), or Isocrates (436–338 B.C.). The writing of Lysias, Isaeus, Demosthenes, and Isocrates passed as the last word in polish and harmony. As speech writers, they had perfected the craft of character betrayal (ἠθοποιΐα) and offered a model of clarity (σαφήνεια).

Other Attic models were the historian Thucydides (460–c. 399 B.C.), the philosopher Plato (427–347 B.C.), and **Aristotle** (384–322 B.C.). The fashion for Atticizing flourished with the books on rhetoric, grammar, composition, and history of Dionysius of Halicarnassus (fl. 30 B.C.). It became popular in educated circles across the Roman empire and soon reached the eastern frontiers. The original concern of Atticists was to replace the disjointed prose of the **Hellenistic** period (that is, after the death of Alexander the Great, 323 B.C.) with a style that was tenser. Comparing Polybius (c. 200–c. 118 B.C.) with Thucydides reveals radical alterations of grammar. In Polybius, there are more nouns, many of them abstract, fewer verbs, more verb compounds, and many compound words that gain no extra meaning from their prepositional prefix. Dionysius of Halicarnassus scorned these elements and regarded them as "Asian."

Many thought that correctness (καθαρότης) was achieved by avoiding unusual words, hiatus, or poetic rhythm and by striving for polished syntax and vocabulary. The Greek lexicon could be widened by adding Ionian forms, poetic terms, and compound words, but non-Attic tendencies were to be avoided, such as the sequence "and moreover." In the second century A.D., Attic Greek was taught for imitation, in forensic practice,

letters, and the drafting of speeches (see **Oratory**). Any Greek syntax or vocabulary found in the text of a classical writer was esteemed. This led to a taxonomy, which aligned "correct" next to "incorrect" words for a given concept. Byzantine historians cultivated the archaic turns of phrase in the Attic idioms so elaborately that they could distort the logic of their syntax. Neo-Atticism was supported by teachers of the Greek race during the **Enlightenment,** men such as Panayotis Kodrikas, **Evyenios Voulgaris, Neofytos Doukas, Neophytos Vamvas,** K. Oikonomos (1780–1857), Kommitas, and S. Vyzantios. Writers such as **P. Soutsos** actively espoused it. Attic prescriptivism lurked behind the rearguard action fought by linguistic purism (καθαρίσμος), against the **Demotic** (mid-twentieth century). They did not, of course, expect the common people to write Attic in daily business. Atticism was a matter for poets, biographers, orators, historians, or government: "An extreme adherent of this movement is caricatured by Athenaeus under the nickname *Keitoúkeitos;* he refuses to eat any dish at a banquet unless its name is attested [*keîtai*] in an Attic text" (Browning 1989: 106).

See also DEMOTIC; LANGUAGE QUESTION; PURISM; VULGARIZERS

Further Reading

Babiniotis, G. "A Linguistic Approach to the 'Language Question' in Greece." *BMGS* 5 (1979): 1–16.

Browning, Robert. *History, Language and Literacy in the Byzantine World.* Northampton: Variorum Reprints, 1989.

Bubenik, Vit. "Dialect Contact and Koineization: The Case of Hellenistic Greek." *International Journal of the Sociology of*

Language 99, "Koines and Koineization" (1993): 9–23.

Russell, D. A. *An Anthology of Greek Prose.* Oxford: Clarendon Press, 1991: xiii–xxxviii.

AUTOMATIC WRITING In automatic writing (at the outset of the twentieth century), the hand was supposed to be guided by forces beyond the writer's planning or volition. The hand and pen were self-moving, and acted mechanically, perhaps stimulated by opium or sleeplessness. This avant-garde manner of composition, imported into Greece from France after surrealism in the 1930s, was later popularized by Maurice Blanchot. It produced attempts at automatic, random writing in Greek twentieth-century literature. **Beratis** was praised for elements of automatic writing in his *Whirlwind,* 1961. The poet **Sinopoulos** classified automatic writing, with "fireworks, the absurd, the dream world," as a part of early surrealism, which progressed to a second level, in Greece, when the surrealism of Embirikos ended by "writing in a rational fashion."

Further Reading

Karampetsos, E. D. and Donald Maddox. "Greece's Poet-Chronicler Tákis Sinópoulos (1917–1981): An Interview." *WLT* 57, no. 3 (summer 1983): 403–408.

AUTOPSY. See BIBLIOGRAPHY

AVGERIS, MARKOS (1884–1973; pseudonym of Yeoryios Papadopoulos) The brilliant intellectual Markos Avgeris did his high school at Ioannina and went on to study medicine at Athens. From 1922 to 1927, he was superintendent of textbooks at the Ministry of Education and from 1927 to 1946 was superintendent of workplace health. He married Galateia Kazantzaki (**Alexiou, Galateia**) in 1933. His first poems came out before he was aged 20. In 1904, his play *In Full View of Men* was put on, to critical acclaim, by New Scene, the avant-garde company of **Christomanos**. Pieces by Avgeris came out regularly in *Noumás, Akritas,* **Hegeso,** *Panathinaia, Young Writers,* and *Art Review.* Many of his essays, some showing his **Marxist** orientation, were collected in a 1959 volume entitled *Criticism, Aesthetics and Ideological Matters.* He published a book on **A. Sikelianós** and many articles, on **Kalvos, Solomós, Kazantzakis, Palamás, Seferis,** Tolstoi, Chekhov, Dostoyevksi, Hugo, T. S. Eliot, Maupassant, Shaw, and others (2 vols., 1964–1965). Avgeris was a keen translator. He did the *Peace, Acharnians* and *Wasps* by Aristophanes, *Antigone* and *Electra* by Sophocles, Aeschylus' *Suppliants,* Goethe's *Faust,* Hugo's *Les Misérables,* and Zola's short stories. Avgeris added a plain, utilitarian touch to literature. In 1970, he published his complete poems, *Crossing and Parallel Paths,* which included *The Song of the Table,* popular since it first came out in 1907. He promoted the use of the **demotic language,** composing booklets on arsenic and lead poisoning, as well as on safety and public health.

AVANT-GARDE. See PROTOPORÍA

AXIOTI, MELPO (1905–1973) Melpo Axioti's father was a musician and composer. He founded the arts journal *Kritikí* (1903). Her mother left the family, so consequently she was brought up at home by her father. Axioti went to a boarding school run by Ursuline nuns on the isle of Tinos, and she gained a grounding in French language and literature. She lived and was married for a while at Mykonos. She won a prize with the novel *Difficult Nights* (1938). She brought out the long poem, *Coincidence* (1939). In 1940, she joined the Communist Party, and later was a member of EAM (see **Resistance**). Four collections of realist stories, interviews, and documentary pieces, which she called *Chronicles* (1945), deal in *engagé* manner with events from the war.

Her novel *Twentieth Century* (1949) highlights the contribution to the struggle against Fascism by Greek women and contains a hallucinating description of women and men being transported to execution after the bloodshed of 1 May 1944. During the roll call, the people selected to die hold their breath or take a step forward. In the van, on their final journey to a trench, they toss a torn scrap of their dress or an engagement ring or their name scribbled on a slip of paper, out onto the road behind them. From 1947 to 1964, Axioti was in enforced exile outside Greece (see **Censorship**).

Contraband (1959) was a powerful poem with a left-wing sense of commitment. It gained for Axioti the friendship and collaboration of **Yannis Ritsos.** Her traumatic displacements (France, East Berlin, Poland) and her eventual return to Greece just before the **Colonels' Junta** are expressed in the metaphor of smuggled goods brought back by an age-bound traveler: "The night has opened the skylight, / You, my lady, are brave, / They call you 'mother country' because you shall hide / My contraband for me."

Further Reading

Kakavoulia, Maria. *Interior Monologue and Its Discursive Fomation in Melpo Axioti's Δύσκολες Νύχτες.* Munich: University of Munich, Dept. of Byzantine and Modern Greek Literature, 1992.

Robinson, C. "[Women's Literary Traditions: Regional Essays.] Greece." In *Longman Anthology of World Literature by Women: 1875–1975,* edited by M. Arkin and Barbara Shollar, 420–424. New York: Longman, 1989.

B

BABBLING Callimachus, who hated language as mere babbling, said "A big book is a big misfortune" (frag. 465). In our own time (1970), M. Yialourakis says: "Babbling is the curse of our literature." Excess length (περισσολογία) refers to any verboseness. Greek critics show censure and animosity to all babbling or multiplication of words (πολυλογία). Another term used in **stylistics** is gabbling (φλυαρία). A writer with excess verbiage has a "gabbling style." **Kavafis** says: "When a tale that should be told in fifty pages is written in thirty, it's better. If the author leaves something out, that's not a fault. But if he does it in more than a hundred pages, that's a dreadful fault!"

Further Reading

Kennedy, George A. *Greek Rhetoric under Christian Emperors*. Princeton, NJ: Princeton University Press, 1983.

BALKANS; BALKAN WARS The rulers of Byzantium knew that control of the Balkans was necessary in order to govern out of **Constantinople.** The term "Balkans" designates a chunk of central Europe that includes the present-day Albania, Macedonia, southern Yugoslavia, Bulgaria, southern Romania, Greece, and western Turkey. The Byzantines had seen Bulgars reach the pastures of the south Balkans and set up camp under the ramparts of Constantinople. After their defeat by the "Bulgar-Slayer," Basil II (976–1025), Byzantium's defense was based on a west-to-east belt of untilled plain or heavy woodland that ran from Stara Planina and the Albanian foothills to the River Danube. Passing through this belt of land, inhabited by nomadic Vlachs and pastoralist Serbs, became a nightmare for **crusaders** or pilgrims. The so-called first Balkan War of 1912 refers to the campaign by Montenegro, Serbia, Greece, and Bulgaria to drive out the residue of the **Ottoman** Empire from the Balkan Peninsula.

In the second Balkan War (1913), these four minor powers squabbled among themselves and with Turkey over the territories that they had gained. The chief battles of the first Balkan War were at Scutari, Salonika (that is, **Thessalon-**

iki), and Adrianople (all 1912). The fighting was closed by the treaties of London (1913) and Bucharest (1913). The Balkan Wars led to huge refugee displacements. The Treaty of Lausanne in 1923 sanctioned an exchange of these populations. Turks or Muslims changed places with Greeks, whereas Bulgarians were swapped for Greeks and also Turks. More than 2 million people may have been uprooted during the Balkan troubles of 1912 to 1923. Between 1924 and 1933, about 100,000 ethnic Turks left Yugoslav Macedonia, or its immediate circumference, to emigrate to Turkey. In February 1938, a conference was held at Istanbul by Turkey, Yugoslavia, and Romania to find ways to dispatch Muslim settlers to Turkey in order to replenish the territories vacated by Greeks. This policy liquidated the **Great Idea** forever. The ultimate failure of the Balkan Wars, from Greece's point of view, is reflected in the literature of the **Generation of the Thirties** and the persistent musing of modern Greek poets on the **Asia Minor Disaster.**

See also DRAGOUMIS; THEOTOKÁS; VENIZELOS

Further Reading

Anthias, Floya and Gabriella Lazaridis. *Into the Margins: Migration and Exclusion in Southern Europe.* Brookfield, VT: Ashgate Publishing, 1999.

Stephenson, P. *Byzantium's Balkan Frontier: A Political Study of the Northern Balkans, 900–1204.* Cambridge: Cambridge University Press, 2000.

BALLAD A ballad (μπαλλάντα) is a poem of varying length on an epic or lyric subject, with a rhythmic, lilting treatment, repeating names or descriptions. Shorter Greek ballads had four strophes, each made up of 8 lines, which were equal in syllabic length. These three octaves were then followed by a single strophe of four lines, called a "dispatch" (αποστολή). The last line of each of the four strophes of the ballad is repeated. This pattern is called "return" (γύρισμα). The ballad, familiar in French poetry, was used by writers such as **Karyotakis** and **Vizyinós** (1849–1896). The latter introduced the title βάλλισμα to translate the Western term.

See also DEMOTIC SONG; PARALOGÉS

BARAS, ALEXANDROS (1906–1990; pseudonym of Menelaos Anagnastopoulos) The poet and diplomat Baras, who served in Turkey, came under the influence of **Karyotakism** in the early 1930s and the pessimistic, fantasist escapism of **Ouranis.** The abiding existential gesture of Karyotakis's suicide and the departing of ocean-going vessels fascinated him. The illuminated harbor at night is a topos in his poetry, as is the distant place name, with its promise of foreign fruits and intangible oriental mystery. By these means, he sought to internationalize the fundamentally parochial nature of Karyotakis's pessimism. In Baras's poems of 1933, *Compositions,* Mario Vitti suggests that the poet finds a partial solution to the *impasse* imposed on Greek verse by Karyotakis. From **Kavafis,** Baras acquires an inoculation of new language and new cosmopolitanism.

Further Reading

Baras, Alexander. *The Yellow House and Other Poems,* trans. by Yannis Goumas. Winchester, UK: Green Horse Publications, 1934.

BARBARIAN Greeks were superior, foreigners were "barbarians." Greeks have always been convinced of the intrinsic superiority of their language. "Any non-Greek is a barbarian," said the ancients. Barbarians speak gibberish, so the modern word *barbarian* (βάρβαρος) signifies "uncivilized." **Kavafis** (1863–1933) creates a model in his poem, "Waiting for the Barbarians," of the frontier settlement, dreading an onslaught from abroad. He has a poem about a pupil of Ammonius Sakkas: "Their Greek was disgusting, what blockheads they were." A boyfriend, in Kavafis's poem "Myris: Alexandria, A.D. 340" is a comely youth "reciting verses / With *his perfect feel for Greek rhythm.*" The Christian barbarian is *nicer* because of his Greek. A Syrian, in Kavafis's "To Have Taken the Trouble," declares his pride at not being barbarian: "I'm young and in excellent health. / A prodigious master of Greek."

BARBERINÓS The Barberinós is the name of a codex containing a history of Turkish sultans up to 1512. The text, by an unknown writer around 1515, has a graphic section about the fall of **Constantinople.** Events are seen through the eyes of a simple man of the people. He observes the sordid speculation of nobles, who sold bread that was distributed charitably by the Emperor, before the city fell. He uses plain similes, comparing the entering Ottomans to "a sea roused by a great wind," or "a measureless swarm of bees," whereas Konstantinos Palaeologus is an "Achilles."

BARLAAM AND JOSAPHAT P. Kasimatis (early eighteenth century) translated the *Story [Life] of Barlaam and Josaphat.* This is the only **romance** in prose, or embryonic novel, from Byzantine times. It contains the tale of the three caskets, which Shakespeare later inserted in *The Merchant of Venice. The Story of Barlaam and Josaphat* is based on a biography of Buddha, which had gradually filtered into Christian sources from the East. It was adapted from the Indian *Lalitavistara* in the first half of the seventh century by an unknown monk, Ioannis, from the Mar Saba Monastery, near Jerusalem (Palestine). Tradition made John Damascenus, the saint and hymnographer, its author, but this attribution was refuted by Zotenberg, in *Notices sur le livre de Barlaam et Josaphat,* Paris, 1886, and by Hammel in 1888. Translated into 17 languages, the work was called "popular" (δημοφιλής) in Greece and Asia Minor. It was adapted for Christian **homilies** by changing the names of the characters. The main characters are Abenner, Hindu king of India in the fourth century, prince Josaphat his son, and Barlaam, a hermit from Senaar. The king has been persecuting the Indian Christians, converted once upon a time by St. Thomas. Astrologers forecast that his son Josaphat will be converted to Christianity, so Abenner keeps the boy under guard. Barlaam manages to find and instruct him in the faith. Abenner cannot dissuade Josaphat, so they govern jointly until first father, then son, abdicate. Abenner also adopts the faith and retires as a monk. Josaphat seeks out Barlaam, so that they may pass their declining years in piety. Later, their joint grave causes various miracles. The **Greek Orthodox** calendar celebrates this legend on 26 August.

Further Reading

Boissonade, F. *Anecdota Graeca,* vol. 4. Paris: Royal Printery, 1832.

Migne, J. P., ed. *Patrologiae Cursus Completus . . . Series Graeca in qua prodeunt patres, doctores scriptoresque Ecclesiae*

Graecae a S. Barnaba ad Photium, vol. 96, Paris: Migne, 1857–1866.

BASIC LIBRARY, THE The Basic Library was a fundamental library of texts, completed at Athens in the years 1952 to 1958. The projected aim of Basic Library was to make Greek literature accessible to a new, increasingly educated readership in scholarly reprints. The series was devised and carried out mainly by the publishing house Aetós in 48 volumes, consisting of anthologies, select editions, or typographical reprints of essential texts. The publisher Zacharopoulos carried through the project under the editorship of a writer and literary historian (I. M. Panayiotopoulos) and a philosopher (L. Papanoutsos), together with 53 university professors or literary figures. It is still considered the best tool for the study of modern Greek literature, from its Byzantine origins to the early twentieth century. Volume 1 (Athens, 1956) presents an anthology of the Byzantine poets (ed. Y. Zoras); volume 2 (ed. E. Kriarás, 1955) offers an anthology of the medieval chivalric **romances**; volume 3 presents texts by Byzantine chroniclers and historians. Volumes 4 and 5 (1956) cover texts by scholars and savants from the period of the **Turkocracy.** Volume 6 (1957) gives an overview of literary texts from **Cyprus.** Volume 7 (ed. Faidon Bouboulidis, 1955) covers literary texts from **Crete.**

The philological and discursive writings of **A. Koraís** are selected and glossed by K. Dimarás, in volume 9 (1953). Volume 10 (1954) contains the literary works of Greece's first political martyr, **Rigas Velestinlís.** Volume 11 (1955) presents a selection of texts by the pioneers of the **demotic** movement, Greece's linguistic **renaissance**, including **K. Dapontis.** Volume 12 covers the **Phanariot** writers and the Athenians who developed and expanded their conservative tradition, including **A. Antoniadis.** The poets **Sp. Vasiliadis** and **D. Paparrigopoulos**, such close friends and passionate writers that contemporaries referred to them as "Castor and Pollux," are in volume 13 (1954). Volume 14 (1953) contains prose and poetry from the **Ionian School.** The complete works in Greek by **Solomós** make up volume 15. Primary texts of some of the more important writers mentioned in the present study may be located, for a first convenient reference, in the following volumes of the Basic Library: **I. Vilarás**: vol. 1. **S. Sachlikís**: vol. 7. **Y. Sakellarios**: vol. 11. **A. Soutsos, A. Rangavís, P. Soutsos, S. Koumanoudis, A. Vlachos, D. Kambouroglous**: vol. 12. **A. Kalvos, L. Mavilis, Iakovos Polylás, Ioulios Typaldos**: vol. 14. **A. Valaoritis**: vol. 16 (1954). **A. R. Rangavís**: vol. 17. **Y. Vizyinós**: vol. 18. **E. Roidis**: vol. 20. **Y. Drosinis, A. Provelengios**: vol. 24. **A. Sikelianós, K. Kavafis**: vol. 25. **A. Pallis, A. Eftaliotis, Y. Psycharis**: vol. 26. **G. Xenopoulos, M. Mitsakis**: vol. 27. **A. Papadiamantis, A. Karkavitsas**: vol. 28. **K. Karyotakis, Maria Polydouri, Tellos Agras, I. N. Gryparis**: vol. 29. **K. Theotokis**: vol. 31 (1955). **Ion Dragoumis**: vol. 39. Volumes 46–47 of the Basic Library present a broad selection of demotic songs and ballads; volume 48 presents a selection of **folklore** in prose.

BASIL Basil, the humble plant that girls place at their window, is an icon of Greek domestic life in the nineteenth century. Basil provides the starting point for a miniature by **Souris** (1852–1919) "To the Girl Next Door": "At times you water some jar of yours which / Contains a flowering basil; / At times you set your gaze above the stars, / Or at some gallant bird of passage." **Z. Papantoniou** (1877–1940) focuses on basil and the same verb for "watering" in the five sentimental, laconic quatrains of his poem "Sorrowing Afternoons": "My mind returns / To the narrow, gloomy / Afternoons of a poor area. / I imagine Sunday, there. / In the sun's red glare / The reduced lady, / Without hope or speech, / Waters her basil." **Elytis** talks of girls' dreams ". . . in which basil and mint shed their fragrance." Basil is the symbol of a patrician girl's determination to marry a commoner, in the play by **Matesis,** *The Basil Plant* (c. 1830). The nationalist writer **Ion Dragoumis** commented: "A pot of basil may symbolize the soul of a people better than a drama by Aeschylus." A **demotic song** addressed to a young woman living overseas (part of the *xenitiá* subgenre) offers to dispatch a trio of foods. The last, and the most pathetic, is basil: "An apple would rot. A quince would shrivel. / Basil, unwatered, would wither. / I shall send you a tear in a handkerchief."

BATTLE OF VARNA (fifteenth century) Paraspondylos Zotikós is the unknown author of *The Battle of Varna,* a poem in 465 unrhymed **decapentasyllables** about a campaign (1444) in which the Turks under Sultan Mourat II defeated combined Hungarian and Polish troops, led by the hero Janos Ounuadis (1385–1456), whom he praises fulsomely. The author calls himself "a philosopher desirous of poetic matters" and claims he was an eyewitness of the battle, hidden in a wood. He loads his verse with inserted speeches and letters (in the learned style of the time).

BAWDY. See CENSORSHIP

BEAKIS, AIMILIOS (1884–1951) The greatest male lead in modern Greek **theater** is still considered to be Aimilios Beakis (1884–1951). He was an accomplished writer, publishing *The War Sketches of Aimilios Beakis—An Actor* (Cephalonia, 1914), based on his experiences as a sergeant in the 1912–1913 **Balkan** campaign, and wrote *Songs of Love and the Tap-Room,* verse in varied **meter** (date unknown). His *Villages of the Passes,* a narrative poem in free verse, appeared in 1945. Its title refers to five mountain villages on the shortcut from Thebes to Athens.

Beakis was the darling of Greece, from classical tragedy to farce, boulevard skit, and comic idyll, a virtuoso lead in Hugo's *Les Misérables*; **Shakespeare**'s *King Lear, Othello,* and *Hamlet*; the *Agamemnon* of Aeschylus; Sophocles' *Oedipus Tyrannus*; Eugene O'Neill; Pirandello; Molière; Hauptman; **Ibsen**; Zweig; Grillparzer; Kleist; *The Barber of Seville*; and others. He was in plays by several modern Greek writers: Pantelis Horn, Dimitrios Bogris, *Judas* and *The White and the Black* by Spyridon Melás, the four-act **Palamás** tragedy *Royal Blossom or Trisefyeni,* **Terzakis,** N. Nikolaïdis, and **Koromilás.** His acting was admired by the hard-to-please Fotis Politis.

BEARDLESS MAN, THE MASS OF THE. See SPANÓS

BEAUTY The cult of physical beauty (ομορφιά) extends from the postadolescent human body of the Karyatids on the Acropolis, to various spear carriers, discus throwers, nude Aphrodites, and full-chested sculptures of Zeus that every Greek has seen since childhood. The extensive connotations of "beauty" in Greek literature cover the glamour of friendship, the enchantment of youth, the loveliness of the Attic countryside, and the handsomeness of soldiers and athletes. One line from the poet Konstantinos **Kavafis** expresses the agony as beauty wanes: "he knows he has aged considerably, he senses the fact, he stares at it." The poet **N. Lapathiotis** (1888–1944) wonders if beauty is an illusory wisp, from elsewhere: "And anyway, what exactly does Beauty mean? The secret, distant promise of a happiness that awaits us."

L. Mavilis (1860–1912) in a famous sonnet on Beauty, suggests that a passing girl of the people, coarsely watched at the crossroads by toiling laborers and traders, is nevertheless a creature that can pacify with her looks. Though far from flowering gardens and unlit by the radiance of art, her beauty gives hope and her watchers end up praising her relation to the Holy. This impulse flows through all five periods of Greek literature: ancient, classical, **Hellenistic**, Byzantine, and modern. Each of these five periods shows the same energy and concern for art, which offers beauty when it displays "unity in diversity" (ἑνότητα στήν ποικιλία). The thrust in Greek thought and art is that all things should arrive at form.

BELISARIUS, THE TALE OF (fifteenth century)

A late medieval verse **romance** relates the exploits and unjust punishment of Belisarius, a general under Emperor Justinian I (505–565). Entitled *The Attractive Tale of the Astounding Man Called Belisarius,* this poem amounts to a statement of Byzantine ethnic pride. It is written in a **demotic** idiom, peppered with archaic words. It shows no specific Western influence. Scholars have attributed to **Emmanuel**

Georgillás the second of its three surviving versions, also known as *The Historical Account about Belisarius.* This latter is written in a broader demotic and runs to 840 mixed (that is, rhyming and unrhymed) lines. If Georgillás did write it, he probably adapted a source written down in c. 1390–1399. The first and oldest version of *The Tale of Belisarius* consists of 556 unrhyming **decapentasyllables.** The third version is in 997 rhyming decapentasyllables (Venice, 1525). The unknown author may be aware of certain medieval **chronicles.** The historical dates of some of his characters do not match the narrative date of his poem. Critics call this "anachronism."

The author shows he is no historian: Belisarius is accused, imprisoned, and released so he can head a Byzantine army. Belisarius takes the army to England, defeats the king, and brings him in triumph to Constantinople. The more Belisarius is magnanimous, the more his adversaries become petty. Courtiers spread rumors that Belisarius has designs on the throne. He is falsely accused, imprisoned, and condemned to **blinding.** The work's aim was to arouse in contemporary listeners pity and fear at the pitfalls of political destiny: "The Emperor, when he heard these matters, lost his head and changed completely: / All the fondness which he used to display to Belisarius, / Was now so much spite and fury directed against him."

Further Reading

Van Gemert, A. F. "The new manuscript of the History of Belisarius." *Folia Neohellenica* 1 (1975): 45–72.

Wagner, Guilelmus [i.e. Wilhelm], ed. *Carmina Graeca Medii Aevi,* Leipzig: B. G. Teubner, 1874 [reprint, Athens: Spanos, 1961]: 304–378.

BENTRAMOS, TZANES (sixteenth century) The Greek (Epirot) mother of T. Bentramos may be related to Mercurios Bovas, hero of a text by **Koronaios.** Bentramos was a captain from **Nafplion,** who traded on his own account. He often sailed to Venice. Here he printed (evidently without having the text proofread for errors) *An Account of Virtuous Women and Others Who Were Wicked* (Venice, 1549). This supposedly ethical and didactic work consists of 148 couplets of jovial misogyny, advising "sensible sisters" not to be offended. He says "making an enemy of a crafty woman / Is worse than keeping company with a lion or dragon," warning that the sign of "loose women" (πόρνες) is that they part hair, wash face, fix eyebrows, use pincers, and handle a mirror.

In his *On Avarice Accompanied by Arrogance* (Venice, 1567), Bentramos gives examples of men favored initially by fortune, then brought low by their pride or cupidity, some from ancient history, others from his own acquaintance, with didactic asides and advice on how to avoid miserliness.

BERATIS, YANNIS (1904–1968) The gifted novelist Yannis Beratis published *A Greek Diaspora* (1930) and a fictional biography of Baudelaire (1935), *The Self-Punisher,* and the short stories of *Moments.* He volunteered for military service on the Albanian front (1941) after a crisis following his wife's death. Beratis covered war themes in a diary style, drawing on the details of his experience to compose *The Broad River* (1946). This work, revised in subsequent editions, related day-to-day events during the Albanian campaign. In a similar manner, his *Itinerary of 1943* (1946) depicted the Resistance in the mountains, on the side of the anti-Communist EDES (National Republican Greek League). In October 1943, ELAS had attacked EDES, alleging that the latter was collaborating with the **occupation** forces. In the winter of 1943–1944, Britain attempted to bolster EDES by cutting off the pro-Communist ELAS from supplies and munitions. Beratis later produced an experimental novella *Whirlwind* (1961), with elements of **automatic writing.**

Further Reading

Mackridge, Peter. "Testimony and Fiction in Greek Narrative Prose 1944–1967." In *The Greek Novel: A.D. 1–1985,* ed. Roderick Beaton, 90–102. London: Croom Helm, 1988.

Vasilakakos, Yannis. Ο Ελληνικός Εμφύλιος Πόλεμος στη Μεταπολεμική Πεζογραφία *(1946–1958)* [The Greek Civil War in Post-War Prose, 1946–1958]. Athens: Hellinika Grammata, 2000.

BERGADIS. See APOKOPOS

BERNADIS, ARGYROS (1659–1720) Bernadis studied, like other seventeenth-century Greek scholars, at St. Athanasios College (founded 1581), in Rome. He converted to Catholicism. Later he returned to the Orthodox creed. He composed the foundation rules for the Monastery of Mega Spilaion (at Kalavryta). Bernadis wrote lives of two Thessaloniki brothers, St. Symeon and St. Theodoros, who founded the hermitage (362 A.D.), a place steeped in Orthodox piety, built where an icon by the Evangelist Luke depicting the Mother of God was found.

BESSARION, IOANNIS (c. 1403–1472) Bessarion was at one time a candidate for the Papacy. Carpaccio (c.

1455–1526), in *The Vision of St. Augustine,* paints St. Augustine with the face of Bessarion, posing him as a pensive **humanist**. Initially, Bessarion took a number of Greek manuscripts to Italy. Later, he made a living as an itinerant humanist and teacher of Greek. Bessarion was the most famous pupil of **Plethon.** He was appointed Cardinal (1439) by Pope Eugenio IV and also worked to unite the **Orthodox** and Roman churches. Plethon's attack on **Aristotle** brought Scholarius into the issue, and also the Archbishop of Nicaea, Bessarion himself. He composed a treatise in four books, *Against a Detractor of Plato* (1469, *In calumniatorem Platonis*) to refute the neo-Aristotelian stance taken by **Trapezuntios** against **Plato**. From 1444 to 1450, Bessarion was engaged in translating Aristotle's *Metaphysics,* Theophrastus, and the *Memorabilia* of Xenophon. Bessarion's lifelong project was a *concordia filosofica,* the harmonizing of Plato and Aristotle. He was a possible candidate for Pope in two conclaves. He donated 800 classical codices to St. Mark's in **Venice.** His bequest became the nucleus of the renowned Marciana library collection.

Further Reading

Copenhaver, B. P. and C. B. Schmitt. *A History of Western Philosophy: 3. Renaissance Philosophy.* Oxford: Oxford University Press, 1992.

Lautner, P. "Theophrastus in Bessarion." *JHS,* no. 115 (1995): 155–160.

Wilson, N. G. *From Byzantium to Italy: Greek Studies in the Italian Renaissance.* London: Duckworth, 1992.

BIBLE In 1493, Yeoryios Choumnos (in **Crete**) circulated *The Creation,* a paraphrase in 15-syllable verse of the first two books of the Old Testament (*Genesis; Exodus*). This work consists of 2,800 rhyming **political verses.** In the mid-sixteenth century, Ioannikos Kartanos (see **Prison**) produced an **encyclopedic** work on the doctrinal, historical, ethical, and ceremonial aspects of Scripture, namely *The Flower and Essence of the Old and New Testament* (Venice, 1536), with passages transposed into simplified Greek. The problem in the period before Greece's independence was this: Should the Bible be translated? Translations of the Gospel, and other religious texts, by **Catholic** or Lutheran missionaries, who were spreading their own religious cause among the repressed Greek population of the seventeenth and eighteenth centuries obliged Greek clerics (hoping to head off these foreign zealots) to insist that translation of the Gospel was an anti-religious matter. Indeed, they declared that the Greeks, in order to save their religion and their ethnicity, ought to stick to the ancient language, the treasury of their forebears. So the truth was to be found in the archaic and unspoilt Bible, and the New Testament would not need a translation till the Gospel Riots of 1901 (see **Pallis**). In modern times, **Seferis** made sensuous translations from "Revelation" and "The Song of Songs." Iosef Eliyiá (1901–1931), Greece's most famous Jewish writer, sought refuge in the pages of the Bible, cultivating in his moody poetry the idealized, peaceful, deserted spots of Old Testament stories. He developed a kind of Israelite "idyll" to counter his personal anguish. He also made sensitive translations from psalms, or "The Song of Songs," and wrote poems about Jesus, Ruth, and the festival of Purim. The doctor-savant Kostas Frilingos (1882–1950) was known for his verse versions of "The Song of Songs"

(1912), "The Book of Job" (1931), and "The Psalms" (1947). Leontios Chatzikostas (b. 1918), a religious write and Orthodox priest in London, Djibouti, and Cyprus, composed *Sursum corda* (1965), *Jeremiad* (1962), versions in verse from books of the Old Testament with prefaces and commentary, as well as *Ecclesiastes* (1966), and *The Immaculate* (1967). The poet Panayotis Sinopoulos (b. 1928) translated from ancient Hebrew poetry and also turned his attention to biblical translations such as *The Revelation of John* (1965) and to simple songs on Isaiah, Job, and Jeremiah.

BIBLIOGRAPHY (as literary activity) Bibliography, the description and listing of books by subject, is a Greek invention. At first the word *bibliography* signified "writing of books." Born in E. Libya, and a student at Athens, Callimachus (c. 305– c. 240 B.C.) worked in the great library of Alexandria (Egypt) and is said to have written 800 books. Ptolemy II commissioned from Callimachus a list of the papyri in his library. The resulting Catalogue (Πίνακας) amounted to 120 volumes "about those who have shone in all areas of learning." It is seen as the foundation of all future cataloguing and bibliography. **Photius** (820–891) was an avid reader and describer of books (in his *Amphilochia* and *Myriobiblos*). Studying at different monasteries during his various periods of exile, Photius read and annotated hundreds of authors in different texts. He used to mark pages he had seen with the note "has been read" (ΑΝΕΓΝΩΣΘΗ).

A handful of scholars like Photius, or the unknown compiler of the **Suda, Psellus,** or **Plethon** labored to master access to the whole of classical writing. Since those times, the invention of printing (c. 1440) and the growth of publishing have transformed book citation. "Self-sighting" (αὐτουία) is the actual viewing of any book or manuscript that the bibliographer is describing. If a bibliographer cannot look at the volume cited, there is a risk of copying a "misprint" (τυπογραφική αβλευία) in the front matter (date, publisher, printer, city, title, author's name). One Greek bibliographer writes that "the * in front of a comment on a book shows that it has *not* been physically seen."

BIBLIOGRAPHY OF MODERN GREEK LITERATURE Y. I. Fousaras's *Bibliography of Greek Bibliographies from 1791 to 1947* (Athens: Estía Bookshop, 1961) is an essential tool (see **Gkinis; Katsimbalis**). To capture information on a national culture, one starts with Th. Besterman, *A World Bibliography of Bibliographies; and of Bibliographical Catalogues, Calendars, Abstracts, Digests, Indexes, and the Like* (Lausanne: Societas Bibliographica, 1966). The *Bulletin analytique de bibliographie hellénique* (Athens: Institut français d'Athènes, 1947–) contains data on mainstream publishing, and some 500 periodicals. Petros Kasimatis (d. 1729) assembled *The Catalogue of Most Frequently Used Church Texts,* an essay on the fear of God (1718) and a catalogue of hymns, introits, and glorificatory chants "from the most solemn religious festivals."

In 1845, Vretos Papadoupoulos (see **Kapodistrias**), a father of modern Greek bibliography, completed his *Catalogue of Books Printed from the Fall of Constantinople to the Year 1821 by Greeks, in the Everyday Spoken or the Classical Greek Language.* He even published an appeal to the people of Levkas to collect funds for the foundation of a Greek printing press (1859). Faidon and later Glykeria Bouboulidis drafted from 1958 to the 1980s an annual bibliography of works in modern Greek literature and of works about them. The Bouboulidis series attempts complete capture and deals with books, or articles on books, published in the year surveyed.

An initiative from the Department of Modern Greek, University of Sydney (1998), is Michael Jeffreys and Viki Loulavera, *Early Modern Greek Literature: General Bibliography (1100–1700).* This census, with over 4,000 entries, is the second volume of a project that the authors began (Sydney, 1997) with *1,500 Facsimiles* [πανομοιότυπα] *Drawn from the Plates of Greek Manuscripts Containing Folk Literature.* It is reviewed in *The Literary Journal* (Φιλολογική, 17, no. 66: 64). The *MLA Bibliography* (USA) briefly describes articles, chapters, books, and proceedings printed about modern Greek literature by a very large sample of publishers and journals. Modern Greek literature, in the *MLA Bibliography,* had its own section from 1968 to 1983; since 1984, it has been classified under Balkan. *MLA*'s boundary dates for the Byzantine period are 300 to 1499, by no means a conventional **periodization.** It lists works on authors, by century, from 1500 to 1999. There are 11,500 titles relevant to recent Greek items collected in Heinz Richter's *Greece and Cyprus since 1920: Bibliography of Contemporary History* (Nea Hellas Verlag, 1984).

See also CHRESTOMATHY; ENCYCLOPEDIA; EPITOME

Further Reading

Blum, Rudolf. *Kallimachos: The Alexandrian Library and the Origins of Bibliog-* *raphy,* trans. by Hans H. Wellisch. Madison: University of Wisconsin Press, 1991.

BIOGRAPHY The genre "Lives of Illustrious Men" goes back to antiquity. Xenophon (also the first novelist) wrote an *Agesilaos.* Isocrates composed a life of Evagoras. Biography flourished in **Hellenistic** times and was popular reading matter at Alexandria. The key work in this genre is Plutarch's *Parallel Lives.* Among the earliest exponents was Dicaearchus (third to second century B.C.), who wrote biographies of earlier Greek writers. Other biographers are Fanias, Clearchus, Hermippus, Idomeneas Lampsachinus, Aristoxenos, and Antigonos Karystios. In the sixth century, Theofilos wrote a biography of the Emperor Justinian; Hesychius of Miletus composed a **nomenclature** (Ὀνοματολόγος), which collects the kind of biographical information that was agreeable to Byzantine readers and became, in turn, a source for the **Suda.** Under Turkish rule, Greeks devoured biographies of Napoleon, Peter the Great, or the Wallachian prince Nikolaos Mavroyenis.

Fundamental biographies covering four centuries of modern Greek authors are in K. N. Sathas's *Modern Greek Writing: Biographies of Those Greeks Who Achieved Distinction in Letters from the Time of the Overthrow of the Byzantine Empire to the Greek National Uprising, 1453–1821* (Athens, 1868, photographic reprint by I. Chiotellis Editions, 1969).

The tradition remains ingrained in modern culture. Potted biographies of many Greek writers can be found on the school syllabus for literature. In his *The Greek Mirror,* D. Alexandidris, an **Enlightenment** scholar, compiled elevating biographies of Greek achievers prior to the fifteenth century and of various ecclesiastical writers (see **Encyclopedia**). In 1865, E. Stamatiadis published his collection, *A Biography of Such Greeks as Worked as Grand Interpreters for the Ottoman Government*. Between 1958 and 1964, Konstantinos Bobolinis edited *The Great Greek Biographical Lexicon,* in five volumes (published by *Industrial Review* editions). Of similarly wide scope is the *Biographical Encyclopedia of Greek Writers,* by D. P. Kostelenos (four vols., Athens: Pagoulatos Brothers, 1976). A supplement to this is D. Siatopoulos's *Literary and Biographical Encyclopedia of Greek Writing* (Pagoulatos, 1981). In the early twentieth century, the fictional biography became popular. Its leading exponent was Spyros Melás. With the centenary of the Greek Uprising (1930), he embarked on texts such as *Adamantios Koraís, The Lion of the Epirus, Manto Mavroyenous, The Friendly Society, Blooded Cassocks, Admiral Miaoulis,* and *The Old Man of the Morea* (that is, **Th. Kolokotronis**).

Further Reading

Malclès, L. -N. *Les sources du travail bibliographique,* Tome II, *Bibliographies specialisées (Sciences Humaines).* Genève: Droz, 1965: "Grèce Moderne," pp. 795–799.

BIRD STORIES (c. fourteenth century)

The *Discussion of Birds* is an amusing attempt at a medieval *ornithologicum compendium* (digest of bird science). It runs to 668 **political** lines and is preserved in eight different manuscripts. The king of the birds, "golden eagle the great," summons all kinds of birds to the wedding of his son, and they appear at the feast in pairs. They describe their own virtues while criticizing the defects of others. The text reflects the way Byzantine observers tried to account for different characteristics of animal behavior. Why, for example, does the goose waddle from left side to right, with its neck pointed upward and its body shortened? This strange gait is due to the fact that the goose was once a slave, stole thread from its mistress, hid the thread in a purse under its legs, and had to wobble like this to conceal the theft. The animals' dispute causes the eagle, as ruler, to threaten to send in the falcon and the hawk to attack his guests. In this plot (unlike other **animal stories**), the birds settle down. The marriage celebration can be completed. A nautical compass, mentioned in the text, dates this work not to the early thirteenth century (with K. Sathas), but to the first half of the fourteenth. There are allusions to contemporary Byzantine church and society.

Further Reading

Tsabaris, Isabella, ed. Ὁ Πουλολόγος [Critical edition with introduction, notes and a glossary]. Athens: Cultural Foundation of the National Bank, Βυζαντινὴ καὶ Νεοελληνικὴ Βιβλιοθήκη [Byzantine and Modern Greek Library], no. 5, 1987.

BLINDING

Byzantium's rulers used blinding (τύφλωσις) to punish treason and check usurpers. Constantine V won a civil war (742–744) against Artavasdus (Leo III's son-in-law) and obeyed the precept "Thou shalt not kill" by blinding, rather than executing, the rival claimant, his two sons, and a handful of officers. Later he had his own supporter Sisinnius blinded. Irene (of the Isaurian dynasty) arranged for her young son to be removed from the Imperial throne and blinded, so that she could be Empress (797–802). Basil II (the "Bulgar Slayer," 985–1025) turned from fighting the Fatimids to the Bulgarians (1001). After defeating them at Kleidion in 1014, he caused thousands of prisoners to be blinded. Their king died of horror.

Ambelás won a **Lassaneios** prize with his play *Schlirina,* based on Constantine IX Monomachus's mistress, rival to his wife Zoe (980–1050; reigned 1028–1050). Zoe's adopted son Michael had been blinded (1042) so Zoe might reign with her sister Theodora. When Zoe married her fourth husband, Monomachus (1042), she lost most of her power and retired to the women's apartments, where she shared a gilded prison with girls favored by her husband. Manuel Olobolos (b. c. 1250), who is known from the *History* of **Pachymeris,** succeeded (1267) **Akropolitis** as head of logic and rhetoric at the University, founded by Michael VIII Palaeologus. Olobolos taught there for six years. He was condemned by Michael VIII to have his nose and lips removed because he criticized the Emperor for having the nominal successor to the throne blinded. Olobolos's lips were partly spared, as he needed them to teach.

Further Reading

Treadgold, Warren. *A History of the Byzantine State and Society.* Stanford, CA: Stanford University Press, 1997.

BLUE AND WHITE The colors on the Greek nation's blue and white flag (η γαλανόλευκη) are seen as a symbol of its land and sea: chalk-white houses over the deep-blue Aegean. **Elytis** wrote about houses that become more white because of their surrounding of blue, and cries "My God, how much blue you waste just to keep us from seeing you!" A character in the novel *Argo* (1933) by **Theotokás,** exclaims when he sees the Greek flag fluttering over the Palace that it is "a re-

ally pleasing combination of colors and lines."

BOGOMILS. See **ORTHODOX CHURCH, GREEK**

BOOK Books were first written on Egyptian papyrus. Ptolemy VI prohibited export of papyrus from Egypt, in an attempt to choke the **Hellenistic** library at Pergamum, which had begun to rival the **library** of Alexandria. In 196 B.C., King Eumenes II, who had founded the Pergamene library, foiled Ptolemy's edict on papyrus by ordering the farming of sheep and calves for the mass production of their cured skins. This introduced the making of "parchment" for books and was the last major step in book production before the **Renaissance** used paper rolls. For hundreds of years after the German invention of printing types (c. 1440), Greeks looked to Venice, Vienna, or the patriarchate of **Constantinople** for the printing, binding, and publication of books. Aldo Manuzio (1449–1515), the Venetian printer of Greek classics and other texts, was the first to issue lists of book prices (τιμοκατάλογοι) to attract orders from overseas. When Napoleon disembarked his invading forces in Egypt (1798), he took with him types for a Greek printing press. D. K. Vyzantios's popular play *Babylon* (**Nafplion**, 1836) was initially scorned in literary circles. But up to 1879, the printed version went through 11 editions. The play was hawked by itinerant booksellers at crowded street corners, along the sidewalks, and even in church vestibules.

Nikos Nikolaïdis (1884–1956) was a bookbinder before he became a writer. Orphaned, and of poor family, he worked at a bindery (βιβλιοδετείο) and then became an **icon** painter (αγιογράφος). He used his skill at painting to illustrate books. He circulated *The Monk's Book* (1951), a condemnation of the monastic life, as a manuscript in 150 copies, photocopied, with post-Byzantine characters and the writer's own illustrations. Many publishers, in nineteenth-century Greece, broke up their texts with engravings or illustrations inside leather-bound books (δερματόδετα βιβλία). The cloth-bound book (πανόδετο βιβλίο) came later, with the larger market created by Greeks studying beyond elementary school. Books with hard backs were followed in the 1950s by the first paperbacks (χαρτόδετα βιβλία). Soon came slim volumes to fit in the pocket (βιβλία τσέπης). Some Arabized Greeks printed their books with pagination from right to left, for example, Kostas Foteinas of Cairo with his prose composition *The Governance of Souls* (Athens, 1955).

Further Reading

Baskozos, Yannis N. "The Book in Greece the Last Twenty-Five Years: From Ideology to the Marketplace." *Hellenic Quarterly*, no. 9 (June-August 2001): 21–24.

BOOK OF TROY, THE The **Byzantine romance** called *The Troy Book* is based on a twelfth-century *Chronicle* (by K. Manassís). This poem, of just over 1,000 lines, was found in a sixteenth-century manuscript. The Trojan hero is reinvented as a courtly interloper. Shipwrecked on his way to Helen's castle, he inveigles the Greek queen after adopting the disguise of a monk. Their love is thwarted by a retaliatory expedition of Greek forces.

Further Reading

Bianchi Bandinelli, Ranuccio. *Hellenistic-Byzantine Miniatures of the Iliad*. Olten: Graf, 1955.

Scherer, Margaret R. *Legends of Troy in Art and Literature*. New York: Phaidon Press, 1963.

BOOKSHOP Grouped on or around Solonos Street near the University in Athens, many bookshops publish, or act as a front window for publishers, like the bookstore of the journal *Estía*, said to be the oldest in Greece.

Further Reading

Winters Ohle, E. *Buchproduktion und Buchdistribution in Griechenland: Probleme und Eigentümlichkeiten des griechischen Buch und Verlagswesen*. Bochum: University of Bochum Press, 1979.

BOOKS IN PRINT. See PUBLISHING

BOUBOULIS, ANTONIS (seventeenth century) The Cretan intellectual Antonis Bouboulis was inspired by the zeal and Hellenism of the Flanginianon College (Venice). While working as a priest of St. George's (the Orthodox community's church), he composed what is in essence the first Greek **patriotic** poem. With the title "Lament of the Glorious City of Athens on the Cruel and Grievous Death of her Beloved, Loyal, Well-Born Citizen Michail Libona, of Lasting Memory, Unjustly and Unrequitedly Killed in her Service" (Venice, 1681), Bouboulis's poem, in 532 lines, makes the city cry out for its favorite son, his dear friend, murdered by the Turks: "how much my heart is in pain." The lines convey a new vigor of patriotism: "so these matters may reach the ears of every nation and race." He also wrote an "Epistle to the Athenians," in 96 lines of verse.

BOULEVARD. See COMEDY

BOUMI-PAPPÁ, RITA (1906–1984)

The versatile author Rita Boumi-Pappá wrote stories about the **German occupation** (*When We Were Hungry and Fought*). She married the militant critic and poet Nikos Pappás, with whom she produced a two-volume *Anthology of World Poetry* (1952, 1963). She became a prolific literary figure, running journals, writing for children, publishing her own verse collections (seventeen, between 1930 and 1977), contributing a number of entries to the Greek *Encyclopedia of Women* (1969), and translating: Carducci, *Poems,* Carlo Levi, *Christ Stopped at Eboli,* Sholokhov's *And Quiet Flows the Don* (see **Pengli**), Pasternak, Anna Akmatova, Brecht, Neruda, Gabriela Mistral, and Samuel Beckett. She adapted Victor Hugo's *Les Misérables* for the theater (1952). Her verse collection *A Thousand Murdered Girls* (1963) represents the last words of women sent to court-martial and executed after participating in **the resistance,** some of them defended by her husband Nikos, who was also an attorney.

Further Reading

Ἐγκυκλοπαίδεια τῆς Γυναίκας, τόμος Δ΄, μέρος ἕβδομο [Woman's Encyclopedia, vol. IV, Part 7] . Athens: Encyclopedic Knowledge Editions, 1964.

BOUNIALÍS, MARINOS TZANES (d. 1686)

The struggle between the Venetians and the Turks (1648–1669) is told in 12,000 lines by Bounialís, in his *Relation in Verse of the Fearful War Which Took Place on the Island of Crete.* This narrative poem in **political** couplets is full of striking scenes and relates atrocities at which Bounialís was an eyewitness, such as the capture of Rethymno, his town. He fled to the Heptanese and then **Venice** (where he was ordained a priest) when Chandace was handed over to the Turks.

BRAILAS, ARMENIS PETROS (1812–1884)

The itinerant intellectual P. Armenis Brailas studied law and philosophy at Paris. He was the first Greek to teach natural theology as a discipline in its own right. At Kerkyra, in 1848, he founded a political party opposed to the Radicals, who wanted to wrest the **Ionian Islands** from British control by force. He ran a **newspaper** called *Hellas* (with **Alexandros Rangavís**, at Athens). He published a stream of articles and books on ontology, on the great German philosopher Immanuel Kant (1724–1804), on religion, and on epistemology. In 1852, he was elected President of the Ionian Senate. In 1854, he was made professor of philosophy at the Ionian Academy (founded 1824). After unification of the Heptanese with the mainland, Brailas became an impassioned advocate of Kerkyra, which he represented at Parliament. He became Minister of Foreign Affairs (1865) and published newspaper pieces in favor of the Cretan insurrection of 1866. He held ambassadorial posts at London (1867), Constantinople, Petrograd, and Paris. He represented Greece, together with Theodoros Deliyannis, at the Congress of Berlin (June 1878).

Further Reading

Moutsopoulos, Evanghelos. *Petros Brailas-Armenis.* New York: Twayne Publishers, 1974.

BRAVE YOUNG MAN. See PALIKARI

BRAVE YOUNG WOMAN

Any brave young man (παλικάρι) shot in **the re-**

sistance or the **Civil War** might have a female counterpart. A song of the late 1940s recognized this, declaring that each girl who fell for the cause had earned the right to be called "a red lily of the field." J. Hart calculates that as many as a third of all Greek women took some part in the resistance. Hundreds were shot. The poet Victoria Theodorou declared in one of her poems that she was "only a sparrow inside the river reeds," but would not be among the birds who flew away in winter. Argiro Koklovi tells of "Noble Katerina" (from Fourne, Crete). This woman, a war widow at 21 and mother of two, took hold of an old man's gun while her children huddled in a cave. After the liberation, she was tried and executed for "antinational" activities. Nausika Flenga-Papadaki tells, in "Save the Children," about a group of four women who staged Aristophanes, or skits on war, or shepherdesses in distress, to ensure the supply of relief to villages where kids were starving.

See also FEMINIST ISSUES

Further Reading

Hart, Janet. *New Voices in the Nation: Women and the Greek Resistance, 1941–1964.* Ithaca and London: Cornell University Press, 1996.

Fourtouni, Eleni, ed. and trans. *Greek Women in Resistance. Journals—Oral Histories.* New Haven, CT: Thelpini Press/Chicago: Lake View Press, 1986.

BRIENNIOS, NIKIFOROS (c. 1062–1138)
The eminent historian Nikiforos Briennios came of a celebrated Byzantine house. The family originated from Adrianople and established itself in Constantinople halfway through the eighth century. The Briennios family disputed the imperial throne in the eleventh century. His father was **blinded** by the successful Alexius Comnenus, but allowed to continue his court functions as a non-threatening general. Nikiforos, also a general, was considered charming and was selected by the Emperor to marry his learned daughter, **Anna Comnene.** He was given the exalted title *Kaisar.* He composed his *Annals* about Alexius in the form of praise and careful commemoration. **Psellus** in his *Chronographia* covered the period 976–1077, that is, almost to the end of the reign of Michael VII Doukas (1078). His closing period is also covered by Briennios, who manages to reach the period before his admired and beloved father-in-law came to the imperial throne (1081). He sets events out in a reliable way, using standard administrative and political sources.

BRIGAND STORIES Stories based on rural brigandage (λησteia) were popular in nineteenth-century Greece. There was a fusion between **Klephts,** sea pirates, brave young men, and romantic loners. The typical brigand is a crook with a heart of gold. Alexis Politis points out that once the **Independence** struggle was over, the armed irregulars broke up and went home in the 1830s. However, people went on reciting bandit songs as before, adapting them to the evolving reality of brigandage under King Otho. Bandit songs in the free kingdom carried forward the outmoded Klephtic songs, especially those that honored the brigand who stole the richest foreign herd. The writer **D. Paparrigopoulos** published an anonymous essay, before finishing high school, entitled "Reflections of a Brigand: Or the Condemnation of Society" (1861). In this pamphlet, he declared that the law may deplore the phenomenon of brigands, but it will not curb them. From

1834 till the early years of King George I, the mountains of Greece were riddled with brigands who were given help, and even support, by the peasants. The atmosphere was redolent with nostalgia for the Klephts and *armatolí*.

In Andreas Moskonisios's essay *The Mirror of Brigandage in Greece* (Ermoupolis, 1869), we meet the notion that two-thirds of a typical band would be Vlach shepherds and only one third would be Greeks (either peasants or runaway soldiers!). In 1853, 92 percent of Greeks lived outside towns or cities. Brigandage was regarded as a response to oppressive taxation by the **Greek monarchy,** which led members of the population literally to "take to the mountains." In the 1920s, brigand stories in pulp fiction serials began to flourish.

The most frequently met bandit hero is Aimilios Athenaios; others are called Pavlos Argyros or Aristotelis Kyriakos. Often the Vlach peasant girl falls at the feet of the local brigand chief. Ever compassionate, he avenges her rape, or forces a cruel property owner to marry her, or restore money that is used to give local maidens a nuptial dowry. The villagers appeal to the brigand as "Oh my Protector," "my captain," and even call his mother "Mrs. Captain." His relatives explain that he is a rebel or crossed in love, but not a crook. In one story, the village priests pass round the offertory plate at a church service, "to help Yannis Tsoulis and his lads."

In April 1870, a day trip to Marathon by a band of British and Italian tourists that included Lord Muncaster led to capture by the brigands Takis and Christos Arvanitakis, who demanded a ransom and amnesty. The Prime Minister (Thrasyboulos Zaïmis) refused, the male tourists were put to death at the village of Dilessi (in Boeotia), and the European press raised a hue and cry. Gladstone and his Foreign Secretary, Lord Granville, averted an Anglo-Hellenic crisis, the Zaïmis cabinet resigned, and future Greek governments moved to suppress the phenomenon of banditry.

Further Reading

Dermentzopoulos, C. A. Το ληστρικό μυθιστόρημα στην Ελλάδα [The Bandit Novel in Greece]. Athens: Plethron, 1997.

Koliopoulos, John S. *Brigands with a Cause: Brigandage and Irredentism in Modern Greece, 1821–1912.* Oxford: Clarendon Press, 1987.

BYRON, GEORGE GORDON NOEL, SIXTH BARON (1788–1824)

The writer Lord Byron is the foreigner most associated with Greek literature. He is the subject of odes by **Solomós** (1824), **Kalvos,** and Achilleus Paraschos. From a modern collection of poems, Nasos Vayenas's *Roamings of a Non-Traveler* (1986), he appears as "Lord Byron at Rethymnon." Before the final Turkish capture of **Missolonghi** (April 1826), the activity of the European **Philhellenes** and particularly the death of Byron "shamed the Christian rulers of Europe into recognizing that the war in Greece was a disgrace to civilization" (Woodhouse 1991: 143). At the age of 19, Byron had published translations from Euripides. Between 1809 and 1811, he roamed Portugal, Greece, and Turkey. In Albania, he commenced *Childe Harold*. Poems on Greek themes drawn from this journey are *The Bride of Abydos, Giaour* (1813), and *The Corsair* (1814).

Scandal and romantic devilry drove him out of England. This appealed to the Greeks, who still name children after him. *Don Juan* (1824) describes his hero's journeys from Seville through Greece and Turkey. **Love of nature** inspired Philhellene passages in *Don Juan,* for example, the hymn to the "Islands of Greece" in Canto IV. Byron's enthusiasm for national liberation movements made him well known to the political insurgents of Europe. In 1823, he was elected a member of the Greek Liberation Committee. In *The Corsair,* Byron contrasts Greek civilization with Turkish villainy, by way of erotic passion, imprisonment, disguised Dervishes, and drunk Muslims. In January 1824, he joined the uprising at Missolonghi, in a gesture to aid the Greek struggle by money and personal example. He died of malaria on 19 April. The writer **D. Kambouroglous** translated Byron's famous ballad with its Greek title "My life, I love you," which starts "Maid of Athens, ere we part." Goethe cast Byron in the figure of Euphoria in the second *Faust.* Byron is the subject of paintings by J.M.W. Turner and Eugene Delacroix; of music by Schumann, Berlioz, and Tchaikovsky; of operas by Donizetti and Verdi; and of poems by Alexander Pushkin, Heinrich Heine, and Alfred de Musset.

Further Reading

Tsigakou, Fani-Maria, ed. *Lord Byron in Greece.* Athens: Ministry of Culture and British Council, 1987.

BYZANTINOLOGY There is a huge body of scholarship round Byzantine literature and antiquities. This is known as Byzantinology and covers the study of icons, heresy, army, tax, magistrates, liturgy, chanting, and palace ritual from the whole period of imperial rule (395–1453). It includes analysis of what today are the less-flattering aspects of the fabled Byzantine culture, its hair-splitting logic (as A. R. Littlewood phrases it) and theological conundrums such as "the indivisibly divisible and divisibly indivisible," and the Byzantine chronology of the world, which numbered years from 5508 and not 5492 B.C., and began the solar year from the vernal equinox, until it was altered to 1 September. Also there is the Byzantine Rite, which coalesces elements from Antioch's patriarchs, Emperor Justinian, Theodore the Stoudite, and revisionist monasticism in Palestine. This is juxtaposed with the study of rampant popularism, as when a Byzantine writer sums up Basil the Bulgarslayer (976–1025) and his successor, Konstantinos II (1026–1028), as "A cross and a shovel made from the same piece of wood." Next to the monasticism, too, is coarse satire, like the pig in one poem who boasts that the bristles in his mane are used for the sprinkling of holy water, or the cat who chides a mouse for eating, defecating, kicking, and littering in the same space.

Byzantinoslavica: revue internationelle des études, a biennial journal issued by the Československá Akademie of Prague, started in 1929 and covers recent work on Byzantium in every number. The bibliography in Krumbacher's monumental *History of Byzantine Literature,* translated from German (1897, 1900) by **Soteriadis,** runs to several hundred pages, across three volumes D. M. Nicol's *A Biographical Dictionary of the Byzantine Empire* (London: Seaby, 1991) refers to notable figures in the Byzantine empire, from the year 330 to 1453. *The Oxford Dictionary of Byzantium,* ed. A. P. Kazhdan (New York: Oxford University Press, 1991, 3 vols.), covers writers, rulers, ecclesiastics, and administrators from eleven centuries. Serials, journals, or encyclopedias on Byzantium include J. P. Migne, ed. *Patrologia series Graeco-Latina,* the "Bulletin of the Historical and Ethnological Society of Greece," *Byzantinische Forschungen, Byzantine and Modern Greek Studies, Corpus Scriptorum Christianorum Orientalium, Byzantinische Zeitschrift, Realencyclopädie der classischen Altertumswissenschaft, Patrologia Orientalis, Bibliotheca Hagiographica Graeca, Byzantinoslavica, Dumbarton Oaks Papers, Byzantion-Nea Hellas* (published in Chile), *Annual of the British School at Athens, Byzantinische-neugriechische Jahrbücher, Revue de l'Orient Chrétien,* the Greek "Annual of the Society of Byzantine Studies," *Greek Roman and Byzantine Studies, Revue des Études Byzantines, Jahrbuch der österreichischen byzantinischen Gesellschaft, Corpus Scriptorum Historiae Byzantinae, Orientalia Christiana Periodica,* and *Corpus Fontium Historiae Byzantinae.* The Center for Byzantine Studies (Dumbarton Oaks) has produced an *Author Index of Byzantine Studies* (Zug: IDC, 1986), which covers author entries for Byzantine topics in 77 Slavic periodicals issued prior to 1917, as well as citations from bibliographies in the journal *Byzantinische Zeitschrift* (1892–1981). Krumbacher refers to the great mistake of many Byzantinologists: "the finer the style and language of a work, the older they think it is; the poorer its style, the more recent it must be."

Further Reading

Kazhdan, Alexander (with Simon Franklin). *Studies on Byzantine Literature of the Eleventh and Twelfth Centuries.* Cambridge: Cambridge University Press, 1984.

Littlewood, A. R. "Byzantium." *FD:* 275–276.

Tomadakis, Nicola B. *Miscellanea Byzantina—Neohellenica. (Saggi, note, articoli, ricerche di Filologia, Letteratura e Storia Bizantina e Neogreca).* Modena: Memor, 1972.

BYZANTIUM, HISTORY OF Byzantium began as the eastern Roman Empire, one of two segments (eastern and western) in which Theodosius the Great divided the Roman Empire at his death in 395. These two segments remained united until 476, when the western Roman Empire was destroyed by barbarian invaders. At this point the Roman Empire of the east was established as an autonomous state under the name "the Byzantine empire," with its capital at Constantinople, the former Byzantium. Constantine (who reigned 306–337) had believed that imperial victories were granted by God. He convoked the first Christian council (at Nicaea, in 325), which approved the Trinitarian creed of Athanasios. He also built a new Rome on the Bosphorus straits: **Constantinople.**

Emperor Theodosius I left Christianity (by 395) the dominant force in the civilized world. He had kept his capital at Constantinople (380). He imposed the Nicaean Creed on all Christian worship (28 February 380) and convoked a second Ecumenical Council. One of its effects was to include ecclesiastics in civil offices (381). Edicts were promulgated against Manichaeism (the dualist heresy) and **Arianism** (which denied, following the theologian Arius, that Christ is monophysite, that is, of one nature with the Father). Theodosius also canceled the **Olympic Games** (394). He prohibited sacrifices, consultation of oracles, and temple worship.

On his deathbed, Theodosius assigned the empire of the East to his elder son, Arcadius, and the empire of the West to his younger son, Honorius. In the reign of Theodosius II (408–450), a military prefect called Anthemius added the massive "Theodosian walls" to Constantinople's ring of defense. A school of higher learning was founded inside the capital, and the Theodosian code became the first imperial epitome of law to be issued (438). The fall of the West to Odoacer in 476, caused by the deposition of Romulus Augustus, was reversed by the emperor and scholar Justinian (who reigned 527–565). He pursued the Vandals in Africa, harassed Arians wherever they controlled **Orthodox** worshippers, attacked Ostrogoths in Italy, and repulsed Persian armies in the east. Justinian waged short, decisive campaigns, using his generals **Belisarius** and the eunuch Narses.

Emperor Herakleios (610–641) further checked Persian forces in the East and made some gains to his North. The rise of **Islam** established a new threat to the Eastern empire, which was by now Hellenic in language, Roman in law, and Orthodox in religion. From Emperor Herakleios to Michael III stretch the dark centuries of Byzantium (610–843), during which the metropolitan areas of Antioch and Alexandria were cut off from the empire. There were two doctrinal battles between church and emperor: the monothelete heresy, which argued that there was only a single will in Christ, and **iconoclasm**, the abolition of bowing to images (προσκύνησις).

With the partial settlement of the iconoclast issue in 843, the gulf between **Catholic** and **Orthodox** became too wide to bridge, and the churches of East and West became separate tools in the politics of empire. In military campaigns, the successors of Herakleios engaged the Lombards in Italy, Bulgars and Slavs north of Greece, and Arab power in Anatolia. The victory of Poson (863) opened up the Balkans to Hellenic influence. War and plague caused a shortage of Byzantine subjects, who were replaced as soldiers or farmers by settlers conscripted from beyond the frontier. The imperial purple was usurped by Basil I the Macedonian (867–886), a soldier who sponsored art and missionary expansion and annexed Armenia, Georgia, and Bulgaria, earning the title of "Bulgar-Slayer." In the tenth century, the Varangians (Russia) and southern Slavs were converted. By 1025, the East of Europe seemed like a mosaic of Byzantine Orthodox communities.

After Basil II's expansionist reign (976–1025), Byzantium stumbled through reverses until 1071, when it lost the crucial battle of Manzikert (Armenia), which brought the Seljuk Turks into the Mediterranean arena. Emperor Alexius vowed to revenge Manzikert and asked the Vatican and royal courts of the West to summon **crusades** for the liberation of the Holy Land. The crusades failed to bind the Western knights to their Byzantine allies, whom they despised as heretics and whose territories (Athens, Morea) they ploughed up into feudal holdings. The Byzantines, in turn, failed to check Seljuk advances and lost (1176) the battle of Myriokefalon, a fortress that they held in Asia Minor, near the source of the Maiandros. The Angelos dynasty exposed Constantinople to the crusaders (1204). Emperor Michael VIII Palaeologus (1259–1282) recaptured Constantinople (1261), but Byzantium's decline accelerated. Hope of Western aid was in vain. The Ottomans advanced each decade into a shrinking patch of land. Emperor Constantine XI and 7,000 defenders were defeated inside Constantinople, at the end of a 20-year siege (May 1453).

Further Reading

Hanawalt, Emily Albu. *An Annotated Bibliography of Byzantine Sources in English Translation.* Brookline: Hellenic College Press, 1988.

Impellizzeri, Salvatore. *La letteratura bizantina da Costantino agli iconoclasti.* Bari: Dedalo Libri, 1965.

Obolensky, Dimitri. *The Byzantine Commonwealth: Eastern Europe, 500–1453.* London: Weidenfeld and Nicolson, 1971.

Pinto, Emilio. *Guida allo studio della civiltà bizantina.* Naples: Libreria editrice Ferraro, 1973.

BYZANTIUM, LITERATURE OF
The ethos of Byzantium struck awe and reverence in Greek writers. L. Machairás states, in his **Chronicles,** that the Byzantine emperors are "sole natural rulers of our world." While the West groped for a kingdom of heaven on earth, the Byzantines believed they had reached it (Kazhdan 1984: 285). For Machairás, a Frankish subject in **Cyprus,** the emperor is humanity's political leader. The Patriarch of Antioch is its spiritual head: "these are the two true rulers of our world." Settled by Greeks around 650 B.C., Byzantium was named Constantinople and declared the New Rome (in 330), by Constantine, when control over the empire was moved to the East.

Until the accession of Emperor Herakleios I (610), Byzantium seemed poised both for an oriental mission and a Western, Latin restoration. Its rulers incarnated glory: Greek had been chosen for the revelation of one religion to all mankind. In Greek, God had ordained that no further knowledge was required for salvation. The modern poet **Kavafis** was entranced by this dualism: "Shining amid the adornments of their priestly vestments; / My mind keeps reverting to the great honors of our race, / To the glorious Byzantinism that is ours" (in the poem "At the Church").

In the period 395–610, intellectual life was divided between the old centers of **Hellenism**: Alexandria, Antioch, Gaza (with its school of rhetoric), and Athens (where the pagan university gradually shed its prestige). *Leucippe and Clitophon,* by Achilles Tatius (?c. 300), or the 61 narrative letters of Aristaenetus (sixth century) cultivate certain pagan values, which now began to seem inadequate beside the new, growing religion. Tryphiodorus composed a *Capture of Troy* (late fifth century), in 691 hexameter lines. Following the reign of Justinian (527–565), pagan aesthetics disappeared, but the fascination with **Hellenistic** values was not completely choked. Lingering glances at antiquity are displayed by writers of the **epigram,** which became the main genre of poetry. The University of Athens closed in 529, but Greek philosophy adapted to Christian dogma and the new metaphysics. A Christian convert (in 520), John Philoponus composed a treatise rejecting the world's eternity. He wrote a grammar, theological works, commentaries on **Aristotle,** and his main work, *The Arbiter,* in which he adopted the role of umpire and tried to bring solutions to the dispute between monophysitism and belief in the Triune God. Ranging between literature and science, Philoponus also suggested that heavy objects fall no quicker than light ones and improved the theory of inertia.

Leontius of Byzantium (475–c. 542) developed a theory of the dual nature of Christ. Emperor Justinian wrote essays on the problems of monophysitism, and on **Origen,** whom he called the worst of all the heretics (543). Under the Macedonian dynasty, the renewal of literature was marked by **Photius** (820–891). His *The Library* (Μυριόβιβλος) is an **epitome** of cultivated and selective reading. He lists and comments on 280 works, of which 120 are by secular authors. *The Li-*

brary is full of passages from **orators, grammarians, romances,** religious works, **chronicles** (some lost), and judgments on **style.** Photius's pupil, Emperor Leo VI the Wise (866–912), revised and hellenized the law, wrote treatises, and was a patron of the arts. His son, Konstantinos Porphyrogennetos, was a poet, essayist, antiquarian, and possibly artist (see **Russia**). His **encyclopedia** of history and political matters has, in its opening remarks on vice and virtue, a striking motto: "The conflict of history includes the immense and the bewildering." This emperor's prestige contributed to a large production of hagiography and saints' lives by Symeon Metaphrastes (late tenth century; see **Synaxarion**).

Under Constantine VII came the reference work *Suda* and also a poetic *Anthology* compiled by Kefalás. A later version became the *Palatine Anthology* (see **Epigram**). In the tenth to eleventh century, church literature became more mystical after the orthodox monks' victory over the **iconoclast** high clergy. The master of this movement toward deification (union with God) and holy quiet (ἀπάθεια) was Symeon New Theologian (c. 949–1022). The period 1025–1204 constitutes a golden age in Byzantine culture. The high period of the Comneni began with the decline of the Macedonian dynasty after the death of Basil II, in 1025. Constantine IX reorganized the University of Constantinople, with a view to drawing civil servants from its graduates. Civilians obtained access to power, and the influence of the literate bourgeoisie began to grow.

This was the moment of the so-called consul of philosophers, **Psellus** (1018–?1081). The versatile author of the *Chronographia* was entrusted with the rectorship of the University. This period of scholarship promoted cultural relations with the West, while eleventh-century literary language made one of its periodic shifts back to **Atticism.** The Comneni court encouraged an aristocratic manner of conversation and speculative thought. Psellus revived **Platonism** and fused neo-Platonist inquiry with the logic of **Aristotle.** John Italus, Michael Italicus, and Soterikos Pantevgenos were among the foremost neo-Platonists of the period. In 1082, John Italus was condemned as a heretic, under Alexius I Comnenus, for having taught "the foolish wisdom of the heathen." Eustratos of Nicaea, a commentator on Aristotle, was also condemned as a heretic, under the Comneni, as much for political as theological motives because the Comneni needed legitimization by the Church.

Mikhail Glykás, seemingly an imperial secretary to Manuel I Comnenus (1143–1180), embellished his *Chronography* with digressions on natural history and theology. Imprisoned on the Emperor's orders, he responded with *Poetic Lines by M. Glykás Which He Wrote during the Time He was Detained Because of a Spiteful Informer.* Konstantinos Manassís (early twelfth century) wrote a **Chronicle** in **political verse** (15-syllable lines) exalting Manuel I and his vision of a revived Roman empire. The **political decapentasyllable** provides the metrical form of *Syntipas,* a story of Indian origin that surfaced in Armenia, and concerns Siddhapati, known to the West as **Sindibad** in *The Thousand and One Nights.* Another fable that has Buddhist origins is the saga of two jackals, **Stephanitis and Ichnelatis,** who teach correct behavior.

See also MIRROR OF THE PRINCE

Constantinople was captured and looted in 1204 by the Fourth **Crusaders,** and the seat of Byzantine power went to

Nicaea for the 57 years of the Latin occupation. Byzantium's displaced center of gravity at Nicaea, in this transitional age (1204–1261), saw an intensification of the Comneni's commitment to scholarship and literature. The Laskaris emperors then restored the university and oversaw the repair of libraries ransacked by war. Under the Laskaris dynasty, the move toward classicism and rhetoric was accentuated. The taste for Atticism in language grew pronounced. Theological debate swung against the West. Dispute was engaged with philosophers belonging to the **Catholic** tradition. Monks shifted to **hesychast** positions. The monk Nikiforos Blemmydes (thirteenth century) wrote on the ideal philosopher-king, for Theodore II, and restored the study of Aristotle, with an abridgment of the *Physics,* which was used as a manual in the West and a digest of Aristotle's logic. His pupil, Theodore II (1222–1258), became the greatest scholar–Emperor of all. Theodore was a **humanist,** philosopher, and mathematician. His mathematicians knew about Arabic numbers and the figure zero and determined to improve the Byzantine system, which used letters of the alphabet as numerals.

A growth in popular literature saw Nicholas Irenikus's *Epithalamium* on the marriage of John III. Then came the first **romances,** coinciding with Frankish incursions. These romances, partly descended from the **classical novel,** mixed Western elements, such as duels, with oriental magic, as in *Velthandros and Chrysantza.* The last flowering of Byzantine literature runs from 1282 (the death of Emperor Michael VIII) to 1453. The Palaeologus dynasty reorganized the university (under Manuel II) and attracted students from Italy. The Patriarchate's school increased in prestige, whereas Thessalonica and Mistra grew as centers of learning. The spiritual movement of hesychasm (withdrawn monachism) deepened its influence. The scholar Maximus Planoudis (1260–1310) edited the *Palatine Anthology.* At the beginning of the fifteenth century, the university at Constantinople, reformed by Manuel II, became a **humanist** center, offering classical law, history, and science. The school at Mistra was next in prestige, with the neo-Platonist teaching of Yemistos **Plethon** (c. 1360–c. 1451). The growth of a **renaissance** in the East was stopped in its tracks by the advance of Sultan Mehmet. His siege spelled the end of Byzantium and the worst disaster to literature since fire consumed the library of Alexandria (47 B.C.). Perhaps 40,000 scrolls went up in flames when Julius Caesar occupied the palaces of Alexandria and was attacked there by Egyptians. Isidore of Kiev estimated the number of manuscripts destroyed during the **Ottoman** sack of Constantinople at around 120,000.

See also FALL OF CONSTANTINOPLE; HELLENISM; RENAISSANCE; ROMIOSINI

Further Reading

Berschin, Walter. *Greek Letters and the Latin Middle Ages: From Jerome to Nicholas of Cusa.* Washington, DC: The Catholic University of America Press, 1988.

Cantarella, Raffele. *Poeti bizantini.* Milan: Vita e pensiero, 1948.

Maguire, Henry, ed. *Byzantine Court Culture from 829 to 1204.* Washington, DC: Dumbarton Oaks, 1998.

Niebuhr, B. G., ed. *Corpus scriptorum historiae byzantinae.* Bonn: Imprensis E. Weber, 1828–1897, 50 vols.

Zakithinos, D. A. Ἡ Βυζαντινὴ Ἑλλάς *(292–1204)* [Byzantine Greece, 292–1204]. Athens, 1965.

C

CAESURA A single line of poetry generally has a caesura, or cut (τομή). This creates a breath, or grammatical pause at its midpoint. The division often occurs after the seventh or eighth syllable in a long line such as the **decapentasyllable.** Caesura gives great effect to a dragon in "The Crystal Song" by Panos Spalas (1909–1970): "Black is what he is, black is what he wears, // and black is what his horse is."

CAFÉ A coffeehouse (καφενείο) often becomes fashionable as a place for writers and artists to meet. **Gatsos** (1911–1992) was a fixture at the Café Floca (Athens). The impoverished **S. Martzokis** (1855–1913) spent most of his time at the coffeehouse, where he was addressed as "Maestro," gave Italian lessons, and translated Italian poetry for **Phexi** editions. Gryparis (1870–1942) was said to be a prisoner of his wife: hanging out at Zacharato's, he exhibited taciturn and moody behavior (Kordatos, 1962: 395), but took no interest in social issues. In the nineteenth century, the Café Caramikon on Constitution Square was the haunt of **A. Paraschos** and his fellow Romantics. Round the turn of the century, the Café New Center was the stamping ground of **N. Lapathiotis, R. Filyras,** Y. Simiriotis, **N. Velmos** (1892–1930), **S. Skipis, A. Karkavitsas,** A. Kambanis, K. Chatzopoulos, and **Periklís Yannopoulos.**

In Alexandria (Egypt), **Kavafis** would drop in at the Pallas Billiards in Misala Street. **Voutyrás,** Yioséf Raftopoulos, and D. Tangopoulos (founder of the journal *Noumás*) were habitués of the Black Cat, run by Yannis Spatalás, which opened in 1917 at the corner of University and Asklepios Streets (Athens). Yerasimos Spatalás (1887–1971) started a literary monthly in 1919, which had the title *Black Cat* and was housed in his brother's homonymous coffeehouse. It ran for a year or so and expressed "the heroic age of Greek literary bohemianism" (Tsakonas). The Black Cat coffeehouse was a meeting place for members of the Artistic Society, founded by Y. Papayotopoulos. Nearby was the Café Euboea, where, from 1923, younger writers congregated, among them **Tellos Agras,**

Petros Charis, **K. Karyotakis,** M. Filintas, M. and Sp. Panayitopoulos. At this café, the journal *Us* was launched and the periodical *New Altars*. It was the young vogue writers of the time who clubbed together to produce *Us*. They held a meeting at which Karyotakis refused to endorse a successful writer to the committee, even though the man was present. Why? According to Papadimas, "because Karyotakis didn't like him."

CALLIOPE Among the nine **Muses,** the goddess Calliope was senior, patron of epic and heroic poetry, protector of fine arts and rhetoric. Statues and pictures show her sitting in thought, with a tablet on her lap, a stylus in her raised right hand. *Calliope,* among the very early Greek periodicals, founded at Vienna (1819) by Athanasios Stagirite, is named after this muse. Running for a year, with 24 issues and a total of 256 pages, *Calliope* played a determining role in the Greek **Enlightenment.**

CANON The canon is a hymn form, usually consisting of nine odes, each ode having the same number of short, metrically similar strophes. The canon thus resembles a long poem of many strophes. Its odes (**troparia**) are interpolated into two or more of the nine canticles of the morning "canon of psalmody" (Alexander Lingas). Around the beginning of the eighth century, the canon began to replace the **kontakion,** becoming the preferred Byzantine form of liturgical verse, especially when the church vetoed any further additions to its official **hymnography.** Each feast had acquired its accompanying hymn, and there was no room for others. Canons permitted variations of rhythm and melody and made room for dogmatics in the Divine Office.

The canon was a purely lyric composition, unlike the dramatic kontakion. Andreas of Crete (660–720), originally from Syria, was its oldest acknowledged master. His *Grand Canon* consisted of 250 strophes and led to a definitive hymnography, poised between the two main traditions of the following century, the Syrian school of John Damascenus and the Stoudite Convent of Constantinople, which boasted the work of Theodore the Stoudite (759–826) and Theofanes Graptos (c. 775–845). Their work forms the basis of the modern Orthodox **liturgy.**

Meletios Syrigos (1585–1664), a Cretan writer who studied maths and literature in Italy, was condemned by Venice and fled to Alexandria, and then Constantinople, where he took administrative posts in the church. Syrigos was a delegate at the Jassy synod, which examined the profession of faith by Kyrillos Loukaris, and he wrote an essay on Calvinist doctrine. He composed a service (ἀκολουθία) for Makarios of Kios in Bithynia, who was martyred in Russia (1590). While living in Kiev, Syrigos composed canons on saints of the ascetic tradition, on the holy martyr Paraskevi (with her bizarre, apocryphal story of imperial Roman cruelty), on the Mother of God, and on the laying down (κατάθεσις) of the Savior's tunic.

CASIA This ninth-century nun, also known as Ikasia or Kassiani, composed **canons** and **tropária.** Casia's powerful **hymn** "Lord, the woman fallen in many sins" conjures up the unknown woman in the Gospel story who washed Christ's feet and dried them with her own hair at the house of Simon the Leper. It is still sung on the Wednesday before Easter in the **Orthodox** church. Around 850 A.D., Casia's beauty and wit supposedly attracted Emperor Theophilos. She took part in a display of possible brides and was invited to a conversation, where her brilliance impressed and annoyed him. Tradition has it that she lost her chance to share the Byzantine throne and therefore built a monastery and retired to a life of pious scholarship.

Further Reading

Tillyard, H.J.W. "A Musical Study of the Hymns of Casia." *Byzantinische Zeitschrift* 20 (1911): 420–485.

CATALEXIS In the analysis of poetic meter, *catalexis,* the word for "termination, ending" (κατάληξη) refers to the cutting away of the final syllable of one segment of verse in relation to another. In grammar, it means the changed syllable at the end of nouns (declension), or the changed endings for tense, person, and number in verbs (conjugation).

CATALOGUE; CATALOGUER Any catalogue is a list of names or soldiers (κατάλογος). The word is not related to the medieval love poem (καταλόγι). The catalogue of a **library** is a πίνακας (see **Bibliography**). Diogenes Laertius drafted a catalogue of the works of **Aristotle,** listing 150 items, covering the equivalent of 6,000 pages. The 30 works by Aristotle that we now have are those edited by Andronicus (a peripatetic philosopher). Catalogues within an actual literary text exploit the devices of length and detail, often depending on repetition, a common device in Greek style (see **Figure of Speech**). Catalogues are frequent in Byzantine writing. As with **ekphrasis,** a catalogue seeks to win the reader's belief that the events being narrated are colorful but true. In *Iliad,* book 2, **Homer** inserted an inventory of Greek ships,

technically an interruption of the subject matter. The catalogue of ships was inserted in the story so that "no Greek state should be left out of that roll of ancient glory" (Geddes & Grosset 1995: 46). We note that it is preceded by a much longer invocation to the **Muses** than the one that opens the *Iliad.* If *that* much help is needed from above to recite a catalogue of ships, then clearly the catalogue is a key factor in **poetics.**

See also GKINIS

CATECHISM Many essays and treatises have been composed, down the centuries, by Greek writers on catechism (κατήχηση) and on Sunday School doctrine in general. In Greek, catechism means the teaching of the prime elements of Christian faith. It is a form of initiation; the verb κατηχώ means "catechize" but has a nuance of "indoctrinate." This subgenre becomes part of an education for the Greek masses, rather than a branch of theology. Typical is Iakovos Rikis, born in Kerkyra, a seventeenth-century doctor and writer who composed *An Orthodox Catechism.* Neophytos Rodinós (seventeenth century; **Cyprus**), a translator of religious texts and lives of the saints, composed catechistic books. Ioannis Prinkos (eighteenth century; b. Zagorá) was a self-taught merchant who built up one of the richest libraries of his age; Prinkos had a deep belief in the value of education, wrote his own catechism in the **Demotic**, and sponsored the reissue (Amsterdam, 1760) of **I. Miniatis,** *Stone of Scandal* (first published at Leipzig, 1718), and of the *Orthodox Confession* (1767) by **Voulgaris.** Each Greek catechistic text differs, but the pattern is always expository and linear. There are questions with set answers, repetitions of points of faith, and metaphysical definitions.

A school catechism (1956) by Ioannidos and Skouteris runs through "Faith as a Means of Knowledge of God," "Proofs for the Existence of God," "Essence and Nature of God," "Natural Characteristics of God" (for example, His Universal Presence, Omnipotence and Eternity), "Logical and Ethical Properties of God," "The Triune God," "God's Foreknowledge of the Universe," "Angels," "Man," "The Birth of our Savior," "Preparation of Mankind for His Advent," "Teaching and Works of Christ," "The Passion and Resurrection of our Lord," "The Ascension and Second Coming of the Lord," "Disputes about the Essence of Christ," "The Redemptive Function of our Lord," "Divine Grace," "The Concept, Effect, and Procession of the Holy Spirit from God" [n.b. not "*and from the Son,*" as for the **Catholics**], "The Church," "The Seven Mysteries" (Baptism, Confirmation, Divine Eucharist, Repentance, Priesthood, Marriage, and Unction), "The Life Hereafter," "Christian Ethics," and so forth. The catechism also expounds the liturgy, church festivals, priestly offices, and the eighteen "best hymn writers" between the fourth and eleventh centuries.

Further Reading

Ioannidos, V. Chr. and V. K. Skouteris. Κατήχησις καὶ Λειτουργικὴ τῆς Ὀρθοδόξου Ἀνατολικῆς Ἐκκλησίας [Catechism and Liturgy of Greek Orthodox Church]. Athens: Organization for the Issue of Scholastic Texts, 1956.

CATHOLIC; CATHOLICISM The catholic ("universal") church is held to be not only the church of the western segment of the Byzantine empire, but the true and apostolic church founded by St. Peter (c. 40 A.D.). By tradition, this church passed on to a line of Popes (bishops of Rome). The patriarchal see of Rome was only defined and set up as such by a decision of the Council of Nicaea (325). The Greek word *papas* ("Pope") was, from the third century, an honorific of bishops of Antioch, Alexandria, Jerusalem, and certain western dioceses. Most "Popes" in the first 300 years of Christianity were Greek. In this period, the Popes used Greek as an official church language. The first Council of Constantinople (381) made Rome the most prominent Christian see, but awarded the same honors and rites to the Patriarch of Constantinople. The synod of Chalcedon (451) reaffirmed all this, and Rome rejected it. From then on, the two faiths were bound to be divided, and despite various efforts in their history, Orthodox and Catholic church were never reunited.

After the year 1081, the word "Pope" refers only to the spiritual leader of the western church. The Popes of Rome gained prestige and power after Charlemagne (crowned Holy Roman Emperor in 800) codified their temporal power. When Pope Leo III made Charlemagne emperor, he caused polemics in the East, by toppling the Byzantine concept of one empire, one God, one world. In the medieval period, five doctrinal differences kept the Catholic and Orthodox apart: (1) perpetual Procession of the Holy Spirit ". . . *also* from the son" (Latin *filioque*); (2) Primacy of the Pope over all bishops in the world; (3) use of unleavened bread as material for the Eucharist; (4) cleansing of sin by Purgatory; and (5) complete beatitude of the Saints. The struggle was exacerbated by the pressure of Jesuits, the foundation (1516) of the Greek college of St. Athanasius at Rome, and missionary work in the East.

Ilias **Miniatis** (1669–1714) in *Stone of Scandal* (Leipzig, 1718) argued that the greatest disgrace was the **schism** between eastern and western Christianity and held that there was only one real divergence, "Procession of the Holy Spirit *filioque*" ("*also* from the Son"). Manuel Margounios (1549–1602), a poet and scholar born at Candia (Crete), was a fellow student of **Meletios Pigás** at Padua (Italy). He published a Latin version of *Dialogue of John Damascenus against the Manicheans* (Padua, 1572) and was accused of heresy for his three-volume study *On the Procession of the Holy Spirit,* written around 1583 (dedicated to Patriarch Jeremias II). Margounios departed from St. Augustine's doctrine; he aspired to the union of the two churches. Despite his Orthodox stance, Margounios showed favor, on some points, to Catholic opinions. After 1584 and a trip to Constantinople, he was named bishop of Cythera. He passed the rest of his life at **Venice.** In more modern times, Takis Papatsonis (1895–1976) wrote verse that fuses the spirituality of the two churches. He joked about how he was thought, by some Orthodox monks, to be Papist (λατιν- όφρων) during his six months at **Mount Athos** (1927). Some of the "majesty of Rome" filters into Papatsonis's verse.

Further Reading

Svoronos, Nicolas G. *Histoire de la Grèce moderne.* Paris: Presses Universitaires de France, 1964.

CENSORSHIP The Greek noun λογο- κρισία has a more euphemistic ring than the word **censorship.** It means the judgment, or approval, of words. A decision by the state to sift texts for printing or broadcast is a periodic phenomenon of Greek life, not one that is exclusive to the **Colonels' Junta.** "Scrawling his black marks in a government office or skulking in the back of the writing mind, the censor is one of the shaping presences of twentieth-century literature" (Margaronis, 1998). Under the control of the Colonels, the word "has been censored" was stamped on a text to confirm that a set of rules for its passage had been followed (K. Van Dyck, 1998). It signified "passed by the censor with any alterations that might be necessary." For seven years, Russian names were banned, and a writer could not highlight the adjective "red." In the nineteenth century, **Makriyannis** had to hide the manuscript of his *Memoirs* on the isle of Tinos (1840). In his 1954 volume of verse, the left-leaning author Menelaos Loundemis (1912–1977; pseudonym of Yannis Balasiadis) has the poem "I'm well," which is, of course, any Greek convict's stereotyped phrase to get a letter past prison censorship. At the end of the poem, Loundemis proposes that HE IS WELL should be carved on his grave.

In 1975, **Victoria Theodorou** published a memoir entitled *Women's Concentration Camps,* which included the transcription of nine notebooks that had been buried in the ground by inmates of the prison at Trikeri. These contained accounts of the camps at Chios and Makronisos. It was a primitive way to sidestep the Junta's censorship. In the 1860s, A. Laskaratos produced a satirical journal on the island of Cephalonia, *The Lamp,* which landed him in **prison.** The antiwar memoir by **S. Myrivilis,** *Life in the Tomb* (1924), was banned during the Metaxás dictatorship (1936–1940) and the **occupation.** Under Metaxás, bonfires of books were organized. Sophocles's play *Antigone* was banned and so were the works of Heine, Shaw, Freud, Anatole France, Zweig, Darwin, Dostoyevski, and Gorky.

At times, religious pressure was brought to bear on Greek writers. Their jobs were threatened by their choice of topics,, or by a stance on the radical side of the **language question. Emanuel Roidis** lost the headship of the Greek National Library, to which he was appointed in 1880. **Palamás** temporarily lost his salary at Athens University. Myrivilis lost his job at Greek Radio. Censorship has affected the distribution and reception of works by **Ritsos, Varnalis, Kazantzakis, Chatzís,** and **Vasilikos,** leading at times to detention or exile. While Tatiana **Milliéx** was living in **Cyprus,** the Junta confiscated her papers, which included the final manuscript of four novels. Her 1973 novel, *Distress,* was stitched together from confiscated papers after she regained possession of them. Preventive censorship was relaxed in November 1969 by the introduction of the Press Law, which placed on writers or editors the onus of vetting their own work. To prevent subversive messages creeping into print, this law required that headlines and titles should exactly match the content of a text. **Elli Alexiou** was deprived of her Greek citizenship in 1950. A play by Alexiou was banned by the Colonels in 1972. **Melpo Axioti,** a writer and member of the Communist Party, had to leave Greece for France (1947). She was later forced, by Greek leverage in Paris, to move on to East Germany.

A set of five one-act plays by Kostas Mourselas was dropped from television in 1973 because of the censor's intervention. His play *Bus Stop* showed two educated tramps rejecting society's values and debating the philosophical implications of a bus stop. In *The Egg,* the same tramps reckon that longevity is a government plot to squeeze work out of the aged. For these gags, Mourselas found his plays banned. **Menis Koumandareas** (b. 1931) was arrested under the Colonels on a charge of immorality, arising from stories published in 1967. He was acquitted at trial. A scene in G. Xenopoulos's play *Only Daughter* (1913) shows a middle-class mother marking articles in the newspapers that her 18-year-old Emma can be permitted to read. Ironically, the mother marks the acceptable articles with red ink; Emma is distressed to see there is no red ink at all on the current number of **Estía**. The term for filthy writing that induces repulsion or disgust is *bdelygma.* Licentious language (αἰσχρολογία) and coarseness periodically undergo censorship. There is an exhortation against such language in the twelfth-century work *The Beardless One* (see **Spaneas**). Here a father, or courtier, tells a young prince how to conduct his life: "You should not utter bad words, or be prepared to listen to them. / Since anyone who is willing to listen to foul language, / Will not be ashamed to talk vulgar, or afraid to do coarse things. / Avoid, if possible, vacuous licentious language."

See also CHORTATSIS; EMBIRI-KOS; FEMINIST POETRY; HAVI-ARAS; HOMOSEXUALITY; KAKEM-FATON; KARAPANOU; THEATER, SEVENTEENTH CENTURY

Further Reading

Margaronis, Maria. "Black Felt Pen." *TLS* 29 (May 1998): 35.

Mourselas, Kostas. "This One and . . . That One," trans. by Andrew Horton. In *Selected Plays.* Athens: Anglo-Hellenic Publishing, 1975: 19–91.

Van Dyck, Karen. *Kassandra and the Cen-*

sors: Greek Poetry since 1967. Ithaca, NY: Cornell University Press, 1998.

CHALKOKONDYLIS, DIMITRIOS (1423–1511) The **Renaissance** scholar D. Chalkokondylis descended from Athenian nobility. He lived in Italy from 1471. He was professor at Padua (Italy) and later Florence, where he was succeeded (in 1492) by Ianos Laskaris. The latter, who had even bluer blood (descending from the imperial dynasty of Nicaea), advised Lorenzo de' Medici as curator of the Laurenziana Library, procuring Greek manuscripts from two journeys to Asia Minor (1490, 1491). Chalkokondylis published *Grammatical Questions* and supervised the first printed editions of *The Surviving Works of Homer* at Florence, 1488, of the *Suda* (1494), and of Isocrates (Milan, 1493).

CHALKOKONDYLIS, LAONIKOS (1424/?1430–1490) Like his relative **Dimitrios Chalkokondylis,** Laonikos lived in Italy (from 1453). His refined **Attic** idiom, now seen as stilted, sets apart his *A History of the Turkish Assault and the Last Phase of the Byzantine Empire* (10 vols.) as a signal achievement in Greek historiography.

CHARITOPOULOS, DIMITRIOS (late seventeenth century/early eighteenth century) The peripatetic writer D. Charitopoulos composed (1708) a **chronicle** in the form of a personal will (διαθήκη), after being forced to leave Roumeli for refuge on Zakynthos. He details the heroic actions of his brother, Filotheos, Bishop of Salona, whose neck swells after a battle wound and causes his death in 10 days. He describes other Greek leaders, like Kourmas, who try to resist the Turks after the Venetians aban-

don the Roumeliot towns, which the Turks wanted. He begs that his brother George have his bones carried back to his childhood home and asks to be buried only "in his breeches and the black shirt," next to the bones of Filotheos, which Charitopoulos has hidden in a bag in a cave. He wills that his own burial occur only when "the all-merciful, all-bountiful God allows our ill-starred race to go free."

CHATZÍS, DIMITRIS (1913–1981) Born in Ioannina, in the year of its incorporation with Greece, the novelist Dimitris Chatzís went into exile at the end of the **Civil War** (1949). A **Communist** in the early war years, he became a leader in the democratic liberation army and could only return to Greece after the fall of the **Colonels,** in 1975. His first published novel, *The Fire* (1946), deals with the mountain **resistance** during the **occupation.** Chatzís defines the cruelty of war, writing from the point of view of the pro-Soviet EAM and ELAS forces in the **resistance.** Most of his stories were written in Hungary or later in East Germany. They offer a chronicle of the humblest aspects of Greek country life, as in *The End of Our Small Town* (1960). Tales like "Sioulas the Tanner" look back nostalgically to a world of village craftsmen. Other reflective stories are collected in *The Defenceless* (1965) and *Studies* (1978). His novel *The Double Book* (1975) is an opaque account of Chatzís's experience of exile, with an intellectual consciousness split between a narrator, Kostas, and a *less* competent "Author." A volume of essays, *Language and Politics,* came out in 1975. In his literary journal *Prism,* shortly before his death, Chatzís made efforts to introduce foreign literature to contemporary Greeks.

Further Reading

Chatzís, Dimitris. Τὸ διπλὸ βιβλίο [The Double Book]. Athens: Kastaniotis, 1977.

Hatzís, Dimitris. *The End of Our Small Town,* trans. by David Vere. Birmingham: University of Birmingham, Centre for Byzantine, Ottoman and Modern Greek Studies, 1996.

Mackridge, Peter. "Testimony and Fiction in Greek Narrative Prose 1944–1967." In *The Greek Novel: A.D. 1–1985,* ed. Roderick Beaton, 90–102. London: Croom Helm, 1988.

Ricks, David. "Tales from Epirus." *TLS* 20 (Dec. 1996): 23.

CHIASMUS The figure of chiasmus, known as "letter X structure," was cultivated in learned or ornate writing. Chiasmus occurs when antithetical or corresponding elements from two successive clauses are not placed in matching sequence when repeated. So we read the grammar as AB/BA, for instance, noun + verb / verb + noun, rather than the more pedestrian, or logical, AB/AB. Dionysios Tsakasianos (1894–1963), in passages from his hymnlike "By Palms and Branches," shows how chiasmus can be made to work effectively with rhythm and repetition: "The poorest among the wise, the wisest among all Teachers," "Raise high the palm branches; the branches, lift high!"

CHILDREN; FAMILY Plenty of sentimentality (αισθηματισμός) creeps into Greek writers' picture of kids in the family, as in the quatrain "Blond lad / Snoozes in silence / An angel looks on, / And sends him a smile." Kostas Piyadiotis (b. 1915), in his poem "Mother's Fingers," falls into bathos: "As I hold the pencil / Between my three fingers, / I remember your fingers, Mother. / With one / You showed me how. / With two you wiped away / My tears. / And with three / You made a sign of the cross / For me." Childlessness is seen as an evil, in all Greek literature: even the hero of the epic **Diyenís Akritas** pines with his wife over "the unquenchable and grievous flame of childlessness."

A *Life of St. Ignatios* tells about a woman whose child could not be delivered from the womb because of its wrong fetal position. Just as the doctors were on the point of carrying out an embryotomy, a patch of material from the cloak of St. Ignatios was placed on the mother's belly. The child was saved. A recurring feature of the lives of saints (see **Hagiography**) is the infertility of the future saint's parents. They intercede for divine help before the wife can conceive. The parents of the saint and empress Theofano viewed their childlessness as a "fate worse than death" and were saved from it by supplication to the Virgin in a Constantinople church. A *Life of Antony the Younger* relates how a landowner offered a share of his estate to the doctor if he could intervene and help him father a child. The doctor is actually the saint in disguise and requests 10 stallions in exchange for this fertility treatment. By the late twentieth century, children are seen as a bore as well as a blessing. In Vangelis Rapotopoulos's novel *The Cicadas* (trans. Fred Reed, Athens: Kedros, 1996), the parents are comically alienated by their unreliable sons and their blasphemous, smoking girlfriends with "cool" behavior unacceptable to all previous generations of Greeks.

Further Reading

Campbell, John Kennedy. *Honour, Family and Patronage: A Study of Institutions and Moral Values in a Greek Mountain Community.* Oxford: Clarendon Press, 1964.

CHILDREN'S LITERATURE Nowadays Greek literature for the young is a niche market. It also has a strong historical tradition. Greek literary texts aimed at kids and adolescents have well-defined rules and categories. These books are expected to incorporate some higher ideal such as altruism (αυταπάρνηση), while also offering amusing situations, some convincing humor, and "adventures galore." There is usually some depiction of the Greek countryside. This reflects the attitude to fauna and flora that characterized Greek nineteenth-century writing for adults. The nineteenth-century magazine *The Moulding of the Young* (from 1879) was popular with kids, and it encouraged just this **love of nature** (φυσιολατρεία). Children like to read "holding their breath," so their authors provide **suspense,** often with "disclosures" of a significant secret and a sprinkling of unlikely events. The **plot** must always bear some relation to children's contemporary reality, and there must be authenticity of detail (αυθεντικότητα των λεπτομερειών). The overall purpose goes back to classical aesthetics: the text must procure for its young readers both enjoyment and instruction (απόλαυση and μάθηση). The book should have a **happy ending**; the bad guys have to be punished and the good guys rewarded for their braveness or their good deeds.

In 1897, the ship's doctor **Karkavitsas** published sea yarns in his *Sayings from the Ship's Bow,* which still enchants junior readers with its marine detail and nautical descriptions. In the period 1918–1920, Karkavitsas devoted himself to composing a number of elementary school **readers.** The chief innovator in the children's genre in Greece was **Penelope Delta** (1872–1941). She wrote highly regarded **historical novels** for kids, as well as books in which a pet talks to the reader about his human family (*Mankas the Dog*) or *Antonis the Crazy,* in which her hero turns into a better boy when he starts school. Delta, among many other texts, wrote *Fairy Tales and Other Matters,* and *The Life of Christ.* The latter presents the Gospel to young readers by analyzing Jesus' birth, his relations with his disciples, the events of Golgotha, and the lasting effect of Christian doctrine. She also wrote books directed at parents and educators, one on the bringing-up of kids, another on the issue of discipline. A typical children's book in contemporary Greece is Nitsa Jorjoglou's *Difficult Steps* (published by E. Mokas Morfotiki), aimed at children from the age of 12 up. A father leaves his family, and the daughter, a sensitive adolescent, tries to draw him back. She discovers a family secret, a nice boy helps her through the subsequent adventure, and after a car accident comes marital reconciliation. The modern plot ingredients of precocious adulthood, urban mobility, parental separation, and youthful *tendresse* are here combined with a dose of sentimentality to try to win children away from Greek TV serials.

"The Scare" by **Vizyinós** is the first Greek children's story to be written in the **demotic** language. Vizyinós produced his classic miniature for a children's magazine. There it remained, out of sight until its "discovery" (1948) and a scholarly reprint by Pigis ("Source Editions"), in their series "Monuments of Neohellenic Literature." Among the first Greek adventure books suitable for reading by children are *Gero-Stathis* by **L. Melás** (1858, *Old Man Stathis*), which contains many retold classical stories and fables. A nephew of Leon Melás, **D. Vikelas,** translated the fairy tales of Hans Christian Andersen (1805–1875). Vikelas also wrote his own novel *Loukis Lara,* familiarizing young readers with events and ideology from the **War of Independence.** Pavlina Pampoudhi (b. 1948) is a prolific practitioner of this competitive literary genre. Often illustrating her own books, Pampoudhi brought out *15½ Strange Little Fairy Tales, The Fantastic Circus Picasso* (1980), *By 1 and 2* (1991), *The Quiet One Who Speaks to Objects* (1982), *Stories for Laughter and Colors* (1987), *Apostolis and Annabella, The Milkman and the Mermaid, Miss Despina and the Dragon* (1988), *The Mouse Book, The Cat Book,* and *The Dog Book* (1989). She translated *Winnie the Pooh* (1982), *Alice in Wonderland,* and *Through the Looking Glass* (1988).

Further Reading

Kanatsouli, M. "Religious Syncretism in Modern Greek Children's Literature." *Children's Literature Association Quarterly* 24, no. 1 (1999): 34–39.

Kanatsouli, Meni. "Aspects of the Greek Children's Novel: 1974–1994." *Children's Literature Association Quarterly* 20, no. 3 (1995): 121–125.

Loty, Petrovits Androtsopoulou. "A Report on the Current State of Greek Children's Literature." *Phaedrus: An International Annual of Children's Literature Research* 12 (1986–1987): 45–47.

CHORTATSIS, YEORYIOS (fl. c. 1590)

The Cretan author Y. Chortatsis may be the author of three major plays from the so-called Cretan **Renaissance.** In this late sixteenth-century period, early modern Greek literature reached its zenith in a regional flowering under Venetian administration. The *Erofili,* by Chortatsis, is a five-act tragedy imitating the Italian play *Orbecche* (1541) by Cinzio

Giraldi. Giraldi was himself an indirect source for **Shakespeare,** with the short stories collected in *Ecatommiti* (1564). Giraldi's play follows Seneca. He imitates the classical Roman author's rigid observance of the **Aristotelian** unities of time, place, and action, while indulging his own Counterreformation taste for passion and horrific events. Into this erudite tradition, Chortatsis introduces a tone of popular wisdom, even **folklore.** The *Erofili* has a prologue spoken by Charos, the Greek plebeian **personification** of **Death.** The nurse laments Erofili's death with the grim verve of Greek demotic poetry. How can these lovely eyes and body "become food for worms"? The nurse tells her mistress: "Without you, I am wronged and tricked." Fiercely sentimental, she declares: "I had hoped to hold your child, and see your heir one day. Instead, I shall bury these scattered limbs of Panaretos, follow you in suicide, and become your servant and beloved nanny in Hades." Gloomy presentiments are highlighted: "How could you have it in mind, how could you know you should fear what you dreamed?"

The neoclassical plot features a king, Philogonos of Memphis, and his daughter, Erofili, who marries a paragon of military virtues, Panaretos. This prince was supposed to broker her marriage to a suitor king, but falls in love with her instead. The brother of King Philogonos appears as a ghost and tells how Philogonos had him assassinated and stole his throne. The king kills Panaretos (see **Hyperbole**). In a revenge typical of Boccaccio's *Decameron,* he serves the dismembered corpse to his daughter as a wedding gift, while pretending to promote their marriage. Erofili kills herself. A chorus, consisting of her nurse and young women of the palace, avenge her by slaying Philogonos. During the performance, there were four interval playlets (ἰντερμέδια) between the acts, modeled on Italian *intermezzi.* For *Erofili,* these consist of episodes from Tasso's *Gerusalemme liberata:* the enchanted garden, the rescue of Rinaldo, the plea of Armida, and the freeing of the Holy City. Supposedly by Chortatsis is the five-act comedy *Katzourbos* (or *Katzaropos*), which uses a contemporary setting, at Kastro (that is, Iraklion, or Candia). In his "Dispute between Candia and Rethymnon," Bounialís, author of *Relation in Verses of the Dreadful War Which Took Place on the Island of Crete,* cites a supposed colleague of Chortatsis, "Katzaropos," as a playwright: "There was a child born in time past, born in my city; / He would later cover me with great honour. / They proclaimed him Yeoryios Chortakis by name, / And he wrote his *Panoria* with sugared lips, / Together with a Katsaropos, and the worthy play *Erofili.*"

This is now considered a reference to the actual *Merry Comedy of Katzourbos,* which consists of a short prologue, five acts, and four interval playlets. The action takes place over the course of a day. It presents a **happy ending** to a love affair, together with the discovery that the principal girl (Kassandra) is the long-lost daughter of the old man (Armenis). Clearly she can no longer be sold in marriage to him. Koustoulieris, the braggart soldier, has a slave named Katzourbos. The young lover, Niccoló, is served by the parasite Katzarapos, who is related to the issue of the play's title. Katzarapos is not a key figure in the cast of characters, where he is called "clowning or witty slave." The comedy features a final reconciliation of the principals, set pieces by stock characters, and the antics of a glut-

ton (δοῦλος φαγάς). So *Katzourbos* follows the Italian sixteenth-century comedy type (*Commedia Erudita*). It may be dated to about 1595–1601.

See also ALLATIOS; TROILOS

Chortatsis wrote a five-act pastoral play (c. 1592), *Gyparis,* also known as *Panoria,* which L. Politis holds "in all probability" to be based on *La Calisto,* by Luigi Groto. The original story is from the Latin poet Ovid: Zeus and Hermes prey on two shepherd girls, using metamorphosis as a disguise. The girls yield to their apparently human suitors. Chortatsis puts aside the motif of the divine lovers and their Arcadian surroundings. In *Gyparis,* one Frosyne intervenes to scold Panoria and Athousa for spurning the love of the two shepherds, Gyparis and Alexis. The boys ask Aphrodite to help them. The goddess of love, in turn, tells her son, Eros, to fire his arrows at the girls. Frosyne chides the girls, once they have fallen in love, pretending that their male admirers have turned elsewhere. Panoria induces her father to arrange her marriage with Gyparis and sets up the other couple. This pastoral play is a skillful adaptation to Cretan reality, with topical names and a rustic innocence, despite its learned Italian source. The comedy *Stathis* may also be by Chortatsis.

See also THEATER, SEVENTEENTH CENTURY

Further Reading

Marshall, F. H. (trans.), with an introduction by John Mavrogordato. *Three Cretan Plays: The Sacrifice of Abraham, Erophile and Gyparis.* London: Oxford University Press, 1929.

Vincent, Alfred. "A Manuscript of Chortatses' *Erophile* in Birmingham." *Univer-*

sity of Birmingham Historical Journal 12, no. 2 (1970): 261–267.

CHOURMOUZIS, MIKHAIL (1801–1882) The **Phanariot** intellectual and playwright M. Chourmouzis came from **Crete.** He studied at **Constantinople,** and lived, after the **Uprising,** at Athens, where he satirized postindependence society in plays like *The Clerk* (1836) and *Gambler* (1839). He fought in Crete with the German Philhellene Eduard Rainek (1795–1854) and recorded his experience in *Cretan Affairs* (1842). Later he was elected to Parliament. He began his career as a social satirist with *Seven Dialogues* (1838), first published in the newspaper *The Age,* 1834. He mocks the hybrid community of Greece rulers after liberation, as a Bavarocracy, with foreign customs, importing new injustices.

CHRESTOMATHY The chrestomathy (χρηστομάθεια) is a sort of collection of texts that is different from a literary garland like the *Palatine Anthology.* The chrestomathy compiles information that aims for "the learning of useful matters." Influential, from **Byzantium** till after the end of Turkish rule, the chrestomathy harvests passages, from classical or approved authors. These excerpts may be religious, historical, philosophical, **gnomic,** or **proverbial.** In 1529, the *Flower of Virtues* was published in Venice on the model of the Italian chrestomathy (1477). This Greek text is the only school manual that we have from the sixteenth century. It lists, under 36 headings, the principal adornments of character and their corresponding vices. Each chapter closes with sayings from the Church Fathers or philosophers. Such texts assist in the acquiring of language and serve the ethical development of the common reader. An-

tonios Vyzantios, an eighteenth-century scholar from Constantinople, published his *Chrestomathy* at Venice in 1720. Panayís Skouzés (1776–1847), in *A Chronicle of Athens Enslaved* (written 1841, revealed by **Tertsetis** in 1859), describes how as a child in the 1780s he passed from "Greek school, to a tutor, Samuel Koubelanos, and proceeded as far as the *chrestomathy,* as it was then called." Such texts offered training in useful matters, in one didactic volume. It was valued as a classroom text in the nineteenth-century monarchy, because primers were in short supply. It was eventually supplanted by initiatives like "Association for the Promulgation of Useful Books" (see **Drosinis**). Typically, Y. Dimitriou (eighteenth century) compiled *A Greco-Latin Grammar Containing Personal Observations, Epistles, and Maxims in Greek and Italian, with the Lives of Various Famous Men and Definitions of the Sciences,* such as a **chrestomathy** in the guise of a bilingual **grammar.**

CHRIST Byzantine literature venerated Christ and held a poor view of any alleged originality. The only "new thing" in the world, according to John Damascenus, is the Incarnation of Jesus. In early Byzantium, some devout believers became "fools in Christ" (σάλοι), literally adapting a New Testament precept that "the wisdom of this world is foolishness with God." Some ascetics acted like crazed animals, as told in a popular biography of Symeon the Salos, by Leontius Bishop of Neapolis (**Cyprus,** seventh century). Greek medieval "fools in Christ" paved the way for Russian *yurodivi,* or the "mad saints" of Islam. Certain images of Christ were called "not made by human hand" (αχειροποίητοι). Christ himself supposedly created the famed veil of Edessa, as a gift for the pious King Abgar. In the tenth century, the Mandylion of Edessa betook itself to **Constantinople** and later vanished.

CHRISTIAN Greeks use the noun "Christian" and the adjective "Orthodox" to signify a sacred, dominant affiliation. This is considered the unmediated, historical Christianity, closer to the truth of the Gospel than being **Catholic** or Lutheran. The Roman empire was, for Byzantine writers, the sole political system sanctioned by God, mandated by Heaven to bring "the whole world into the ecumene of Orthodoxy" (Haldon). Greeks have clung to the Greek Orthodox Church, and some 99 percent of them today are members of that flock. In the twentieth century, there was a loose grouping of writers recognized by literary critics as aspiring to make "religious poetry." Papatsonis (1895–1976), in his poem "White Greek Chapel," invokes a rural church surrounded by a choir of melons, fig trees and olives, lashed by the **sun.** The poet imagines how this chapel, instead of angels, has cicadas that "sing the Canon of Mercy, / In their own way, each afternoon till late." **Psycharis** once joked that religion, for a Greek, meant nothing more than his fatherland. **Roidis,** in the prologue to his novel *Pope Joan* (1866), says that anyone who has gone into one of our churches is occupied by one desire: to get out. Roidis makes five constructively witty criticisms of the **Orthodox** Church: a service may last two hours, so nobody listens to it; the priests are chosen from the scourings of the Earth, so nobody accepts their advice; the fasting is only suited to "big shot monks," so nobody fasts; **icons** are freakish, so nobody wants to embrace them; and the Church speaks through its nose.

See also ORTHODOX CHURCH

Further Reading

Beaton, Roderick. "'Our Glorious Byzantinism': Papatsonis, Seferis, and the Rehabilitation of Byzantium in Postwar Greek Poetry." In *Byzantium and the Modern Greek Identity,* edited by David Ricks and Paul Magdalino. Aldershot: Ashgate, 1998.

CHRISTOMANOS, KONSTANTINOS (1867–1911) The writer and theater director K. Christomanos was traveling companion and tutor to the Empress Elizabeth of Austria. After the second of his journeys with her, he stayed in Rome (1892), became **Catholic,** did voluntary work in the Vatican libraries, aspired to reconcile the **Orthodox** and Catholic churches, and toyed with becoming a monk at Monte Cassino. He cofounded the Viennese review *Wiener Rundschau,* settling eventually in Athens (1899). On 27 February 1901, he set up New Scene (see **Theater Companies**). In ten years he lost all his savings in expenditures for this theater. He wrote several books in German (including *Book of the Empress Elizabeth: Pages from a Diary*). *The Wax Doll: A Novel of Athens,* his only Greek fiction, was published as a serial (επιφυλλίδα) in the daily paper *Homeland.* It is a colorful and lugubrious tale of a wedding, infidelity, funeral, second wife, and allied urban misery. Mascaro called the novel "a pure record of manners, which vividly and faithfully describes the life, atmosphere and gaiety of the Athens of the time" (1973: 21). Christomanos's niece, Lilika Lourou, organized an archive of his papers after his death.

CHRISTOPOULOS, ATHANASIOS (1772–1847) Christopoulos was at once poet, scholar, translator, grammarian, and jurist. The son of an impoverished priest who emigrated to the Danubian provinces, Christopoulos published a *Grammar of Aeolo-Doric or of the Spoken Greek Language* (1805). He composed one of the first milestones of Greek popular poetry, *Lyrics* (1811), which went through several editions in his lifetime, influencing the **Ionian School** poets and enhancing the revival of a national language, with refined, simple pieces such as "Let there be no vacuum in Nature, / No emptiness in Creation, / No void anywhere,/Let our wine barrels be full . . . ," and "Cheerfully, harvest advances, / And the world is off to party." He studied in Bucharest and Padua, and then spent most of his life in Wallachia, Moldavia, and Transylvania (the Danube provinces) and virtually as a court poet at **Constantinople**. He helped draft a modern legal code for the principality of Wallachia (1816) and was involved with the secret society **Philikí Hetairía** (1819).

See also ENLIGHTENMENT

Further Reading

Christopoulos, A. Γραμματικὴ τῆς Αἰολοδωρικῆς, ἤτοι τῆς ὁμιλουμένης τωρινῆς των Ἑλλήνων γλώσσας [*Grammar of Aeolo-Doric or of the Spoken Greek Language*]. Vienna: 1805, publ. together with Δραμα ἡρωϊκόν[Heroic Drama], better known as the Ἀχιλλεύς [Achilleid].

Christopoulos, A. Τὰ ποιήματα (ἐρωτικά, βαγχικά, ποικίλα) [Verses about Love, Drinking Songs, and Divers Other Matters]. Athens: Phexi, 1916.

Christopoulos, A. Ἄπαντα [The Complete Works of A. Christopoulos], ed. Y. Valetas. Athens: Friends of the Byzantine Monuments of Kastoria Editions, 1969.

An issue of the journal *Greek Creation* (no. 100: l, April 1952) deals with A. Christopoulos.

CHRISTOVASILIS, CHRISTOS (1860?–1937)

Christovasilis's date of birth, in a remote Souli village (Epirus), where his father was a prominent landowner, is given as 1855, 1861 or, more credibly, 1860. Like the Epirot writer, **Krystallis,** Christovasilis was a collector of rural and **folk** material. His stories and poems are steeped in local lore, and his life was fueled by anti-Turkish, pro-Epirot nationalism. As a boy, he ran away from school (in Constantinople) and led a band of teenage patriots to take part in the uprising of the Epirus (1878). He was caught, released, and later arrested; he escaped again. He hailed the Greek army's capture of Trikala (capital of Turkish Thessaly) in a patriotic ode of 181 lines, which was circulated widely in a pamphlet. For this, he was arrested (on the day of his marriage) and sentenced to death by the Bey (1882). His family bribed his way out, and he hid on a farm. From 1885, he was in Athens, publishing, studying, and compiling local history. He won the *Acropolis* literary **competition** (1889) with a countryside tale. In 1897, he fought in the campaign for N. Epirus, and for 30 years he advanced the cause of Epirus, while composing ethnocentric works. He was twice a member of parliament. He edited the Ioannina paper *Freedom*. His best prose is gathered in *Stories from the Stockyard* (1898), which contains 11 pieces recalling his rural childhood, and *Stories of Exile* (1889). He later won first prize in a competition promulgated by **Psycharis,** and the result was the publication of *Stories from Mountain and Field* (1901). He died on 21 February 1937, the day they celebrated the liberation of Epirus.

CHRONICLE, HISTORY

"Chronicles" from the medieval period of modern Greek literature are often in the nature of a summary epitome or "digest" (περίληψη) of a huge span of years. The compiler could not have access to all the sources on which a real chronicle would depend. The writers of these historical digests were usually monks, aiming to provide their brother monks with manuals of universal knowledge. At times they used one source for an entire chapter or followed it much too closely. Ioannis Antiocheus ("from Antioch") wrote, probably in the seventh century, a historical digest to the year 610. *The Paschal Chronicle* is a seventh-century work that gives a digest of the years between Adam, the first created man, and the tenth year of the reign of Herakleios (610–641).

The eighth-century author George Synkellos ("cell companion") became ill (c. 810) while composing a history from the creation to his own time and asked St. Theofanis the Confessor (c. 760–818) to complete his work. Theofanis was born under Emperor Constantine V (741–775), a powerful **iconoclast.** A worshiper of icons himself, Theofanis compiled a *Chronographia,* which amounts to a digest of sources and borrowings concerning the years from 284 right up to the accession of Emperor Leo V (813–820). The so-called *Scriptores post Theophanem* are anonymous writers who were commissioned by Konstantinos VII Porphyrogennetos (945–959) to continue the treatment begun by Theofanis.

A *Chronicle* by Simeon Master and Logothete runs from the Earth's creation to the death of Romanos Lekapinos (948). It was written in the first years of the reign of Nikiforos II Phokas (963–969). **M. Psellus** (1018-?1081) covers, in his *Chronography,* the reigns of 14 emperors over the years 976–1078. He offers real explanation of politicians' acts and rejects any idea of the intervention of providence in human affairs. Ioannis

Skulitsis was a contemporary of Psellus, and his *Chronicle* also covers events of the late eleventh century.

Ephraim is the author of a verse chronicle (c. 1313) that is 9,564 trimeters in length and deals with Roman and Byzantine history. He confuses all invaders under the name "Scythians" and deals with the reign of Justinian in 33 lines. Mikhail Panaretos was the partial eyewitness of some events in his chronicle of the emperors of Trebizond (1204–1426), evoking the Anatolian attempt to recreate Byzantium, crushed by the **Ottomans**.

The *Sathas Synopsis* is a digest published by K. N. Sathas (1842–1914), an itinerant discoverer of early Greek texts, in his *Medieval Library* (Venice, vol. 7, 1894: 1–556). The book, written probably in the thirteenth century, covers history from the creation to the reconquest of Constantinople by Emperor M. Palaeologus (1261). The author suppresses his name, but he may be Theodoros Skoutariotis, the metropolitan of Kuzikos (the ancient city of Propontis destroyed by earthquake in 1063). He owned Greek codex 487 of the Marciana Library (Venice), which also contains our digest. Konstantinos Manassís (mid-twelfth century) wrote *A Historical Digest* (Leiden, 1616), a work in 15-syllable lines setting out world history from the creation to the death of Emperor Nikiforos Botaneiatis (1081).

In the 1160s, **M. Glykás** composed a *Chronography* in four volumes, dealing with the creation, Jewish and Anatolian history, Rome till Constantine the Great, and Byzantium till the death of Alexius Comnenus (1118). He fills the work with digressions on natural history and theology, and the writing is a monument of early **demotic.** *A Chronicle from the*

Creation of the World up to 1629 is attributed to Dorotheos of Monemvasia. This digest, made from an array of separate authors, became a source on Greek history during the Turkocracy and one of the first popular readers. Its earliest version covers events up to 1570. Manuel Malaxos is the author or scribe of a *Universal Chronicle* written around 1580.

CHRONICLE OF ANTHIMOS The *Chronicle of Anthimos* is by the late eighteenth-century educator Ioannis Venizelos and relates the history of Athens to 1800. **Perraivós** took material from this chronicle for his *History of Souli and Parga* (Venice, 1815). The 300-page manuscript was acquired (1822) by Kyriakos Pittakis, the Athenian archaeologist who saved lead material in the Acropolis ruins from the Turks (1821) by advising the Greek rebels to donate their own lead to the enemy. Pittakis published the *Chronicle of Anthimos* (1853) in the archaeological review, which he coedited with **Rangavís.**

CHRONICLE OF GALAXIDI The text of the *Chronicle of Galaxidi* was discovered in archaeological diggings (1864) at the imperial monastery of Christ the Saviour. According to the manuscript, the chronicle was written by a monk called Euthymios. Composed in **plain** language, it draws on archival documents (in parchment, skin, seals, and bulls) once stored at Christ the Saviour's. Highlighting a small town in the Gulf of Corinth (see **Vlami**), the chronicle goes from the first century to 1690. In 981, Galaxidi was deserted because of an invasion by Bulgars, "who cut what they found alive to pieces." In 1211, its citizens supported the founder of the Despotate of Epirus, Michael Angelos Comnenus. John the Il-

legitimate, duke of New Patras, was Galaxidi's leader. They twice defeated the Catalans.

CHRONICLE OF MOREA (fourteenth century) We meet the name "Morea," for a wild area of the western Peloponnese, at the start of the thirteenth century. In western Europe, it was known as the isle of Greece. The Vatican called it "Achaia," like the classical Roman province. Geoffroy de Villehardouin, nephew of a man who wrote *Chronicle of the Conquest of Constantinople,* was blown from the main body of a **Crusader** navy onto the coast of Morea. After his Frankish troops took over, it was consolidated as the princedom of Morea, with the Duchy of Athens-Thebes attached as feudatory. Between 1204 and 1205, he annexed Morea, where Italian merchants had already traded. He recognized existing property and social practices. The *Chronicle of Morea* is an anonymous poem of 9,219 unrhyming **political** lines, narrating events in this territory up to 1292: "The sons of the nobility, owning fiefdoms, / Were expected to retain them, relative to the rank they possessed, / With their liege homage and their military dues. / All that was left fell to the Franks. / People in the countryside kept the same status as before." The text displays Gallicized, or chivalric, vocabulary. Therefore editors like P. Kalonaros (1940) accept that the author is a Frankish-Greek (Γασμουλος), probably the son of a Greek mother and a French father, as he seems to be a Catholic. His anti-Greekness can be seen from passages like "who can be confident of trusting an oath from these Greeks, / As they don't respect God or love their master? / They have no esteem for each other and just act out of cunning." The notables of Morea petition Geoffroy for religious freedom, refusing to accept "France's faith" in place of Orthodoxy. The first part of the poem covers the fourth Crusade and the capture of Constantinople and closely corresponds to Villehardouin's *Chronicle.*

Further Reading

Buchon, J. A., ed. *Chroniques étrangères relatives aux expéditions françaises pendant le 13e siècle. Anonyme grec: Chronique de la principauté d'Achaïe.* Paris, 1841.

Schmitt, John, ed. *The Chronicle of Morea. Tὸ Χρονικὸν τοῦ Μορέως. A History in Political Verse, Relating the Establishment of Feudalism in Greece by the Franks in the 13th Century. Edited in Two Parallel Texts from the mss. of Copenhagen and Paris, with Introduction, Critical Notes and Indices.* London: Methuen & Co., 1904.

CHRONICLES OF LEONTIOS MACHAIRÁS AND GEORGE BOUSTRONIS

Medieval civilization in **Cyprus** is highlighted in these historical chronicles. Leontios is the son of a Stavrinos Machairás, who in 1382 attended the election of the successor to Peter II (1359–1369) and voted for Iakovos I Lusignan. Leontios was a favorite in the Frankish court. He went with King Ianos (1398–1432) on an ill-fated mission to attack Arabs invading Cyprus. In 1434, he acted as an envoy to Sultan Ikonios. Machairás's chronicle opens with a survey of older Cypriot history, reviews the island's main monasteries, bishops, and saints. It sets out the period of Peter II and then takes events down to 1432, that is, the death of King Ianos. He respects the Catholicism of his island's rulers, but criticizes those Greeks who abjured **Orthodox** beliefs to embrace the Latin church. Machairás complains about the corruption of the Greek language under Latin administration. One of his sources is a lost history by King Hugo IV (1324–1359). Machairás's work is continued by Boustronis, a Hellenized Frank. Boustronis was a friend of Cyprus's last king, Iakovos II, and in 1458 he served as an envoy, though he later incurred the displeasure of Queen Carlotta and was imprisoned in the keep (Leucosia).

Further Reading

Dawkins, R. M., ed. and trans. Leontios Makhairás. *Recital concerning the Sweet Land of Cyprus entitled "Chronicle."* Oxford: Clarendon Press, 2 vols., 1932.

CHRONICLE OF SERRAI

The name of the supposed author of this chronicle, Papasynodinós of Serrai (1600–1670), seems to merge the surname of an author ("Synodinós") with the word for "priest" (παπάς). He describes events of 1598–1642 in a chronicle of **mixed language** about a Macedonian provincial town. We see the hero, Manolis Bostantsoglou, captured because he was dawdling on a street where Turks had died. He is punished by impalement. The plane tree where he is hanged shrivels in horror at such treatment of a Christian, who yelled at his captors from the stake and refused to abjure his religion. The Turks who bore false witness against him are struck blind. Such touches display the typical osmosis, in chronicles, from fact to fabulous. A "Lament on Constantinople" attributed to Papasynodinos was shown by D. Roussou (*Nea Estía,* 1938) to be a variant by **Mathaios** of Myreon of another text of his own.

CHRONICLE OF THE TOCCO FAMILY OF CEPHALONIA

The historical poem that comprises the Tocco chronicle

contains 3,923 unrhymed **political** lines (from the fifteenth century) and is preserved in Vatican codex Greek 1831, folios 1r to 80r. It covers the period 1375–1422. Its purpose is educational. In fact, the codex contains a version of the *Spaneas* and was owned by the despots' family. Author and original title are unknown, but the text gives a clear account, in **plain Greek,** of the role in Frankish government played by this family, which had its origins in Florence. Members of the Tocco dynasty become dukes of Levkas, despots of Epirus, or Palatine Counts of Zakynthos and Cephalonia. The perspective expressed by the Tocco chronicle is partisan: our Byzantine poet extols his masters, Charles I Duke of Leukosia and Leonard II Count of Cephalonia. He shows affection for the despotate of Epirus and the city of Ioannina, but is hostile to Albanian elements in the fiefdom of Arta. His style recalls the breathless, conventional lexicon of **Akritic** poems: "Nobody could believe the thing which had happened; / He greeted the leaders and he embraced them, / Then he started to speak to them in sugared words."

Further Reading

Schiró, Giuseppe, ed. *Cronaca dei Tocco di Cefalonia di Anonimo.* Rome: Accademia dei Lincei, 1975.

CHRONOGRAPHER. See DIGEST

CHRYSOLORAS, MANUEL (c. 1350–1415) This author from **Constantinople** was the first to flee to the West (πρῶτος φυγάς) and teach Italians Greek. He spread the knowledge of classical manuscripts across Europe. Manuel II Palaeologus sent him to Rome (1391) on a mission to seek military assistance from the Pope against the Turks. This le-

gation met with failure. In 1394, Chrysoloras accompanied the Emperor on a tour of European countries. In 1408, the Emperor sent him to Paris and London. Chrysoloras enjoyed life in the West. He lectured on classical Greek at Florence (1396–1399), Milan, and Venice. He translated **Homer** and **Plato** into Latin. He was entrusted by Pope Alexander V with preparations for a proposed council on the Union of the **Catholic** and **Orthodox** churches. He wrote the first Greek book ever published, an easy-to-use **grammar** textbook entitled *Questions* (Venice, 1484). This book was translated into Latin by the humanist Guarino da Verona and perhaps printed as early as 1471. Chrysoloras also produced letters, the *Comparison of the Old and New Rome* (that is, Rome and Constantinople), and a translation of Plato's *Republic* and was made Cardinal by Pope John XXIII.

See also LASKARIS; PUBLISHING

Further Reading

Thomson, J. "Manuel Chrysoloras and the Early Italian Renaissance." *Greek, Roman, and Byzantine Studies,* no. 7 (1966): 63–82.

CHURCH. See ORTHODOX CHURCH, GREEK

CINEMA. See FILM

CIVIL WAR The Greek civil war that followed the Second World War was full of tragic, fratricidal incidents. Thus the poet Y. Tsoukalás (1903–1975) confesses that he betrayed and led his daughter, Aliki, to her death in 1949. She was executed by a firing squad: "our kid's grave: an armful of earth." The Greek penal code carries the death penalty for acts promoting civil war (ἐμφύλιος πόλεμος), under art. 18, 1864; art. 17 of the present constitution. The years of fratricidal strife run from 1946 to 1949. Some historians define them as starting in 1944. Athens was freed from the **German occupation** on 18 October 1944. M. Papandreou then ordered the demobilization of guerrilla forces. Trouble broke out in Athens on 2 December 1944. An armistice was concluded between the British Forces in Greece and the central committee of ELAS (see **Resistance**) on 12 January 1945. The hard-line left refused to recognize the results of a plebiscite on 1 September 1946, which reinstated royal rule (King George II). Leaders like Aris Velouchiotis, Nikos Zachariadis, and Gen. Markos (Vafiadis) drifted into legend or disgrace: "Golden swords are gleaming / Gunfire resounds from all quarters / Aris is going to war with his brave partisans" (P. Koumoukelis, in Scarfe 1972: 161). The writer **Kotzioulas** recorded a memoir of his comradeship with Velouchiotis in the hills: *When Aris and I Were Together* (1965). Another song went: "Markos, what mountain ridges are you treading / Now? In what town is your swift step heard?"

Accounts of battles or reprisals in the Civil War were angled from every perspective. American aviators "fried" the Greek mountain peaks with napalm. The British gave a bounty of £1 for the head of every dead partisan. Jailers on Makronisos tied naked detainees up in bags with a cat and dipped the bag into the sea, so the animal went berserk against the human body, as it struggled to avoid drowning. G. Katsamas wrote about the execution of Nick Beloyannis and three other KKE officials (1953) by the Greek police: "They were killed before dawn and on Sunday, both strictly prohibited by Greek law." There were 40 doctors in Greece to care for the wounded of the resistance. An eye hanging out of its socket, ears cut away to steal earrings, men burned alive, breasts hacked off women, gouged intestines severed by a rusty razor blade: these may be set pieces for a resistance memoir. Egli Ioannidis wrote: "They raped Anastasia and then stabbed her to death with knives. A dog howling awakened us and we went outside and found her body." Of course, the dog failed to wake them earlier.

The British made parachute drops with "boxes of shoes that were left foot only" (E. Ioannou). This was designed to tell ELAS members without boots that their Leftism was known to Churchill. If government troops caught men or women suspected of being Communist, they put their heads on poles outside the village. Later, in peacetime, ex-partisans were the ones who were obliged to obtain a certificate of civic responsibility. Some claimed they were victims of discrimination if their house was not painted white or their dog was off its lead. Brutality turned into marvel or prodigy: "An east wind was blowing and the howling of tortured men could be heard distinctly from Lavrion, ten kilometres away across the water, until dawn" (*distinctly; from 10 kilometres?* see Eudes, D. 1972: 358). Greece is the country where fewest intellectuals protested against the fate of the Republicans in Spain. The **Metaxás** dictatorship was grandiosely called "The Third Greek Civilization." With the **Occupation** and the Civil War, opposition intellectuals had the choice of flight or fight, from 1936 to 1949. The close of the Civil War left an emaciated country with a necklace of detention islands. The Greek Communist Party (KKE) supposedly made three attempts to take over the country: (1) during the Occupation; (2) in December 1944, and (3) in the Civil War (1946–1949). Up to 100,000 defeated Communists eventually left Greece to go to the other "People's Democracies" (1949), an exodus described in the film *Happy Homecoming, Comrade* (1986).

Further Reading

Iatrides, John A. and Linda Wrigley, eds. *Greece at the Crossroads: The Civil War and Its Legacy.* University Park: Pennsylvania State University Press, 1995.

Scarfe, Allan & Wendy Scarfe. *All That Grief: Migrant Recollections of Greek Resistance to Fascism, 1941–1949.* Sydney: Hale & Iremonger, 1994.

CLASS STRUGGLE The **Marxist** explanation of society and history is often delineated by authors who write for less-privileged readers or describe the class struggle between laborers and proprietors. Dimitris Raftopoulos (1890–1923) has an arresting poem called "Proletarian," with an image of the poor man in a cellar, intently watching wealthy youths emerge from a mansion to celebrate in the garden after dusk. The main theme of politically committed (στρατευμένοι) writers is inequality. Egli Ioannidis, born 1939, writes (1994): "Greece was class-ridden right through and I could see the injustice. Everywhere you went you could see it: at high school, at university. They looked up the record of who your parents were and what their occupations were and who your grandparents were and what their occupations were."

Deeper themes are the struggle between workers and bourgeoisie for control of resources, the theory of value and surplus value (της υπεραξίας), the redistribution of capital, and the abolition of private property. So the class struggle (πάλη τῶν τάξεων) pits the owners against the working class. The transitional stage from capitalism to **communism** is a dictatorship of the proletariat. All social classes contest the material means of production. Conflict over the modes of production (τὰ παραγωγικὰ μέσα) and the abolition of class discrimination is reflected in the **modern Greek novel** (1880–2000). Kostelenos, among other twentieth-century historians of Greek literature, commends (1977) the "historical–materialist method of analysis of a literary work." This may lead to the observation of significant voids in a conservative author's texts. Tofallis (1976) notes, for example, that there are no revolutionary echoes in any story by **Papadiamantis.**

Further Reading

Shrader, Charles R. *The Withered Vine: Logistics and the Communist Insurgency in Greece, 1945–1949.* Westport, CT: Praeger, 1999.

CLIO The **muse** Clio was the protector of history and rhetoric. She is depicted sitting on a bench, holding a roll of parchment. Modern Greek periodicals have taken the patron of history for their masthead. *Clio* was a daily newspaper in Cairo (1916–1937). *Clio* was also an illustrated fortnightly in Smyrna, issued by Tsoukaridis and Takis Simos. The best-known *Clio* was a Greek weekly that circulated at Trieste (1861–1883), edited by Dionysios Therianos. A weekly *Clio* was produced for Greek expatriates at Leipzig (1885–1891).

CODEX. See PALAEOGRAPHY

COLLAGE Collage is a technique by which experimental poets imitate the scissor-and-paste activity of small children, gluing bits of newspaper, tickets, or pamphlets onto pages that also contain verse. **Elytis** uses collage (καρτοκολλητική) in the dialogic poetry of *Maria Nepheli* (1978), inserting phrases from foreign languages, trademarks, and business words into his verse. Also, the alternating voices of the poet and a girl paste the physicality of womanhood onto the ideology of youth. The novelist **Vasilikós** devised a similar collage, by stitching together documents and articles in his two-volume work *K* (1992) to present a scandal in public life caused by the banker Yorgos Koskotás. The use of collage lends a gritty authenticity to other thriller and detective (θρίλερ, ντετέκτιβ) stories.

COLONELS' JUNTA, THE Greece came to the Colonels' Junta by a tortuous route. After the 1950s, the country moved from a long period of rightist government to a centrist union. In the mid-1960s, a moderate Prime Minister with broad support, George Papandreou, tried to restore further civil rights and lessen army interference in Greek public life. King Constantine was not sympathetic, and Papandreou resigned. Elements of his Center Union were charged with setting up new democratic elections for May 1967. With only 11 political detainees now left in jail, the army suddenly acted. On 21 April 1967, a cadre of Greek colonels staged a coup, possibly with political support from the United States. Thus began the so-called Colonels' Junta, of seven years' duration.

Greek cultural life was severely affected by the seven-year dictatorship of 1967–1974 and its "National Government." Symbols of the regime were placed near airports, harbors, and the en-

trance to towns. One highway sign featured a phoenix resurrected out of flames. The name "Greece" and the date "21 April 1967" were prominent on these hoardings. The poet Menelaos Loudemis (1912–1977) has a poem called "Homeland," with the lines "Greece, I am shocked that / I, an idolator of Beauty, / Can see your Karyatids ridiculed, / And not go mad." Books were subject to **censorship,** or banned. The Cretan writer **Lilí Zografou** lampoons this political hiatus in her book *Occupation: Whore* (1978). **Kostoula Mitropoulou** (b. 1927) describes the November 1973 uprising against the Colonels in her bestseller *A Chronicle of Three Days* (1974). In 1969, a gazette of prohibited books contained 760 titles by over 200 writers, Greek and foreign, including Aristophanes and **Shakespeare.** In November 1971, a list of prohibited books was produced by the Directorate of National Security, proscribing Chekhov, Brecht, Deutscher, Peter Brook, and Tomasi di Lampedusa.

Some editors, writers, or musicians were arrested (see **Torture**) or placed in detention (like **Douka, Ritsos**). Others went into exile or were obliged to stay out of Greece (see **Vasilikos, Chatzís**). Some, like the female writer **Milliéx,** who had been a militant in the EAM (see **Resistance**), were deprived of their citizenship. Another female writer, **Elli Alexiou,** was prevented by the Ministry of the Press and Information, in 1972, from mounting a production of her play *A Day in the Secondary School* (1973). When the 58-year-old poet Yannis Ritsos was arrested in the summer of 1967 and became ill in detention on Samos, a hundred French writers staged a protest campaign. Consequently, the government permitted him to return to Athens. In 1970, a book neutrally titled *Eighteen*

Texts was published with the covert aim of gathering reactions by Greek writers to the Colonels' rule. By the Press Law of 1969, editors and publishers were obliged to attend to the censorship of their own works, and a book's title had to match exactly its contents.

The title *Eighteen Texts,* therefore, generically masked a statement by Greek writers, linking literature to political commitment. Here were a much-discussed **Seferis** poem "The Cats of Saint Nicholas," Kay Cicellis's "Brief Dialogue," Takis Koufopoulos's "The Actor," a story by **Spyros Plaskovitis,** "Going Home" by **Kotziás,** "Nights" by **Takis Sinopoulos,** "The Plaster Cast" by Thanasis Valtinos, and texts by **Stratis Tsirkas, Menis Koumandareas,** Nora Anagnostaki, **Rodis Roufos,** Yeoryios Chimonas, **Th. D. Frangopoulos,** "Athos" by **Nikos Kasdaglis,** and "Traffic Lights" by Lina Kasdagli, with Alex. Argyriou's ambiguous "The Style of a Language and the Language of a Style," Maronitis's "Arrogance and Intoxication," and Manolis Anagnostakis's "Target," in which poetry is compared to a pack horse, toiling for the resistance, even if its lines are too flimsy to enter politics: "Today verses will not mobilize the mass, / Nowadays verse will not overthrow regimes."

In April 1970, 300 political prisoners were released, including the composer Theodorakis. On 17 November 1973, the Junta dispersed students occupying the Polytechnic of Athens. **Ioanna Tsatsou,** in her poem "Protest," recalls the galloping horses and the intimidation: "Perhaps, on some righteous day, / All is left from this will be a flute." This confrontation between the right and the left is reflected in various literary works, such as *The Mystery* (1976) by **Margarita Limberaki,** or *Fool's Gold* (1979) by

Maro Douka. The Colonels condemned American culture, but wanted American imports. So poets and songwriters stuffed their texts with consumer trademarks. A sculptor handed out carnations in plaster to mock an article by colonel Papadopoulos, the Junta's strongman, which said that Greece was a crippled body needing a cast.

Further Reading

Clogg, R. and Yannopoulos, G., eds. *Greece under Military Rule.* London: Secker & Warburg, 1972.

Papadopoulos, Yeoryios. Το πιστεύω μας [*Our Credo*], vols. 1–2. Athens: Press Office, 1967–1968.

Woodhouse, C. M. *The Rise and Fall of the Greek Colonels.* London: Granada, 1982.

COMEDY Comedy has been fairly restricted in modern Greek cultural life. The term *revue* (επιθεώρηση) corresponds in meaning to the skit, or "boulevard." This was the only kind of comedy current in Athens at the turn of the twentieth century. It became very popular, adapted from the racy stage hits of nineteenth-century Paris. The idea was to entertain the public with a satirical view of current events, using songs, choruses, dance, spectacles, and mime. Some revues were annual events, like *Cinema* (1908), *A Bit of Everything* (1894), or *Panathenaia* (1911). It has been shown (by G. Yalamvanos, in *JHD* 6, no. 1, 1979) that only 384 plays on original Greek subjects were produced in Athens between 1800 and 1908. The main thrust of comedy was to imitate western European forms. The French model was still being copied between 1907 and 1922, in Athenian revues aiming at sociopolitical subjects in and around World War I. The texts from this boulevard theater have a three-act structure and one central actor who is on stage in most scenes.

Thus in the late nineteenth century, Greek comedies were lowbrow, compared with western European productions. Social comment reached the Greek stage in the form of revue. Farce and swooning emotions were provided by slapstick (φαρσοκωμωδία) and the **komeidyllio.** The stock characters "joker" and "boaster" returned in nineteenth-century comedy, where craftiness beat arrogance. The joker starts out as the underdog, like Fasoulis, in **puppet theater.**

See also THEATER PERFORMANCES

COMMITMENT, POLITICAL. See MARXIST

COMMUNISM; COMMUNIST PARTY
The Communist Party of Greece was formed in November 1918, on the heels of the Russian Revolution, and called initially the Socialist Labor Party of Greece (SEKE). In 1920, the name was altered to Socialist Labor/Communist (SEKE/K), and in 1924 to Communist Party of Greece (KKE). In April 1920 it joined the Third International, adopting 21 clauses passed by the Third International. In 1923, an internal crisis broke out. Following a plenary assembly, the party's first leaders, Ar. Sideris and I. Yeoryiadis, were excluded as right-wingers. In 1924, Evangelos Papanastasiou was proscribed as an extremist. After the Pangalos dictatorship collapsed (1926), a further split in the KKE was caused by the "liquidationist opposition." The liquidationist faction of the KKE wanted a purge. They believed the Greek party was threatened by (1) leadership with no ideological homogeneity, (2) low party numbers, and

(3) a gulf between the spontaneous (αὐθορμήτο) and conscious (συνειδητό) movement. The faction failed, withdrew as a group, and issued the journal *Spartacus.* In 1929, they formed an opposition called "Spartacus" and were viewed as followers of Trotsky. In 1933, a joint resolution condemning German Nazis was signed by Greek nationalists, liberals, and Communists.

The loyalty of some writers to the hammer-and-sickle is unswerving. **Ritsos** wrote: "Bulgaria has the complexion of an open door, / The color of an open, freshly printed book, / Where you can read freely: 'Chapter 1, Peace; / Chapter 2, Factories. Justice.'" The *Communist Manifesto* by Marx and Engels (1848) was first translated into **plain Greek** by the writer K. Chatzopoulos (selected passages, 1908). In 1919, a new, complete translation was issued (anonymous). In 1921, a third Greek translation, by I. Sideris, came out. A translation, preface, and commentary by Yannis Kordatos followed in 1927. General-Secretary of the KKE from 1945 was Nikos Zachariadis, who had a determining function in party internal politics from 1931. A popular rhyme of the war years went: "The people are victorious, / Can snap their chains with ease / The leader of their Party / Is Zachariadis." The journal *Idea* was put out in 1933 as an anti-Communist flagship of civic freedom, fighting dialectical materialism more urgently than Fascism. Among the staff of *Idea* were the young writers **Terzakis** and **Theotokás.** The young **Seferis** refused to contribute. A Communist Youth League (OKN) had a branch in Greece from 1920. A novel by **K. Kotziás,** *Condemned for High Treason* (1964), concerns confusion caused in the Left (1950), when the communist N. Ploubidis was executed. Kotziás uses the character Ilias Sandas to depict Ploubidis as a rising cadre in the party who continues illegal activity in the wake of the Civil War and is branded a "provocateur" by the party.

In fact, after the end of the Colonels (1974), archives were opened, history courses were modernized, and the Centre-Left government of Papandreou recognized the EAM and ELAS **resistance** struggle. The end of the demonization of communism in the 1980s led to TV films or books about a struggle that was controversial on both sides. They discredited (as Marion Sarafis says, 1990) the story that Britain saved Greece in the late 1940s from a left-wing putsch, or that ELAS would have "marched on Athens." Ageing Communist intellectuals are studied with understanding and poignancy in the novel by **Alkis Zei,** *Achilles' Fiancée* (Athens: Kedros, 1987). Her characters still believe in the *cause,* traveling between Athens, Rome, Paris, Tashkent, and Moscow. Euro-communism and consumerism have passed them by. Lila Champipi's novel *Passing Out in the Acropolis* (Athens: Exantas, 1997) analyzes the emotions felt by the daughter of a Greek political exile, who feels alone and stateless when he dies. The Party's share of the national vote has not been better than 12 percent, in recent times. Its support of the anti-Gorbachev coup in the Soviet Union (1989) alienated some intellectuals.

Further Reading

Critis. "Mort et Renaissance d'un Parti communiste." *Politique d'aujourd'hui,* no. 4 (April 1969).

Dounia, Christina. Λογοτεχνία και Πολιτική. Τα περιοδικά της Αριστεράς στο μεσοπόλεμο [Literature and Politics: Periodicals of the Left in the Inter-War Period]. Athens: Kastaniotis, 1996.

Sarafis, Stefanos. *ELAS: Greek Resistance Army.* London: Merlin Press, 1980.

COMNENE, ANNA (1083–c. 1148)

Anna Comnene used to complain bitterly that she had not been made a man. The eldest daughter of the Byzantine emperor Alexius I Comnenus and Irene Empress of the East, she withdrew from political life to a convent after a failed attempt to prevent the imperial succession of her brother (Alexius Ioannis). She then composed the *Alexiad* in 15 books, a history of her father's exploits, covering the historical period 1069 to 1118. This completes the work of her husband, **Nikiforos Briennios,** a soldier and diplomat. Her *Alexiad* is an erudite work, infused with loyalty to her father, whom she praises as the "Thirteenth Apostle." She makes use of contemporary sources, in a style that Krumbacher calls "an entirely mummiform school language which is diametrically opposed to the popular spoken language which was used in literature at that time." She even apologizes for using barbarian personal names or Russian place names in her text.

COMPETITIONS, POETRY; PROSE

In the latter part of the nineteenth century, competitions for prizes in poetry, prose, and **folklore** studies were sponsored by the state or founded by individuals to enhance the new Greek kingdom. Such benefactors were **St. Rallis** (1850), K. Tsokanos (1855), Th. P. Rodokanakis (1860), G. Melás (1857), V. Soulinis (1878), D. Oikonomou (1877), **G. Lassanis** (1884), K. Soutsos (1893), K. Sebastopoulos (1895), D. Theofanopoulos (1923), and E. Benakis. **Estía** and **Philadelpheios** were other major awards. Societies like **Parnassós,** Evangelismos, or the Society of Friends instituted contests and periodicals. Because the press was not yet fully developed, competititions gave poets and dramatists a chance to act as a mouthpiece for public sentiment. G. Pappageotes surmises that the prohibition of contact between the two sexes found solace in the submission of passionate fictional diaries. The hundreds of thousands of lines that reached the annual poetry competition judges between 1851 and 1877 were mainly patriotic or lugubrious. They offered a plethora of youthful deaths and writers opting for suicide. From the 1850s, large numbers of plays were submitted to the poetry competitions, and the concentration on comedy encouraged an interest in folklore and the **demotic.** In 1858, **Tertsetis** entered the Rallis competition with a play entitled *Triumph of the Poetry Contest.* His intention was to ridicule the competition and defend the right to use everday demotic.

The **Voutsynas Poetry Prize** was awarded from 1862 to the year 1876, when it was stopped, because unsuccessful contestants began to publish articles denouncing the members of the committee. In 1873, for the first time, a collection of lyric poems composed in the demotic was honored, *The Voice of My Heart,* by **D. Kambouroglous.** Up until this time, entries for literary competitions had been required to follow the rules of classical drama, or be **purist** and use **Katharevousa.** The troubled **Ioannis Karasoutsas** (1824–1873) entered his poems for three of the poetic contests (1855, 1857, 1867). Karasoutsas never won and later committed suicide. In December 1889, **Christos Christovasilis** (1860?–1937) unexpectedly took first prize in a competition started by the newspaper *Acropolis* with his story "Pastoral New Year," and this decided his career for

journalism and letters. Other literary prizes of the late nineteenth century were awarded under the names **Lassaneios** and Pantelideios. The Pantelideios also ran a drama prize, to which the indefatigable competitor **Timoleon Ambelás** (1850–1926) submitted his *Prince of Morea,* which had already gone to other competitions under the title "Prince of Achaea." In 1907 **Kazantzakis** entered his play *Day Breaks* for this prize. Its theme was a woman who rejects her husband. This subject was in advance of its time, but controversy reached the pages of the journal *Noumás* because of the fact that *Day Breaks* was written in the demotic. The editor of *Noumás* expressed delight that Kazantzakis's play received an honorable mention from the adjudicators. The judges could not award *Day Breaks* their prize because it broke the rule that the play be composed in Katharevousa and consist of iambic dodecasyllables. There were also foreign and national prizes for the literature of the new Greece. The translation of Homer's *Iliad* into demotic **decapentasyllables** by **A. Pallis** (Paris, 1903) won the prize of the French Society for the Promotion of Hellenic Studies.

Ioannis Gryparis (1870–1942), a classicist, poet, and literary editor, won the National Prize for Arts and Letters. Miltiadis Malakasis (1869–1943), who wrote about his native **Missolonghi** and composed light, Romantic lyric verse, was another winner of the National Prize. The annual Kalokairineios Prize of 2,000 drachmas was instituted in 1919 by a Cretan benefactor, called Kalokairinos, and a committee appointed by the literary society "Parnassós" was entrusted with its management. The Theodoropoulos was a prestigious mid-twentieth-century prize, promoted by the Union of Greek

Writers. In 1953 it gave honorable mention to the volume *Captain Yannakis,* short stories by the Cypriot author Xanthos Lusiotis. In 1961 the Academy of Athens awarded **Tasos Athanasiadis** its major prize for a prose work, on the completion of his trilogy *The Panthei,* which took fifteen years in the writing. The Women's Literary Society awarded Angeliki Barella its 1968 prize for her children's book *Greece and Ourselves.* In more recent times, **Vasilikós** has won The Award of the Group of Twelve, for his prose fiction.

Greek **science fiction** has its own prize named "Icaromenippus," after a journey to the moon in the Hellenistic writer Lucian (170 A.D.). Silver medals have gone to Dionysis Kalamvrezos for *Sickness and the Lotus Flower* (1995) and to his *Stories of the Solitary, the Banished, and the Shipwrecked* (1995). The Icaromenippus gold medal for best **science fiction** story (1995) went to Makis Panorios for "Actor," and K. Athanasiadis took a silver medal for "Punishment." In 1996, M. N. Antonopoulos won the Icaromenippus medal for *Hyperborea: Struggle with the Shadows,* and D. Papadopoulos took the gold medal, for his space opera *The Planet of Revenge.* The best stories entered in the 1996 *Elle Magazine* SF competition came out as a book.

See also ESTÍA; PARNASSÓS; PHILADELPHEIOS; RALLIS; VOUTSYNAS POETRY PRIZE

Further Reading

20 + 1 ιστορίες: από τον διαγωνισμό του *Elle* [Twenty plus One Stories from the *Elle* Competition]. Athens: Kastaniotis, 1996.

COMPOUND ADJECTIVE The use of compound adjectives, some incorporating strings of other words, is a feature that sets Byzantine and modern Greek writing apart from Latin. In the fifteenth century *Story of Achilles,* praise of the heroine's beauty uses the kind of strings of compounds that were sought after in Byzantine style: "crystal-column-necked, red-lips-adorned, full-moon-eyed, pearl-white-toothed." In his **Homer** translations, **Kazantzakis** used original compound forms about Helen: "laughing like an almond tree," or "on whom roses drip," or "shoulders on which desire glides." In his early writing, **Palamás** was a "hunter" after compounds (Papadimas 1948: 241). In the newspaper *Town* (December 1899), Palamás writes: "I think the use of compounds is, and ought to be, *unlimited* in poetic expression. The Greek language has always been immeasurably susceptible to compounds, and the ancient Greek poets exploited this priceless good fortune boldly and unstintingly."

CONJUNCTION; RELATIVE PRONOUN According to **Kavafis,** the monosyllable που, meaning "that, who, which," with its various grave and circumflex accents in pre-1980 Greek, had an ugly effect, repeated over and over again. He thought the disappearing participle was bound to come back and save Greeks from the hideous sound of *pou.* But participles (*saying; having said; about to say*) faded from modern Greek writing. This is because **parataxis** (a row of main clauses) became commoner than **hypotaxis** (a cluster of subordinate clauses). Kavafis's aspiration for the Greek **sentence** is the mark of a linguistic conservative. He did not foresee the language reforms in which the accent on all monosyllables would be abolished.

CONSTANTINOPLE   The   world's most famous city, Constantinople, was founded on the site of the ancient Byzantium in 330 A.D., by Emperor Constantine. The city sits on a strategic peninsula, surrounded by water on three sides, between the channel of the Golden Horn to its north and the sea of Marmara (Propontis) to the south and east. Asia faces it on the opposite coast. This was the imperial Byzantine capital for over 1,000 years, until its **fall** to the Turks in 1453. It was protected from inland by a system of gates and fortifications: the three wall systems were the formidable ramparts of Theodosius, Constantine, and Severus, protecting the inner city more tightly, as one came close to the great Christian cathedral of **Hagia Sophia,** which sat up against the coast inside the old walls of Byzantium. In the tenth century, Venetian traders gained a foothold inside Constantinople, and the Genoese assumed control of Galata, just north of the Golden Horn.

In 1204 the **Crusaders** sacked the city with great force and parceled out its territory, for temporary exploitation, between Baldwin of Flanders (five-eighths), and Venice (three-eighths). The few travel books or city guides in Byzantine literature tend to start, or end, in the city: the fourteenth-century scholar Andreas Libadenus composed a *Tour from Constantinople to Egypt, Palestine and Trebizond.* Possibly of the tenth century is a work known as "The Homeland of Constantinople" (*Patria Constantinopoleos*). Ioannis Kananos wrote an account of Sultan Mourat's first unsuccessful siege of the city in summer 1422. He used the spoken language, so that we learn real and not **Atticized** names of enemy officers or of the siege engines aimed at Constantinople's walls. The eventual relief of the city is described as a Divine intercession by Mary Mother of God.

Medieval sermons also link Constantinople's security to the intercession of the Virgin, who protected Christians by helping them defeat sieges of their capital (between 626 and 718). Hymns were sung along the city walls to honor the Mother of God, and one defender of Constantinople (Patriarch Sergios, in 626) may have composed the poem "To thee, Champion and Commander." From Thrace come demotic lines about an old lady who was frying fish, when a voice whispered to her from above "Stop cooking, or the City will become Turkish. If the fish leaps up and comes alive, then the enemy will come and Turkify the City." The fish comes alive, so an Amir rides in. From another text, Niketas Akominatos (author of a *Thesaurus of Orthodoxy*) addresses Constantinople with ecstasy: "O! City! City, cynosure of all cities, / Renown of this world and marvel of the next." Niketas Choniatis (c. 1150–1213), who wrote on Emperor regimes in the eleventh century, gives an account, in *De Statuis,* of the Latin troops' pillage of art, statuary, and relics in the 1204 crusade.

Demotic songs are patterned on a line of 15 syllables, which was called "political" verse, because it came from *The* City ("Poli"). It became the governing verse of demotic poetry, for Constantinople stood for every *polis,* and calling it "the City" was a paranomasia (or nickname). From c. 1392 comes the anonymous *Poem about the Capture and Reconquest of Constantinople,* in 759 political verses, preserved in the Marciana (Venice) codex 408. Its first lines are like an epigraph: "How the queen of all cities was taken by Italians, / And later handed back to the Greeks, / Is written here for you to find out, if you wish." Our poet calls Akominatos his guide, and draws on

Yeoryios Akropolitis. The closing lines fix a date of composition by saying the Palaeologi had held the throne for 131 years.

After Constantinople's fall, and its Islamicization as Istanbul, Greeks mourned the lost center of all that was wise and fair, which Athens could never replace. Byzantium's conqueror, Mehmet II, fashioned a court culture at his Istanbul palace (*Seraglio*). This led to the literature of the *Divan,* so named for the Sultan's council.

See also BYZANTIUM, HISTORY OF; FALL OF CONSTANTINOPLE

CONSTITUTION. See POLITICIANS

CONTRACTION In Greek poetry or grammar, contraction (συναίρεση) is the important principle by which two light syllables are replaced by one heavy (long) syllable. In practice, this means that two vowels are merged into one diphthong, or one vowel. This is sometimes the same as the consequence of **hiatus.** Examples of contraction are in the verb *dilo-o,* which becomes *diló* ("I clarify"), or the noun *no-os,* which becomes *nous* ("mind").

CORINTH Corinth had one of the most powerful locations in ancient Greece, poised on the isthmus between the Peloponnese and the mainland. It controls sea trade to the west and the east, as well as movement between the two halves (northern and southern) of Greece. In 1395 the Byzantines dislodged the Franks and sold Corinth (in 1400) to the Knights of Rhodes, a pious order of left-behind **Crusaders.** Corinth, with the Peloponnese, was annexed by the Turks in 1458. After 1612, it was held by the

Knights of Malta, among others. **Venice** took possession of Corinth in 1687, but lost it to the Turks in 1715. The Turks were ousted in the **War of Independence** (1822). This colorful city and region has produced many writers, among them **K. Karyotakis** (1898–1928), the unexpected, melancholy innovator of twentieth-century lyric poetry, and the female novelist **Lina Kasdagli** (b. 1921). From the city or its region come the theologian Siphis Kollias (b. 1921), and the poet Vasileios Lazanás (b. 1916), who wrote an essay (1972) calling Goethe's "Maid of Corinth" an important ballad, with its move from the classical to romantic and its heroine from a time when Paul was founding Christianity at Corinth. The productive writer Kostas Lazanás (b. 1915) experienced political persecution for his certain **Resistance** stances. Kostas Stamatis, a lawyer and civil servant who published several volumes of poetry (as well as legal material on the concept of harbor policing), was born at Brachati, in the countryside near Corinth. Antigone Bouleki-Galanaki was also born in the city (1912). She did not complete her law degree (Athens), published her first poems in *The New Corinthian,* and later produced several collections of verse and a volume of stories, *The Stroll of Bitter Length,* in 1963.

Further Reading

Thomopoulos, Sozon. Κορίνθιοι συγγραφεῖς *1863–1963* (βιογραφικά—βιβλιογραφικά) [Corinthian Writers 1863–1963: Biographies and Bibliographies]. Athens: 1962.

CRETE Crete, which became part of Greece in 1913, is a flat finger of land with a surface area of 8,400 sq. kilometers, descending slightly from west to east along latitude in the Aegean, south of the **Cyclades.** It has two universities, founded in 1973 and 1977. Its art and literature have tended to be rebellious, subversive, decentralized, and dialect based. In the medieval period, there were innumerable uprisings (for instance, 1213, 1365, 1570, 1603) against Venice, after it had bought Crete for 10,000 silver franks from the crusader Boniface of Montferrat (1212). The Turks controlled all of Crete by 1717, so next came uprisings against the Turks, in 1770, 1821, and 1841, because, even after the **War of Independence,** Turkey held on to control of Crete. More or less violent flaring-up of Cretan nationalism occurred in 1858, 1869, 1905, and 1912, when E. Venizelos appointed Stefanos Dragoumis to administer Crete in the name of the King.

Since Thales, the astronomer, and the writer Riano (c. 275 A.D.), who appears in the *Palatine Anthology,* Crete has produced generations of chroniclers, songsters, novelists, and poets. The island was conquered by Venice in the early thirteenth century, but from the end of the sixteenth century shed its Venetian and Byzantine ethos and began to acquire a culture of its own. The early work, *Voskopoula,* was surpassed by the later *Erotokritos*. Then came a surge in works for the stage: **George Chortatsis** wrote three well-known plays in the period between 1585 and 1600, a tragedy, *Erofili,* a comedy, *Katzourbos,* and an Arcadian play entitled *Gyparis.* The capture of Candia by the Turks in 1669 halted this golden age in its tracks.

Yet Crete, with its White Mountains and other continuous hill chains, remained a haven for bandit haunts, and its village culture (masculine, and highly prone to blood feuds) was seen as obstreperous and audacious. A **demotic** song portrays most of the ships on the Greek **sea** fleeing before threats by Mr. North Wind: "To him said a ship that came from Crete: / 'North Wind, I fear you not, although you bleat; / My masts are bronze, my rigging steel, / With sails of silk above my keel'." Crete possessed a **demotic** literary language that was fully formed in the early seventeenth century. Thinking of **Dante,** Petrarch, and Boccaccio, who molded Italy's literary idiom, **Psycharis** called Crete the "Tuscany of Greece." Around 1493, Yeoryios Choumnos set to verse Byzantine pseudo-biblical stories in his *Creation.* From the last quarter of the fifteenth century comes the first text in vernacular Greek, printed at Venice (1519), a dream visit to the nether world conventionally known as *Apokopos*. From the early fifteenth century come the autobiographically laced prison and **bawdy** poems of **Stefanos Sachlikis.**

The *Lament on Bitter and Insatiate Hades,* by **Ioannis Pikatoros** of Rethymno, written after 1519, shows features of *Apokopos* and reminiscences of Dante. It describes a visit by Pikatoros himself to the nether world. From this period comes the anonymous *Story of a Girl and a Young Man,* and also an *Exile,* concerning life far from home (see **Xenitiá**). The Cretan war between Venetians and Turks (1648–1669) is narrated in the *Relation in Verses of the Dreadful War which Took Place on the Island of Crete* (publ. Venice, 1861), by **Bounialís.** Previously (1681), a similar poem was printed by his imitator from Cephalonia, Anthimos Diakrousis.

A *War of Crete,* in 9,287 iambic verses, was written by the doctor–scholar known as Pikrós, namely Athanasios Skliros (1580–1664). He completes his account of the Turkish conquest at line

307 of the 23rd section of this anguished, eyewitness poem. From about 1635 is Crete's major dramatic work, *The Sacrifice of Abraham,* now believed to be by V. Kornaros. A date placed speculatively at about 1640 marks the acme of Cretan writing, the chivalric romance by Kornaros, *Erotokritos*, later published at Venice (1713).

The Cretan Grigorios Palamidis composed a versified history of Michael the Brave, in Poland (1607). Originally from Crete are the authors **Leonardos Dellaportas,** Markos Mousouros (c. 1470–1517), Andreas Sklentzas, and **Antonios Achelis** (who composed a *Siege of Malta* in the late sixteenth century). Cretan, too, are the unattributed "Pretty Shepherdess" (see **Voskopoúla**), the groundbreaking plays of **Yeoryios Chortatsis,** and the tragedies of Ioannis Mormoris (seventeenth century). Chortatsis's pastoral play *Gyparis* presents a mixture of **Hellenistic** elements and Italian pastoral motifs. The mannerisms of Longus and Achilles Tatius are spliced with the renaissance values of Torquato Tasso's *Aminta,* Sannazaro's *Arcadia* or Guarini's *Il pastor fido* (*The Faithful Shepherd*). Guarini's play was translated into 15-syllable lines, and **plain Greek** by Mikhail Soummakis (1658), a learned doctor from Zakynthos, who managed to transfuse into his version much of the freshness of the Cretan poems. Chortatsis has the hero, a shepherd, fall for a beautiful shepherdess. She spurns him to pursue her devotion to the huntress divinity, Artemis (that is, chastity). By various stratagems, the girl's virtue is compromised. Chortatsis's cast, contrary to the Italian model, is from a late-sixteenth-century Cretan setting, sporting names like Frosyne, Alexis, Panoria, and Yiannoulis.

The play *King Rhodolinos,* by **Ioannis Andreas Troilos,** was first printed in Venice, 1647. The neoclassical comedy *Fortounatos,* by Markos Antonios Foskolos, was written and performed during the long Turkish investment of Candia (1648–1669). *That an Old Man Ought Not Marry a Young Girl* is an early sixteenth-century poem in 198 **political** lines, offering a mildly indecent variation on the stock theme of the grey-haired cuckold: "When you are old, and over seventy, / You lose your wits, and your head grows empty; / As time goes by and the old get older, / Their head must melt upon their shoulder."

The demotic poetry of Crete has various subgenres, such as *paralogés* and *mantinádhes* (see **Lianotrágouda**). The "songs of the foothills" (ριζίτικα) come from the *roots* of the White Mountains. Feasting songs (συμποσιακὰ) come mainly from the period of Turkish rule and were sung by a male chorus. There is an interesting tradition of wayfarer chants, known as "songs of the road" (τραγούδια της στράτας). After the fall of Crete's capital (Iraklio) to the Turks (1669), the island's literature was characterized by historical poems (**Meletios Pigás, Kyrillos Loukaris**).

Turkish administration of Crete had been much harsher than the preceding Venetian rule. Some scholars argued that waves of refugees carried Crete's literary and popular culture away to the **Heptanese** and the Morea. There is a faltering continuation of the great Cretan tradition in the poetry of Michalis Vlachos (around 1705). In 1786, a cheese-maker called Pantzelios composed the *Song of Daskaloyannis,* a formative text in 1,032 lines, about exploits under the renowned leader Daskaloyannis (1730–1771) and his swashbuckling Sphakiot rebels (see **Orloff**). Ioannis Mourellos (1886–1963) is the first modern journalist and chronicler of the emancipated island. He wrote a three-volume *History of Crete*. Michalis Diallinás (1853–1927) declared that he used the "bile of Juvenal" in his satire, wrote historical pieces on Cretan events or legend, poems on such subjects as **E. Venizelos,** or the **Balkan Wars,** and verse plays based on incidents from Crete's recent past.

Diallinás's *Girl from the Village of Kritsá* is a short epic about a maiden who fought the Turks disguised as a man. The poem became popular reading matter. The heroine's identity is not discovered till she is wounded in battle. Iannikodaskalos (1864–1917), teacher and notary, wrote verse in **dialect.** This was recited by the common people of Lasithi, a bowl-shaped plain in the Dikti mountains, which for centuries had been cut off. So steeped in **folk** tradition is the satirical verse of Iannikodaskalos, that some thought it a collective work by the Cretan peasantry. His *Kalamaukiad* was written in the dialect of the villages round Ierapetra, the most southerly city in Europe, the "crossroads of Minoan and Achaian civilization," according to Arthur Evans, restorer of Knossos.

See also KAZANTZAKIS; KONDYLAKIS; PREVELAKIS; THEODOROU; ZOGRAFOU

Further Reading

Holton, David, ed. *Literature and Society in Renaissance Crete.* Cambridge: Cambridge University Press, 1991: 102–128.

Zachariadou, Elizabeth A. *Trade and Crusade: Venetian Crete and the Emirates of Menteshe and Aydin, 1300–1415.* Venice: Istituto Ellenico di Studi Bizantini e Postbizantini, 1983.

CRITICISM, GREEK LITERARY
The unrelenting beautification of the writer's text, after early drafts, has always been prized by Greek literary critics. Dionysius of Halicarnassus, who wrote the first classical criticism (Rome, 30–8 B.C.), says that Plato "combed, and curled and rebraided his pages," while his own *On Composition* taught **orators** how to arrange words. He was admired by Longinus, the author of *On the Sublime.* By the seventeenth century, Longinus himself was considered second to **Aristotle** as a guide to literature and criticism.

In modern times, "style" (ύφος) has been regarded as the sum of "expressive devices" that define an author or a text. In nineteenth-century Greek criticism, much attention was given to the "force," "coloring," "vitality," "sincerity," and especially "coolness" of a writer's use of figures of speech like **simile** or **metaphor. Konstantinos Asopios** (1785–1872), professor of Classical Greek at Athens, produced a *Critique of Soutsos* (1853), which was an analysis of the **purist** poetry of **Panayotis Soutsos** and a response to his manifesto, *New School of The Written Language.* Asopios's book ranged over the stylistic values of Soutsos's vocabulary and word order. It offered prescriptions for modern Greek writing, while also arguing the validity of the contemporary **demotic.** It is seen in retrospect as the first modern critical work.

The preferred mode of analysis for subsequent critics was the close reading: phrase-by-phrase explanation of a prose passage or poem. They use many quotations from the text and proscribe anything under the heading of slavish imitation (δουλική μίμηση). Direct quotation of the writer's words is particularly the case in Greek critical practice. This is due to the educational impulse behind the history of Greek prose. During the **Enlighten-**

ment, the student would not possess the original, so he copied down the teacher's quotations, thus forming a **chrestomathy.**

Further Reading

Frangopoulos, Theofilos D. Κριτικὴ τῆς κριτικῆς. Δοκίμια [The Criticism of Criticism: Essays]. Athens: Diogenes, 1978.

Longinus. *On Great Writing (On the Sublime),* trans. with intro. by G. M. A. Grube. New York: Bobbs-Merrill, 1957.

CRUSADES The crusade was an armed pilgrimage by the Christian West against the pagan East. It was first called in 1095 and made attractive by papal indulgences (guarantees of purgation, or forgiveness), or glimpsed possibilities of annexation and conquest. The purpose of the movement was to release Christians in Palestine from Muslim pressure, or to free Jerusalem as the center of Christianity. The crusading journey was undertaken on separate occasions, with wildly diversified commanders in the eleventh to thirteenth centuries by soldiers known as crusaders (σταυροφόροι), so-called because they carried a red cross on their garments. Their mission was to rescue Christians in the East, or recapture the Holy Sepulchre.

The first crusade (1096–1099) was convoked by Pope Urban II at the Council of Clermont (1095). Two expeditions were sparked off. First was a plebeian rabble led by Peter the Hermit, which was neutralized by the Turks. Then, a federation of feudal armies captured Antioch. The Byzantine emperor Alexius I became alarmed by the crusaders' rapacity. He did not assist the Christian victors, who sacked Antioch and put its inhabitants to the sword. In 1097, Alexius prevented the crusaders from destroying Nicaea, the Seljuk capital, but they took Edessa (modern Urfa, in southern Turkey near the Syrian border), and finally Jerusalem (1099).

The victorious crusaders conducted a massacre of the defeated population of Jerusalem. This military success generated, to the horror of Alexius I and the Greeks, a ribbon of Latin states across the Middle East: a Principality of Antioch, a County of Edessa, a Kingdom of Jerusalem (which went to Godfrey Bouillon), and a County of Tripoli. The second crusade lasted from 1147 to 1149 and resulted in a failed siege of Damascus. It was led by Emperor Conrad III and King Louis VII of France. The third crusade (1189–1192) was intended to deliver Jerusalem from the Kurdish sultan Saladin, who had recaptured it from the Franks in 1187. It was led by Frederick Barbarossa and Richard I the Lionheart of England. It succeeded in capturing **Cyprus** and Acre, a town northeast of Haifa (Israel's port).

Geoffroy de Villehardouin, nephew of the author of *Chronicle of the Conquest of Constantinople,* was blown with his crusader ships into Morea, and his Frankish troops then carved out a private princedom, from the year 1204, annexing the Morea, a huge area where Italians were already trading. He recognized existing property and social practices. The ***Chronicle of Morea*** is an anonymous poem, narrating events in this territory, which he first controlled, right up to 1292.

When the fourth crusade captured Constantinople in April 1204, after altering its course to seize Zara on the Adriatic coast, the Christian warriors halted. They burned, raped, pillaged, and looted **Hagia Sophia.** Baldwin of Flanders became Byzantium's first Latin emperor.

The Pope expressed no regret for the **Orthodox** capital. The calamity of 1204 astonished Islam and appalled the Greeks. Some Greek writers speculated that Greece's enemy might have come from the West rather than the East, and **Anna Comnene** records in her great book of memoirs about her father (Alexius I, 1081–1118) the circulation of false rumors that he had detained certain Western commanders or the feeling by Alexius that the crusaders should have handed Antioch back to Byzantium.

Further Reading

Atiya, Aziz Suryal. *The Crusade: Historiography and Bibliography.* Bloomington: Indiana University Press, 1962.

Mayer, Hans Eberhard. *Bibliographie zur Geschichte der Kreuzzüge.* Hannover: Hahnsche Buchhandlung, 1960.

CYCLADES About 24 of the 56 Cyclades islands are inhabited. They are so named because they form a circle (κύκλος) round the sacred isle of Delos. The main islands are Amorgos, Andros, Sikinos, Mykonos, Syros, Folegandros, Kea, Milos, Kythnos, Serifos, Santorini, Sifnos, Paros, Ios, Naxos, Delos, and Tinos. From Tinos, which has a temple dedicated to Poseidon (because the god drove away its snakes), comes the poet Bianca Romaiou (pseudonym of Niki Kollarou). This writer had her schooling at the nuns' convent on Tinos and later moved to Athens, where she won a number of literary prizes. The poet **N. Gatsos** wrote a famous surrealist poem about the Cycladic isle of Amorgos, without even going there. **E. Roidis** is the most famous writer from Syros, but there are many others: **Dimitrios Vikelas** (b. 1835, in Ermoupolis, capital of Syros), **Rita Boumi-Pappá** (b. 1906), who from 1830 began publishing her own journal called *Cyclades,* **Yeoryios Sourís** (satirical poet and journalist, b. 1853), and Leon Koukoulas (1894–1967), National Theater organizer, translator of Ibsen, and one of the poets of the so-called minor tone.

From the isle of Naxos came the women writers **Melpo Axioti** (1905–1973) and Dialechti Zevgoli-Glezou (b. 1907). The poet Maria Yeoryiou-Falangá (b. 1912) came from two of the great sailing families resident on the island of Andros and wrote for several leading Greek journals before publishing volumes of her own work. The famous modern Greek editor and satirical journalist who founded *Rabagás,* Kleanthis Triantafyllos, was from Sifnos. Also from Sifnos came Greece's great lyric poet, **I. Gryparis** (1870–1942).

CYPRUS The demotic literature of Cyprus commences with the topical **chronicles,** composed between 1448 and 1458, of Leontios Machairás (c. 1390–c. 1455), who belonged to a prominent family that had performed services for its French overlords, the Lusignan dynasty. Machairás was secretary, like his elder brother Nikolaos, to the feudal ruler Sir Jean de Nores. He perhaps accompanied de Nores on a mission to end Genova's hold on Famagosta. Cyprus has a violent history. In 58 B.C., the island became a Roman province. In the fifth century A.D., it was absorbed into the Byzantine empire. From the seventh to tenth centuries, it was invaded by Arab forces. In 1191, it was conquered by Richard the Lionheart and subsequently purchased by Gui de Lusignan (1192). Cyprus became a kingdom (1197). For nearly three centuries (1192–1473), it was ruled by Lusignans. It became the chief Christian center in the East after the defeat of the **Crusaders.**

In 1571, Cyprus was conquered by the Turks. Solomon Rodinós (1516–1586) composed a chronicle of events from the first appearance of the Turkish fleet up to the final conquest of the island. In diary format, using prose and verse, Rodinós evokes the catastrophe, but colors it with calamities deriving from locusts, plague, and **earthquake. Orthodox** worship was restored, but the fall of Cyprus caused a decline in the Cypriot tradition of poetry and prose **chronicles.**

Neophytos Rodinós (d. 1669) wrote a **biography** of great men of Cyprus up to the seventeenth century, *Concerning Heroes, Generals, Philosophers, Saints and Other Figures Who Came from the Isle of Cyprus* (Rome, 1658). In the late seventeenth century, Ioachim Kantzelleris composed a poem on the war (1645–1669) between Turkey and **Venice.** In 1788, the archimandrite Kyprianos Kouriokourineos (c. 1750–c. 1803) composed a history of the island, in **plain Greek,** with vivid evocations of its capture: "Though he had received great favors from her, the Pasha did not keep faith with the Countess; perhaps she was the unluckiest of all: her slaves and possessions were loaded on a barge and dumped at sea."

See also PARALOGÉS

Folk songs from Cyprus include "Valiantis and Maroudkia," "The Willowy Girl and the Nobleman," "The Pedlar," "Diyenís and Charos," "Return of the Traveler from Foreign Lands," and "Triantafyllenia." In 1878, the administration of Cyprus was delegated to Britain, and in 1925 it became a British colony. In the 1950s, Greece backed Union with Greece (*Enosis*), and the Papagos

government asked Britain to hold a referendum on the island's future. In 1955, there were trilateral talks (between Turkey, Greece, and Britain); in 1959 there was agreement against a backdrop of secessionist gunfire; on 16 August 1960, the island became an independent republic. On the infamous 15 July, Turkish forces occupied northern Cyprus and still hold it militarily (2002). Greeks print "I can't forget" (Δεν ξέχνω) on a map of Cyprus with the north in black. The Cypriot D. K. Tofallis writes: "Actually it is hard for anyone to draw a line and then say that from this line commences our modern Greek literature" (1976: 9). It is even harder to say when a new country's literature begins.

If some historians of Greek literature argue that a country's literature only starts when it is independent, then Cypriot literature would start in 1960, which is absurd. Mid-twentieth-century poetry from Cyprus, vigorous and widely reviewed, includes work by such names as Z. Efstathiou, Y. A. Makridis, Nikos Kranidiotis (a leading writer, b. 1911, who was also a critic, publicist, and politician), Pythagoras N. Drousiotis (b. 1908, lawyer and educationist), A. Pernaris, T. Anthias, K. Kryssanthis, M. Kralis, S. A. Sofroniou, X. Lissiotis, P. Michalikos, P. Krinkos, and Glavkos Alithersis (1897–1965; author of a *History of Modern Greek Literature,* 1938). A clearinghouse for information and bibliography on Cyprus is The Inter-University Research Committee on Cyprus, run by Modern Greek Studies, University of Minnesota.

Further Reading

Books by writers from Cyprus are under headings (with full bibliography) in Zafeirios, L. H. νεοτερή Κυπριακή λογοτεχνία· γραμματολογικό σχεδίασμα [*Modern Cypriot Writing: A Literary Sketch*]. Leukosia: Kostas Libouris, 1991, illus.

Dalmati, Margherita. *Poeti ciprioti contemporanei.* Milan: V. Scheiwiller, 1967.

Gregoriou, George. *Cyprus: A View from the Diaspora.* New York: Smyrna Press, 2000.

Kitromilides, Paschalis and Marios L. Evriviades. *Cyprus* [revised edition]. Oxford and Santa Barbara: Clio, 1995.

Montis, C., and A. Christophides, eds. *Anthology of Cypriot Poetry.* Nicosia: Proodos, 1974.

CYRIACUS OF ANCONA (di Pizzicolli; 1391–1452) The Italian archaeologist Cyriacus of Ancona was the first Western scholar to visit Greece. He described its antiquities in several volumes, recording plans of buildings, coins, and inscriptions. It was once thought that Cyriacus wrote the earliest Greek sonnet, but the attribution is now rejected.

D

DAFNI, EMILIA (1887–1941) Dafni's date of birth is given variously as 1881 (Mirasgezi) or 1887, according to *Great Encyclopedia of Greece* (1926–1934). Godfather, at her baptism, was the fashionable writer A. **Paraschos.** Her 1923 collection of verse, *Goblets of Gold,* had a preface by Palamás. Her father was the writer Ioannis Kourtelis, her husband the poet Stefanos Thrasuboulos Zoïopoulos (1882–1947). Her first verse collection, *Chrysanthemums,* came out in 1903. She wrote two politically **committed** novels on troubled, talented women (Smaro and Drosoula), *The Gift of Smaro* (1924), and *Foreign Land* (1937). She wrote six one-act plays (not performed) and several short stories.

Further Reading

Rekas, Jan. "How I Discovered the Real Emilia S. Dafni (1881–1941)." *Antipodes* 29–30 (1991): 96–104.

Rekas, Jan, ed. *Echoes of the Old Athens: Short Stories and Poems from the Works of Emilia S. Dafni.* Sydney: University of New South Wales Press, 1988.

DALAKOURA, VERONIKA (1952–) Veronika Dalakoura wrote book reviews for *Daybreak,* a newspaper that followed the **Communist** Party of the Interior's line, *The News,* a large-circulation afternoon tabloid, and *Tribune.* She published prose pieces in *The End of the Game* (1988). Her verse includes *Poems 67–72* (1972), *The Decadence of Love* (1976), *The Sleep* (1982), and *Days of Pleasure* (1990). She translated *The Diary of Nijinsky* (1981), Saint-Exupéry's *The Little Prince* (1984), *The Letters of Arthur Rimbaud* (1984), J. Kessel's *The Lion,* stories by Flaubert and Balzac, and Bunuel's *The Andalusian Dog.*

Further Reading

Anghelaki-Rooke, Katerina. *Ten Women Poets in Greece.* San Francisco: Wire Press, 1982: 10–11.

DAMODOS, VIKENTIOS (c. 1679–1750, perhaps 1752) Coming from Cephalonia, V. Damodos studied with **I. Miniatis** and lived at Venice and Padua. His date of birth is uncertain; his name is spelled Δαμωδός or Δαμοδός. After graduating in law (in Italy), he worked as a judge at Cephalonia. In 1720, he started a school in the village of his birth, Chabriata, and taught philosophy there for the rest of his life. His most celebrated pupils were **Evyenios Voulgaris** (1716–1806), and Moschopoulos. He tried to break the influence of **Korydalleús.** Damodos's *Epitome of Aristotle's Logic* (1759) and his own *Art of Rhetoric* (1759) were published posthumously. He wrote the essays *Dogmatic Theology, On the Ten Commandments, Metaphysics, A Synopsis of Moral Philosophy, Physics,* and *For a More Extensive Logic,* drafting them as handbooks, in **plain** language. As an educator, he held that Greek philosophy should be discussed in contemporary, **demotic** Greek. A devout **Orthodox** Christian, Damodos still expounded Descartes and insisted on the mutual independence of philosophy and religious teaching. He admits that **Aristotle** taught that happiness was the ultimate good, whereas the Orthodox hold the ultimate good to be blessedness.

DAMVERYIS, IOANNIS (1862–1938)

The versatile journalist Ioannis Damveryis, born at Iraklion (**Crete**), was exiled in 1916 for pro-**Venizelos** activities. His published verse includes *The Songs of Prison* (1916) and *The Songs of Exile* (1920). His main prose work is *My Cretans* (1898), which tells of eighteenth-century uprisings on the island. He wrote articles on the antiquities of Athens and composed a *History of Crete.*

DANCE; DANCING

Dance has always featured prominently in Greek cultural life. In *Firewalking and Anastenaria* (1994), the writer Jason Evangeliou (b. 1926) uncovers mystic rites that survived until the twentieth century in Thrace and date back to Dionysian orgies. The Anastenaria were held to honor Constantine and Helen at a festival of several days beginning on 2 May, with frenzied dancing, rushing up hills, and the phenomenon of walking on fire without manifest burns. Elsewhere, **demotic songs** were accompanied by dances conducted in lines, called rounds (συρτοί). The writer **Theotokis** captured a moment of the dance in his short story "Village Life": "Violinists began to play the unvaried tune of the syrto." Rounds are dances in which the performers stand in a line, face turned to the side, holding each other's hands, and making light, sideways steps. The lead dancer is expected to draw the whole chain and to prompt any changes of rhythm or step for the line. He performs left or right shifts and devises other variations, picked up by the front dancers, for the others to follow.

Aegean island *syrtoi* commonly have a 2/4 time and may be danced in promenade style. *Syrtoi* are for family or party occasions. A recently married couple moves clear of celebrating kin to perform an Anatolian dance called *karsilamás.* The Klephtic (τσάμικος) dance was performed at festivals, or marriages. At times, the Klepht gives a display of elegance and grace, wearing the kilt (φουστανέλα). This dance is executed in 7/8 time, with eight steps to the right and four to the left, or eight to the right, four to the left, and four more to the right. The main dancer may cause the *tsamikos* to pause, while he performs high leaps or falls backwards, clapping hands to belt. This dance could be accompanied by **Klephtic songs,** consisting of single **strophes** of 1½ lines, or popular songs like "Once upon a time an eagle," or "Below, in the country of Valtos." At times, a singer interrupted his text with variations like *turns,* or *folds,* names given by the people to musical refrains (επωδόι) that could be inserted at the middle or end of a song. These refrains required the addition of words to match the tune. A simple, repeated 15-syllable verse might give rise to metrical patterns with 8- or 6-syllable lines, as in: "At the windows of the priest's house . . ." / "I am ruined, I am dead!" / ". . . Two black eyes, he saw." This jingle, referring to seduction, forms a six-syllable verse inside the story told by the eight-syllable verses on either side. The *kalamatianós* is a dance in 7/8 time, where males and females form a chain, with characteristic clasped wrists.

DANTE ALIGHIERI (1265–1321)

Dante, greatest of Italian poets, from the city of Florence (Tuscany), first mastered amorous and autobiographical poetry in the vernacular, with his *Vita Nuova* (c. 1292, *Young Life*). Dante then forged a powerful vernacular Italian, in his vision of humanity and how it earns its afterlife, *The Divine Comedy* (c. 1321). This ambitious, encyclopedic poem (containing much of contemporary culture and politics) consists of *Hell* (Κόλασις), *Purgatory* (Καθαρτήριο), and *Paradise* (Παράδεισος). These three canticles making up *The Divine Comedy* (1321) were translated by **Kalosgouros** (1853–1902), **Kazantzakis, Papatsonis,** and others. Dante was imitated by **Pikatoros** and Bergadis. Voutieridis holds that there is no similarity between Dante's treatment of the nostalgic dead and Bergadis's *Apokopos,* as I. Skulitsis, Legrand, and Krumbacher have argued. Kazantzakis notes how the structure of Dante's vision is "a mathematically architectural body, where the imagination is strictly subordinated to the austere intellect of its creator." He was fascinated by Dante's structuring power of triads, noting how the Italian writer's *terzina* is "a strict rhyming pattern which weaves the verses tight, and binds them in bundles of three." Papatsonis expands the words uttered by Odysseus (*Hell* XXVI, vv. 118–120), where he exhorts the Homeric sailors to ponder honor and cross the ocean toward new discovery and possible danger: "Consider the seed you were born from: / You were not created to exist like brute animals, / But for the pursuit of valor and knowledge." **A. Rangavís** (1809–1892) is another major modern Greek writer who tested himself by translating Dante (as well as Goethe and Tasso). Kambanis judges these versions "frigid and improvised." The poet **Yeoryios Stratigis** (1860–1938) wrote an essay *On Dante's Comedy.* **K. Krystallis** (1868–1894) composed a youthful epic, *The Shades of Hades,* which shows the influence of the Florentine poet.

DAPONTIS, KONSTANTINOS (1711/13/14?–1784; also known by religious name, Kaisarios)

The prolific popular writer Konstantinos Dapontis joined the monastery of Xeropotamou, on Mount Athos, in 1757, after a series of journeys and political vicissitudes in the service of patrons like the **Phanariot** K. Mavrokordatos, Prince of Wallachia, who commissioned a historical account of the Russo-Turkish War (1736–1739). This was published in the nineteenth century. Another posthumous work is Dapontis's *Garden of the Graces* (after 1765), which describes in 6,000 **decapentasyllables** and **plain,** accessible vocabulary a mission through the Danube provinces to raise money for his monastery. Works published in his lifetime circulated widely and were read or quoted by the humble, as well as the educated. He wrote *Spiritual Table* (1778) and *Chrestoetheia* (Venice, 1770). Politis says that he "put all he heard or saw into thousands of careless, prosaic lines." His work a is a blend of Enlightenment ideas and Byzantine tradition. The several thousand lines of *Mirror of Women: Vol. I* (1766) were written in jail. Its digressions, which leave the ostensive theme (women in Scripture and history), exhibit dashes of wit and rehashed erudition, alongside a popularizing Christianity. There is a similar mix in Dapontis's *Talisman of Reason, or Hymns to the Hymn-Celebrated Virgin* (Venice, 1770). A rare communicator in perilous times, Dapontis passed on to his readers a **digest** of contemporary events and piety.

Further Reading

Historical works by K. Dapontis are collected in Sathas, K.N., ed. Μεσαιωνικὴ Βιβλιοθήκη [Medieval Library Series], vol. 3. Venice: Typois tou Chronou, 1872, pp. 1–70; 71–200.

DARAKI, ZEPHY (1939–) Zephy Daraki is a prolific poet, with 14 volumes of verse from 1967 to 1986 and the novel *Martha Solger* (1986). Daraki belongs to the "second post-War generation," as Tsakonas calls it, referring to writers born a little before World War II, like **Kiki Dimoulá** and **Anghelaki-Rooke**. As such, there is an undercurrent of dark, smudged, antilyricism in much of her work, with poems that court the subject of death, and others that evoke the "exile of sensation" and the gloom of dreams. Daraki received the Ford Prize (1973), together with left-wing writers who had been targeted during the regime of the **Colonels** (1967–1974).

Further Reading

Daraki, Zefi. "Dark on Dark"; "Freedom"; "The Hanging Kites"; "Suicide," trans. by Kimon Friar. *The Coffeehouse*, no. 5 (winter 1977): 38–41.

DATES Much symbolism is attached in Greece to certain dates: 21 April 1967 marks the start of the **Colonels' Junta.** It was once displayed on placards, together with the name "Hellas." In Cyprus, 1 April is the anniversary of the uprising against the British mandate. Mere mention of 15 July 1974 arouses memories of the Turkish occupation, which is recalled by a sticker with the two words "I can't forget" written over a map of Cyprus. Throughout Greece, 25 March stands for the Greek revolt against Turkish rule at the beginning of the **War of Independence.** Eleni Gousiou, the nineteenth-century Greek-Egyptian woman poet, celebrates this hallowed date in an ode that was composed for a patriotic banquet (c. 1860): "Today's the date / That Greece was reborn, / When she put off her black garb / And again dressed in shining white." The date 28 October is called "No! Day" (OXI), because during the night from 27 to 28 October 1940, **Metaxás** said "no" to Italy's request for an invitation to occupy Greece. He restored his wavering prestige, and was commended by the nation. The date later became a national holiday.

DATES. See PERIODIZATION

DATING (OLD STYLE or NEW STYLE) Officially the Greek dating system changed on 16 February 1923, when 13 days were added to Old Style dates in the twentieth century, and twelve days were added to Old Style dates from before the twentieth century. This modification of days or month results from Greece's late discarding of the Julian calendar in favor of the Gregorian system. In the present volume, dates are changed to New Style in order to fit with European history. Actual dates placing boundaries round subdivisions of modern Greek literature are much debated

See also PERIODIZATION

DAVID (early eighteenth century) The *David* is a verse play in five scenes, composed by an unknown writer from Chios. It was found among the papers of **L. Allatios** (1588–1669), himself a prolific writer and dedicated antiquarian. The play consists of 629 **decapentasyllables,** in rhymed couplets typical of **Crete.** The plot is from the *Old Testament:* the biblical protagonist sins, repents, and thus constitutes an ethical lesson, typical of a Jesuit drama performance. Because the Greek words are written in Latin letters (the script called **Frangochiotika**), the text may have been intended as a language exercise for scholarship students at the Greek College at Rome, or even a proselytizing document directed at potential **Catholic** converts on Chios.

DEATH Death is a key theme and often personified in Greek literature. A **demotic song** from the Peloponnese runs: "'What is it like in the underworld?' the Fates ask a little bird who flies up from there. 'Do the young men bear arms, do the women have jewels, and the kids have toys?'" The answer is: "They don't wear jewels, they don't bear arms, / And the poor little kids just search for their mums." Another text says: "I had put the sun to guard the mountain pass, the eagle over the fields, / And the fresh north wind on the sea. / But the sun went to bed, the eagle fell asleep, / And some ships stole the north wind, / So Charon had time to come and take you away." Both Χάρος (from the classical Greek ferryman Charon) and death (θάνατος) are theme words in Greek literature, exposing the **diglossia** in the national vocabulary and highlighting the personification of death. The writer Agis Theros said that Greeks thought death was merely an act. What follows it is the Underworld, where Greeks continue an existence without life's joys. The Greek mourning song (see **Mirologia**) consoles the recent dead as they move to a place where survivors *may well forget them.*

In popular song, it is a place where "Daughter does not speak to mother, nor mother to daughter, / Nor children to their parents, nor parents to children; / The king is equal to all the rest. / Houses there are dark, their walls are covered with spider's webs, / Great people and simple mix." A dirge about Charos was translated by Goethe: "Old folk implore him, young lads fall to their knees before him: / 'Charon, halt in a village, halt near a fresh spring, / So the old ones may drink water, so the young may throw quoits, / And so the small children may pick flowers.' / 'I do not halt at a village, or near a fresh spring, / For then the mothers come to the water and recognize their kids, / And couples recognize each other too, and one can't prise them apart.'" Greek folk songs still called the underworld Hades, but Charon, ferryman of the dead, becomes "Charos," who duels with the living like a heroic warrior, stern and thin, despite his age.

The dead long for the light of day. **Folklore** depicts them hoping to steal the keys of the Underworld from Charos, to regain the warm world above. Death's wife, the so-called Charontissa, is pictured having supper with him. Charontissa even feels pity for the dead, whom Charos is obliged to transport on a black horse. In a poem by **Christovasilis** about the **King Turned to Marble,** Charos is seen chatting with his black mother, ". . . who asks him with joy about the measureless thousands and thousands of dead subjects he is escorting." Charos may wait to play a game of quoits with his prey. The Greeks' fascination with the personification of death informs a poem like "The Dance of the Shades" by K. Chatzopoulos (1871–1920): "Come and we shall sing—do not shiver in fear—a slow, long and eternal lullaby for you; do not be afraid to join in the slow, never-ending dance of death." Chatzopoulos mixes into this cauldron a *lamia* (witch) and an owl (γλαύξ), "which plays a nostalgic music for us from the ruins yonder."

Further Reading

Garland, Robert. *The Greek Way of Death.* Ithaca, NY: Cornell University Press, 1985.

Lawson, John Cuthbert. *Modern Greek Folklore and Ancient Greek Religion: A Study in Survivals.* Cambridge: Cambridge University Press, 1910.

DECAPENTASYLLABLE The unrhymed, 15-syllable line (δεκαπεντα-σύλλαβος) was the favorite **meter** of popular poetry and first appeared in the fourth-century writer Gregory of Nazianzus's "To the Virgin." It is based on rhythmic return of the tonic accent, as in the old prosody of the **Kontakion.** Imitating the pitch of daily speech, it became the first popular expressive form in medieval Greece. Greek **demotic song** is cast in these 15-syllable lines, subdivided into 8, then 7, syllables, or extended to a 16-syllable line subdivided 8–8, without

rhyming. The line pauses slightly on a **caesura** at its middle, like most **political verse**: "I grew old, imagine boys! // a klephtic brigand for forty years." This virtually splits the line into two hemistychs, making it resemble the iambic of classical writers. Decapentasyllables may be in rhyming couplets, as in *Erotokritos*.

DEFEATIST POETRY The "poetry of defeat" (της ήττας) is the work of young left-wing writers who felt lost in their time. It became the dominant manner after 1949, with the disillusionment that crept in at the end of the **Civil War**, through the Cold War, and into the reality of the modern concrete jungle (τσι-μεντούπολη). Other groups flourished: there was a Christian circle, a "far right" or "conservative" group, and an active Thessaloniki circle round the journal *Diagonal* (1958–1983). The New Left gathered round the journals *Departure* and *Criticism*. It included names like **M. Anagnostakis,** his friend Kleitos Kyrou (b. 1921), Panos Thasitis (b. 1924), Thanasis Fotiadis (1921–1991), Vasilis Frankos (b. 1924), Yoryos Kaftanzis (b. 1920), and Steryos Valioulis (1914–1986), born at Serres to Thracian parents expelled by the Turks, who was variously an importer, contractor, salesman, cashier, proofreader, and "wounded child of our era," as he was called by a Serres columnist (1960). These are some of the disillusioned (διαψευσμένοι) poets, and they left the most acrid flavor of all on modern Greek.

They observed the broken idol of a socialist Utopia and recorded the stagnancy of Existentialism, while watching the dreams and clenched fists of the **Resistance** dissolve into a consumer society. Often this is a seen as a literature of *Angst.* Human relations and social progress are blocked in an impasse (αδιέξ-οδο). There was a partial move to anarchy, with thinkers like Renos Apostolidis, but by 1956, with the invasion of Hungary, the crucial twentieth Plenum of the Soviet Communist Party, and the repudiation of Stalin, the stalemate sensed by the defeatist poets became binding. Zachariadis, who had dismissed (1930) the first Greek socially conscious novelist, Petros Pikrós (1895–1956), as a "pseudo-Marxist," was consecrated leader of the Greek Communist Party. Now intellectuals like M. Lampridis, **M. Avgeris,** Y. Kordatos, Michalis Papaïoannou (b.1912), **Aris Alexandrou,** Soteris Patatzis (1914–1991), Yannis Youdelis (b. 1921), and others were obliged to choose between the swan song of past, heroic times and the new hedonism of "beat, bar, and nicotine addicts."

Further Reading

Frangopoulos, Th. D. "Modern Greek Literature." *Greek Letters,* no. 2 (1983): 275–283.

DELLAPORTAS, LEONARDOS (1350–1419/1420) The Cretan lawyer and diplomat Leonardos Dellaportas was born in Candia and became a reliable agent of Venice. He was, however, sent to **prison,** apparently in connection with the matter of a natural child, some time after 1403. During his incarceration, which dragged on for eight years, Dellaportas composed his *Words of Entreaty* to the Virgin Mother and Christ and some didactic poetry. He is best known for a long poem in 3,166 unrhymed **decapentasyllables,** which is set in the form of a dialogue between the writer himself and a beautiful young woman, who stands for the virtue of truth. It includes the narration of scriptural episodes, as well as motifs from contemporary **romances.** There is an autobiographical component, involving commentary on recent political events and on items concerning his own misfortune and the neoclassical theme of response to adversity. Dellaportas is the one poet of this period whom we know by name; his work was discovered, during research at Mount Athos in 1953, by M. Manoussakas. Dellaportas is also the author of a "Passion" (in 800 lines) and of the devotional work on contrition *Concerning Repayment.* He was probably Greek **Orthodox,** with an Italian father and Greek mother. He took part in fourteenth-century military campaigns that established the Venetian Republic in the Aegean; in the north of Italy he fought against the Genovese militia and Hungarian mercenaries. In Crete he was a businessman and diplomat. He conducted legations to various Ottoman and Christian courts, negotiating treaties with Sultan Mourat I (1359–1389), Th. Palaeologus (1383–1407, Despot of Morea, see **Plethon),** the Emir of Milet (in the year 1403), and the Sultan of Tunis (1389)

DELTA, PENELOPE (1872–1941) Penelope Delta was born in Alexandria and became a familiar figure in the Greek community of Egypt. Her father was the well-known benefactor Emmanuel Benakis. She earned a special reputation with her stories and novels for children, was fiercely patriotic, and supported the movement to universalize the use of the **demotic** in school. Her **historical novels** are for adults as well as children, but were written chiefly to replace the defective school texts and **readers** of the period. *In the Time of the Bulgar-Slayer* (1911) is a historical novel dealing with the expansionist emperor Basil II. *The*

Secrets of the Marshes (1937) is another historical classic, dealing with the absorption of Thessaly and Thrace into mainland Greece during the heyday of the **Great Idea.** She wrote *Fairy Tale without Name* (1910) concerning a kingdom with an unjust ruler, later redeemed by the return of Prudence and Knowledge. It was adapted for the theater by **Iakovos Kambanellis.** *Antonis the Crazy* is about a kid who lives with a strict aunt and good-natured uncle. Three siblings admire the crazy scrapes he gets into, but when the time comes for him to go to school, Antonis makes up his mind to gain adult approval. *Mankas the Dog* is the story of a friendly little pedigree. Its novelty in **children's literature** rests on the fact that the pet tells the story about the dog-loving family (not the humans about the dog). Delta committed suicide when German forces entered Athens (in April 1941), perhaps an unusual gesture for an old lady. She was buried in her garden, with the word "silence" (ΣΙΩΠΗ) on her grave. Arsinoi Papadopoulou (1853–1943), another children's writer, is said to have made the same act against the occupation, at the extraordinary age of 90.

Further Reading

Sachinis, Apostolos. Τὸ ἱστορικὸ μυθιστόρημα [The Historical Novel], 3rd ed. Thessaloniki: Konstantinidis (Μελέτη [Study Series], no. 15), 1981.

Storace, Patricia, ed. *Dinner with Persephone: Travels in Greece.* New York: Pantheon, 1996: 319–355.

DEMOTICISM. See VULGARISM

DEMOTIC LANGUAGE Demotic means "of the people," and so demotic Greek is both a linguistic and political definition. Demotic Greek is the language that is spoken by the common people, as opposed to the "learned" (*loyia*) or "purist" (*katharevousa*) idiom, which was officially adopted as the state language of the new Greece in 1829. Written demotic Greek is based on the rules and **grammar** of the common, spoken language, rather than on those of the purist idiom. "Demotic" language is also called "plain," "common," "spoken," or "folk" (δημῶδης). The reasons for this pervasive **diglossia,** for the existence of two language registers in the same country, go back to ancient Greek history and culture.

Modern writers like **Psycharis** argued that Demotic was the real descendant of Classical Greek. In the first and second century A.D., a movement called **Atticism** began to make urban Greek speakers self-conscious about their Greek vocabulary and grammar. No word or phrase was to be used, in contemporary Greek, unless it had an attested provenance in an Athenian text of the fourth or fifth century B.C. These approved idioms with a classical pedigree were called "Attic." Unacceptable terms were rejected as "Asian" or "Hellenic" and were treated with contempt (Browning 1989: 50). In the fourth century A.D., Atticizing idiom became the natural vehicle for ecclesiastical writing and later for legal, administrative, sacred, historical, and philosophical texts. Thus began the long, slow slide of Byzantine literature away from the grasp of the common people, who by the time of the **Enlightenment** were only reading prayer books and prophecies.

In the Byzantine period, the only genres that consistently used the demotic were the sermon or the digest of religious rules. By mid-tenth century A.D., the

Byzantine taste for neoclassical Greek caused a redrafting of works of popular piety. In the last two centuries of Byzantine rule (1261–1453) and the **Turkocracy,** some nonlearned literary texts were written in the plebeian, spoken language. These were manifestations of a tradition in the demotic. They belong to nonprestige genres, such as medieval prose **romance,** song, popular sermon, and lyric poem. At times, a simplificatory tendency was at work. A writer would himself know the classical forms, but avoid them so as not to confuse his readers with, for instance, inflected forms of the participle, noun declensions, optative mood, or the four oblique noun cases, accusative, genitive, dative, and ablative. R. Browning notes an encyclical letter of Gregory V (1819), in which the Patriarch condemns the neglect of classical grammar and disapproves use of the demotic in popular education. Yet he does so in a Greek that features demotic elements, adopting the contemporary use of the classical present infinitive, *einai,* for *esti* ("it is") and enclitic personal pronouns (*mou, sou, mas:* "my," your," "ours"), rather than the possessive adjective. Gregory avoids the dative indirect object, the classical Greek future tense, and the optative mood.

With the adoption of **Katharevousa** as the language of the unified new Greece, erudite items from the ancient language crept back: at first, some people wanted a classical model for the education of the country at its rebirth. Optative mood, infinitive endings, pluperfect tenses, and even the ultra-archaic (and linguistically superfluous) aorist imperative were encouraged. The old Greek particles, once used as fillers to give nuances of mood or logic (*gar, te, de, ara*) were resuscitated. As time went on, political and so-cial forces tipped the scales back to the demotic. From 1880 to the end of the century, the prestige of writers like **Palamás, Papadiamantis,** and Psycharis opened up for the less-educated reader a new world of popular poetry and genre novel (for instance, the portrayal of local manners). When **A. Pallis** published a demotic translation of the *New Testament* (1901), the Ecumenical Patriarch, Ioakeim, protested in an encyclical. Outraged students rioted because a sacred text had been rendered in the vernacular. Some blood was shed (November 1901). After the riots (though not as a direct consequence) the Greek government fell. In the same year, a judge issued the first written decision of the law courts using the demotic.

In November 1903 there were again riots in the Athenian streets, because Aeschylus's *Oresteia* plays were to be staged at the Royal Theater in a demotic translation (by **Soteriadis**). This modern Greek version was "considered to contain certain vulgar expressions" (Dicks, 1980: 182). In 1911, the writer **Kostís Palamás** was dismissed (temporarily) from his position as Registrar of the University of Athens for endorsing the use of demotic. The seesaw movement toward complete adoption of the demotic, or partial retention of Katharevousa, lasted to 1976. At that date, after the conservative years of the **Colonels,** demotic was established as the official language of the state. Demotic now became the language of all school classes in education, and not just of the first four grades (as was the case from 1945 to 1964). After the 1976 legislation, Demotic became the language of most sites of privilege and authority, such as the universities and the media. A few exceptions survived for a while, as in military circles with a jingoist ethos, the

Orthodox Church hierarchy, corporate documents, or plebiscites.

Further Reading

Schwyzer, Eduard. *Griechische Grammatik,* vol. 1, *Lautlehre, Wortbildung, Flexion.* Munich: Beck, 1939.

Schwyzer, Eduard and Albert Debrunner. *Griechische Grammatik,* vol. 2, *Syntax und syntaktische Stilistik.* Munich: Beck, 1950.

Thumb, Albert. *Handbook of the Modern Greek Vernacular: Grammar, Texts, Glossary,* trans. by S. Angus. Edinburgh: T. & T. Clark, 1912.

DEMOTIC SONGS The so-called demotic song is present in Greek life from the end of the first millennium. It became the popular verse of the Greek-speaking territory long before Greece was a country as such. Demotic songs were composed or recited in the **demotic language** and draw, in part, on the heroic, antiauthoritarian model of the **Acritic** cycle. These songs, epics, or *paralogés,* based on fine exploits, are composed in an idiom and grammar close to the vernacular tongue. It helped the uneducated listener to identify patriotically with the Byzantine heroes or Christian issues shown in the text. From the time of **Diyenís Akritas** to the kingdom of Otho, Greek popular culture accumulated a treasury of 20,000 demotic songs.

The first reports that Westerners had of the Greek demotic song came from eighteenth- and nineteenth-century travelers, but Greece itself began to formalize their study only after **Independence.** Some of the early Greek folklorists tended to render uniform the spelling or lexical features of certain demotic songs as they edited them. Consequently, the resultant homogeneity of the demotic songs cannot be used as an argument for a common national language. Historians and critics do agree that the supreme poet of modern Greek literature is the Greek people (Y. Valetas 1966: 18). These folk songs are without a known author (αδέσποτα). They may have been carried to Greece from sources in Asia Minor. They were always sung, generally with **dancing,** and thus constitute a genuine, oral literature.

After the fall of **Crete** to the Turks (1669), a **renaissance** of Greek literature as such was stifled. Only the demotic songs continued as a creative genre. The poet **Apostolos Melachrinós** argues that "the Greek race survived its hard experience because it did not stop singing." Demotic songs were interesting to European folklorists, particularly to those who argue the uninterruptedness of **Hellenism.** The songs began to be edited and printed during the **War of Independence.** They expressed hatred of the Turks and of the old Frankish enemy: "Death lashes me from within, / From dry land, the Turks assail me, / From the sea, the Franks."

The demotic songs were revealed to the West in two volumes dated 1824 and 1825 by Claude Fauriel (1772–1844), the French Romantic scholar, a friend of Schlegel and Mme de Staël. Among the **Ionian School** poets, collections of demotic songs were made by Antonios Manousis (1828–1903) and **Spyridon Zambelios** (1815–1881) in the years 1850 and 1852, respectively. **N. G. Politis,** the founding father of Greek **folklore,** attempted (in 1914) a critical edition *Selections from the Songs of the Greek People,* comparing alternative lines or passages and refusing to make any conjectural additions of his own. Although the text of N. G. Politis's edition may be authentic (as L. Politis has observed, based on a critical survey by Yannis Apostolakis in 1929), the knitting together of its segments into a whole does not represent an original composite work. It does not reflect the way in which the component parts were once sung.

As manifestos of the demotic idiom, the songs became a rallying point in the nineteenth century, especially in the **Ionian Islands,** for the forging of a popular, national language, and consequently a revived Hellenic literature. The songs influenced poets like **Solomós** and **Palamás** and such prose writers as **Argyris Eftaliotis** (1849–1923) and **Y. Psycharis** (1854–1929). Dimarás notes the vitality of formulaic expressions in the folk song, such as "three birds were a-sitting," "the word was in suspense," "it offended him," and the use of binary opposition, as in "high-low," "soft-hard," "snow-sun." Some songs draw staple topics from the sea, like the "Master North Wind," or "The Traveling Girl." Others find stock themes in the Godmother, a bridesmaid who turns out to be the bride.

The modern Swallow Song (χελιδόνισμα) is sung on 1 March to celebrate the return of migrating birds. It begins with the same words as the classical poem on this theme: "He's come, he's come, the swallow!" In the demotic song, Greek writers found a granary of idioms and proverbial expressions. They also observed the dynamic preference for verb and noun, epic themes, lyric raptures on nature, and rural festivities. If it originates in Anatolia or Cyprus, the demotic song seems to spread across the Dodecanese (thirteenth century). From the thirteenth to the fifteenth centuries, it flourished in Crete and during the seventeenth century, the Aegean. In the eighteenth century, it was present in mainland Greece, particularly in Epirus. Tentative classifications by region and theme have been suggested: Could demotic songs be grouped under the human activities to which they refer? Work, fighting, village festivals, herding sheep, rocking babies, the **lullaby,** or a child imitating the swallow. Other demotic songs may be didactic, or they reflect on fatalism and the passing seasons. Some songs list the qualities that are praiseworthy in a man or woman. They may be satirical or deal with exile. There are carols, **gnomic** rhymed couplets, and festival songs, which exhort young people to adopt hedonism and seize the day, mindful that Death (rather than the Last Judgment) lurks ahead: "Enjoy life, young boys and girls; / Who's to know who'll be alive next year, / Since Death has decided / To take us all?" We also find love songs and laments on death, known by the Byzantine name *mirologia*. Other important demotic types are prison chants and **Klephtic** songs. The latter come from before and during the **War of Independence.** Historical songs, such as the **Akritic** cycle, go back further, referring to the Anatolian frontiers or to the medieval **Diyenís Akritas.** The type and style of demotic singing also varies by region or province. Pastoral songs are associated with mountain regions; satirical songs with the **Ionian Islands.** A melancholy vein of demotic song is commonly found in the **Cyclades** and Asia Minor; a more joyful variety is familiar from Crete. In the Peloponnese and Epirus, the heroic song tends to predominate. The **meter** is generally the **decapentasyllable,** mostly divided into segments of 8–7 syllables, or a 16-syllable line divided 8–8. There is no rhyming.

Typically demotic, the "Song of Daskaloyannis" consists of 1,032 lines. It describes the revolt of the hero in Sfakia, on the southwestern coast of Crete in 1770 and the sacrifice of this leader. As in many forms of Greek writing, the insurgents are incited by promises of help from **Russia:** "Lord, give me thought and mind in the head / To sit and think of Master John / Who was the first in Sfakia, the first lord, / And with all his heart wished Crete to be Greek. / Every Easter and Sunday he put on his hat / And said to the headpriest, 'The Muskovite I'll bring / To help Sfakia and chase the Turks / Along the way to The Red Apple Tree'" (see **King Turned to Marble**). This song was apparently written by Anagnostes Sephes from the dictation of Barla Pantzelios in 1786, 16 years after the abortive Sfakian revolt that it narrates: "But if the letters are faulty, the words without grace, / It is the education of a cheese-maker and the pen of a shepherd."

Demotic ballads often contain maxims for a homespun philosophy: "Lucky mountains, lucky fields, / They have no fear of Death. / They don't expect that killer, / They only wait for lovely spring, / For summer to make the mountains green, / To strew the field with flowers." A recurring figure is the "brave young lad" (see **Palikari**), which dominates modern Greek, through **Palamás** and **Myrivilis** to World War II stories and the modern novel. The stock demotic figure of Death battles the brave youth in one ballad: "They went away and wrestled / On the marble threshing-floor. / Nine times the youth threw Death, / And the ninth time Death was hurt." At times the "moody atmosphere" (Pappageotes, 1972) of the love song is increased by the participation of nature in the individual's crisis, in a grand pathetic fallacy: "I kissed some red lips and mine were painted red. / I wiped them with the handkerchief / And it was painted red, / And when I washed it in the river / The river was painted red. / The seacoast and the middle of the sea turned red. / An eagle came to drink; / His wings were painted red. / Even the sun became half red / And all of the full moon." P. Koumoukelis recalls (in Scarfe 1994: 162): "Songs are the best history. Songs are the cementer of the people. The best song we had for stirring up your blood was 'The Locusts.' The Germans were the locusts spreading over our earth devouring everything in their path: 'It's a shame for the sun and stars and the dawn to look upon. / Let's all join hands and let's all grab swords / And let's get rid of the locusts.'"

See also MIROLOGIA; PARA-LOGÉS

Further Reading

Clark, Richard. "Modern Greek Literature: Bibliographical Spectrum and Review Article." *Review of National Literatures* 5, 2 (fall 1974): 137–159.

Fauriel, Claude C., ed. and trans. *Chants populaires de la Grèce moderne,* 2 vols. Paris: Dondey-Dupré, 1824; 1825.

DENDRINOS, YEORYIOS (? –1938)
Born in Cephalonia, Yeoryios Dendrinos completed his studies at elementary school and became a jack-of-all-trades and even a pedlar. He always aspired to be a writer. He caught tuberculosis and died very young, leaving the satire *Mammoth* and the stories *The Man Who Accepted Everything* (1933).

DETECTIVE NOVEL. See THRILLER

DIALECT
The dialect is a topical variation in language, differing from the eth-

nic language in a specific range of sounds, grammatical forms, and word types. The distinction is often arbitrary, because all languages have their source in a dialect. The difference between modern standard Greek and the plethora of Greek dialects is not always clear-cut because many dialect forms enter the national idiom. Classical Greek was itself subdivided into several dialects. The main ones were **Attic,** Aeolian, Ionian, and Doric. The Attic dialect became the prestige variety of written Greek. Some modern dialects have been cut off so radically from the mainstream that they are no longer related to a Greek model, namely Tsakonian, Pontiac, and South-Italian. The Cretan and Cypriot dialects, on the other hand, showed such a strong flowering of poetry and chronicles in the seventeenth century that one of their dialects might well have formed the national language. Political power eventually gravitated to the Peloponnese (in the war for **Independence**) and Athens, making their widely understood dialects the natural basis for modern spoken Greek.

The Cypriot fourteenth-century legal text *Assizes* is the first fully fledged modern Greek text in dialect, though we know it was translated from a French original. The **Phanariot** writer **A. Christopoulos** (1772–1847) was so enamored of the illustrious dialect of Constantinople that he proposed that it alone might shape the future written language and suggested it was probably the "fifth dialect of ancient Greek." His contemporary, the great national poet **Solomós,** writing his "Dialogue" on language about 1825 (publ. 1859), knew that it was desirable that an established dialect emerge as a national Greek tongue, but he distrusted Phanariot support for the

Constantinople *koiné,* or courtly dialect, because it was still too close to Turkish dominance.

Further Reading

Dawkins, R. M. *Modern Greek in Asia Minor: A Study of the Dialects of Silli, Cappadocia and Pharasa, with Grammar, Texts, Translations and Glossary.* Cambridge: Cambridge University Press, 1916.

Tsopanakis, Agapitos. *Essai sur la phonétique des parlers de Rhodes: contribution à l'étude des dialectes néogrecs.* Athens: Verlag der Byzantinisch-Neigriechischen Jahrbücher, 1940.

DIALOGUE　　Dialogue is the key component of Greek fiction next to description (περιγραφή) and narration (αφήγηση). In the novel *Exodus* (1950) by **Ilias Venezis,** there is a stream of dialogue linking rural characters in the **resistance,** and this gives the fighting a fairy-tale dimension. Critics refer to other types of dialogue in the modern Greek novel as a "faithful transcription" of real speech. They recognize the artifice that is needed to keep dialogue simple, to copy "the natural flow of speech," as when a Greek character in a novel set in Anatolia produces sentences with the verb trailing at the end (like conversational Turkish). Fictional dialogue also employs the "self-answered question" (ανθυποφορά), a figure by which an orator puts a question and then provides the answer. Dialogue is also set in question-and-answer passages, in which characters, who know more than the reader (see **Irony**), fill out their story.

DIASPORA　When the Romans conquered Greece in the first century B.C., they accelerated a process called *diaspora* ("dispersion"), which pushed conquered Greeks from their place of birth.

This whole phenomenon of departure and absence is seen as a "scattering" (διασπορά). The historical millions of Greeks who have lived outside Greece (as with modern Palestinians) make up "the Greeks of the diaspora." The Romans took captured Greeks back to Italy as slaves or tutors to their children. This enslavement within the diaspora exported Greek ideas elsewhere in the world (Jane and Wood, 1995: 46). After the **War of Independence** came an expansion of Greece's territorial boundaries, but the reality of emigration soon increased. Newly created jobs were not adequate in a country with few railways and backward agriculture. Males began to emigrate, especially at the end of the nineteenth century, though the political mass of Greece had swollen since 1830.

Greek descendants residing in foreign countries, or exile, produced books, songs, poetry, theater, and art. There has been a distinctive Greek culture in America, Australia, Egypt, France, Romania, Slavic Macedonia, Bulgaria, Turkey, and certain outposts of the Ottoman empire, Albania, Cappadocia, Pontus, and the Danubian principalities, Wallachia and Moldavia, run by **Phanariots,** well-born Greeks from **Constantinople.** Literature by **Hellenism** abroad proposed stories of emigration, displacement, and nostalgia, as well as new homeland themes.

From about 750 to 550 B.C., Greeks founded colonies from the Black Sea to Spain. They took with them a ready-made culture, municipal institutions, and education. After the decline of Greek political power and conquest by the Romans, Greeks were scattered in communities across the Mediterranean. Their Roman masters were averse to trading by sea, and the Greeks provided instructors in rhetoric, librarians, teachers, and sec-

retaries to Roman noblemen or governors. When the early medieval period saw the collapse of the West, the Greeks of **Byzantium** found ways to maintain a trading sphere in the East. After the Ottomans crushed Byzantium in 1453, diaspora Greeks managed to hang on for centuries, as bankers, ministerial advisers or governing princes, translators to the Sublime Porte (Ottoman court), merchants, and shipowners. The Ottoman ruling class disliked trade and shunned civil administration. Bureaucracy was left in the hands of Greeks, especially at Constantinople. The diaspora communities outside Hellas proper, in the Ottoman Empire, became prosperous. Homogeneity was created by the practice of **Orthodox Church** worship and an autonomous Greek school system. The worst event that befell Greeks in 2,000 years of *xenitiá* was the loss of Smyrna, the most populous Greek city in the world, to renascent Turkish nationalism (1922). The so-called **Asia Minor disaster** became a central theme of diaspora writing and of modern Greek literature.

Further Reading

Hussey, J. M., ed. *The Cambridge Medieval History. Volume IV: The Byzantine Empire. Part II: Government, Church and Civilisation.* Cambridge: Cambridge University Press, 1967.

Jane, K. and Priscilla Wood. *Ancient Greece.* Dunstable: Folens, 1995.

Papanikolas, Helen. *A Greek Odyssey in the American West.* Lincoln: University of Nebraska Press, 1997.

Walker, D. S. *The Mediterranean Lands.* London: Methuen, 1960.

DICTIONARIES Compiling dictionaries was a key task for **Renaissance** and **Enlightenment** writers, at times when the scholar merged with the **teacher.** M. Mousouros (c. 1470–1517) advised the Venice printer Aldus Manutius on Greek books, in manuscript or codex, from 1494, and he produced the *Dictionarium Graecum Compositissimum* (Venice, 1497), an authoritative Greek–Latin dictionary, with an introductory **epigram.** Mousourus and Zacharios published the *Comprehensive Dictionary of Word Roots* (1499). In the last century, a celebrated nine-volume text was *Great Lexicon of the Greek Language (Demotic, Katharevousa, Medieval, Later, Classical;* Athens: Dimitrakos, 1936–1950). It had a second edition in 1958 and was then reissued as a new edition in 15 volumes, by a publishing enterprise called "Hellenic Learning," under X. Tegopoulos and B. Asimakopoulos.

The other key text in the lexical genre, from mid-twentieth century, is Ioannis D. Stamatakos's *A Dictionary of the Modern Greek Language, Katharevousa and Demotic, and from Modern Greek Words into Classical* (Athens: Petros Dimitrakos, 1952; 1953 and 1964). The third volume of this project came out late: printing began in 1955, but it was available only in 1964. Greatest of the modern dictionaries of medieval Greek writing (covering words in popular texts in the period from 1100 to 1669) is the 14-volume project by E. Kriarás (see references). It was partly overtaken by George Babiniotis, *Dictionary of the Modern Greek Language* (Athens: Center for Lexicography, 1998). This massive volume of 2,064 pages was met with huge public debate and became a bestseller. It offers 150,000 "words and phrases" and is credited (by Goutsos) with giving the fullest picture of Greek since the demise of **diglossia** and having the most scientifically arranged lemmata, trying not to give synonyms as definitions, and including comment boxes with both prescriptive and descriptive mini-essays.

Further Reading

Goutsos, Dionysis. [Essay Review]. *JMGS* 17, no. 1 (May 1999): 163–170.

Kriarás, E. Λεξικὸ τῆς Μεσαιωνικῆς Ἑλληνικῆς Δημώδους Γραμματείας *1100–1669* [A Lexicon of Medieval Greek Popular Writing from 1100 to 1669], 14 vols. Thessaloniki: Royal Hellenic Research Foundation, 1969–1997.

DIDASKALOS. See TEACHER

DIET. See MEDICINE

DIGEST. See CHRONICLE, HISTORY

DIGLOSSIA The word *diglossia* refers to the coexistence of two languages, like **Attic** Greek alongside **plain Greek,** or **Katharevousa** next to the **Demotic.** Diglossia denotes the case when a community uses two morphologically and lexically distinct forms of one language. It tends to create a permanent, simultaneous use of two registers in a country. The term also describes communities in which two idioms actually flourish, one "high" (educated), the other "low" (outside formal education). The loss of a hundred plays by Menander can be blamed on diglossia, for Menander was not allowed on the school syllabus after the fifth century, because his comedies had not been written in Attic, but in an everyday language known as the *koiné* (κοινή = "common to all").

Further Reading

Kriarás, E. "Diglossie des derniers siècles de Byzance: naissance de la littérature néo-hellénique." *Proceedings of the XIIIth In-*

ternational Congress of Byzantine Studies. Oxford 1966. London, 1967.

DIMINUTIVE The adjective *diminutive* (υποκοριστικός) refers to modification of a word by suffixes that denote small size, affection, cajoling, teasing, or scorn. When the poet **Ritsos** published *Morning Star* (1955) for his newborn daughter Eri, he added the subtitle *A Small Encyclopedia of Diminutives.* In this verse, we are struck by the abundance of words like "little girl; mumsy; mini-hills, shoelets."

DIMOULÁ, KIKI (1931–) The major modern woman poet Kiki Dimoulá was born in Athens, worked as a bank clerk, and published collections of experimental and **feminist** verse, among them *Darkness of Hell* (1956), *In Absentia* (1958), *The Bit of the World* (1971), which won the second State Prize, and *The Last Body* (1981). Her writing was seen by critics as a careful mixing of **purist** tones with demotic directness and some archaic diction that touched on the irony of Kavafy, such as "No, I am not in grief / That at the appropriate hour it should darken," or "Have you observed my phenomenon? / The total eclipse, in the end, of me?" Meraklís calls Kiki Dimoulá "one of the most unobtrusive, noiseless, solitary, unbelievers in Greek poetry," and Holst-Warhaft has referred to the way "she surveys her situation with wonderfully ironic self-detachment." Her blunt, concrete style was effectively adapted and recast in the volumes written after the death of her husband, the poet Athos Dimoulás (1921–1985). Many of these poems inventively but unmourningly reconstitute the dead beloved as a talking presence in her life: *Farewell Never* (1988) and *Lethe's Adolescence* (1994).

Further Reading

Dimoulá, Kiki. *Lethe's Adolescence,* trans. by David Connolly. Minneapolis: Nostos, 1996 (reviewed by G. Holst-Warhaft in *JMGS* 17, no. 1 [May 1999]: 192–196).

DIONYSOS **(1901–1902)** *Dionysos* was a short-lived, but influential, literary journal that promoted the style and imitation of the French Symbolist poets. Founded and edited by Dimitrios Chatzopoulos and his brother Konstantinos Chatzopoulos (1871–1920), with **Yannis Kambysis** (1872–1901), *Dionysos* continued where the journal *Techni* left off. A special number of the periodical *Greek Creation* (no. 102: 1 May 1952) deals with K. Chatzopoulos.

Further Reading

Chatzopoulos, K. Πεζά [Prose Writings]. Athens: Ikaros, 1956–1957.

DIRECT SPEECH Most Greek narrative uses direct speech, in the second person, but the **demotic songs** use it instinctively, instead of indirect speech (πλάγιος λόγος). In "The Widow's Son Cherishes Three Fine Horses," the hero goes to battle on a steed called Black and dies. The horses called Grivas and Pipanos start moaning: "Well, where is our Master, Black you fool?" Black says, without any transitional phrase: "Let me sing you my part, / And the pain of my heart."

DISTICHON (COUPLET) The *distichon* is a rhyming couplet. It appears for the first time in verse from Venetian-occupied Crete, in the work of **Stefanos Sachlikis** (c. 1332–c. 1403). The term *couplet* (λιανοτράγουδο) also refers to a **folk** form. Verse couplets date from the medieval period. Some are forceful enough to be knitted together into longer texts, where they construct so-called **alphabets. Rhyme** was employed in earlier, for example, Syrian, poetry. Rhyming lines were later used by the Troubadours (thirteenth century) and brought with the Crusaders from Provence. Sachlikis sprinkles **rhyme** across the account of his imprisonment, occasionally using it in three to five consecutive lines. The increasing presence of the rhymed *distichon* in Cretan verse leads to the gradual obsolescence of the old, nonrhymed **political verse.** The rhymed couplet became a separate unit of thought, or stood alone as an **epigram.** The only extant examples of rhyme in earlier Greek poetry are the hymn *Acathistos* and the **kontakion** by St. Romanus on Judas.

DIYENÍS AKRITAS *Diyenís Akritas,* also known as *The Two-Blood Border Lord,* is the greatest of the Byzantine sagas. It is preserved in fourteenth-century manuscripts and known to be considerably older. It deals with events and types that can be dated to the ninth or tenth century and was probably written down in the eleventh century in Asia Minor. It is composed in unrhymed 15-syllable verse. The anonymous poet responsible for the prototype of this widely copied work lived far from any metropolis, possibly among the border guards in east Turkey. Perhaps he was the educated vassal, or administrator, of some nostalgic baron. This text is the first to use demotic Greek for a popular Byzantine story. It is the first text in modern Greek and became known to the literary world in 1875, with the publication of a manuscript that had been found at Trebizond.

Differing manuscript versions were discovered in the following decades. A total of six Greek manuscripts became available, and each of these constituted a different recension of the same story. A critical edition of the Escorial version was published in 1985 by Stylianos Alexiou. Alexiou deduces, from the mention of the Hashish-Assassins sect in Syria, a twelfth-century date of compilation. He shows that the Escorial manuscript is superior and earlier, if less "learned," than the Grottaferrata version. The saga originates in Asia Minor and refers to a historical background, possibly set in 788 A.D. Some scholars date the subject to the period 928–944; others propose a later time setting, 1042–1054.

The hero, Basil Diyenís Akritas, is of mixed Greek and Arab blood. He fights on the borders between the Byzantine and the Islamic empires. He is "a Cappadocian hero" (Beaton). The story begins with the abduction from her home in Cappadocia of the hero's mother by an Arab invader, the Syrian emir Mousour. She is the daughter of a Byzantine prince from the Doukas family. She has five brothers. The abductor proposes a duel with one of the five. The youngest is selected by lot, is coached by his eldest brother and wins the duel. The defeated Arab turns Christian, settles on the Byzantine side, and marries the girl. In the next generation, the eponymous hero born to this couple is of mixed Islamic/Christian parentage. He embraces the Christian faith. His father, the emir, goes back to the Muslim side and brings across his Muslim mother and relations. The two-blood border lord, Diyenís Akritas, is trained in letters and arms bearing. He learns, like young Hercules, to tear apart wild animals. In his first hunt, the boy kills a lion and two bears. As a young man, he has some adventures with a band of *Apelates.* When adult, he elopes with Eudokia, the daughter of a general who rules as a Byzantine border baron. Diyenís is pursued by a band of soldiers and by the girl's five brothers. He wins the battle, spares the brothers, and is granted the right to marry the general's daughter. He receives three sets of gifts from his new relatives. Living with his beloved, in territory on the border, he pacifies the region and hunts down bandits. The Byzantine emperor summons Diyenís to his court, but Diyenís refuses to go. The Emperor visits him in order to witness his feats of physical accomplishment. Diyenís excels in a first-person narrative of his previous adventures, including the rescue of his wife from a dragon. In one version, he meets a girl abandoned in the desert. While accompanying this girl back to her seducer (on the pretext of enforcing their marriage), he rapes her.

When Diyenís defeats the Amazon warrior Maximó, she offers to surrender and have sexual intercourse with him. He slays her, though accepting her plea. Our border lord is a settler as well as a wanderer. He constructs a castle with an enchanted garden (two features of later, Western romances). Details are narrated, with picturesque **ekphrasis,** concerning the amenities at his palace, including fountains, cellars, linked reservoirs, welcoming parrots, animal statues pouring fresh water out of their mouths, all topped by a mausoleum on a one-arch bridge over the river Euphrates. As he grows old, his bodyguard of 300 favorite warriors flies back to base every day, chattering like sparrows (σπουργίτες): "And so like charming fledglings on the wing / They send a charming echo of their wondrous king." He is brought low by a wasting disease. He calls his beloved to his side and recalls the happy vicissitudes of their union (which has no offspring). While she prays for him to be spared, he dies, enjoining her never to marry again. In a feature common to *The Thousand and One Nights,* she promptly joins him in death. This great saga, with its emphasis on triple occurrence, may perhaps (Baldick) symbolize the three classes of Byzantine society: one to fight, a second to pray, a third to work. One scholar argues (in Thorlby 1969: 191) that the poem is not a true historical epic: "It may have been built out of shorter, orally transformed lays dealing with particular persons and events." There is a formal description of the border lord's funeral and a grandiose ekphrasis concerning his tomb. The saga closes with **gnomic** reflections on the rise and fall of human ambition. The theme of abduction is fundamental to the Diyenís story, as it is in the genre of **romance,** and **Akritic song.** In 1670, Ignatios Petritsis composed a variant on the *Diyenís Akritas.*

Further Reading

Alexiou, S., ed. Βασίλειος Διγενὴς Ἀκρίτας (κατὰ τὸ χειρόγραφο τοῦ Ἐσκοριάλ) καὶ Τὸ Ἆσμα τοῦ Ἀρμούρη [Lord Diyenis Akritas (According to the Escorial Manuscript) and the Song of Armouris]. Athens: Ermis, 1985.

Hull, D. B., trans. *Digenis Akritas: The Two-Blood Border Lord.* Athens: Ohio University Press, 1972.

Kalonaros, Petros, ed. Βασίλειος Διγενὴς Ἀκρίτας. Τὰ ἔμμετρα κείμενα Ἀθην ῶν . . . Κρυπτοφέρρης καὶ Ἐσκοριάλ [Lord Diyenis Akritas: The Verse Texts from Athens, Grottaferrata and the Escorial]. Athens: D.N. Papadimas Editions, 1970.

Mavrogordato, J., ed. *Digenes Akrites.* Oxford: Clarendon Press, 1956.

DONÁS, PASCHALIS IOANNIS (late eighteenth century) The medical figure Paschalis Donás represents, with his arts background, an **Enlightenment** hybrid that Greek critics often refer to as the "doctor sage" (ἰατροφιλόσοφος). Donás was born in Epirus and at Ioannina became one of the doctors of **Ali Pasha.** He studied medicine at Bologna and worked for a merchant while in Italy. He wrote a *Refutation of the Ravings of Abbot Compagnoni on the Greeks* (publ. in Italian, Leipzig, 1773), which came out in Greek at Venice in 1802. He translated verse by Tasso and Petrarch from Italian to Greek and wrote poetry himself. Perhaps he, or **Mavrommatis,** could be the **Anonymous Greek** who published in Italy (1806) the **patriotic** text *The Greek Rule of Law, or a Discourse on Freedom.*

DONKEY, LEGEND OF THE *Legend of the Donkey* is a fifteenth-century tale in 393 unrhyming **decapentasyllables.** A differing story (of fifteenth-century origin) is the *Tale of the Donkey, the Wolf, and the Fox* in 540 unrhyming lines. A rhymed version was first printed in 1539 (Venice). A donkey hides from his cruel master in the woods. A fox and a wolf insist on accompanying him, so the donkey tells them his master is close by, with bloodhounds. The animals embark on a boat, and the donkey has to row, while the wolf appoints himself captain, and the fox takes the tiller. The fox proposes that each of them should confess the animals he has eaten, and thus obtain remission of sins. The wolf and the fox admit having eaten all manner of flesh. The donkey admits that he once stole a lettuce leaf, so his master beat him. The fox and the wolf do not intend to absolve the donkey, so he risks being eaten by them. The donkey escapes by cunning: he says he must reveal a secret before he takes his punishment. He has magic powers in his back hoof (it lets him hear enemies from a great distance). He makes the wolf kneel to recite a *Paternoster* in the prow, then kicks him into the sea. The fox takes fear and dives in. The **allegory** in these donkey tales, with predators trying to outwit a patient victim, is anticlerical.

DON'T GET LOST The magazine *Don't Get Lost* (Μὴ χάνεσαι) was founded in 1880 by an adventurous and independent journalist called Vlasis Gavriilidis (1848–1920), who was born in Costantinople and sent by a benefactor to study political science and philosophy at Leipzig. Back in Constantinople, Gavriilidis founded the short-lived journal *Concord,* which was soon merged with *Neologus.* Later, he fell under the suspicion of the Turkish masters of Constantinople, with his paper *Reform.* He found out that he was likely to be arrested for a seditious article on charges that carried the death penalty. To the Turkish police, who called round at his newspaper office, asking for Mr. Gavriilidis, he is supposed to have said, "He just stepped out; I'm waiting for him myself." He then complained to the policemen that he was wasting his time waiting and left. A week or so later he was in Athens (1877) and doing editorial work for *The Daily Debater.* In 1878, he and Kleanthis Triantafyllos founded the radical, pro-Demotic journal *Rabagás*. Soon (1880) Gavriilidis moved to his pet project, the twice-weekly magazine *Don't Get Lost.*

A hackneyed phrase by the contemporary politician Alexandros Koumoundouros was the source of the journal's title. When Koumoundouros's wife became distressed at political opponents' attacks on him, he apparently consoled her with the admonition "Don't get lost!" The journal soon evolved (1879) into a firmly nonpartisan daily newspaper called *Acropolis.* In 1890, he brought the rotating cylinder for the first time to Greek newspaper printing. Gavriilidis was in his element and for 40 years poured out, in his laconic manner, articles on finance, **feminism,** farming, art, language, business, society, women's clothes, mixed education, the army, and politics. He pictured the poet **Sikelianós** as "a beautiful chaos of a virgin Hellenic soul." Gavriilidis's ideology was uncompromisingly pro-progress. He supported a new classless, demotic Greece. It was said that a critical article by Gavriilidis could topple a Greek government. At age 28, he roared his *Credo* from the columns of his paper: "Our goal is the national regeneration of Greece; our means are absolutism, constitutionality, democracy, revolution, theocracy and anarchy. [. . .] Observe how much we dissent from the multitude. They want Hellenism to die an orderly death and be solemnly buried; we prefer that Hellenism live, albeit in disorder, even with mutual slaughter!" Gavriilidis stood as best man at the wedding of **Kostís Palamás** to Maria Valvis.

DOSITHEOS   OF   JERUSALEM (1641–1707) The patriarch Dositheos staked his tenure (from 1669) on Greek **Orthodox** stewardship of Jerusalem's shrines. He wrote religious essays, variously attacking Calvinism and chastising the Latin church. He gained the nickname "scourge of the Papists" (Λατινομάστιξ). Dositheos composed a *His-*

tory of the Patriarchs of Jerusalem, published by his successor in the post, 1715) and an *Orthodox Confession of the Faith of the Catholic Apostolic Eastern Church, Followed by an Exposition Concerning the Three Chief Virtues, namely Faith, Hope, and Charity.*

DOUKA, MARO (1947–) Maro Douka became well known as a novelist and political prisoner under the **Colonels' Junta** (1967). Douka, born in Haní (Crete), studied from 1966 at Athens University, where she became a left-wing militant. Her first novel, *Fool's Gold* (1979), tells the story of Mirsini, a girl from a bourgeois family, whose father is involved with several women. Mirsini's family possesses shares in a mine, inherited through a great-grandmother's extramarital love affair. Mirsini's mother commits suicide; the protagonist herself has unsatisfactory love affairs, one with a comrade in the Left movement who cannot, in practice, accept the equality of women. The narrative, which moves back and forth in time, highlights the so-called Generation of the Polytechnic and its political activity. This leads up to the Polytechnic revolt of 1973, in which the students occupied the buildings in November and put up graffiti banners proclaiming NO TO THE JUNTA. In the ensuing repression by the **Colonels' Junta,** troops and tanks on the night of 16 November ended the Polytechnic occupation. There were casualty figures (disputed on both sides) of about 30 killed and several more injured. In Douka's narrative, Mirsini refuses to typecast her commitment to political activism by responding to a questionnaire about whether to join a political organization. The crux presented by this questionnaire detonates a series of chronological and narrative breaks in sequence. Douka's second novel *The Floating City* (1984) moves between Paris and Athens and between three different subtexts, while telling the apparently conventional story of an affair between a married man in Paris and his actress girlfriend in Athens.

Further Reading

Douka, Maro. *Fool's Gold,* trans. by Roderick Beaton. Athens: Kedros, 1991.

Yannakaki, Eleni. "The Novels of Máro Doúka." In *The Greek Novel: A.D. 1–1985,* ed. Roderick Beaton, 110–119. London: Croom Helm, 1988.

DOUKAS, NEOPHYTOS (c. 1760–1845) Neophytos Doukas was a prominent classical scholar, **Enlightenment** teacher and fanatical exponent of **Atticism.** "The whole of Hellenism existed inside his head," D. Vernardakis once said of Doukas. From the Epirus, Doukas lost his father when young, and he took orders in a monastery. He later studied at Bucharest, where one of his teachers was the scholar Lambros Fotiadis (1752–1805). In 1803, Doukas was invited by the Greek community of Vienna to work and teach in that city. He stayed there 12 years. He then took over the directorship of Fotiadis's school in Bucharest (1815), but was forced to resign (1817) after an attempt was made on his life. He was found beaten one morning on the street. The attack was made by opponents of his conservative stance on the **language question** and his support of Atticism, possibly by Alexandros Mavrokordatos. Doukas wrote over 70 volumes in his lifetime, including a 10-volume summary, with commentaries, of the history of Thucydides. His collected correspondence of over 1,500 letters is extant. His

influence on modern scholarship is such that he is credited with setting the form for classical editions in the Budé series (with facing French translation) and the German Teubner texts.

See also HELLENISM

DOXARÁS, PANAYOTIS (1662–1729)
The painter and writer Panayotis Doxarás called himself Peloponnesian, signing "Lakedaemonian" on some of his canvases. He lived and worked on Zakynthos. As a soldier, he campaigned with a group of mercenaries on the island of Chios (1694), paying for their services on behalf of **Venice.** In 1696, he helped to organize the defense of Venetian positions in the Peloponnese. He translated Leonardo da Vinci, *The Art of Painting,* from the Italian, making polite excuses for his own uncultivated grammar. Doxarás wrote his own treatise, *On Painting,* in the **plain** language. Here he exalts the **Renaissance** and its painters, in contrast with the ossified Byzantine art. He sought to adapt the techniques of Western art to Greece while imitating the painters of Venice and producing fine portraits.

DOXAS, ANGELOS (1900–1985; pseudonym of N. N. Drakoulidis) Born at Constantinople, the critic, essayist, poet, novelist, short story writer and film director Angelos Doxas wrote a notable antiwar novel *Human Blood* (1946). Doxas is a modern version of that durable and versatile Greek species, the medical doctor with literary talent and energy. He studied at Athens, Paris, and Vienna. He qualified as a lawyer and psychoanalyst. He was also professor of nature study at the Athens School of Art and Crafts (1929–1938). He published verse (*Libation to the Wind; The Hours of Greyness*), stories, plays, novels, psychobiographies

of Orestes, Plato, Shakespeare, Michel-angelo, Cervantes, Rimbaud, Baudelaire, and (in 1968) a psychoanalysis of Aristophanes. He collected travel impressions in the volumes *Enchantment of the Tropics* and *In the Dizziness of America.* He produced 360 articles or book contributions (in Greek and other languages) and over 30 books of his own. In 1937, Asteris Kobbatzis noted that **Xenopoulos** and Doxas, between them, had created a brand-new reading public in twentieth-century Greece.

Doxas's novels, many of them cosmopolitan slices of life from Paris, *Lizetta* (1923), *Eva, Dora, Eight-Thirty This Evening, Turn the Switch, Surprise Party, Three Drops of Petrol, Naked Woman,* and such stories as "Party," "Jean," and "Vana," confronted modern readers with a racy cocktail of psychology and human emotion, in an ambiance of cash, comfort, and cabaret. His *Waiter, a Whisky!* (1932) ran to 20,000 copies and six editions by 1950. This was an unprecedented figure for a collection of prose stories at the time. Later came the novels *The Planet, After Midnight,* and *Love for Mankind,* which turned to wider, post–World War II problems. Doxas was a joint editor of the literary journals *The Greek Review* and *Eve.* Xenopoulos commended Doxas, in an essay of 1944, for being the first writer to renew the Greek genre novel (see **Ithografía**) and for becoming "Greece's most widely read prose writer between the Wars." Doxas's study *A Psychoanalytic Analysis of Palamás* won the gold medal and State literary prize in 1960. It makes Greece's modern icon of poetic gravity into a rather more fiery figure.

DOXASTIKÓN The term *doxastikón,* or "glorificatory" (δοξαστικόν), refers to a *troparion* chanted after the Praises, based on psalms of David that use the words "praise the Lord" (Αἰνεῖτε τὸν Κύριον). The *doxastikón* is sung before the doxology (eucharistic hymn) and begins with the words "Glory be to the Father, the Son and the Holy Ghost." Saint Gregory of Nazianzus "Theologos" (c. 329–381?), whose works are a major source for Byzantine **hymns,** writes in a discourse on Easter and his late priesthood: "on the day of the Resurrection, let us shine with the festival, embrace, and say, brothers, even to those who hate us, we forgive all misdeeds at Resurrection." These phrases return later in a Byzantine hymnographer's work, a *doxastikón* of the Praises of the Feast of Resurrection.

Further Reading

Karavites, P. "Gregory Nazianzinos and Byzantine Hymnography." *JHS* 113 (1993): 81–98.

DRAGOUMIS, ION (1878–1920) The unswerving irredentist Ion Dragoumis put together, in his novel *Samothrace* (1908), a passionate investigation into the sources of contemporary **Hellenism.** *Blood of Martyrs and Heroes* (1907) was drafted to shock Greek youth out of complacency and to kick-start Philhellenic nationalism by a narration of the Macedonia campaign. He also wrote a blatantly irredentist account of the outposts of Hellenism in Anatolia, and ways to conserve them, namely *All Those Alive* (Athens, 1911). Diplomat, political writer, and social philosopher, Dragoumis had been a volunteer in the war of 1897. In 1902, as vice-consul at Monastir, Dragoumis organized the defense of the **Orthodox** communities in western Macedonia against the so-called Bulgarian Committees. He helped to organize

Greek community outposts in eastern Macedonia, eastern Roumeli and Thrace (where he held consular positions up to 1907). As first secretary at the Constantinople embassy (1907–1908), he took measures toward political equality and self-affirmation for Greek **diaspora** communities in the **Ottoman** territories. In 1909 he was involved in planning for an army insurrection. In 1911, when the Italians occupied the Dodecanese, he urged union with Greece, or autonomy, at a conference on Patmos.

He enlisted in the first **Balkan War** (1912) as a corporal. When sent on a team of negotiators to discuss terms for a handover of **Thessaloniki** to Hassim Tahsin Pasha, Dragoumis on his own initiative raised the Greek flag at the Metropolitan's palace. Two months later, he tried to organize the occupation of Kastellorizo. In 1915, he was elected as independent deputy for Florina (northern Macedonia). In Parliament, he opposed neutrality, supporting Greece's entering World War I on the side of the Allies and forecast the territorial rewards for this policy in a postwar realignment of Anatolian frontiers (a robust formulation of the **Great Idea**). He expounded his policies in the weekly *Political Review,* which he founded in January 1916. He was deported to Corsica with other politicians and served out the war in exile. He was pardoned at the end of 1919. When an assassination attempt was made on **E. Venizelos** in Paris (31 August 1920), Dragoumis was picked up by security police and gunned down in the street. He was a cofounder of the pro-Demotic **Educational Society,** where he exerted a deep influence on **N. Kazantzakis.** Kazantzakis, in turn, published an overblown, chauvinist poem in the special issue of the literary journal *Néa Estía*

(no. 342: 15 March 1941) devoted to Ion Dragoumis. Kazantzakis's poem imagines the grey head of Dragoumis held high at the gates of Paradise, standing erect after preserving the race. He used the romantic pseudonym "Archer."

See also BALKAN WARS; DIASPORA; PROGONOPLIXÍA

DRAMA; DRAMATISTS Nineteenth Century; Twentieth Century. See GERMANY; KARAGHIOZIS; OPERA; PUPPETS; ROMAS; SHAKESPEARE; TERZAKIS; THEATER

DRAMATIC PRESENT The dramatic present tense is the use of present time to relate acts from the past as though they are happening simultaneously with the act of writing the text. In the famous **demotic song** *The Dead Brother* (see **Paralogés**), the narrator breaks into his past tenses with phrases like "The eight brothers are against, but Kostantis is in favor" (of their 12-year-old sister's marriage and life in Babylon, line 8), or "the slab which rumbles and the earth that booms" (line 68).

DREAM INTERPRETATIONS The five volumes of *Dream Interpretations* by Artemidorus Daldianus (second century A.D.) provide instruction on how to explain dreams. This was not so much literature for the superstitious, as occultism for the educated: the ὀνειροκρίτης is an "explainer of dreams." Artemidorus wrote (lost) books on *Bird Divination* and *Reading Hands.* The works of Galen and Aristides, contemporary with Artemidorus, show that **Hellenistic** writers in early Empire society believed that dreams offer forecasts and rules for future behavior.

DROSINIS, YEORYIOS (1859–1951)
Yeoryios Drosinis worked for the leading journal called *Hearth* (Ἑστία) until 1898. He published the magazine *National Uprising* (1898) and a literary annual, *Calendar of Great Greece,* from 1922. Drosinis was one of the main figures behind The Association for the Distribution of Useful Books (see **Melás; Vikelas**). He edited the Association's journal, and he compiled its volumes on Natural History, Birds, The Blind, Fishing, Hunting, and Bees. He was one of the first members of the Academy of Athens (1926) and is believed (Pappageotes, 1972) to have controlled policy in its literary section up to the day he died. A special issue of the literary journal *Néa Estía* (no. 583: 1951) is devoted to Drosinis, as also are two monographic numbers of *Greek Creation* (no. 44: 1 Dec. 1949, and no. 71: 15 Jan. 1951).

E

EARACHE. See MEDICAL TRACT

EARTHQUAKE The sixteenth-century
writer Manolis Sklavos composed a
poem on the Cretan earthquake of 1508,
The Disaster of Crete. One of many types
of lay **medical treatise** is the *Prognosis
from Earthquakes* (Σεισμολογιόν). A
characteristic seventeenth-century tract
advises: "If the sun is in Scorpio, and an
earthquake occurs by day, this augurs
great danger, and if it occurs by night, it
foretells the sickness and death of many."
Abbatios Hierotheos uses elegant **demotic** in his *Account of the 1637 Earthquake in Cephalonia.* He came from
Cephalonia, was prior of a monastery
(1631–1664), and built a museum in the
Strophades, guarding the relics of St.
Dionysios, patron of Zakynthos (see
Martzokis, A.). An anonymous writer
from Santorini shows the power of simple evocation in his **chronicle** of the effects of the 1650 earthquake: "The
earth's foundations shook and with the
earthquake came a stench as of herbs and
sulphur. The sea swelled and ran a distance of two miles onto the island. A mist
lay flat like smoke over the whole of Santorini, striking men in the eyes, blinding
them. And likewise few livestock and
few birds survived, and the fields were
filled with the carcasses of the rest."

ECCLESIASTICAL POETRY, BYZ-
ANTINE Early church verse glorifies the
Divine or intones passages from Scripture. Because all authority is vested in the
divinely appointed emperor, it is his exalted church and his court circles that determine what shall or shall not be sung
in verse. Certain models are followed,
and originality of content is not itself a
goal. This body of medieval Greek poetry preserves the old meters, but the
quantitative principle of long or short
vowels falls away. Accent becomes an in-
dication of where stress in pronunciation
should fall. The verse is based on the
number of syllables and the tone of the
words. Whether syllables are long or
short does not concern the writer. He disregards **elision,** does not bother to elim-
inate **hiatus,** and no longer distinguishes
between acute or circumflex accent.

The very early Byzantine figure Bishop

Methodios of Philippi (who died in 311) composed a *Banquet* (following Plato's *Symposium*) that introduces a choir of virgins intoning a poem in praise of chastity. This text has stanzas followed by a refrain, a structure more typical of later Byzantine **hymns,** like the **kontakion.** Dölger shows how the last writer to use classical meters for ecclesiastical poems is Synesius Bishop of Cyrene (?370–c. 413), and by the sixth century the poet and the musician of a kontakion were generally the same person, and he was called a *melodos.* The work of Symeon the Theologian (late tenth century), displays an adherence to mysticism and penance that excludes all sources except Holy Scripture, as in his *Catecheses* ("Monastic Sermons"), his *Theological Chapters,* and his *Loves of the Divine Hymns.* He was the first writer to use **political verse** in religious poetry. Symeon left 10,700 lines of poetry that were published after his death by a pupil, Niketas Stathatos. **Psellus** (eleventh century) composed about 37 poems on ecclesiastical or philosophical matter, running from a couplet to 1,400 lines. Much of the remaining ecclesiastical poetry is homiletic in nature, that is, it could be adapted to a sermon and recited as a lesson.

Further Reading

Dölger, F. "Byzantine Literature." In *The Cambridge Medieval History.*

Volume IV: The Byzantine Empire. Part II: Government, Church and Civilisation, edited by J. M. Hussey, 207–264. Cambridge: Cambridge University Press, 1967.

EDUCATION.   See   LANGUAGE QUESTION; READERS; SCHOOL

EDUCATIONAL SOCIETY The Educational Society was established by a group of 36 writers, public figures, and intellectuals (including **Kazantzakis, Dragoumis, Mavilis,** A. Delmouzos, and **Karkavitsas**) on 10 May 1910. Its program was to give Athens a model demotic school and to constitute the springboard for the use of **demotic** language in a reformed Greek school system. By 1923, the dominant leaders in the group were M. Triantafyllidis (author of the influential Greek grammar of 1941), Delmouzos, and the (Marxist) **D. Glinós.** They worked with I. Tsirimokos, who became Minister of Education, to get Parliament to approve the Demotic as the sole teaching language in the first four classes of primary school. The Educational Society issued a trimonthly *Bulletin* from January 1911 and grew so rapidly that an amendment to the statutes (November 1914) devolved control of the Society from its founders to the assembly of its members. One of the main needs in the school system was for textbooks in the demotic. Authors were urged to submit draft volumes. **Z. Papantoniou** (1877–1940), who published his first short story, "The Baker," in *The Illustrated Estía* (1895), was invited in 1918 by the Ministry of Education to produce a general reader for the first four primary grades, in the demotic. The result was *The High Mountains,* which was attacked by the **Purists** and championed by the **Vulgarizers.** It is a saga about a group of schoolboys who organize their summer vacation at a mountain retreat. In 1917 the Greek government called on the Educational Society's experts to initiate school reform. This was carried out in the politically favorable periods of 1918–1920 and 1922–1925, when Glinós and Delmouzos headed teacher training colleges. Delmouzos and other founders withdrew (1927) when the Educational

Society adopted a sociological program. K. Bastiás issued a combative, demoticist journal, *Greek Letters,* at this point to house the Delmouzos group after the "split."

EFTALIOTIS, ARGYRIS (1849–1923, pseudonym of Kleanthis Mikhailidis) Eftaliotis translated the *Odyssey* into modern Greek in nine long years of unremitting concentration. The last three books (22–24) were unfinished at his death, and later translated by **N. Poriotis.** Eftaliotis became an enthusiastic **Vulgarizer** with the encouragement of **A. Pallis,** whom he knew personally after rooming together on trading missions. While in India, both men learned of the language reforms associated with **Psycharis** and adopted them with gusto. In 1889 Eftaliotis sent his debut poems, *Songs of an Expatriate,* to the **Philadelpheios Poetry Competition.** He gained the prize, with a very high mention. He lived outside Greece as an entrepreneur and a clerk to merchants (Manchester; Liverpool; India). He was the first author after Psycharis to use the **demotic** in all his published prose. His stories are quite conservative and respectful of Greek customs and **folklore.** He wrote with an appreciation of old furniture, courtyards, parties, dowry boxes, and handsome but virtuous women. When he described Bombay or his travels in Ceylon, he commented on the caste system, the shawls, cremation, the weather (always), the danger of snakes to the unshod, the less-visible Muslim women, the downpours, and the plurality of gods. Negative comments (on cleanliness, or religion) drew him to compare Indians with Turks. A special issue of *Néa Estía* (no. 537: 1948) is devoted to Eftaliotis.

See also PALIKARI

Further Reading

Thrilos, A. Μορφὲς τῆς ἑλληνικῆς πεζο-γραφίας καὶ μερικὲς ἄλλες μορφές [Figures of the Greek Prose Tradition, and Various Other Figures]. I. Athens: Difros, 1962.

EFYENA The *Efyena* is a play by a seventeenth-century author, Theodoros Montseletze. Nothing is known about this man, but dialect features and certain locations enumerated in a comic dialogue from the play make it clear that he was from Zakynthos, in the **Ionian Islands.** This in turn constitutes a proof that drama was alive and active there in the mid-seventeenth century, and not merely an export of the Cretan **theater,** thought to have arrived with scholars fleeing to the Heptanese from the Turkish conquest of Crete (1669). The drama is based on a fairy tale about a girl whose hands are cut off by order of her stepmother. The Virgin Mary restores the hands miraculously, the wicked stepmother is beheaded, and so "Lopped Hands" becomes an icon of divine grace. It was familiar all over the West from the thirteenth century. The text was apparently possessed by the scholar **Allatios** but rediscovered three centuries later in his archive by M. Vitti (1960). *Efyena* contains well-orchestrated interludes between the acts, the lopped head is shown on a salver to the audience, and there are rambunctious squabbles between cunning servants.

1821. See WAR OF INDEPENDENCE

EKPHRASIS The term *expression* (*ekphrasis*) denotes the formal praise of a building or its decoration, written as a tribute to its patron. In Byzantine **romance,** for instance, *Livistros and Ro-*

damni, the alternating vicissitudes of the principal lovers are relieved by *ekphraseis,* or ornate love letters. The *ekphrasis* in romance may describe a garden, frieze, sculpture, or a series of paintings on a palace wall. The writing of narrative poems in this manner, often describing art in eloquent tones, flowered with Paul the Silentiary (sixth century), an usher (*silentiarius*) at the court of Justinian. He was influenced by the circle round Agathias and wrote a *Description of the Church of the Hagia Sophia,* 887 hexameters in length, with a majestic *ekphrasis,* "Description of the Pulpit," as an added pendant in 275 lines (years 552–565). His contemporary, John of Gaza, composed an *ekphrasis* on a pagan wall painting as an accompaniment to Paul's Christian text.

Further Reading

Maguire, H. "Truth and Convention in Byzantine Descriptions of Works of Art." *Dumbarton Oaks Papers,* no. 28 (1974): 111–140.

ELEABOULKOS, THEOFANIS (sixteenth century) Eleaboulkos is a heroic type of scholar–priest. From 1543 to 1551, he inflamed congregations at Constantinople, preaching with a prophet's eloquence and forging a generation of pupils who set about clearing the historical obscurantism of the surroundings. They revived the study of theology and provided from among their number several future Patriarchs of Constantinople. Among them was Damascenus the Stoudite, an early writer of the **demotic,** and Jeremias II Tranos (c. 1530–1595), who was Patriarch three times between 1572 to 1595, survived 35 tumultuous years in ecclesiastical politics, invited Manuel Margounios (1549–1602) to his court, worked with **Meletios Pigás,** met Lutheran theologians to discuss tendentious items of **Catholic** dogma, and recognized the Tsar as the "only Christian sovereign in the world" (1589).

ELGIN MARBLES. See ATHENS

ELISION The elision of syllables (ἔκθλιψη) is used in verse as a way of avoiding **hiatus.** Hiatus is caused when a word ending with a vowel stands directly in front of a word beginning with a vowel. One of the two words drops a letter. Elision is made by blending (κράση): two successive words are combined into one, with the loss of a syllable. A simple adjustment, to create euphony, was "subsidence" (συνίζηση), whereby two vowels are "sunk" together to form a single syllable. They are sounded in this collapsed form, though they are written as two. At times, the doubling up of vowels in one word was eliminated by a contraction called synaeresis (συναίρεση). Poets also employed "subtraction" (αφαίρεση), which was the removal of one syllable to avoid hiatus. Another adjustment was the addition of euphonious consonants, a form of interpolation (παρεμβολή). The consonant γ, or *v,* was inserted between two vowels, in order to soften their contiguity. When the critic Korphis mentions the corrections that Nikos Chantzaras (1884–1949) made to his otherwise simple poems, he adds that "the verse was purified of parasites like excess adjectives and hiatus" (*MENL [Great Encyclopedia of Modern Green Literature],* XII, 674).

ELYTIS, ODYSSEAS (1911–1996; pseudonym of Odysseus Alepoudelis) Poet, essayist, graphic artist, translator, biographer, and Nobel Prize–winner for

literature (1979), Elytis was born at Iraklion (Crete), where his father went, while young, from Mytilene. In 1914 the Alepoudelis family, including six children of whom Odysseus was the youngest, went to live in Athens. The writer spent his summers living on different islands in the Aegean (Crete, Spetsai, Lesbos), which he celebrated in light and color: "as the sun rises, the guns of all great world theories are silenced." He took his high school diploma (1928) and enrolled in law two years later. He studied till 1935, but did not complete his degree. In November 1935, encouraged by **Katsimbalis,** he published his first poems in the new periodical *Ta Néa Grámmata* (*New Writing*). Later he collected his verse in a volume entitled *Orientations* (1940). His pseudonym was devised to avoid associations with the Alepoudelis soap made by his family. It unites different aspects of the author's mythology (Hellas, Helen, Freedom, Hope), as well as the word for "vagabond" (ἀλήτης). In October 1940, with the outbreak of the war with Italy, Elytis went to the Albanian front, and his experience as a young officer in Greece's First Army Corps marked him deeply and was later recast in the form of a long poem with the title *Lay Heroic and Funereal for the Fallen Second Lieutenant in Albania.* Another collection of lyric verse came out in 1943, with the title *Sun the First.*

There is an embryonic silence of 15 years between the publication of the *Lay* and Elytis's masterpiece *Dignum Est* (Ἄξιον ἐστίν). This work came as a considerable surprise (1959) and had a mixed reception from critics. Elytis's interest in Cubist art explains some of the geometry in its structure. The material is spliced into psalms, odes, and prose passages. The poem commences with a Genesis and ends with a Gloria. There are 30 poetic fragments, 12 odes, and 18 psalms, grouped around six readings. The composition is in three parts: (1) The campaign in Albania; (2) The enemy occupation; and (3) The Civil War. In each, the turn of events is sketched by two prose Readings, framed by the four Odes and the six Psalms. The sixth and last Reading is marked by the subtitle "prophecy" and deals with a coming "change" in a hymn of glory: "Worthy is life, worthy is light, worthy is the struggle and recompense for the sacrifice." At the center of the triptych is a Passion, fragmented into "Here Then Am I . . ." (verse), "The March Towards the Front" (prose), and "A Single Swallow" (prayer in verse), followed by an assemblage of odes, a story "The Great Sortie," the prophecy (fairy tale and speech). It is set among portraits of men, girls, soldiers, and endless landscape. The Gloria challenges us with the panoply of the Universe: "Now the incurably black hue of the Moon. / And always the blue-gold glitter of the Galaxy."

Elytis traveled in Europe, living five years at Paris (1948–1953). The art collector Tériade introduced him to Matisse, Chagall, Giacometti, de Chirico, and Picasso (1948). He met Breton, René Char, Eluard, Tzara, and Pierre-Paul Jouvé. He studied at the Sorbonne and contributed articles in French to the magazine *Verve.* Later he visited the United States (1961) and the Soviet Union (1962), tabling Greek viewpoints at international meetings.

Elytis received the State Prize for Literature in 1960, an honorary doctorate from the University of Thessaloniki (1975), and the Nobel Prize (1979). He called the famous opening line of

"Drinking the Corinthian sun" a tourist catchphrase, and he scorned his own "Mad Pomegranate Tree," that ever-popular poem in which others have seen a pageant of delirium battling evil. In *Open Documents* (1974), Elytis declared that the purpose of his poetry was to wake up objects and hear the echo of phenomena. Language is not the sum of word symbols that denote objects, but a force unleashed by the intellect. In his later essays, *Private Path* (1991), Elytis gave prominence to the sea journey, for the challenge of the wide sea was 6,000 words, and his little boat was maybe fifteen steps in length, rising and falling with a wave's swell.

See also COLLAGE

Further Reading

Decavalles, Andonis. "Time versus Eternity: Odysseus Elytis in the 1980s." *WLT* 62, no. 1 (winter 1988): 32–34.

Decavalles, Andonis. "Elytis's Sappho, His Distant Cousin." *WLT* 59, no. 2 (spring 1985): 226–229.

Elytis. *Maria Nephele: A Poem in Two Voices,* trans. by Athan Anagnostopoulos. Boston: Houghton Mifflin, 1981.

Ivask, Ivar. *Odysseus Elytis: Analogies of Light.* Norman: University of Oklahoma Press, 1981.

Odysseus Elytis. *Journal of an Unseen April* [bilingual text], trans. by David Connolly. Athens: Ypsilon, 1999 (reviewed in *TLS,* 24 Sept. 1999: 25).

Odysseus Elytis. *The Oxopetra Elegies,* trans. by David Connolly. Reading: Harwood Academic Gordon and Breach, 1997 (reviewed in *TLS,* 30 May 1997).

Odysseus Elytis. *Collected Poems,* trans. by Jeffrey Carson and Nikos Sarris. Baltimore: Johns Hopkins University Press, 1997 (reviewed in *TLS,* 19 Dec. 1997: 5–6).

Odysseus Elytis. *The Sovereign Sun: Selected Poems,* trans. by Kimon Friar. Philadelphia: Temple University Press, 1974.

Odysseus Elytis. *The axion esti,* trans. and annotated by Edmund Keeley and George Savidis. Pittsburgh: University of Pittsburgh Press, 1974.

Odysseus Elytis. "*Analogies of Light:* The Greek Poet Odysseus Elytis." *Books Abroad* 49, no. 4 (autumn 1975): 627–716 [with an appreciation by Lawrence Durrell].

Odysseus Elytis. Ιδιωτική οδός [Private Path]. Athens: Ypsilon, 1991.

EMBIRIKOS, ANDREAS (1901–1975) The **surrealist** poet, psychoanalyst, and novelist Andreas Embirikos was born in Romania to a family of international shipowners. Embirikos worked for a while at the London branch of his father's shipping company. He gave up this job out of solidarity with his family's jobless dockyard laborers. For a while he lived in France, reading Hegel, Marx, Freud, and Tolstoy while he studied psychoanalysis (1925–1931). He met André Breton and members of Breton's surrealist fraternity. He soon gave up socialism and declared that "Marxism, once it gained power, chose to fence the intellect inside narrow bounds of political expediency." In Greece (from 1932) Embirikos set up a group of psychoanalysts with Maria Bonaparte and other colleagues. He believed that unbridled sexual energy, together with poetry, could create the goal of most young intellectuals of the Depression years, a better world.

He made a sensation in 1935 with his volume *The Kill of High Heat,* which featured **automatic writing** and haphazard gobbets of prose. Some of the material was a deliberate recycling of **purist, Katharevousa** elements, as well as formula items from the media and scientific clichés. The resulting **collage** was a late transplant to Greece of the implications of Breton's first surrealist manifesto (1924). Eventually, Embirikos published marginally more conventional verse, *Hinterland* (1945). Of this volume, Trypanis remarks that its "strange, exotic, erudite language can be considered a real contribution to modern poetic diction." There was also the posthumous volume *Oktana* (1980).

Rumors circulated about a licentious prose work (composed by Embirikos in the period 1945–1951). This was finally brought out in the 1990s because of doubts by Embirikos's widow as to whether such material was fit to print earlier: *The Great Eastern* (2 vols., 1991) is the longest, most sexually explicit of all Greek novels. The book concerns the maiden voyage of a ship of this name (on 21 May 1867), a story once told by Jules Verne. The modern text is an experiment in prose (more playful than Pasolini's *100 Days of Salò*). It presents, in a page-to-time correlation, sequenced acts of fornication, voyeurism, bestiality, incest, and masochism related by, to, and about the passengers on their journey, with a playful, pseudopsychoanalytic emphasis on orality and ejaculation.

Further Reading

Embiricos, Andreas. *Amour Amour. Writing or Personal Mythology,* trans. by Nikos Stangos and Alan Ross. London: Alan Ross Editions, 1966.

Friar, Kimon, ed. and trans. *Modern Greek Poetry.* Anixi: Efstathiadis, 1995: 290–291.

Ricks, David. "Charting a Maiden Voyage." *TLS* 10 May 1991: 18.

Themelis, Y. Ἡ νεώτερη ποίησή μας— Πρῶτος καὶ δεύτερος κύκλος [Our Modernist Poetry: The First and Second Cycle]. Athens: Phexi, 1963.

EMPIRICISM The empiricism of classical thought lies embedded in much modern Greek writing. Thales showed that the planet is round by observing a stick's shadow. Anaximander inquired how the universe began. He believed, but could not prove, that humans evolved from another sort of animal. These writers understood the need for research to be followed by proof, a process known as empiricism (ἐμπειρισμός). Though Greek philosophers proposed theories, even **myths** and **metaphors,** to explain reality, for them "true significance lay in experience, and not in theory." Before **Plato,** philosophers already valued the collection of empirical data. **Aristotle** and his successors recommended use of scientific method and empirical confirmation of a theory. In the fifteenth century, **Plethon** recommended Strabo as a supplement to information in Ptolemy. He detected apparent imperfections in Strabo's *Geography.* Strabo had commented on Eratosthenes's attempt to measure the planet, and Plethon adds: "If the great size of the Atlantic did not prevent us, we could sail from Spain to India along the same parallel." Plethon's attention was caught by an assertion in Posidonius: "If you sail from the west using the east wind, you will reach India at a distance of 70,000 stades."

ENALLAGE *Enallage* (meaning "exchange") is the swapping of one word with another in forensic writing or poetry. The trope of *enallage* (ἐναλλαγή) includes the alternation of one part of speech by another part of speech, usually the adjective in place of the adverb, or one tense (the present) in place of another (the future). **Chrysanthe Zitsaia** dwells, in her evocation of the isle of Thasos ("Pan the Great Never Died"), on how the satyr "half-closed his sensual eyes." The last word may be either an **adjective** or adverb, but shifts, perhaps against logic, to the latter.

ENCYCLOPEDIA An essential source on Greek topics, including literature up to the early twentieth century, is P. Drandakis, ed., *Great Encyclopedia of Greece* (*MEE*, 24 vols., 1926–1934, with a 4-vol. *Supplement* of 1957). This national project is of great use because (a) most of the entries on modern Greek writers are by other authors, and (b) all articles end with a select bibliography. The earliest Greek encyclopedia (Vienna, 1806) was compiled by a doctor who came from Tirnavos (Thessaly) and learned his **medicine** in Germany, D. Alexandridis: *A Mirror of Greece* (see **Biography**). Alexandridis did a *Synoptic Collection of Accounts by the Ancient Geographers* (Vienna, 2 vols., 1807–1808). Modern Greek encyclopedias were composed rather late, in comparison with the West: next we meet Stavros Voutyrás (1841–1923) and his *Dictionary of History and Geography, Containing a Digest of History, a Geophysical and Political Survey, the Lives of Illustrious Men, Legends and the Traditions of Every Nation from the Most Ancient Times till the Present* (9 vols., Constantinople, 1869–1890).

A *Greek Lexicon* (3 vols., Venice, 1809–1916) by A. Gazís, editor of *The Scholar Hermes* (Vienna) and a member of the insurrectionist **Friendly Society,** was followed by a *Synopsis of the Sciences* (Vienna, 1826). This was composed by another **Enlightenment** sage, **Konstantinos Koumas**. These pedagogic nineteenth-century initiatives were improved on in the early twentieth century by the sophisticated tools of Drandakis and by K. Elevtheroudakis, editor,

The Encyclopedic Lexicon (12 vols., 1927–1932). Benét, editor of *The Reader's Encyclopedia* (1972), considers his own encyclopedia "one of the most complete and practical in existence." Benét does not cite the encyclopedias mentioned earlier or *Suda*, though he scoffs that the French *Encyclopédie, ou dictionnaire raisonné des sciences, des arts et des métiers* (1751–1780), has one column devoted to artichoke recipes (p. 314). Modern Greek is well served by the *Concise Orthographic and Encyclopedic Lexicon* (Athens: Ilios), which runs to 4,498 pages, and *Short Encyclopedic Dictionary* (Athens: Eleuthoudakis, 1935), 3,099 pages, with 1,726 pictures.

ENGONOPOULOS, NIKOS (1910–1986) Engonopoulos came from a **Phanariot** family, but was totally disengaged from the ruling class. Hostile to convention and the academy, Engonopoulos was a painter, designer, and poet, who admitted that **Embirikos** influenced his work, but drew ideas and attitudes from outside Greece. He dabbled in **automatic writing,** exploring the intellect, rather than the subconscious, to tease some logic out of this fad. He studied at the School of Fine Arts in Athens and was a pupil of **Fotis Kontoglou.** Later he showed canvases at national, European, and American exhibitions. He was commissioned to do sets and costume design for theater productions such as Plautus's *Menaichmoi* (1938), Aeschylus's *Prometheus Bound,* and Sophocles's *Electra.* He illustrated contemporary writers' books and translated verse by García Lorca, Picasso, Lautréamont, Mayakovsky, Baudelaire, De Chirico, and Tzara. He brought out several volumes of poetry that tended to irritate or even shock his readers: *Don't Talk to the Driver* (1938),

The Pianos of Silence (1939), *Seven Poems* (1944), *Bolivar* (1944), *The Return of the Birds* (1946), *Advent* (1948), *The Atlantic* (1954), and *The Valley with the Rosebeds* (1978). He published a *Lecture* (1963) on his career in art and a monograph entitled *The Presentation of Futurism* (1961). Engonopoulos's poem "News about the Death of the Spanish Poet Federico García Lorca on 19 August 1936 in a Ditch of Camino de la Fuente" is brisk and casual, compared with its solemn title: "for a while, now, / Above all in our present, crippled years, / They've had this habit / Of gunning down / The poets."

Further Reading

Engonopoulos, Nikos. *Bolivar,* trans. by James Laughlin. New York: New Directions, 1960.

McKinsey, M. "Language Questions: Diglossia, Translation and the Poetry of Nikos Engonopoulos." *JMGS* 8, no. 2 (1990): 245–261.

ENJAMBMENT The French word *enjamber* refers to extending a leg over an obstacle before putting down the foot. Enjambment (διασκελισμός) is the device in poetry that makes the grammar of a line, or a whole strophe, stride over into the beginning of the following line (= "run-on line"). In Greek lyric verse, enjambment creates an effect of enhanced continuity. In a **Markorás** poem that sanctifies "Work," the third quatrain runs three of its four lines into the following line: "Away over there let our cares / Fly, like / Startled bats / That have spotted the light."

ENLIGHTENMENT The years of the age of Enlightenment (Διαφωτισμός), c. 1700–1830, came later than the rise of encyclopedic knowledge and sociopolit-

ical thought in the West. **Drosinis** said of nineteenth-century schools in Greece: "Of our masters there was none to give us more than his conscientious, formal teaching, without soul or enthusiasm. We learnt dry letters and nothing else." The Greek Enlightenment was really a string of educational initiatives: conscientious teachers or clerics translated the classics, composed **grammars,** compiled dictionaries, wrote commentaries, founded schools, and in some cases gathered a band of disciples, whom they then dispatched to the four winds. They are known by the phrase "mentors to the nation" (διδάσκαλοι τοῦ γένους). Their work was carried forward by scholars, like Koraís, who lived in Western cities, and educators in the **Ionian Islands** or cities of the **Ottoman** empire imbued with the **Phanariot** tradition and the financial backing of the Greek merchant shipping class, cultivated sponsors who lived abroad.

Who, then, were the precursors of this movement? Men like Hierotheos the Hybirite (b. 1686), **Konstantinos Dapontis** (1713/14?–1784), Iosipos Moisiodax (1725/35?–1785), **Neophytos Doukas** (1760–1845), **St. Kosmas the Aetolian** (1714–1779), Konstantinos Vardalachos (1775–1830), **Anthimos Gazís** (1764–1828), Grigorios Zalikoglou (1776–1827), **Konstantinos Mikhail Koumas** (1777–1836), and **Neophytos Vamvas** (1770–1856) toiled to promote the education of Greeks, which they saw as the key to freedom from the Turks. Each considered himself an enlightener of the enslaved nation (διαφωτιστής).

The antisecular tradition, however, was deep rooted. Yerasimos Spartaliotis thought it preferable (mid-seventeenth century) that there should be "ignorance with piety rather than science with impiety." From the period of Ptochoprod-romos (twelfth century) comes the invective: "O Christ, accursed be letters and accursed whoever cultivates them." An unknown wit of the fifteenth century declared that clerics are people who "swallow the camel and filter the mosquito." In the eighteenth century, Moisiodax fought for the twin causes of science and letters. Though affected by consumption, he studied at Ioannina, Smyrna, Athens, **Thessaloniki, Mount Athos,** and Padua (in Italy). He taught at Jassy (Romania) and later traveled to **Venice,** Trieste, and Vienna. Among his many pupils were **Rigas Velestinlís** and P. Kodrikas. To better serve those to be enlightened, Moisiodax published his work in a **mixed** learned and demotic idiom (μιχτή). He taught in several schools of the Danubian principality, but resigned various times in order to uphold pure science or the content of the classics, rather than grammatical form.

Alexandros Mavrokordatos published anonymously (in **Russia**) a poetry collection entitled *Bosphorus in Borysthenia.* Rigas Velestinlís, **Ioannis Vilarás** (1771–1823), and **Athanasios Christopoulos** (1772–1847) each devised reading matter for the unmediated access of common people. A cleric from Pelion, Grigorios Konstantes (1753–1844) published a *Modern Geography* (1791) with another Thessalian, Daniel Filippidis. A leading role was taken by the scholar **Dimitrios Katartzis** (also known as Fotiadis). It was understood that education could not be imparted by language or textbooks that were incomprehensible in school. The progressive merchants sponsored classes for "the culture-starved Greeks" (Pappageotes). They endowed libraries and orphanages, raised subscriptions for hospitals, and subsidized learning by sending the two best pupils each year from schools in their province to the West for graduate training.

See also KORAÍS

Further Reading

Henderson, G. P. *The Revival of Greek Thought, 1620–1830.* Albany: State University of New York Press, 1970.

Koumolides, John T. A., ed. *Greece in Transition: Essays in the History of Modern Greece, 1821–1974.* London: Zeno, 1977.

ENTHUSIASTS The "Enthusiasts" (Ἐνθουσιασταί) were a gnostic group of zealots who adopted beliefs held by the Euchites (Εὐχῖται). The Euchites were heretics from a remoter period, who revered God and minor deities. **Photius,** in chapter 52 of his *Library,* says that the Euchites resided in Thrace in the eleventh century. They preached a triune authority: God the Father is lord of all things transcendental. His elder son, Satanail, is lord of the earth. His younger son, Christ, is lord of heaven. When the Enthusiasts became influential, an imperial delegate, perhaps **Psellus,** was sent to negotiate with them. He wrote a *Dialogue* about their withdrawn mysticism, which was later linked with the Bogomil movement.

See also ORTHODOX CHURCH

EPARCHOS, ANTONIOS (1491–1571) The family of the nobleman Antonios Eparchos were from Kerkyra. His father was a colleague of Laskaris. The house had lost its fortune (1538) when Suleyman I the Magnificent (1494–1566) attacked the island. Eparchos escaped and went to Venice and was helped financially by benefactors. He became a teacher, calligraphic copyist, and itinerant manuscript importer, carrying out commissions for popes and French royalty. He wrote "Lament on the Disaster of Greece," consisting of 200 couplets, printed in 1544, and bound with letters to three friends.

EPIC An epic (ἔπος) is a long poem in stately verse (of 11-, 15-, or even 17-syllable lines), generally subdivided into books (ραψωδίες). It has a heroic or patriotic subject. In classical Greek, the epic included gods. In Byzantine and modern Greek, the epic deals with themes of war and national resurgence. **Stefanos Koumanoudis** (1818–1899) wrote up to 7,000 lines of an incomplete epic entitled *Stratis Kalopichiros.* **Alexandros Rizos Rangavís** (1809–1892) composed an epic entitled *The Demagogue,* evoking Dimitrios, the Tsarist pretender of the seventeenth century.

See also AKRITIC SONGS; ALI PASHA; ANTONIADIS; DIASPORA; DIYENÍS AKRITAS; EROTOKRITOS; IONIAN ISLANDS; KAZANTZAKIS; KRYSTALLIS; MARKORÁS; MARTZOKIS, A.; SOLOMÓS; VALAORITIS, A.; VIZYINÓS; VOUTSYNAS POETRY PRIZE; ZALOKOSTAS

EPIGRAM An epigram is a concise verse summary of some important issue, written with serious or satirical content and composed in the manner of captions carved on works of art. Verse epigrams are the only secular poetry that lasts to the end of **Byzantium** (1453). A literary circle that gathered round Agathias the Rhetorician (c. 536–582) produced the *Cycle,* a collection of epigrams arranged by subject. They represent the kernel of the future *Palatine Anthology,* containing such gems as "you can forgive cows for fleeing before a lion," to justify the Per-

sians' flight from **Alexander.** Callimachus was master of the **Hellenistic** epigram, which gave writers license to relate small, daily occurrences to large, religious traditions. These reflective observations in verse (ἐπιγράμματα) were written in the middle Byzantine period by **Ptochoprodromos,** Konstantinos Kefalás, Konstantinos of Rhodes, Kometas, **Photius,** Leon Choerosphactes (ninth century), Ioannis Geometres Kyriotes (tenth century), Ioannis Mauropous (eleventh century), **Psellus** (1018–?1081), Manuel Philes, Christoforos of Mytiline, Nikolaos Kallikles (eleventh–twelfth century), and others.

Further Reading

Cameron, Alan. *The Greek Anthology from Meleager to Planudes.* Oxford: Clarendon Press, 1993.

EPILLION The word *epillion* is a **diminutive** of epic (ἔπος) and denotes a poetic miniature, in the Alexandrine period, usually a heroic narrative, of 100 or more hexameter lines. In the *epillion,* the focus is on refinement and detail. The vogue returned for a short while in **Romantic** poetry. Its popularity recalls Callimachus (c. 305–c. 240 B.C.), who decreed "a big book is a big misfortune."

Further Reading

Pontani, Filippo Maria. *L'epillio greco.* Florence: Sansoni, 1973.

EPINIKION The *epinikion* is a song or poem to celebrate the occasion of a victory (νίκη). Its plural (ἐπινίκια) denotes sports, or sacrifices, held in antiquity to give thanks for winning. The **personification** of victory, Nike, was seen as a charioteer or winged maiden. She advised the gods, who dispensed victory, or was herself the goddess of winning. In the **Orthodox Church,** the phrase "victorious hymn" refers to the triumphal "Holy, holy, holy, Lord God of the Sabbaoth," which occurs in the **liturgy.**

EPISKOPOPOULOS, NIKOLAOS (1873–1944) Episkopoulos, the future "French" author known as Nicolas Ségur, began his fairy-tale career at a humble pharmacy on Zakynthos, where he listened to the gossip of intellectuals who used to foregather there. In his teens, he moved to Athens and wrote for the **newspaper** *Town* and contributed to *Techni* and *Panathinaia,* edited by Kimon Mikhailidis. Attracted by Western, symbolist influences, Episkopopoulos went to Paris (1902) and stayed there till his death. He gained the support of the novelist Anatole France and wrote neoclassical, pseudohistorical prose, partly influenced by d'Annunzio, A. France himself, and the decadent, occultist Villiers de L'Isle-Adam (1838–1889). He wrote a five-volume history of European literature (publ. 1953).

EPISTOLOGRAPHY Gregory of Nazianzus (fourth-century theologian and divine) gave early models of letter writing (ἐπιστολογραφία), intended for publication, among the 250 letters from him which survive. In a letter to Nikoboulos, he gives a guide to the genre, saying that a letter should be neither long, nor short, and its impression should be conveyed through clarity, as though the sender were chatting with the recipient. There should be some elegance of style, yet without any abuse of its effect. **Photius** also wrote on method in letter writing. **Phanariot** writers also composed letters for communication and effect. They inserted **Turkish** words to spice up

their text (ἰντικάμι, "revenge,") or they might give the date and place in verse, as in a 1744 letter that starts with the couplet "Written February third, this letter's brought / From Bucharest, that noble court." The salutation "I bow to you" (προσκυνῶ) expresses the writer's obedience and reflects a clerical usage that dates to the fourteenth century. Later, the adverb "worshipfully" might be used to close a letter to the Patriarch. The word could be put under a triangle of printed crosses or outside the envelope. Other salutations for use in letters are "neck respectfuly bent," "your devoted slave," "humbly yours," "with filial devotion," or "with brotherly wishes." Among the possible titles to letters was the expanded formula "I kiss the hand of my respected Bey."

Aelian (c. 165–c. 222), in his 22 *Rustic Letters,* expounded opinions on the pastoral life (see **Korydalleús**). **Palamás** used the formula "sweet Koraism" to commend the prose style of **Koraís,** by whom we have more than 1,000 letters. Koraís's epistolary writing often went off in the form of a circular. This was then transcribed to another copy and passed to other correspondents. His letters gave advice on rebellion against the **Turkocracy,** education, cultural projects, and so on. The epistolary novel comes late to Greek, compared with the example of Goethe, Foscolo, and Smollett. **Mimika Kranaki** (b. 1922) crowned her career with *Nostalgia for Greece* (1992), a novel in letters describing the life of Greek intellectuals who fled to the West at the time of the **Civil War,** growing into **Philhellenes** during their expatriation. **Rhea Galanaki** (b. 1947) forges a romantic, socialist hero from the previous century, in the novel *I'll Sign as Louis* (1993). She depicts his life and surroundings by having him post letters to a woman in the days before his suicide. Renos Apostolidis (b. 1924), who saw regular army service (1947–1949) in the Civil War, taking part in 35 battles but never firing a bullet against his humanitarian convictions, made a record of his experiences in *Pyramid 67* (1950), an epistolary novel that centers on a bespectacled narrator who loses his glasses and moves myopically on many battlefields, in a text full of reported interpolations, like the digression that demonstrates the need for a new form of writing.

EPITAPHIOS   The 1936 poem by **Ritsos** under the title *Epitaphios* can be fully appreciated if it is understood that the adjective "funereal" (ἐπιτάφιος) suggests an epitaph. Ritsos's use of the word *epitaphios* recalls the embroidered image of the dead Jesus. It is made still more somber by being composed in the couplets of the demoric lament known as *mirologia*. Ritsos dramatizes a mother's threnody over a son killed in a demonstration quelled by army and police units among striking tobacco workers. These events took place in Thessaloniki in May 1936. Ritsos rushed home and drafted the work in two nights. 10,000 copies were rushed out. Later, the 250 remaining copies in People's Bookshop were publicly burned by the Metaxás regime, together with texts by Anatole France, Gorky, and Karl Marx.

The noun *epitaphios* refers to a strip of embroidery representing Jesus Christ after his Deposition from the Cross. This cloth was unfurled only for Good Friday. It has acquired an aura of uniqueness in Greek **Orthodox** ceremonials. It tended to remain in pristine condition, unlike more frequently exhibited relics. Various poets, as well as Ritsos, have used the word *Epitaphios* as the title of a volume of their work, for example, Alkis Tropaiatis (1949) and Takis Varvitsiotis (1951).

EPITHET. See ADJECTIVE

EPITOME   Till the nineteenth century, literature came to most Greek readers by way of the epitome, a **digest** from many works, or an abridgment of one work. It offered a distillation (short or long) from a body of laws, facts, or prayers. The major part in earlier Greek literature is played not by an individual author's book, but by his appearance in an epitome of several such books. The **chrestomathy** is related to the need, sensed by most Greek educators, to provide much "by way of the little." The ideal of the epitome was to provide an abstract of the book in question (α περίληψη). Such works, some in **anthology** format, conveyed an entire *corpus* of writing by way of their essential content. In the year 920, during the reign of Emperor Romanos, an unknown law teacher drafted an *Epitome of the Laws,* under 50 headings. This model is seen in other Byzantine handbooks. In the **Hellenistic** age, it tempted intellectuals to toy with cosmic sympathy and a "unitary conception of all departments of knowledge." Long (1986: 221) compares the philosopher Posidonius (c. 135–50 B.C.) with **Aristotle** or Eratosthenes: "A critical synthesis of existing knowledge may be highly original and a most fruitful source of new discoveries." Eratosthenes (born, according to *Suda,* c. 276 B.C.) was appointed by Ptolemy II (246–221) head librarian at Alexandria, where he succeeded Apollonius Rhodius.

Further Reading

Long, A. A. *Hellenistic Philosophy: Stoics, Epicureans, Sceptics.* London: Duckworth, 1986.

EPODE In the classical period, the epode was a refrain that followed the **strophe** and **antistrophe** in an ode by Pindar, or in his imitators. In postclassical Greek, it refers to a lyrical piece in which short verses cap longer ones. In modern Greek, the word *epode* means a refrain in which certain lines are repeated at the end of successive strophes (as in **Ballad**). Other such refrains, in nineteenth-century oral and written poetry, were termed pleating (τσάκισμα) or return (πιστρόφι).

ERATÓ Among the nine **Muses,** Erató was the special protector of love poetry, marriage, and dancing. She is often depicted holding a lyre. Erató discovered how to compose hymns for the immortals and was therefore credited with inventing poetry.

***EROTOKRITOS* (c. 1640–1650?)** In 10,052 lines, subdivided into five books, the *Erotokritos* is an **epic** love story. It comes down from an unknown, mid-seventeenth-century author, using the eastern dialect of the island of Crete. He gives his name as Vitsentzos Kornaros. The *Erotokritos* shares a few elements, and repeated lines, with the Cretan religious drama, *The Sacrifice of Abraham* (c. 1635) and appears to be modeled on a translation into Italian prose of the French romance by Pierre de la Cypède, *Paris et Vienne.* N. Cartojan identified *Paris et Vienne* as the prototype (in 1935). Whereas L. Politis considered the derivation an established fact (in 1973), he noted that the medieval French spirit of the source is completely Hellenized, in *Erotokritos.* The Cretan narrator's account of a war between Athenians and Vlachs is new, and his text abounds in attractive **demotic** touches. Kornaros's work may also draw on a version of the same romance, in *ottava rima* strophes (ABABABCC), by Angelo Albani, namely the *Innamoramento di due fedelissimi amanti Paris e Vienna* (publ. 1626). Depending on which of these two derivations is accepted, the period of composition of *Erotokritos* is placed at 1600–1610, or as late as 1640–1660.

It is written with a sure touch, in a robust 15-syllable line, with deft asides: "For whoever can speak with awareness and style / Will make the eyes of men fill with laughter and tears." It has been quoted for centuries by Cretan peasants, recited by bards, and sold by peddlers. It has symbolic touches that delight the critic as much as the common reader: Aretousa, the heroine, sends an apple when Erotokritos, her admirer, is pretending to be sick. Is this a therapeutic gift, or a signal of love? When he has to escape from her father's kingdom, his sigh makes the earth shake. The girl, alone with her nanny, swoons as if dead on the old woman's lap.

At the **happy ending,** the "birds, flying low, sang sweetly." This compound verb turns a random flock into playful celebrants. Readers note the armor of the prince from **Nafplion,** who on his helmet affects an opaque sun next to a shining girl. This is code for the concept that his lady's radiance shines brighter than the sun. Can *Erotokritos* be a "long and tedious romance saturated with Italian influence," as J. B. Bury once asserted? In the *Poetics* (1449b17), **Aristotle** states that "anybody who can tell a good tragedy from a bad one can do the same with epics." **Seferis** sees the *Erotokritos* as "rural rather than seafaring." Though the battle scenes are powerful, he finds they are not the best part of the poem, which is simply a love story. The warrior Karaminitis "makes war for war's sake," whereas the other champions make war in a cause led by love. The unifying force of their story is passion: "Note how Love works many magic spells, / And forces mortals sick with love to act." In the *Erotokritos,* Holton and others have detected the *Comedy* of **Dante** (1321), Boiardo's chivalric epic, the *Orlando innamorato* (1494), Ariosto's *Orlando furioso* (1516–1532), and to a lesser extent Tasso's *Gerusalemme liberata,* 1565–1575.

The poet **Typaldos** in 1880 (publ. 1911) considered it the greatest poem in modern Greek literature. Synadinós staged it as a play in 1929. Miss Marika Kotopouli (see **Actor**) was a sensation playing Aretousa in a funnel headdress, like a damsel from the days of romance, lamenting like the dirge-singers of Mani. The *Erotokritos* is also a work in the genre of fictional narrative, borrowing from the Greek tradition of popular storytelling. Seferis calls the duels not just "repetitions" but "encores." He finds the influence of courtly writing minimal: there is only one learned word in the poem, namely "self-governance" (φταξιούμενο), whereas there are 10 Arabic and 40 Italian words. Its prosodic form is the **decapentasyllable** in rhyming couplets. In the fourteenth century, this kind of narrative made use of the trochaic octosyllable (that is, $-\breve{} \times 4$).

A recurring theme of *Erotokritos* is the mutability of Fortune, often allied to the image of a turning wheel. The work shows a significant resemblance, in its opening statement, to the declaration of theme in Yioustos Glikós's *Mourning for Death* (1524). The tragedy *Erofili* (by **Chortatsis**) is another apparent source. The names of the male and female protagonist, Erotokritos and Aretousa, make a neat etymological match with Erofili

and Panaretos. The nurse's name, Frosyne, may be borrowed from Chortatsis's pastoral comedy *Panoria.* The second book of *Erotokritos* is almost wholly given over to a tournament mounted by King Iraklis to entertain his daughter Aretousa. Three previous Greek narrative poems make a tournament into a major plot component. As in the Greek *Theseid* (itself an adaptation of Boccaccio's *Teseida delle nozze di Emilia,* c. 1340), so in *Erotokritos* each of the tournament treatments includes a villain, a paragon of beauty, and a rough countryman. The trio of Kromis, Nestor, and Evander, in *Theseid,* is reflected by three characters in *Erotokritos:* the Karamanitis, the Prince of Byzantium, and the Lord of Patras. In both works, the hero is banished and returns under an assumed name. The romance **Apollonius of Tyre** (perhaps late fourteenth century) also features a tournament. Holton argues that the creation of a mystical setting links *Apollonius of Tyre* and *Erotokritos.* The tournament episode in each has similarities with the other: the description of the prize, the proclamation, the narrative detail.

The **Alexander Romance** by pseudo-Callisthenes offers possible sources for episodes in *Erotokritos:* Alexander's steed roars and drops dead on hearing its master's death. In *Erotokritos,* the horse of the Karamanitis dies at the moment of its master's death. The *Alexander Romance* may provide the author of *Erotokritos* with a knowledge of the place name Macedonia. Funerals in both works are similar, for Darius and Alexander in the *Romance,* and for the death of Aristos, in *Erotokritos:* "When his soul departed, leaving the body, / A great thundering took possession of the skies, / And people saw a darkling whirlwind / Swirl round the corpse of the young warrior."

The early Greek saga *Diyenís Akritas* is not a direct source of *Erotokritos,* though both Diyenís and Erotokritos serenade their beloved, both play a lute for her, both sing like a nightingale, both face the danger of being discovered by the girl's parents, and in both works the song functions as a means for the hero's recognition by the heroine. Kornaros uses **enjambment,** as in Italian narrative poetry, to break up the potential monotony of his **political** meter. Kornaros probably read some of his popular Greek narrative material in vernacular chapbooks (φυλλάδες), and common folk were the first to give a reception to *Erotokritos.*

Most writers of the eighteenth century, with the exception of **Konstantinos Dapontis** in a condescending reference, ignore the work. **Adamantios Koraís** was too stern to recommend it, but covered his censure by referring to a "Homer of **vulgar** literature." European travelers at the beginning of the nineteenth century, men like Leake, Depping, and Clarke, did discuss the work. Foreign scholars praised the poem, among them the editor of **demotic songs,** Fauriel, and Iken, who translated passages into German. Pouqueville and Brandis offered unfavorable views, and **Rangavís** was lukewarm about the *Erotokritos.* Neroulos, in his lectures on Greek literary history, was scornful, claiming (in 1828) that *Erotokritos* had fallen "into a just oblivion." Today it is easier to see the greatness of a work in which form and content completely coalesce; one whose fortune Seferis compared with the painter **El Greco** ("how many icon painters had to toil so that one day a Theotokopoulos could emerge"). The *Erotokritos* does not coincide with any cultural zenith, and it lacks an artistic milieu. Seferis sees it as a sign of the obliqueness of neo-Hellenism:

"This is the unfinished dialogue of Greek history: always, at the boundaries of areas and periods; this is the fate of our race: that one floruit should be totally ready, that a complete ruin should be totally imminent."

See also CRETE; RENAISSANCE; VENICE

Further Reading

Holton, David. "*Erotokritos* and Greek tradition." In *The Greek Novel, A.D. 1–1985,* ed. Roderick Beaton, 144–53. London: Croom Helm, 1988.

Holton, David. *Erotokritos.* Bristol: Bristol Classical Press, 1991.

EROTOPAIGNIA The "Playthings of Love" (Ἐρωτοπαίγνια) are mid-fifteenth-century songs, usually short. They may have been written down in Rhodes. They come from the same song collection, the so-called Καταλόγια, as the *Alphabet of Love*, and the "Song of the Hundred Words."

See also HEKATÓLOGA; KATALÓGIA

ESTÍA The weekly Athenian periodical *Estía* was started by Pavlos Diomidis on 4 January 1876. In a simple statute, it proclaimed the dissemination of useful knowledge. It was to provide "reading material for the heart and mind of the public, in a simple style that is, as far as possible, comprehensible to all." Subsequent directors of *Estía* were Y. Kasdonis and **Y. Drosinis.** It gained a weekly circulation of about 3,000 and was the first Greek periodical to go on sale by the single copy, showing its price on each issue and not reserved for subscribers. Drosinis converted it into an illustrated daily in 1894, with **G. Xenopoulos** as assistant editor. *Estía* held an important short story competition in 1883. This competition marks the inception of the genre story (that is, the portrayal of homely scenes), using the technique and content called *ithografía* ("recording of manners"). The *Estía* competition also called for the treatment of national plots and the recording of the national Greek character. The panel of judges consisted of the Greek folklorist **N. G. Politis, Emmanuel Roidis,** and Spyridon Lambros (see **Olympics**). **Papadiamantis** wrote his short novel *Christos Milionis,* based on an old **demotic song** about the **Klephts,** in a calculated effort to fit the requirements of the 1883 prize.

The journal printed (1890) a striking piece by **Mikhail Mitsakis,** "A Wall." This foregrounds part of a castle that has lasted through time, but whose history calls into question the usual narrative of time and place. In 1895, *Estía* published an even more unusual short story by **Vizyinós,** "Moskov-Selim." A blurring focus turns its Turkish protagonist, who has fought in all the Sultan's wars, into a paradoxical admirer of **Russia.** He lives on a windswept steppe, a psychological crossing between Greece, Russia, and Turkey. He is a family scapegoat from the unstable nightmare of kidnapping (see **Janissaries; King Turned to Marble**), yet his story runs counter to the Chauvinist mood following the Russo-Turkish war (1877–1878). *Estía* published the long novella by Palamás, *Death of the Brave Young Man,* in 1891. This periodical became, for nearly 20 years, the mouthpiece of a generation (see M. Chryssanthopoulos, under **Novel, Greek Modern;** also **Competitions; Bookshop**). It was the first Greek **newspaper** to publish small ads.

ETACISM. See PRONUNCIATION

EUPHEMISM The trope of "attractive sound," or euphemism (ευφημισμός) was originally used for flattery. It becomes a **figure** by which a distinguished term is used to portray an unpleasant reality. A. Tropaiatis (b. 1909), in *Tale of the Occupation,* has a boy wave from a lorry that drives a load of condemned Athenian men to a shooting range. His girl is left behind. He sets off "for the journey which has no return." This is less harsh than saying "to be shot."

EUTERPE Among the nine **Muses,** Euterpe was the goddess who protected music and lyric poetry and was the patron of wind instruments. She is often depicted holding a double flute. Greece's first purely literary periodical took its name from this Muse: *Euterpe* was issued at Athens, from 1848 to 1874, by a coterie of joint editors and distinguished intellectuals: Grigorios Kambouroglous, Konstantinos Paparrigopoulos, Nikolaos Dragoumis, **Alexandros Rangavís,** and Konstantinos Pop (see **Money**). Pop introduced the novelty of the current events column (χρονογράφημα). In each issue of this popular, innovative nineteenth-century journal, he discussed intellectual trends in Greece, comparing them deftly with events and ideas from contemporary Europe.

EVANGELIKÁ The "Gospel disturbances" or *evangeliká* (Εὐαγγελικά, or Εὐαγγελιακά) is a term referring to riots that took place in Athens (8 November 1901) after a translation of the New Testament into **demotic** Greek, rather than **Katharevousa,** by **Pallis.** The demonstrations were stirred up by academic theologians, as well as by conservative elements close to Professor **Mistriotis,** at the University. The rioters broke down the offices of *Acropolis* (which from 9 September 1901 had been serializing Pallis's allegedly impious version). They demanded that the Metropolitan bishop of Athens, Prokopios, excommunicate the **Vulgarizers.** The Gospel disturbances resulted in the death of eight students and the wounding of up to 70 others. The government, headed by Theotokis, resigned; the Metropolitan was dismissed. The royal family was indirectly involved because Queen Olga had patriotically urged the cause of such a translation after the country's military reverses of 1897.

See also DEMOTIC; PALLIS

Further Reading

Carabott, Philip. "Politics, Orthodoxy and the Language Question in Greece: The Gospel Riots of November 1901." *Journal of Mediterranean Studies* 3, no. 1 (1993): 117–138.

EXPATRIATION. See XENITIÁ

EXPERIMENTAL NOVEL. See BERATIS; NOUVEAU ROMAN; KARAPANOU

F

FAIRY TALE A fairy tale (παραμύθι) is a fantastic account of amazing events that are not specific to any one time or place. Sofia Mavroeidi-Papadaki (b. 1905, in a Cretan village) is one of many writers who adapt these tales to literary form, albeit as **children's books,** in her *The Fairy Tale of Olympus* (1943) and *Atalanta, Water Nymph of the Forest* (1957). Greek fairy tales include speaking animals, magic spells, repeated challenges, a rat who wants to marry his beautiful daughter to the sun, a snake who wants to be friends with a reluctant crab, a fox who wants to be a bird so he can catch prey on the wing, an exile who receives three wise words of advice from his foreign master instead of wages, an owl who thinks her child is prettier than the partridge's at bird school, or a king who gives two litigious peasants a week to calculate the quickest, the heaviest, or the most needful thing in the world (mind, fire, earth). Fairy tales often deploy a "happily ever after" motif as their ending: "so they married and lived happily, and we even happier!" or "So they lived and they died / With kids and grandkids besides." The opening formula "Once upon a time" is equally common (Μια φορά κι έναν καιρό).

Further Reading

Kioulafidou, Eirini and D. Papaioannou, eds. Ελληνικὰ Παραμύθια [Greek Fairy Tales]. Athens: Nostos, 1998.

FAKINOU, EVYENIA (1945–) The gifted writer Evyenia Fakinou was born in Alexandria and grew up in Athens, where she studied as an artist and tour guide. Fakinou is married to the Athens-based writer Michalis Fakinos (b. 1940). In 1974, at Belgrade, she learned the art of puppet theater. In 1976, she set up her own dolls' theater at Athens. She worked at this for five years, while writing and illustrating her own children's books. She gradually turned to fiction for adults. In *The Seventh Garment* (1983), she deals panoramically with major events in Greek history from the **War of Independence** to the military dictatorship of the 1960s, narrating the responses to memory and the clash with present values of a mother, her daughter, and a granddaughter. In *Who Killed Moby Dick?* (2001), Fakinou explores the exotic idea of a writer who seeks to compose the history of a city called Accra, which no longer has the national highway going through it. This writer courts his collaborator's beautiful girlfriend (Helen). His friend's stepfather wants him to complete the book quickly and be gone (to save own his son's hold on Helen). So he gives the writer a copy of *Moby Dick,* which is supposed to contain a memoir by a citizen of Accra who had been in the nineteenth-century hunt for the famous whale. The convolutions of this postmodern plot show that the backwater town can stay in the national headlines, despite the confusions of a text-within-the-text.

Further Reading

Fakinou, Evyenia. Το έβδομο ρούχο [The Seventh Garment]. Athens: Kastaniotis, 1983.

Fakinou, Evyenia. *The Seventh Garment,* trans. by Ed Emory. London: Serpent's Tail, 1991.

Fakinou, Evyenia. *Astradeni* [1982], trans. by H. E. Kriton. Athens: Kedros, 1991.

Fakinou, Evyenia. Ποιος σκότωσε τον Μόμπυ Ντικ [*Who Killed Moby Dick?*]. Athens: Kastaniotis, 2001.

FALIEROS, MARINOS (c. 1395–1474)

Falieros, a dilettante writer from **Crete** in the mid-fifteenth century, nobly connected, was involved in the island's civil government. Among his extant works in political **rhyme** are two dream sequences based on erotic themes: "An Amorous Somnolence," in 130 lines and the more substantial "History and Dream." The treatment of his beloved is interwoven with the figure of Fate and Pothoula, love personified. Falieros wrote a dirge in rhymed political lines, with dramatic settings for the Virgin Mother, entitled *Lamentation on the Passion and the Crucifixion.* He also composed two ethico-religious, admonitory texts: the "Instructive Speeches" (before 1430) are set out in 326 rhymed **decapentasyllables** and the "Consolatory Rhyme" (c. 1425) is admonitory verse in 302 such lines.

FALLMERAYER, J. P. (1790–1861)

The Austrian historian Fallmerayer, in the 1830s, enraged Greek **patriots** after their struggle for **independence** by suggesting that the inhabitants of contemporary Greece were not linear descendants of the older, classical Greeks. Fallmerayer espoused a theory of Slavic origins for modern **Hellenism. N. G. Politis,** father of modern Greek **folklore** studies, attacked this theory with his prize-winning essay (written in 1869 when he was still a teenager) "Modern Greek Mythology."

P. Sherrard (1978: 10–11) quotes from an essay by Robert (1929), which puts Fallmerayer's theory in its harshest form, namely that the modern Athenians were "the unmoral refuse of mediaeval Slav migrations, sullying the land of their birth with the fury of their politics, and the malformation of their small brown bodies." George **Byron** had cried in *The Giaour* (1813): "Approach, thou craven crouching slave: / Say, is not this Thermopylae? / These waters blue that round you lave, / Oh servile offspring of the free." There can be no dispute, as Sherrard points out, concerning the Albanian origin of certain Greek populations. The nineteenth-century Scottish historian George Finlay showed how ethnic Albanians had occupied the familiar areas of classical Greece: Attica; Megara; most of

Boeotia; parts of Locris, Andros, and Euboiea; Marathon; Plataea; Salamis; Mantinea; Olympia; Poros; Hydra; and Spetsai. Finlay wrote: "To me Greece is a second country, the scene of my boyish enthusiasm and the hope of my maturer years." Though a typical **Philhellene** (he took part in the Greek independence struggle), Finlay accepted Fallmerayer's thesis that contemporary Greeks were not the descendants of classical Greeks.

Further Reading

Fallmerayer, J. Phil. *Geschichte der Halbinsel Morea.* Stuttgart and Tübingen: J. G. Cotta, 1830.

Finlay, George. *History of the Greek Revolution and of the Reign of King Otho,* 2 vols. London: Zeno, 1971.

Hussey, J. M. "Jakob Philipp Fallmerayer and George Finlay." *BMGS* 4 (1977): 79–87.

FALL OF CONSTANTINOPLE In the mid-fourteenth century, Ibn Battuta counted 13 townships inside the walls of the so-called City. The loss of Constantinople to the Turks (1453) was seen in Greek literature as a calamity, a dreadful split between East and West. The post-Byzantine writers who chronicle the Capture (Άλωση) include George Sphrantzes, Laonikos Khalkokondyles, Michael Kritoboulos, and Doukas. Pius II called the fall of Constantinople "the second death of Homer and Plato." Sphrantzes, more realistic, put it down to errors in Byzantine politics, and not to "sins," Divine Providence, or Fate. The Athenian Khalkokondyles is one of the first modern Greek authors to suggest that the sack of Constantinople was an Asiatic revenge for the siege of Troy in preclassical times. This rationalizing argument (αἴτιον) for the city's capture was accepted in some Western texts. For the historical setting of his 1907 poem, *The Dodecalogue of the Gypsy,* **Palamás** chooses the eve of the invasion of the capital. The gypsy's mixed lays include an account of the flight of Byzantine scholars toward the West and the destruction of the Utopian writings of **Yemistos Plethon.** The siege of the city founded by Byzas lasted 31 years. The day on which **Ottomans** penetrated the city wall, Tuesday 29 May 1453, is a symbolic **date** in Greek culture. Isidore of Kiev calculated that around 120,000 manuscripts were destroyed in the Ottoman sack of Constantinople.

Popular songs detailing the Fall are full of grandiose, stupefied mourning. In one lament, "The Last Palaeologus," the speaker refuses to believe the Emperor is dead: "No, he rests, / He is only sleeping; with a gold crown at his head and a sceptre in his hand." In the darkness of a wide cave, fitted like a palace under a tower at Golden Gate, the Emperor is bathed in a blue radiance, emanating from a star lit by the hand of God as a sacred flame. In a demotic lament from Trebizond, "Capture of Constantinople," two birds bring a special message that no erudite cleric can read or interpret. A little boy comes forward and deciphers the code: "Woe is me, alas, the Turks have taken the City, / Captured the royal seat; our suzerainty is changed." The Emperor arms himself with a sword and pike, then cuts to pieces 300 Turks and 13 Pashas, until his weapons are broken.

In fact, Byzantium was defeated in a waiting game, and its ramparts were breached with a cannon made by a Hungarian and offered for sale to both sides. Constantine XI Palaeologus, the last emperor, no longer had funds for artillery. He was killed in the street, as the empire dwindled into nothing. The unknown writer of *Lament on the Fall of Constantinople* (late fifteenth century) relates, in 118 **political** lines, the enslavement of the captured defenders, the looting of Christian churches, and the pillage of the capital, with an encomiastic memoir on the greatness of **Hagia Sophia.** He tells the sun and moon to dim their light, but he also weaves "a little allegory" about Justinian (the sun) and his city (the moon), asserting gnomically that "the moon cannot shine without the sun." The Emperor asks some attendants to cut off his head (a motif seen in **Klephtic** poetry), so he may not fall alive into the hands of Muslims.

The city's capture is reported in a discussion between two boats at Tenedos, using the form of stichomythy (στιχο-μυθία), alternation or sharing of lines by two speakers. Though the news comes to Crete, this poem is probably of Cypriot origin. The earliest artistic lament on *The Capture of Constantinople,* once attributed to **Emmanuel Georgillás** of Rhodes, consists of 1,045 mixed rhyming and unrhymed decapentasyllables that beg concerned rulers of Western Europe to help the ruined empire. These texts explain that it was brought low by "envy, miserliness and empty hoping." A *Lament* by another unknown hand consists of 128 unrhymed decapentasyllables that culminate in a dialogue between Venice and Constantinople. Here, the Italian voice expresses its compassion, and the Byzantine voice rehearses its nostalgia. The anguish can be felt over five centuries: "You, mountains, will mourn and, stones, you will crack; / You rivers will shrivel, and, fountains, you will run dry, / Because the key of all Creation has been lost, / The precious eye of Anatolia and Christiandom; / And you, moon of the sky, should no longer light the earth."

Dated around 1500, the *Lament of the Four Patriarchates* gives voices to Constantinople, Jerusalem, Alexandria, and Antioch, as they bemoan the calamity. Jerusalem tries to console Constantinople, by saying "Look what I've been through." Alexandria recalls the many "beautifully adorned churches" that stood open every day. Antioch calls on God's consolation because its own castles, monasteries, and Christians have begun to vanish.

One of the most famous of the Greek folk songs, extant in various forms and differing in length from 11 to 18 political verses, recalls the last mass celebrated in Hagia Sophia and ponders whether the church can survive the Sack. These *Laments* illustrate the merging of Byzantium with all world religion: "The time has come for Christians, for Latins and for Romans, / For Russians and for Vlachs, Hungarians, Serbs and Germans, / [. . .] to raise on high the Cross, the sign of Christ." Nature itself is caught up in the paroxysm: "Heavenly moon, grant no light to earth. / Flowing waters, cease running and stand still. / Sea, announce the calamity, the fall of Constantinople." The fall of the city is a modern motif, from the story by **Thanasis Petsalis**'s "The City Is Captured," to Angelos Simiriotis's poem "The Unfading Rose," with women crowding Hagia Sophia, as the "dogs" close in: "The choir is chanting, the candles are blazing—O weep, mothers and offspring!— / The City is taken! As the dogs trampled the place of fragrance, / And stood near at hand, the temple's floor was strewn with roses."

See also MATHAIOS

Further Reading

Bréhier, Louis. *The Life and Death of Byzantium.* Amsterdam: North-Holland Publishing, 1977.

Dieterich, Karl. *Geschichte der byzantinischen und neugriechischen Litteratur.* Leipzig: C. F. Amelangs Verlag, 1909.

Philippides, Marios. "Early Post-Byzantine Historiography." In *The Classics in the Middle Ages. Papers of the Twentieth Annual Conference of the Center for Medieval and Early Renaissance Studies,* edited by A. S. Bernardo and S. Levin, 253–263. Binghamton, NY: Center for Medieval & Early Renaissance Studies, 1990.

Rodley, Lyn. *Byzantine Art and Architecture: An Introduction.* Cambridge: Cambridge University Press, 1994.

FALL OF CRETE. See CRETE

FALL OF CYPRUS. See CYPRUS

FANATICISM, DEMOTIC. See VULGARISM

FASCISM Xefloudas, in his novel *Men of the Myth* (1944), makes a soldier, trudging through ice and rain toward the Albanian front, speak words to justify Greece's war against Fascism: "We'll fight Mussolini's Fascism and Hitler's Nazism, since they joined forces to enslave us. We'll go to war to prevent the existence of fascism in the world." Greeks saw Mussolini (1883–1945), the *Duce* (ἀρχηγός), as a warlord occupying Albanian territory. The National Socialism (Ναζισμός) of Hitler (1889–1945) represented starvation and **occupation** (1941–1942 and 1944). What they thought of the fate of the Greek **Jews** is less certain.

Further Reading

Tsoucalas, Constantine. *The Greek Tragedy.* Harmondsworth: Penguin, 1969.

FASOULIS. See PUPPETS

FEMINISM AND GREEK WRITERS
In the early nineteenth century, some women intellectuals produced essays or translations, verse, and drama. **Evanthia Kairi, Elizabeth Moutzan-Martinengou,** Aikaterini Rasti, Rozana Samourkasi, Fotini Spahti, Mitio Sakelariou, Rallou and Aikaterini Soutzou, for example, published work in the period 1816–1832. A paper aimed at promoting the interests of Greek women was founded in 1871 with the title *The Newspaper for Ladies.* It was published until 1918 and contributed to a reassessment of the role of women in marriage, education, property rights, and inheritance. An active woman prose writer of the period, **Kallirrhoe Parrén** (1861–1940), was editor and took up the cause of girls' schooling. In an essay of 1913, **Emmanuel Roidis** suggested that women's writing should be confined to topics like needlework and cooking, because women become imitators if they try to enter the public domain.

Athena Rousaki Germanou was the first Greek woman to print a volume in modern Egypt, namely *Fragrant Flowers* (1902), and the first principal of the Female Workers' College. This later became the (Night) School for Working Girls, an initiative run by the Union of Greek Women, in the city of Alexandria. Also in Alexandria (1920), Rousaki Germanou published a sociopolitical essay on feminist action, *Concerning the Rights and Activity of Women,* and much later, in Athens (1953), the volume *Boundaries in Flames.* In the early twentieth century, a tiny number of girls proceeded from basic literacy instruction to secondary schooling. The ideal agenda was to get a dowry, be chaperoned, then get engaged, and stay in marriage. If they wrote, women were expected to confine themselves to sentiment and landscape. The subject matter of the poetess was seen by most readers as "lyric verses full of butterflies, dewy mornings, and maternal affection." A job in the theater was considered compromising for a woman. This applied to **Myrtiotissa,** despite her anticonformism. The First Panhellenic Women's Conference was held in Athens, on 26–29 May 1946.

A survey by *The News* (2 March 1992: 26–27) showed recently that, in cultural activities, only 7 percent of participants were female. In scientific fields, women made up 3 percent of workers. In the arts, women made up to 25 percent of the workforce. About 10 percent of key figures from the period 1950 to 1990 cited in the Greek *Who's Who* are women: 457 out of 4,856, by one index. The 300 members of Parliament have included 13 or fewer women. Some women's collectives emerged in Greece, and one published the journal *Broom,* which ran from 1979 to 1981 and carried information about the international women's movement, for example, an interview with the German author Christa Wolf. Not all female writers approved of the term *feminist* or agreed that there was a specifiable "women's writing." **Kostoula Mitropoulou** rejected the category of "women's prose" and said that she found it "a rather humorous term."

See also DELTA; FEMINIST POETRY; NAKOS

Further Reading

Anastasopoulou, Maria. "Feminist Discourse and Literary Representation in Turn-of-the-Century Greece: Kallirrhoe Siganou-Parren's The Books of Dawn." *JMGS* 15, no. 1 (1997): 1–28.

Cowan, Jane K. "Being a Feminist in Contemporary Greece: Similarity and Difference Reconsidered." In *Practicing Feminism: Identity, Difference, Power,* edited by Nickie Charles and Felicia Freeland Highes. London: Routledge, 1996.

Prinzinger, Michaela. *Mythen, Metaphern und Metamorphosen: Weibliche Parodie in der zeitgenössischen griechischen Literatur.* Stuttgart: J. B. Metzler, 1997.

FEMINIST ISSUES George Tornikis stated in his funeral oration for the Empress **Anna Comnene** that women are "born for spinning and weaving." In Byzantine times, making cloth was considered the most suitable occupation for females. **Psellus** criticized Empress Zoe, in the eleventh century, because she did not weave or spin. Rich women, or females in the imperial family, founded nunneries, usually as intended homes for themselves or daughters when widowed. A few Byzantine women wrote lives of **saints,** a genre popular with all **Orthodox** believers. Abbess Sergia (seventh century) described the transportation of the remains of St. Olympias, the woman who founded her convent. Theodora Raoulaina wrote the lives of two brothers who defended the reverence paid to **icons** (see **Iconoclasm**), Theodoros and Theofanis Graptoi. Theodora collected rare manuscripts, owned a Thucydides codex, and exchanged letters with Patriarch Gregory II (of Cyprus) and Nikiforos Choumnos. Well-connected women did act as patrons: Empress Irene Comnenus fostered the work of **Theodoros Prodromos,** Manganeios Prodromos, Ioannis Tzetzis (c. 1110–1180), and Konstantinos Manassís, who composed a *Chronicle* in **political verse** praising Manuel I and his vision of a classical revival. He dedicated the work to Irene Comnenus and called her "a foster child of learning." For eight more centuries, women were chaperoned, exchanged for a dowry, and confined to the house. A centrist government (1950–1952), headed by General Plastyras, gave Greek women the vote in March 1952. Women began by voting in separate polling booths, which were supervised by female political workers. The dowry (προίκα) was abolished in 1982, by the Family Law Bill. Hart (1990) points out that it was female participation in the **resistance** (EAM/ ELAS) that led to women's liberation in twentieth-century Greece. The parents of one partisan said: "Really a girl should be tended like a hot-house flower."

Further Reading

Hart, Janet. "Women in Greek Society." In *Background to Contemporary Greece,* edited by M. Sarafis and M. Eve, 95–121. London: Merlin, 1990.

FEMINIST POETRY The acknowledgment of "women's writing" is commonplace in Greek criticism from the 1980s. **Kiki Dimoulá** composed a modern Greek feminist manifesto in the poem "Mark of Recognition" (1971) about a statue of a woman with her hands tied. The text closes in the vocative: "I call you woman / Because you are a captive." In a newspaper interview, Dimoulá compared the permanent struggle to avoid contradiction in her poetry with a distant childish recollection: wanting a pair of shoes from her parents but afraid the shop would no longer have the ones that she liked in the size that she took. A lasting principle unrolls from beginning to end of Dimoulá's poetry: "I am much too exhausted by a certain reality, to want to reveal any other. I think that I am more exhausted because I am a woman. It is a difficult, tiring and hazardous task for a woman to avoid being merely her sex, or a complete renunciation of it." In the 1980s, some poets like **Mastoraki** and

Laina rejected the term *feminist*. Their work, as shown in *Tales of the Deep* (Athens: Kedros, 1983) and *Hers* (Athens: Keimena, 1985), displays a woman's story as narrated outside the male-colonized canon.

In *Hers,* Maria Laina's ninth book of poems, she dramatizes, in miniatures, the female glance and the room in which the female feels she goes mad while everyone sleeps: "She had forgotten: / The others will be asleep, / While she whispers frenzied words to her mirror." **Rhea Galanaki** shocks us by foregrounding the use of formerly unprintable words: "and amongst my clothes in the wardrobe is a pitch-black vagina, with no trace of red" (from *The Cake,* Athens: Kedros, 1980). In an anthology of 1979, Andia Frantzi proposed the same poetic foregrounding: "In the midst of the poems / The pudenda of Penelope gape" (Το αιδοίο της Πηνελόπης χάσκει). These writers signal their distance from the "ghetto of tender sentiment" (K. Van Dyck) and their closeness to a period (1981–1983) when the government abolished dowries, instituted divorce by consent, and legislated equal pay. J. Campbell evokes another, rural Greece: "Unmarried girls on an errand should walk briskly. Those who habitually loiter on corners, and look around, endanger their reputations."

Further Reading

Vakalo, Eleni. Γενεαλογία [Genealogy], trans. by Paul Merchant. Exeter: Rougemont, 1971.

"Women and Men in Greece: A Society in Transition." *JMGS* I, no. 1 (May 1983).

FICTION. See NOVEL, GREEK CLASSICAL, MEDIEVAL, and MODERN

FIGURES OF SPEECH A figure of speech (σχήμα λόγου) may compel attention or be made visible by informed reading or by a critic describing the text. Figures of speech (or **tropes**) have been the sinew of Greek writing. Clearly, the study of literature is susceptible to cyclical fashions that downgrade the importance of **rhetoric.** The figures include many terms, such as **allegory, ekphrasis, euphemism, irony, litotes, metaphor, onomatopoeia, oxymoron, pun, sarcasm,** soriasmos, and **zeugma.** Longinus analyzed figures, linking them both to **style** and composition.

Further Reading

Heath, Malcolm. *Hermogenes on Issues: Strategies of Argument in Later Greek Rhetoric.* Oxford: Clarendon Press, 1995.

Worthington, Ian, ed. *Persuasions: Greek Rhetoric in Action.* London and New York: Routledge, 1994.

FILM It has been calculated that around 2,100 movies were produced in Greece during the twentieth century (Constantinidis, 2000). The initial period, early Greek film (1900–1925), starts with a documentary directed by the talented Manakis brothers (Miltos and Yannakis, b. 1878 and 1882), called *The Weavers,* set in Abdela, a small village south of Kastoria in northern Greece, inside what was then Ottoman territory. A film version based on the classical play by Aeschylus, *Prometheus Bound,* followed in 1927, directed by Dimitris Gaziadis (1899–1965). Gaziadis produced the first large-scale box office success with *Love and Waves* (1927), which sold many thousands of tickets. Around 1937, a Law on Cinema was brought in by General **Metaxás,** with a view to tightening controls, and this compromised the freedom of movie expression through the **Occupation** and **Civil War** years.

Technology came into the cinema in the interwar period, notably in the soundtrack overlay of The *Lover of the Shepherdess* by P. Dadiras (1932), which was itself an adaptation of the successful 1891 operetta (***komeidyllio***) *The Lover of the Shepherdess* by **D. Koromilás** (1850–1898), based on a poem by **Zalokostas.** The film (ταινία) tended to make it more obvious that the catchy songs in this production were "folkish rather than folk" (Franklin Hess), dressed-up Italian fare rather than Greek. *Mean Streets,* based on a **Xenopoulos** play of that name, was made in 1933 as a joint Greek–Turkish production, in Istanbul studios. G. N. Makrís, in a 1933 review for *Néa Estía,* called *Mean Streets* "the first truly Greek film." Throughout the 1930s an exacting Greek tax levy made it easier to produce films abroad, and so Greek productions moved to Cairo and elsewhere.

Together with such dramatic idyll films as *The Lover of the Shepherdess,* there was the genre of the mountain film, such as *Ali Pasha* (1929) or *Maria Pentayiotissa* (1930). Here, as in the literature of the period, we meet lovers of different social rank at remote, rural settings, with folk dances and happy endings consecrated by a village fete. The genre opens up into mountain adventure films that feature violence tinged with cowboy western effects: *The Ground Was Stained Red* (1965) and *The Bullets Don't Come Back* (1967).

Yorgos Tzabellas (b. 1916), who wrote the operetta *Brigand of My Heart* (1936), made his screenplay *The Applause* (1944) into the first significant movie of postwar Greece. Tzabellas also made *Forgotten Faces* (1946) and *Marinos Kontaras* (1948), the latter based on a story by **A. Eftaliotis.** This was the first Greek film to be seen at an international festival (Brussels, 1949). Later came his hit *The Drunkard.* He collaborated with Finos Films and also with Anzervos, for whom he made the European hit, *Counterfeit Money* (1955). He adapted his theater play of 1959, *And Let Woman Fear Her Husband,* into a film with this title (1969), winning the International Chicago Festival prize for directing. The first modern adaptation of a classical Greek play is by Tzabellas: *Antigone* (1961). Meanwhile, Michael Cacoyannis's film *Stella* (1955) offered a stark representation of contradictions in postwar society in the story about a singer called Stella who protects her bar, "Paradise," and takes the road of personal freedom rather than marriage, and this road is fatal to her when the lover she turns down (Miltos, a football player) takes her life. In the Iakovos **Kambanellis** play on which the film's screenplay is based, *Stella with the Red Gloves,* Miltos was a lorry driver.

Since 1975, the Greek art film industry has been dominated by the director Theodoros Angelopoulos. He made such masterpieces as *The Traveling Players,* which shows how a repertory touring group might have responded to the rural province in prewar years and also how the historical theater company took care to negotiate its way into potentially hostile towns. Angelopoulos explored in *Alexander the Great* (1980) the relation between leadership and dreams of social improvement. Pantelis Voulgaris, in *Acropole* (1995), pointed Greek cinema toward the experimental and the hypermodern, by setting the movie in a theater that shows a politician seeking out a showgirl, Lakis, both in reality and in a dressing room, while the spectators see desire and alternative objects of desire in reality and in a mirror.

In 1997, an impoverished actor in his 20s, Renos Haralambidis, made a film for less than $10,000, with mostly unpaid actors, called *No Budget Story.* He showed with the actual film, and the film within a film, how the making of a feature film without finance or big studio support is still possible in an urban situation and called into doubt traditional plotting and locations. But this was due also to commercial and social pressures. The period from 1975 to the present has seen movie theaters in Athens and Thessaloniki disappear in their scores. **Television** has exploded from 2 channels to 35 (including cable TV and commercial).

Further Reading

Constantinidis, Stratos E. "Greek Films and the National Interest: A Brief Preface." *JMGS* 18, no. 1 (May 2000): 1–12 [also introduces 13 essays on twentieth-century Greek cinema].

Horton, A. *The Films of Theo Angelopoulos.* Princeton, NJ: Princeton University Press, 1999.

Kolovos, Nikos. *Cinema: The Art of Industry.* Athens: Kastaniotis, 2000.

FILYRAS, ROMOS (1889–1942; pseudonym of Yannis Oikonomopoulos) It was his father, a writer and headmaster, who taught Romos Filyras the ABC. Filyras, who came from **Corinth,** attended high school at Piraeus and studied law at Athens University. He was an eternal student, never obtaining his degree. He became a grade-two clerical employee in the army's justice department. He lost his sanity after complications arising from syphilis and spent 15 years, from spring 1927 to his death (1942), at the Dromokaiteion Psychiatric Institution (near Dafnion, 10 kilometers west of Athens).

He published his first poems, *Roses in the Foam,* in 1911 and a darkly satirical prose piece, *The Showman of Life,* in 1916. The slim verse volumes that followed, from 1911 to 1923, departed from the contemporary, exalted tone of **Palamás**: *Returns* (1919), *The Women Who Are Next* (1920), *Sandglass* (1921), *Pierrot* (1922), and *Sacrifice* (1923). Filyras composed the social column for certain newspapers. He wrote articles for other papers and for leading periodicals, for example, *The Evening, The Artist, Young Greece, Advocate,* **Parnassus,** *The Illustrated Parnassus,* **Noumás, Hegeso,** and *Panathinaia.* At various times, he was chief editor of *The Moulding of the Young, Parnassus,* and the famed *Néa Estía.* There is a harrowing account of a visit (3 October 1931) that Kostis Bastiás made to interview Filyras in the psychiatric institution: the poet says that he gets on well with the mad patients, but the hospital routine is unvarying, and his friends will not travel out from Athens to visit him: "So what's Marika Kotopouli up to? Remind her that since the time she got the notion to have me locked up, she hasn't come to see me here."

Further Reading

Filyras, R. Ἅπαντα. (Ἔμμετρα καὶ πεζά) [Complete Verse and Prose of Filyras], ed. by A. Hourmouzios. Athens: Gkobostis, 1939.

Korfis, Tasos. Ῥῶμος Φιλύρας. Συμβολὴ στὴ ζωὴ καὶ στὸ ἔργο του [Romos Filyras: A Contribution to the Study of his Life and Work]. Athens: Prosperos, 1974.

FLAG. See BLUE AND WHITE

FLORIOS AND PLATZIA-FLORA The *Love Story of Florios and Platzia-Flora* is an early fifteenth-century Greek **romance** in unrhymed **political verses,** indirectly derived from a French twelfth-century romance, *Floire et Blanchefleur.* A wealthy Roman knight has no heir, so he and his wife travel to ask the intercession of St. James. Saracens attack and kill them all, except for the now pregnant wife. She is protected by their queen, because of her beauty, and gives birth to Platzia-Flora, while the queen has a son on the same day: Florio. Brought up together, the boy and girl fall in love. The king sends Florio away, but a magic ring keeps the couple united. If Platzia-Flora is in danger, the tarnishing of the ring will warn Florio to rescue her. The girl is accused falsely and condemned to be burned alive. Florio returns and saves her. Next, she is destined to be sold as a slave. Helped by a new ring, he finds her in a tower at Babylon. A magic spring under the tower can reveal by the purity of its waters whether the maiden inside is pure or not. Florio slips into the tower together with a box of roses sent by the king. After the young couple's first day of passion, the king can tell from the spring's waters that Platzia-Flora is no virgin. He finds them in the tower, embracing. They are sentenced to be burned. Their ring keeps them alive. The king learns that Florio is of royal lineage, so he sends the pair to Rome.
See also HAPPY ENDING

Further Reading

Spadaro, Giuseppe. *Contributo sulle fonti del romanzo greco-medievale "Florio e Plaziaflora."* Athens: Texts and Studies of Modern Greek Literature Series, no. 26, 1966.

Spadaro, Giuseppe. "Note critiche ed esegetiche al testo di "Florio e Plaziaflora." *Byzantion* 33 (1964): 449–472.

Spadaro, Giuseppe. "Per una nuova edizione

di 'Florios ke Platziaflore.'" *Byzantinische Zeitschrift* 67 (1974): 64–73.

FLOWERS OF PIETY (1708) The *Flowers of Piety* (1708), a miscellany edited by boarding students at the Phlanginian College in Venice, was an important step on the road to a Greek vernacular literature.

See also SONNET; SYNONYM

FOLKLORE Folklore played an ideological role in Greek thought, especially after Independence (1828). It was no longer seen as an unsophisticated thing of talking birds and magic spells. It was recorded, and handed down as a treasury of **Hellenism.** Greek folklore studies acquired great prominence in the twentieth century. Folklore weaves in and out of the genre novel (as in **Papadiamantis, Vizyinós,** and **Karkavitsas**), the novella, the **demotic song,** and Romantic poetry. Thus Vizyinós's story, "The Only Journey of His Life," is told in the first person by a young boy sent to find his dying grandfather at the top of a house. The old man embarks on an account of his travels, which never took place, except in his imagination. His wife found a chaperon, saddled the horse, and went in his stead. **Constantinople** was his unattainable destination. The apprentice tailor boy wanders through the vizir's seraglio, ordered by fierce eunuchs not to look up at women's faces. In this narrative, a courtyard wall seems the end of the universe, and the panel in the palace slides open by itself.

Greek folklore looks back to the religious syncretism of the Greco-Roman period, rather than to classical antiquity. The islanders of Paros, in the **Cyclades,** venerate Hagia (Saint) Theoktisti, a girl caught by pirates in the ninth century.

She escaped and hid in the forest for 35 years, leading an edifying life. When a huntsman found her, she asked him to bring her a communion wafer, sank to the ground, and died. The huntsman tried to take her hand as a relic, but some force prevented him from leaving Paros unless he restored the corpse's hand.

Among demotic songs, those for children, like the swallow song have an ancient heritage. The **Akritic** songs are medieval in origin and hark back to aristocratic feudalism, in remote locations, against a backcloth of banditry and the troubling **personification** of Death *(Charos)*. Among narrative songs with no clear date of origin is "The Return of the Exile." In this type, a wife asks for proof and signs that the repatriated man standing before her is really her husband. In the "Dead Brother" type, one of nine brothers, who have all died in an epidemic, comes briefly alive and rides across the clouds to bring a sister to their dying mother. The young woman lives with her foreign husband, in another country (for example, Babylon). The girl asks her brother why his boots are muddy and his features pale. She wonders if he really exists, while they journey home. When they reach their destination, the brother cannot enter. He must return to the grave, instead of joining her inside the home. Vizyinós draws on this folk repertoire in a poem such as "The Dream," where a lad in his sleep imagines a boy just like himself, standing at the side of a river, and prays: "May God not make / This dream come true!" When he leaps forward to save the boy, he sees his own corpse in the current.

Another folk type is the rhymed **distich,** or two-line stanza, considered as a single poetic unit. These couplets were common in the Aegean islands and tended to contain sententious, popular wisdom, as did semilearned versifiers (ποιητάρηδες) from Cyprus, or the "rhymesters" (ῥιμαδόροι) of Crete. Some legends passed between Greece and Turkey, but then crossed back, enriched or altered by the neighbor. Chunks of medieval mythology broke off and formed the tales of Florentin, of **Apollonius of Tyre,** or *The Sun-Born Maiden,* who defies all the traps set for her except one, devised with the aid of magic, by the mother of a knight who loves her. Many Greek **proverbs,** local superstitions, or regional tales contain references to semideities. These nymphs (see **Nereids**), goblins, and sprites may be derived from Greek classical poetry. But they attest the anthromorphic thrust of Greek religion in the Byzantine period. Female demons shaped like donkeys are Ἀνασκελάδες.

It is better not to fall in love with a witch who adopts the form of a beautiful girl, for she is a *lamia.* Though she takes you to a sumptuous palace or a wedding, it is all fake. She may be a snake (as in Keats's poem, "Lamia," drawn from a romance set in **Corinth**). **Palamás** composed his poem "Black Lamia," about a witch who "contained / All Hell in her heart, / And made me depart / To the bed of a dried-up well, / To find her ring / Which supposedly dropped in." Certain old hags (στρίγλες) can become invisible, grow wings, fly into houses at night, disturb mothers in childbirth, and drink the blood of neonates. In his memoir *The Real Zorba and Nikos Kazantzakis,* Yannis Anapliotis tells how the Maniot peasants thought **Kazantzakis** was consulting a book of sorcery because he was seen walking about reading. Peasants propitiate the Fates (Μοῖρες), who, in classical times, wove the thread of a person's life. To modern Greeks, the *moires* are demonic figures who ordain their future, so they must be won over at a child's birth. Roman and medieval beliefs supply the ghosts called "shades" (στοιχειά), thought to be souls of murdered people. The statue placed at a classical city gate to prevent invasion (τέλεσμα) mutates into the modern Greek ντελεσίμι, which is a mass of shards, each representing an evil that the villagers desire to escape from. The objects are then buried at a distance from the village, and a pillar is erected above them.

The elfin sprites (καλλικάντζαροι) are deformed and idiotic Little Folk, human goblins who will pollute your Christmas festivity unless the housewife puts sausage and omelet on the roof. A priest can banish the sprites by sprinkling your house with holy water at Epiphany. During the twelve days from Christmas to Epiphany, you put a gold coin in a "royal biscuit" (βασιλόπηττα), and the guest who gets the biscuit with the coin also gets most good fortune in the coming year. Special carols are required for certain dates on the calendar, like 1 January and 1 March. When the Greeks go out for a picnic on Ash Monday, they may greet the reawakening of Mother Nature. In many areas, fires are lit at Easter to banish evil spirits. You burn an effigy of Judas, and the girls play on rope swings, like their ancestors 2,000 years ago. Purificatory fires are lit on the Day of St. John (24 June). On the isle of Aegina, people used to recite "I have averted evil and found good." Soothsaying may be practiced by girls to divine who is to be their bridegroom. For the Presentation of the Virgin (21 November), country people prepare a soup from many vegetables to invoke a benediction on their crops, like the classical πανσπερμία.

Some modern Greek folklore has pagan antecedents, like the belief that certain days at the beginning of August are a time of ill omen.

Further Reading

Cowan, Jane K. "Women, Men, and Pre-Lenten Carnival in Northern Greece: An Anthropological Exploration of Gender Transformation in Symbol and Practice." *Rural History* 5, no. 2 (1994): 195–210.

Dawkins, Richard M., ed. and trans. *Forty-five Stories from the Dodekanese.* Cambridge: Cambridge University Press, 1950.

Hesseling, Ch. *Charos, Ein Beitrag zur Kenntnis des neugriechischen.* Leiden/Leipzig: S. C. Van Doesburgh, 1897.

FOLK MEDICINE. See MEDICAL TRACT

FOOD. See MEDICINE

FOREIGN INFLUENCE, NINE-TEENTH AND TWENTIETH CENTURIES In the **Renaissance,** and the **Enlightenment,** the main European influences on Greek literature were indirect, coming via the printing presses of **Venice** or by intellectuals traveling abroad. Friedrich Nietzsche (1844–1900) exerted a decisive effect on Greek writing. Nirvanas (**pseudonym** of the Russian-born writer Petros K. Apostolidis, 1866–1937) published *The Philosophy of Nietzsche* in 1896. The term *Nietzscheism,* in Greek Νιτσεϊσμός, refers to the classical apothegms, the Apollinean versus Dionysian polarity, and the Superman theories ascribed to the German thinker. A significant stream in modern Greek literature is the line from Hegel to Schopenhauer and Marx. A further influence that floods nineteenth-century Greek writing is Ibsenism, the life-view and

stagecraft of the Norwegian playwright Henrik Ibsen (1828–1906). Greeks translated or imitated the Norwegian writer Knut Hamsun (1859–1952, Nobel Prize in 1920), who read Nietzsche and was an ardent Germanist, professing some Nazi leanings.

Dante and Leopardi (for **Solomós**), Foscolo (for **Kalvos**), and Gabriele d'Annnunzio (himself influenced by Wagner and Nietzsche) are the main Italian currents that poured into nineteenth-century Greek writing. From the United States, a parallel force was exerted by W. Whitman and E. A. Poe. From Paris came the inebriating effect (on the poets of the **New School of Athens**) of the Parnassians: F. Coppée and S. Prudhomme, with echoes from Musset. Other more generalized French influences were Béranger, Lamartine, Anatole France, A. Dumas, Baudelaire, Valéry, and Mallarmé (but not Proust); from Belgium, Maeterlinck; from Russia, Tolstoi; from England, **Shakespeare, Byron,** Walter Scott, Ruskin, and Oscar Wilde. Greek literature was soon illuminated by the uneven reflections of Freud, T. S. Eliot, Joyce, Camus, and Samuel Beckett. By mid-twentieth century, modern Greek literature traveled on experimental paths of its own in novel, song, and lyric poetry.

See also NATURALISM; NIETZSCHEISM; NOVEL; ROMANTICISM; SYMBOLISM

Further Reading

Denisi, Sofia. Το Ελληνικό Ιστορικό Μυθιστόρημα και ο *Sir Walter Scott (1830–1880)* [The Greek Historical Novel and Sir Walter Scott: 1830–1880]. Athens: Kastaniotis, 1994.

FOREIGN INFLUENCE, PRE-NINETEENTH CENTURY The oldest Greek literary documents to survive the disruptions of medieval history date to the eleventh century. So there is a key question: Are these works influenced by contact with western Europe? Did early Greek writers in the **demotic** imitate Europeans after clashing with **Crusaders,** who carried exemplars of song, dance, or vernacular literature? Voutieridis says "no" to this hypothesis, arguing that Greeks did not believe that the year 1000 would mark the world's end or the advent of the Antichrist. After year 1000, European kingdoms begin to emerge from barbarism, but this was too late to influence Greek civilization. The Greeks, in fact, had wandering storytellers earlier than the West. The Bishop of Caesarea (ninth century), annotating a copy of Philostratus's *Apollonius of Tyana,* mentions "these accursed Black Sea Paphlagonians who compose their special songs about events which befall great and glorious men, and then sing them at each door for a coin."

In the twelfth century, the returning Byzantine interest in classical Greek caused a slowing down in the use of the popular language, which in turn reduced the effect exerted on Greek popular literature by Western vernacular literature. The revival of classicism ended in Byzantium and the West, during the thirteenth century. The standoff between the Latin and Greek church meant that by the end of the fourth Crusade, before the beginning of the **Turkocracy,** there was no reason for Frankish influence to linger in Greek vernacular culture.

Further Reading

Legg, Keith R. and John M. Roberts. *Modern Greece: A Civilization on the Periphery.* Boulder, CO: Westview Press, 1997.

FORTOUNATOS (c. 1662) Written between 1665 and 1662, the Cretan comedy

Fortounatos consists of a dedication, a prologue, five acts, and four interval playlets (ιντερμέδια). The author is Markos Antonios Foskolos, probably a Cretan, despite his Italian name, or a Hellenized Venetian. He is known to have died in 1662. His play was written at Kastro, that is, Candia (Iraklion), in the dialect of Eastern Crete, but with all the Greek words transcribed into the Latin alphabet. Perhaps the author's purpose, in this lively rendering of a standard Roman plot, was to lift the spirits of the defenders of Candia at some stage in the city's long siege by the Turks (1648–1669). The text was transliterated into Greek characters by Stefanos Xanthoudidis, in his critical edition (1922). The plot is unashamedly lowbrow: it features a doctor from Cephalonia, Louras, who loses his only son, Nicoletto. While the child is on the beach, with his nanny, pirates catch and abduct him in their vessel. A merchant from Kastro, Yiannoutsos, comes into possession of the boat, purchases the child, and raises him as his own son, with the name Fortounatos. Meanwhile, Louras travels far and wide to recover Nicoletto, is widowed, settles in Kastro, and falls for an unscrupulous widow's daughter, Petronella, who just happens to be the beloved of his biological son, Fortounatos. The old man's infatuation is indecent. The young man is tangled up in hope and jealousy: "I tremble in fear that she may observe the grand affairs / Of Louras, and get fed up with her mother's nonsense, / And then perhaps change her mind and take Louras as husband, / And drop me, poor wretch, like a fish on the stones." This is blocked by a recognition scene (**Anagnorisi**) between the dotard and his son. The formula leads to a **happy ending,** the nuptials of Petronella and Nicoletto. It permits the dose of **bawdy** acceptable in contemporary Crete, as in the loose talk (ἐλευθεροστομία) of the pimp, Petros.

FOSCOLO, UGO (1778–1827) The poet, playwright, novelist, and scholar Ugo Foscolo was born on Zakynthos, lived in Italy and England, and wrote chiefly in Italian. Foscolo is the author of 12 graceful and felicitous **sonnets** (including "To Zakynthos"). He composed *Dei sepolcri,* a complex anti-Napoleonic ode concerning funeral celebrations, the neoclassical poems *Le grazie,* and a romantic epistolary novel, *Le ultime lettere di Jacopo Ortis* (1802). Foscolo wove together the themes of flight from Napoleonic war, the extenuating love affair, dreamy rural interludes, and suicidal resolve in this book, establishing a Mediterranean equivalent of Goethe's *The Sorrows of Young Werther* (1774). He was the mentor and friend of **Kalvos,** influencing **P. Soutsos, Laskaratos,** and other nineteenth-century Greek writers. On perusing Kalvos's "Ode to the Ionian Islands," Foscolo wrote: "Dear Andreas: You are dreaming, because dreams are what you write about your country, the arms and the virtues of the Greeks. Greece is a corpse and Italy is also a corpse, but a very fat one. Let's leave the dead in peace and let's try to live quietly ourselves."

FOSKOLOS, MARKOS ANTONIOS (d. 1662). See *FORTOUNATOS*

FRAME STORY The narrative frame is a way of rendering the central story more precious and formally adorned, at the center of one or more of a series of stories-within-the-story. The protagonist will happen on a situation where he hears or sees a story about his antagonist, or future wife, or enemy told by another character. The **romance *Livistros and Rodamni*** is the first fictional text in modern Greek to explore the device of the frame story. The framing device (*Rahmenerzählung* in German, *conte à tiroirs* or *mise en abîme* in French) is familiar from *The 1001 Nights* (ninth–eleventh centuries, from Egypt, Iran, or India) and present throughout the Sanskrit *Hitopaedesa.* The frame story in *Livistros and Rodamni* has the added novelty of being told by a *first*-person narrator.

Further Reading

Manussacas, M. "Les Romans byzantines de chevalerie et l'état présent des études les concernant." *Revue des Etudes Grecques* 10 (1952): 70–83.

FRANGOCHIOTIKA Frangochiotika (Φραγκοχιώτικα) is the phonetic spelling of Greek using the Latin **script.** It was adopted in Papal propaganda sent to Greek **Catholics** in Crete or the **Ionian Islands.** It may have been used by Jesuits operating out of Rome to draft the early eighteenth-century play ***David*** to fish for potential Catholics among the **Orthodox** at Chios. Indeed, the play is free of foreign vocabulary and has lively dialogue and **proverbs,** all of which makes it accessible to an audience of proselytes.

Further Reading

Lock, Peter. *The Franks in the Aegean, 1204–1500.* London and New York: Longman, 1995.

FRANGOPOULOS, Th. D. (1923–1998) In 1954, the novelist Th. Frangopoulos published the first edition of the anti-Communist *War about the Walls.* This innovative novel about the World

War II period deals with the development of a young man during the German **occupation** and the **Civil War.** It contains various characters *à clef,* including his friend and fellow writer, **R. Roufos** and the figure of K. Maltezos, killed by Communists in 1944.

See also CIVIL WAR; RESISTANCE

FRATERNAL TEACHING The anonymous pamphlet *Fraternal Teaching* put out in Paris, 1798, is certainly by **A. Koraís.** It is an attack on an encyclical of 1798 supposedly signed by Anthimos, Patriarch of Jerusalem from 1789 to his death in 1808. Anthimos secured concessions for the **Orthodox** in their claims over the Holy Sepulchres, by two decrees of Sultan Selim II. He consequently maintained good relations with the Turkish court. The faked encyclical stigmatizes the atheism and diabolical principles behind the French revolution. He attacks rival churches, such as the Latin heresy and its protestant offshoot in England. His purpose is to support Turkish rule of Greece. To this end, he blends passages from Scripture and contemporary social thinking to prove the legitimacy of Ottoman rule as a salvation for Greeks. Scholars now rule out Patriarch Anthimos or his successor, Gregory V, as authors. They point to the conservative cleric, Athanasios Parios.

Koraís reacted with fury, for freedom was in the air: the new French republic was preparing military action against Egypt. **Rigas Velestinlís** and other Greek conspirators had just been arrested in Vienna. Koraís directs his pamphlet "to Greeks across the entire Ottoman Empire, a refutation of the Patriarchal teaching recently published at Constantinople, falsely issued under the name of the Blessed Patriarch of Jerusalem." He sum-

mons his compatriots to show the "inhabited world" (the Hellenocentric Οἰκουμένη) how the Patriarchal document is nonsense. The rest of Europe must not think this Turk-loving bishop represents the feeling of Greeks. He is an "official enemy of the Nation and of Religion." Koraís analyzes the rights of man and discusses the nature of a just society. He improvises verses, to rebut the clumsy poem, which the "Patriarch" pens to embellish his tract. Athanasios Parios wrote a counterattack on *Fraternal Teaching* (1798), but friends of Koraís arranged that it remain unpublished.

FREE BESIEGED, THE (c. 1830; 1833–1844) *The Free Besieged* is an unfinished **epic** on the battle of **Missolonghi** by **Solomós.** It contains intense moments of beauty, seeming like a modern assault on the sublime, the greatest Greek poem *never* written. The scraps of *The Free Besieged,* which Solomós's friend **Polylás** reconstructed, are a handful of syllables, rehashed phrases of rarefied grandeur. Just when the vocabulary of the sublime seemed depleted, Solomós endowed it with deep ideas and the force of contrast: a cannon gun, a wandering butterfly, the bewitchment of nature, the enemy's ferocity, a child dying of hunger, women torching their beds, April, the murmur of the turtledove, a season of spring and yet despair. The sublime lies in his cajoling mix of peace, war, fear, hope, life, death, radiance, and extinction. The reader wonders from what century Solomós's chosen words fall. To the honey-suffused and dewy cosmos he asks: "What mysteries?" The sublime plays on the impossibility of a verbal answer and the seduction of ineffability.

FREE VERSE Free verse (ελεύθερος cτίχος) represents the huge swathe of poetry since the 1930s that displays syllabic inequality (ανισοσυλλαβία), in which each line has a different number of syllables. In free verse, prosody and rhythm do not follow the format of poetic tradition, that is, regular **meter.** The crucial aspect of free verse is that it dispensed with **rhyme** (ομοιοκαταληξία), a feature that was previously thought to give the cohesion necessary to modern Greek poetry.

FRIENDLY SOCIETY. See PHILIKÍ HETAIRÍA

FRUIT, SCHOLAR OF Story of the *Scholar of Fruit,* whose first version is from the twelfth century, is a satirical display of pseudolearned notions. A short tale in prose, ostensively to illustrate fruits, it follows the model of the **animal story,** staging the trial and sentencing of a grape for the evil crime of causing intoxication, clumsiness, and confusion in humans who take wine. Here the quince is King, the pomegranate is Counsellor, the pear is Protonotary, the apple is Lo-

gothete, the orange is Head of Wardrobe, the yellow peach is First Guard, the lemon is Grand Droungarios, and other fruits follow, descending the Byzantine court hierarchy. The grape appears and accuses many fruits in the realm of high treason. "Princess" Vine, and the Housekeeper Lentil, a Nun who is a raisin, the owl-nosed chickpea, and the black-eyed bean come forward as witnesses. The evidence of fruits of the field, like a garlic, finds the grape at fault. This text is especially entertaining in its **allegory** of the ceremony of the Byzantine imperial court. The grape's punishment is to be hung from crooked beams, cut by a knife, and have its blood drunk by humans till they hardly know what they are doing.

See also WINE

Further Reading

Zoras, Y. Th. Ὁ Πωρικολόγος (κατ᾽ ἀγνώστους παραλλαγάς) [The Scholar of Fruit: Following Unknown Textual Variants]. Athens: Dept. of Byzantine and Modern Greek Literature at the University of Athens, 1958.

G

GALANAKI, RHEA (1947–) Rhea Galanaki is an objective, dispassionate narrator and a highly experimental poet, one of contemporary Greece's most discussed writers. In her debut volume of verse, *Albeit Pleasing* (1975), she produced "cryptic fragments" (Karen Van Dyck) that hinted at the possibility of mythic scenes from a classical Greek past that the author was prepared to put behind her, but had the knowledge to play with. Her verse in *The Cake* (Athens, 1980) showed a pregnant woman baking a cake and more successful, free of duty, and myth, than a male hunter who hangs up his spoils and is still caught in them. Her collection even highlights the idea of a modern that is "non-myth-consoled." Her first historical novel (1989), *The Life of Ismail Ferik Pasha: spina nel cuore* (trans. by Kay Cicellis, London: Peter Owen, 1996), is an example of the new Greek fiction. It plays in the volatile margins of shifting identity and nonaligned alliance. In the 1821 Cretan uprising against **Ottoman** rule, two peasant brothers are captured, one carried to Egypt and rising to become Minister of War, the other fleeing to Odessa and making his fortune at Athens.

The long journey by Emmanuel (Ferik) by way of Egypt to the cave where he was once captured, or to the family house in Crete is spliced with images of his mother's destiny and his own return, with the possibility of ending back at his beginning (that is, the Lasithi plain where he was born to a humble Christian on Crete). Emmanuel can either meet or oppose as an ethnic enemy his newly Hellenized brother, Antonis. The story of this polarity teases the modern reader by opaqueness and doubling: Emmanuel— or should he be called Ferik?—dies, leading the Egyptian army against Crete's second insurrection (1866–1868), while his lost or regained brother, Antonis, finances a Cretan revolt.

Further Reading

Calotychos, Vangelis. "Thorns in the Side of Venice? Galanaki's *Pasha* and Pamuk's *White Castle* in the Global Market." In *Greek Modernism and Beyond: Essays in Honor of Peter Bien,* ed. Dimitris Tziovas, 243–260. Lanham, MD: Rowman & Littlefield, 1997.

Yannakaki, Eleni. "History as Fiction in Rea Galanaki's *The Life of Ishmail Ferik Pasha*." *Κάμπος: Cambridge Papers in Modern Greek*, no. 2 (1994): 121–141.

GALAXIDI. See VLAMI

GALAZI, PITSA (1940–) The patriot, essayist, and broadcaster from Cyprus, Pitsa Galazi published several volumes of verse between the 1960s and 1990, refusing a first prize in the Cyprus Poetry Competition as a protest against the factions in poetry awards. Best known among her collections are *Signalmen* (1980–1982) and *Learning Asleep* (1978). Her 1963 collection *Moments of Adolescence* bore witness to Cyprus's freedom struggle in 1955–1959. It was written in a fever of anger over events of 1974, when **Turkey** invaded Cyprus, annexed the northern section of the island, and according to Galazi, caused "the second Asia Minor catastrophe."

GATSOS, NIKOS (1911–1992) Born in the village of Asea (Arcadia), Nikos Gatsos moved to Athens at age 16 and studied literature and philosophy. He later went on to France. Gatsos has translated Garcia Lorca, Tennessee Williams, Eugene O'Neill, and other playwrights for television, radio, and theater. A surrealist poet in the 1930s and 1940s, Gatsos wrote the lyrics for pop and protest songs in the 1960s. His songs were set to music by such well-known composers as Chadzidakis, Charhakos, and Mikis Theodorakis, who also set songs by the writer **Kambanellis.** From 1953, Gatsos contributed to National Radio. His stature rests on a single collection of verse, *Amorgos* (1943), which is entitled after a minor Aegean island that the writer had never visited. This verse flows in and out of inconsequential bravura, nightmarish and tender in turns: "Heracleitus saw two little cyclamens kissing in the mud, / So he stooped to kiss his body, that had died in the welcoming soil." In the abstract compositions of *Amorgos,* there are allusions to **Klephtic** ballads, **folk stories,** biblical rhythms, and dreaming. The whole assemblage is sutured with a deft touch: "A step light as a thrill on the meadow, / Or a foam-trimmed sea's kiss." After 1943, Gatsos made a living by writing pop songs and gambling (D. Constantine).

Further Reading

Capri-Karka, Carmen, ed. *The Charioteer,* no. 36 (1995–1996): Special Double Issue for Nikos Gatsos, 285 pp., with essays by E. Aranitsis, A. Argyriou, O. Elytis, D. Karamvalis, A. Karandonis, K. Kouri and T. Lignadis, pp. 178–254.

GAZÍS, ANTHIMOS (1764?–1828) The **Enlightenment** figure and patriot Anthimos Gazís became a monk after his schooling in Thessaly and went to Constantinople (1796), where he gained ecclesiastical promotion. He was invited to Vienna by its Greek community (1797) to become curate of the chapel of St. George's. He studied math and science there, publishing (1799) a translation of Benjamin Martinus's *Compendium of Philosophical Science* and founding (1811), on behalf of a fraternity in Jassy, the radical journal *The Scholar Hermes* (see **Koraís**). While on a fund-raising trip to Odessa (1816), Gazís was initiated into the **Friendly Society.** Under cover of an educational visit to Delphi (1818), he enrolled many **Armatolí** leaders in Phocis. In the following years, Gazís became a key figure in the **Uprising.** Gazís's other main works are *A Geographical Ta-*

ble of Greece, with Old and New Place-Names (Vienna, 1800), a *Chronological Constitution* (1803), a two-volume *Greek Library* (Venice, 1807), and a three-volume *Greek Lexicon* (Venice, 1809–1816). He was succeeded as editor of *The Scholar Hermes* (1811–1821) by K. Kokkinakis (1781–1831) and Theoklitos Pharmakidis (1784–1860). In the **War of Independence,** Gazís represented Thessaly at the various national conventions.

Further Reading

Chatzifotis, I.M. Ἄνθιμος Γαζῆς, 1758–1828. Νέα θεώρηση τῆς ζωῆς καὶ τοῦ ἔργου του, μὲ ἐπιλογὴ κειμένων του [Anthimos Gazis, 1758–1828: A New Examination of His Life and Work, with a Selection from His Writings]. Athens: Estía Bookshop Editions, 1969.

GENERATION OF 1930. See GENERATION OF THE THIRTIES

GENERATION OF THE EIGHTIES (OF 1880). See NEW SCHOOL OF ATHENS

GENERATION OF THE SEVENTIES The term "Generation of the Seventies" was widely used, after the 1970s, to describe poets living in the shadow of the **Colonels' Junta** who had reacted against right-wing values and **censorship.** A more topical term for these writers was "lucky-dip and pinball kids" (ἡ γενιὰ τῶν γερανῶν καὶ τῶν φλίπερς) because they seemed to write about a generation that liked to hang out in game arcades, playing pinball or banging away at machines to lift prizes (with a model crane).

These young writers seemed to pass swiftly from their first book to a national reputation. Nana Isaïa made her debut in 1969, Vasilis Steriadis in 1970. In 1975,

Tasos Denegris published *Death in Canning Square: Poems from 1952 to 1969,* a collection from two decades. Dimitris Potamitis, an actor and poet, produced a first collection of poetry, *The Banquet,* in 1964, followed by an ironic *tour de force,* "The Assassination of the Angels by Westerns and Formica, plus the Migration of the Petitbourgeois Citizen Dimitrios Potamitis through the Borough of Dreams," in 1967. In 1970, he brought out *The Other Dimitrios,* making a pun and a variation on his pseudoself, the antihero of the preceding volume.

One group of the seventies generation, namely **K. Anghelaki-Rooke,** Isaïa, Steriadis, Dimitris Potamitis, Lefteris Poulios, and Denegris, entitled their 1971 anthology *Six Poets,* making their identity into the book's label, thus obeying the Colonels' ruling that new books had to describe their contents (see **Censorship**). Dimitris Iatropoulos, in 1971, published an ambiguous *Anti-Anthology,* showcasing other poets of this generation, hinting at an anthology of *opponents,* rather than an *alternative* selection. Stefanos Bekataros and Alekos Florakis brought out a collection of 1970s poets entitled *The Young Generation: A Poetic Anthology* (Athens: Kedros, 1971). Poulios juxtaposed modern consumer elements and nostalgic values, like the kilt (φουστανέλα) of Greek warriors, with the capitalist reality of the supermarket. The juxtaposition in Poulios's line "Boeings and angels tear you apart" is an example of the mixed affiliations of the 1970s generation, part militant, part hippy.

The journal *Anew* (1964–1967) issued a manifesto praising new printed formats for verse and a mixture of stylistic values (modernist, avant-garde, countercultural); one of the leading lights of *Anew* was the transvestite **K. Tachtsis,** who has been unfairly called "author of a single book," the gossipy *The Third Wedding* (1962). Poetic texts of the 1970s had a flair for irregular margins, blank space, or unorthodox lettering on the printed page.

Further Reading

Siotis, Dinos and Chioles, J., eds. "Twenty Contemporary Greek Poets." *The Coffeehouse,* nos. 7–8 (1979): 3–130.

"Three Young Poets: Jenny Mastoraki, Haris Megalinos and Lefteris Poulis," trans. by N. C. Germanacos and others. *Boundary 2* 1, no. 2 (winter 1973): 507–518.

Williams, Chris, ed. and trans. *A Greek Anthology: Poetry from the Seventies Generation.* Peterborough: Spectacular Diseases, 1991.

GENERATION OF THE THIRTIES

The term "Generation of the Thirties" is used to group together writers and intellectuals who were born around 1910 and who started publishing in the early 1930s. The modernism they represented is seen as coming to Greece almost a generation later than it came to Western Europe.

Novelists like **Y. Theotokás, K. Politis,** and **S. Myrivilis** fleshed out their own idiosyncratic versions of the perceived avant-garde manner of James Joyce's *Portrait of the Artist as a Young Man* (1914). Prose writers like Karagatsis (1909–1960), on whom *Nea Estía* published an obituary issue (no. 823: 1961), **Th. Petsalis** (b. 1904), and **A. Terzakis** (1907–1979) constructed family sagas from the new, urbanized Greece and offered psychological analysis of the bourgeoisie. Two poets of this group, **Seferis** and **Elytis,** won the Nobel Prize for Literature (1963; 1979). **Yannis Ritsos** is the group's most political poet, whereas

Andreas Embirikos, Nikos Gatsos, Nikos Engonopoulos, and **Nikiforos Vrettakos** introduced **surrealist** elements, psychoanalytic themes, and a humbler view of the classical heritage.

The 1929 essay *Free Spirit,* by Yorgos Theotokás, was seen by many as the intellectual manifesto of the Generation of the Thirties, with an impetus that was centrifugal and modernizing. Whereas the Generation of the Thirties reacted against reverence for the demotic song, genre narrative (*ithografía*), and **Byzantinology**, Theotokás hailed the urbanization of Athens, technology, jazz, and the airplane. He castigated Greek thought since **Independence** because the new nation had failed to add to the **Great Idea** of widening Hellas to its medieval frontiers and had really debated only the **language question.**

GENNADIOS, YEORYIOS. See YENNADIOS, YEORYIOS

GEORGE THE AETOLIAN (?1505–c. 1580)

The birth and death dates of the sixteenth-century teacher and intellectual, George the Aetolian, born in Corinth of Aetolian background, are scarcely known. A popular tradition has it that he died at age 55. He is one of the forerunners of the **Enlightenment** during the time of the **Turkocracy.** When young, he may have been in exile at Constantinople. He studied later in Venice. He returned to Greece to teach in various cities and perhaps at the Patriarchate's Great School of the Nation, in Constantinople. His importance for literature is that he wrote letters in the formal language, but was equally at home in the vernacular. He translated Aesop's *Fables* (at least 144 of them) into **plain Greek** and 15-syllable lines. An early commentator (1888) on these Aesop versions is Spyridon Lampros, of the **Parnassós** Society. He edited them, as too a little later did E. Legrand (1896). George also wrote encomiastic poems to contemporary celebrities like Mikhail Kantakouzenós and Iosaf Argyropoulos (Bishop of Thessaloniki) and is thought to have copied or collected older codexes.

Some unknown intrigue led to a dispute between George and a court protonotary and metropolitan, Theodosios Zygomalás (1544–1614). George may have jeered at the class of notaries, then influential in the Patriarchates. He appears to have been defended against a series of scurrilous charges by the interposition of a comic dialogue entitled "Lover of Truth" (Φιλαλήθης), composed by Alexandros Fortios, of Kerkyra. Only the prologue to this work has survived.

GEORGILLÁS OF RHODES, EMMANUEL (?1445–c. 1500)

To Emmanuel Georgillás (born c. 1445), a narrative poet from Rhodes, is rightly attributed the work *The Plague of Rhodes* (1498). This author and his writing are typical of "government by knights" (Ἱπποτοκρατία), a stage when Rhodes was held by the Order of Knights of St. John (1308–1522). Perhaps also correctly attributed to Georgillás is one of three surviving versions of *The Tale of Belisarius,* in 840 mixed verses (rhyming and unrhymed). Our author states his surname as "Limenitis" (from a settlement on Rhodes called Limenio). He has sympathies with the Latin church and believes that Franks and Greeks live in religious harmony on the island of Rhodes. He tells the reader that he lost his spouse, all his children save one son, and three married sisters, plus their children, as a result of the plague, which beset his island in the years 1498 and 1499. His mother and two or three orphans of his sisters appear to have survived.

This devastation is reflected in a narrative of 644 rhymed **political verse,** which abound in cautions that Rhodes' morals were the cause of its destruction and injunctions to its islanders to mend their way of life. Georgillás interests the historian, in this sententious and asymmetrical poem, with his touches of everyday life, ranging from housekeeping, clothing, shoes, and jewelry to the wedding garlands sewn out of vines and slips of paper, which remained a custom on Rhodes till the early twentieth century. We see the clothing of the great ladies woven from expensive finery "in the Frankish style" and the village maidens with their "white faces and apple-red cheeks and lips," who wear a long skirt and affect slippers with gold thread (παντόφλες) while maintaining demure attitudes on the threshold of their houses. The earliest lament on the fall of **Constantinople** (published by Legrand in 1880) is by an author who suppressed his name for fear of reprisal, once thought to be Georgillás.

GERMAN OCCUPATION. See OCCUPATION

GERMANY; GERMAN PHILOSOPHY

Yearning and sublimity in the great German writers (Goethe, Schopenhauer, and Wagner) struck a chord in their humbler Greek counterparts. **Chatzopoulos** (1868–1920) saw Wagner's *The Flying Dutchman* in Dresden with his wife-to-be (1900). So their daughter was given the name of the heroine, Senta. Kleon Paraschos and **Skipis** scoff at the soaring agnostic melancholia of "Windmill" by **Mavilis,** calling this sonnet a "poison imported from Germany." Greek Romantic writers elaborated the link between yearning and death, which they admired in Wagner, especially the cult of doomed beauty in *Tristan and Isolde* (1865). Studying in Germany during the nineteenth or early twentieth century, they underwent the "enormous impression" of Nietsche's thought (Tsakonas, 1999: 212), and they absorbed the idea of the beautiful in Novalis and Platen-Hallermünde (1795–1835): "Wer die Schönheit angeschaut mit Augen / Is dem Tode schon anheimgegeben" ("He who has witnessed essential Beauty / Is already vowed to Death").

Further Reading

Veloudis, Yorgos. *Germanograecia: Deutsche Einflüsse auf die neugriechische Literature, 1750–1944.* 2 vols. Amsterdam: Adolf M. Hakkert, 1983.

GKINIS, DIMITRIOS S. (1890–1978) The indefatigable scholar Dimitrios Gkinis studied law and literature. From Athens, he went for further studies in law at Leipzig. He gained a doctorate from Thessaloniki University (1960) and wrote several monographs on Byzantine law, including a learned essay, published in German, on the correct dating (741?) of the Isaurian legislation known as *Ecloga.* He also analyzed the unsigned works of **A. Koraís** (1948) and brought to light an unknown ode by **Kalvos** (1938). Gkinis chose to use the terms *catalogue* and *bibliography* to describe his major project, *A Catalogue of Nineteenth Century Greek Newspapers and Periodicals from 1811 to 1863* (2nd ed., Athens, 1967), and the *Lists of Greek Codices Accessible in Greece and Asia Minor* (1935). With Valerios Mexas (1904–1937), Gkinis drafted a three-volume

Greek Bibliography: 1800–1863 (1957). This large repertory was printed serially in Academy of Athens Editions: *A Greek Bibliography* (vol. I, *1800–1839,* publ. 1939, vol. II, *1840–1855,* publ. 1941, and vol. III, *1856–1863,* with an index, publ. 1957).

GLINÓS, DIMITRIS (1882–1943) Glinós, an activist and intellectual from Smyrna, gained a considerable reputation as an educationist. He studied, often in poverty, at Constantinople, Athens, Jena, and Leipzig. In 1936, he entered parliament in the Pan-Populist (that is, Communist) Front. He was then exiled to the isle of Santorini under the Metaxás regime (December 1937). During a stroll round the island, he heard a seven-year-old girl reciting her Greek homework. He described the scene in the sketch "Mr Teacher Takes a Walk," and saw in it the relentless vacuity of Greek **education**: "Nominative O-, O-, O-. Genitive TOU, -OU, -OU. Dative TÔ, -Ô, -Ô. Accusative TON, -ON, -ON. Vocative: Ó, Ó, Ó." Among his many books are *Nation and Language* (1920), *The Crisis of Demoticism* (1923), and most significant, a model revolutionary pamphlet for the 1940s, *What Is the National Liberation Front? What Does It Want?*

See also EDUCATIONAL SOCIETY; RESISTANCE

GLORY BE TO GOD. See DOXASTIKÓN

GLYKÁS, MIKHAIL (twelfth century) The poet and chronicler of the Byzantine period, M. Glykás, thought to be from Kerkyra, probably had the rank of imperial secretary (γραμματεύς) to Manuel I Comnenus, who reigned from 1143 to 1180. Apparently Glykás was denounced by a friend and convicted in a case with political ramifications. He was thrown, on imperial orders, into the dreaded Noumera **prison** (Constantinople), where he was held in 1158–1159. A young man at the time (born c. 1130), Glykás composed a petition in 581 unrhymed **political verses,** *Poetic Lines by M. Glykás Which He Wrote during the Time He Was Detained because of Some Spiteful Informer.* Addressed to Manuel I Comnenus, this vernacular text uses both **demotic** and classical vocabulary (not in the same lines). It is replete with proverbs, dark observations on his detention, and pleas for forgiveness, as well as some chatty satire and borderline jokes about priests and their wives.

It seems that the judges condemned him to **blinding** (on orders dispatched from the Emperor, in Cilicia. This punishment must have been commuted. When he was released from jail, Glykás became a monk and joined in typical theological skirmishes of the period: on the significance of "because the Father is greater than me . . ." (*John,* 14, 28), the importance of unleavened bread, or the issue of the imperishability of the Holy Communion. In 1164, still impoverished by the effect of his trial, he dispatched a further supplicatory poem to the Emperor, as the epilogue to a collection of **proverbs** with religious glosses in political verse. This got him nowhere. But he forged on with 95 theological letters. Here he borrowed copiously but was not shy to mention sources. In one of the letters he opposed the Emperor Manuel's defense of astrology. His *Chronography* starts with a volume about world history from the creation and continues with one on Jewish and Oriental kingdoms; in the third book, he features Roman history up to Constantine the Great. His fourth book

takes Byzantine events up to the death of Alexius Comnenus (1118). His chronicle is leavened with digressions on natural history (for example, from Aelian) and theology.

GNOMIC The gnomic saying (γνωμικόν, γνώμη) annotates an event or sketches an opinion. Such utterances were compiled in antiquity as the *Wisdom of Jesus Son of Sarah,* or *One Line Sayings of Menander.* The latter are improving lines from Menander's classical comedies. The learned **Photius** informs us that Ioannis Stobaios compiled his *Anthology* (fifth century) for a son named Septimius. The first book draws on heresy, praise of philosophy, and philosophers' opinions on geometry, arithmetic, and music. The second book starts with logic; its bulk is on ethics. The third book is all ethical sayings; the fourth is politics and home management. Stobaios seems to be building his treasury on the remains of a collection by the grammarian Orion for Empress Eudokia, wife of Theodosius the Lesser. A post-eighth-century monk known as Ioannis Yeoryiadis compiled sayings from the Old Testament, classical poets, and other writers. Aristoboulos Apostolis (1465–1535), who became Arsenios, the Catholic Archbishop of Monemvasia (1514), made the anthology *Ionia* out of material assembled by his father, Mikhail. It was published in Latin after Mikhail's death (1519). The Greek version came to light in 1832 and was published by Balts (Stuttgart). A thousand paradoxes and mottos are collected in *Numbered Sayings* (1967) by Heraklis Apostolidis (1893–1970). Apostolidis was a prolific writer, who cofounded the Greek Socialist Party and left when it turned to Communism. Further volumes of his gnomic sayings, *Tailpieces* and *Last Sayings,* came out in 1968. His poetry *Anthology* (1933) went through 13 editions and became a standard work. He contributed to *Great Encyclopedia of Greece* (1926–1934).

GOLFIS, RIGAS (1886–1958; pseudonym of Dimitrios Dimitriadis) The father of Rigas Golfis, poet, critic, and journalist, had married a girl from a famous literary family (**Drosinis**). Rigas himself, born at **Missolonghi,** studied law at Athens and worked there for 46 years as a notary. He was a committed **demoticist,** close intellectual ally of **Palamás,** and contributor to *Noumás*, writing many of that combative journal's book and play reviews. He published the play *Monster from the Deep* (1908) and a collection of essays *Imagination and Poetry* (1935). Golfis was well regarded as a lyric poet and had several volumes to his credit: *The Songs of April* (1909), *Hymns* (1921), *At the Turn of the Rhyme* (1925), *Lyric Colors* (1930), and *Tetrameters* (1953).

GOUZELIS, DIMITRIOS (1774–1843) Gouzelis, nephew and pupil of **Martelaos,** from a noble Zakynthos family, wrote heroic verse, was a fanatical democrat, and fought as an officer in Napoleon's army. He was imprisoned in Constantinople for a while. Later he joined the **Friendly Society** and gathered volunteers to go to the Peloponnese to fight in the **Uprising.** He published a translation of Tasso's *Gerusalemme Liberata* (1807), dedicated to Napoleon. His play *Chasis* (1795) is a teenager's work that became popular all over Greece. It was first performed by young amateur actors during the 1800 carnival. Gouzelis uses paired **political verse** and makes a central character of the braggart warrior type. It precociously continues the Zakynthine comic tradition, which itself develops from illustrious Cretan precedents.

GRAMMAR, MANUALS OF MODERN GREEK The impulse to write manuals of modern Greek was felt chiefly by intellectuals living outside Turkish-ruled Greece. Until the Enlightenment, there were few publishing centers or distribution networks on the Greek mainland for improving books. The scholar Markos Mousouros (c. 1470–1517), who worked in Italy, published an influential grammar of Greek (Venice, 1515). He was preceded by **Chrysoloras** and **Laskaris,** also in Italy. Konstantinos Laskaris's *Grammar* went through six editions in the seventeenth century and remained in use two centuries later. A simplified digest of the Laskaris grammar (Rome, 1608) was printed for pupils at the Greek College in Rome. Nikolaos Sofianós, working in Venice (1550), compiled a *Grammar of Plain Greek,* eventually issued by E. Legrand (1874). Simon Portius (b. 1606), a Chiot residing in France, produced a Greek grammar in the early seventeenth century. Girolamo Germano (1568–1632) published a *Grammar of the Spoken Language* (Rome, 1622) and an *Italian-Greek Dictionary* for use by Jesuit missionaries bound for Anatolia. Ioannis Paradisios (Paris, 1637) produced a grammar for use by French students. Bessarion Makris devised a manual with questions and answers on grammar (a σταχυολογία, or "set of gleanings"). **Antonios Katiforos** of Zakynthos wrote a grammar and poetic method (after 1735) that had several more editions (Venice, 1769, 1778, 1784). Theodoros Gazís (1400–?1475/

1478) composed *A Grammar in Four Parts* (Venice 1756, 1758). Nikiforos Romanos composed in Latin a *Grammar of the Vernacular Greek Language* (France, mid-seventeenth century). Yeoryios Rousiadis from Kozani, a member of the **Friendly Society,** taught in the communities of Vienna and Budapest and contributed to ethnic welfare by writing a Greek grammar, as well as translating texts from French, German, and the classical *Iliad.*

GREAT IDEA, THE The dream beneath the Great Idea was to reincorporate the Aegean, Balkan, and Anatolian territories inside the boundaries of a widened Hellenic nation. Thus the Great Idea was the crucial plank of Hellenic **nationalism** in the nineteenth century. In 1838, on the occasion of Independence Day festivities, the cry "To the City" (Constantinople) was heard in the crowds. What was the history behind these territorial fantasies? Greece had gradually expanded the area won from the Turks (1821–1829) by territorial gains in 1832, 1864, 1881, 1913, 1923, and 1947. Inside these annexures and frontier extensions lay the irredentist lure of the Great Idea. The most "unredeemed" Hellenes of all were those that dwelled in such enticing, prosperous areas as Constantinople and Smyrna. These Ottoman cities were central to the dream of a Greece of "Two Continents and Five Seas."

So piece by piece, Greece gained the northern areas of Epirus, the **Ionian Islands,** Thessaly, Macedonia, Thrace, then Crete, the main Aegean Islands, certain Anatolian islands, and Cyprus. North of a line drawn from Arta to Othrys lies a new mainland Greece. It is twice the size of old Greece, and all of it has been acquired since 1881, most of it

added since 1913 (see **Balkan Wars**). The term "Great Idea" (μεγάλη ιδέα) was coined in 1844 by Ioannis Kolettis, a Hellenized Vlach. Kolettis had worked in the court of **Ali Pasha's** son and emerged in the first years of the newly created Greek kingdom (1832) as a theorist and later as Prime Minister. He argued for the rights of all Hellenes who lived in the old **Ottoman** Empire, not just the titular Greeks who lived inside the boundaries of the recent kingdom (see under **Diaspora**): "The kingdom of Greece is not Greece; it is merely a part, the smallest, poorest part of Greece."

The irredentist passion identified with this idea in the early twentieth century was fomented by **E. Venizelos,** at the head of the Greek Liberal Party. The so-called *heterochthons* would be amalgamated into a version of the old Byzantine empire, whose capital was Constantinople, with a geographical catchment running from the northern Epirus to Trebizond, Samos, and Crete. Before World War I, the average Greek patriot or nationalist believed in this irredentist ideal. The areas of Macedonia, Thrace, Istanbul, and Asia Minor had to be reconquered, so their population could reside inside a greater Greece. Burning at the core of the Great Idea was a fantasy that Constantinople could again be made the capital of Greece, just as once, in 1261, it had been recaptured by the Byzantine court after its exile at Nicaea. The novel *Christ Re-crucified* by **Kazantzakis** contains (as Bien noted) an elaboration of *topoi* associated with the Great Idea. We have a nationalist speech to his flock by the character Fotis, who announces that one of the entrances to their reconstructed (Anatolian) village will be called the Gate of Constantine Palaeologus. Associated with the Great Idea is the **myth**

of a "**King turned to marble**" (μαρμαρωμένος βασιλίας) who will
emerge from the North, perhaps **Russia,**
to liberate Greece. Like Palaeologus, this
liberator is expected to break into Istanbul (that is, Constantinople) and drive the
Turks (in a phrase derived from a folk-
tale) "as far as the Red Apple tree." As
early as 1617, this idea of succor from
the "blond peoples" was ridiculed in a
poem by Mathaios of Myreon.

An example of the pride that accompanied the Great Idea into the twentieth
century is the feeling for the 12 islands
of the Dodecanese, Greece's most southerly archipelago, its most remote territory, and the one with the most Anatolian
culture. The Knights of St. John captured
the area in 1309 and were ousted by Su-
leiman the Magnificent (1522). Held by
Turkey until 1912, the Dodecanese was
annexed by Italy after the Italo-Turkish
war, then taken over by the British after
World War II, and so became the last territory ceded to Greece (7 March 1948).

Further Reading

Alexandris, Alexis. *The Greek Minority of Istanbul and Greek-Turkish Relations,
1918–1974.* Athens: Centre for Asia Minor
Studies, 1983.

Carabott, Philip. "'Pawns That Never Became Queens': the Dodecanese Islands,
1912–1924." *Κάμπος: Cambridge Papers
in Modern Greek,* no. 4 (1996): 1–27.

Mavris, Nicholas. Δωδεκανησιακὴ Βιβλιογραφία [Bibliography of the Dodeca-
nese]. 2 vols. Athens: Dodecanese History
and Folklore Society, 1965–1974.

GREEK The Greek alphabet was the
first in which each letter stood for a
sound. Greek (Ελληνικά) is now a language used by 12 million speakers; 2 million live in the **diaspora.** Some form of
Greek has been used from 1400 B.C. to
the present day. There are four main divisions along its historical continuum:
Mycenaean (c. 1400–300 B.C.), **Hellenistic** (c. 300 B.C.–300 A.D.), Byzantine
Greek (300–1453), and Modern Greek
(1453 to the present). Mycenaean, deci-
phered from clay tablets excavated at
Knossos, is not a progenitor of any modern dialect. Hellenistic Greek is the language left in the train of **Alexander the
Great** and of the *Septuagint* (c. 250
B.C.). In the New Testament, Hellenistic
becomes a broad, omnibus idiom called
"common to all" (κοινή). It became an
illustrious vernacular in postclassical
writers, like the historian Polybius (c.
200–c. 118 B.C.); Dionysius Thracian,
the first codifier of **grammar** (c. 170–c.
90 B.C.); Epictetus (c. 50–c. 120), a freed
slave who became a philosopher; and Lucian the satirist (c. 115–c. 180).

Byzantine Greek becomes the vehicle
for many literary types: sermon
(κήρυγμα), speeches, **biography, kontakion, canon, hymn, epigram, acrostic, verse, alphabet, demotic song, romance,** fable, **letter, satire, chronicle,
allegory, synaxarion,** and **reader.** Up to
and beyond the **Enlightenment** period,
the **language question** made Greeks
aware of the inherent **diglossia** in their
culture. Thus the modern language had
to emerge from a long ideological contest
between the purist **Katharevousa** and the
vernacular **demotic,** which was gradually
won by the latter. That is to say, modern
Greek is a mixture of learned elements,
some classical heritage, and the broad
vernacular idiom. Modern Greek then
moved quickly in the late twentieth century, with national newspapers, uniform
television parlance, and simplified accents (see **Accent Reform**) to become a
plastic language that could coin its own
terms for **science fiction,** the Internet,
and theory of literature.

Further Reading

Finlay, George. *A History of Greece from Its Conquest by the Romans to the Present Time*, B.C. *146 to* A.D. *1864.* [7 vols., 1877]. New York: AMS Press, 1970.

GREEKNESS. See ROMIOSINI

GREEK RULE OF LAW 1806. See ANONYMOUS GREEK; DONÁS

GREGORÁS, NIKIFOROS (1295–1360) N. Choumnos (1255–c. 1327) and Th. Metochites (1269–1332), chancellor to Andronikos II Palaeologus, are leading philosophers of the late Byzantine age, and Nikiforos Gregorás was a pupil of Metochites. Metochites reintroduced the study of astronomy. Gregorás, became an equally versatile scholar, well regarded in Andronikos's court. He taught at the school of Chora in a convent of Constantinople and composed **humanist** dialogues in the manner of **Plato.** Krumbacher calls Gregorás "the greatest polyhistor of the last two centuries of Byzantium." Gregorás noticed how the discrepancy between the Julian calendar and the spring equinox made it problematic to decide when Easter falls. He advised the emperor, in *On the Date of Easter,* to devise a new calendar. As a conservative reaction was mooted, the plan was shelved. Gregorás anticipated Pope Gregory XIII's reform of the calendar by over two centuries. Gregorás appears to have supported the Zealots (loosely identified as the party of the poor) against the **Hesychasts** (party of the rich); he disputed with Barlaam, an intransigent opponent of the unification of the two churches. In 1351, he lost favor and was imprisoned in a monastery for two years. After the downfall of his former friend **John VI** Kantakouzenós, then leader of the Hesychasts (1355), Gregorás was released from detention. He devoted himself to completing the *Romaic History,* a **digest** in 37 books that starts at 1204 and covers the empire of Nicaea and his own times (1320–1359). He wrote 10 books in 1352, while in confinement, in under 40 days. The work constitutes a chronicle of fourteenth-century Byzantium, despite some loss of objectivity on issues where he took a stance and procured his ruin. He wrote prolifically: **homilies, consolatory addresses,** prayers, encomia, **letters,** dialogues, obituaries, testaments, biographies, grammatical essays, notes on errors in the orthography of the *Odyssey,* scholia, commentaries, astronomy, and even an essay on how to prepare an astrolobe.

Further Reading

Webster, J. C. *The Labours of the Months in Antique and Mediaeval Art.* Evanston and Chicago: Northwestern University Studies in the Humanities, 1938.

GRITSI MILLIÉX, TATIANA. See MILLIÉX; TATIANA GRITSI

GRYPARIS, IOANNIS (1870–1942) The amateur painter and poet Gryparis, close to the **New School of Athens,** wrote some of the finest **sonnets** in the modern Greek tradition, especially the cycle of 12 "Scarabs" in the 15-syllable line (publ. in *Estía,* 1895) and the later hendecasyllabic sonnets of "Terracottae" (1919). He translated all of Aeschylus's tragedies and a number of other classical plays, some **Homer,** Catullus, and Goethe. Gryparis had his schooling in Constantinople and went on to study classics (1888) at the University of Athens. In 1893 he published his first poems, *Eve-*

ning Matters, and for a while took up schoolmastering because of reduced family circumstances. In 1895, Gryparis took on the editorship of the Constantinople journal, *The Literary Echo,* making it strongly pro-**demotic.** In his mature years he taught and worked in the Ministry of Education at Athens, also serving as director of the National Theater (see also **Café**). He collected his "Intermedia" (written 1899–1901) and his three "Elegies" (written between 1901 and 1909) for the only volume printed in his lifetime, *Scarabs and Terracottae* (all 1919).

H

HAGIA SOPHIA Sleek Islamic minarets were added to Constantinople's basilica Hagia Sophia after it was de-Christianized in 1453 by the conquering Turks. In Greek literature, Hagia Sophia is the ultimate symbol of piety and the legitimacy of empire. A plain demotic song evokes its 400 bells and 62 chimes, which used to peal "round our Emperor on the left and our Patriarch on the right." A voice comes from heaven and from the mouth of an Archangel: "send word to Frankish Land for three ships, one to transport the cross, another, the Gospel and the third, the finest, to carry overseas our holy altar." **A. Moraïtidis** (1851–1929) attended an all-night vigil at Mount Athos, where Patriarch Joachim III was present. The chanting, vestment, candelabras, and icons induced a swooning nostalgia in our writer, who described the scene in the mountain monastery as though he were back in the capital: "You'd think you were back in the charmed era of Byzantium, in Constantinople, at Hagia Sophia." The eighteenth-century historian Gibbon drew on Procopius, Agathias, Paul the Silentiary (see **Ekphrasis**), Evagrius, and Pseudo-Codinus to describe Hagia Sophia, yet called it dull and insignificant.

Further Reading

Louth, A., J. Haldon, Ruth Webb, J. Lowden, and D. Womersley. "Taking a Leaf from Gibbon: Appraising Byzantium." *Dialogos: Hellenic Studies Review* 6 (1999): 141–155.

HAGIOGRAPHY Hagiography is the composition of documents that adorn the cult of saints and the writing of saintly lives (see **Synaxarion**). The *Monthly Ritual* (Μηναῖον) was a book with entries for each day of the month and described the relevant festival or martyrdom of any saint that was to be commemorated. The *menologion* (Μηνολόγιον) is an almanac of entries for all 12 months of the year, with biographical and devotional information about their associated saints. The lives of men who had gone into desert or mountain retreat was of special interest to later congregations, because therein could be learned their acquisition of gifts and *charismata* (endowment by the unction of the Holy Spirit). Eighth-century collections of saints' lives contain the biography of those martyred for the cause of **icon** worship, like St. Gregory Spatharios and 12 who died with him around 730 or the death of 60 Christian martyrs in Jerusalem c. 724, or of 20 monks in Sabba (Palestine) killed by Arabs (787), and of 42 in Syria (around 841).

Symeon Metaphrastes (mid-tenth century) was admired by **Psellus** for his ability to turn such lives into art. Later he was followed by such literary men as Theodoros Prodromos with his twelfth-century *Life of St. Meletios the Younger* (1035–1105) or Ioannis Tzetzes (c. 1110–1185), with a *Life of Lucia*. Even in the Greek settlements in Calabria, this religious fervor was turned into literary art with the life of *St. Nilus of Rossano,* who founded the monastery of Grottaferrata. At the end of the twelfth century the fervor of hagiography abated and gave way to the historicized lives in **Y. Akropolitis,** N. Choumnos, and **N. Gregorás.**

Recently a more radical perspective has emerged: L. Papadopulos and G. Lizardos arranged selected lives in *New Martyrs of the Turkish Yoke* (Seattle, 1985). They used the artistic form of a *menologion* to present some 90 saints who gave their lives for their faith in the "Greek" territories during the Turkocracy. Eva Catafygiotu arranged the subjects of her *Saints and Sisterhood: The Lives of Forty-Eight Holy Women* (Minneapolis: Light & Life, 1999) as a modern *menologion* for a sorority that has been silenced in the first 18 centuries of the modern era.

Further Reading

Delehaye, Hippolyte. *Les Légendes hagiographiques.* Brussels: Société des Bollandistes, 1955.

Galatariotou, Catia. *The Making of a Saint: The Life, Times and Sanctification of Neophytos.* Cambridge: Cambridge University Press, 1991.

Hackel, S., ed. *The Byzantine Saint.* London: Fellowship of St. Alban and St. Sergius, 1981.

Meinardus, Otto F. A. *The Saints of Greece.* Athens: George Scouras, 1970

Wood, Diana, ed. "Martyrs and Martyrologies." *Studies in Church History,* no. 30 (1993).

HAPPY ENDING Emphasis on the happy or unhappy ending of a plot has been paramount in Greek literature since **Aristotle** (384–322 B.C.) and the analysis of alternating fortune in his *Poetics.* Characteristic of the classical Greek **novel** are "the separation of the two lovers, hairbreadth escapes from a series of appalling perils and adversities, and final reunion and a happy ending" (Howatson and Chilvers: 1993). Typical is the close of the thirteenth-century **romance Velthandros and Chrysantza,** where the narrator sums up the text and all of life: "If the commencement was good, and recent events turn sour, / Then the wise proverb tells us that everything is spoiled. / But if good things follow and crown the end of a life, / Then all is good and a thousand times blessed. / I declare 'Amen to that' and hereby close my tale." Ending the romance **Florios and Platzia-Flora**, a fifteenth-century author commented that his heroes have survived condemnation to death "so that they may go on to live and prosper." The seventeenth-century comedies from **Crete,** *Stathis,* Foskolos's **Fortounatos,** and *Katzourbos,* are in the manner of classical Roman comedy: Voutieridis observed that "the plot of the drama is bound to terminate happily." `

HAREM For a Greek woman to end up in a **Turkish** harem caused morbid horror. In the early seventeenth century, **Triantafyllos Ypsilantis,** whose descendants took part in the **War of Independence,** left Trebizond to prevent a pasha from taking his 15-year-old daughter for his harem. Fantasy about the harem reached back to **Byzantium** and forward to **Roidis** and **Vizyinós.** The soldier, ambassador, and historian Yeoryios Frantzis (1401–c. 1479) was captured more than once by the enemies of the Palaeologus dynasty. He was captured by Catalans while returning from Akarnania (1430) and by the Turks at the **fall of Constantinople** (1453). In 1458, he took refuge in Kerkyra, where he composed his *Chronicle.* This was completed in 1467 and relates events since 1258 from an imperial perspective. He married (1437) the daughter of Emperor Alexis Palaeologus. She was captured at Adrianople (Edirne) after the fall of Constantinople. He managed to ransom her from the Turks, but mourned forever the abduction of his daughter for the Sultan's harem and the killing of his son. He died as friar Gregory, in the monastery of Tarchanioti, where his wife also took the veil. When **Karkavitsas** comes to describe Smyrna (in his *Diary,* publ. *Estía,* 15 Feb.–5 Apr. 1895), he stressed that "everywhere its hellenism bubbles over impetuously," yet his attention is caught on the Quays by "a whole harem with the fantastic colours of their robes, gazing all round them and twittering like a flock of thrushes."

HAVIARAS, STRATÍS (1935–) The novelist and poet Haviaras, when he emigrated from Greece to America (1967), had already published three volumes of verse in the 1960s. This was followed in 1972 by a fourth volume in Greek, *Apparent Death,* which explored the life of a young boy faced by war, immature witness to the violence and reprisals of military occupation. After a few years in the Anglophone environment, Haviaras published a further volume of poems, this time in English, *Crossing the River Twice* (1977). Also in English were Haviaras's two subsequent, well-received novels about the German **occupation** and the ensuing Greek **Civil War,** *When the Tree Sings* (1979; publ. in Greek, 1980), and *The Heroic Age* (1984). Some of his narrative scenes seem to push the limits of descriptive propriety, as when an adolescent boy, Dando (in *When the Tree Sings*), has sex with a little cow, tied to a peach tree while he is leaning off a branch. Levcas, the village informer, gets a dog to lick butter off a red-head woman's feet while she is supine, tied naked to a four-poster bed, observed by adventurous boys through her cottage windows at night.

These aesthetic explorations are quickly surpassed by the violence of war between Greek irregulars and the occupying German Commandant, who shunts a cage with civilian hostages at the front of his supply train convoys in order to prevent the train from being blown up. Apart from his collections of poetry in Greek, *The Lady with a Compass* (1963), *Berlin* (1965), *The Night of the Stiltwalker* (1967), and two in English, *Apparent Death* and *Crossing the River Twice,* Haviaras edited two anthologies, *35 Post-War Greek Poets* (1972) and *The Poet's Voice* (1978), with cassette recordings of 13 American writers reading from and commenting on their own works, including Marianne Moore, Sylvia Plath, and Ezra Pound. His "Millennial Afterlives, A Retrospective" (in *Mondogreco,* spring 1999: 54–62) is a minimalist set of sketches of Greece. One is about a customs clerk at Patras who checks on a Greek princess who has become a nun (and has an oversized rubber object in her luggage). He tells a clerk that the queried import is "a collector's item; ephemeral art." The nun-princess winks in gratitude.

Further Reading

Demas Bliss, Corinne. "The Heroic Age." *Boston Review* 9, no. 3 (June 1984): 31–32.

du Plessix Gray, Francine. "Germans in Greece." *The New York Times Book Review,* 24 June 1979: 14–15.

Kalogeras, Yorgos D. *"When the Tree Sings:* Magic Realism and the Carnivalesque in a Greek-American Narrative." *International Fiction Review* 16, no. 1 (winter 1989): 32–38.

Myrsiades, Kostas. "Nekrofánia." *Books Abroad* 48, no. 1 (winter 1974): 195–196.

Thiébaux, Marcelle. "Children Changed to Stone." *The New York Times Book Review,* 10 June 1984: 14–15.

HEGESO Hegeso was the first modern Greek periodical devoted solely to lyric poetry. Its name was based on a memorial column that had been recently transferred from Kerameikós to the National Museum. *Hegeso* was founded by **Nikos Karvounis** (1880–1947), Fotos and Yiorgos Politis, **Kostas Varnalis,** Dimitrios Koumarianós, Mitsis Kalamás (pseudonym of D. Evangelidis), **Leandros Palamás, N. Lapathiotis, Romos Filyras,** and N. Chantzaras. *Hegeso* ran nine months, from 1907 to 1908 and was supported by the so-called Generation of 1905, "the poets who follow Palamás," including **Sikelianós, Sotiris Skipis, Myrtiotissa** (1883–1968) and Emily Daphne (1867–1941).

HEKATÓLOGA (mid-fifteenth century) The *Hekatóloga,* or "Songs of a Hundred Words" (Ἐκατόλογα), are included in the collection of love songs known as Καταλόγια, possibly from the isle of Rhodes. Such exchanges were also called numerals. In them, challenges and responses go from number 1 to 10, then by decades up to 100. They were found, in 1952, to be of Chiote origin (Lavagnini, 1969).

See also ALPHABETS OF LOVE

HELLENISM; HELLENIC The word *Hellenism* (Ελληνισμός) designates the whole Greek people and also the period of Greek intellectual life following Alexander the Great, in which the Hellenic language and civilization spread outside Greek boundaries to the Macedonian territories, Asia, and Egypt. In classical times, there was no political unit called Hellas as such, though Panhellenic festivals brought together Greeks from the different cities, which were then states. Indeed, the Greeks identified the whole world with what was inhabited by them (ἡ οἰκουμένη). The Olympic Games attracted 40,000 people, more than an average city–state. In much of the **Hellenistic** period, the true international center of Hellenism became Alexandria (Egypt).

Bishop Eustathios of Thassaloniki (c. 1115–c. 1195) stated that the world could be separated into "Hellenic" or "barbarian." However, the term *Hellenism* is not conventionally applied to culture of the Byzantine period, which repudiated the classical tradition (παράδοση) of gods, games, and theaters. Around 1450, **Plethon** still called for the remaking of a "Hellenic" nation with its own secular law system and contingent deities. After the fall of Byzantium, an intermittent hellenizing force emanated from the **humanist** and early Enlightenment writers that left the **Turkocracy** for the West. Travelers and exiles, like **Chrysoloras, Bessarion,** Plethon, Argyropoulos, and the post-Renaissance commentators on Aristotle like **Voulgaris** or **Vamvas** were the ones who kept Hellenism alive. Later, in the modern period, Greek writers began to see an obvious discontinuity between the "Hellenic ideal" and Greek actuality (Herzfeld, 1986). Who were these modern beneficiaries of classical knowledge, morality, and art, with their oafish Turkishness, deserters from battles they thought they might lose? The irony is that Western **Philhellenes** counted it a duty to come to the rescue of a country with such beautiful ruins. **Nikos Gatsos** writes of Hellenism in the poem "This Land": "It is a myth / Furnished from color and light, / A hidden myth / Tied to the world of the sun. / At daybreak this land charges forth / To join again / Its own immortal nation."

Further Reading

Bowersock, G. W. *Hellenism in Late Antiquity.* Ann Arbor: University of Michigan Press, 1990.

Hammond, N.G.L. *Alexander the Great: King, Commander and Statesman.* Bristol: Bristol Classical Press, 1989.

Momigliano, Arnaldo. *Alien Wisdom: The Limits of Hellenization.* Cambridge and New York: Cambridge University Press, 1975.

HELLENISTIC The term *Hellenistic* is used as a conventional epithet to define culture and history from the death of **Alexander** (323 B.C.) to the early fourth century A.D. As Greece expanded its boundaries, it met an enlarged audience, able to swallow myriad books: "We know the names of eleven hundred Hellenistic authors; the unknown are an incalculable multitude" (Durant, 1939). The decline of the Hellenistic is often taken to start with the destruction of Cleopatra's fleet at the battle of Actium in 31 B.C., followed by the Egyptian queen's suicide. Ineluctably, the Roman Empire developed out of the ruins of this Hellenistic world, which lost its Anatolian and Macedonian possessions to Rome by treaty and defeat. Because it was never a political unity, the Hellenistic world shows a startling, promiscuous interrelationship of cultures. As long as its literature was judged to be patchy and inferior, its manuscripts were no longer copied by Byzantine scribes. This led to the loss of many volumes of the greatest Hellenistic historian, Polybius, who had a commanding interest in how chance *(tyche)* can be controlled in human affairs and who judged that the historian should not copy the tragedian "mastering the emotions of his audience for the moment by the plausibility of his words."

R. Pfeiffer comments unsympathetically that this period shows "no original magnitude of subject or gravity of religious and ethical ideas." Moses Finlay found its literature "cold, lifeless, and essentially rhetorical." Yet Hellenistic writers posed the notion of "charity towards mankind" (φιλανθρωπία) in the ideal ruler, and the Christian divine, Eusebius, picks up this important idea in his eulogy of Constantine. K. Dover said of the Hellenistic poets of the third century that "they had a sharp eye and ear for how human beings feel and talk and act." Their taste for **epigrams** was absorbed into the work of Proclus of Athens (410–485), Palladas (end fourth century), Claudian (fifth century), and others. This flowed on into the great Byzantine collections of epigrams by Constantine Cephalas (ninth century) and **Maximos Planoudis** (1260–1310). Hellenistic authors show a marked respect for writing, from the elementary mastery of letters to the use of rhetoric. A **demotic song** tells how St. Basil the Great (c. 330–379) once scratched the alphabet in the gravel for some urchins at the side of a road. Hellenistic belief in demons was pent up by subsequent Christian writing, but Theodore of Santabaris's belief in hypnotic persuasion affected the imagination of Emperor Basil I (867–886), just as the occult practitioner Michael Sikiditis was active in the reign of Manuel Comnenus (1143–1180).

Further Reading

Burstein, Stanley M. *The Hellenistic Period in World History.* Washington, DC: American Historical Association, 1996.

Onians, John. *Art and Thought in the Hellenistic Age: The Greek World View, 350–50 B.C.* London: Thames and Hudson, 1979.

HEPTANESE. See IONIAN ISLANDS

HERMONIAKÓS, KONSTANTINOS (early fourteenth century)

The scholar Konstantinos Hermoniakós, who lived in court circles in the despotate of Epirus, produced a version of Homer's *Iliad* around the year 1330 in 8,799 unrhymed trochaic octosyllables (lines of four feet, stressed/unstressed: $-\smile$). It is divided into 24 rhapsodies (that is, books) and 142 chapters. The work was apparently commissioned by John II Angelos Doukas, Despot of Epirus (1323–1335). As a compilation, it errs by including pre- and post-Homeric material. It is partly a paraphrase in **plain Greek** of an intermediate Homeric adaptation by the Byzantine poet Ioannis Tzetzes (c. 1110–1185), one of his *Allegories of the Iliad.* Both appear to be based loosely on the romance of Troy by Benoît de Saint-More. Hermoniakós falsified events so as to introduce characters who are alien to the Trojan legend. Thus he gives Achilles a regiment of Bulgarian and Hungarian troops. His language is a mix of learned and popular idioms. Hermoniakós's Homer was published by E. Legrand in 1890. Later Voutieridis mocked the way he loads his overshort lines with the Greek particles "for," "therefore," and "namely," whereas Kambanis considered it "dull and poorly crafted."

See also LADDER POEM; TROJAN WAR

Further Reading

Jeffreys, E. "Constantine Hermoniakos and Byzantine Education." Δωδώνη [Dodoni], no. 4 (1975): 81–109.

HESYCHASM Hesychasm, which became a great spiritual movement in fourteenth-century **Byzantium,** encouraged physical intensity of prayer and an aspiration to see the pure, uncreated light of Mount Tabor, as the Apostles saw it irradiating Christ, during his Transfiguration. Hesychasm is derived from the word for quietness (ἡσυχία). It denoted a state of ecstatic spiritual withdrawal, when the worshipper's devotion was invested in a search for grace (χάρις). The theological sources of Hesychasm are to be found in such authors as Gregory of Nissa, Evagrios Pontikos, Diadokos of Foticea, and Maximus the Confessor (fourth to sixth centuries). Its driving force came, however, from the monk Grigorios Palamás (c. 1296–1359). Some of his mystical acolytes on **Mount Athos** would sit cross-legged, sink their jaws on the chest, and focus on the navel till they fell into a trance caused by dizziness. The point was to partake in the "uncreated" light that once upon a time bathed Christ. Consequently, there were sharp doctrinal disputes about the distinction between uncreated and created light until the mid-sixteenth century.

The Hesychasts held that prayer should be an unceasing monologue, as in "Lord Jesus Christ, have mercy on me," uttered again and again, so as to actualize St. Paul's precept "Pray without ceasing" (I *Thessalonians* 5, 17). Such prayer was integrated with special positions of the body and control over the breathing, so that "the mind might be unified with the heart." This method was thought to facilitate the perfect contemplation of "Taboritic light." It asserted a belief in man's psycho–physical unity. It also posited the unknowability of God, as opposed to un-created forces, which may be perceived in the mystic raptus of contemplation. The Calabrian monk Barlaam opposed Hesychasm by denying the distinction between essence and energy. The movement was legitimized by two Councils of the Eastern **Orthodox Church,** held at Constantinople in 1341 and 1351. An anonymous work of the mid-nineteenth century, *Tales of a Russian Pilgrim,* promoted a revived Hesychasm for the modern era. The pious novelist **A. Papadiamantis** was influenced as a young man by the *Kollyvades,* who opposed the increasing secularization of the Orthodox Church and yearned for a contemporary return to Hesychasm.

Further Reading

Hart, T. "Nicephorus Gregoras: Historian of the Hesychast Controversy." *Journal of Ecclesiastical History* 2 (1951): 169–179.

HIATUS Two adjacent vowels, standing at the end of one word and the begin-ning of the next word, cause hiatus (χασμῳδία), which has a displeasing effect, as in "merry yet" (χαρὰ ἀκόμα). To avoid this supposed cacophony, poets adjusted the ending, the phonemes, or the stem in the offending pair.

See also ELISION

HISTORICAL NOVEL The historical novel was established and influential in mid-nineteenth-century Greece. Yet there is no mention of Greeks writing this genre in Georg Lukács's *The Historical Novel* (1937). In 1850, the aristocratic writer **Rangavís** produced Greece's first historical novel, *The Lord of Morea,* showing how the **crusaders** of the thirteenth century came to the Peloponnese. Konstantinos Ramfos (c. 1776–1871), from Chios, took part in the **Uprising** and after the liberation was appointed by **Kapodistrias** to be governor of Messenia and later Poros. Ramfos published the novella *Dhespo of the Epirus,* which tells of the abduction of Dhespo Tagou by Ali Pasha's troops and her release by her own warriors. He also wrote the novel *Katsantonis* (1860), which ranges over the mountains of Epirus, using **Klephtic** songs to frame the figure of the warrior-brigand Katsantonis, tactician of guer-rilla battle, promoter of schools for the fledgling Greeks, and martyr of the Up-rising, gasping for water as **Ali Pasha** stalks him to death, shrieking: "I give the finger to your God, fool. I spit on Him."

A key historical author is **Stefanos Xenos** (1821–1894), whose *The Devil in Turkey or Scenes in Constantinople* (Greek ed. 1862; 3 vols., London, 1851), earned him the large sum of £1,200. Xenos also wrote a novel entitled *Heroine of the Greek Uprising* (1851), so widely read that it taught a generation of Greeks an outline of their own liberation struggle. He created, in his female protagonist, a girl from Arcadia called Andronike, an icon of modesty and **patriotism,** whose saga covers all the events of the Uprising. She is present at several of its battles, taken prisoner by the Muslim enemy, sold at the Constantinople slave market, and dies at a monastery in Russia. Xenos did archival research in London to prepare the historical matter for this documentary novel. His data on the conflict of 1812–1828 is still considered useful. **Spyridon Zambelios,** the critic, historian, and folklorist, wrote two broad works of historical fiction based on Crete's Venetian period: *Historical Scene Paintings* (1860) and *Wedding at Crete* (first publ. in Italy, 1871), the latter noted for its **patriotism.** From this high period of the Greek historical novel comes Nikolaos Makrís (1827–1912), a career soldier and later Police Chief at Athens, who left a *Story of Missolonghi,* with narrative surrounding the exploits of the sortie. His book was later published by Protopsaltes (see **War of Independence**). A modern writer who dealt exhaustively with Byzantium and Turkocracy was **Petsalis-Diomedis** (1904–1995). He wrote over 10,000 pages, mostly historical fiction. His two-volume account of life under the Ottomans, *The Mavrolykos Family* (1947–1948), was adapted for Greek radio and recommended for school libraries and high school classes.

The first book by **P. Delta,** *For the Homeland* (1909), tells young readers about the tenth century and how the Tsar of Bulgaria, Samuel, fights the Byzantine general Gregory Taronitis at the battle of Thessaloniki, and how this patriotic general was killed. His son Asotis was taken prisoner, but connived with Samuel's daughter to escape back to Byzantium. In 1938, Angelos Terzakis made a strong bid to revive the historical novel, which had ailed in the twentieth century, with his *Princess Ysabeau.* Here we see Princess Isabeau de Villehardouin married on 28 May 1271, to Prince Philippe, a son of Charles d'Anjou. His political ambitions included annexation of the Frankish possessions in Greece, known as the Morea. Ysabeau was widowed young. She was regent of the principate of Morea from 1297 to 1300. In the latter year she traveled to Rome for the Jubilee celebrations decreed by Pope Boniface VIII. Ysabeau (aged over 40) then found a new husband (aged 22) in the Count of Piedmont (February 1301). With him she returned to Morea, but he allowed his entourage of barons to enrich themselves at the expense of the feudatories. Ysabeau attempted to strengthen the claim of her sister, Marguerite, on the principate, before dying in 1311.

Further Reading

Mitsakis, Karolos. "The Contemporary Greek Historical Novel 1974–1997." *Hellenic Quarterly,* no. 9 (June-August 2001): 37–41.

HISTORICAL PRESENT. See DRAMATIC PRESENT

HISTORIES OF MODERN GREEK LITERATURE The initial problem in setting out a historical description of modern Greek literature is periodization. The German scholar Ulrich Moennig points out that it has long been a subject of dispute where the actual beginning of modern Greek literature should be situated. The histories of Greek literature by L. Politis, K. Th. Dimarás, and M. Vitti start at the earliest texts in a Byzantine vernacular that materialized around the twelfth century. The **Phanariot** writer Iakovakis Rizos Neroulós (1778–1849), on the contrary, emphasizes the eighteenth century, in his history of modern Greek literature (publ. 1827). Between 1750 and 1800, schools were transformed into *lycées* or colleges. Greek intellectuals, like his grandfather ("Jackovaky Rizo, mon aïeul"), of whom he is extremely proud, came back from study abroad and accepted "la tâche honorable de l'enseignement public." Thus culture finally set sail in the eighteenth century, thanks to schooling. Men of high sentiment endeavored to promote a language that would render Greece a civilized nation. Here Rizos Neroulós is using code for "Let's speak and write neo-classical." He praises the civil servant "Panajotaky of Trebizond," that is, Panayotis Nikousios, who gained great favor with the Turks in Constantinople, wrote on the natural sciences, and was succeeded in 1673 by his young secretary, Alex Mavrokordatos (called "he of the Secret Counsels," ὁ ἐξαπορρήτων).

Rizos Neroulós lists Mavrokordatos's peers as **Miniatis**, Kakavellas, **Meletios Pigás, Sougdouris,** Kritias, Hourmouzios, Panayiodouros, and **Antonios Katiforos.** The latter taught the philosopher **Evyenios Voulgaris** (1716–1806), whose hope of inducing **Russia** to free Greece was dashed by the death of Potemkin (1791). Mavrokordatos's literary successors tended to publish at Bucharest, **Venice,** or Leipzig. A further wave of Enlightenment writers included Benjamin of Lesvos (1762–1824), Athanasios Psalidas (1767–1829), and Daniel Filippidis (1758–1832), the author, with **Grigorios Konstantas** (1753–1844), of *The Modern Geography* (Vienna, 1791), a text that has been compared with the **anonymous** *The Greek Rule of Law, or A Discourse on Freedom* (1806).

Others who constellate this strand of literary history include Lambros Fotiadis (1752–1805), **Neophytos Doukas,** Konstantinos Vardalachos (1775–1830), who met **Kapodistrias** (future President of Greece) while the latter was studying medicine in Italy, and Stefanos Dounkas (d. 1830), who was appointed (1813) headmaster of the royal college in Moldavia, but was obliged to send a formal recantation to the Ecumenical Patriarch after linking theology with physics and chemistry (1813) in his philosophy lessons. Other contributors to this financial, polemical **Enlightenment** are the Zosimas brothers and that adversary of **Ali Pasha,** father Evthymios. D. P. Kostelenos (1977) declared that good histories of modern Greek literature can be counted on the fingers of one hand. Kostelenos only approves the history of modern Greek literature by Kordatos, but he quotes from those of Dimarás and Voutieridis and admits that K. Thrakiotis (1965) is "useful." He finds all of them dated and condemns the histories of modern Greek literature by Kambanis and Nikos Pappás. He says the latter (1973) displays an inexplicable immodesty (ἀμετροέπεια). Kostelenos rejects time limits like "Generation of 1900," or "Generation of the 1930s." He takes up the centrality, for Greek literature, of education. The first community school founded after 1453 was at Athens (1647). Here Grigorios Soterianos taught. A century later, Greece and expatriate Hellenism was crisscrossed by schools, that is, in Bucharest, Jassy, Russia, and areas under Venetian control. These schools had names like "home of the Muses," "academy," "gymnasium" (Μουσεῖα, Ἑλληνομουσεῖα, Γυμνάσια, or Ἀκαδημίες) and were located at Larisa, Ioannina, Turnavos, Ampelakia, Zagorá,

Milies in the Pilio, Dhimitsana, or wherever Greek communities had became reasonably secure. The Epirus was the most evolved area, with three colleges at Ioannina and local schools at Metsovo, Zagoria, Kalarrytes, and Syrrakos. Many schools sprang up in Asia Minor: Chios, Patmos, Andros, Hydra, Naxos, Paros, and Mytiline (c. 1650–1750).

Nikos Pappás embarked (1973) on his "truthful" history of Greek literature to fulfill a dream and counter the rigid, partisan, conservative efforts of Dimarás. Pappás ridicules any classifications like "school of the Heptanese" or "Circle of Mt Taïyetos," saying they are *invented* in most histories of modern Greek literature. Among the older efforts, he commends Voutieridis and Papadimas; among the newer authors, Thrakiotis and Valetas. Pappás gives only a cursory account of the "distant years of our medieval period," because "our literature's *real* history starts from Solomós and Kalvos." This fact is lost in the 500 pages of Dimarás, "who swims to its sources and protoplasms, and actually halts at the point where our literature and history began." I. M. Panayotopoulos, in other areas a decent thinker, has produced a "limited" and "crippled" history of modern Greek literature. Linos Politis's effort is "catastrophic." Foreign Hellenists beg for an updated history of our literature, but Dimarás's tome, with its frequent reprints, serves no purpose (!). The phrase "Heptanesian School" is an oft-repeated stereotype about a mainly unrelated group of authors. To be a "school" (like the Cubists, Romantics, Futurists), you need a manifesto, a magazine, a center, or a program. Pappás says the only sources of modern Greek literature are *Erotokritos,* the **demotic song,** the *Sacrifice of Abraham,* a play by **Chortatsis,**

and none of the Skoufos, Rodinos, and Sofianós that critics push into their histories to pump out the bibliography. Karantonis and Dimarás (that "library rat") maliciously cut the space for **Moraïtidis** and his cousin **Papadiamantis.** Their purpose was to compromise the Papadiamantis legend. Dimarás exalts **Kazantzakis** in order to downgrade **Sikelianós.**

Karantonis declares that **Kavafis** is the most "erotic" of all our poets, but only for his usual purpose, which is to magnify **Palamás** and **Seferis.** Pappás says that Kavafis's poems have no connection with love. They incubate, rather, a lurking "obsession with good looks." Our literary historian dismantles the posturing of *poésie pure,* which he calls "guileless lyricism." Did **Elytis** really fight in Albania (p. 224)? How can we survive the acrid and dehydrated climate of Seferis (p. 238)? "As for George Seferis, I declare this frankly, nobody can say, either with ease or with difficulty, why he gives the impression of being a great poet" (p. 173). Does anyone realize that the forerunner of Seferis is the underestimated **Apostolos Melachrinós** (p. 205)? Is not the imagery of **Yannis Ritsos** "a hideous tangle of naturalism and melodrama, at an abysmal level of aesthetic and poetic execution" (p. 209)? Gloomily we gaze on the "Sahara Desert of modern fiction" after 1930, and on noncommitted modern writing, which labors for "the intellectual Teddyboyism of our age, which is a licence that bears no resemblance to the allure of revolutionary Bohemianism in the last century." This historian of literature holds that "the true renewers of poetry are the realists, for they refer art back to man."

HISTORIOGRAPHY Historians of the twelfth to fourteenth centuries adhered to the polished grammar and vocabulary of **Atticism.** Constantine VII Porphyrogennetos (son of Leo the Wise) may have composed the works *On Military Districts* and *Ceremonies of the Imperial Court.* The latter contains, in 800 pages, an account of Byzantium's court procedure. Sections of this work are prefaced by songs, one of which is the earliest example of **political** meter: "Behold, sweet spring bringeth back / Joy, health, life, affluence, / And valor from God to the Greeks' ruler, / And God-given victory over his foes." Constantine VII may have inserted parts of a *Life of Basil I* (867–886) in the work of Joseph Genesios, who composed (945–959) the four *Lives of the Rulers,* covering the period of Leo V (813–820), Michael II (820–829), Theophilos (829–842), and Michael III (842–867). The author tries to gloss over the darker elements in Basil I's life and has a weakness for marvels and proclamations. **Nikiforos Briennios** (c. 1062–1138) began a history of his father-in-law, Emperor Alexius I, making use of sources, in a confident imitation of Xenophon. He died after covering the period 1070–1074, so his chronicle does not deal with Alexius's reign. His wife, **Anna Comnene,** completed his work in the *Alexiad,* which was, in turn, continued by two former imperial secretaries: Ioannis Kinnamos (c. 1142–1203), born to an illustrious family, who composed a history in seven books of the period 1118–1176, and Niketas Choniatis Akominatos (c. 1150–1210), who in 21 books related events of the years 1180–1206. Both these writers show hostility to the West, and Kinnamos defends Byzantine claims to world primacy.

Greeks also had a taste for universal history, covering events from the creation to the author's time, or the current emperor (see **Digest**). Such books carry lists of people and occurrences, relating epidemics, earthquakes, food shortages, comets, meteors, shooting stars, construction projects, and even rumors from the Hippodrome, where the crowds went for races or riots. The **Turkocracy** produced other types of historians. Manuel Malaxos, a sixteenth-century scholar who moved to Thebes from Nafplion after it fell to the Turks (1538), wrote a *History of the Patriarchs of Constantinople* (1577), published in Martin Crusius's *Turkish Greece* (1584). Angelos Christoforos (1575–1638), from Gastouni in the old Frankish fiefdom of Morea, lectured in Greek at Cambridge and Oxford (1608–1612) and wrote *Companion to the Present State of the Greeks,* which contains a history of the **Orthodox Church.**

Païsios Ligaridis (1609–1678), who studied at St. Athanasius College in Rome, embraced **Catholicism,** worked in the East, and reverted to Orthodoxy, turned out to be a combative teacher and traveler (Chios, Jassy, Jerusalem, Gaza, and Russia). Ligaridis quarreled with his masters and wrote an unfavorable history of the Patriarchs of Jerusalem. Chrysanthos Notarás, Patriarch of Jerusalem from 1707 to 1731) wrote a history of the conquest of China, *The Suffering of Cathay* (1694). Yeoryios Zaviras (1744–1804), a Macedonian merchant who lived much of his life in Hungary, wrote *Modern Greece* (1872), which contains a biographical register of Greek scholars in the Turkocracy. The aristocrat Ioannis Palaeologus Venizelos (1730–1807) was a teacher who was devoted to Athens. He wrote a history of the city, not favoring its élite. Another historian from the aristocracy, Athanasios Comnenus Ypsilantis (d. 1789), studied in the West, became a doctor to grand vizier Rajip Mehmet, for whom he performed confidential missions, and wrote *Affairs of Church and State in Twelve Books* (completed c. 1789). This sketches a history from Julius Caesar to Ypsilantis's time, with Greece at the center. Ypsilantis deals with the older period by synchronizing his account of different countries; he divides the post-1453 period into narratives from separate localities and takes them in order. Dimarás calls it a work for Phanariots, as it sports a parade of women, relatives, factions, intrigue, clerical bribery, and inserted Turkish words.

Sergios Makraios (1750–?1819) wrote *Triumph against the Copernican System* (1797) and *Memoirs of Ecclesiastical History from 1750–1800*. Konstantinos Paparrigopoulos (1815–1891), professor at the University from 1851, published a *History of the Greek People from Antiquity to the Present* (1853) and completed his *History of the Greek Nation* in 1877. His tripartite division of Greek history into ancient, Byzantine, and modern was attacked by **Sp. Vasiliadis** (1845–1874), but his theory of a continuous Hellenic tradition dominated the course of Greek historiography well into the twentieth century and makes him the sovereign figure in this ideological minefield. Nikolaos Vlachos (1893–1956) was one of a group of historians who followed. Vlachos studied in Germany and went on to publish *Theoretical and Methodological Problems in History* in 1925.

A near-contemporary was Yeoryios Aspreas (1875–1952), who had a dashing career in popular journalism and the theater, but also wrote an interpretation of the immediate post-Independence years, *The Political History of Modern Greece (1821–1928),* a work in three volumes

(unfinished), issued in 1930. Kostas Kairofilas (1878–1961), born on Zakynthos, where as a youth he took Italian lessons from **M. Martzokis,** moved in anti-Fascist circles in Rome, acted as a foreign correspondent in London, and was a colleague in plotting with **E. Venizelos,** but he found time to gather substantial historical data: *The Heptanese in the Venetocracy* (1943), *Zakynthos and the Greek Revolution* (1935), and a *History of Athens* (1935).

Yannis Kordatos (1891–1961) moved to the left, following the implicit directives of Soviet theory, in his massive corpus of work. This includes a history of modern Greek literature (1962) and books on modern Greek political history (1925), the vernacular versus scholarly tradition (1927), the 1821 revolution in Thessaly (1930), Rigas Velestinlís and the Balkan federation (1945), a history of modern Greece (1957–1958), *History of Ancient Greece* (1956), and *History of the Byzantine Autocracy* (1960). His voice is serious, and his tone is often accusatory. Nikos Svoronos (born Levkas 1911–1990) was an intellectual Marxist historian, trained for many years in France. He wrote historical accounts of material referring to the Klephts and *armatolí* at Levkas (1939), the Byzantine fiscal and tax system, the economic effect of tax on Thebes (1959), and *Histoire de la Grèce moderne* (1953), called by R. Ehaliotis (2000) "the first Marxist-slanted short history of Greece." **Ritsos,** another Marxist, asks in his *Survey of Modern Greek History* (1976) what was the effect of the 1940s: "Human losses rose to 7 or 8 percent of the population; agricultural production was lowered by over 70 percent, shipping lost 73 percent of its tonnage." This implicitly accepts that the ideological battle of the **Civil**

War was not worth fighting. Much modern history tends to follows this revisionist line, linking Greek events to the rise and fall of its fractured revenue, as in the work of Serafeim Maximos (1895–1962), a prolific journalist and sociological commentator, who examined Greece's economic weakness.

Further Reading

Gardikas, Katerina. "Greek Historical Periodicals Related to Modern Greek History." *Modern Greek Society* 5, 2 (May 1978): 22–29.

Havelock, Eric A. *The Literate Revolution in Greece and Its Cultural Consequences.* Princeton, NJ: Princeton University Press, 1982.

Macrakis, L. and N. P. Diamandouros, eds. *New Trends in Modern Greek Historiography.* Hanover: Modern Greek Studies Association, 1982.

Topping, Peter. "Greek Historical Writing on the Period, 1453–1914." *Journal of Modern History* 33 (1961): 157–173.

HOLOCAUST. See JEWS AND GREEK LITERATURE

HOMER Homer is the supposed eighth- or seventh-century B.C. author of two **epic** poems in several thousand lines, the *Iliad* and *Odyssey,* one on the war at Troy, the other on a hero's difficult return from that war. Long after their composition, these two texts were each divided into 24 books, matching the number of letters in the Greek alphabet. Smyrna, Chios, Colophon, Ithaca, Pylos, Argos, and Athens all then claimed the honor of being Homer's birthplace. Dio Chrysostom already referred in the first century to Homer as being "first, middle and last for every youth, man and veteran."

In the Byzantine period, children had to learn long passages from Homer by heart because he was thought to be an example of fine style and moral sentences. Indeed, the thirteenth-century Greek version of *The Trojan War* runs to over 11,000 lines, approaching the great length of Homer's own poems. **Dimitrios Chalkokondylis** (1423–1511) was the first scholar to print the *Iliad.* N. Loukanis, an eclectic scholar and champion fencer from Zakynthos (seventeenth century), made a version of the *Iliad* in unrhyming eight-syllable lines. His distinguished successor, **I. Polylás,** made a translation of Homer's *Odyssey* into the **demotic** (1875–1881). Polylás also produced a version of book 7 of the *Iliad* for the **Parnassós** society (1890); two more books of the *Iliad* were published in his lifetime, and other versions were found among his papers at his death.

In the modern age, poets like **Seferis** grapple with the Homeric archetypes: ". . . so much life, / Joined the abyss / All for an empty tunic, all for a Helen." Seferis playfully follows Euripides in suggesting that Helen never went to Troy, so the whole of the *Iliad* might be in vain: "Paris lay with a shadow as though it were a solid form. / We killed each other over Helen ten long years." All Greek writers take up the Homeric theme of transience: "A day will come when sacred Troy shall perish, / And Priam and his people shall be slain" (*Iliad,* book 6, vv. 448–449). In *Iliad,* book 17, vv. 426–440, Achilles' horses, Balius and Xanthus, lower their heads to the ground and weep. In the *Alexander Romance* and *Erotokritos,* a horse grieves over its master's death. Not being immortal, like the horses in Homer, it dies of grief. A phrase in Homer can be enough to create an obsession. Thus a reference in *Iliad* (book 2, v. 560) mentions certain lords who held "Hermione and Asine." This inspires the grandeur of "The King of As-iné" by **Seferis**: "Do then such things still exist? That is, the movement of face, the shape or affection / Of people" (1938–1940). **Elytis** talks of his own writing as "my poor house on the sandy shores of Homer." Andreas Mothonios asks, in a poem to Cephalonia (1948): "Who will bring you water, / And help you plant your story, / When your youngest deck-hand / Makes despairing circles in the sky over Vancouver?" Of course, the an-swer is "Odysseus."

See also HERMONIAKOS; PALLIS

Further Reading

Merchant, Paul. "Children of Homer: The Epic Strain in Modern Greek Literature." In *Aspects of the Epic,* edited by T. Win-nifrith, P. Murray, and K. W. Gransden, 92–108. New York: St. Martin's Press, 1983.

Notopoulos, James. "Homer and Cretan He-roic Poetry: A Study in Comparative Oral Poetry." *American Journal of Philology* 73, no. 3 (1952): 225–250.

Ricks, David. *The Shade of Homer: A Study in Modern Greek Poetry.* Cambridge: Cam-bridge University Press, 1989: 119–158.

HOMILY In Byzantine Greece, the homily dealt with the current religious festival and its particular significance. Some homilies offered teaching (διδασ-καλία) on the virtues of a given saint. Others formed part of a discourse called *homiletics* (ὁμιλητική). The etymologi-cal meaning *company* (ὁμιλία) had al-ready given way to that of *preaching* (κήρυγμα). Within a congregation, the preacher offered a homily on a sacred text, creating a spiritual dialogue with the listeners, who could then try to interpret the Gospel for themselves. Homilies were educational and provided the only explanation heard by the common peo-ple. Canon 19 of the council *in Trullo*

called on bishops to give homilies daily. Themes included the fate of the deceased, liturgy, monastic life, morality, scripture, saints, or doctrine.

The homilies of John Chrysostom of Antioch (c. 344–407), Patriarch of Con-stantinople from 398 to 404, were the fa-vorite reading of the early Byzantine world. Other famous composers of hom-ilies were Cyril of Alexandra, Germanos of Constantinople, Makarios Chrysoke-falos, **Photius,** and Theofanis Kerameús. St. Basil Bishop of Caesarea (c. 330–379) wrote nine homilies on the world's creation (*Hexaemeron*). His "Homily to Youth" was influential in determining the later Christian reacceptance of the pagan past. Handbooks called *homiliaries* (ed-ited anthologies of sermons by the pa-tristic writers) were used by medieval preachers to sift out suitable homilies for liturgical festivals.

Makarios Patmios (1650–1737), a strong spokesman for the use of the **de-motic** so that uneducated people might have access to religious knowledge, left over 2,000 sermons, composed in a homespun, accessible language.

Further Reading

Nock, A. D. *Conversions: The Old and the New in Religion from Alexander the Great to Augustine of Hippo.* Oxford: Oxford University Press, 1961.

Ware, Timothy. *The Orthodox Church,* 2nd ed. London and New York: Penguin, 1993.

HOMOSEXUALITY In the medieval period, the relationship of *adelphopoiia* ("adoption of a brother") included the possibility of same-sex familial relation-ships that somehow permitted passionate physical contact. Explicit homoeroticism was always frowned on by the church. Dion Smythe points out that the term often used in late Byzantine canon writers for homosexuality was "man-madness." Greece now has various gay papers, which come and go, but not as a result of any official censorship. Over the last century, a number of homosexual writers have taken up a self-declared camp posture. The best known of all Greece's homosexual writers is **Kavafis,** who writes with camp egoism and aesthetic longing about young men's looks and their pagan, fugitive liaisons. As a young man in Constantinople, Kavafis supposedly found time to meet men at night by flitting between his mother's house and a relative's lodgings because each thought he was sleeping at the other's. In a notebook entry for 13 December 1902, Kavafis observes: "I do not know whether perversion gives strength, sometimes I think it does. But it is certain that it is a source of splendor." He was followed by the figures of **N. Lapathiotis,** D. Christianopoulos, and **Kostas Tachtsís** (1927–1988), who traveled and lived all over the world, known for his Epicurean pose and his provocative attitude. Dinos Christianopoulos (b. 1931) is a leading poet of the **Thessaloniki** school and his 1996 poems show echoes of Baudelaire and Kavafis. Christianopoulos's work displays a candid, postmodern homoeroticism, which M. Raizis detects in the poem "Persecuted": "I love you, brothers, like the leftists; / We and they are always persecuted: / They for bread, and we for our body."

Further Reading

Alexiou, Margaret. "Cavafy's 'Dangerous' Drugs: Poetry, Eros, and the Dissemination of Images." in *The Text and Its Margins: Post-Structuralist Approaches to Twentieth-Century Greek Literature,* edited by Margaret Alexiou and V. Lambropoulos, 157–196. New York: Pella, 1985.

Boswell, John. *Marriage of Likeness: Same-Sex Unions in Pre-Modern Europe.* London: HarperCollins, 1995.

Christianopoulos, Dinos. *Poems,* trans. Nicholas Kostís. Athens: Odysseas, 1996; reviewed by M. Raizis in *WLT* 71, no. 3 (summer 1997): 629.

Jusdanis, Gregory. *The Poetics of Cavafy: Textuality, Eroticism, History.* Princeton, NJ: Princeton University Press, 1987.

HONOR Courtship and love are controlled in Greek folklore by the community and family's need to uphold honor and *filotimia* ("esteem"). Up until the 1930s, many fictional plots turn on the theme of a girl's chastity (τιμή), compromised even if she is seen talking with a young man on her way to draw water at the village well. This presumption of patriarchal stewardship continues in some narrative up to the present day. Thus in Kostas Arkoudeas's *Mind You Don't Turn to Stone* (Athens: Nea Synora, 1996), the female protagonist expresses the anguish of countless women who see life slipping away, with no prospect of adventure or change. In the story "Village Life," by **Theotokis,** a farmer takes revenge on the daughter of a wealthy family, who refused his son's hand in **marriage.** He notes that the girl likes another man. He arranges for this couple to be shamed after an all-night tryst in her family's country hut, and they are then unable to marry (to redeem her honor), because they had been baptized by the same godfather. The paramount consideration for unmarried girls is honor and for married women perceived fidelity. Konstantinos Chatzopoulos (1868–1920) in his short story "Tasso" (1910) dedicated to **Psycharis,** delineates a young heroine, beautiful but poor, who falls in love with a local doctor, who is from a rich family. The doctor narrates the way the relationship is choked by family and custom. In Achilleas Kyriakidis's *Music* (Athens: Ypsilon, 1995), the hero has all the inhabitants of the village killed for the sake of his image of a girl. In Tzimis Panousis's *Girl Hunt* (Athens: Opera, 1996), the hero dare not speak to the 18-year-old girl next door, so he takes pictures of her unposed body in hundreds of telelens photo shots from intrusive viewpoints, removing her honor metaphorically. Subterfuge and science replace honor eventually, for in Stella Karamolegkou's *Lonely Venus* (Athens: Psychogios, 1996), the heroine discovers love on the Internet. Two men answer her e-mails, and she is caught in a love triangle that the guardians of honor can no longer detect.

Further Reading

Safilios-Rothschild, Constantina. "Morality, Courtship, and Love." *Southern Folklore Quarterly* 29, 4 (1965): 279–308.

Stewart, C. "Honour and Sanctity: Two Levels of Ideology in Greece," *Social Anthropology* 11, no. 2 (1994): 205–228.

Walcot, Peter. *Greek Peasants, Ancient and Modern: A Comparison of Social and Moral Values.* New York: Barnes and Noble, 1970.

HUMANISM In the **Renaissance,** the so-called humanities (*literae humaniores*) replaced the division of schooling into *quadrivium* (music, geometry, arithmetic, astronomy) and *trivium* (rhetoric, logic, grammar). The Greek word for *humanism* is thus derived from the Italian word *umanista,* which refers to a citizen and scholar who has skill in translation and **paleography,** the accurate editing of old texts. Greek humanists took part in Catholic–Orthodox church negotiations, taught classical Greek in Italy, or translated ancient texts for noble patrons. Up to the nineteenth century, many cultural historians assumed that the Renaissance was the creation of Hellenists from Byzantium, who traveled to Italy around the time of the fall of Constantinople (1453). In fact, **Ioannis Bessarion,** Ioannis Argyropoulos, **Yemistos Plethon, Dimitris Chalkokondylis,** M. Mousouros, **Anthimos Gazís, Manuel Chrysoloras** and others, like **Leon Allatios** and **Janos Laskaris,** did play a central role in the interpretation of ancient texts. Yet there were humanists, before the Renaissance who influenced Bessarion and Plethon: men from the fourteenth century like Manuel Moschopoulos, Thomas Magister, Dimitrios Triklinios, and Maximos **Planoudis.** The Renaissance ideal of "striving for excellence and surpassing all others" went back to preclassical times to the text of **Homer** (*Iliad,* book 6, line 208). The humanists inherited the bibliophile education of Byzantine scholars, like **Photius,** John Italus, Demetrios Kydonis, **Psellus,** the great Homer commentator Archbishop Eustathios (of Thessaloniki), and Ioannis Tzetzes (c. 1110–1185), who wrote commentaries on many classical writers and on his own learned letters. These figures indirectly taught the Renaissance courts and universities of the West to read classical Latin and Greek in the original and to revere history rather than dogma. In the humanist revival that embellished the reign of Manuel I Comnenus (1143–1180), there was a fashion for using writers of the second and third century A.D. as rhetorical models, but distancing the resultant book from its prototype. Thus Psellus wrote a poem to explain legal terms, and Tzetzes wrote erudite commentaries, but in verse.

Further Reading

Kelly, L. G. *The True Interpreter: A History of Translation Theory and Practice in the West.* New York: St. Martin's Press, 1979.

Makdisi, George. *The Rise of Humanism in Classical Islam and the Christian West.* Edinburgh: Edinburgh University Press, 1990.

Setton, Kenneth M. *Europe and the Levant in the Middle Ages and the Renaissance.* London: Variorum, 1974.

HYMN; HYMNOGRAPHY Greek hymnography was originally simple and plain. It began, in the fifth century, with short poems consisting of a few **strophes** (see **Troparion**). Early hymns were a form of rhythmic ecclesiastical poetry, without classical meters. By 1830, the Greek scholar Oikonomos had demonstrated the melody underlying Greek hymns. Manuscripts containing Byzantine hymns preserve their particular musical indications (νεύματα). These markings differ from classical or medieval forms because they only show how heavy or sharp is the next tone compared with the preceding one. The main principle of rhythmic poetry is the number of syllables and the tone of the words. The syllables are counted without relation to their length and shortness. **Hiatus** (*synezesis*) is allowed without restriction. Elision is ignored. The slow recitative manner tends to lengthen syllables and make words stand apart from each other. The difference between acute and circumflex accent, unknown to the living language, is absent. The prototype strophe of early hymns is called a "hirm" (εἱρμός). The troparia have to maintain the pattern of a model strophe (both in tone and number of syllables). The most serious "hirms" were collected in a specialized booklet, called εἱρμολόγιον. One important type of rhythmic church poetry consisted of 10, 20, or more matching strophes, prefaced by a proemium of 1, or 2, shorter strophes. Another kind, canons (κανόνες) consisted of eight or nine different chants. At the end of strophes, there might be chanted a hymnal refrain (ἐφύμνιον). Hymnography contained the **acrostic**; thus if, as in Laodicea, the chanting of psalms by unknown authors was forbidden, having the writer's name in an acrostic woven into 24 or 30 lines was an advantage. Krumbacher calculated that a third of 300 distinct composers (μελῳδοί) are only known by name because of this acrostic. Obviously an acrostic cannot be perceived by the ear, whereas tone and rhyme can.

See also DOXASTIKÓN; KONTAKION

Further Reading

Barker, Andrew, ed. *Greek Musical Writings,* 2 vols. Cambridge and New York: Cambridge University Press, 1984–1989.

Strunk, Oliver. *Essays on Music in the Byzantine World.* New York: Norton, 1977.

Wellesz, Egon. *A History of Byzantine Music and Hymnography,* 2nd ed. Oxford: Clarendon Press, 1961.

HYPALLAGE Substitution, or hypallage (ὑπαλλαγή), is a **figure of speech** in which the logical relation between words is altered. Hypallage features an agreement, or syntactic modification, that unsettles the reader, as in the famous **demotic song** "About Parga," which refers to the sale of the island by the English to **Ali Pasha** in 1819 (for £156,000). The speaker evokes the islanders' past bravery, and how they must dig up and burn their ancestors' remains to avoid Turkish desecration before they all move to Kerkyra. Line 15 (of 16 lines) dramatizes the order after the historical fact: "And now disinter the valiant bones of your ancestor," where the poet means "the bones of your valiant ancestors."

HYPERBATON The stylistic device of hyperbaton literally means "stepping over" (ὑπερβατό). Two related clauses in a sentence are separated by an intrusive phrase. To interpret its meaning, we have to find the clause's continuation, as in **Kalvos** (Ode 8, strophe 11): "Surely they walk, / With arrogant, / Scornful feet over *the golden* /—Now shattered—/ *scales* of the law?" Here the epithet "golden" is separated by an intrusive phrase from its logical noun partner "scales." Emphasis is powerfully weighted in the hyperbaton sprinkled across the story "The Seaman," by Panayotis Axiotis (1840–1918), where a sailor who brought sums of money across the sea for friends is shamed for losing it in a wreck and blows his brains out with his family's rifle: "in a single poor dwelling, what a fearful contrast, *of catastrophe* reigned *the gloom*," and "the money stayed down there, in, *of the insatiate sea,* the *darkness unlit.*"

HYPERBOLE The **figure** of overstatement, hyperbole (ὑπερβολή) is used to indicate any exaggerated vocabulary, as in a phrase like "highly colored tale," or more precisely to indicate an extravagant effect by way of words, as in the demotic couplet "If the sea doesn't swell, then the rock does not foam, / If your mother doesn't bewail you, then the world doesn't cry." In the **demotic song,** hyperbole is found everywhere, almost a standard mode of expression: "Love burns through rocks and tames wild beasts, / And I have it in my heart, and it's killing me." In the play *Erofili* by **Chortatsis,** the heroine laments the murdered Panaretos with the following conventional exaggerations: "Most tasty and fragrant-smelling mouth, / Source of all virtues, kneaded with sugar, / Why don't your sweet, embroidered lips / Cry out, alas, for your slave, your Erofili?"

HYPOTAXIS Hypotaxis (ὑπόταξη) is a literary artifice in which the sentence builds up several subordinate clauses. As such, it is the direct opposite of **parataxis.** Hypotaxis may display many conjunctions, connective words, and the use of the subjunctive (seen as a stylistic marker of erudition, or **Atticism**). Kourtovik cites (1995) the novels of Nikos Kachtitsis (1926–1970), whose heroes express themselves "with the harmonious, ponderously rhythmic, long-sentenced language manner of a bygone time."

I

IAKOVIDI-PATRIKIOU, LILI (1899–1985) Iakovidi-Patrikiou became well known as a playwright: her *Fair Game* (1937) won the annual Kalokairinos **competition** for a dramatic work and was played at the K. Mousouris Theater. *Angelina* (1943) was played during the **occupation** by the Miranda Group. The play *Girls* (1938) won a prize from the Athenian Academy. *There's a Way for Everybody* took the state prize awarded by the Ministry of Education in 1963. After law studies in Athens, she married the theater designer Mikis Iakovidis. Iakovidi published some early poems in *Noumás* (1920) and soon joined its editorial board. She became a protegée of **Palamás,** publishing a monograph on his *Greetings of the Sun-Born* (1900). Later she produced a study on events surroundings Palamás's death in 1943 (40 days after his wife's death): *Kostís Palamás: The Sortie* (1964). Her verse collections are *Hours Full of Light* (1932), *Forty Songs* (1934), *Skylarks* (1940, winning a State Prize), and *Retrospection* (1957, also winning a State Prize). The volume *Earth Without Water* (1969) deals with the un-

timely death of her daughter and has parallels with Palamás's *The Grave* (Τάφος, 1898), which were meditations on the death of his son, Alkis. *Idols of the World* followed in 1973. She also published (1940) a study on the poet Karthaios.

IBSENISM *Ibsenism* is a label for human issues observed in urban, modern situations in the plays of the Norwegian writer Henrik Ibsen (1828–1906). It rests on an awareness of the harsh struggle by men to make a living within the rules of society, the inheritance of family guilt, the gulf between dream and reality in love, the freedom to marry or separate, the conflict between integrity and dishonor in business, and the contrast between the hesitant, cautious lady and the wilder, implacable, modern woman. The New Stage company put on plays by Ibsen at Athens between 1901 and 1905, and these were admired and absorbed by **Palamás,** among others. Ibsenism affected Greek writing from this time on. **Kazantazkis,** in his early play *Day Breaks* (1907), shows the effect of Ibsen's reflections on a woman's freedom of choice. When Ibsen's *The Ghosts* was put on in Athens (29 October 1894), **Gr. Xenopoulos** stood up before the performance and delivered a speech attacking the previous course of modern Greek drama. He declared that Ibsen was a better model than Byzantine historical plots or boulevard theater, and that the taste for the past had to be changed. His own first plays in the manner of the Ibsenist social question, *Third Party* and *Foster Father,* were performed in 1895. The "third party" of that play's title is not a lover, but a husband, and this spouse is shown as the obstacle against the union of his young wife with a youth who worships her. Alkis, the husband, commits suicide in front of the couple, and his ghost keeps them apart, posing an Ibsenesque problem of marriage and idealism in symbiosis. **Yannis Kambysis** (1872–1901) was another exponent of Greek "social drama," in plays like *The Farce of Life, The Secret of Marriage* (1896), and *Miss Anna Coxley* (1897).

ICON Modern Greek literature constantly refers to the "image," or "icon," of a sacred face. This is a flat painted artifact on a small rectangle of wood, used since the fifth century A.D. as a symbol of veneration and an aid to devotion. Icons depict Christ, the Virgin Mother, Saints of the Greek **Orthodox** church, or episodes from Scripture. Miraculous properties are associated with some icons, and their value seems enhanced by the intricate gold tracery that framed or covered them. The self-suppression of the painter leads to a conservative and dematerialized style, in tune with the withdrawn expressions on the obliquely impersonal features. The faces are remote and detached, seen in three-quarters profile, or gazing fixedly out of the center of the picture, not engaging with the eye of the viewer. Icons were to be venerated, but not adored. This was always a key distinction.

An "unmade-by-hand" (αχειροπο-ίητος) is an icon, or even a church, created by God rather than humans. If miraculous cures occurred in front of it, pious Greeks attributed this to the observer's faith rather than the Saviour's grace. In the middle ages, icons were classified according to the miracles that they had caused. Some icons were considered productive of miracles (θαυμα-τουργόί); some were declared "unmade by hand" (αχειροποίητοι). Monasteries were named after such icons. Icon painters took to fasting and all-night vigils before starting their work, hoping to render it miraculous. Legends about these "unmades" proliferated: it was believed that the Divine image was smeared onto a tile, scarf, towel, or shroud. Sometimes, the Virgin would imprint her own image on a surface. One icon of Mary, painted by the apostle Luke, turned into three copies of itself, then nine, and was multiplied all over the monasteries of Greece. Stories exist of icons that saved themselves during the **iconoclast** period by sailing down river and across to **Constantinople.** Others saved themselves in the fire but were blackened by flame.

Unlike the mosaic or fresco, an icon can be carried around by the traveler. It may be used as an object of devotion, like a relic, or as a subject of contemplation by the pious illiterate, who is unable to read the Gospel. The high-quality wood for the icon (beech, walnut, or oak) had to be prepared in advance of painting. The religious artist (άγιογράφος) generally left a frame of about two centimeters at the perimeter, so that his subject would emerge in relief from its flat, unpromising surface of wood. In some icons, the area to be painted was scooped out so as to sit slightly lower than the framing perimeter. The paint was not applied directly to the wood: a layer of protective gauze was laid over it. This made the icon long-lasting. A mixture of putty and glue was, in turn, applied over the gauze. This constructed surface was smoothed over with sandpaper. An outline, without shading, was sketched on. Round contours were added, and gold leaf was glued over some or all of the surface. At times, waxed colors were burned onto the wood or marble, which also made it long-lasting. The paints in Byzantine **hagiography** were chiefly ochres, mixed with egg yolk, water, or vinegar. The subject's face and limbs were rendered in dark greens or browns. The shadowing of face or body was conveyed by lighter versions of the same colors. Finally, a protective varnish was added. The icon was usually highlighted from the center of the picture. Its artistic effects lessen as they radiate outward to the wooden perimeter.

See also ICONOCLASM; ICONO-GRAPHY

ICONOCLASM From the seventh to ninth centuries, Greek literature dwindled, partly because of the great doctrinal struggle of iconoclasm. The so-called war on icons (εικονομαχία) was a movement to abolish the revering of religious images (εικονολατρία). Patriarchs were flogged or blinded; torture or execution was visited on monks who retained icons, and this led eventually to military edicts and the ransacking of monasteries or religious houses with suspect pictures. The iconoclast movement in the Empire was supported by Muslims. The Caliphs at Damascus fomented ac-tion against images among their own Christian population (680–724). A kind of excess, perhaps, had been reached in the eighth century, when a family might choose a picture rather than a human as a godfather for the baby, or when people might crush an icon and drink its powder with water as a sacred potion. The three famous defenders of images are John Damascenus (died c. 749), who composed the great work of Christian apologetics, *The Fount of Knowledge,* Germanos of Constantinople, and the monk George of Cyprus. Another anti-iconoclast is the monk Theofanis of Sygriana (died 817), who composed a celebrated *Chronography,* which was translated in the West.

Relics were thrown in the sea, the intercession of saints was denied, and churches could be decorated only with items like flowers, birds, or fruit. The persecution, apparently pushed on by army officers, began with Leo III the Isaurian (716–741) and was stepped up by his son Constantine V (741–755), to whom the monks gave the injurious epithet "name of a turd." An iconoclast Synod (753) ruled that representations of Christ must be Nestorian or Monophysite and show Him only as man, because a likeness of His Divinity is impossible to create. Therefore, the only lawful picture of Christ was the Eucharist, and it was blasphemy and idolatry to use bits of dead matter to depict the saints who abide with him. The theological solution was familiar to all parties, despite a second iconoclast campaign that began in 1814. In 787, the Seventh General Council (Nicaea, in Bithynia) had ruled that icons may receive a veneration (προσκύνησις), which is "relative," but not adoration (λατρεία). The iconoclast controversy was settled at a ceremony on 11 March 843, and from that day, images and icons were restored: the date marked a renascence of Byzantine literature (843–1025) and ushered in a wave of hymn writing. Even an emperor joined the poets in this genre. The son of Leo VI the Wise, Constantine VII Porphyrogennetos (lived 905–959), composed a series of *Exapostilaria* on the appearances of Jesus Christ after His resurrection.

ICONOGRAPHY Iconography, or the making of an **icon,** involves not so much a picture as a figurative approximation to the Divine. It invites reverence by not assuming an exact likeness (ἀπομίμησις), for the only true image of Christ is in the Eucharist **liturgy.** "Behold, the lamb of God," said John. Thus in icons he may be seen pointing his hand at a sheep, a symbol of Jesus. Another typical subject of iconography is the petition (δέησις) with St. John, Christ, and Mary. A *mandorla* ("almond") may be present. This is a curved slice of heaven at the top of the icon, where the resurrected Christ appears. The Virgin Mary lights a candle when informed by an angel of her approaching death. Many of the icon's subjects, drawn from the dodecaorton (or 12 main feasts of the church), are posed in *orans* ("praying") posture. A head nimbed by a halo represents sanctity. Artists drew a partridge as a sign of the coming of the Holy Spirit. Candles could be shown to represent the supernatural star at Christ's birth. The nativity is conveyed by a baby and litter. By the ninth century, Christ had an appearance that was described as youthful, three cubits in height, frowning, clear-eyed, long nostrils, full-haired, forgiving, soft-complexioned, black-bearded, wheat-colored in appearance, of average stature, long-fingered, pleasant-voiced, sweet-speaking, meek, peaceful, and tolerant. The chief symbols of Byzantine iconography are the lily, cross, cell, and nimbus. Its main features are the circle, dome, and rounded arch. There are three ways of depicting Christ's garments: modestly clothed while living, naked when dead, or swathed in Syrian purple in resurrected glory. The general color system of icons is related to a kind of alchemy: green and brown represented the earth and its vegetation. Blue was a sign of heaven and contemplation. Scarlet red meant strength, or the blood of the martyrs. Deep red stood for the imperial purple, or the blood of Christ. White indicated purity and the invisible presence of God. Gold meant magnificence, the light of the sun, and hence Divine energy.

ICONOSTASIS The iconostasis screen (εικονοστάσι) is a wood or marble structure that separates the nave from the altar in a Greek **Orthodox** church. Icons owned by the church were attached to this carefully wrought barrier. In some cases, the iconostasis gave access to the sanctuary by three doors: a central, or "royal," one for bishops, one on the right for deans, and the other for ordinary clergy. It acted as a powerful symbol of the division between earth and heaven.
See also RITSOS

IDEALISM   Hegel, Kant, and other German writers taught idealism. They held that the physical world might be determined or even replaced by the construct of the observing mind, and that ideas were logically prior to material objects. **Solomós** accepted this concept with relation to the pure work of art, which he saw consecrated in German idealism. His poetry became increasingly idealist throughout his career, as he concentrated on the themes of religious worship, fatherland, duty, love of humanity, and the contemplation of nature brought to an apogee of devotion. **Provelengios** (1850–1936) was another modern Greek writer who followed these precepts, picked up during his studies in Germany. **Markorás,** strongly influenced by Solomós, devoted himself, in all his poetry, to the triple ideal of fatherland, love, and nature. Idealism generates in these authors a kind of grave melancholy, which hovers at the edge of mysticism.

IMAGE; IMAGERY The feminine noun εικόνα means **icon** or "likeness." It refers to any literary device that elicits a picture, or series of pictures, of the reality being described in verse or prose. Greek critics speak of the "imagery" (εικονοπλασία) of a text, which is the total sum of its dominant images. Many an image is visual (οπτική), or auditory (ακουστική), and so appeals to two or more of the reader's senses, as in lines from *Sun the First,* by **Elytis**: "The *whitewash that bears on its back* the noontimes, / And the *cicadas, those cicadas in the ears* of the trees."

IMPERIOS AND MARGARONA The verse **romance** *Imperios and Margarona* emerged in the sixteenth century, an apparent imitation of the twelfth-century adventure *Pierre de Provence et la Belle Maguelonne.* The original Greek version is believed lost. The story known to us has 893 unrhyming **political** lines. It features the son of the Lord of Prebentza. When the prince is removed from royal nurses, aged four, his " . . . father sets him to the study of letters." Imperios studies Holy Scripture, Plato, **Aristotle,** Palamedes (sic), and **Homer,** "that excellent poet and foremost of wise men."

Like **Diyenís Akritas,** he is a skilled warrior by the age of 12. He defeats a wandering knight who challenges the local youths to joust. After a quarrel with his father, he roams various countries, protected by an amulet donated by his mother. At Naples, he falls in love with Princess Margarona. The king proclaims a tournament, and by the rules the victor can have Margarona's hand in marriage. Imperios wins, weds Margarona, and acquires the kingship. Later he desires to return to his former country. He leaves with his wife in secret. As in the romance *Velthandros and* **Chrysantza,** they are pursued, and their escort perishes. An eagle snatches Imperios's amulet. It is found, later, in the belly of a large fish by Margarona, who has founded a convent. After capture by pirates, Imperios lives for seven years in the court of the Sultan of Cairo. This saga of pan-Mediterranean vicissitudes goes back to *Pierre de Provence,* by the French cleric Bernard Trivier (1178), which has not survived. A French novel of 1453 is extant. The eighteenth-century memoirist **Dapontis** adds to the story in his *Flowers for Meditation* (Άνθη Νοητά), suggesting that Margarona founded the Monastery of Daphni (situated on the road from Athens to Eleusis): "Here love of the Lord was in charge, / And Imperios was the abbot, and by him / That monastery was inaugurated, and increased in beauty."

IMPOSSIBLE; IMPOSSIBILE (Lat.). See ADYNATON

INDEPENDENCE The single event that arouses positive and unalloyed imagery in Greek literature is the fact of Independence (ανεξαρτησία). This was initially achieved by the military defeat of the Turko-Egyptian forces in Greece

(1828). It was only confirmed after mopping-up operations, the assassination of Greece's first president (1831), and a patchy, but bloody, civil war (1833).

See also HISTORICAL NOVEL; KAPODISTRIAS; MISSOLONGHI; MONARCHY; ORLOFF REBELLION; POLYZOIDIS; WAR OF INDEPENDENCE

INTERIOR MONOLOGUE In interior monologue (εσωτερικός μονόλογος), the writer gives a telegraphic account of the thoughts that pass through the mind of a fictional character, often the protagonist. The device was introduced late to Greek fiction, mainly by **Thessaloniki** school writers. It is developed by the technique of "internal focusing," which dominates a remarkable book by Stratis Doukas (1895–1983), *Prisoner of War's Story* (1929). Here a fugitive from a column of Greek prisoners in Turkish Anatolia ponders, while narrating, his flight, his residence in caves, burglaries, and denial of identity, adding hints at future events and allusions to what in modern critics is classified as "the horror of war" (η φρίκη του πολέμου). It is rendered chiefly behind the narrator's eyelids, as an event in his mind. To authenticate this narrative manner, the hero, Nikolas Kozakoglou, is called on by the writer to sign a shorthand manuscript of events at the end.

See also ASIA MINOR DISASTER; NARRATIVE ANALYSIS

Further Reading

Kakavoulia, Maria. "Interior Monologue: Recontextualizing a Modernist Practice in Greece." In *Greek Modernism and Beyond: Essays in Honor of Peter Bien,* ed. Dimitris Tziovas, 135–49. Lanham, MD: Rowman & Littlefield, 1997.

INTERPRETATION The **Hellenistic** writers set out to interpret many phenomena that **Aristotle** was the first to observe. Aristarchus of Samothrace (c. 217–145 B.C.) invented literary criticism and may have written 800 commentaries. Dionysius the Thracian says that Aristarchus knew by heart the whole of classical tragedy. Aristophanes of Byzantium fixed the Greek alphabet and invented proofreading. Zenodotus attempted a critical edition (διόρθωσις) of the text of **Homer.** These writers began to make lists of "nine historians," "ten lyric poets," "the ten orators," "the four heroic poets," draft **epitomes** of "best books." Their outlines of drama, science, and philosophy show how the first step toward interpretation in Greek literature was selection.

INTROSPECTION Fotis Politis stated, at the start of the twentieth century, that the new Greek reading public was justified in wanting to see "a mirror *of themselves,* as in real life, in writers' works." They wanted a view into themselves, not a description of the surroundings. The reflexive pronoun "oneself" (εαυτός) is masculine in modern Greek and often followed by a pronoun in the genitive, for example, "the self of *you.*" Writers, to refer to the self, must use three or more words: "self of him," "with the self of her." Modern poets like Vafopoulos have been praised for their inspection of the inner self, where the ego conducts relations with himself or ourselves, and the Greek phrases seem to bear an added charge, suggesting "my inner me," or "our inner being." Most writers perform some measure of "introversion." In Greek, it may turn into omphaloskepsis ("navel gazing"), a word favored by polemical antimodernists.

IOANNOU, FILIPPOS (1796–1880)

The died-in-the-wool royalist Filippos Ioannou was born at Zagorá, on the island of Andros. He was for a while an aide to Admiral Miaoulis and later studied at Münich. He was appointed professor at Athens University (1839) and sustained a hard-line reverence for antiquity (*arkhaiolatría*), composing the *Philosophical Pastimes* in classical Greek and giving vent to an oddly Homeric cry against Turkish rule when translating a "bogus folk song" (D. Ricks, 1989: 42). While in Germany, he gave Greek lessons to the future spouse of Otho, and queen of Greece, Amalia. In 1842, Ioannou was elected to Parliament. He was also, for a while, director of the Royal Library. In 1862, King Otho meddled with the selection of certain ministers designed to execute a reform memorandum presented by Admiral Kanaris. The king tried to push nonentities or timeservers into portfolios, so his prerogative and the constitution might hold sway. The king's banishment led to the fall from favor of Ioannou, who had meantime risen to the Senate.

IOANNOU, YIORGOS (1927–1985)

Yiorgos Ioannou was an experimental poet and prose writer, born in Thessaloniki, who was eventually compared with James Joyce. Ioannou began his career with slender verse offerings, *Heliotropes* (1954) and *The Thousand Trees* (1963). Here brief lyric episodes are a foretaste of Ioannou's later prose production, with themes taken from the lost world of childhood and the torment of city life. A first collection of short stories, *Out of Self-Respect* (1964), was well received by critics, with its unusual mixture of self-analysis and intimate realism, set out by a first person narrator in short narrative segments. Some of the stories in his subsequent collections, *The Sarcophagus* (1971) and *The Sole Inheritance* (1974), refer to the German occupation and its effect on an adolescent who survived it. M. Meraklís criticizes Ioannou's work for always offering "personal incidents" and the "private history" of the narrator. Indeed, he traveled widely and conducted field work on **demotic songs** and folk tales, which he published with commentary or illustrations (1965, 1966, 1970). Periods spent abroad or the atmosphere of the city of his birth return as themes in *Our Blood,* Ioannou's third collection of prose. In 1978, Ioannou founded a literary journal, *The Pamphlet.* His critical work includes essays on Thessalonian popular culture. In 1982, Ioannou published *Multiple Fractures,* a personal narrative based on a stay in a hospital.

Further Reading

Germanacos, N. C. "An Interview with Three Contemporary Greek Prose Writers (May 1972): Stratis Tsirkas, Thanassis Valtinos, George Ioannou." *Boundary 2: A Journal of Postmodern Literature and Culture* 1, no. 2 (winter 1973): 266–313.

IONIAN ISLANDS The Ionian Islands (or Heptanese), home of a disproportionately large swathe of modern Greek literature, consist of Corfu (Kerkyra), Levkas, closest to the Greek mainland, Cephalonia, Zakynthos (Zante), Cythera, Ithaca, and Paxos. They were under Venetian rule from the fourteenth century to 1797. The Treaty of Campo Formio (1797) put Napoleonic forces in charge of the Heptanese, as well as the four Venetian towns on the Greek mainland: Préveza, Vonitza, Parga, and Bultrinto. **Ali Pasha,** tyrant of Ioannina, took back the latter one from the French, earning Nelson's admiration. The islands came under the British from 1815 to 1863. They were transferred to Greece by Britain as part of the wedding settlement on King George I. The seven islands were home, or birthplace, to many Renaissance-influenced and Romantic writers, who are now conventionally referred to as the **Ionian School.** The Heptanese was a hotbed of revolutionary sentiment before the **War of Independence** of 1821.

Ithaca is the mythical home of Odysseus. Of this most famous island in world literature, **Kavafis** wrote the proverbial verses: "Do not expect Ithaca to give you riches. / Ithaca has given you the wonderful journey. / Without Ithaca you would never have embarked on this journey. / Now Ithaca has nothing more to give you." For **Homer,** "wooded Zakynthos" belonged to the kingdom of the **epic** hero Odysseus. Zakynthos, in the late eighteenth century, was "a nest of singing birds." From Zakynthos, under Venetian administration, come the writers **Ugo Foscolo, Andreas Kalvos,** and **Dionysios Solomós.** From Kerkyra came the sonneteer and patriot **Mavilis.** The French poet Charles Baudelaire referred to Cythera in a couplet from *Les fleurs du mal:* "The ship rolled under a cloudless sky, / Like an angel intoxicated by dazzling sunshine." From Levkas came **Valaoritis,** who wrote his *Fotinós* (1879, publ. posthumously in 1891) to celebrate an uprising by his island's inhabitants against a medieval Frankish ruler.

Further Reading

Tziovas, Dimitris. "A Telling Absence: The Novel in the Ionian Islands." *Journal of Mediterranean Studies* 4, no. 1 (1994): 73–82.

IONIAN SCHOOL, THE The nineteenth-century Ionian School, and the **Ionian Islands** in general, play a changing role in Greek culture. The islands had a limited, local importance in literature, until the eighteenth century. Their role became national after 1820. In the sixteenth and seventeenth centuries, some lyric poetry existed alongside a didactic or hagiographical prose tradition. The works of important Ionian writers were printed in Venice. Ioannikios Kartanos, from Kerkyra, published *The Flower and Essence of the Old and New Testament* (1536). **Ilias Miniatis** (1669–1714), of Cephalonia, issued volumes of *Sermons.* Alexios Rartouros, from Kerkyra, devised a prototype of popular preaching in his *Sermons* (1560). From c. 1540 come Markos Defanaras's *Didactic Words of a Father to His Son.* Defanaras wrote a *Story of Suzanna,* in 788 rhymed **political** lines. *The Story of Tagapietra* by Iakovos Trivolis, of Kerkyra (died c. 1547), describes a noble Venetian captain who fought Muslim pirates in the Adriatic and has an Italianate eight-syllable line. Trivolis's *History of the King of Scotland and the Queen of England* is an imitation, in rhymed **political verse,** not of Boccaccio's licentious novella (*Decameron,* VII, 7), but of its reworking by an anonymous Venetian, *Historia de li doi nobilissimi amanti* (1524). Sofianós called Trivolis "full of grace and gaiety." P. D. Huet called him *miserrimus imitator* ("a wretched imitator"). Nikolaos Loukanis (of Zakynthos) produced a paraphrase translation of Homer's *Iliad* (seventeenth century).

During the nineteenth century, Italian influence in the Ionian Islands persisted, with Venice cultivating businesslike relations with an indigenous aristocracy. The emancipated Ionians contributed to the development of bilingualism, which prevailed on the islands and created Greek access to Italian culture. As late as

1851, the English authorities tried to demote the use of Italian and make Greek the official language in the Heptanese. Italian influence was countered by the absorption of Greek refugees from Morea or Crete. The islands offered periodic asylum to **Klephts,** who brought their characteristic **demotic songs.** These influences, and a Western atmosphere of free thought, contributed to the first aspirations for a national culture. The lesson of past and present events pushed the Ionian School into the avant-garde of the independence movement. Many of these writers, together with **Solomós** and **Kalvos,** form a roll call of patriots and visionaries: **Antonios Matesis** (1794–1875), **Andreas Martzokis** (1849–1923), Y. K. Romas (1796–1867), Spyridon Melissinós (1823–1888), **Antonios Manousis** (1828–1903), P. Panás (1832–1896), **Yeoryios Tertsetis** (1800–1874), **Ioulios Typaldos** (1814–1883), **Andreas Laskaratos** (1811–1901), **Iakovos Polylás** (1826–1896), **Aristotelis Valaoritis** (1824–1879), **Spyridon Zambelios** (1815–1881), **Yerasimos Markorás** (1826–1911), **Lorentsos Mavilis** (1860–1912), Yerasimos Mavroyannis (1823–1906), Stylianós Chrysomallis (1836–1918), and **Konstantinos Theotokis** (1872–1923).

IOTACISM. See PRONUNCIATION

IRONY Aristotle explains that irony is a pretense tending toward the underside of truth. The disparity between what the characters know of their situation and what is known by an opposite character, or by the reader, is called "tragic irony" (τραγική ειρωνεία). S. Doukas (1895–1983), in his novel *Prisoner of War's Story* (1929), uses this device when the Turkish farmer Hatzimemetis puts the

disguised Greek fugitive in charge of his flocks of sheep and says, "Here we had Greeks [Ρωμιούς]. With your skill, I reckon you're next to them. Now you can take their turn." Hatzimemetis does not know that the man called Bechtzet, to whom he will offer clothes, food, and a niece in marriage, is actually a Greek. The reader knows this all along, hence there is tragic irony when the fugitive actually deceives his kind employer.

ISLAM The Byzantine emperor Herakleios, after defeating Persia (627), was visited by Mohammed's envoys and saw Islam at its infancy. The prophet died in 632, Damascus fell to the Arabs in 635, Jerusalem in 637. Herakleios was defeated by an Arab army at the River Yarmuk, in 636. By 641, the Arabs held Syria and Palestine. In his last years as a theologian, Herakleios saw Islam as an "attractive new heresy." Islamic law held that a city that would not surrender to a Muslim army was fit to be plundered. In the sack of 1453, some townships of **Constantinople** were spared because they voluntarily submitted. The Muslim invaders then refrained from attacking certain Christian churches.

According to Islamic faith, the three revealed religions are Jewry, Christianity, and Islam, in that order, therefore one can convert forward, along this historical line, but not back. To do so is to commit apostasy and risk death, because the most recently revealed religion must be right. In Greek, the term is "Mohammedanism," and the Muslim religion was of little account to **Orthodox** Christians when they were under Ottoman masters. Greek post-Independence literature links it to cruelty, effeteness, and luxury. Neither Greek Islamic nor Christian practice was really understood by the other, though both religions have crucial points in common, such as veneration for holy shrines, burial of holy men, and worship of saints. Under the Turkocracy, Christians could not ring church bells, repair a church, or dress like Muslims. They could not marry a Muslim or give evidence in a law court against a Muslim. Nor could they ride a horse, carry firearms, or build a house higher than a neighboring Muslim house.

Christians were prevented from entering the Acropolis area of Athens, because it was a Muslim living quarter. The Venetians assaulted the Acropolis in 1687, because the Ottomans stored gunpowder in the Parthenon, and when the Ottomans recaptured this arsenal, they built a mosque in the shell of the classical temple. One male child in every four or five was taken from Christian families to serve as a **Janissary,** and he was immediately circumcised, for to be otherwise was considered unclean in Islam.

When Constantinople fell (1453), the scholar **Trapezuntios** (George of Trebizond) tried to persuade sultan Mehmet II the Conqueror to become Christian and maintain the imperial tradition. Trapezuntios argued that between Christianity and Islam there were no substantial dogmatic discrepancies and so the existence of a unified community was possible, allowing Greeks and Turks to coexist with equal honor. He addressed *On the Truth of the Christian Faith* to the Sultan in 1453, and later met him personally. As an envoy of Pope Nicholas V, he went to Crete and Constantinople to study political conditions (1465). His contacts with the Muslim leader were considered criminal, and he was jailed on his return.

Further Reading

Ladas, Stephen P. *The Exchange of Minorities: Bulgaria, Greece, and Turkey.* New York: Macmillan, 1932.

O'Leary, De Lacy. *How Greek Science Passed to the Arabs.* London: Routledge and Kegan Paul, 1949.

Rosenthal, Franz. *The Classical Heritage in Islam.* London: Routledge and Kegan Paul, 1975.

Walzer, Richard. *Greek into Arabic: Essays on Islamic Philosophy.* Cambridge, MA: Harvard University Press, 1962.

ISSAIA, NANA (1934–) Nana Issaia is a writer and painter who held five Panhellenic exhibitions between 1960 and 1975. She became a central figure of the 1960s and was influenced by the **surrealist** writer **M. Sachtouris.** Fatigue and self-annihilation serve as an underpinning for Issaia's bleak poetics, especially in *Meaningless Days and Nights* and *Alice in Wonderland* (both published in 1977), *The Realization of Forgetting,* and *The Tactics of Passion* (both publ. 1982); she translated Margaret Drabble's *The Waterfall* (1989), Thomas Mann's letters, T. S. Eliot's *Notes Towards the Definition of Culture* (1980), Herman Hesse's essays, and Sylvia Plath's poetry (1974). The American poet also had a strong effect on Issaia's early verse.

ISTANBUL. See CONSTANTINOPLE

ITHOGRAFÍA The staple material of the genre novel is the recording of manners, or *ithografía* (ἠθογραφία). This type of narrative, prominent in the late nineteenth-century novel, consists of a moral sketch and some description of a traditional or rustic environment. R. Beaton highlights the controversial nature of the word and the critical debate that has subsequently surrounded it (1994: 72), suggesting that the category "short folkloric realism" fits only a restricted num-

ber of works by **Papadiamantis, Vizyinós, Karkavitsas, Palamás** (*Death of
the Brave Young Man,* 1891), and **Kondylakis,** in *The Big-Foot* (1892). He observes that the unifying factor in prose
fiction published in Greece between 1880
and 1900 was the "detailed depiction of
a small, more or less contemporary, traditional community in its physical setting." An earlier example of this writing
is the story "Karaiskakis's Adoptive Son"
(by the nineteenth-century writer N. An-
tonopolous), which shows a girl stopped
at night by an old man who inquires why
she is rushing from Arta to Athens, and
why she is cast down by sorrow. Garou-

phaliá ("Carnation") says that her beloved is an honorable man, who stole but
one kiss from her in three meetings, as
she went to draw water from the village
fountain (where else could a Greek girl
meet a young man?). This man stopped
a fight over her reputation at a village festival. They fall in love at sight; he will
not abduct her to hasten marriage in the
rural way, for he must go to Athens to
expel the Turk. Now she tells the old man
she dreamt that two birds wounded an eagle, and she woke to find a cat had pushed
his neckerchief into the fire. So she must
hurry away to learn if the gallant lad is
dead or alive.

J

JANISSARIES Each Greek living under Turkish rule might be enlisted as a janissary. As a member of the so-called foreign *millet,* he was a *rayah* (ραγιάς). This Turkish word (signifying "cattle") meant any bondsman. A leading citizen or priest was obliged to offer his best-looking son as a janissary, a trainee of the Sultan's élite military corps. The Janissary system (Γιανιτσαρισμός) lasted until 1676 and stripped one in five male children from Greek families. Dimitrios Kambouroglou published the play *Kidnapping of Boys* (Athens, 1896) to propose a historical view of the conscription of Greek boys under **Ottoman** rule. There is a disturbing account of child kidnapping in *The Mavrolykos Family* (1948) by **Petsalis.** Families with only a single son are not required to hand him over, so Nikolakis Matapás and his wife decide to kill one of their two sons in order to save the other from recruitment. The Pasha decides to select the surviving one anyway. Nikolakis draws a dagger, a guard cuts off his hand, and another kills his second son.

In Epirus, a popular **demotic song** railed against this kidnapping of boys (παιδομάζωμα): "Be damned, O Emperor, thrice be damned / For the evil you have done and the evil you do. / You catch and shackle the old and the archpriests / So you can take children as janissaries." In the Cretan tales of **Kondylakis** (1916; 1919), a villager buys pigs and lets them harass his Muslim neighbors. Warned that this provocation may lead to his death, he retorts: "the age of janissaries is over." Kondylakis's narrator observes that villages like Modi are being emptied of Turks. Some of those left behind have taken to wine or sausages. "The feudal pasha no longer existed and the age of janissaries had passed so far back that it risked oblivion."

Recruiting officials, generally corrupt, came through a town or village. They checked parish records and submitted a list (duplicated to prevent substitutions) to the Aga of Janissaries in Constantinople. The Greek boys were destined for Anatolia or Roumeli, far from their home region, to deter absconding. Parents had to pay for the janissary's red cap and coat, sewn by the Jewish community in **Thes-**

saloniki. In 1826, Sultan Mahmut II decided to put an end to the power of the janissary corps. On 14 June, the janissaries revolted. They were besieged in their barracks and quickly demobilized (17 June 1826).

JEWS AND GREEK LITERATURE

Greece has always had a significant Jewish population. The Byzantine hymnwriter Romanos the Melodist (sixth century) was Jewish, and the Christian program of Romanos is a blend of Syrian poetics and Greek devotion. The culture and worship of Israel was never proscribed in Greece, except briefly under the Nazis. Bishop Theoklitos Bibos (1832–1903) published the *Elements of Hebrew Gammar* (1866) and in his theology course at Athens University conducted Old Testament studies in Hebrew. The persecution or extermination of Jews is not a prominent theme in Greek literature. The word in contemporary writing for *holocaust* does not refer to the anti-Semitic campaign. The Greek word ὁλοκαύτωμα means a "slaughter," such as the German treatment of the town population of Kalavryta on 13 December 1943. At 2:34 (the Church clock still stands at this hour and minute), German troops killed 1,436 men over the age of 15. A memorial garden bears the signature "Holocaust of 1943." Greek stories from the historical Holocaust (1939–1945) do not show much Greek awareness of the fate of their Jews. An exception to this indifference is the Rabbi Pessah from Volos, who used contacts with the Greek **resistance** to shelter 752 Greek Jews so that when a German column came to Volos to round up Jews for deportation, they only collected 130 individuals. A seventeenth-century narrative poem, *Story of Markas the Jewish Girl,* was popular reading among uneducated people during the years of Turkish rule and rudimentary education. Published at Venice in 1668, it was reprinted several times. It tells an implicitly anti-Semitic story: Dimos, a Christian baker, falls in love with the Jewish girl, kidnaps her, and brings her to Christian salvation in the neighboring principality of Vlachia. Karatzás, the prince in person, baptizes her and marries her to Dimos. The dastardly pursuit conducted by her Jewish family is foiled. The poem (by an unknown writer) is in 810 rhyming 15-syllable lines.

JOHN VI KANTAKOUZENÓS (1292–1383)

John VI was proclaimed Emperor by an army in Thrace. He ruled from 1341 to 1355, needing Bulgarian and Turkish aid to become coregent of the teenaged John V Palaeologus (1332–1391). This was followed (1347) by further civil war, in which the Turks made gains throughout Thrace. John VI placed himself as chief protector of the **Hesychasts** when their opponents, the Zealots, took Thessaloniki (1346). In 1349, John VI intervened to end this self-made state, but was forced to abdicate (1355) after John Palaeologus entered Constantinople. He retired as the monk Joasaph to **Mount Athos** and later Mistra, where he devoted himself to theological essays, a commentary on Aristotle's *Ethics,* and his own *Histories,* four volumes covering the period 1320 to 1356, providing an account of the turbulent fourteenth-century events.

JOURNALISM, LITERARY, NINETEENTH CENTURY

Greek journalism started as a vehicle of patriotic consciousness on foreign soil wherever there were communities of Greek businessmen who wanted to read newspapers about Hellenism: among such papers were *The Hellenic Telegraph* (1812–1829), *The Scholar Hermes* (see **Gazís**), and *Ephimeris,* published by the Poulios brothers in Vienna (from 31 December 1790). The latter counted **Rigas Velestinlís** as a subscriber. The first newspaper produced in Greece (at Kalamata; from 1 August 1821), *The Clarion,* was used by Dimitrios Ypsilantis for revolutionary purposes in the Mani. Its ambitious proclamation says that it will cost 50 piastres (γρόσια) per day and will not be printed on Sundays or feast days. It quickly folded because the general editor, Th. Farmakidis, refused to accept censorship (by Ypsilantis). Greece's second newspaper, *The Hellenic Mirror,* was founded in Hydra (from October 1821) and ran two years, reporting on naval clashes in the **uprising.** By 1836, there were at least 10 Greek newspapers in circulation: *Hope, Athens, Savior, Progress, The Spectator, Iris, The Klepht, The Courier, Greece Reborn,* and *The People's Friend.* In the period from 1833 to 1843, the number of daily papers issued in Athens and all other Greek cities rose to 62. In 1861, there were 41 dailies, 26 at Athens and 15 in the provinces. In 1870, there were 68 daily newspapers in Greece and 16 in areas subject to Turkey or foreign countries.

Parnassus was the main literary periodical produced at Athens between 1877 and 1895, and had a long print run. *Bomb* was a fortnightly satirical paper. It started in Athens on 29 May 1849 and closed with its issue of 2 August in the same year. *Euterpe,* published by Grigorios Kambouroglous, came out fortnightly from 1848 to 1855. This was Greece's first literary periodical. It boasted a new

item, K. Pop's feature column on intellectual developments in Greece or the West (see **Money**). Among its regular contributors were **A. R. Rangavís** (a cofounder), Nikolaos Dragoumis, and Konstantinos Paparrigopoulos (see **History**). *Pandora* a fortnightly run by **Dragoumis,** Paparrigopoulos, and Rangavís, gained a circulation of a thousand, was produced at Athens, and later became monthly. It printed 24 supplements in a print run from April 1850 to April 1872. It featured Dumas and other French novelists in translations by Dragoumis. Equally influential was *The National Library,* which ran from 1865 to 1873. **Theodoros Orfanidis** put out a satirical periodical called *The Archer* (1840–1841). The author **D. Koromilás** (1850–1898), inheriting his father's publishing company, ran *The Daily,* Greece's first newspaper with telegraph reports, from 1 October 1873. Its success forced its competitors to go daily. It counted six future Prime Ministers and eleven Ministers among its early contributor talent. *Asmodaeos,* the literary and humorous weekly, ran from 1875 to 1885. The politico-satirical paper *Light* (1860–1878) was edited by the humorous writer Sofoklis Karoudis, who was a target of **censorship,** hounded by authorities, often in hiding, firing invective from his retreats (see **Prison**). Ioannis Ververis began on *Light* and then progressed to his own paper, *Rogue.*

Most versatile was **Sourís** (1852–1919), who brought out his weekly, *Romios,* in verse for 36 years and used it to comment on every facet of contemporary life (see ***Don't Get Lost***, and its successor, *Acropolis*). Other journals that flourished in this period include *Chrysallis* (1863–1867), *The Week* (1884–1891), and *Estía* (1876–1895). In 1888, the writer **A. Papadiamantis** (1851–1911) was appointed to Athens' first daily, *Ephimeris* (see previously), in charge of serials and translations. In 1892, Papadiamantis changed papers to join the staff of *Acropolis,* which was Athens' second daily (established 1884). This newspaper printed many of his stories on feast days, as Papadiamantis specialized in potboiler fiction for Christmas, Epiphany, and Easter. In 1884, *Acropolis* started the serialization of his *The Gypsy Girl.* His historical novel *Merchants of Nations* was published in *Don't Get Lost,* under his pen name, Boem (1882). Yeoryios Molfetas (1871–1916) edited the satirical paper *Weed* at Cephalonia (1892–1916). Angelos Kantounis edited the politico-satirical paper *Gouzelis* at Zakynthos in the same period. Other weekly or fortnightly magazines became daily newspapers, like *Kairoi, Scrip,* and *The Town,* aiming at the huge, potential readership of Athens and Piraeus, a population of 55,000 (1870), which had expanded to 141,000 by 1889. A singular position was occupied by *The Moulding of the Young.* Started in 1879 by Nikos P. Papadopoulos as a monthly, the magazine aimed to provide pleasant, improving material for children. Until 1893, the chief editor was A. P. Kourtidis (using the **pseudonym** Aimilios Himarmenos). He was followed by **Xenopoulos,** using the familiar pseudonym Phaedo. *The Moulding of the Young* proved popular and went to fortnightly, then weekly issues. Many of its contributors were established prose writers and poets: **Vizyinós, Drosinis, Palamás,** Themos Anninos, **D. Kambouroglous,** and **Sourís.**

JOURNALISM, LITERARY, TWENTIETH CENTURY Greek journalism in the last century was an indigenous, locally mushrooming enterprise. **Aposto-**

los **Melachrinós** (1883–1952) produced the magazine *Life* in Constantinople. In Athens, he published the literary magazine *The Circle* (monthly 1931–1935). For his journalism, he used the pen name "Klimis Porphyrogennetos." *Thesaurus* is the title of an illustrated weekly (Athens, from 1938) that was directed by I. Papayeoryiou (b. 1904), who later gained a seat in Parliament, and put out the journals *Spectator, Atlantis,* and *Fancy,* and the newspapers *Free Speech* and *The Athenian.* Other journals cultivated a utilitarian stance, like *Renaissance,* which was founded in September 1926 at Athens, directed by **D. Glinós,** and written entirely in the **demotic,** as the monthly organ of the **Educational Society.** Equally utilitarian was *Greek,* founded in 1928 by the Association for the Distribution of Useful Books, with K. Amantos and S. Kougeas as editors (see **Drosinis**). The increased intellectual activity of the 1930s can be gauged from the plethora of periodicals with avant-garde programs in this decade: *New Letters* (1935–1940, 1944–1945) and *The Circle* (see earlier), which first introduced the poetry of T. S. Eliot to Greeks in its issue of July 1933, antedating the influential translation by **Seferis** of *The Waste Land* (1936), and *The Third Eye* (1935–1937), *Idea* (founded 1933), *Young Pioneers* (1931–1936), and *Today* (1933–1934). The periodical *Exercise Book* came out from 1945 to 1947, was edited by A. Xydis, and featured the work of younger poets from the 1930s: **N. Valaoritis, Miltos Sachtouris,** Eleni Vakalo. *Greek* was issued after 1937 by the Society for Historical Research and then suspended because of the war. It was taken up again (1954) by the Society for Macedonian Studies, with two university professors as editors, L. Politis and S. Kyriakidis. Renos Apostilidis edited the influential *New Greek* (1952–1967), and there was another bunching of literary journals in the 1960s: *Periods* (1963–1967), which balanced modernism and brash experiment, *Testimonies* (1964–1967), *Art Review* (1954–1967), and *Anew* (from 1964), which responded to a new counterculture made possible by "the democratic liberalism of George Papandreou's government" (E. Arseniou, 1997).

Anew exaggerated the current mode for small journals: a coalition of friends in a bar, rather than an editorial board. It ran alternative material: anecdotes, games, the recitation of Christakis, mythical parties at Simos the Existentialist's, and promoted the revelations of A. Shinas, who suggested a writing machine called "narrative apparatus AS38f," echoing the Beat generation's initiation into creative patterns, and radical icons, such as the inventor "Bennett" in Panayotis Koutroumbousis and the author as shaman in Alexandros Pop. *Thracian Annals* (from 1960) was conceived as a general periodical by Stefanos Ioannidis in Xanthi and came out trimonthly until issue number 28, when it was halted by the inception of the **Colonels' Junta.** It reopened in 1972, with the partial lifting of **censorship,** but became a large-format annual, going from volume 29 to 46 before it closed in 1986, addressing topics outside the Thracian definition of its title.

See also TSOKOPOULOS

K

KAIRI, EVANTHIA (1799–1866) The intellectual and poet Evanthia Kairi is the author of *Nikeratos,* a play based on a hero of the defense and fall of **Missolonghi,** incarnated in the warrior Christos Kapsalis. Printed in **Nafplion** (1826), it is the first play published by a Greek woman. It was staged at Ermoupolis, but out of modesty, Kairi declined to appear. *Nikeratos* was plagiarized in 1870 by another female writer, Elpida Kyriakou, in a pirated version. Evanthia Kairi translated French texts on the woman question, many sent to her by **Koraís** from Paris (see **Epistolography**). She first wrote to him at the age of 15. She corresponded with European **Philhellenes,** appealing to women's groups abroad on behalf of the Hellenic cause. Kairi also wrote a short history of Greece. She refused many offers of marriage, some from princes, declaring that she was "betrothed to Christ." Her brother, Theofilos Kairis (1784–1853) died in **prison** after being held for using his teaching to promote liberal ideas.

See also KALLIGÁS

Further Reading

Patsalidis, Savas. "Greek Women Dramatists: The Road to Emancipation." *JMGS* 14, no. 1 (1996): 85–102.

KAKEMFATON Anything that has an indecent meaning, deliberate or unintentional, is *kakemfaton* (κακέμφατον). The term is used in rhetoric or criticism to denote fortuitous **bawdy,** in which a chance group of syllables can produce indecency.

KALAMOGDARTIS, ILIAS G. (?1820–1848) I. Kalamogdartis was born in Patras and died in Cairo at dates that are still uncertain. Dimarás gives his life as 1817–1849. The *Great Encyclopedia of Modern Greek Literature* opts for 1817–1848. After school he joined the public service. Because of consumption, he went to Egypt. The story is told that he asked King Otho's personal forgiveness after pursuing antimonarchist intrigue (between 1845 and 1848). He was retired from the Ministry of Foreign Affairs by Prime Minister Kolettis. In 1838, he published a translation of *Le ultime lettere di Jacopo Ortis* by **Foscolo,** and this was attributed to his uncle. He also contributed poems to periodicals, among them *Parnassus* (1868), and anthologies. Kalamogdartis was one of the first poets to use **demotic.** Some of his poems were set to music and sung in Greece up to the end of the nineteenth century.

KALLIGÁS, PAVLOS (1814–1896)

The versatile Kalligás was a historian, lawyer, novelist, and member of Parliament. His father (from Cephalonia) with his mother (of Smyrnian origin) fled Turkish rule and settled in Trieste, where Kalligás started his education. He continued his studies at Geneva, Munich, and Berlin and in 1837 received a doctorate from Heidelberg. A year later, he was appointed Professor in Natural Law at Athens University, but dismissed in 1845 by the Kolettis government. In 1851–1854 he was an assistant district attorney. Over the late 1850s and the 1860s, Kalligás contributed to the drafting of the Greek civil code of law. He failed to gain a parliamentary seat in the elections of 1865, but became a deputy in 1879. In 1882, he was appointed Minister of Economic Affairs. Later, twice, he became president of the Chamber and was administrator of the National Bank from 1885 to his death. He wrote legal and historical essays, including *A Critique of the Gnostic System of Theofilos Kairis,* in the fortnightly *Pandora* (1851). In *Thanos Vlekas* (1855), Kalligás set his hand to what is now considered one of the pioneering (modern) Greek novels. His topic was the young Greek kingdom, shorn of the Romantic melodrama that stultified nineteenth-century pictures of the **War of Independence** and its aftermath. In *Thanos Vlekas,* sharecroppers struggle against their old adversaries, the "big landowners" (τσιφλικάδες). The peasants are sapped by inequity: they cannot buy their land. The mortgage, which must be paid in kind, is oppressive. They are beaten by a bailiff, who uses a troop of armed attendants to impose the required tribute. Their animals are counted at their watering holes. The town notable, who pretends to help them, demands a large sum of money to advance a fictitious lawsuit. The book's protagonist, Thanos, tries to blunt the effect of his elder brother's depredations. This antihero, Tasos, is his mother's favorite, but he turns out to be an unscrupulous landgrabber, acting worse than a traditional brigand. The persecuted Thanos remains magnanimous, supported only by his betrothed bride and her protective father. The main characters of the novel, Thanos and Eufrosyne, are clearly delineated. Its rural setting, with the inequality embedded in Greece under King Otho, is described in strong folkloric tones. Twentieth-century commentators (for example, Beaton, 1994: 333) pick out its dated language. This puts the same spoken idiom in different characters' mouths and is, for Kordatos (1962: 274), "hyper-purist, with many archaic sayings."

Further Reading

Doulis, Thomas. "Pavlos Kalligas and *Thanos Vlekas:* The Lack of Common Sense among the Greeks." *JMGS* 17, no. 1 (May 1999): 85–106.

Kalligás, Pavlos. Θάνος Βλέκας, [Thanos Vlekas] ed. and intro. by Stelios Phokos. Athens: Odysseus, 1989.

KALLIMACHOS AND CHRYSORRHOE (c. 1310–1340)

The best-known Greek **romance** is *The Story of Kalli-*

machos and Chrysorrhoe. It tells, in 2,605 **political** lines, of a king's son who releases a princess from her guardian ogre, but is prevented by a rival from marrying her immediately. Kallimachos is one of three sons, and each tries to show exceptional prowess in order to become the king's sole heir. Kallimachos enters a dragon's castle and sees a girl hung by her hair in a beautiful chamber, packed with sumptuous foods. This fulsome, Byzantine scenario elicits a conventional **ekphrasis**. The dragon turns up, and the girl advises the hero to hide in a silver jar. The dragon feeds and tortures the girl. He is slain by the hero when he falls into a deep sleep. Another young prince falls in love with the girl. This youth raises an army and acquires a golden apple with certain magic powers in order to win her.

Kallimachos is slain, and revived, by the apple. He tracks down Chrysorrhoe and places his personal ring on a tree in the palace gardens, which she is allowed to visit. One day she wanders toward the tree, and a scene of recognition (see **Anagnorisi**) is facilitated: "She holds back the foliage and spots the little ring. / She grasps the ring, and wears it, and feels an immense shock." Chrysorrhoe gains freedom for herself and her newly recovered Kallimachos by addressing a set speech to the king, posing a symbolic question: Who should be allowed to enjoy the fruits of a cultivated vineyard? This chivalric romance with love interest has Anatolian elements (magic apples, helping brothers, the mortal spell) spliced onto Byzantine forms (rhetorical discourse, court etiquette). It displays few Frankish or chivalric motifs. It is hard to determine the author. Tradition holds that Andronikos Palaeologus (son of Konstantinos, nephew of Michael VIII, first cousin of Andronikos II) composed it.

Further Reading

Perry, B. E. *The Ancient Romances: A Literary Historical Account of Their Origins.* Berkeley: University of California Press, 1967.

Tsolakis, E. Th. "Κριτικὲς παρατηρήσεις στὸ κείμενο τοῦ μυθιστορήματος Καλλίμαχος καὶ Χρυσορρόη" [Critical Observations on the Text of the Romance *Kallimachos and Chrysorrhoe*]. *Greek* 25 (1972): 414–419.

KALLIPOLITIS, MAXIMOS (seventeenth century) Kallipolitis helped **Patriarch Loukaris** produce one of the major translations of the age (1638), rendering the *New Testament* "into simple idiom and common tongue, so that anyone may hear Holy Scripture." The church at Constantinople tolerated the translation of the *Gospels* into Slavic languages, but rejected the same for demotic Greek because Greeks could follow the original. This view is stated by A. Helladios, who studied at Oxford and rejected the idea that contemporary Greeks were ignorant, in his *Present State of the Greek Church: Why Modern Greeks Should Refuse to Accept Editions of the New Testament Made in Barbaro-Greek Idiom* (1714). Kallipolitis was suspected of devising his translation on behalf of the Dutch for Protestant missions. The **Orthodox Church** opposed any modification whatsoever of Scripture, as it had been revealed and therefore received in one sole form.

KALOSGOUROS, YEORYIOS (1853–1902) The *Great Encyclopedia of Greece* (1926–1934) and other sources give his birth as 1849. He was born on Kerkyra. When young, he met **I. Polylás** (custodian of the **Solomós** manuscripts, translator, and pro-demotic scholar). Polylás exerted a great influence on Kalosgouros, recommending that he be sent to supervise beneficiaries of the Montesenigeios bequest in Switzerland. Kalosgouros used his time to study languages and work on translations: Aeschylus's *Prometheus Bound,* the Italian poems of Solomós, and Foscolo's *Dei sepolcri.* In 1891, he published his *Critical Observations on the Translation of "Hamlet" by I. Polylás.* He also published an essay on the **language question,** adopting a rational, normative stance, *On the Nation's Language and National History* (1889). He influenced the prosody of subsequent verse production around the turn of the century, with his development of the 13-syllable line. After Kalosgouros's death, more of his translations came out in periodicals, among them V. Alfieri's play *Saul* and Dante's *Hell.* He published an interesting review in *Estía* (1893) of Palamás's volume of poems, *Eyes of My Soul.*

KALVOS, ANDREAS (1792–1869) The great **patriot** Andreas Kalvos was revealed to the literary world, 20 years after his death, by **K. Palamás.** Kalvos may be the only modern Greek writer of whom we do not possess a picture. His literary production is slight but his influence on how we assess nineteenth-century Greek culture is considerable. Born at Zakynthos, Kalvos was taken away as a child aged 10 by his adventurous father. He was never again to see his mother, an impoverished aristocrat. His third Ode, "To Death," was a later recollection of her. Father and two sons went to Livorno, on the west Italian coast. Here there was a prosperous Greek colony that included the Zosimas brothers, well-off merchants devoted to the Greek cause. Nostalgia for his childhood home, and the distance from his mother, colored Kalvos's adolescence, but his meeting with **Ugo Foscolo** in Florence, at the age of 20, changed the course of his life. Kalvos published 10 patriotic odes called *Lyra* (Geneva, 1824).

A further set of 10 odes was later published in Paris (1826). His poetic voice then fell silent. Like other intellectuals from the Venetian islands (see **Heptanese**), Kalvos was more at ease writing in Italian than in Greek. He had a standard Italian education, and the first language in which he wrote was Italian. From a linguistic viewpoint, Kalvos was an exception among the **Ionian School** of writers. He was neither a **vulgarizer** nor an innovator. His language is a composite idiom, which admits living, dialectal forms alongside archaic words. Next to nouns from popular Greek, Kalvos ranges adjectives drawn from **Homer** and Pindar. His poetic diction is determined by necessities of rhythm and the demands of his subject matter, which stretches from the world of classical antiquity to Kalvos's contemporary surroundings. He was affected by the trauma of the **War of Independence,** which he observed close at hand. He took no part in the fighting nor was he welcomed by the patriots.

In his odes, Kalvos evokes the sacrifice and abnegation of the Greek people, the suffering of the freedom fighters, the grandeur of their actions, and their sense of justice. He has an elevated conception of the poet's role. The writer guarantees immortality to the heroes of a cause by celebrating their exploits. Kalvos was for a while Foscolo's companion and private secretary. Tutored or bullied by Foscolo, Kalvos adopted the older writer's devotion to classical Greek, his liberal politics, and his distrust of the "clash of sceptres."

Kalvos set his hand to two neoclassical Greek tragedies: *Danaides* (about the semidivine daughters of Danaus) and *Theramenes* (based on one of the Thirty Tyrants of Athens, who was killed by Kritias). He followed Foscolo, first to Switzerland (June 1816) and later to London (September 1816). Here the two poets are known to have quarreled, and they had a parting of the ways. In May 1819, Kalvos married an English woman, Marie Thérèse Thomas. She died some months later. Kalvos published a special method for the teaching of Italian to British pupils, *Italian Lessons in Four Parts,* which included his translation of a volume of Robertson's *History of the Reign of Emperor Charles V* and extracts from Alfieri, Ariosto, Petrarch, and Tasso. His theory that modern Greek and ancient Greek were basically the same language was expressed in lectures reported in the London *Times* of 9 June 1818, and in *The Gentleman's Magazine.* Kalvos thought that modern Greek, though a partial debasement of ancient Greek, was pronounced the same as the classical tongue. In 1820, he retraced his steps to Florence and joined a conspiratorial society. Expelled from Florence in 1821, he again took asylum in Switzerland. By 1826, he was ready to join the Greek struggle against the Turks. He settled in Corfu (Kerkyra), where he lived for the next 26 years. He taught philosophy and Italian at the Ionian Academy (founded 1824), counting the poet **Andreas Laskaratos** among his pupils. He became misanthropic. His publications were a thing of the past. He carried on feuds with literary people. He took to dressing in black and had his furniture painted black. The lit-

erary circle gathered round **Dionysios Solomós** took no interest in Kalvos. He returned to England in 1852. Here he married a woman 20 years his younger, Charlotte Augusta Wadams, who ran a school for girls. He went on teaching and published some theological tracts.

In his verse prosody, Kalvos strove to avoid what he called the monotony of the Cretan poems. He split the popular verse form of 15 syllables into two hemistychs, a classical practice that recalls the Aeolian manner, that is, an iambic meter ($\breve{}\,-$) interspersed with anapests ($\breve{}\,\breve{}\,-$). This invented **meter** was based, he said, on "vowel contractions and stresses." It was designed to "imitate the movements of the soul and express everything that senses and spirit come up against in the physical or imaginary universe." His lyric odes display a uniform structure. One strophe of four lines, each composed of seven syllables (akin to the Italian *settenario*), is followed by one line consisting of five syllables (the Italian *quinario*). He provided numerical charts for the elucidation of his verse. He also used Homeric images to give it a patriotic, Hellenic, quality. In rendering a passage from book III of the *Iliad,* Kalvos comes close (as Ricks observes) to reviving the vocabulary of **Homer.** The Homeric "Achaeans breathing anger in silence" become, in Kalvos, "the Achaeans with silence breathing great power." The same line in both poets begins with the masculine definite article, in the plural, followed by the particle "δ'." In the last of the 1824 odes, Kalvos refers, by using the title "The Ocean," to the Homeric father of all Gods, and this confers an especial eloquence on its references to a sea battle with the Turks. **Odysseas Elytis** said that Kalvos was able to capture any lyric possibility in a flash. The writer

Stratis Tsirkas quotes Kalvos's "Rain still suspended / While the winds of the universe / Slumber" and mentions the sharpness of **imagery** drawn from such day-to-day observations as "The sun, moved in a circle, / Encloses me, like a spider, / With light and with death, / Unendingly," and his unexpected analogies: "Free, unbridled, the horses canter / Through the vineyard, and on their back / The whistle of the winds / Rides alone."

Pappageotes picks out as Kalvos's masterpiece "To the Sacred Battalion," an ode to the 300 students of the Greek communities in Romania, who formed a regiment modeled on the Sacred Battalion of classical Thebes and were later killed almost to the man in the **War of Independence.** Kalvos's *Odes* were hailed by Népomucène, Lemercier, Firmin, Didot, *Le Constitutionnel,* and the *Revue encyclopédique* as a revival of Greek literature and a hymn to liberty. So fundamental questions remain about Kalvos: his odes to Canaris, Botzaris, **Byron** ("the British Muse"), and Psara were taken up by postrevolutionary France. But why did their author stop writing? Did Kalvos complete all his work precociously, like a prototype of Rimbaud (1854–1891) or Lautréamont (1846–1870)? Did the severance from his mother make him self-destructive? Was his lugubrious romanticism too far removed from the **brigands** who built Greek nationalism? Perhaps the disciples of Solomós were right: Kalvos described the present by clothing it in the past. His poetry disappeared from view, unquoted by the very revolution that it tried to celebrate, from the outside looking in. He was only rediscovered around 1888.

Further Reading

Andreiomenos, George. "The Reception of Kalvos by Modern Greek Criticism: Some Introductory Remarks." *Balkan Studies* 32, no. 2 (1991): 209–215.

Kalvos, Andreas. *Odes,* trans. by George Dandoulakis. Nottingham: Shoestring Press, 1998.

KAMBANELLIS, IAKOVOS (1922–)

Born on Naxos, Kambanellis came to be considered the father of post–World War II Greek theater and an innovator of its mid-twentieth-century forms. He was held prisoner by the Germans (1943–1945) at the Mauthausen concentration camp. His first play produced on stage was *Dance on the Ears of Grain* (1950), followed by *The Seventh Day of Creation, Courtyard of Miracles, The Age of the Night, Fairy Tale without Name* (see **Delta**), *Long Live Aspasia, Odysseus Come Home, The Colony of the Punished, Our Big Circus, The Enemy People, Faces for Violin and Orchestra, The Four Legs of the Table,* and other plays. Kambanellis made his mark on Greek cinema as a screenwriter. He joined hands with young, avant-garde directors to cooperate on projects like *Stella,* by Michael Cacoyannis (who made *Zorba the Greek* in 1964, starring Anthony Quinn). He did the screenplay for the black-and-white film *The Dragon,* by Nikos Koundouros (1956), in which an inoffensive clerk is mistaken for a serial killer called "Dragon," and for *The River,* by Koundoros. Kambanellis directed one movie treatment of his own, in black and white, *The Canon and the Nightingale,* which is a collage of three separate stories, fusing **surrealist** elements and black humor, as when a Greek barks at the German officer billeted on his house, and the officer barks back. Kambanellis wrote *Mauthausen* (1963) in prose. This was to be an authentic story: "I relived it in the hours during which I looked back at old

notes and made an effort to recollect it."
He teamed up as a songwriter with the
composers Manos Chadzidakis, Mikis
Theodorakis, and Stavros Charhakos,
raising the prestige of Greek pop song.
See also GATSOS

Further Reading

Kambanelis, Jacovos. "Courtyard of Miracles," trans. by I. Murdoch. *Thespis* nos.
2–3 (1965): 127–151.

Kambanelis, Jacovos. "He and His Pants,"
"The Woman and the Wrong Man," trans.
by G. Valamvanos and K. MacKinnon. *The
Charioteer* no. 26 (1984): 9–15; 17–35.

Kambanelis, Jacovos. *Tale Without Title*,
trans. by Stratos E. Constantinidis. Box
Hill: Elikia Books, 1989.

Kambanellis, Jakovos. *Mauthausen*, trans. by
Gail Holst-Warhaft. Athens: Kedros, 1995.

KAMBÁS, NIKOLAOS (1857–1932)

Verses (1880) was the sole volume of poetry published by this fleetingly influential figure, in the watershed year of 1880
when the so-called **New School** of Athenian poets seemed to form itself in a
small, influential group. Later **Palamás**
would say: "Friend Kambás and I opened
the way; third came Drosinis." Kambás
went on to Egypt, where he became a
judge in the court of appeals. He wrote
verse for scattered periodicals there, but
grumbled that his poetic career was over.
Trypanis includes Kambás in his history
of Greek poetry (1981: 652) on the
grounds that it was chiefly through him
that **Palamás** and **Drosinis** first learned
of literary developments in France.

KAMBOUROGLOUS, DIMITRIOS

(1852–1942) Aged 20, Kambouroglous
sent his play, *Good and Evil Conscience*,
to the **Voutsynas poetry competition,**
attacking the chief enemies of his father

Grigorios Kambouroglous (1809–1868),
who had battled to found a National Theater (1857) and started the **journals** *Euterpe* and *Week*. 1873 was the first year
in which verse composed in the **Demotic**
won the **Voutsynas prize**. The winner
was D. Kambouroglous, with a volume
entitled *The Voice of My Heart*. Dimarás
draws attention to the vigorous, earthy,
anti-Romantic tone of its first composition: "I only love two things on earth, my
friend: love and candy. It is for these that
I live. It is for these that I die of envy. All
the rest is nothing to me!" Kambouroglous found success with two of his plays
submitted to the **Lassaneios drama
competition,** and he also won the Retsi-
naios Prize of Piraeus (1896) with his
historical play *Kidnapping of Boys*. In his
career as a journalist, he became so involved with Athenian antiquities that
people called him "scribe of Athens,"
and fellow citizens referred to him as Little Mr. Dimitrios. In 1927, he was elected
to the Academy and in 1934 became its
president. A special issue of *Néa Estía*
(no. 141: 1932) is devoted to Kambouroglous.

Further Reading

Iacovides, Anna-Olivia. *Le personnage du
Turc dans la littérature grecque du XIXe
siècle*. Montpellier: Mimeographs, 1978.

KAMBYSIS, YANNIS (1872–1901)

The writer Yannis Kambysis studied law
at Athens and (like many intellectuals of
the period) went to Germany for postgraduate studies. He was influenced by
German and northern European writers
(Strindberg, Hauptmann) and became a
versatile playwright, poet, and short
story writer. His play, *The Mother's Ring*
(1898), has always been popular. The
composer Kalomiris took the theme for

his **opera** from the Kambysis text. He founded the journal *Dionysos* with K. Chatzopoulos and other colleagues. He saw two collections of verse into print, *The Shadow of Wisdom* and *The Book of Fragments* (1900).

KANELLOPOULOS, PANAYOTIS (1902–1986) Panayotis Kanellopoulos is yet another writer and Prime Minister (1945 and April 1967). He was also Minister of National Defense and other portfolios, in governments after the **Civil War.** He was born at Patras, studied in Athens and Germany, published his first poem in *Noumás* at age 16, and joined K. Tsatsos and I. N. Theodorakopoulos to found the Archive for Philosophy and Theory of the Sciences (1927), an educational institute promoting alternatives to **Communist** ideology. From 1927 to 1936, he established himself as one of the founders of Greek sociology. The dictator **Metaxás** kept Kanellopoulos in internal exile (1937–1940) at Kythnos, in the Cyclades, Thasos, south of mainland Xanthi (Thrace), and Karistos, on Euboea. At these outposts, he prepared his first book of poetry. Because he was in exile, this had to come out under a **pseudonym** (Aimos Aurelios): *Simple Sounds Set in Lines* (1939). He also composed *History of the European Mind* (2 vols., 1941–1947). At Karistos, Kanellopoulos wrote a five-act play, *Oliver Cromwell.* He was in Egypt (from 1942), with Tsouderos's cabinet in exile, as Vice-President and Minister of Defense. In 1951, he published *Twentieth Century;* in 1953, *Christianity and Our Age: From History to Eternity;* in 1956, *The End of Zarathustra.* Kanellopoulos became a driving force in the Popular Party (1958). From 1959, he was organizer of the National Radical Union, serving as Vice-

President in a Karamanlis cabinet. In 1964, he became leader of the Radical Union. Once Paraskevopoulos lost his mandate in 1967 (when the Radical Union left his parliamentary coalition), Kanellopoulos, the Radical Union leader, became Prime Minister. Amid countrywide turbulence, Kanellopoulos called national elections in May, but was upstaged by the *coup d'état* of the **Colonels** (21 April 1967). He compiled a three-volume history of Greece, *From Marathon to Pydna* (1963), and composed the **historical novel** *Born in 1402,* a swan song of **Byzantium** (1958).

KANELLOS, STEFANOS (1792–1823) Kanellos came from Constantinople and, after his schooling, was a schoolteacher at Bucharest and a passionate adherent of the **Uprising.** Kanellos wrote verse in which he appealed directly to sword, warrior, or rifle, urging Greeks to fall on the Turks as one, not to expect help from the West, nor to await the mythical support of **Russia:** "The hour has come, the trumpet cries: / Our blood leaps up and boils with joy! / The bang of the gun, the swish of the sword / Begins to thunder abroad, / And as I slaughter the Turks, /—Hail Greece!—I cry." Two of Kanellos's marching songs were used by the conspirators of the **Friendly Society.**

KAPODISTRIAS, IOANNIS (1776–1831) Count Kapodistrias, the first President of Greece (murdered in 1831), came from the island of Kerkyra of a noble family that originated in the Dalmatian city of Capodistria. For a long period, he was in the service of Tsar Alexander I; he was Russian Ambassador to Switzerland, where he helped organize the separate cantons into a federal system.

He was a representative at the Councils of Vienna and Paris, where he sponsored the autonomy of the **Ionian Islands** as a British protectorate. In 1815 he became the Russian Foreign Minister. In 1827, the Troezene constituent assembly of rebel Greece appointed him governor (κυβερνήτης) of the new nation. He arrived in 1828 at Nafplion and went on to Aegina, where he took power from 21 January 1828. He was faced by a chaotic, anarchic administration. There was no national revenue, as no taxes had been collected. He founded schools, a College of Education, an agricultural college at Tiryns, and a National Bank. His first, provisional government had 27 members, but he tended to confer authority on a privy council that included some **Independence** heroes (like Th. **Kolokotronis,** N. Botzaris, and Nasos Fotomaras). This led to the anger of other Independence warlords, such as the brothers Konstantinos and Yeoryios Mavromichalis (feudal chiefs in the Peloponnese), who assassinated Kapodistrias as a tyrant at Nafplion on 27 September 1831.

As an author, Kapodistrias left letters and wrote *Mémoires biographiques sur le président de la Grèce le comte Jean Capodistrias* in French (Paris: Papadopoulos-Breton, 2 vols., 1837–1838). They were published by A. Vretos Papadopoulos (1800–1876), the first systematic bibliographer of modern Greece and the cataloguer of the Heptanesian administrator Lord Guildford's library (on Kerkyra). Kapodistrias's *Memoirs* were translated into Greek by Mikhail Laskaris. **Ioannis Zambelios** published a play entitled *Ioannis Kapodistrias* around 1843, whereas in the last century both **N. Kazantzakis** and Theofilos Frankopoulos wrote theatrical works entitled *Kapodistrias* (1946, 1959).

Further Reading

Mendelssohn-Bartholdy, Karl. *Graf Johann Kapodistrias*. Berlin: Mittler, 1864.

KARAGHIOZIS Under Turkish rule, the only theater allowed in Greece was the Karaghiozis shadow show. Karaghiozis theater used cardboard puppets to represent Greek or Turkish stereotypes. It was adapted from Turkish models, but has faint echoes from rebels in the comedies of Aristophanes (Dikaiopolis, Xanthias, Strepsiades). There were still about 60 puppeteers operating across Greece in 1936. The word *Karagöz* signifies *Dark Eyes* in Turkish. It was supposedly invented by a certain Sheikh Kishteri in the medieval period. In Turkish theater, he is a stock character who misinterprets Hacirat, the braggart, and his wife Lachampiyya. After the **War of Independence,** upper-class Greek audiences inclined to Western values, so Karaghiozis became a pursuit of rural or lower-class Greeks, who maintained a residual **Muslim** culture. The Turkish *Karagöz* had been performed at night, in coffeehouses during the month of Ramadan. It was assimilated into Greek popular literature, while preserving its Anatolian satire and bawdy humor (Myrsiades, 1986). The Karaghiozis became a sort of moral spokesman, traveling the country attended by musicians, satisfying the popular appetite for word games. Each character might have his own idiom, from **Katharevousa** to a "childish lisp" (K. Van Dyck, 1998:14). There is the good-natured Sultan from Asia Minor. There is the braggart **Heptanesian** islander and petty aristocrat in high hat and frock coat, Sior Dionysios, pilloried for flirting with the French. Barbayorgos ("Uncle George") is a rustic from Roumeli. Dervenaias is the personal adjutant of the Vizier. Like Karaghiozis's fire-eater Uncle George (or Yorgaros), the bodyguard gives Karaghiozos regular beatings. Veli-Gekas is an apostate, Islamicized hit man for **Ali Pasha.** The source of his character is the homonymous Albanian from Skodra, a warlord sent against the legendary **Klepht** Katsantonis (1770–1807), only to be killed by him in a duel.

The standard recurring plot in Karaghiozis is straightforward: a Turkish deputy in Greece needs a clever person in town to carry out some task. He asks the collaborator Hatziavatis to get the person. Hatziavatis is a comic incarnation of the **Phanariot** citizen. He says, with the duplicity of experience and ingratiation: "I revere Ye, my Lord; earth, ground may I be, for Ye to tread on; may God cut back my days so Your years become longer." He runs into Karaghiozis, who passes himself off as the right man for the job. The protagonist dons the relevant costume and hoodwinks the stock characters. His actions are unethical, and his fraud is exposed. He nags his kids to speak correctly, but they answer with cheeky puns. His rebellion fails, and he accepts the penalty. He clearly represents Greek subservience to the Turks, as exemplified in **kidnapping** (παιδομάζωμα), but his arms are artificially lengthened so he can scratch his back or his head, and his hands are mobile enough to explore other people's pockets. For a brief moment, he reverses the Greek's subordinate status and seems to expropriate Turkish power. But he is also resigned to their surrounding tyranny, like the Cappadocian Christians. He says in one play: "So what can they do? They'll beat me, and get tired, and catch a cold, and drop dead." The puppet questions the Greek principle of social precedence, by being an unreliable underling who alters the hierarchy of prestige with his native cunning (πονηρία). Typical plays are Kostas Manos's *The Hero Katsantonis,* Markos Xanthos's *The Seven Beasts and Karaghiozis,* or *A Little of Everything* by Andonis Mollas (1871–1948), pseudonym of A. Papoulias, one of the shadow theater greats, who wrote, set, and printed many comedies in the tradition: *The Man-Eaters, The Cardplayer, Robbery at the Palace,* and *Arson at the Prisons.*

The shadow theater has room for post-1960 adaptation, like *Karaghiozis as James Bond* or *Karaghiozis as Astronaut.* These subjects show the effect of comic strips and television on the bedrock of **folklore.** Great Karaghiozis puppeteers (listed by R. Gudas) include Yannis Roulias, Dimitris Sardounis, Sotiris Spatharis, and Andreas Kyriazopoulos. The Anatolian *Karagöz* had a sparse diffusion in Greece during the eighteenth century because of resistance from the **Orthodox Church.** Its spread may also have slowed down, after Independence, because anti-Ottoman attitudes were cultivated by Greek nationalists. It filtered down from northern Greece, where most Turks were settled. Performances in **Nafplion** and Athens (1841, 1852) show how far south the influence of *Karagöz* had reached by midcentury. In the 1890s, there was a fully Hellenized Karaghiozis shadow theater at Patras. Male dominance is not questioned in Karaghiozis plots, either by the Turkish puppeteers or by their more liberal Greek counterparts. So Karaghiozis theater tends to deploy stereotyped females: the hag, the flirt, the docile wife, the shrew, the gossip, the nag, or the devoted daughter. During the German **occupation** of Greece in World War II, traveling Karaghiozis puppeteers were part of an anti-Nazi information network, exchanging tickets for food and playing beside the agit-prop performances of **resistance** fighters, like Vasilis Rotas (1889–1977). Rotas was the author of *All about Karaghiozis* (1955) and ran a troupe with the EPON resistance brigade in the mountains. He founded the "People's Theater" (1930–1936) and translated **Shakespeare.** Such activists spread left-wing propaganda to the villages of Greece. Some Karaghiozis plays have a literary source (Myrsiades, 1975). Mollas's *Karaghiozis and the Beautiful Gypsy* (1925) recalls Cervantes's *Don Quixote.* Markos Xanthos's *Karaghiozis as Woodcutter* (1924) is reminiscent of Molière's *Le Médecin malgré lui.* In *The Seven Beasts and Karaghiozis,* the Turkish deputy in Greece dies and his mother assumes his job. She announces that whoever kills seven marauding beasts can marry her granddaughter and later become the next deputy. Karaghiozis takes up the challenge, but needs the help of Alexander the Great to overcome the animals. Upon their demise, the granddaughter falls in love with Alexander. The Turkish woman's intrigue causes the girl's death and Alexander the Great's suicide. Poor Karaghiozis is left to pick up the pieces. He manages to kill the grandmother with a penknife, but must bury the hero and his own sweetheart.

Further Reading

Danforth, Loring. "Humour and Status Reversal in Greek Shadow Theatre." *BMGS* 2 (1976): 99–111.

Myrsiades, Linda. "Legend in the Theater: Alexander the Great and the Karaghiozis Text." *Educational Theater Journal* 27, no. 3 (1975): 387–394.

KARAPANOU, MARGARITA (1946–)

M. Karapanou is the daughter of **Margarita Limberaki** Karapanou. Her sketch "My Dog Louka," in the journal *The Word* (1999), is an impressive example of the best modern Greek women's writing: terse, ironic, and universal in scope. A woman who "adores" and who is "adored" by her pet dog brings her home from a clinic to die. They lie down together. She remembers her crazy Dad's death, with a Scottish model in the car, not the gross woman he was living with. She recalls her aunt, who bequeathed, then wanted back, two valuable French paintings, "Landscape with Cattle at Pasture," and "Landscape with Cattle Not at Pasture, but About to Be." The dog kisses her in the ear, dies, and is replaced (after its funeral) by a "soppy hound" who could be son-of-Louka. She gives it half the previous dog's name: *Lou.*

M. Karapanou's first novel, *Kassandra and the Wolf,* made a sharp impression on critics (1976). Coming on the heels of the **Colonels' Junta,** the book appeared to make use of an implied, metaphorical **censorship.** The heroine stutters her name "Ka-ka-ka-ka-s-s-s-sandra," masking (but creating) the infantile word for excrement. Kassandra cuts a doll to shape: "I laid her in her box, after first cutting off her feet and hands, so she might fit. Later, I cut off the head, to make her weigh less. Now I can love her lots." In a documentary format, 56 separate sections and 115 pages of text, a voracious and precocious six-year-old hovers on the edge of morbid sexuality. The episodes, unlinked, have the unsophisticated headings one would expect from an elementary school **reader:** "The Lesson," "Plasticine," "A Picnic Outing." Karapanou compresses vignettes about the child's absorption with violence and the half-perceived role of suicide or butcher played by relatives, servants, even little playmates in Athens. Granny suggests abnegation to our heroine, reminding this child that well-bred Greek women do not understand the act of love. Faní, the kitchen maid, tells her to rejoice that a woman's open legs admit "hurricanes into the abdomen." K. Friar compares the child to a hypothetical Cassandra of Greek **myth** who, instead of being devoured by the wolf, falls behind the sofa for sexual congress with it. The heroine enjoys hanging around the local slaughterhouse: her story reveals the murderous nature of the adults who constructed it. If the child tortures a pet kitten, her text deconstructs the wolfish mask behind which bourgeois Greeks put passion to a lingering death.

Further Reading

Clapp, Susannah. "Nursery Notions." *TLS* 17 (Nov. 1978): 1347.

Friar, Kimon. "Margarita Karapanou." *WLT* 51, no. 2 (spring 1977): 317.

Karapanou, Margarita. *Kassandra and the Wolf,* trans. by N. C. Germanacos. New York: Harcourt Brace Jovanovich, 1976.

KARASOUTSAS, IOANNIS (1824–1873) Karasoutsas came from Smyrna and died by his own hand on the day (20 March 1873) when another short-lived romantic writer, **D. Paparrigopoulos,** was receiving his funeral in Athens. In 1839, at Hermoupolis, Karasoutsas brought out his youthful poms, *Lyre.* A year later came another collection, *The Suckling Muse.* In 1841, he published an *Ode to the Insurrectionists of Crete* and then an *Elegy to the Zosimas Brothers, Greece's Benefactors* (1842). From 1846 was another collection of verse, *Morning Melodies.* The year 1848 saw an *Ode to Charles Albert* and in 1849 came Karasoutsas's *Poetic Selection.* In 1850, he became a French teacher at **Nafplion** and

in 1852 was transferred to Athens. He composed school texts, including a French grammar, a French reader, and a dictionary of French synonyms. Karasoutsas submitted verse to the poetry **competitions** on three occasions in the 1850s without winning. In 1856, he composed the poem "Response to the Poet Lamartine, Author of a Turkish History." The quintessentially Romantic French writer, Alphonse de Lamartine (1790–1869), had published *Histoire de la Turquie* (1854–1855) and other historical works to pay debts. Karasoutsas was a friend of the blind writer **Ilias Tantalidis** and wrote compassionate lines on his blindness, to which Tantalidis responded in the same verse meter. Karasoutsas translated Lamartine's *Le Lac* (1872), Harriet Beecher Stowe's *Uncle Tom's Cabin* (1854), and V. Hugo's *Notre Dame* (1867).

KARELLI, ZOÉ (1901–1998; pseudonym of Chrysoulas Pentziki Argyriadou) The poet, critic, translator, and dramatist known as Zoé Karelli was born in Thessaloniki. Chrysoulas Pentziki (her real name) was the older sister of another influential writer from the Macedonian group, namely Nikos Gavriil Pentzikis (born 1908). At the age of 17, after private tutoring in music and languages, she was married. She was widowed in 1953; her married name was Argyriadou. Karelli's poetry, often Christian and mystical, always enigmatic, was at first associated with that of Yorgos Themelis (1900–1976) and more particularly with the journal *The Snail,* which ran from 1945 to 1948 in Thessaloniki and continued the regional and avant-garde impulses of the periodical *Macedonian Days,* which had started up in 1932. Zoé Karelli published her first collection,

Travel Route, in 1940, and other volumes followed at regular intervals: *Season of Death* (1948); *The Imagining of Time* (1949); *Of Isolation and Arrogance* (1951); *Copper Engravings and Sacred Icons* (1952); *The Ship, Kassandra and Other Poems,* and *Tales from the Garden* (all 1955); *Contrasts* (1957); and *The Mirror of Midnight* (1958). She translated two plays by T. S. Eliot, as well as the *Autobiography of Benjamin Franklin.* Karelli began, in the 1950s and 1960s, to compose verse dramas of her own, seeking a less introspective form to express her metaphysical strivings. Among her theater works are *Suppliants* (1962), *Simonis, Byzantine Prince* (1965), and *Orestes* (1971). The two latter plays were performed by the State Theater of Northern Greece. She wrote essays on several European modernist writers (Samuel Beckett, Luigi Pirandello, Franz Kafka, James Joyce, and Albert Camus) and on American and Russian authors. Her complete poetry was published in two volumes and won first prize in the State Poetry awards of 1974. In 1982, Zoé Karelli became the first woman writer invited to sit in the Academy of Athens.

KARKAVITSAS, ANDREAS (1866–1922)

The short story writer and novelist Andreas Karkavitsas, born in Lechaená, became an army doctor and took to writing genre tales in the *ithografía* manner, based on rural life. He published a collection of stories (1892) that had been written when he was only a teenager for small periodicals. His masterpiece, *The Beggar,* came out in 1897 and is a work of powerful, if bleak, social realism. Karkavitsas's contribution to the genre is to take a conventionally unpopular and negative character, like the Boeotian boor of classical literature, and show how he

works as a professional beggar, tricking other poor or reduced inhabitants in a region that, historically, had only just been incorporated in Greece. W. Wyatt, the book's translator, noted how the force of nature is used as an integral feature in its pages, harnessed by the writer as an instrument to assist in the merging of farm animal, human character, and locality. A public building set on fire or a river in full flood acquires a symbolic, almost Homeric, validity in Karkavitsas's scheme of things. There is also a strong Romantic tendency to paint lyrical effusions of nature, such as the quivering rays of dawn, the wine-blue slopes of mountains "with their ashen tufts of cotton" and the "miasmic exhalations of the marshes." *The Archaeologist* (1904) was his last work. His abrupt silence was perhaps caused by the political disaster of 1897 and the ensuing "bankruptcy of the nation" (Jina Politi). Defending his book, Karkavitsas wrote to a colleague that the time had not yet come, in their "godforsaken nation," for "untrammeled singing. We must also instruct."

The Archaeologist enshrines the lesson of contemporary territorial claims and losses, augmented by threats from Bulgaria and Turkey, in the bourgeois destiny of the Evmorfopoulos family and the survival or dismemberment of their estate lands. Their firstborn son, Aristodimos, represents the classical rights of inheritance and the power of written learning. Aristodimos stands for *arkhaiolatría* ("worship of antiquity"), whereas the second-born son, Dimitrakis, negotiates with the marginalized power of the spoken word. In the tension between these key figures from the Evmorfopoulos saga, we meet an **allegory** of the conflict between **Katharevousa** and the **demotic.** As in G. Verga's *I Malav-*

oglia (1881, a contemporary model of Italian realism), the tough belief system of a once-prosperous family trying to resurrect its fortunes is expressed by many a **proverb.** In Karkavitsas's *The Archaeologist,* two proverbs express the pro-, or anti-, Katharevousa stance: "An illiterate man is rough wood" as against "Letters are fetters" (quoted in Politi, 1988: 49). A special number of the literary periodical *Greek Creation* (no. 82: 1 July 1951) deals with Karkavitsas. He was a member of the **educational** society and composed well-regarded school **readers.**

Further Reading

Politi, Jina. "The Tongue and the Pen: A Reading of Karkavítsas' *O Arheológos.*" In *The Greek Novel: A.D. 1–1985,* edited by Roderick Beaton, 43–53. London: Croom Helm, 1988.

Wyatt, William F., Jr. "Nature and Point of View in A. Karkavítsas' *The Beggar.*" In *The Greek Novel: A.D. 1–1985,* edited by Roderick Beaton, Roderick, 32–41. London: Croom Helm, 1988.

KARVOUNIS, NIKOS (1880–1947) Nikos Karvounis was cofounder of the poetry journal *Hegeso.* As educator, journalist, and "strenuous opponent of the totalitarianisms of the inter-War period" (K. Bastiás), Karvounis became an eclectic theosophist who, in 1933, joined the Greek Communist Party. All his life, he tried to blend his wide, early reading with a syncretistic Christianity. He had a hiker's **love of nature** (the Black Sea, the Carpathians, landscapes of his Romanian childhood) and took his colleagues on long walks into the suburbs at night or on holidays in the snow. He worked for papers like *Scrip, Estía*, and *Republic.* His column in the paper *Morning,* for the period 1931–1934, helped to orientate the patriotic and sociological thinking of the

decade (Y. Valetas). Karvounis was a volunteer in the **Balkan Wars** and sent stories from the military front. One of his articles was a firsthand report on the poet **Mavilis,** who died in his arms. Karvounis was a Garibaldine corps volunteer in the Asia Minor campaign and fought in the **resistance** during the **occupation** (1940–1944).

Further Reading

Featherstone, Kevin and Dimitrios K. Katsoudas, eds. *Political Change in Greece: Before and After the Colonels.* London: Croom Helm, 1987.

Karvounis, N. Ὁ πόλεμος Ἑλλάδος καὶ Βουλγαρίας [The Graeco-Bulgarian War]. Athens: Phexi, 1914.

KARYOTAKIS, KOSTAS (1896–1928) Kostas Karyotakis, the dominant poet of his period, was a sensitive translator of the French Parnassian poets; was a connoisseur of Verlaine, Baudelaire, Laforgue, and Hugo; and suddenly shot himself at age 33. He set a fashion for melancholy and sardonic verse that became known as **Karyotakism.** When only 23, Karyotakis published *The Pain of Man and Things* (1919). In 1921 came his second volume, *Nepenthe.* Some writers (F. Skouras, A. Papadimas) consider him seriously neurotic; he attempted to sue the journal *Noumás* for not publicizing his first volume and wanted to restrain them from publishing any ironic reviews. He advertised an adversary's apartment for sale, causing the same trouble and confusion "as the villain who leaves ox entrails at a neighbour's door." **Nirvanas** thought his court case a sign of "immoral farce." Among early twentieth-century writers, his was the most ambivalent influence on the **Generation of the Thirties.** Karyotakis went against the **demotic** current that was in the air. He forged a personal language. This was much copied, after his swan song *Elegies and Satires* (1927), which adopted verbal acrobatics as readily as archaism: "What divine will governs us, / What tragic destiny holds the thread, / Of the empty days which we currently live out, / As if moved by an ancient, fatal habit?" Perhaps his disposition was exacerbated by turbulence in his emotional life. In 1913 he fell in love with one Anna Skordili, who two years later married another man, though they kept up a relationship for years.

In 1922, Karyotakis became involved with the writer **Maria Polydouri** (1902–1929), who was herself considered unstable. He affected to regard women as "a fallen idol." His pessimism is usually inflected by irony: "Thought and poetry equal / An unsatisfactory burden." His lyricism is always unquestioned: "The sea will caress us like a dream, / Will carry us to lands which do not exist. / The sea breezes will be like cupids in our hair, / And the breath of sea-weed will make us fragrant" (from "Sleep"). Another kind of poem, despairing and satirical, is "Mihalios" ("Young Mike"), which tells of an ignorant, good-natured lad from the village, "taken off" to be a soldier. Away goes this Karyotakist anti-hero, falling in beside his mates Maro and Panayotis. In the first six lines, Mike cannot learn to slope arms, and he asks the Corporal to allow him to go home. In the next strophe of six lines, Mike is lying in a hospital. He stares at the ceiling; he is speechless; but he might be pleading to go home. In the third six-line strophe he is dead; his mates see him off at the cemetery; but his foot is left sticking out of the ground. These three poised, balanced stanzas construct a curt indictment of war. In "Prev-

eza," which Ricks calls "one of the most quoted poems of the century," the reader watches a deadpan summation of all that is provincial. The title conjures up a backwater in eastern Epirus, south of Ioannina. It happens to be the town where Karyotakis killed himself. The text displays an insistent, lilting **anaphora** on the word *Death,* which stands at the beginning of several lines and sentences. It is shot through with a pungent awareness of the gallows, in the tiny mediocrity of life. It anticipates the odor wafting off moribund men in modern texts, like Vafopoulos's poem "Taste of Death." In Karyotakis's "Préveza," mortality is measured against insignificant, black, pecking birds, or the town policeman checking a disputed weight, or identified with futile street names (boasting the date of battles), or the brass band on Sunday, a trifling sum of cash in a bank book, the flowers on a balcony, a teacher reading his newspaper, the prefect coming in by ferry: "If only," mutters the last of these six symmetrical quatrains, "one of those men would fall dead out of disgust."

Further Reading

Agras, T., Petros Charis, and Kleon Paraschos. "Κώστας Καρυωτάκης" ["Kostas Karyotakis"]. *Néa Estía* 16, 17, and 18 (1928): 726–835.

Hadas, Rachel. "Enjoying the Funeral: Constantine Caryotakis." *Grand Street* 3, no. 1 (autumn 1983): 153–160.

KARYOTAKISM The writing of **Karyotakis,** and his spectacular suicide at the age of 33 (in 1928), set the trend for melancholy, sardonic verse, which became known as "Karyotakism." Angheliki Varvitsiotis-Konti has a poem in her *Unclaimed Life* (1933) entitled "To the Corpse of K. Karyotakis." Here she cries out, "How I understand you, o unknown / Hymnist of death," and hails his loss as the soul's response to mortality. The six quatrains of her poem parade an opulent indulgence in despair: "Your life was a bitter-laughed / And secret-drinker sufferance, / A tear-refreshed blossom, / And a song-cycle of sighs. // While you harmoniously chanted / A wildly accented prayer / To unforgiving destiny, / Your lyre was smashed in fragments."

Spyros Gouskos (1911–1941) seems like a virtuoso adept of Karyotakism. Born on Zakynthos, Gouskos went back, after dropping out of his math and physics courses at the University of Athens, and settled to a life of stifling isolation on the island. Gouskos died a premature, sacrificial death as a lieutenant in the reserve, fighting on the Epirot front (January 1941). His short life was seamed with isolation and eccentricity. In fits and starts he became a science undergraduate, tradesman, agricultural clerk, municipal library cataloguer, and grocer. His verse is scattered in various journals, but in his lifetime he did not prepare a volume. Gouskos, while a grocer, must have found this calling incongruous with poetry, for he adopted the **pseudonym** Angel of Twilight. Sotos Skoutaris (1913–1944) was a short-lived adept of the cult of Karyotakism. His father, a stationmaster, died when he was three. The reduced family survived the sack of Smyrna (1922) and went to Piraeus, settling in the industrial extension of Nikaia. Skoutaris labored by day and devoted himself to poetry by night. He once wrote, almost prophetically, about his own alter ego: "He will slip away, all by himself, into non-existence." D. Ricks labels Karyotakism a "vein of maudlin pessimism, as practised by its less talented exponents, which infected a whole generation of poets."

Further Reading

Skouras, F. "Ὁ Καρυωτάκης, μπροστὰ στὸ φράγμα τῆς νευρώσεως" ["Karyotakis, Faced by the Barrier of Neurosis"]. *Néa Estía* 15 (May 1943).

KASDAGLI, LINA (1921–) Lina Kasdagli published a series of verse collections: *Sunflowers* (1953), *The Roads of Noon* (1963), and *A Crown of the Year* (1975); translations from John Steinbeck, Mark Twain, Patrick Leigh Fermor's *Rumeli,* François Mauriac, and André Gide; and a children's book *The Snail Is Traveling.* For 25 years, Kasdagli served as editor of the *Greek Girl Guides* magazine. She edited *Neohellenic Folk Culture* (2 vols., Gnosi).

KASDAGLIS, NIKOS (1928–) The novelist Nikos Kasdaglis came from the isle of Kos (Dodecanese). He moved, when a child, with his family to Athens. He fought in the **resistance** (1943–1944), and after the Liberation worked for the Rural Bank (Rhodes) until 1970. In 1952, Kasdaglis published a collection of four short stories, *Squalls,* describing, in harsh, realist style, individuals striving to manage life on and off the sea, whether by fishing or smuggling, by drinking or riotous behavior. He wrote with similar realism about the clash of ideologies among Greeks who lived through the German **occupation.** In the novel *The Teeth of the Millstone* (1955), an uncouth young man with no ideological commitment and ultimate distaste for his strong-arm comrades is drawn by mere hunger to sign up for the anti-Communist head kickers of the "special security police." In the story of *The Shaven Heads* (1959), Kasdaglis presents the chronicle of a young infantryman doing military service. Private Yiannilos beats up an officer after a quarrel concerning a prostitute. The action moves between the camp and the brothel, but is told in the first person by six different characters. The text is avant-garde, close to the *nouveau roman,* showing that there is no one correct point of view on an event, and that each character is a dossier of the society that generates them. In 1961, Kasdaglis caused lively debate with *I Am the Lord, Thy God,* a polemical novel on the coercion and constraint of all social life. Meraklís commented loftily on Kasdaglis (1972): "Houses of tolerance are his basic locus of inspiration, and art can hardly be released from that source."

Further Reading

Mackridge, Peter. "Testimony and Fiction in Greek Narrative Prose 1944–1967." In *The Greek Novel: A.D. 1–1985,* edited by Roderick Beaton, Roderick, 90–102. London: Croom Helm, 1988.

KASOMOULIS, NIKOLAOS (?1792– 1872) D. Stamelos, in the *Great Encyclopedia of Modern Greek Literature* (vol. 8: 368), proposes 20 August 1795 as Kasmoulis's date of birth. Kasomoulis was a renowned fighter and author of **memoirs** about the **Uprising.** His father and brother were killed in battle and his whole family taken captive (1829). He fought at **Missolonghi** and wrote a circumstantial account of the sortie (1826), in a section of his *Military Memoirs of the Greek Revolution, 1821–1833* (3 vols., 1939–1942).

KASTANAKIS, THRASOS (1901– 1967) The novelist, scholar, and short story writer Kastanakis, born in Constantinople, went to France in 1918. He studied literature and subsequently made a literary career. In Paris he became a pupil and later a close colleague of **Psycharis.** His novel *The Princes* was well received in 1924, when it won a competition prize set up by a publishing house. In the next 20 years he wrote five further novels and many short stories. For a while, he held a job as Lector in Modern Greek at the Sorbonne. He lived the rest of his life in France. Kastanakis was interested in forging a clear distinction between the novel and the short story because it was artistically necessary for the story to rotate round a single individual or to concentrate on a single event. It should not present a collective situation. Kastanakis's own short stories seem to pass through three theoretical stages. First came the anecdote combined with psychological analysis. Second, he turned to the interplay of thought and feeling in his characters' interior drama. Third came emotional adventure. His novels were also theoretically innovative, for they presented a sweep of contemporary Greek social types, from the upper middle class to the laborer and peasant. Kastanakis also dealt with the theme of Greeks' behavior and their way of life overseas. He published over 20 novels or collections of prose stories between 1924 and 1963, including *The Race of Men* (1932), *The Mysteries of Greekness* (1933), and *France Betrayed* (1945).

See also FILM

KATALOGÍA (mid-fifteenth century) The plural noun *Katalogía* is the title of the most prominent late-medieval collection of Greek vernacular love poems, playful and outspoken, Western in outlook. The singular noun *katalogi* (κα- ταλόγι) denotes a popular song with an amorous theme. The plural denotes "a hundred short words" about love.

See also ALPHABET OF LOVE; EROTOPAÍGNIA; HEKATÓLOGA

Further Reading

Hesseling, D. C. and Hubert Pernot, eds. Ἐρωτοπαίγνια *(Chansons d'amour). Publiées d'après un manuscrit du XVe siècle avec une traduction, une étude critique sur les* Ἑκατόλογα *(Chanson des cent mots), des observations grammaticales et en index.* Paris: Bibliothèque grecque vulgaire, vol. 10, 1913.

KATARTZIS, DIMITRIOS (1730/25?–1807; also known as FOTIADIS)

Born in Constantinople, Dimitrios Katartzis was a liberal **Phanariot** and prominent **Enlightenment** sage, who worked as an educator among the parish communities (παροικίες) in Romania. He composed scientific and philosophical works in the manner of the French encyclopedists. He determined that the culture-starved outposts of the **Diaspora** needed textbooks in the spoken language. To an educational essay of 1787 he appends a list of 600 titles of Greek didactic books, manuscripts, or pamphlets. This provides a very early example of technical bibliography. He insisted on the rule "if it is spoken so, then it should be written so." He called his language system (1783) *Modern Greek,* drawing the venom of archaizers, who demanded the retention of classical syntax, among them Lambros Fotiadis (1752–1805), who taught at Bucharest and perhaps influenced Katartzis's choice to write in the learned language from 1791.

KATHAREVOUSA

This word *katharevousa* was originally a metaphor to define the learned form of Greek as "purifying" (see **Purist**). The term is highly charged, as well as technical. It stands for the prestige variety of classicizing Greek, originally fashioned by scholars like **Ko-**raís and **N. Theotokis.** Historically it refers to a scholarly and conservative tendency. In the nineteenth century, the dignity of Katharevousa was adopted by the new Greek state as its national language, after Independence in 1828. Katharevousa gained a further, political significance in the late nineteenth century because Macedonia and other parts of the Balkans were associated with the **Great Idea,** the reintegration of supposedly Greek territories into an ideal, pan-Hellenic geography. If Katharevousa could be maintained as a strict national norm, then Greek claims on Macedonia could be linked to the supposed Greek-speaking reality of that territory. Supporters of the **demotic** risked the charge of being called pro-Slavic. Supporters of Katharevousa passed as anti-Ottoman and pro-unification. Many prose writers in the late nineteenth century continued the tradition of writing in Katharevousa, and some used it for narrative description, switching to the Demotic for plebeian or rustic speech. **Psycharis** was the first to argue that Katharevousa should be completely discarded in favor of demotic. Katharevousa has been awkward at accommodating new concepts (space travel, advertising), forming new words, or modernizing old syntax. Katharevousa can form fresh compounds, like the demotic, to name new realities, as in calques on foreign words, but it cannot make compounds with initial *good-, bad-, white-,* or *bitter-.*

R. Browning notes, in a comprehensive list (1989: 61–66), that Katharevousa cannot form passive participle compounds with a qualifier like *black-, much-, sun-* before the verb element (as in "sun-burnt," "black-clothed," "much-loved"). It insists on different words for many objects and concepts, so Katharevousa and demotic have contrasting words for "house," "mother," "water," "bread," "fish," "I see," and "I stand." The two registers also diverge on structural vocabulary, such as "who," "not," "without," "here."

Katharevousa has a tendency to use subordinate clauses and **hypotaxis.** Demotic prefers **parataxis** of the kind "it began and it rained." Katharevousa continues the classical Greek dative case ("gave to-his-friend . . ."), whereas demotic has verb + preposition "to" (σε) + a single noun case. Katharevousa may use the accusative, genitive, or dative case after prepositions or as the object of certain verbs. Demotic has the accusative. The complex texture of Katharevousa may be used for a mystificatory purpose, as when the urban Greek bamboozles his country cousin. In the late nineteenth century, some journalists and writers, despite radical political views, were proponents of this purified idiom. Y. Hyperidis (1859–1939) called the demotic language "a frightful linguistic construct." He jeered at Psycharis as "an unholy self-appointed philologist" and called him "an Erostratos [love-victim] of language." The journalist A. Chamoudopoulos joked that Hyperidis "would prefer to be hanged from the 30-meter steeple of St. Photini's rather than sacrifice a word-final 'n' from the purist language." Katharevousa encases and thus prolongs certain clichés: "Thanks be to Thee, o God," "a tooth for a tooth," "the apple of discord," "be that as it may," or "the question is posed." Katharevousa has such lexical and morphological depth that some of its elements will survive in science, engineering, politics, law, and religion. No doctor would discard "bladder" (οὐροδόχος κύστη) to find a demotic equivalent.

Further Reading

Dimitrakos, D. Μέγα λεξικὸν τῆς ἑλληνικῆς γλώσσης (δημοτική, καθαρεούσα, μεσαιωνική, μεταγενεστέρα, ἀρχαία [Great Lexicon of the Greek Language: The Demotic, Purist, Medieval, More Recent and Classical], 15 vols. Athens: Helleniki Paideia, 1964.

KATIFOROS, ANTONIOS (1685?/ 1696–1762) Katiforos came from an aristocratic family on Zakynthos and started his illustrious career with studies at the Kouttounianon College in Padua and the St. Athanasios college in Rome. He wrote a Greek **grammar** and cultivated satirical verse, which had enjoyed a long tradition in the **Heptanese.** In 1735, he was invited by the Greek community in **Venice** to teach at the Flanginianon College. He composed a *Life of Peter the Great of Russia,* which was translated into **plain Greek** (1738) by Athanasios Skiás. He was later invited to Russia by the roving talent scout Prince Mentchikov. Taking the sea route, Katiforos was in a shipwreck off Holland and lost his effects. The Duke of Lorraine appointed him tutor to his children. Katiforos translated Cicero, but the manuscript is supposed to have been lost when he posted it to Venice for publication. On the way back to Zakynthos, to assist his sister (widowed with four children), he was entertained by Frederick II in Berlin. At Zakynthos, he embarked on a lexicon, but lost his eyesight when he reached the letter *mu* (M), so halted the project. He dedicated a history of the Old and New Testament, illustrated with brass engravings, to K. Mavrokordatos, prince of Wallachia.

KATSAÏTIS, PETROS (end seventeenth–eighteenth century) The *Lament of the Peloponnese Addressed to Greece* (1716), by Petros Katsaïtis from Cephalonia, is a chronicle in 2,990 rhyming 11-syllable lines. Its subject is the capture of **Nafplion** and other Turkish victories in the Peloponnese in 1715. He finished it in Crete, a year or so after he was taken there as a prisoner from the fall of Nafplion. He was purchased and set free by an Aga. Katsaïtis repaid this benefactor and returned to Argostoli (Cephalonia), where he wrote two neoclassical tragedies, *Iphigeneia,* in 3,858 lines (May 1720), and *Thyestes,* in 2,476 lines (July 1721), published by E. Kriarás in 1950. Despite their Cretan idiom, both are based on plays by Lodovico Dolce (1508–1568). They were written for stage performance, are evidence of amateur theatrical activity in the **Ionian Islands,** and add considerably to our knowledge of an autonomous theater tradition.

KATSIMBALIS, YEORYIOS K. (1899–1978) Katsimbalis was a member of the *Néa Grámmata* group; a scholar, translator, and bibliographer of **Palamás**; and an early compiler of bibliographies on contemporary authors. He was followed, in this exemplary search for documents on a writer's life, ideas and texts, by the bibliographers Valetas, Markakis, N. B. Tomadakis, and Y. I. Fousaras, with more recent researchers such as Adamantios Anestidis, D. Daskalopoulos, Emm. Kasdaglis, Mario Vitti, and Y. Panayotou. Katsimbalis is the central figure of Henry Miller's novel *The Colossus of Maroussi* (1960).

Further Reading

Sharon, Avi. "Katsimbalis: A Life in Letters." *The New Griffon, New Series* [Tribute to George Katsimbalis] 2 (1998): 17–18.

KAUSOKALUBITIS, NEOPHYTOS (d. 1780) The peripatetic intellectual Kausokalubitis (from a Jewish family that had adopted Christianity) taught himself in the Mount Athos libraries, became a teacher at the Vatopediou school there, and later worked on Chios and at Bucharest. He is one of the most conservative **Enlightenment** teachers and tends to disseminate archaizing, **purist** views in the Romania area. Among his students were Lambros Fotiadis and G. Konstantás, who shared his purist position in the developing **language question.** His published works include *Selection from the Complete Psalter* (1759) and a commentary (1768) on the fourth book of the **grammar** by Th. Gazís.

KAVAFIS, KONSTANTINOS PETROU (1863–1933) Kavafis was born and died in Egypt, at Alexandria, and spent most of his life there. The future poet was the youngest of nine children and began his school studies privately at home. His father was a well-off merchant. After the early death of Kavafis senior, the family was short of money, and his mother took them to live in England. They stayed there seven years (1872–1878), so English was the poet's first language. Back in Alexandria, the young Kavafis studied for a while at a business school. From 1882 to 1885, the family lived in Constantinople with his mother's father. His mother died in 1889. For a while Kavafis lived with one of his brothers and then eventually on his own. In 1892 he was appointed to a junior post at the Ministry of Public Works. He occupied a permanent position in the Irrigation Office until he retired 30 years later, with the rank of Assistant to the Bureau Chief. It seems that he only visited Greece twice in his life. He lived for many years in an apartment on rue Lepsius in Alexandria. The novelist E. M. Forster once referred to Kavafis as standing at a slight angle to the universe. A niece asked Kavafis why he did not move to a better address than the rue Lepsius. He replied that there was no better place to live than between "these three centres of existence; a brothel, a church for forgiveness, and a hospital to die in."

He began writing poems in 1883. Throughout his life, Kavafis tended to circulate verses privately, to publish poetry sparingly, and to disown it periodically, or to change versions by hand on his mimeographed, limited distribution pamphlets. He published a mere 14 of his poems, in 1904. The first formal edition of his poetry came out in 1935, two years after his death. Kavafis had issued just 177 poems by himself. The remaining 75 were published by G. P. Savidis in 1968. The formation of his idiosyncratic manner, which gradually transforms itself into a landscape of man's confusion in history and desire, can be seen in masterly brevities from the turn of the century: "Walls," "Themopylae," and "Waiting for the Barbarians." The harsh couplets of "Walls" (1897) grind in asphalt the problem of the individual versus the species: "But I did not hear the noise or echo of the builders. / Imperceptibly they shut me away from the world outside." There is an existential lesson in Kavafis's poem inspired by Dante's reference to Pope Celestine V (*Hell,* III, 60–61: "The shade of one / Who through cowardice made the great renunciation"). Kavafis gives this poem (1901) the title "Che fece . . . il gran rifiuto," slightly misquoting the original. He expands Dante's notion of the abdication into a homily on the gulf between acceptance and cowardice: "To some men there comes a day / When they must utter a towering / 'Yes' or 'No.'"

The Hellenist in Kavafis produces a sermon on honor in "Thermopylae" (1903): "greater glory is earned by those / Who foresee—and there are many who do—/ How Ephialtes will appear at the end; / How the Persians will break through." It is an **allegory** of any politics that holds its principles against a coming doom. An ironic mode peers from behind the classical veil of Kavafis's Hellenistic poems, as in "Alexandrian Kings," with Cleopatra's children, Alexander, Ptolemy, and Caesarion, dressed in silk and jewels at their meaningless coronation. Kavafis dwells on Caesarion's sandals, "tied up by white ribbons, and embroidered with rose-colored pearls," which find their natural end, as empires crack and fall, amid the complicity of courtiers: "they knew what it was really worth, / What empty words those kingdoms were." A tantalizing allegory glitters in "Waiting for the Barbarians" (1904), a source for the South African novel of this name by J. M. Coetzee (1980) and probably for D. Buzzati's Italian novel, *Il deserto dei tartari* (1940). An emperor has awoken early. The Senate is idle. No laws can be enacted. The population loiters on an emblematic Anatolian precinct. Their ruler is awaiting infidels at the main gate, with his consuls and praetors in tasseled, embroidered gowns, bearing rings, jewels, and encrusted staffs. The tableau stands for uncertainty at the accession of an age, a war, or an indecipherable prophecy.

The world according to Kavafis is one where principalities are unable to prevent the decay implied by any future. One day the empire will lie under sand. In a decade, or a century, the precinct will vanish with the accession of what is now unknowable. Are they Circassians, Macedonians, or Egyptians, massing at this remote defile from another kingdom? Will this province detonate a disaster, and then settle back into dust, like Bosnia and Armenia? Kavafis's symbolism sidesteps any conclusion. Night falls, and the barbarians fail to come. Messengers report the enemy has disappeared. Here is Hellenism, pressed at labile border posts by Franks, Turks, Albanians, Bulgarians, Serbs, and pushed later from the rigmarole of nationalism. Three special issues of *Néa Estía* (no. 158: 1933, no. 620: 1953, and no. 872: 1963) were devoted to Kavafis.

See also IONIAN ISLANDS

Further Reading

Forster, E. M. "The Poetry of C. P. Cavafy." In *Pharos and Pharillon* (publ. 1926). London: Michael Haag/Immel, 1983: 91–97.

Jusdanis, Gregory. "Cavafy, Tennyson and the Overcoming of Influence." *BMGS* 8 (1982–1983): 123–136.

Keeley, Edmund. *Cavafy's Alexandria: A Study of a Myth in Progress.* Princeton, NJ: Princeton University Press, 1977.

Liddell, Robert. *Cavafy: A Critical Biography.* London: Duckworth, 1974.

Margaritis, Nicholas. "Will the Real Cavafy Please Stand Up?" *Yearbook of Comparative and General Literature,* no. 40 (1992): 117–134.

KAVVADIAS, NIKOS (1910–1975)

Born in Manchuria to a traveling army supplier, Kavvadias was brought back to Cephalonia as a child and later lived in Piraeus. In 1929, the future poet went to sea in the merchant navy and for several years traveled the world on different ships, with varying nautical duties. He published two popular collections of po-

etic yarns about mariners: *Marabou* (1933) and *Fog* (1947). A typical short composition is "The Pilot Nagel," which tells the story of an old Norwegian mariner, once a captain of cargo vessels, now a pilot in Colombo. It conveys both the excitement, and the monotony, of a life spent on the ocean. The corpus of Kavvadias's poems, written in a jaunty, ballad style, in rhyming quatrains or octaves, appeals to a Greek's vision of the **sea.** His poem "A Dagger" (Ένα μαχαίρι) was made into a song by Thanos Mikroutsikos and became popular in a country of mariners, for whom "the first thing God made was the long journey" (**Seferis**).

Further Reading

Kavvadías, Nikos. *Wireless Operator: Selected Poems,* trans. by Simon Darragh. London: London Magazine Editions, 1999 (reviewed by Shomit Dutta in *TLS,* 24 Sept. 1999: 25).

Kavadias, Nikos. *The Collected Poems of Nikos Kavadias,* trans. by Gail Holst-Warhaft. Amsterdam: Hakkert, 1987.

KAZANTZAKI, GALATEIA. See ALEXIOU, GALATEIA

KAZANTZAKIS, NIKOS (1883–1957)

Born at Iraklion, Kazantzakis liked to say that he was "first a Cretan, then a Greek." Novelist, poet, translator, playwright, traveler, and politician, he was capable of concentrating simultaneously on several literary projects. Kazantzakis translated about 50 books into Greek, including Homer, **Dante,** and Goethe. It is said that he translated Dante's *Divine Comedy* in 45 days (1932) and part I of Goethe's *Faust* in 12 (1936). He wrote nine screenplays, an autobiography, various school textbooks, a history of Russian literature, contributions to encyclopedias, hundreds of newspaper and periodical articles, even an unpublished French-Greek dictionary. He produced over 30 novels, plays, and philosophical books, alongside his life's work, the drafting and revision of *The Odyssey: A Modern Sequel* (1938). In this reworking of **Homer,** the classical soldier and wanderer evolves into a revolutionary saint. The result is a massive, tormented, religious work that has been called "a monument of the age." From 1902 to 1906, Kazantzakis studied at the University of Athens Law School and graduated with top honors. The year 1907 found him in Paris, attending the lectures of Henri Bergson at the Collège de France, and in 1911 he translated the philosopher's book *On Laughter.*

He wrote a thesis on "Frederick Nietzsche and the Philosophy of Justice and Government," which he published in Iraklion, when he returned in 1909. In 1910, Kazantzakis cofounded the Educational Society, with its vigorous program for incorporating **demotic** language into school teaching. In 1911, he married his childhood friend, **Galateia Alexiou,** later a successful novelist in her own right. He and his wife entered a competition calling for primary school textbooks written in the **demotic.** They wrote a primer and five teaching manuals. They won prizes for all their submissions, and Kazantzakis used the money to finance his subsequent travels. In 1912–1913 he was a volunteer in the **Balkan Wars,** serving in the special office of the Prime Minister, **Elevtherios Venizelos.** After traveling throughout Greece and making a journey in the footsteps of Nietzsche in Switzerland, he was put in charge of a mission from the Ministry of Social Welfare (1919 to 1920). His task was to organize the repatriation of Greeks who were being persecuted in the Caucasus. Kazantzakis was appointed on 21 May 1919, carried out his assignment immediately, and in August went on to Paris to report in person to Prime Minister Venizelos, then a delegate at the Versailles Peace Conference. In January 1920 we find Kazantzakis (Bien, 1989: 103) "personally superintending the resettlement of the refugees in the orphanages of Macedonia and the abandoned villages of Thrace." He was later a minister of state (1945).

Kazantzakis wrote a novel in French about the Soviet Union, *Moscou a crié,* changing the title to *Todo-Raba,* after an African magician (1929); a Greek version by Y. Manklís was published in 1956. In this text he declares: "I am a mariner of Odysseus with heart of fire but with mind ruthless and clear." Another of his novels, published in French as *Le Jardin des rochers* (1936: also *The Rock Garden,* 1963), concerns a European traveler who is caught in the war between China and Japan, in the 1930s. His *Serpent and Lily* (1906) received a review by **Palamás,** among others. As P. Bien has pointed out, Kazantzakis abandoned the novel form more or less completely for 30 years. He "begrudgingly" came back to it when international recognition as a writer appeared to depend on fiction. In the early 1920s Kazantzakis paid visits to Germany and soaked up the atmosphere of postwar Communism. In 1924 he joined a group of Communist insurgents on Crete and was arrested for his activities. In the late 1920s he made three visits to the Soviet Union, but despite his Marxist sympathies, he was condemned by the Greek Communist Party and rejected by **resistance** forces when he volunteered in May 1941. His play, *Christ* (published in 1928) immediately created controversy. It was held to be sacrilegious because of his intermixture of Buddhist and Christian views, and a charge was filed with the Athens public prosecutor's office in 1930. Kazantzakis also created theater vehicles for specific actresses. The play *Day Breaks* (1907) was devised for the great actress Marika Kotopouli. *Melissa* (1937) and *Julian the Apostate* (1939) were written as a dramatic vehicle for A. Minotís. These plays did not reach theater production. A play based on the **demotic song** *The Bridge of Arta,* Kazantzakis's *The Master-Builder* (1909), also failed to gain a production, but was adapted into an **opera** by Manolis Kalomiris.

M. Antonakis points out that the legacy of World War II and Greek **Civil War** put Kazantzakis out of step with both ideological values. Peter Bien surmises that the Royal Theater vetoed his work because of its political unacceptability. In 1941, Kazantzakis finished a new play, *Buddha,* and late in life he projected an ambitious "Third Faust." C.-D. Gounelas notes the allusive subtlety of Kazantzakis's plays *Christ* and *Buddha,* the former using duplication and apparition, as in the Greek **icon,** in order to "construct a universally attainable image of Christ" (1998: 323). In *Buddha,* Gounelas sees the Chinese village setting as a dream and thus a symbol of "the mind's illusory contrivance" (1998: 326).

Such plays serve, alongside his *Odyssey,* to present Kazantzakis as a world writer with vaulting ambitions, far removed from the popular author of *Zorba* (Athens: Dimitrakos, 1946). The novel *Zorba the Greek* was based on a larger-than-life, illiterate man of the people. This Macedonian "Zorba" and Kazantzakis himself were involved in a lignite mine project, in the Mani province, be-

tween 1916 and 1917. As fictional characters, the two constitute dynamic and meditative halves of a composite Greek type. They harmonize Dionysiac and Apollinean impulses, familiar from Nietzschean terminology. Zorba scandalizes his "Boss" by womanizing, homicide, and neglect of their mining equipment and aerial cableway. Zorba is also a reflection of the anarchy and starvation of the German **occupation,** when Kazantzakis wrote the book and at times stayed in bed to conserve energy and food. In winter 1941 the famine in Greece caused the loss of nearly a half-million lives. *The Life and Manners of Aléxis Zorbás* was made into the successful American movie *Zorba the Greek* (starring Anthony Quinn) and a musical on Broadway.

The poetic achievement of Kazantzakis is prodigious, creating (as D. Ricks has observed) a new **epic,** in a new epic meter (the 17-syllable line), with a new demotic vocabulary. Especially challenging is the forging, by Kazantzakis, of hundreds of new **compound epithets.** These compete, over thousands of years, with the stock epithets that constellate the hexameters in **Homer.** The universal thrust of Kazantzakis's epic poem is tellingly reflected by its division into 24 books, spanning the same number of letters as the Greek alphabet. This indexing device also links ancient with modern, for the scholar Aristarchus of Samothrace (fl. 156 B.C.) had once divided the *Iliad* and *Odyssey* into 24 books each (putting an asterisk next to lines that he found especially beautiful and a dagger by those he suspected of interpolation; see **Homer**).

Prevelakis records that Kazantzakis scorned his own novel writing, calling it a relaxation after real work. *Christ Re-*

crucified (written 1948) is set in the year 1922, significant in Greek memory for the **Asia Minor disaster.** It portrays an Anatolian village that rehearses a performance of the Last Passion of Jesus. In this setting, Greek refugees are persecuted by their Turkish masters and by profiteering fellow-Greeks from a neighboring village. The protagonist of this multilayered saga, Manoliós, is crucified anew because he enacts Gospel principles in real life outside his performance. Other villagers play out different roles in the violent events from real life, which replace the projected Christmas pageant. *Christ Recrucified* was adapted by the French director Jules Dassin for his movie *He Who Must Die* (1956) and was made into an opera by the Czech composer Bohuslav Martinu. The novel *Freedom and Death* (1950) is set in Crete and transforms the author's father Michalis, a small-scale farmer and seed merchant, into an irredentist hero at the time of the Cretan insurrections of 1889 and 1897–1899. Certain passages in *Freedom and Death* led the Holy Synod of the **Orthodox Church** to accuse Kazantzakis of blasphemy. He was symbolically exonerated by the Greek parliament in 1955, when it upheld the artistic right of free speech. The title words of the book's British translation ("Freedom and Death") are an adaptation of the irredentist rallying cry of Crete, which was added by Eleni Kazantzakis to her 1974 edition of her husband's book: "Freedom *or* Death."

The Last Temptation of Christ (written 1950–1951) creates an iconoclastic hero out of Judas, invited by Jesus to betray him so the Son of God can complete his mission by being crucified. Because of this novel (which the Vatican placed on the Index of Prohibited Books), Kazantzakis was excommunicated by the Greek Orthodox Church. In 1952–1953, he wrote the fictional biography *Saint Francis* (also known as *The Little Poor Man of God*), which is sustained by an elemental religious devotion. This work closely follows historical sources concerning the founder of the mendicant order. Kazantzakis's last published novel, *The Fratricides* (written in 1949), tells the story of another religious figure, a priest caught between the warring Royalist and Communist forces in the **Civil War.** Kazantzakis once observed (in *Report to Greco*) that the writer must "make the decision which harmonizes with the fearsome rhythm of our time," and Gounelas declared that Kazantzakis's concentration on the human mind served him in the way that **myth** served ancient tragedy (1998: 318). Three numbers of *Néa Estía* (no. 729: 1957, no. 779: 1959, and no. 848: 1962) were devoted to Kazantzakis. *Journal of Modern Greek Studies* (vol. 16, no. 2 [October 1998]) is a special issue on the author.

See also VULGARISM

Further Reading

Dombrowski, Daniel A. *Kazantzakis and God.* Albany: State University of New York, 1997.

Gounelas, C.-D. "The Concept of Resemblance in Kazantzakis's Tragedies *Christ* and *Buddha.*" *JMGS* 16, no. 2 (October 1998): 313–330.

Kazantzakis, Nikos. *Christ Recrucified,* trans. by Jonathan Griffin. New York: Simon & Schuster, 1953.

Kazantzakis, Nikos. *The Saviors of God,* trans. by Kimon Friar. New York: Simon & Schuster, 1960.

Kazantzakis, Nikos. *Saint Francis: A Novel,* trans. by P. A. Bien. New York: Simon & Schuster, 1962.

Kazantzakis, Nikos. *The Rock Garden,* trans. from the French [*Le Jardin des rochers*] by

Richard Howard. New York: Simon & Schuster, 1963.

Kazantzakis, Nikos. *The Fratricides,* trans. by Athena Gianakas Dallas. New York: Simon & Schuster, 1964.

Kazantzakis, Nikos. *Report to Greco,* trans. by P. A. Bien. New York: Simon & Schuster, 1965.

Kazantzakis, Nikos. *Symposium,* trans. by Theodora Vasils and Themi Vasils. New York: Crowell, 1975.

Kazantzakis, Nikos. *Serpent and Lily: A Novella* [with a manifesto "The Sickness of the Age"], trans., introduction, and notes by Theodora Vasils. Berkeley: University of California Press, 1980.

Kazantzakis, Nikos. *Two Plays* [*Sodoma kaí Gomora*], trans. with an introduction by Kimon Friar; with an introduction to "Comedy," a tragedy in one act, by K. Kerényi, trans. by Peter Bien. St. Paul, MN: North Central Publishing Co., 1982.

Kazantzakis, Nikos. *Buddha,* trans. by Kimon Friar and Athena Dallis-Damis. San Diego, CA: Avant Books, 1983.

Lea, James F. *Kazantzakis: The Politics of Salvation,* with a foreword by Helen Kazantzakis: University of Alabama: University of Alabama Press, 1979.

Levitt, Morton P. *The Cretan Glance: The World and Art of Nikos Kazantzakis.* Columbus: Ohio State University Press, 1980.

KEDROS MODERN GREEK WRITERS SERIES This was a series initiated (1991) by the Athens publisher Kedros to offer contemporary, often experimental, Greek novels in English and some reissues of classics (such as *Drifting Cities,* by **S. Tsirkas**). Many of the translations were sponsored by the Greek Ministry of Culture. In 1996, Kedros boasted three sets of paperbacks that were "moderately priced" (V. Calotychos). In December 1998, Katia Lembessi, Kedros's chairman, admitted that the series was slowing down, perhaps because foreign sales for Greek books are poor and distribution costly. The translations were lively, though they received mixed reviews. A passage in breezy modern idiom is quoted by Livas from Nikolaïdis's *Vanishing Point:* "Few years in the course of our lifetime, which has seen such strange happenings, have been so disheartening and creepingly tacky as those that succeeded the Occupation" (trans. John Leatham). K. Mourselas's *Red Dyed Hair,* one of various novels adapted as television serials, has a spirited Kedros version: "Louis was . . . the one who broke the sound barrier, who made a mess of all our stinking alibis, and even if we finally admit he's dead then there'll be birds chirping on top of his grave" (trans. Fred A. Reed). Koumandareas's novel *Koula,* a popular TV serial in the 1980s, was chosen for Kedros, though his other novels had stronger claims to a sponsored translation. Plaskovitsis's *The Façade Lady of Corfu* offers a narrative with a slow start, love intrigue under a political spotlight, and a spectacular ending in a bomb explosion.

Texts selected for Kedros give few external clues: the cover has the author's photo, and there is no introduction. Titles include Sotiris Dimitriou, *Woof, Woof, Dear Lord* (trans. L. Marshall), **Aris Alexandrou,** *Mission Box* (1974), trans. Robert Crist, and Costis Gimosoulos, *Her Night on Red.* The original Greek version "A Night with the Red Girl" (1995) becomes a "ventriloquized text" (M. Yanni), that is, written by a male, voiced by a female narrator, merging its heroine by a transvestite process into its author. Other titles in the series are Marios Hakkas, *Kaisariani and the Elegant Toilet* (trans. Amy Mims), Yorgos Ioannou, *Good Friday Vigil;* **Iakovos Kam-**

banellis, *Mauthausen* (1963); Christoforos Milionis, *Kalamás and Achéron* (trans. Marjorie Chambers); Vangelis Raptopoulos, *The Cicadas* (trans. Fred A. Reed); Alexis Panselinos, *Betsy Lost*; and Aris Sfakianakis, *The Emptiness Beyond* (trans. Caroline Harbouri).

Further Reading

Calotychos, V. "Kedros Modern Greek Writers Series." *JMGS* 17, no. 1 (May 1999): 170–179.

Heimonas, Giorgos. *The Builders,* trans. Robert Crist. Athens: Kedros, 1991.

Kotzias, Alexandros. *Jaguar,* trans. H. E. Kriton. Athens: Kedros, 1991.

Koumandareas, Menis. *Koula* [1978], trans. Kay Cicellis. Athens: Kedros, 1991.

Sotiriou, Dido. *Farewell Anatolia,* trans. Fred A. Reed. Athens: Kedros, 1991.

KENTROU-AGATHOPOLOU, MARIA (1930–)

Based in Thessaloniki, Kentrou-Agathopoulou published several volumes of verse after her 1961 debut, *Soul and Art*. Among them are *Crossings* (1965), which won the Municipality of Thessaloniki Prize, *Armillaria* (1973, a word invented for this title), *Landscapes that I Have Seen* (1975), and the collection *Emigrants of the Inner Water* (1985). Critics and anthologists are struck by the pitiless exploration of personal solitude in many of her poems. The texts are full of confessional insight: we learn about the fierce unbidden physicality of her father, a train-driver, or the challenge to any woman of gazing from a window into the street. We watch a woman carrying a pebble from the sea and relating it to a flower, tree, garden, and—death. And presumably the same woman wonders at the way old women seem untouched and the way the old have to go to bed without being tired. Kentrou-Agathopoulou has lectured and written on her friend and fellow Thessaloniki poet, Zoé Karelli.

KIDNAPPING. See JANISSARIES

KING TURNED TO MARBLE

According to legend, an angel snatched the emperor Constantine Palaeologus, as he was about to be slain by a Turk, on the day of the **fall of Constantinople** (29 May 1453) and turned him into marble. The emperor was transported to a cave or to the vaults of **Hagia Sophia.** Here he became the enmarbled king (μαρμαρωμένος βασιλίας). Since then Greeks have waited for the angel to revive him, when the time comes to restore **Byzantium. Christovasilis,** in his poem, "The Enmarbled King," shows "merciful night" spread like a canopy over the dead king's headlong flight toward the King of the Dead, in the Underworld (see also **Death; Folklore**). The emperor rides at full speed, with his army of dead behind him. He pauses when he hears Charos and turns back his **brave lads** (παλληκάρια). The enmarbled king turns to fight like a lion and "drive all the infidels from Constantinople, / and send them, in rows, to the symbolic Red Apple Tree." The narrator in "Moskov-Selim," a mordant tale by **Vizyinós** (1895), accepts that Turks who have been victorious over the Balkans may still withdraw across the Bosphorus to the Red Apple Tree, leaving the Greeks "the keys of Byzantium like a sacred entrustment."

See also ORLOFF REBELLION

KLEPHTS; KLEPHTIC SONGS

The Klephts were a loose organization of mountain brigands with a (romanticized) career of guerrilla resistance to **Ottoman** rule. Whether they were a real historical movement and justify such terms as "Klephtic period" is placed in doubt by some commentators, for example, Kordatos, Lambrinos, and Herzfeld (1986: 61). European nineteenth-century scholars, such as Fauriel, the Romanian princess Helen D'Istria, and Arnold Passow, popularized the idea of a genre of "Klephtic songs." These, like other **demotic songs,** could be accompanied by **dance.** The Klephts suffuse Greek history with an ideal of resistance, but Herzfeld warns that our meager sources cannot locate the familiar famous surnames before 1720. The Tsar wrote a memorandum (1711) that called on the Klephts to help **Russia** in its war against Turkey. The poet **A. Valaoritis** immortalized the figure of Athanasios Diakos (1788–1821), who was captured, taken to Lala, and roasted alive by the Turks. **Rangavís,** in his poem "The Free Klepht Warring Against the Ottomans," evokes a warrior who draws his sword above the rocks. His palace is the mountain; his blanket is the sky. The choice of freedom or death is expressed in staccato, Romantic phrases: "Heavily the earth rumbles; / A rifle falls. / Everywhere (is) trembling, slaughter. / Here (is) flight, there (is) slaughter." The dead Klepht is carried away by his companions, on foot, as they intone a dirge: "The Klepht lives free; / Free the Klepht dies."

Odysseas Androutsos (1788–1825), son of a "Klepht-gendarme" (κλεφταρματολός), was an independence warrior, trapped and murdered by an opponent on the Acropolis. His letters and speeches express granite **patriotism.** Androutsos, aged 15 (1803), was at the court of **Ali Pasha;** later he corresponded with **Byron, Koraís, Vamvas,** and the generals. He founded schools (1824, 1825), started a charitable society, and preserved Greek antiquities. His style displays the noble

brigand: "I spent the main part of my life killing Turks, hunting tyrants. I spent it in caves and mountains. Road ambush, thicket and wild beast can bear witness that scarce one Turk fled my hands alive." Androutsos was written up in poems by **Zalokostas, Zambelios, Y.** and **A. Paraschos, Palamás, Stratigis,** and **Papantoniou.** Rangavís published a romantic verse narrative (1837) in which a young Klepht called Dimos kills the hermit who refuses to marry him to his beloved Elena, whom he has rescued from the Turks. Later he discovers they are siblings, and the hermit was his father. **Valaoritis,** in his poem "Astrapoyannos" (after 1857), gives an account of Lambetis, whose wounded chief, Astrapoyannos, orders his men to kill him and take his severed head so the Turks cannot sully it: "Strike, Lambetis; sever me, take me to your bosom." The obedient Klepht is wounded in a later battle and falls dead over the soil where he interred Astrapoyannos's head. For the Klephts feared one thing above all: to fall alive into Turkish hands. **Gatsos** introduced, in *Amorgos,* a Klepht called Kitsos, idealized in a demotic song. He was on the point of execution by the Turks when his mother asked a river to reverse its course so she might cross the water to join him. This event displays the **trope** of "impossible occurrence" (ἀδύνατον). Quoting from a ballad, Gatsos compared a dust storm to the conflagration caused by two Klephts fighting in the War of Independence: "Is this the noise of Kalivas, or is it Levendoyannis fighting? / No, the tumult comes from Dhespo facing thirteen thousand foes."

Athanasios Lekas (1790–1821), a Klepht from Attica, was tortured to death by the Turks after the battle of Halandri. The Klephts drank to a "welcome bullet" that would save their wounded body from outrage. Chief Katsantonis (1770–1807) and his brother, George, when betrayed to **Ali Pasha,** were condemned to have their bones broken by hammer blows. George lay silent while his legs, from hip to ankle, were shattered in bits. The Klephts prayed to a patron saint of their own, "Panagia Klephtrina," who protected robbers at land and sea. Typical of Klephtic songs is the bird messenger, or the dying chief's testament, and his plan to make a brother his successor in command, as in "The Death of Markos Botzaris": "Three little partridges were perched, high up on Karpenisi; / Their claws with crimson dye were stained, and red were dyed their feathers; / And round about their heads were bound and twisted kerchiefs. / From fall of evening they lament, and cry they in the morning: / 'Skodra Pasha will fall on us with soldiers eighteen thousand, / With him he's bringing Djelad Bey, he's bringing Agha Kïoris, / And Nikothéan's coming too, the dog, the Christian-slayer!'" Dying with a bullet from "an Albanian Latin dog" in his head, Markos cries: "You, my lads, do not cry for me, do not wear mourning black; / Send news to the Franks, send tidings to Ancona; / And write a letter to my wife, that they have killed Marco; / Tell her to raise my boy with care, and teach him letters." Klephtic myths are fused with facts from the **Independence** struggle: Fotos, the Souliot, hit by a sniper during hostilities in which Ali Pasha built 60 forts to contain the Souliot rebels, urged his Souliot companions to cut off his head to prevent his being taken alive to Ali.

Some ballads deal with the feats of one rebel, like Kitsos, who is marched to the gallows, or Christos Milionis, the female warrior Dhespo, Stathas, Gyftakis,

or Boukouvalas: "These are not buffaloes, tearing each other's throats, nor wild beasts at battle. / It is actually Boukouvalas fighting fifteen hundred men, / And the bullets fall like rain, the bullets drop like hail." Songs about the Klepht's life celebrate his arms, his camp, his exhaustion, and his emotions: "Farewell, high mountains, rose-flowering fields, / Farewell, dews of dawn, and night-time, under the moon." One class of songs deals with battles between mountains. These have a classical precedent, in a second-century contest between Mt. Cithaeron and Mt. Helicon. One ballad heard all over Greece was "The Battle between Mount Olympus and Mount Kisavos." The catalogue of Klephts includes fighters in the independence war, or real brigands, after whom folk songs were named, for example, Metsouisios, Diakos, Dimos Skaltzas, Androutsos (which Baggally draws from no. 17 in the **Politis** list), Zidros, Lazos, the Androutsos (drawn from no. 31 in Passow's collection), Athanasios the Vlach, Vlachavas (see **Romiosini**), Koumoundouros, Liakos, Diplas, Syros, Nikas, Zacharias, Niko-Tsaras, **Kolokotronis,** Katsiyannos, Vivas, Grivas, Murtzonis, Tzavelas, and Katsantonis. Historians ask whether the Klephts were social-minded bandits or crooks settling feuds.

Further Reading

Gallant, Thomas. "Greek Bandits: Lone Wolves or a Family Affair?" *JMGS* 6, no. 2 (1988): 269–290.

KNIGHTS OF THE ROUND TABLE

The manuscript of the Greek chivalric text *Exploits of an Aged Knight,* from the late thirteenth or early fourteenth century, has 306 unrhymed **political** lines. The title for this episode from the saga of the *Knights of the Round Table* was proposed by its first editor. Brunet de Presle observed that it should really have been called Ὁ πρεσβύτης ἱππότης, because the meaning "old man; ambassador" requires πρεσβύτης, the form preferred by a learned person, and this text is semilearned. It is a free rendering of a French poem (end twelfth century), *Gyron le Courtois*. The hero is an old horseman who defeats the younger knights of King Arthur's court. Some phrases are straight transcriptions into Greek, such as the expressions for Round Table, or Lancelot du Lac. The author imitates **Homer**: thus Arthur addresses his wife Genièvre (line 139) with the words of Hector to Andromache in the *Iliad*.

Further Reading

Ellissen, A. Ὁ πρέσβυς ἱππότης [The Aged Knight], *ein griechisches Gedicht aus dem Sagenkreis der Tafelrunde*. Leipzig: Wigand, 1846.

KODRIKÁS, PANAYOTIS (1762–1827) Panayotis Kodrikás was a linguistic opponent of **Koraís,** with whom he conducted a "battle of the pamphlets" (1816–1821), which included letters, pseudonymous articles, and aggressive titles like "Suppression of a Goat" (1817). With his essays in French and *A Study on the Shared Dialect of Greece* (2 vols., 1818, dedicated to the Russian Tsar), Kodrikás scorned the attempt by **Katartzis** to identify the national Greek idiom with the "domestic style of Constantinople nobles," since he mistook "a trite domestic idiom" for an archetype. Kodrikás argued that Greece preserved its national integrity through adversity because it preserved the language of its "forefathers" and rejected **Enlightenment** attempts to simplify Greek. He was

vain about his parents' lineage, and he tended to inflate the importance of his secretarial positions in Romania and Moldavia. In Bucharest and Jassy, he was asked by Prince Mikhail Soutsos to gather sensitive information (1795) on the French Revolution. He was effectively the key figure in an **Ottoman** delegation to Paris to establish diplomatic relations with the Napoleonic court (1797). He later became an agent of the French secret services and in 1800 was recalled by the Supreme Porte, by now suspicious of him. Kodrikás ignored the call and stayed on in Paris, working for Foreign Affairs. Dimarás thinks it a pity he did not leave history something more than the memory of an "adroit libeller."

KOGEBINAS, NIKOLAOS (1856–1897) Born on Kerkyra, Kogebinas became sickly and was tutored at home (in classics and modern European languages). He later took up the professed principle of **Polylás,** that emergent Greek intellectuals must devote themselves to translating all of classical and the best of modern literature. Kogebinas drafted or completed versions of Theophrastus's "Flattery" (from *The Characters*), Virgil, Aeschylus, Tibullus, Goethe's *Iphigineia,* and Schiller's *The Diver* and left an unfinished essay of his own, *On the Literary Works of Vilarás*. With his poor health, he died after a move to Athens, during tumultuous rallies for the 1897 Balkan campaign. His complete works came out posthumously (Athens, 1916).

KOKKOS, DIMITRIOS (1856–1891) Kokkos was a noted poet and writer of operettas (*komeidyllia*). Born at Andritsaina, he was shot dead in Athens by a mentally disturbed army sergeant who imagined his father had been insulted in the play *Old Nicholas's Lyre*. Kokkos's family came from Naxos. He gained a degree in law (1886) and from 1887 was secretary to the Greek consulate of Trieste. He subsequently published travel impressions of Italian cities in the magazine *Don't Get Lost*. On his return to Athens, he was appointed to a secretary-ship in the Ministry of Economic Affairs. He submitted articles, mainly satirical, to papers like *Town, Rabagás, Don't Get Lost,* and *Acropolis*. He assisted the humorist and poet **Yeoryios Souris** with the magazine *The Greek,* which Souris put out, crammed with verse commentary on every topic, from 1883 until 1918. Kokkos soon went his own way, publishing four collections of satirical verse, *Laughs* (1887), *Daisies* (1891), *Memories and Hopes,* and *Poems*. Most popular of all were *komeidyllia* for which he wrote the words and songs himself, *Old Nicholas's Lyre, Captain Jacob,* and *Uncle Linardos*. The protagonist's role in these three plays, which were revived repeatedly from 1888, proved a popular vehicle for the actor Evangelos Pantopoulos. The songs woven into the story were a hit with the general public and so, too, were stock types like Manuel, which people soon identified as anyone behaving stupidly. *The Fortune of Maroula* was a joint project by Kokkos with **Dimitrios Koromilás** (1850–1898), another successful contemporary playwright. *The Village Bride,* left half-finished by the author, was completed and performed after his death.

KOLOKOTRONIS, THEODOROS (1770–1843) The **memoirs** of Theodoros Kolokotronis tell how the extirpation of the entire Kolokotronis clan was ordered by the Turkish Porte (1804). Theodoros escaped to Zakynthos in 1805 (see **Martelaos**). He then gained the grade of major in the British army. In the **War of Independence,** he retained the loyalty of the Maina; at times, like Achilles in **Homer,** he sulked when rival factions belittled him. When he marched on Kolettis, in the power struggle after the murder of President **Kapodistrias** (27 September 1831), a situation of anarchy arose. By 1832, outside Nafplion, Kolokotronis governed virtually the whole of Greece. When he was tried for treason (1834), the judges **Tertsetis** (who later edited his memoirs) and **Polyzoidis** refused to sign the death sentence.

KOMEIDYLLIO Operetta, called in Greek *komeidyllio* (κωμειδύλλιο), was greatly in vogue around the 1880s. Literally "comedy with idyllic elements," it appealed to an audience mystified by the neoclassical or Byzantine plots of nineteenth-century theater, cast in what is now considered their frigid **purist** idiom, with their lingering adherence to the so-called Aristotelian unities (time, place, action). The comedy idyll turned reluctant readers into willing theatergoers, who lapped up its farce and sentimentality. The operettas played out their stories in an idealized neck of the woods or at the kind-hearted laborers' end of town. The language was openly **demotic,** often contained in songs. Their popularity spread the habit of attending plays among Athenians and led to the foundation of the Royal Theater (1901). **Dimitrios Kokkos** (1856–1891), killed by a deranged theatergoer who thought his father had been lampooned in a Kokkos play, wrote the songs and music for several *komeidyllia,* such as *The Fortune of Maroula* by **Koromilás,** *Old Nicholas's Lyre, Captain Jacob,* and *Uncle Linardos*.

See also THEATER COMPANIES

KONDYLAKIS, IOANNIS (1861–1920) Kondylakis was a Cretan journalist, freelance writer, and essayist. He had a spell of teaching (after 1885) at a rural school in Crete and subsequently drew on contrasts and surprises from this part of his life for the sketches of *When I Was a Schoolmaster* (1916). Later, in Athens, he had a regular column in a newspaper. Like his friend **G. Xenopoulos,** Kondylakis produced some gritty urban realism, dealing especially with the poor of the big city in his novel *Les Misérables of Athens* (1894). Here he adapted, for Greece, the French serial story of urban realism, crime, and trade, the so-called *feuilleton* novel. His book shows some of the social awareness that was beginning to affect Greek circles at the turn of the century and would flow into the foundation of the Socialist Labor Party (1918). The best of Kondylakis's localized fiction is *The Big-Foot* (1892). R. Beaton (1994: 73) picks out in this work an ingredient typical of contemporary rural characterization, "the gentle mockery of the heroic simpleton." Here Kondylakis made use of the **demotic,** to which he was generally opposed, for the first time. His early short stories, set mainly in Crete, also belong to this folkloric manner, essentially genre narrative, the homely portrayal of everyday scenes. A special issue of the literary journal *Néa Estía* (no. 851: 1962) is devoted to Kondylakis.

See also JANISSARIES; SATIRE

Further Reading

Kondylakis, Ioannis. "The Funeral Oration," trans. by Alice-Mary Maffry. *The Charioteer,* no. 4 (1962):117–123.

KONEMENOS, NIKOLAOS (1832–1906) Konemenos studied at the Ionian Academy (the first university in the Near East, founded 1824) and lived many more years on Kerkyra, publishing social satire in verse, *Things I Imagined* (1867) and producing a literary magazine from 1858, namely *Morning Star.* He also drafted an essay on Italian philosophy, *On the Family* (1876), a study written in Italian, *Thieves and Murderers* (1893), and a kind of intellectual "testament" (1901). In 1873, he published a pamphlet on the **language question,** showing that he was carrying forward on the **Ionian Islands** the radical program of **Solomós,** an "exceptional achievement" (Krumbacher), because Konemenos had no training in linguistics.

KONSTANTÁS, GRIGORIOS (1753–1844) Konstantás was an **Enlightenment** teacher, coauthor with D. Filippidis (1758–1832) of *The Modern Geography* (1791). He translated philosophy and history from minor authors (Francesco Soave, Millot). In 1788, he went to study in Vienna, Germany, and Padua (the usual stopping place for Greek intellectuals in Italy). In 1803 he negotiated with his friend **Gazís** over funding a scientific academy with a 4,000-volume library for Milies of Pilio (his birthplace). In 1814–1816, this dream was realized, though the Sultan limited the school's functions. Konstantás rejected Gazís's invitation to join the conspiratorial **Friendly Society,** but joined the **Uprising.** Later, he worked at a boarding school on Aegina founded by **Kapodistrias.**

KONTAKION In the sixth century, there arose a new form of Byzantine hymn, the *kontakion* (κοντάκιον), which probably came from Syrian models adapted to a Greek public. The *kontakion* provides a solemn poetic **homily** after the lesson based on the Gospel. It usually consists of 18 to 22 stanzas, each ending with the same refrain. These stanzas are chanted in the same melody, with a rise and fall of accentuation at corresponding lines in each stanza. The metrical structure was not, as in other poetic genres, based on lines of equal length with a series of long or short syllables. The *kontakion* is set in a series of **strophes** with lines of varying length. Their rhythm was provided by the alternation of stressed and unstressed syllables, and each was to be linked by some alphabetical device to the next, or they might form an **acrostic,** which revealed the name of the individual who wrote the hymn. The Nativity Hymn by St. Romanus (fl. c. 510 A.D.) was sung every Christmas up until the twelfth century at dinner in the imperial household of **Constantinople.** The proemium of this *kontakion* ("The Virgin on this day gives birth to the Supra-Essential one") survives in modern **Orthodox** services. The Syrian composer Romanus may have composed up to 1,000 *kontakia.* The *kontakion Funeral Chant* by Anastasius is well known. Most famous is the "unseated hymn" (ἀκάθιστος), sung standing. It is of uncertain authorship. It has 24 stanzas linked by an **acrostic** and evokes the Redemption, while making a **liturgy** to the Mother of God in the fifth week of Lent.

See also HYMN; ICON

KONTARIS, YEORYIOS (floruit 1670)

Kontaris, a seventeenth-century cleric from Macedonia, was inspired by the wars between **Venice** and **Turkey** to write Greece's first patriotic historical work, *Ancient and Highly Instructive History of the Glorious City of Athens* (Venice, 1675). It was drafted in **demotic** language, to appeal directly to the common reader.

KONTOGLOU, FOTIS (1895–1965)

Fotis Kontoglou came from Ayvali (on Lesvos) and was the author of 20 volumes. He worked as novelist, critic, art professor, restorer, icon painter (for example, of scenes from **Homer**), and eventually technical superintendent at the Byzantine Museum of Athens. He studied fine arts in various European centers, particularly Paris. His first book, *Pedros Cazas,* came out in a limited edition at Paris in 1918 and Kydonia (Asia Minor) in 1920; the first Greek edition was printed (by Chr. Ganiaris) in 1922 and was well received. This novel deploys the narrative fantasy of a manuscript "which fell into the hands of one Fotis Kontoglou, at Oporto," offering the themes of adventure, treasure, and piracy. The blend was unfamiliar to Greek fiction readers at the time. Writing about his home, in "The Straits of Ayvali," Kontoglou says that when you see a schooner, drawn up for repainting on the beach, you would think the ship is Argo, and the sailors are "curly-haired Jason and his comrades."

Further Reading

Kontoglou, Fotis. "Preface," "Palamidi," "Mystra" [from *Journeys*], trans. by Jo-Anne Cacoullos and Katherine Hortis. *The Charioteer,* no. 5 (1963): 86–103.

KORAÍS, ADAMANTIOS (1748–1833)

In 1800, the great publisher, **Philhellene,** and critic Adamantios Koraís wrote that the Greeks had fallen silent and dared not whisper under his Muslim oppressor. Koraís was a driven, anxious man, "small in size, but all gold." He went from a middle-class background to fame at Paris (see **Kodrikás**). Born in Smyrna, son of a merchant from Chios, he was introduced to classical literature by a Dutch pastor at Smyrna. From 1771 to 1778, he worked as a trader in Amsterdam. From 1782 to 1786, he studied **medicine** at Montpellier. As physician and scholar, Koraís resided in Paris from 1788 until 1833. He experienced the French revolution and the setbacks of Napoleon, whom he censured as a "despot of despots." Perhaps influenced by Edward Gibbon (1737–1794), Koraís developed an aversion to the **Orthodox Church** and the Byzantine period. The holdings in his library show a predilection for **Enlightenment,** scientific authors. Koraís read J. F. Cooper, P. Bayle, D. Hume, Lafayette, Saint-Simon, Montgaillard, Bousset, Fleury, Saint-Croix, and others. He quotes from the French translation of Gibbon's *History of the Decline and Fall of the Roman Empire* (Paris, 1819). In 1798, he produced the anticlerical pamphlet *Fraternal Teaching.* He then worked on patriotic themes, issuing the *War Hymn of the Hellenes Fighting for Freedom in Egypt* in 1800. In 1801 he published the nationalist manifesto *Martial Trumpet-Blast:* "Serve the French with enthusiasm, take their troops the necessary victuals. With your ships, with your hands, with your hearts, and with your very life, if need be, help those dear friends of the Greek race to achieve the seizure of Egypt, whose freedom will entail the salvation of Greece entire." The frontispiece shows a Turk with sword threatening a woman in rags, symbol of Greece's enslavement.

In 1802 Koraís translated *Crimes and Punishments,* by the Italian penologist Cesare Beccaria. Koraís dedicated this translation to the **Heptanese** Republic. In Paris, he brought out the *Forerunner of the Hellenic Library* (1805), which includes the artfully conversational "Improvised Reflections on Greek Education

and the Greek Language." As scholar, critic, and thinker, Koraís contributed to the **language question** by developing an eclectic solution (in essays and prefaces written from 1805 on). He accommodated the radical position of some **Vulgarizers** (supporters of the **demotic,** or of **plain Greek**). He accepted some views held by conservative linguists, who wanted Greek to retain a tincture of **Atticism,** of "pure" elements from its past. Koraís considered that the artificial idiom that he espoused was a communal spoken language (κοινὴ μιλουμένη). In the preface to his *Hellenic Library* edition of Isocrates, he explains why he believed this communal idiom was a national mother tongue. He sought to cut out conspicuously demotic terms and replace them by learned forms. **Vlachoyannis** later lampooned these as "curious linguistic monsters" and quoted Koraís's prescription of the forms "little table," "small food serving," and "my will is to say," "my wish is to write" for the future tense. Koraís favored the rejection of foreign loan words, especially Turkish, and thought spoken Greek was already corrupted by "foreign words" and "degenerate formations."

At long distance, Koraís gave advice on the founding of the radical periodical *The Scholar Hermes,* begun in Vienna (1811, directed by **Anthimos Gazís**), with its links to the **Friendly Society,** which conspired to overthrow Turkish rule of Greece. After 1805, Koraís conceived the plan for his *Hellenic Library,* designed to present classical texts to a modern Greek readership, with accessible information in scholarly introductions. He saw into print the *Greek Library* (in 16 vols., Paris, 1807–1826). He edited nine volumes of *Subsidiary Texts of the Greek Library* (Paris, 1809–1827). His prefaces to the first four books of Homer's *Iliad* are known as *The Running Reverend.* They mark a launching pad for modern prose narrative (1811–1820). Affecting the fashionable blend of letter and dialogue, Koraís employed "the convention that whoever is speaking in a letter is the same person from first to last" (M. Vitti). This gives the illusion of stable perspective in a pretended epistle to "My friend." Koraís used dialogue to flesh out the narrative letter, as in contemporary prose by Goethe, Friedrich Schiller, Chateaubriand, Benjamin Constant, and Madame de Staël. The purpose of Koraís, in his vernacular prefaces to the *Iliad,* is to show how education can be brought to common islanders, inspiring pride that **Homer** lived in an obscure parish on Chios or that villagers can help save Greek antiquities from export. The village priest, by name so fast that he "runs" through the psalm on Sunday, watches a parishioner draft a translation of Homer. This priest, who swipes a pinch of tobacco while serving the consecrated bread at Communion, has seen all 64 parishes on the isle of Chios. Though less well traveled than Odysseus, the running reverend is in touch with the feelings of his simple people. He donates two piastres, the cash he has earned for conducting a wedding, to the costs of the author's *Homer.* When funds are donated to enlarge his church, which is three times larger than its rural congregation, the Reverend counters that the money should be invested and the interest used to pay a teacher for reading and writing lessons.

A classicist throughout his life, Koraís despised Byzantine history as "Hellenism in decline." The only true Hellenes were the ancient Greeks. Koraís used the term *graikoí* for modern Greeks. For him, the decline of the Greeks dated from the Roman conquest, when they were dismissed as *Graeculi.* Their inept, "Graeco-Roman" rulers bequeathed an emasculated, feeble empire. They kept on declining, till they gave in to the Turks. Thus the Greek inheritance was plucked "from the paralysed hands of despots, the Graeco-Roman emperors." He remarked that reading a page by a Byzantine author could give a man an attack of gout and reckoned that when the Sultan assaulted Byzantium in the fifteenth century, "[i]nstead of an army on the alert he found monasteries and monks squabbling over points of dogma, and learned men dabbling with paper and inkpots" (Fassoulakis). Koraís was an armchair revolutionary from afar. He thought that if the Greek **Uprising** had came 30 years later, primary education for the whole nation might have been achieved, and its government could have avoided trouble caused by the Western powers, "by that Anti-Christ Holy Alliance." In a letter of 1827, he maintains that the Uprising was "still untimely since it did not leave us sufficient time to learn how our teachers might be changed." He blamed the Orthodox Church (rivals of the Vatican) for solidifying Greek subservience to the Ottomans. Koraís remarked in his autobiography that for him the words *Turk* and *wild beast* had the same meaning. He tried to serve the nationalist cause by publishing further volumes in his *Hellenic Library* that would sustain the ideals of Greek freedom. Koraís even regarded Ioannis Kapodistrias (1776–1831), the first president of Greece (1828–1831), as a tyrant.

See also FRATERNAL TEACHING

Further Reading

Fassoulakis, S. "Gibbon's Influence on Koraes." In *The Making of Byzantine History:*

Studies Dedicated to Donald M. Nicol, edited by R. Beaton and C. Roueché, 169–173. Aldergate: Variorum, 1993.

Vitti, Mario. "The Inadequate Tradition: Prose Narrative During the First Half of the Nineteenth Century." In *The Greek Novel: A.D. 1–1985,* edited by Roderick Beaton, 3–10. London: Croom Helm, 1988.

KORAN It is believed that the *Koran,* the holy book of **Islam,** in 114 chapters or Surahs, was revealed by the Angel Gabriel to Mohammed in the early seventh century. The collection of this material began under Caliph Abu-Bekr in 634 and was completed under the third Caliph, Osman (644–656). John Damascenus (c. 676–c. 757) knew Arabic and used the text of the *Koran* to write the first serious treatise against Islam. A Byzantine theologian, Nikitas Vyzantios, wrote three essays, which contain rebuttals of passages from the *Koran.* Vyzantios analyzes points of Muslim theology in *Against the Muslims.* In the fourteenth century, a former Emperor (**John VI Kantakouzenós**) wrote a similar exercise against Islam, which was considered a Christian heresy, like any form of dualism. Yerasimos Pentakis (b. 1838) published the first systematic translation of the *Koran* into Greek (Alexandria, 1878), in a comprehensive edition of 700 pages, and there were two further Athenian editions (1886, 1921), the last dedicated "to my Muslim co-citizens in Greece," for Pentakis, a prolific writer and diplomatic interpreter, had lived in Egypt.

Further Reading

Hasluck, F. W. *Christianity and Islam under the Sultans,* ed. Margaret M. Hasluck. New York: Octagon, 1973.

KOROMILÁS, DIMITRIOS (1850–1898) The all-round writer Dimitrios Koromilás, who took over his father's publishing company when young, co-founded the youthful society **Parnassós** (1865), wrote the first Greek hit musical, *The Fortune of Maroula* (1889), edited the newspaper *The Daily,* and produced 23 serious theatrical works between 1874 and 1888, eventually treating his journalism as a hobby next to the business of breaking the stranglehold of French taste on contemporary Greek theater. His operetta (*komeidyllio*) *The Lover of the Shepherdess* (1891), based on a poem by **Zalokostas,** was his last success with the Athenian public.

KORONAIOS, TZANIS (b. 1480) The only extant work by Koronaios, a writer from Zakynthos, is *The Exploits of Mercurios Bovas* in 4,500 rhyming political lines divided into 19 "songs" (c. 1520). It celebrates an Albanian-Greek officer who traced his mythical lineage back to Pyrrhus, king of Epirus. Bovas led Greek mercenaries who fought beside Venetian forces in the 1495–1517 war against the Turks. The poem boasts that he wanted "to enter battle and increase his honor." He died in 1527 with the rank of Commander-in-Chief of the Venetian democracy. Koronaios gives considerable detail and displays many sources to validate the poem's historical authority.

KORYDALLEÚS, THEOFILOS (1563–1646), Korydalleús gained fame in the early **seventeenth century** as the trailblazer who initiated Greeks in the analytic study of **philosophy.** He studied at Padua and taught at Venice, Athens, Zakynthos, and Constantinople. Among his books is *On Diverse Styles of Letters* (1624, with many later reprints), which gained wide diffusion as a model of letter writing. He wrote an *Exposition of*

Rhetoric (1624) and *Annotations and Queries on the Complete Logic of Aristotle* (Venice, 1729). He supposedly had a bad temperament, made enemies, and was accused of Calvinist sympathies.

See also DAMODOS

KOSMÁS, THE AETOLIAN (1714–1779)

Kosmás, the Aetolian (declared a Saint in April 1961) was a "teacher of the race" and an itinerant evangelist throughout the **Balkans.** He memorized sermons for delivery. Some improvised **admonitions** were transcribed by the pious. A letter to his brother Chrysanthos, headmaster of a Naxos school, tells how he traveled across 30 prefectures in Greece and Asia Minor to found 10 secondary and 200 primary schools: "Better, my brother, to have a Greek school in your province than fountains and rivers." He is said to have pulled down one or two churches in order to build a village school out of their masonry. Kosmás was caught and hanged from a tree by the Turks in 1779, allegedly on information supplied by Jewish or Venetian traders, who saw his nationalist message as deleterious to their interests. His body was thrown into the river Hapsus (near Kolontasi). **Ali Pasha,** the future despot of Epirus, who saw his own interests at play, later caused a church to be raised in Kosmás's name.

KOTOUNIOS, IOANNIS (1577–1658)

Born at Beroia (Macedonia), Kotounios later wrote and taught at various Italian institutions. He went to Rome to study at the Greek college and later taught at the universities of Bologna (from 1617) and Padua (from 1627). Kotounios made a *Collection of Greek Epigrams,* corresponded with the polymath **Allatios,** and left all his effects to the University of Padua for use by Greek scholarship students. The legacy lasted until 1798.

KOTZIÁS, ALEXANDROS (1926–1992)

The novelist and critic Alexandros Kotziás published a novel about a group of **Civil War** diehards, trapped within an Athenian gangland, *The Siege* (1953). The protagonist, Minás Papathanasis, is a special battalion activist in the **occupation,** typical of the anti-Communist without any ideology, when Greece's government was in exile in Egypt (see Mackridge, 1988: 96), and the country suffered a fatal power vacuum. His unorthodox novel, *Brave Telemachus* (1972), confirmed his reputation, followed by the stream-of-consciousness manner of *Usurped Authority* (1979). Kotziás translated (from the English) Nicholas Gage's world bestseller *Eleni* (1983), which dealt with unsolved atrocities and residual guilt from the **Civil War.** Another Kotziás novel, *Jaguar* (1987), reinterprets that violence by posing a confrontation over the ownership of a family house. Two women, once members of the **Resistance,** the sister and the widow of a Communist hero, are presented through the sister's monologue. One critic calls it a "a torrent of party-pietism, self-righteousness, fallen ideology and false idolatry." It was made into a successful color film (1994) by Katerina Evangelakou.

Further Reading

Kotziás, Aléxandros. *Jaguar,* trans. by H. E. Kriton. Athens: Kedros, 1991 [reviewed by Julietta Harvey in *TLS* 27 (Dec. 1991): 17].

Mackridge, Peter. "Testimony and Fiction in Greek Narrative Prose 1944–1967." In *The Greek Novel: A.D. 1–1985,* edited by Roderick Beaton, 90–102. London: Croom Helm, 1988.

Makrinikola, Ekaterini, ed. Αφιέρωμα στον

Αλέξανδρο Κοτζιά [A Tribute to Alexandros Kotziás]. Athens: Kedros, 1994 [reviewed by Sophia Denissi in *WLT* 69, no. 3 (summer 1995): 625–626].

Romanos, Christos S. *Poetics of a Fictional Historian*. New York: Peter Lang, 1985.

KOTZIÁS, KOSTAS (1921–1979)

Kostas Kotziás was the elder brother of Alexandros mentioned previously. He fought with EAM (see **Communist**) during the **resistance.** K. Kotziás went to live in Moscow (1967) and died there. Much of his fiction was inspired by his partisan background. Among his novels are *The Sooted Sky* (1957), *Gallery no. 7* (1960), *The Illegal* (1974), and *The Unyielding One* (1978). His play *The Awakening* (1946), also based on the resistance, was performed with Aimilios Beakis in the lead role.

Further Reading

Mazower, Mark. *Inside Hitler's Greece: The Experience of Occupation, 1941–44*. New Haven, CT: Yale University Press, 1993.

KOTZIOULAS, YORGOS (1909–1956)

Kotzioulas was a very withdrawn writer from a rural family in Epirus. He suffered harsh, almost self-chosen deprivation. He produced many translations, from Dickens, Hugo, Maupassant, Gide, the *Chanson de Roland,* Gorky, Zweig, ten collections of verse, and travel notes on **Mount Athos** (1940). During the **Occupation,** he fought with EAM, and later wrote memoirs of the **Communist** leader, Aris Velouchiotis (publ. 1965). In the war, he composed plays for a traveling agit-prop theater troupe affiliated to ELAS, among which are *Wake up, Slave, The Policeman, The Sufferings of the Jews, Women of Epirus, The Party Representative,* and *The Forest Ranger.* The schematic model for Kotzioulas's street theater plots is (1) village's initial suspicion of the Communists from the hills, (2) the Communists win the villagers' trust, and (3) the villagers realize their best interest is to join them (analysis by Valamvanos). Kotzioulas nurtured books and discarded jobs; a colleague once said that at one time Kotzioulas ate a lettuce for supper and then slept under a fir tree. He contracted tuberculosis in 1934, but rejected what he called the "foolhardiness" of a suicide solution, like **Karyotakis.**

Further Reading

Gerolymatos, Andre. *Guerrilla Warfare and Espionage in Greece, 1940–44*. New York: Pella, 1992.

Valamvanos, G. "Θέατρο στα βουνά— Theater in the Mountains, by George Kotzioulas. Athens: Themelio, 1976." *JHD* 5, no. 4 (1979): 91–93.

KOUMANDAREAS, MENIS (1931–)

Koumandareas was a versatile realist, dedicated to the short story form. He described middle-class kids of the 1950s in the **socialist realism** of *The Gadgets* (1962) and torpid, corrupt manners among the upper class in *The Navigation* (1967), for which he faced immorality charges under the **Colonels' Junta.** Meraklís comments (1972): "Without any filtering process, he adopts bawdy material, slimy with sexual discharge and nausea. This brought him before the courts." He published several titles in the following years, notably the novel *Glass Engineering* (1975), which won a state prize for fiction, and *Roving Trumpeter* (1989). Of his own writing, he said: "When I was very young I learnt by reading to love and respect authors that I sensed were worthwhile. I rejected the rest instinctively.

Later, better equipped and less innocent, I tried to be more fair."

Further Reading

Houzouri, Elena. "Menis Koumantareas *Dio Fores Ellinas* (Twice a Greek)." *Hellenic Quarterly* 9 (June-August 2001): 73.

KOUMANOUDIS, STEFANOS (1818–1899) The scholar and poet Koumanoudis studied in Germany and France and later was appointed professor of Latin at Athens University (1851) and served as judge in the **poetry competitions.** Koumanoudis was chairman of the **Rallis** committee (1857) when Dimitrios Vernardakis (see **Language Question**) entered his play *Maria, Daughter of Doxapater,* based on scenes from the Venetian occupation of the **Heptanese.** Vernardakis did not win a prize and launched a sharp attack on the whole committee for its decisions. **K. Asopios** (see following) defended the committee, and Vernardakis returned to the attack in notes prefacing the German printed edition of his play (1858), where he discussed contemporary theater and praised **Shakespeare** as a people's poet. This debate and others were teased out by Koumanoudis, who also reminded his overzealously **nationalist** nineteenth-century readers that **Venice,** with its printing presses, was the chief agency that had kept Greece enlightened during its dark ages. Koumanoudis favored the use of the **demotic,** especially in lyric poetry. With his prestige as a scholar, lexicographer, and historian, he was able to speed up the slow development of **literary criticism** in nineteenth-century Greece. Dimarás (1972: 347) associates criticism with a group around **K. Asopios** (1785–1872).

KOUMAS, KONSTANTINOS (1771–1836) Born in Larisa, Konstantinos Koumas was a traveling **Enlightenment** intellectual. When he inserted an autobiography in volume 12 of his *History of Human Accomplishments* (Vienna, 1832–1838), he did not mention that the Austrian authorities imprisoned him for a while after he fled to Vienna from Smyrna in 1821 as a member of the **Friendly Society.** Clearly the Viennese **censor** would not have permitted this detail to show up in Koumas's life story. In 1835 Koumas was appointed director of the Greek School in Trieste (then in Austria).

KRANAKI, MIMIKA (1922–) In postwar France, Mimika Kranaki wrote a striking "novel of adolescence," *ContreTemps* (1947). She collected her short stories under the title *Circus* (1950). She then wrote in French for several decades, until the wide-ranging saga of her exiled generation is told in *Nostalgia for Greece* (1992, see **Epistolary**). In 1958 she was made professor of philosophy at the University of Nanterre (Paris).

Further Reading

Farinou-Malamatari, Georgia. "The Novel of Adolescence Written by a Woman: Margaríta Limberáki." In *The Greek Novel: A.D. 1–1985,* edited by Roderick Beaton, 103–109. London: Croom Helm, 1988.

Kranaki, Mimika. *Contretemps.* Athens: Estiá, 1975 (first publ. 1947).

KRYSTALLIS, KOSTAS (1868–1894) The bucolic, rural poet Kostas Krystallis always extolled the surrounding fauna and flora like a farming countryman, with a simple love of **nature.** He was a supremely pictorial writer, far removed from anything that might be described as a "thinker" (Trypanis). Krystallis attended the Hellenic high school at Ioannina (a province not yet incorporated into Greece). As a schoolboy, he published a verse epic under the title *The Shades of Hades,* which exhibits obvious borrowings from Dante's *Hell* and the underworld narrative in Homer's *Odyssey.* Its anti-Turkish feeling forced him to flee to Athens (1886), where he worked as a typesetter, copyeditor on the Bart and Hirst children's encyclopedia, secretary for the periodical *The Week,* and later ticket inspector on the Athens-Piraeus railway line. He lost this post in 1893, developed consumption, and died at Kifissia, yet one more prolific poet from this period to perish very young. Others were **Y. Kambysis,** 1872–1901; Ioannis Raptarchis, 1838–1871; **D. Paparrigopoulos,** 1843–1873; and **Spyridon Vasiliadis,** 1845–1874. He was the darling of his generation and is recognizable in the stage figure of Yannakis from the **Kambysis** play *The Mother's Ring.*

L

LABDACISM. See PRONUNCIATION

LADDER POEM The verse artifice of the "ladder poem" goes back to the classical historian Polybius (c. 200–after 118 B.C.). In a ladder poem, the last word of each line is adopted as the opening word for the next line, in such a way that the whole composition appears to be in the form of a progressive movement upward to a lofty conclusion. A noted ladder poem in 91 iambics was composed to mourn the death of Emperor Manuel Comnenus (1143–1180) by the prolific twelfth-century versifier and translator Ioannis Tzetzes (c. 1110–1185). C. Trypanis (1981: 479) comments that Tzetzes is trying to make the form "lift the tragic pathos ninety steps high!"

LAND; LANDSCAPE. See NATURE, LOVE OF

LANDOS, AGAPIOS (c. 1600–c. 1671?) Born in Crete around 1600, the ordained monk Agapios Landos gave generations of deprived Greeks some of their favorite reading. He wrote in an accessible style, signing his pages "from Friar Agapios," or "one who trained at Mount Athos." His *Of Agronomy* (Venice, c. 1620) is a digest of farming and medical advice; his *Salvation of the Sinful* (Venice, 1641) is an edifying discussion of miracles, virtue, penance, fasting, and money: "Second cause of blasphemy: gaming, especially at cards. So you must avoid it like a snake. Namely, do not play for cash, or other goods. Reflect that this is what your worst losses come from."

LANGUAGE QUESTION, THE The so-called language question has been embedded in Greek culture since Byzantine times, when learned **Attic** already vied with a vernacular idiom, a distant precursor of the modern **demotic** (*dhimotiki*), in writing. The speech of prelates and officials was also different from that of the common people, as we can see in dialogue from folk songs, laments, and **hymns.** It has been debated whether this is a form of bilingualism or an actual **diglossia.** Certainly the question became pressing around 1830, when Greece became a state. A new state requires an official language, so the government and education system (see **Kapodistrias**) had to adopt one of the many varieties of written and of spoken Greek. Officialdom had to promote a prestige variety, a national language, if only for its news bulletins, **constitution,** and the drafting of laws. Previously the language question had been felt as a matter of facilitating communication and readership. Now for historical reasons, in the nineteenth century, it became urgent.

The choice was between a learned language, a **Katharevousa** (that is, **purist**), a vernacular idiom, or a mixture of these and other solutions. In the twentieth century the question became political. Standardization of the educated Peloponnesian dialect had successfully replaced the Old Athenian dialect, because the Peloponnese was the first area to be "redeemed" from the Ottomans and because it had links to merchants and shipowners with international standing. Certainly the language question was always hard to solve. Symeon Kavasilas (who translated **Aesop** and the speeches of Isocrates) wrote to Martin Crusius at the end of the sixteenth century that there were more than 70 modern dialects of Greek, but among them the Athenian variety was the worst.

The coexistence of two idioms had afflicted Greek territories since the first century B.C. Accents, breathings, subscripts, subjunctives, and declensions created a natural gulf between the privileged and the populace, who could hardly understand, let alone write, them. One tendency, among certain **Enlightenment** scholars, was to approve the use of a day-to-day language spoken by the common people. This is the source of the adjective "demotic." In the seventeenth century, E. Yiannoulis (see **Education**) used the adverbs "in proper Greek," "in mixed vernacular" (μιξοβαρβαριοτί), and "in the low tongue" (χυδαϊστί) to express the main sides of the question.

Katartzis (1783) used the terms *select* (αἱρετή) and *natural* (φυσική) to express the difference between prestige and vernacular Greek. Gradually the demotic acquired a patriotic value, becoming, in a series of fits and starts, the dominant form of Greek. The contrary tendency was to react against manifestations of the Demotic and replace it with expressions and syntax that had disappeared from use. This line meant imposing Katharevousa, the idiom that, prompted by **Koraís,** was thereafter associated with expository prose, lectures, legal circulars, and army documents. A fanatical preference for Katharevousa may even be mystically related to **Atticism.** Some literary theorists in the mid-nineteenth century were pleased to abandon the learned tradition. **Solomós** said: "The writer does not teach the language; he learns it from the people." Solomós thought that the corrections by A. Koraís to contemporary diction were as ridiculous as trying to upgrade the first line of Dante's *Divine Comedy* from "Nel mezzo del cammin di nostra vita" to *In medio camini nostrae vitae.* Solomós advised writers as follows: "First surrender to the language of the people and then, if you are able, conquer it." He uses a model poet as spokesman in a debate to confound a pedant, pointing out that the existence of dialects never prevented the evolution of a national language.

Solomós could see that differences between the various Greek dialects were minor, compared with Italy. Prose was slower than poetry to accept the logic of his argument in favor of a *koiné*. Throughout the nineteenth century, the campaign for a "mixed language" (μιχτή) envisaged a fusion of simplified Katharevousa and Demotic, removed from its natural morphology and syntax. The mixed language was associated with the journal *Panathinaia,* edited by Kimon Mikhailidis, whereas the Athens University professor A. Skiás battled against the mixed language, calling it a "linguistic monstrosity." Th. Frangopoulos observed (1983) that the language question still affected the way novels were written between 1830 and 1930, and only after 1920 was the Demotic really approved over Katharevousa for prose, the way it had been for poetry since 1820.

Writers were naturally among the first to look to the Demotic as a vehicle of expression (see **Vilarás**). It began to be accepted as the linguistic form in which new texts could be published. A weighty contribution to the language question was offered by D. Vernardakis in his *Report on Pseudo-Atticism* (Trieste, 1884). He asked: "What is it to us whether or not the ancients had this or that particular form? These language questions refer to ancient scholarship and can have no possible reference to our own situation and the contemporary language we speak." He argued that "what the ancients discussed was in different speech, on different science, Lord help us, from the real task of our own science and discussion as it ought to be carried out nowadays." Opposition to this emergence of the Demotic came from **Purists, Phanariots,** and civil servants who did not fully understand that there are no sharp boundaries between dialect and learned forms in modern Greek, because they have grammatical structures in common. Merging of the two idioms also arises

from ambiguity about the domains where they belong. Greeks felt unsure whether street names, municipal signs, and shop fronts should be put up with purist or demotic words. Historically, the dispute has even led to tragedy: the "Oresteia riots" (*Oresteiaká*) of 8 November 1903 were the consequence of an attempt to stage Aeschylus in a mixed rather than classicizing idiom. Three demonstrators were killed and seven wounded.

Under the **Junta,** dropping purist values was deemed unpatriotic and therefore pro-Communist. So in the mid-twentieth century, different idioms again coexisted for a short while, each corresponding to a different stage of intellectual sophistication. The situation was partially rectified by legislation of 1976, which confirmed *dhimotikí* as the language of school, university, and state institutions. The learned language survived, however, and was still preferred by some academics, military officers, or ecclesiastics, who rejected living parlance as a model for linguistic usage. There was a corresponding push, in demotic theory, to extend living parlance to all written usage. There was an ultrademotic form, the result of a rigid codification by scholars. A mixed language might be located somewhere between the learned and demotic model. This was a compromise position. Another compromise lay in the so-called language of fluent speech. This makes major concessions to the Demotic. But it does not admit demotic neologisms, which it avoids by recourse to vocabulary drawn from the learned language. K. N. Sathas produced an early treatise on the issue: *Modern Greek Writing: A Supplement on the History of the Modern Greek Language Question* (Athens, 1870, reprint Athens, I. Chiotellis Editions, 1969).

See also KONEMENOS; KORAÍS; VULGARISM

Further Reading

Browning, Robert. *Medieval and Modern Greek.* London: Hutchinson University Library, 1969.

Householder, Fred W. "Greek Diglossia." *Georgetown University Monograph Series on Languages and Linguistics,* no. 15 (1962): 109–132.

Irmscher, J. "Über die neugriechische Sprachfrage" [On the Modern Greek Language Question]. *Wissenschaftliche Annalen,* no. 1, (1952): 583–590.

Irmscher, J. "Über die neugriechische Sprachfrage" [On the Modern Greek Language Question]. *Wissenschaftliche Annalen,* no. 2, (1953): 44–52.

Mirambel, André. "Les états de langue dans la Grèce actuelle" [Language Conditions in Present-Day Greece]. *Conférences de l'Institut de Linguistique de l'Université de Paris,* no. 5: 1937.

Vernardakis, Dimitrios. *Report on Pseudo-Atticism.* Trieste: Lloyd, 1884.

LAPATHIOTIS, NAPOLEON (1888–1944) The father of Napoleon Lapathiotis was general Leonidas, the first minister of the army after the Goudi uprising, in the government of **E. Venizelos;** his mother was a relation of a former Prime Minister, Charilaos Trikoupis. What of their son, the poet? Versatile, a nocturnal butterfly and socialite, conspicuous for his sexual deviance, Lapathiotis was the quintessence of the uncommitted esthete and urban aristocrat of his time, a **Romantic** to his very roots, a nocturnal dilettante in **music, painting,** and the grasp of foreign languages. Mundanely, as was common at the time, he began with law studies. He produced a single collection of verse in 1939: *Poems.* He contributed to many journals, like *Hegeso,* and was

admired for his refined translating. His mother was the only woman he ever loved, and he tells her in one poem that there is nothing in their house that does not bring his mind back to her, nothing in his life that she has not indelibly marked. After his father's death, Lapathiotis felt dashed by poverty and hard times. He killed himself in January 1944; money was raised by friends to cover his funeral costs.

Superficially, the solitary life and its ending remind one of the poet **Karyotakis** (1896–1928), but the verse and stories are more morbid, less violent. "At the Night Club" is a poem of two quatrains that show a violin playing and two men drinking in warm fellowship, as if they are "tied in a madness of love." When the violin ceases its sweet huskiness, and the friend leaves, then the heart of the poet feels "the coughing song of death." In one of his **epigrams,** he says he is "in favour of anything new," for the new is movement and life, whereas the old is mere expediency. Lapathiotis declares: "Nothing, nothing in the world or in death is fairer than the glance and smile of love." He says that kindness and "dignity for dignity's sake" are the two duties of Man. There is no third duty. In the short story "Stefanos and His Complaint," a man at a sanatorium is revived, for one summer season, by walking in the gardens with a boy ten years younger. As he regains health, they plan to write, and then meet in Paris. The boy goes away, the letters become infrequent, and the hero drifts back to death.

Fever, blood, books, and heightened sensuality are fused in this writing, with touches from French authors like Baudelaire and Proust. He adored painting and he used narcotics for many years. In a poem entitled "With What Craving I

Await You," he says that his mind is maddened and his lips baked dry since the darling with pretty velvet lips went away. He writes of boys that he met on the streets, or of a penniless lad that walks by his side, incurious of the fine garments of others. One day he drank from the lips of his beloved, when "The curtains were red, / And the bed was white." Despite the extreme bleakness of his final period, he managed to publish a fragmented story of his youth, *Bouquet* (1940). In an article, Lapathiotis declares, predictably, that the maturity, intellect, and consciousness of **Kavafis** give him the first place in modern Greek literature.

LASKARATOS, ANDREAS (1811–1901)

The poet, freethinker, and social gadfly Andreas Laskaratos produced a prose **satire** entitled *Mysteries of Cephalonia* (1856). Its account of the clergy's avarice, superstitions of the faithful, and icons that shed tears caused an immediate charge of heresy. Though he came from an aristocratic Heptanesian family, Laskaratos was excommunicated. He left Cephalonia and went to England. In 1857, at Zakynthos, he issued his satirical newspaper, *The Lamp*. He attacked churchmen who traded on the naïveté of their flock and demagogues who preached union of the Ionian Islands with Greece. He issued an "Answer to the Excommunication" (1868), but the anathema was not removed until 1900. In 1872, he dedicated his collected poems, *Various Verse Pieces*, to **Yeoryios Tertsetis**. His prose works include *Behold the Man* (1866), an *Autobiography* (written in Italian), *Characters, Story of a Donkey*, and the *Meditations*, of which he said ". . . they are wholly me," a phrase which later impressed **Seferis**. Laskaratos's *Complete Works* came out in 1959.

Further Reading

A special issue of *Néa Estía* (no. 827: 1961) is devoted to Laskaratos, as also a special number of the periodical *Greek Creation* (no. 73: 15 Feb. 1951).

LASKARIS, JANOS (1445–1535)

In Rome, as director of the Greek College with its own printing press, Laskaris was able to edit and publish the earliest works of modern Greek scholarship: *Ancient Scholia on the "Iliad"* (1517), *Ancient Scholia on the Extant Tragedies of Sophocles,* and *The Philosopher Porphyry's Homeric Questions* (1518). He produced editions of the plays of Sophocles and of the Greek orators (1508–1509). It was said: "To be like Laskaris is to Hellenize." While director of Lorenzo de' Medici's libraries (Florence), he gathered classical manuscripts from **Mount Athos** and the East. Among several commissions that he undertook in western Europe was the setting in order (1518) of the Royal Library of Paris. He composed an epigram on the death of the painter Raphael.

LASKOS, ORESTIS (1908–1992)

Born at Eleusis, by the age of 20 Orestes Laskos was established as an actor and subsequently played in several movies. His first collection of poems, *The Film of Life* (1934), established him, in Meraklís's vigorous phrase, as the publicist of "variety halls and dancing salons." His poetry, facile and popular, spoke tellingly of the petit-bourgeois vanity of the capital and, as a distant second best, the anxious striving of provincial city centers. His poetry collection *Wild Geese* came in 1936, followed by *Táa-Póa* (1938), *Frigate* (1947), *Captain Laskos* (1950), *Africa* (1956), *Naked Muse* (1975), and others. The critics A. Karantonis and

C. A. Trypanis call Laskos one of the "coffee-house cosmopolitans," associating him with **A. Baras** and Caesar Emmanuel (who was the quintessential poet of the Athenian nightlife between the wars). But Laskos was better able to see the vagaries of his life as showman, actor, and Bohemian writer. In the poem "Wild Geese" he satirizes himself, ordered to rest by a doctor, and staying in the small parental house, which has gone to rack and ruin. His life is like rowing a boat without oars. When the wild geese fly north and ask him to join them in their seasonal flight to peace, he says "Not this year," until one year, when he asks the migrating geese to take him away, they give the same answer back.

LASSANEIOS DRAMA COMPETITION Two annual prizes, one for a play with a contemporary subject and the other for a period piece in a Byzantine or pre-Independence setting, were endowed by **Yeoryios Lassanis** from his estate, to be administered, after his wife's decease, by Athens University. The competition ran from 1888–1907, when the legacy ran out. Winning the prize did not guarantee a stage production of the successful script. One criterion of the bequest was that the contemporary play should deal with a relevant (Greek) plot and not be an "aping" of French theater. Nine comedies won prizes in the two decades of the Lassaneios competition, among them D. Kambouroglous, *The Key of the Chest,* and **Timoleon Ambelás,** *Five o'clock.* Eleven historical subjects won prizes, including plays (see **Voutsynas Poetry Prize**) by the indefatigable **A. Antoniadis,** and *The Girl from Lemnos,* by **Aristomenis Provelengios,** four pieces by P. Dimitrakopoulos, including *Irene the Athenian,* and significantly, in the wider

context of twentieth-century Greek literature, an early version of the play *Master-Builder* by **Kazantzakis,** with the title *Sacrifice,* submitted under his Cretan pseudonym Petros Psiloritis.

LASSANIS, YEORYIOS (1793–1870) Yeoryios Lassanis studied in Germany, taught in Greek schools at Moscow and Odessa, joined the **Friendly Society,** persuaded Ypsilantis to lead the **Independence** campaign, and fought alongside him in the Sacred Battalion routed at Dragatsani. He was held for a while in **prison** by the Austrians and released after the direct intervention of the Tsar (1827). He joined D. Ypsilantis as a camp commander for the East Greece campaign. He took part in the last battle of the war, at Petra, between Levadhia and Thebes (September 1829) and later rose to political prominence. He was prefect of Attica, a tax inspector, and Minister of the Economy under **King Otho.** He published a **patriotic** pamphlet, *Greece,* in Moscow (1820), under the rather transparent **pseudonym** of Gorgiadas Lusanios. His play *Greece and the Outsider* was published there in 1822, but the Russian censors would not allow it to come out with his intended dedication to Rigas Velestinlís. He also wrote the tragedy *Harmodios and Aristogeiton.* With **Yennadios,** he collaborated on a six-volume *Preparatory Encyclopedia,* for schools. At his death, Lassanis endowed many foundations, including funds for a **Lassaneios drama competition.**

LEO THE WISE (866–912) Son and successor of Basil I of Macedon, tutored by **Photius,** Leo cleaned up and issued the *Imperial Decrees,* statutes enacted since the reign of Justinian. Leo was the author of **homilies** and **addresses,** which he declaimed at religious gatherings. There are 33 such speeches, and the longest is on John Chrysostomos. Leo VI earns his nickname "the wise" from a letter of dogmatics sent to Caliph Omar.

Further Reading

Antonopoulou, Theodora. *The Homilies of the Emperor Leo VI.* Leiden: Brill, 1997.

Tougher, Shaun. *The Reign of Leo VI, 886–912: Politics and People.* Leiden: Brill, 1997.

LESBIANISM Was Sappho a seventh-century B.C. dyke? The first medieval use of "Lesbian" in this sense may be traced to a marginal note (σχόλιο) by Arethas (850–932) on the *Educational Guide* by Clement of Alexandria (160–220). Photius is the only **Byzantine** writer between the seventh to tenth centuries who quotes the poetess from Lesbos, though there are traces of Sappho's moon and stars motif in hagiographies of St. Eufemia, by Theodoros Bestís (who was commissioned in 1090 to revise the Byzantine legal code), and Symeon Metaphrastes. Fragments of Sappho's poems are found in texts by **Anna Comnene,** Isaac Tzetzes, his brother Ioannis Tzetzes, **Michael Psellus** (eleventh century), the twelfth-century historian K. Manassís, the rhetorician Michael Italikos, Grigorios Pardos, renowned for his *Annotations on Hermogenes's Treatise concerning Rhetorical Skill,* and Nikitas Choniatis Akominatos (who wrote a history of the years 1180–1206).

Efstathios of Thessaloniki, a twelfth-century scholar, cites Sappho's notion of love motivated by pure friendship, as opposed to love of a "fair whore." In the 1990s, the journal *Amfi* (short for *amfisvitisi,* "questioning") dealt with modern female homosexuality in material that included both erotic stories and social critique. Its open-ended title suggested the bi- and the dual. In 1987, The Greek Homosexual Liberation Movement (AKOE) as well as *Amfi* helped bring before the European Parliament's first Public Commission on male and female homosexuality the case of a Greek man who had killed a lover who made him solicit in women's clothes. But Lesbian issues did not become visible at the same period. The law considers such erotic acts incodifiable or unprovable. They are disregarded by the **Orthodox Church.** They may be consigned to the image of the manly woman or man-woman, familiar from nineteenth-century stories about women with facial hair and muscles hardened by farmwork. Greek women may be attracted to each other but they are "phallically inactive." Lesbians are not a cause, in contemporary Greece (Faubion, 1993), because they cannot "jump" (*pidhai*) the partner, or "strike," or "penetrate," or be the energy force, like "real men" (*andres*). Olga Broumas, born in Greece (1949), writes poetry in her adoptive America on lesbianism and feminist themes. Her "Twelve Versions," in the robustly homoerotic volume *Beginning with O,* are linked with a series of paintings by Sandra McKee.

Further Reading

Colby, Rob. "Caves of Sexuality." *The Village Voice* 29 (Aug. 1977): 41–42.

Pontani, F. "Le cadavre adoré: Sappho à Byzance?" *Byzantion: Revue Internationale des Études Byzantines* 71, no. 1 (2001): 233–250.

LETTER WRITING. See EPISTOLOGRAPHY

LIANOTRÁGOUDA The *lianotrágouda* are very brief poetic compositions, sung by the common people in different situations, generally couplets. They are known by other names, for example, *mantinádhes* and *amanádhes*, verse-pairs or serenades. A set of couplets consists of one or more **distichs** in 15-syllable **meter** and **rhyme.** Several modern Greek writers have imitated this folk form, for example, **Palamás, Drosinis,** and **Polemis,** but their learned versions of the demotic manner do not match the raw immediacy of "Bright eyes no longer seen, those lips now silent made, / And bodies no more passing by, from memory quickly fade," and "Whosoever loves the rose must steel himself, / When its thorns prick him, not to say it hurts."

LIBRARIAN; LIBRARIES Ptolemy I and II created the library of Alexandria (third century B.C.), using a catalogue system devised by **Aristotle.** It eventually possessed up to 700,000 papyri rolls. The library of the kings of Pergamum, in **Hellenistic** times, may have had 200,000 texts. How does Greece fare later? During the **Turkocracy,** there were no public libraries. Several monasteries of **Mount Athos** and Meteora managed to retain their medieval collections. The library of John the Theologian Monastery, at Patmos, founded by the venerable Christodoulos (as stated in his will), gathered 890 manuscripts, 2,000 ancient editions, and 13,000 documents. In the **Enlightenment,** philanthropists endowed school libraries with holdings that now have historical value (at Patmos, Ioannina, Miliés, Zagora, Andritsaina, and Chios). The National Library was inaugurated on the island of Aegina (1829). It was later combined with the university library at Athens (1842). Since 1943, it has been entitled to receive a copy of every text printed in Greece. In 1980, 60 percent of Greek publications actually reached the National Library. Athanasios Skliros (1580–1664), who left Crete to study in Italy, inscribed an ex libris couplet in each volume of his personal library: "One who was bitter, by nickname, like the immortals, by forename, / And a doctor by trade, owned this book." In 1796, the first catalogue of the Patriarchal Library of Alexandria was drawn up by Parthenios II of Patmos. In 1947, it had a three-volume catalogue, in 1948 a new building, and in 1952 celebrated its millennium. Dimitrios Ainián (1800–1881) was the first modern scholar to demand public libraries in regional communities. The Ionian Library was founded in 1852 and in two years acquired 30,000 volumes. It was destroyed by fire in World War II. Alkis Tropaiatis (b. 1909) has a poem called "What a lot of books in libraries" about the array of books along the sun-kissed shelves of a library, where a child tries to shape his letters, and Tropaiatis begs God not to endow him "with the scorching knowledge of books, / With their narrow and fruitless wisdom." The library of the Greek Parliament was founded in 1845, with the right of legal deposit. **Psycharis,** having lived in France, left a personal library of 35,000 volumes to it.

Further Reading

Wilson, Nigel G. "The Libraries of the Byzantine World." *Greek, Roman and Byzantine Studies,* no. 8 (1967): 53–80.

LIMBERAKI, MARGARITA (1919–2002) Granddaughter of the publisher **G. Phexis,** Margarita Limberaki is the author of *The Straw Hats,* which went through 19 editions between 1946 and 1985, attracting the label "novel of adolescence" (μυθιστόρημα εφηβειάς). Limberaki relates the summer seasons of three sisters who live with a divorced mother, an aunt, and a grandfather abandoned by his wife. The main focus is the relationship of the sisters with men, whom they variously marry, pursue, or reject. Limberaki's first novel, *The Trees* (1946) was published under her maiden name, **Karapanou.** In the 1950s, she wrote plays both about left-wing issues and the status of women. Limberaki adapted her experimental novel *The Other Alexander* (1950) for the stage. Both play and novel offer an analogy of the **Civil War,** for the plot shows how the legitimate and illegitimate children of an industrialist either own, or work for, his mine. They choose intrigue and thus self-destruction. The heroine of *Kandavlis' Wife* (1954) declares: "I have hair and eyes that are mine, and I am nobody's." She takes control of her life, though married, and seeks her own context in it, similar to the later heroine in *Zvü* (1982), who defines her role to a point where her husband, a Roman king, cannot understand if she is "healer or poisoner."

Further Reading

Farinou-Malamatari, Georgia. "The Novel of Adolescence Written by a Woman: Margaríta Limberáki." In *The Greek Novel: A.D. 1–1985,* edited by Roderick Beaton, 103–109. London: Croom Helm, 1988.

Lymberaki, Margarita. *The Other Alexander,* trans. by W. and H. Tzalopoulou Barnstone. New York: The Noonday Press, 1959.

LITERAL SENSE A word, phrase, or passage that follows strict dictionary meaning is said to have literal sense (κυριολεξία). As an expressive mode, literal sense is relatively austere. The verb κυριολεκτῶ means "speak literally." Exemplary is the patriotic hymn "Thourios" by **Rigas Velestinlís**: "How long are we to leave the world, for bitter slavery? / How long are we to lose brothers, fatherland and parents, / Our friends, our children and all our relatives? / Better would be one of hour of the life of free men / Than forty years of slavery and imprisonment. / What does it profit you, if you should live, and you are in slavery?"

LITERARY ANALYSIS; LITERARY CRITICISM Modern Greek culture seems little affected by fads in literary analysis that absorb Western universities or publishers. It is generally immune to **Marxist** analysis, the New Criticism, psychobiography, structuralism, semiotics, deconstruction, and the hybrid verbiage of postmodernism. Modern Greek writers have been *also* critics. This dual calling of writer/critic is conspicuous over the last 200 years of Greek literature. It makes modern Greek literature an arena in which the writer and the critic are merged.

In Greece, a book tends to be reviewed in such a way that an average person with high school education can understand the discussion. Greek critics do not write *only* for a school-age reader. However, they generally have interested youth in mind. So simplicity becomes a feature of Greeks who write on their own literature. They are removed from fashionable "discourse," and they have the passing of school exams in mind. The writer Kondylakis (1861–1920) declared he envied the "simple narrative" of the classical historian **Xenophon. K. Varnalis,** in *Living Men* (1938), said of **Psycharis** that he "brought to Greek letters the famous *clarté* of the French language, which is the masterpiece of all the Latin languages." The guiding motto was: "being clear is being wise" (Σοφὸν τὸ σαφές).

Further Reading

Lambropoulos, Vassilis. *Literature as National Institution: Studies in the Politics of Modern Greek Criticism.* Princeton, NJ: Princeton University Press, 1988.

LITERARY HISTORY. See HISTORIES OF MODERN GREEK LITERATURE

LITERATURE The word for *literature* (λογοτεχνία) combines "art" with "word." Historically, oral literature is prior to written literature (γραπτός λόγος). Greek oral literature has always run along an inside track, closer to **nationalism** than its signed, written counterpart. It is an anonymous, unsigned literature, which has produced, the **demotic song**, the **alphabets**, the **Klephtic** ballads, *paralogés*, and *amanés*. These subgenres are accepted by modern scholars as a component of neo-Hellenic culture. The writer **Fotis Kontoglou** even said that a man who does not appreciate demotic songs cannot understand the **Uprising of 1821.** Greece's written literature is divided into the categories writing in meter and writing in prose (πέζος λόγος), a binary opposition expressed by the modern words *poetry* and *prose* (πεζογραφία).

Further Reading

Davidson, Thomas. *The Education of the Greek People and Its Influence on Civilization.* New York: AMS Press, 1971 [repr. of 1894 ed.].

LITOTES The noun *frugality* (λιτότητα) also contains the meaning "litotes," the **trope** of understatement. What is *litos* in style or expression is frugal and simple, qualities much admired by Greek writers, who condemn **babbling.** Andreas Muaris (in *Flowers of Piety,* 1708) writes: "No time can ever / Wither the glory that was Greece / *Because wisdom is an amaranth.*" This **metaphor** is also a litotes, because wisdom is actually 20 centuries of **Homer, Aristotle,** and **Plethon.**

LITURGICAL BOOKS The monk and scientist Nikiforos Theotokis (1731–1800) was one of a number of educators to compile a Sunday almanac (κυριακοδρόμιον). His first, *Interpretation and Instruction on the Sunday Gospel,* is used by priests today (publ. Moscow, 2 vols., 1796). It contained **addresses** on the passages from the Gospels assigned to the Sundays of the church year. His second Sunday almanac (Moscow, 2 vols., 1808) was an *Interpretation Chiefly of Passages from the Acts of the Apostles Assigned for Sundays.* The *Pentecostal Service Book* (Πεντηκοστάριον) originally contained the services running from Easter Sunday through the 50 days to Pentecost Sunday. Later, services up to All Saints and the morning Gospels were added.

The rites administered by the church's priests are set out in the *Prayer-Book* (Εὐχολόγιον). This text contains the order for baptism, engagement, marriage, unction, consecration, sprinkling of holy water, and prayers for the sick, the confessional, ordination, the building of a new house, or the blessing of a vineyard. The *Timetable* (Ωρολόγιον) lists the prescribed services for the day, like Matins, Vespers, and the lesser Hours.

Further Reading

New Martyrs of the Turkish Yoke, trans. by L. J. Papadopulos and G. Lizardos. Seattle, WA: St. Nectarios Press, 1985.

The Pentecostarion, trans. by the Monks of the Holy Transfiguration Monastery. Boston: Holy Transfiguration Monastery, 1990.

LITURGY The year's liturgical services in the Eastern Orthodox Church run to 5,000 pages in 20 volumes. Functions on the **Orthodox** calendar are repeated over the week, the month, or the year. Greek writers like **Papadiamantis** tend to fall under the rhythmic fascination of this opulent, architectonic liturgy. The prayers had to be declaimed in a loud voice (by an edict of the year 564) or recited in a tone of "cantillation," which was also used for reading the lessons from Scripture. Canticles and chants were woven into the Byzantine liturgy with a hypnotic variation that later affected the verse of **Elytis** and **Seferis,** as in "Song from Exodus," which is ordained for Good Friday, where the precentor (*psaltis*) and the congregation alternate lines such as: "Let us sing unto the Lord, for he has triumphed gloriously," "The horse and the rider has he thrown into the sea." "For he has triumphed gloriously." "The Lord is my strength and my protector, and he is become my salvation." The last great mystical work of the Byzantine period was *The Explanation of the Divine Liturgy,* by Nikolaos Kabasilas (c. 1319–c. 1391). This work professes a spiritual life based passionately on the Sacraments, like the setting out of the bread, the offertory, and the communion. Kabasilas sees the liturgy as an interplay between the human and the transcendental, as it appears in **icons** showing angels celebrating mass and in the way liturgical practice merges participation with intercession by the dialogue between congregants and celebrant.

Further Reading

Schulz, Hans-Joachim. *The Byzantine Liturgy: Symbolic Structure and Faith Expression.* New York: Pueblo, 1986.

LIVES OF THE SAINTS. See SYNAXARION

LIVISTROS AND RODAMNI An extended medieval **romance** in 3,481 unrhyming **decapentasyllables,** the *Story of Livistros and Rodamni* may have been composed between the fourteenth and fifteenth centuries by an unknown popular writer in one of the islands under Frankish control. Two male heroes, Livistros and his ally Klitovós, rescue Livistros's wife Rodamni from another king who has abducted her, helped by a witch. The story of Livistros is framed inside the narrative of Klitovós, who is telling a widow, formerly his beloved, that he met Livistros traveling on a remote road. The young Latin prince revealed his name and told how he learned the nature of love after killing a bird in a hunt. In a dream, he is led to the Temple of Love, where two maidens, Justice and Truth, initiate him. According to Klitovós, Livistros learned that he was to marry Rodamni, daughter of King Chrysos, but that a witch would seek her doom. He takes an escort of noble warriors, reaches Chrysos's Palace of Silver, and uses bow and arrow to dispatch eight messages of love (medieval πιττάκια) to the princess. He wins a joust, gains her hand, and becomes heir to the king.

One day the couple is out hunting, and passing traders offer him a ring. When he wears it, he seems to fall dead. His friends revive him by removing the ring, but Rodamni and her escort disappear. Klitovós, himself the nephew of a king, now tells his own story: he once loved the widow's daughter and the king imprisoned him. Later he marries Rodamni's sister Melanthia. They rescue Rodamni from her captor, the king of Egypt. Melanthia dies, and Klitovós returns to spin this twinned narrative to his listener. The tale is decorated by colorful lists (καταλόγια). A symmetrical **catalogue** of the year, running from March to February, shows each individual month as shepherd, harvester, or hunter, carrying a written motto in two lines that state his symbolic relationship with time. Thus November is depicted as a farmer carrying wheat in his apron and clasping a paper that says: "I'm the one who sows the earth and I reap the seed that I hold. / For all that I give to the earth, it gives me back threefold." These lists, and the love messages (πιττάκια) give the verse a tone reminiscent of **demotic song.**

See also FRAME STORY

Further Reading

Di Benedetto Zimbone, A. "Gli ottonari nel *Libistro* della redazione escurialense" [Eight-Syllable Lines in the Escorial Version of the *Libistro*]. *Folia Neohellenica* 7 (1985–1986): 7–32.

Lambert, J. A. *Le Roman de Libistros et Rodamné. Publié d'après les manuscrits de Leyde et de Madrid avec une introduction, des observations grammaticales et un glossaire* [The Romance of Libistros and Rodamni. Published according to the Leiden and Madrid Manuscripts, with an Introduction, Grammatical Notes, and a Glossary]. Amsterdam: Verhandelingen der Koninklijke Akademie van Wettenschappen te Amsterdam, 1935.

Rotolo, Vincenzo, ed. and trans. *Libistro e Rodamne. Romanzo cavalleresco bizantino.* Athens: Κείμενα καὶ Μελέται Νεοελληνικῆς Φιλολογίας [Texts and Essays in Modern Greek Literature], no. 22, 1965.

LONG-HAIRED LITERATURE The modern Greek word for "shaggy" or "thick-haired" is μαλλιαρός. At the turn of the century, it became the habit for partisans of **Katharevousa** to apply this adjective to outspoken supporters of the **Demotic.** The brothers Spilios Pasayannis (1874–1909) and Kostas Pasayannis both sported long hair. Spilios Pasayannis used a deliberately marked **demotic** in his verse, which his brother issued in a posthumous collection (1920, *Echoes*). In his prose, Spilios made a habit of employing robust or unusual popular vocabulary, drawn at times from the area near Sparta where he was born. **Ioannis Kondylakis** first called the Pasayannis brothers "hairy" in 1898. He and some fellow writers associated with the avant-garde periodical ***Techni*** were chatting together when the Pasayannis brothers passed by. Kondylakis commented ironically: "There goes long-haired literature." The epithet subsequently passed from an ironic quip about the **Vulgarizers** to a label for critics and writers who choose a markedly demotic diction. It was remembered, 40 years later, in the pejorative phrase "long-haired communists" (μαλλιαροκομμουνιστές).

LOUKARIS, KYRILLOS (1572–1638) Loukaris is the central figure in Greek religious and round him gravitated some of the great writers of the age, **Kallipolitis, Yerasimos Vlachos,** Yerasimos Spartaliotis, Meletios Syrigos, **Agapios Landos,** and Athanasios Varouchas. Born in Crete, Loukaris studied at Padua and followed **M. Pigás** as Patriarch of Alexandria. In 1620, Loukaris was ordained Patriarch of Constantinople. He held the post three times. Finally, the Turks put him to death (1638). His personal mission was to guard **Orthodoxy** against its doctrinal enemy, **Catholicism.** Because of Loukaris's writings, the Catholics gave up missionary plans to convert the Greek population. He founded a printing press at the Patriarchate. It was the first printery in Greek territory under the Turks. He sponsored a translation into **plain Greek** of the *New Testament* (1638; see also **Kallipolitis**) and modernized the Patriarchate's school, turning it into a college of advanced studies. Loukaris donated the fourth-century *Alexandrine Codex* (from the Patriarchal Library of Alexandria, where it is first mentioned in 1098) to King Charles I Stuart of England. It is now in the British Library.

Further Reading

Roberts, R. J. "The Greek Press at Constantinople in 1627 and Its Antecedents." *The Library,* no. 22 (1967): 13–14.

LULLABY The cradle lullaby (νανούρισμα) is a genre of the Greek **demotic song.** In one type, the mother asks Sleep to take her tiny child and bring him back tall as a peak and straight as a cypress with branches spread to East and West. A variation is the cradle-rocking song of the provident mother: "Sleep, child, for I've ordered your dowry from Constantinople, / Bought your clothes and jewels from Venice. / My only babe, little babe, is asleep, / Leaf of my heart, apple of my eye." **Yeoryios Sourís** makes a cruel satire on this subject in his "Lullaby": "A mother is sending to bye-byes / Her new little babe, / And a slender fellow is idling his time / Away beside her. // 'Go to sleep, so I don't burst, / O hidden boast of mine: / Go to sleep, so I can fix / Another brother for you.'"

M

MACEDONIA Muslim and Christian enmity was always fused with **nationalist** rivalry in Macedonia and the **Balkans.** When the Turkish Empire crumbled at the turn of the century, Bulgaria, Romania, and Serbia hatched designs on Macedonia. The year 1903 saw a Slavic uprising in Macedonia, so Greece aided **Turkey** by attacking Vlachs and Slavs on Macedonian soil. In 1912, Greece, Montenegro, Bulgaria, and Serbia joined in a common cause. Turkey was defeated in this round of **Balkan Wars.** In the Treaty of London, Turkey dropped all claims on **Crete** and its other holdings west of **Istanbul.** After Bulgaria's military defeat by Greece and Serbia (1913), the Treaty of Bucharest awarded Greece a large slice of Macedonia (with Kavala and **Thessaloniki**), almost doubling the territory owned by Greece. When Macedonia broke off from the Yugoslav federation (1991) and became an independent republic, Greece claimed "Macedonia" was a Greek name, and therefore Macedonia's flag illegally used a Greek symbol; also its constitution appeared to authorize annexure of the Greek province called Macedonia. In 1993, the UN accepted the new Balkan member under the name Former Yugoslav Republic of Macedonia. Greece imposed sanctions (1994) on FYROM because its concerns had not been settled. Bilateral tensions on border definition, the flag, and the republic's name have not yet been resolved.

Further Reading

Danforth, Loring M. *The Macedonian Conflict: Ethnic Nationalism in a Transnational World.* Princeton, NJ: Princeton University Press, 1995.

Karakasidou, Anastasia N. *Fields of Wheat, Hills of Blood: Passages to Nationhood in Greek Macedonia, 1870–1990.* Chicago: University of Chicago Press, 1999.

MACEDONIAN SCHOOL OF WRITERS, THE. See THESSALONIKI

MAKRIYANNIS, GENERAL (1797–1864; usual style for Yannis Triandafillos) Makriyannis was a military leader and memoirist of the **War of Independence.** Though illiterate, like many of the patriots who went to war for Greece in the Romantic period, Makriyannis taught himself to read and write at the age of 32 in order to set down his experiences in the Greek struggle for independence. At the end of this conflict, he was appointed a Chiliarch by Kapodistrias, the first president of Greece, and took the post of General Director of the Executive Authority of the Peloponnese and Sparta. Makriyannis settled down to work, determined not to waste his leisure time, recording the events in which he had served his country since childhood and after joining the clandestine movement **Philikí Etairía.** For a while his manuscript notes were hidden by a friend on Tinos, out of fear that royalist agents might ransack his house. After 1840, he was involved in a conspiracy aimed at forcing the imposed Bavarian **monarch of Greece,** King Otho, to grant his country a **constitution** (forced by a coup of Sept. 1843). When Makriyannis wrote the section of his *Memoirs* dealing with this period (1840–1844), he drew on notes that he said had been kept hidden under the ground.

The manuscript of the famous book was actually discovered in a tin under the house of his son Kitsos Makriyannis by Yannis Vlachoyannis in 1901 (who published it in 1907). Makriyannis's robust style slips easily into **demotic song:** "The Sun spins round, and tells them, spins round and says: / Last night, when I set, I hid myself behind a little rock / And I heard the weeping of women, and the mourning of men / For those slain heroes lying in the field." His *Memoirs,* not published until more than four decades after his death, were the first book in demotic prose by an unlettered person, in modern Greek culture. When they came out, they caused a sensation for the new century. In the mid-1830s, Makriyannis commissioned a series of **paintings** by Panayotis Zografos about subjects from the **War of Independence** and events from the conflict between Turkey and Greece, such as the **fall of Constantinople** (1453). He wrote detailed captions for the 26 pictures, which he called "the thoughts of Makriyannis." He hoped, by this commission, to put the record straight on events from the Uprising, which in his opinion had been obscured by controversy and factions. The fall of Constantinople shows an allegorical figure of Greece, burdened by chains, pointing a finger of reproach at the victorious sultan, who is depicted reclining on a despot's throne, ordering defeated clergy and conciliators to be placed under a yoke signifying bondage.

Despite his **patriotism,** Makriyannis was tried for acts of treason, sentenced to death, and amnestied after three years in prison. Thus the ex-hero died a broken man. **Seferis** once said that he considered Makriyannis the "humblest and also the steadiest" of all his teachers. Makriyannis had outgrown his time, deploring the aftermath of a struggle that created as much rivalry between fellow Greeks as with their historical adversary, Turkey. In 1983, his *Visions and Miracles* was published posthumously. They alter our focus on the self-taught hero of the 1821 struggle to an image of Makriyannis as Christian sinner–saint.

Further Reading

Sherrard, Philip. "General Makriyannis: The Portrait of a Greek." In *The Wound of Greece: Studies in Neo-Hellenism,* 51–71. London: Rex Collings, 1978.

MALAKASIS, MILTIADIS (1869–1943) The poet Malakasis was born in **Missolonghi** and lived in Athens from 1875. He studied law at the University but then spent a long period abroad, mostly in Paris, coming under the powerful influence of his cousin, the writer Jean Moreás (Ζὰν Μωρεάς), **pseudonym** of **I. Papadiamantopoulos.** Malakasis won the National Prize for Arts and Letters, translated (1920) Moreás's *Stances* from French to Greek. and worked for many years in the library of the Greek Parliament. He placed some of his first literary efforts in the journal *The Week,* whose secretary was an impoverished fellow-poet, **Kostas Krystallis** (1868–1894). Malakasis married the daughter of the Prime Minister of Greece, Deliyioryis. A story is told of the poet's last illness: Malakasis and the writer **Antonis Travlantonis** were in beds near each other at The Hospital of the Annunciation, and they shouted "Good day" across the ward to each other until, one morning, Malakasis did not respond. Travlantonis died a few days later.

MANGANARIS, APOSTOLOS (1904–1991), The poet Manganaris was born at Smyrna and eventually settled at Athens, where he published several volumes of poetry, *In the Bonds of Verse* (1920), *At the First Station* (1929), *The Other Road* (1943), *The Cycle of the Journey* (1973), and *The Twelve-Vertebrate Ones* (1975). When he returned to poetry, after a silence of 30 years, with his *Driving By: Thirty-three New Poems* (1972), he was often sarcastic, introducing metapoetic themes in a way accessible to the general reader. He jeers at the fat socialists and blasé millionaires, the street boys, the cliques, and the audiences who applaud before they boo at a poetry reading. He drew on fellow coffeehouse poets like Caesar Emmanuel and **Orestis Laskos,** but his sharp and versatile outbursts are not, as in their case, mere glances at life on the stage.

See also CAFÉ

MANOUSIS (also MANOUSOS), ANTONIOS (1828–1903) Born in Kerkyra, Manousis went to Venice (1843) and later to Padua to study medicine. He reached the rank of Major in the Italian Army, but failed to gain parallel rank in the Greek forces. In 1852 he accepted an invitation from the Metropolitan of Ioannina to found a chair of Italian in that city, and he taught for four years. In 1850, he published *The National Songs,* an important collection of **demotic songs.** In 1848, he produced *Death of the Blind One,* with a dedication to **Solomós,** inspired by his own mother's case. From 1857 came the volume *Sighs* and from 1876 his collection, *Lyric Pieces—Recollections,* including Italian verse and imitations of Dante and Petrarch. Some critics see him as a mere devotee of Solomós.

MANTINÁDHA The "morning song" comes from the Italian word *mattinata,* and its Greek plural is μαντινάδες. They were mostly serenades sung by the male lover beneath a girl's window. In Crete, the *mantinádha* might take the form of a rhymed couplet, or *dístichon,* and was often improvised. By mid-twentieth century it was no longer restricted in subject matter. From Crete comes a *mantinádha* for January 5, Epiphany Eve: "Oh! My sunk cross, / Your grace is superb, / Do you think I shall be helped by God / Next year to get hold of you again?"

Further Reading

Charis, Manos. ᾿Αντες αμάν: πρωτότυπες κρητικές μαντινάδες [Antes Aman: Original Mantinadhas from Crete]. Athens: Dorikos, 1996.

MANTZAROS, NIKOLAOS (1795–1873) A friend of the Ionian poet **Solo-**

mós, Nikolaos Mantzaros, set a Petrarch sonnet and several of Solomós's poems to music, including the "Ode to Byron." He composed the "Hymn to Liberty" as a four-part ensemble of male voices with orchestral accompaniment, thus creating the national anthem of Greece (1865), which was adopted from its two opening strophes. Solomós's text and Mantzaros's music officially replaced the Greek translation of the Bavarian national anthem, which was used as the Greek anthem under King Otho. It is said that Solomós's personality bewitched his inner circle of cultivated friends, like **Typaldos, Markorás, Polylás, Matesis, Trikoupis,** and Tommaseo, but Mantzaros was his devoted acolyte. Mantazaros studied in Italy (Naples), became life president of the Kerkyra Philharmonic, and wrote a treatise on music.

MANUSCRIPT. See PALAEOGRAPHY

MARATHON It is supposed that a foot soldier named Pheidippides ran to Marathon, in 490 B.C., to fight against the Persians. He created a legend by running back to Athens to announce the victory, a distance of about 24 miles. After declaring "Hail, we won," he fell to the ground and died. According to Herodotus, Pheidippides also ran to Sparta (and back) to call reinforcements. The writer Sokratis Lagoudakis (1864–1944), who edited the journals *Immortal Hellenism* (1939) and *Hellenism* (1942), ran the marathon (now 26 miles) in the first Olympic Games (1896) and came in second. Lagoudakis P. Papastamatis (b. 1908) has a poem "Marathon-Runner" that sanctifies this legend: "The Elders at Athens awaited your coming, / O wing-footed Marathon-runner! / They expected that you might bring victory news. / You,

who saw the rear of the Asian invader crushed / Far from his sacred soil, / Ran, / To carry your final gasp!" John Buckler remarks that the "Athenians celebrated their victory in an outpouring of literature and art that still inspires today." The battle is supposed to have cost the Persians 6,400 soldiers and the Athenians just 192. It symbolizes a heroic fight against very high odds and is recalled in memoirs of **Missolonghi** and the **War of Independence.**

MARKORÁS, YERASIMOS (1826–1911) The **Ionian Island** poet Yerasimos Markorás, much influenced by **Solomós,** was both neoclassical and modernizing. He translated Homer's *Iliad* book III and book VI, lines 1–74. His 1,624-line poem *The Oath* (1875) deals with the nationalist insurrection of 1866 in Crete, centering on the defense of the monastery of Arkadi against Turkish besiegers. **Palamás** called it "the Song of Songs of contemporary heroism." From August to October 1866, the Cretan revolutionary committee refused Moustapha Pasha's ultimatum to disband and evacuate the monastery. Many defenders were blown up or shot. Those who surrendered were summarily tried and executed. The prisoners were marched to their death. Some 964 insurgents were besieged at Arkadi; a handful survived. **Galateia Alexiou,** in her play *Arkadi,* dramatizes this campaign. It ended with the Abbot's blowing up the gunpowder store in the inner fort and has become an icon of Cretan irredentism. Markorás concentrates on the plight of a group of women and children, led back as slaves to their villages after the end of Arkadi's resistance.

A Cretan orphan girl, Evdokia, had visited her lover at the place of battle. He has sworn her an oath that they will live together happily, after the war. She returns to the island and visits the monastery, where her fiancé, Manthos, now lies buried under the ruins. In a vision, she sees Manthos, and he tells her the story of the siege. Over the ruined bricks, Evdokia expires, in the disembodied presence of her lover. Markorás invests this miniature epic with Homeric overtones (Richardson, in Mackridge, 1996: 15). Palamás later referred to Markorás as "Demodocus," the name of the bard who tells the saga of Odysseus after the Fall of Troy, without realizing that Odysseus was a guest at the very banquet where he was reciting it.

Further Reading

Greek Creation, 103: 15 May 1952, is a special number of the periodical, on Markorás.

MARRIAGE Christian women have the same subordinate situation as Muslim women in Greek writing of the nineteenth century. Marriage was arranged, and married women stayed indoors. In earlier centuries, the daughter of the priest and the son of the widow were key characters in **demotic songs** and destined to become the bride and groom. In one modern story, "The Wedding," a former sponge-diver (1940s) who turned writer, Yannis Manglis, shows rural matchmaking in action. Those involved are a sailor, his rough pal, and a rural spinster aged 35. As so often in Greek fiction, we have a duper and a duped. "When you marry, choose a girl from our island. If she's not your equal in station, find one from the neighbouring islands" (Manglis, in Gianos, 1969: 250). The nuptial ceremony is an anticlimax, for the men plan to make off with the dowry. Nothing is so forlorn as a jilted bride.

Typically, the Greek fictional heroine of the early twentieth century, as in the work of **Mimika Kranaki,** could find no meaning in her surroundings, unless she accepted solutions such as marriage, childbearing, and subservience. What this still meant in 1980 is sketched by Winterer-Papatassos: "Always the object of respect, the traditional woman's prestige increased with age. Unhappy marriages ended upon the death of the spouse, not by divorce" (1984: 6–7). With new social freedom, the issue for marriage in the late twentieth century is infidelity. In Lena Divani's *The Lives of Women: A Novel* (Athens: Kastaniotis, 1997), a woman is devastated to find out that her husband is having an affair. Her life is completely altered, but her female friends reflect this contested reality back to her in their own versions of conjugal experience. Vasilis Nemeas's *Butterflies in the Stomach* (Kastaniotis, 1997) tells the story of a man in love with the wife of his friend. In D. Christakopoulos's novel *Wholehearted Love* (Athens: Ploigos, 1997), a man cannot prise his beloved out of her marriage to another. There is a transgenerational study of a modern couple, now aged over 40, once high school sweethearts in the carefree days of rock music, in Apostolos Strongylis's novel *Myrto and the Others* (Athens: Odysseas, 1996).

Further Reading

Gianos, Mary, ed. *Introduction to Modern Greek Literature: An Anthology of Fiction, Drama, and Poetry.* New York: Twayne, 1969.

Saint Cassia, Paul and Constantina Bada. *The Making of the Modern Greek Family: Marriage and Exchange in Nineteenth-Century Athens.* Cambridge and New York: Cambridge University Press, 1992.

Van Dyck, Karen. "Women's Poetry and the

Sexual Politics of Babel." *JMGS* 8, no. 2 (Oct. 1990): 173–182.

MARTELAOS, ANTONIOS (1754–1819)

Martelaos lived and died on Zakynthos. He was a typical nobleman, enrolled in the island's Golden Book of aristocrats, and he studied classics and Italian, tutored by Panayotis Palamás. He became a teacher, founded a school, adopted political attitudes opposed to the Venetian administrators of the island, and taught his fellow-citizens Greek, free of charge. Among his pupils were **Tertsetis, Matesis, Foscolo,** the children of the fugitive **Klepht** hero **Kolokotronis,** probably **Solomós,** and perhaps Kolokotronis himself. Martelaos is the first poet of the **Heptanese** who did not use dialect and Venetian vocabulary. He chose to use a "national demotic idiom," apparently after helping to burn the local Golden Book of nobles in the town square. He wrote a *Manual of Greek Grammar* and made translations of it from Latin and of passages from Tasso's *Gerusalemme liberata.* He composed a hymn in 34 quatrains, evoking the French Revolution, Napoleon, and General Gentilly, who came in his stead to the Heptanese. This was evidently read by the young Solomós, who in his "Hymn to Liberty" has an echo of Martelaos's **image** of the heroes' bones. Martelaos's hymn was ridiculed by the writer Nikolaos Logothetis-Iouliaris.

See also PARODY

MARTINENGOS, ELISABETIOS (1832–1855)

Elisabetios Martinengos was a minor Zantiot writer, who published an unusual and important autobiography by his prematurely deceased mother (see **Elisábet Moutzán-Martinengou,** 1801–1832) and added a supplement to his edition of this work containing his own lyric compositions and translations of poems from English, French, Italian, and German. He lived the conventional life of a well-born heir on Zakynthos. He wrote a play, *Lambros,* and verse praising his island's beauty. He published a poem, *The Three Artists: or on the Ideal* (1854; second ed. 1883). He contributed to the Zakynthos periodicals *The Review* and *Bee Hive.*

MARTZOKIS, ANDREAS (1849–1922)

The writer Andreas Martzokis was born (and died) on Zakynthos, fifth son of a liberal Italian *emigré* Ludovico Martzokis and Countess Marina Messalá. A polyglot, he gave private language lessons all his life. He published poetry collections entitled *Night Flowers* (1878), *Roaring of Waves* (1880), and a verse epic with ethnographic aspirations, *The Abbot of Anafonitra* (1889), about a tiny community on Zakynthos, which became popular, had several reprints, and was widely read on the island. It tells the apocryphal story of the local saint, Dionysios, who hid his brother's killer by lying to police. A second part of the saga came out in 1911, entitled *The Holy Man of Strophades* (preface and notes by the author himself). Typically Heptanesian, A. Martzokis also wrote satirical **epigrams** and impromptu verses, often for public recitation.

MARTZOKIS, STEFANOS (1855–1913)

Stefanos Martzokis was the youngest son of Ludovico. He was born on Zakynthos and died at Athens. Martzokis was brought up in his father's household in the atmosphere of a literary salon. He published his first Italian verse, *Poesie: ore di tormento,* in small broadsheets (1878). In 1833 he was appointed

Italian teacher at the school in Argostoli, capital town of Cephalonia. In 1900 his *Sonnets* were put out by a group of Parisian scholars and admirers in a private edition. In 1903 his complete poems were published by Maraslis. Moving to Athens (1897), this impoverished aesthete attracted around himself a distinguished literary group, which frequented the **café** Karatzas or the fashionable coffeehouse "New Center." The government awarded him the Knights' Silver Cross (1910). In 1925 his son Kaisaros published Stefanos's complete works as a posthumous tribute. The writer **K. Varnalis** characterized him as "a belated bard of olden times" and lauded his "fluid verse, simple rhymes, even language, lack of affectation, lack of excess ornamentation." Martzokis earlier contributed the preface to Varnalis's 1904 volume, *Honeycombs.* One of his other prose works was an extended essay on Solomós in the Paris journal *Grecia.*

Further Reading

Martzokis, Stefanos. Ἄπαντα [Complete Works of S. Martzokis]. Athens: Makris and Sia, 1925.

MARXIST LITERARY CRITICISM; MARXISM

Kostelenos, Chourmouzios, and Kordatos are among twentieth-century Greek critics who assess writers by their Marxist awareness of the **class struggle,** the modes of production, the inequity of the capitalist system, and their adherence to **socialist realism** (κοινωνικός ρεαλισμός). The left-wing journal *Free Letters* ran from 1945 to 1950 and operated at the edge of legality, with contributors such as **Avgeris,** Pappás, and **Varnalis.** Up to a point, the earliest Greek Marxists imitated the line of the Soviet cadres, who adopted *klasso-vast* ("the class nature of literature"), *naradnost* ("the need for art to appeal to the masses"), and *partijnost* ("party-mindedness"). Political equality and religious tolerance (ανεξιθρησκεία) were high on the agenda of Greek Marxists. Writers are allies of the workers and peasants, so they practice "Art as political commitment." They have no toleration for books that are not *engagé:* "Art that is not politically committed cannot exist."

Literature is the main organ of social development, and Greek literature must *reflect* Greek society as it evolves. Modern writing must be tied in with Greece's philosophy, science, aesthetics, and sociology. Writers who join the Communist party have to accept the party line (η κομματική γραμμή). They should oppose the doctrine art-for-art's-sake (η Τέχνη γιὰ τὴν Τέχνη). After the **Colonels' Junta,** the ideal of noninvolvement (μή συμμετοχή) seemed untenable. Varnalis once said: "The words which we employ should have a tangible meaning. They ought to correspond to a reality that humans perceive. Abstract and metaphysical items should not be mixed in at all" (interview in Bastiás 1999: 171–175).

See also CLASS STRUGGLE; COMMUNISM; SOCIALIST REALISM

MASTORAKI, JENNY (1949–)

Jenny Mastoraki has translated Edmund Keeley's *Cavafy's Alexandria: Study of a Myth in Progress* (1976) into Greek for the publisher Icaros (Athens, 1979). She has also translated from American, Italian, English, South American, and German authors, including Heinrich Böll, *Auto-da-fé* by Elias Canetti (Nobel Prize Winner, 1981), and Giorgio Manganelli's *Endless* (1977). Her versions of Kleist's

Penthesileia and Goldoni's *The New House* were play texts for productions in Thessaloniki and Athens. Her collections of verse include *The Legend of St. Youth* (1971), *Road Tolls* (1972), *Kin* (1978), *Tales of the Deep* (1983), and *With a Crown of Light* (1989). Her verse repeatedly uses the word *mother,* and it often hints at a lexical relationship between the Mother and the Homeland. She investigates the code of an older, agricultural society, setting it against the harshness of the city, with memories from Greece's recent **Civil War,** depicting the present age as one of anomaly and raving. The armory of this scholar–poet is thus irony, bitterness, and an implicit **feminism.**

Further Reading

Germanacos, N. C. (and others), trans. "Three Young Poets: Jenny Mastoraki, Haris Megalinos, and Lefteris Poulios." *Boundary 2* 1, 2 (winter 1973): 507–518.

MATESIS, ANTONIOS (1794–1875)

Matesis was born on Zakynthos and died at Syros. He studied Italian with Abbot Rossi and wrote patriotic and love poems, elegies, and the play *The Basil Plant,* which mocks the ways of the Zantiot nobility and is a precocious stage vehicle, with partial echoes of Schiller's play *Intrigue and Love* (*Kabale und Liebe*), first performed 9 March 1794. *Basil Plant* is Greece's "first drama of ideas" (A. Terzakis), nor is it an exaggeration to say that it breathes the wind blown from the French Revolution, or that it rivals that manifesto of European **romantic** writing, Hugo's play *Hernani* (1830). Matesis translated *Dei sepolcri* (by **U. Foscolo**). The five-act *Basil Plant* (written about 1830, published in 1855) was first played by a group of amateurs on the island in 1832. The chief actor was

Konstantinos Dragonas. It is set in a period during which a few ruling families on the island were known as "the first houses," whereas lesser aristocrats came from "second houses." Matesis set his play in 1712, when the customs of the first houses on Zakynthos were much more autocratic and when Louis XIV was still King of France! Matesis was an intimate friend of **Solomós.** Perhaps he groomed the future author of the "Hymn to Liberty" with his own lines: "How long, dear friend, / Is our lyre to stay silent? / All around is the clash of war / Which calls it to task." His complete works came out posthumously (1881) at Zakynthos, edited by De Biasi.

Further Reading

Protopapá-Boubolidou, Glykeria, ed. Ἀντ. Μάτεσι, Ἔργα, ἔμμετρα καὶ πεζά [The Verse and Prose Works of A. Matesis]. Athens: Modern Greek Classics, 1968.

Terzakis, Angelos. "Matesis' VASSILIKOS: The First Drama of Ideas." In *Modern Greek Writers: Solomos, Calvos, Matesis, Palamas, Cavafy, Kazantzakis, Seferis, Elytis,* edited by E. Keeley and P. Bien, 93–107. Princeton, NJ: Princeton University Press, 1972.

MATHAIOS, METROPOLITAN OF MYREON (d. c. 1624)

Mathaios, bishop of Myreon, who lived in seventeenth-century Romania, wrote a chronicle of Wallachia, *A Further History of Events That Occurred in Wallachia, from the Time of Servanus up to Voievod Michael, the Present Duke, Done by the Most Reverend among Prelates, the Metropolitan of Myreon, Lord Mathaios, Dedicated to the Glorious Prince, Lord Ioannis the Katritzis* (Venice, 1683). This historical medley contains *The Lament and Grieving for Constantinople* in 459 lines. It begins at line

2,305 of the verse chronicle, complaining that Greeks put their hopes in foreign aid, waiting for the Spanish to sail "with their fat galleys which are at Venice" or a blond race to come to their deliverance from Moscow: we Byzantine Greeks embraced futile oracles, prophets, and fantasies of salvation, for "the bird we held in our hand has flown far away." He expresses conventional grief that **Hagia Sophia** became a mosque, a multitude of churches and colleges were smashed, and children were made Muslim. The *Lament* contains a long prayer to God, full of vocative **address,** pleas, and exclamations, expressing bewilderment that the Creator can tolerate such a spectacle, pleading with Him to repair it.

MAVILIS, LORENTSOS (1860–1912) The poet and patriot Lorentsos Mavilis was born in Kerkyra to an aristocratic family. His grandfather on the maternal side was Count Kapodistrias Souphis, cousin of the first President of Greece. His grandmother was sister to the mother of Y. Theotokis, member of one of the leading families of the island. As a child, Mavilis spoke Italian and learned Greek at school. He later studied for 15 years (1878–1993) at universities in Germany. He was involved in nationalist intrigue on the island of Kerkyra (early 1890s). With his close friend, **K. Theotokis,** Mavilis organized a brigade of military volunteers to join insurrectionists in Crete (1896). He also saw action in Epirus (1897). In 1910 he was elected to the Greek parliament as representative for Kerkyra. In electioneering speeches, he stated his reverence for the writer **Polylás** and promised to follow Polylás's "honorable politics of restoration." He began an Assembly speech of 26 February 1911, on the **language question** with the words: "I am a pupil of Polylás and for many years was his friend" and coined the memorable phrase: "There is no such thing as a vulgar language; there are only vulgar people." Mavilis expressed his philosophical ideas, in part drawn from the philosopher Schopenhauer (1788–1860), in poems such as "The Secrets of the Unknown."

There are some 58 extant **sonnets** by the poet, all in the **demotic,** of which he became a vigorous standard-bearer. Among his most polished sonnets are "Fatherland," "Olive Tree," "Beauty," and "To the Demotic." Here, in the contrast between the **demotic** virgin and **Katharevousa** as a slatternly hag, is a lyric manifesto for **Vulgarizers:** "Let other men gather to kiss an aged / Woman, covered with make-up, ugly and cold, / Who can only lament the wilting of her youth." The sonnets came out one by one in his lifetime and were published in a slim volume after his death. His best-known poems, such as "Twilight" and "Forgetfulness," date from the late 1890s. Out of this slight corpus came a far-reaching effect. Mavilis's verse was considered a paragon of exalted meditation in the unsophisticated Demotic. He fought in the Bulgarian war (see **Balkans**), fell on 29 November 1912, at Driskos, and was mourned by the writer **Myrtiotissa.** His last words were: "I expected many honors from this war, but not the added honor that I offer my life for my Greece." Two issues of the journal *Néa Estía* (no. 335: 1940 and no. 803: 1960) are devoted to this writer, as is a special number of the literary periodical *Greek Creation* (no. 91: 15 Nov. 1951).

MEDICAL TRACT The medical tract (ιατροσόφιον) is of uncertain authorship and usually constitutes a kind of prescription for unsophisticated laymen. Popular in **Byzantine** times and also under **Turkish** rule, this medical folklore mixes superstition with practical remedies, like the modern almanac. It was designed for a semiliterate public of laborers who had little capacity to read **romance** or history. One type is the *Prognosis from Thunder* (Βροντολογιόν): "If in March, Aries thunders at night, it spells disaster for the sick, and for people in general." Another is the *Course of the Moon* (Σεληνοδρομιόν), which dispensed lunar data: "On the second day of the moon's cycle, Eve was created from the side of Adam. This is a good day for all business; the sick will be cured," and "On the third day of the moon, Cain was born: this is a bad day, and the sick will expire." On the 16th day of the moon, the patient "takes fear, but gets well."

The quack (ψευτογιατρός) is a stock figure who goes back to classical comedy. A modern version of the bogus doctor is to be found in a famous story by **Palamás** (see **Palikari**). In Greek, the quack feeds on the tradition of the tracts, which might give a cure for orthopnoea (breathing only in an upright posture): "It is a condition which prevents a person from falling to a recumbent position, because then he can't breathe, so he is forced to sleep sitting up. An exceptional remedy is for the patient to drink a cupful of urine from a male child, who should be 6 or 7 years of age, and then the orthopnoea patient will be cured." Cures in these pseudolearned books are given for nonhealth problems: "For a married couple, if they are quarreling, give the buds of reeds, with wine, to drink." From Codex 178 of St. Dionysius of **Mount Athos** comes the verse: "You should get a nice, venomous antidote plus dog's tooth violet, / And plenty of rose-jam, neatly sugar-coated, / And some other potions that are good and tempting, / And whoever buys them, will never lose his money." Incorrect medicine passed into these *iatrosofia*. They guided people on food choices: "Here is a reminder to all people, about what it behooves them to eat each month throughout the year, to suit their health and benefit."

In Bursian, we learn that smelling bay leaves can stop a person getting drowsy. We read: "In May, wash your head frequently and eat warm foods, and draw blood from the liver, and eat fennel, and drink from its juice, in order to get rid of gall." We learn elsewhere: "If you want someone not to get drunk, let him eat, on an empty stomach, the stalk of a cabbage or five bitter almonds." The medical tract is part of an extensive, ephemeral literature for the uneducated, now completely forgotten. In this respect, it has fared less well than **animal stories** or lives of the **saints.**

Further Reading

Dalby, Andrew. *Siren Feasts: A History of Food and Gastronomy in Greece.* London and New York: Routledge, 1997.

Lawson, John Cuthbert. *Modern Greek Folklore and Ancient Greek Religion: A Study in Survivals.* New York: University Books, 1964 [first publ. 1910].

Smith, Wesley D. *The Hippocratic Tradition.* Ithaca, NY: Cornell University Press, 1979.

MEDICINE In the **Enlightenment,** many Greek medical doctors, such as **Koraís,** also became writers. Preeminent in the early years was Alexandros Mavrokordatos (1641–1709), known as "he of the Secret Counsels." He was a doctor, a liberal intellectual, and a cornerstone of the educational progress that gradually led to Greek independence (1821). He understood the blood's circulation through the human body and was accused by the Turks of black magic because they could not understand pulse-taking. Yeoryios Hypomenás of Trebizond (seventeenth/eighteenth century) was sent from the Danubian principalities by K. Bassarabas to study **philosophy** and medicine at Padua (Italy). In 1709 an **anthology** was published in Hypomenás's honor at Venice, with 40 **epigrams.** The term *learned doctor* (ἰατροφιλόσοφος) refers to this intellectual mixture in one man. Ioannis Manis Rizos (of Constantinople, d. 1788) is a typical eighteenth-century doctor–scribe. He studied at Padua and returned as a physician to Greece. He published *The **Epitome** of Dates* and an essay in verse: *Warring Elements* (Venice, 1746). The aspiration to universal knowledge in the Greek medical tradition goes back to the *Hippocratic Writings,* a corpus of 50 treatises composed in Ionian dialect (?mid-fourth century B.C.), which includes a *Book of Prognostics, On Regimens in Acute Diseases,* and *About Epidemics,* which has case studies of 40 patients with life-threatening conditions. The volume *On the Sacred Disease* corrects the layman's view of epilepsy.

K. Palamás's famous story *Death of the Brave Young Man* (1891) plays on an attitude of rural Greeks: their refusal to pay for a doctor, their recourse to herbs, and the misguided courage that causes a man to seek amputation and death, rather than survive as a cripple: "They brought the best doctor in our Seatown: a doctor with credentials, with a name. This fellow had pulled many a patient away from the Grim Reaper. Truth is, most of Seatown only used him at the last minute,

when they had given up on the quacks and women healers. Altogether, Doc was annoyed: not that he missed out, by not being called sooner (so he said), but because the quacks put the gift of life at risk, and they all believed in charlatans. He got on with his job as a doctor. The villagers feared him; when they were on their last legs they got used to him, couldn't do without him; he seemed more like the commander of a boat, than a physician." Such necromancy contrasts with the empiricism of classical Greeks, such as Galen (c. 130–c. 200 A.D.): "There is one entrance for all the various articles of food. What receives nourishment is not one single part, but a great many parts. In cases of jaundice, two things occur at once: the dejections contain no bile at all, while the whole body becomes full of it."

Nikolaos Mavrommatis (1770–1817) studied medicine and literature in Italy; returning to Greece, he was appointed physician of Mouchtar, son of **Ali Pasha** of Ioannina, but left for Levcas because of the Pasha's tyranny. He was appointed by the French (protectors of the **Heptanese**) to teach math and Greek literature at the leading high school of Kerkyra. He was one of the founders of the French-sponsored (1807) Ionic Academy and taught there for several years. In 1814 the Ionic Academy was dissolved by the British general Campbell when he ended the Napoleonic occupation of Kerkyra. Mavrommatis is thought to have written the couplet for the title page of the enlightened Viennese periodical *The Scholar Hermes*: "I [Hermes] am not despatched, as once upon a time, by God. / I am assigned to speak the work of Man." His progressive and educational views tugged him outside the medical field: "A Pindaric Ode to Napoleon," *The*

Drowning of Frosyne (a poem relating to the notorious deed done by Ali Pasha), "Speech to the Youth of these Ionian Islands on the Need to Study Ancient and Modern Greek," and *A Treatise on Greek Words.* His father, Panos, took part in the Greek uprising promoted by Katherine I of Russia (1770) and was killed at Brachorio.

The translation of a popular French favorite, *Paul et Virginie* by Bernardin de Saint-Pierre (1737–1814), was made in 1824 by the doctor–savant Nikolaos Pikkolos (1792–1866), who studied in Bologna, practiced at Bucharest, taught philosophy at the Ionian Academy (Kerkyra), and settled in Paris to follow literary pursuits. He produced a four-act tragedy, *The Death of Demosthenes* (see **Palaiologos**); an anthology, *Sidelines of a Lover of the Arts*; poems; and translations of Descartes' *Discours de la méthode* (1637) and Aristotle's *On Animals.*

Further Reading

Nutton, Vivian. *From Democedes to Harvey: Studies in the History of Medicine.* London: Variorum, 1988.

Temkin, Owsei. *Galenism: Rise and Decline of a Medical Philosophy.* Ithaca, NY: Cornell University Press, 1973.

MEGÁLI IDÉA, I. See GREAT IDEA, THE

MEIOSIS Reduction, or decrease, is created by the **trope** of meiosis; in learned Greek it refers to the **figure of speech** by which an object or concept is made slighter, by stylistic means.

MELACHRINÓS, APOSTOLOS (1883–1952) Melachrinós was born in Romania, lived in Constantinople till 1922, and then went to Athens. As a poet, he cultivated a **symbolist** manner. He edited the journal *The Circle* (1931–1935). He produced verse translations of classical plays and two collections of poems: *The Way Leads . . .* (1904) and *Variations* (1909). **Andreas Embirikos** called him "the first modern Greek poet among us." He produced an edition of **demotic songs** (1946) and was committed to the notion of continuity between the popular and learned tradition. In the three parts of his unfinished *Apollonian* (1938), which he thought the heart of all his verse, Melachrinós embarked on what he calls "the five components of poetry: song, fairy tale, play, sorcery and dream" (interview in Bastiás 1999: 159).

MELÁS, LEON (1812–1879) A childhood enmeshed in nationalist conspiracy brought out the **patriotic** fervor of Leon Melás as an adult. He went to school in Odessa, where the family escaped from Epirus. In 1826 Melás went with his father (who made a living by giving private lessons) to Kerkyra, where he attended the Ionian Academy. Aided by a private scholarship, Melás went to Italy for further studies in law at Pisa. Back in Greece in his 20s, he became a lawyer and later a judge. In 1838, the government appointed him to a professorship in Law. By 1841 he was Minister of Justice, but clashed with King Otho over the muzzling of the press. In 1843 he was Minister of Justice a second time, but went almost immediately to London, where he worked in commerce and wrote the inspirational novel for right-thinking young Greeks, *Old Man Stathis* (1858). Modeled on the French text *Simon de Nantua,* by Laurent de Jussieu, *Old Man Stathis* is a collection of moral sketches and illustrative episodes. Used as a school **reader,** it nourished a generation of

Greek adolescents (see also **Missolonghi**). Melás published another reader, *Christopher,* the *Education Manual, Moral Addresses,* concerning the Church's Sunday *Gospel* readings, and an *Educational Guidebook.* Later he composed a *Lesser Plutarch,* containing 12 famous lives from ancient Greece, published after his death by the Association for the Distribution of Useful Books (see **Vikelas**). On 22 February 1866, he was appointed chairman of the committee set up to choose the new King of Greece. On the outbreak of the Cretan uprising (1866), he raised 9 million drachmas for the Athenian solidarity fund.

MELISSANTHI (1910–1990; pseudonym of Ivi Kouyia) The poet Melissanthi, born in Athens, married the statesman and writer Yannis Skandhalakis (1952). She studied French, German, and English in institutes at Athens and translated widely: poems by Emily Dickinson, Robert Frost, Nelly Sachs, Verlaine, Banville, and Rainer Maria Rilke. She taught French at schools and spoke on literary subjects on Greek radio. She produced poetry with a mainly religious inspiration, in the prewar period, but from the 1940s she became interested in the ideas of Karl Jung on the collective consciousness and the Messianic teachings of Berdya'ev. In the mid-1930s she convalesced from tuberculosis in a Swiss sanatorium. A collection of all her poetry, both religious and analytic, is in *Travel Itinerary* (1986). In one **image** of personified Silence, in Melissanthi's poem "Ancient Shipwrecked Cities," she merges an image of suffering into a sharp existential lesson: "The mirror of the moon is befogged / Like a ransom for the guilt / Of *knowing* and *existing.*" In her 1950 slim volume *The Season of Sleep and Wake-fulness,* Melissanthi slams words deep into the heart of abstract concepts in order to frame a definition of life and thought: "Merciful is sleep / Because of our uncertain existence, / Because of the weakness of our memory, / Which cannot endure great Wakefulness, / Because of the fickleness of our hands, / Because of the carelessness of our heart, / Which cannot endure the dagger of Love, / Which plumbs its depth with soundings, / Yet cannot endure the conflagrations of Existence." In this poetry, rhythmic argument and battering definitions weave in and out of each other. Melissanthi closes the third section of "The Season of Sleep" with a panorama of universality after the repeated question "Who sleeps at the instant when all matter is awake? [. . .] / Say it with me—Love is as powerful as death, / And many waters cannot quench love, / Nor can whole rivers choke it." In 1960 she wrote a prize-winning play for children, *The Little Brother,* and in 1979 she gained first place in the State Prize for Poetry. In 1986 she published *With the Ancient Gods* children's stories.

See also MISOGYNY

Further Reading

Friar, Kimon, ed. and trans. *Modern Greek Poetry.* Anixi: Efstathiadis, 1995: 223–232.

MELPOMENE One of the nine **Muses,** Melpomene was known in ancient times to be mother of the Sirens and patron of ode and song. Her name is derived from the verb *chant* (μέλπω). Later she becomes the protectress of tragedy and is depicted standing erect with a tragic mask in her hand. Melpomene also invented the two-corded cello (βάρβιτος).

She showed her acolytes how to accompany song with instrument.

MEMOIRS The Greek word for *memoirs* means an "autobiography" (the life of an individual written down by himself) and also the narration of events that someone has lived through or observed. This plural Greek noun acquires patriotic significance as a thematic word for first-hand accounts of deeds from the **War of Independence,** as in the title of E. Protopsaltes's *Memoirs of the Fighters of '21* (Ἀπομνημονεύματα ἀγωνιστῶν τοῦ *'21*, 20 volumes, 1956–1959). It is a word that revivifies the memory of warriors like Yeoryios Karaiskakis (1780–1827), the monk Papaflessas (1788–1825), the female sailor Manto Mavrogenous, decorated by President **Kapodistrias** with the rank of Lieutenant-General, or matriarch Laskarina Boumboulina of Spetsar (shot in 1825), or Nikitarás Stamatelopoulos, who was nicknamed "The Turkeater" after the battle of Valtetsi, near Tripolis (May 1821).

Nikolaos Kasomoulis composed *Military Memoirs* (publ. by **Y. Vlachoyannis** from 1940–1942) and hints at cannibalistic scavenging by some of the patriots at **Missolonghi:** "That was the day one of the volunteers cut some flesh from the thigh of a defender who had been killed, and ate it." Kasomoulis completed his memoirs while serving as Head of the Marine Guard at **Nafplion.** The manuscript consisted of 2,701 large handwritten sheets. The first of the three volumes deals with 1820–1827 and the second with 1827–1833; the third is a study of the **Klephts** and **armatolí** (see **Vlachoyannis**). The memoirs of **Kolokotronis,** "Old Man of the Morea," **Klepht** and Independence hero, were dictated by the illiterate general to **Ter-**

tsetis, who was then librarian of the Greek parliament. The style is taut and vigorous. As he rode from the gate to the citadel of Tripolitsa, after the siege and the massacre, on streets awash with gore and bones, his horse's hoof never touched the ground between the city walls and the seraglio. His politics are crisp: "the French Revolution and the doings of Napoleon opened the eyes of the world. The nations knew nothing before and the people thought that kings were gods upon the earth, and that they were bound to say that whatever they did was well done."

Other memoirs, for example, by **Varnalis,** the two wives of **Kazantzakis** (see **Zografou**), **Theodorou** or **Nirvanas,** recall a less nationalist ethos. In the first volume of his memoirs, **Alexandros Rangavís** (1809–1892) tells how his father taught the children to stage improvised plays at home to illustrate Bible or history lessons. Indeed, 1815 to 1816 were still golden years for a wealthy **Phanariot** family among the Turks at Constantinople. Alexandros tells how he and his 14-year-old friends in 1824 performed Voltaire's *Mahomet* (1741) in a barn.

See also HISTORICAL NOVEL; HISTORIOGRAPHY; MAKRIYANNIS; MISSOLONGHI; PERRAIVÓS; PRISON; TERTSETIS

Further Reading

Kolokotronés, Th. *Kolokotronés, the Klepht and the Warrior: Sixty Years of Peril and Daring: An Autobiography,* trans. with an introduction and notes by Mrs. Edmonds. London: T. Fisher Unwin, 1892.

METAPHOR Metaphor (μεταφορά) is the most powerful of all **tropes** and produces a transfer from a word's normal meaning to some other meaning, which may be related to the normal one or not related at all. Metaphor is a **figure of speech** that can convey preeminence or create **paronomasia,** a person, object, or entity *par excellence.* Other metaphors use the association of similarity, as when a writer selects a different name in place of the normal word. In a **Hellenistic** miscellany, Abraham is called "greatsounding." Philo the Younger explains that this occurs because Abraham's name was thought to mean "chosen father of sound." By an association of size or proportion, the writer can create metaphors with understatement (λιτότητα), reduction (μείωση), or exaggeration (υπερβολή). A poetic fragment on **Missolonghi** by **Solomós,** *The Free Besieged,* is tapestried with metaphor, some dreamy, rousing, and evocative, others creating brevity by a string of metaphor and **synechdoche,** as in the line from fragment 2, sketch 3: "Steed of Araby [the cavalry forces of Egypt], mind of a Frenchman [an organizing officer from France], scouting of Turkey [Turkish military spies], cannon ball of an Englishman [and guns of British design]."

Further Reading

Lloyd-Jones, Sir Hugh. *Greek Comedy, Hellenistic Literature, Greek Religion, and Miscellanea: The Academic Papers of Sir Hugh Lloyd-Jones.* Oxford: Clarendon Press, 1990.

METAXÁS, IOANNIS The Army officer and premier Ioannis Metaxás set up a military dictatorship on 4 August 1936 (see **Venizelos**). Metaxás formally confiscated a copy of the **Ritsos** volume *Epitaphios* at a public burning of seditious books. He is famous for saying "No!" (όχι), on 28 October 1940. This "no" re-

jected the Italian ultimatum demanding the passage of Italian forces into Greece. He set up a social security system in Greece during his rule, normalized the payment of pensions, and led Greece in repelling the Italian invasion from Albania (winter 1940). Metaxás's military rule lasted till his death (29 January 1941), but his intervention in the **language question** and his personal belief in the **Demotic** had an important effect on Greek writing. Metaxás commissioned a state-sponsored grammar of the demotic language from Manolis Triantafyllidis, then professor of linguistics at the University of Thessaloniki. The result (1941) has been a popular classic, seen by many Greek intellectuals as a reference point for written usage. The leftleaning government of Papandreou, in the 1960s, introduced Triantafyllidis's grammar officially into the Greek school system.

Further Reading

Vatikiotis, P. J. *Popular Autocracy in Greece 1936–41: A Political Biography of General Ioannis Metaxas.* Ilford: Cass, 1998.

METER Meter (μέτρο) is the heading for all the conventions that cover stress, syllables, and rhythm in a line of poetry. Before the advent of **free verse,** Greek poets handled meter with attention to the harmony between each stressed syllable (τονισμένη συλλαβή) and each unstressed syllable (άτονη συλλαβή) in the line. The study of meter took into account the "foot," which is a single measure, usually consisting of two or three syllables. Up until the explosion of free verse associated with the generation of the **1930s,** five main meters were present in modern Greek poetry. The iambic, represented by the sign ˘ ‾, consists of an unstressed syllable followed by a stressed one, as in the words "a child." Trochaic, $-\breve{}$, consists of stressed followed by unstressed, as in "come now" (ἔλα τώρα). The dactyl has three syllables, $-\breve{}\breve{}$. The anapest also has three syllables, but in reverse order from the dactyl, $\breve{}\breve{}-$, as in "I shall sing" (τραγουδῶ). The median-stressed, $\breve{}-\breve{}$, also known as "amphybrach," has unstressed, stressed, then unstressed syllables, as in "a flower" (λούλούδι). At the end of the line there was usually a conceptual pause (comma, dash, or full stop). If the sense ran over to the next line, it was said to be **enjambment.**

Now the duly arranged words of a poem in meter may constitute 5, 7, 8, 9, 11, 12, 13, 15, or even 17 syllables per line (στίχος). The **decapentasyllable** (15-syllable line) is called **political verse** and was particularly prevalent in **demotic songs** and narrative poems. A line with an accent or tone on the last syllable is oxytone. When the accent is on the last-but-one syllable (παραλήγουσα), the line is called paroxytone. The manipulation of these two cadences causes many sensory effects in Greek verse, as in the first quatrain of P. Soutsos's "Amorous Eventide": "What a lovely *moon*let; / What an amorous *eve!* / Restfully the *breeze*let / Plays all round the *trees.*"
See also HIATUS; PORIOTIS

METONYMY Metonymy (μετωνυμία) is a **figure of speech** that names one object indirectly, by referring to another. Literally, it is an "alteration of the name" (μετονομασία) and is common in Greek lyric poetry. Thus **Myrivilis,** in his poem "Autumn," calls the cyclamen "Turkish woman" because this forest flower is veiled, lurking below nuts. He also calls a shower of rain "the water from God."

Panayotis Soutsos calls God "the poet of Totality."

METRICS. See ARSIS; METER; THESIS

MICHAEL, THE NOBLE, VOIEVOD OF VLACHIA (sixteenth century) A **demotic song** calls Michael "our bey." Michael the Noble was a generic hero to Greeks under Turkish rule. In one poem, he is praised for campaigning from Wallachia (Romania) and fighting a battle in which the Turks lost 3,000 men, while he lost three, "what a shame, they were fine lads, brave warriors." In another song, Voievod Michael tells a brother, fighting beside him, to move away in case he kills *him* with his sword. Y. Stavrinos, a seventeenth-century officer on the staff of the prince of Vlachia, composed *The Gallantries of Voievod Michael,* a list in verse of deeds accomplished by Michael (Venice, 1668), drawing, in turn, on a verse chronicle by **Mathaios.** Stavrinos and his son were put to death by order of the Voievod Stefanos. Y. Palamidis (early seventeenth century) composed a poem in 1,382 rhyming decapentasyllables (1607) about the legendary Michael (publ. by Legrand, 1881).

MILLIÉX, TATIANA GRITSI (1920–) The novelist, translator, and journalist Tatiana Gritsi Milliéx was for a time general secretary of Greek PEN. She had a typical schooling, for a girl of this period, in music and languages. Gritsi gave up university and trained for a while as a dancer. She married Roger Milliéx in 1939 and from 1941 was involved with the Greek **resistance** against the German **occupation.** She first attracted attention with her translation (1945) of the war novel by Vercors *Le Silence de la mer*

(1942), an ideological choice by this young, left-wing partisan because the French book was also composed during a period of clandestine fighting. Milliéx later had trouble with the Greek **censors** under the **Colonels.** Her first novels, *Theseon Square* (1947) and *On Street of the Angels* (1949), deal with young women characters. In a long career, Milliéx became interested in experimental writing, especially the *nouveau roman,* and the challenge of the antinovel as a form of artistic expression. Way-marks in this process of self-invention are *In the First Person* (1950), *Behold a Pale Horse* (1963), *Retrospectives* (1982), and *The Threshing Floor of Hecate* (1993).

MINIATIS, ILIAS (1669–1714) Miniatis became one of the great preachers at the close of the **seventeenth century.** When aged 10, he went from Lixouri, second town in Cephalonia, to **Venice** on a scholarship. Miniatis studied at Flanginianon College, coming under the influence of the rhetorician **F. Skoufos,** and was ordained a deacon soon after graduating. He preached at St. George's, taught at his former college, and had tours of duty at Cephalonia, Zakynthos, Kerkyra (where he was tutor to the nephews of the Venetian administrator), and Constantinople (as aide to the Venetian minister). He carried out a legation to Emperor Leopold of Austria and was later elevated to a bishopric in Venetian-occupied Peloponnese (1711). His *Homilies* (Venice, 1717), combining learned vocabulary with elements in **plain Greek,** were widely admired.

MIROLOGIA The "songs of death" (μοιρολόγια, a Byzantine word) are demotic laments, usually recited as funeral songs. Perhaps their lineage is as ancient as Homer, *Iliad* XXIV, 719ff. Their singers have considerable poetic craft: "What shall I send to you, darling, there in the Underworld? / An apple would rot, a quince will shrivel. / Grapes will fall away, a rose would droop." In his poem "Don't Come," Yeoryios Zervinis (1875–1906) forbids his interlocutor to light a candle at his grave or weep under the willow tree. It is enough to "have the lament of some passing bird at the edge of the cemetery." The laments were chiefly a womanly art and could consist of elaborate poems or "tuneful weeping" (Holst-Warhaft). Some were recited by paid female mourners and others by a relative of the loved one at the wake. Laments from the Maina mountains to the south of Sparta are composed in 8-syllable lines rather than the predominant **political verse** of 15 syllables.

These **demotic songs** gave women the control of mourning in Greek culture. The laments could trigger revenge cycles that challenged the law courts. A Mani lament (1932) by the mother of one Stavrianis, Doureka, lists all the villages where her daughter was admired. A lament for Vetoulas (c. 1830) evokes a mourning sister who is found sitting mute in an old stone quarry. In a text from Kandila (1959), the singer suggests that only a life of suffering gives the singer the natural right to lament: "Whoever knows not death, weeps not over the dead, Vasio, Vasio of mine; / And whoever knows not exile, weeps not for the exiled, little Vasili of mine; / And whoever knows nothing about sickness, moans not over the sick, Vasio, Vasio of mine." Laments focus on the contrast between an idyllic past and the miserable present. They may involve the examination of a hero's dead body and the enumeration of its wounds.

The story *Death of the Brave Young Man* by **Palamás** provides a description of the lament in its relationship with the funeral. The dying hero gets his own mother to sing to him, prompting her with a traditional lament formula: "Youth turns into earth / And youthful joys to grass. / The body, strong as a hawk, / Becomes ground where people walk." Here the mother laments her son while he is still alive. The lament that prompts the poem *Funereal* (Ἐπιτάφιος) by **Ritsos** was based on the death of a striking tobacco worker and inspired by an actual photograph. Ritsos saw in the Communist newspaper *Rizospastis* (10 May 1936) the picture of a mother bending over her slain son's body. "I'll dye my dress red with the blood of the relatives of those who killed you, my boy" (see **Epitaphios**). The furor created by Ritsos's imaginary lament, with its music setting by Theodorakis and the *bouzouki* singer Grigöris Bithikotsis, in 1959, paved the way for protest songs of the 1960s. A small selection of traditional funeral songs is in A. and W. Barnstone (eds., *A Book of Women Poets from Antiquity to Now*. New York: Schocken, 1980).

Further Reading

Holst-Warhaft, Gail. *Dangerous Voices: Women's Laments and Greek Literature*. London: Routledge, 1992.

Motsiou, Y. "Ἑλληνικό Μοιρολόγι. Προβλήματα ερμηνείας και ποιητικής τέχνης [The Greek Funeral Song: Problems of Interpretation and Poetic Craft]." *Dodoni* 31, no. 2 (1992): 165–228.

MIRROR OF THE PRINCE "Mirror of the prince" (κάτοπτρον του ἡγεμόνος) was a conventional term for a book in which an ascetic man or a magic creature instructed a young ruler on how to behave. From the sixth century A.D., Buddhist precepts were contained in stories about anthropomorphic animals who taught moral values to humans. These Indian tales drifted across to Eastern Europe. The edifying genre also goes back to antiquity. The patristic writer Synesius (c. 370–412) composed an address *On Kingship* for delivery before the emperor Arcadius in 399, warning the orientalized monarch that he lived like "a polyp of the sea," wallowing in self-indulgence, remote from his common subjects. In subsequent "mirrors of the prince," a wise courtier fashions the ideal young man, so he may thereafter function as a virtuous king. The genre reached its apogee in *Imperial Statue* (c. 1250) by Nikiforos Blemmydes (c. 1197–c. 1272), composed for his pupil, the future Emperor Theodore II Laskaris.

See also STEPHANITIS AND ICHNELATIS

MISOGYNY Greek literature, despite its fixed reference points in the mother, the sister, and the home (σπίτι), does not grant equality to women and seems misogynous to many outside readers. Folk and **demotic** couplets are full of digs at the fair sex: "A young woman's head turns like a windmill: / The man that she chases off today, tomorrow she makes her friend," or "Never, at the rear end of a vessel, do we fail to see some greenery; / Never, on a maid's fair lip, do we fail to see some red." At the end of the fifteenth century, an unknown author composed in 1,210 lines the *Legendary of Well-Born Ladies and Most Honorable Noblewomen* (edited by K. Krumbacher, Munich, 1905). The first part of this work (475 lines) is in mixed rhyming and non-rhyming **decapentasyllables,** the rest is in eight-syllable lines. These women are crudely insulted, and realistic details are introduced about their bad conduct: "they try everything / To make their hair fair," and they "remove their wretched eyebrows," or choose colors like white or red to paint their faces after they wash them.

Palamás once asked **Vrettakos** his opinion about **Melissanthi:** "Tell me, is it possible for a woman to be a poet, if she's busy with housework?" **Karkavitsas** wrote to K. Chatzopoulos about a disillusionment in love: "That bitterness passed and left nothing else inside me but a hateful contempt for the female sex." The poet **Karyotakis** sneers: ". . . take a fork / And sound the depth of your empty brain! / *Untamed limbs, see-through clothes,* / Cloying, hypocritical mouths, / Unsuspected, negative / Creations, and therefore specially privileged!" The italicized phrases (ἀτίθασα μέλη, διαφανῆ ροῦχα) reveal the problem. Karyotakis cannot allow that a woman has a love life. In his story "Medical Help," Papadiamantis makes his hero say: "My neighbour, Konstantinos Rigas, is a smart and worldly fellow. When a little girl is born in the district and he sees the women and relatives celebrating, Konstantinos will say: 'Rejoice, kids: another drudge is born.'"

A wife can leave, certainly, but not cuckold her husband. This implicit rule is seen in the **Papadiamantis** story "Homesick Woman," where the woman declares: "He knows perfectly well that I cannot betray his honor! But he also knows I can't live in this foreign clime." The father of **Kazantzakis** was said to revere the male sex so much that he refused to look his daughters in the face. In the **Resistance,** parastate groups mocked women who joined the left-wing partisans (EAM), or the Youth Movement

(EPON). They addressed one song to the EPON girls: "Now that the Germans are here, / Your belly is flat / And when the Russians come / Your belly will grow. / Babies and many other gifts / The Greek mountains give you. / With swollen bellies and / Your string of cartridges / *You* are the heroines of ELAS." Yiorgos Markopoulos (b. 1951) published a long poem, in 1987, with the title "Natascha Pandi." It ends with the quip: "a woman, after the first night of marriage, is sure to wake up without the man she had dreamt of marrying."

Further Reading

Kalogeras, Y. and Domna Pastourmatzi, eds. *Nationalism and Sexuality: Crises of Identity,* 135–145. Thessaloniki: Aristotle University, 1996.

MISSOLONGHI The toast of Greek **nationalism,** epicenter of fact and fable from the **War of Independence,** Missolonghi is a former fishing town on the north gateway to the Gulf of Corinth, east of a shallow inland lagoon, the Limnothalassa. The Turkish forces laid siege to this littoral stronghold no less than three times during the war. In 1822 Mavrokordatos held Missolonghi against a force of 10,000 commanded by Omer Vrioni. In 1823 the defense against a second siege was held by the legendary Souliot hero, Markos Botzaris. **Byron** landed at Missolonghi on 5 January 1824 and took a house belonging to Christos Kapsalis on the foreshore. On 22 January 1824, he penned "On This Day I Complete My Thirty-Sixth Year," with the prescient lines "The fire that on my bosom preys / Is lone as some volcanic isle; / No torch is kindled at its blaze—/ A funeral pile." He also made efforts for the town's defense ahead of the third siege (see **Phil-**

hellenes). The provisional Greek government assigned Byron general leadership of an expedition to relieve Naupaktos, but he fell sick and, after a short illness, died on 19 April 1824. When the radical poet **A. Soutsos** came to Greece from Paris (1825), he wanted to join the besieged at Missolonghi, but Admiral Miaoulis, who had him in his ship, would not let him disembark. Reshid Pasha brought a force of 15,000 to invest the town in April 1825. He was reinforced, six months later, by Ibrahim Pasha at the head of 10,000 Egyptian auxiliaries from the Peloponnese. The 5,000 defenders, soldiers and civilians of one mind, held out for 12 months against cannon bombardment (which **Solomós** could hear across the water at Zakynthos). One by one, the Greeks lost the islands in the lagoon.

On the night between 22 and 23 April 1826, the surviving defenders opted for a mass sortie (see **Zalokostas**). Many of these events are idealized in the planned or finished sketches of Solomós's poem *The Free Besieged.* Those who left Missolonghi in the sortie were supposedly betrayed by a deserter. Some of the survivors were ambushed in the foothills of Mount Zygos by a force of 1,000 Albanians. About 9,000 Greeks and Philhellenes emerged from Missolonghi; only 1,800 cut their way out to Amphissa. Those who stayed behind blew themselves up with their gunpowder magazine, killing some of their assailants. Missolonghi remained under Turkish control from April 1826 to 2 May 1829. The town was handed back under a settlement that belied the seven years of blood and drama. Several major literary figures have come from Missolonghi: **Y. Drosinis, Miltiadis Malakasis,** D. Malakasis, Mimis Dymberakis, **Kostís Pa-**

lamás, K. Stasinopoulos, **A. Travlantonis,** and **Sp. Trikoupis.** The writer and government minister **Leon Melás** (1812–1879) wrote the verse drama *Athanasios Diakos* (1859) in honor of his uncle Pavlos, who fell at Missolonghi.

Further Reading

Dakin, Douglas. *The Greek Struggle for Independence, 1821–1833.* Berkeley: University of California Press, 1973.

Garrett, Martin. *Greece: A Literary Companion.* London: John Murray, 1994.

MISTRIOTIS, YEORYIOS (1840–1916) The conservative scholar Yeoryios Mistriotis identified the **Klephts** and the leaders of the Greek independence struggle with the epic heroes of **Homer:** "Each hero of the time of the Klefts and each commander of our great Revolution is the most comprehensive and most eloquent scholium on the Homeric epics" (the passage, dated 1871, is translated in D. Ricks, 1989: 42). Mistriotis followed Hippolyte Taine's theory concerning the atmosphere flowing round any work of art, the "ambient milieu," which it must express if it is to achieve genuineness and inspiration: "Great poets are not born like Athena from the skull of Zeus; they are representatives of the people among whom they live." He upbraided the partisans of the **Demotic** in the language riots of 1901 and 1903 (see **Pallis; Evangelika**). R. Beaton (1994: 316) cites a self-justification by Mistriotis: "The Greek people risks losing its very existence for the sake of a few individuals who call themselves demoticists. I do not know if these people are paid in money or in kind. The Bulgarians are trying to detach from mother Greece her dearest daughter [that is, Macedonia], while others who call themselves demoticists are taking a hatchet to the mother herself."

Further Reading

Kordatos, Yannis. Δημοτικισμὸς καὶ λογιωτατισμός [Demotic versus Learned]. Athens: Boukoumanis, 1974.

MITROPOULOU, KOSTOULA (1927–)

Mitropoulou has written around 40 works, starting in the area of antinovel (αντιμυθιστόρημα: see **Nouveau Roman**) and extending her unconventional manner to one-act plays and librettos for choral drama. Her favored themes are the recollection of a love affair, a woman's struggle for freedom, women's social expropriation, and the fictional character's conflict with the state, yet she felt uncomfortable with the category of "women's fiction." Influenced by N. Sarraute, she chose other modern experimental writers to translate: Harold Pinter, V. Woolf's *Mrs. Dalloway,* Marguerite Duras, Alberto Moravia's *La noia,* and Tennessee Williams. Her debut, *The Land with the Suns* (1958), was followed by a prize (1962) from the Committee of Twelve for *Faces and Figures.* A much later success was the novel *The Antique Shop on Tzimiski Street* (1988).

Further Reading

Lord, Tracy M. "Kostoula Mitropoulou's To παλαιοπωλείο στην Τσιμισκή and the New Novel." *JMGS* 11, no. 1 (1993): 133–148.

MITSAKIS, MIKHAIL (1860–1916)

The writer Mikhail Mitsakis was born in Megara. His date of birth is erroneously given as 1868 in the *Great Encyclopedia of Greece* (1926–1934). He went to high school in Sparta. He briefly studied law in Athens before taking up humorous

journalism, first in the period 1880 to 1885, with Anninos's periodical *Asmodaeos* (see **Roidis**), and then with its successor *Town* (1885–1887). In 1886–1888 he contributed regularly to *Acropolis.* He also wrote for *Don't Get Lost.* He worked for a number of years on D. Koromilás's newspaper *The Daily,* contributing chronicles, gazettes, travel impressions, and book reviews. Later he tried to issue satirical papers of his own, *Noise* and *Capital,* but they had short runs. In 1896, he wrote for *Scrip.* Mitsakis had dealings with almost every broadsheet or satirical gazette of note in the last 20 years of the nineteenth century. He contributed articles to the *Encyclopedic Dictionary.* For the periodical *Estía* he produced local color pieces, considered exemplary in their observation of people and places.

Mitsakis's dazzling but dispersive career was cut short by a mental impairment that overtook him in 1896. He became unproductive, at times a hobo skulking along the Athens backstreets, periodically in an asylum, for the last 20 years of his life. The publisher Yeoryios Phexis was so alarmed by the state of the half-crazed Mitsakis that he gave him one drachma every morning. His scattered work was collected in three posthumous volumes.

Further Reading

Mitsakis, M. Τὸ ἔργο του [His Literary Works]. Edited by M. Peranthis. Athens: Kollaros, 1956.

MIXED LANGUAGE. See LANGUAGE QUESTION

MOATSOU, DORA (1895–1978)

The poet Dora Moatsou, wife of **K. Varnalis,** was born in Constantinople of a family with Cretan origins. She studied French at the Sorbonne. In 1927 she published her first poetry collection, *Lines,* and later came *In Memoriam* (1938), *Songs for Children* (1953), and *Love and Yearnings* (1954). C. Robinson observes how her sonnet "Penelope" employs a traditionalist approach to classical **myth,** using **allegory** to stress a simple moral aspect, in this case the phenomenon of wifely fidelity. A more satirical treatment of classical names is to be found in her poem "Old Man Teacher." Here Antigone and Aphrodite encircle the bed of a bumbling teacher, who coughs and sneezes in the winter, whose spectacles slip from his nose, and who corrects 62 copybooks bent over his table till one in the morning. The old man acts in rage and fuss because Maria carelessly breaks glasses, while a certain Aphrodite is flighty, and Antigone seems to invade his class.

Further Reading

Robinson, Christopher. "'Helen or Penelope?' Women Writers, Myth and the Problem of Gender Roles." In *Ancient Greek Myth in Modern Greek Poetry: Essays in Memory of C. A. Trypanis,* ed., Peter Mackridge, 109–120. London: Cass, 1996.

MODERNISM. See PROTOPORÍA

MONARCHY, GREEK In 1832, the European powers chose a Bavarian prince as Greece's first king, but Otho soon lost the respect of many intellectuals. He was lampooned or fiercely criticized by leading writers, including the **Soutsos** brothers. This opposition may have contributed to his deposition (1862). A Danish prince was elected (1863) and reigned as King George I of the Hellenes. This second monarch was attacked by Yeoryios Hyperidis (1859–1939), a fiery journalist from Smyrna, in a verse mime entitled *On Board the Vessel* (1876). Here King George was represented as a naval commander, the state was a ship, Prime Minister Koumondouros was deputy captain, and the citizens were the crew. The vessel is tossed by storms, in need of Democracy to find a harbor.

A **constitution** was enacted under King George I (1863). Greece acquired the province of Thessaly and much of Epirus (1881), which endeared him to various writers who espoused the **Great Idea** (see **Polyzoidis**). King Constantine favored Greek neutrality in the first World War and abdicated to make way for his younger son, Alexander. Constantine returned to Greece after the death in 1920 of Alexander and was again deposed, in 1922. George II succeeded him and was expelled in 1923. This led to the proclamation of a Republic of Greece. The years 1924 to 1935 were marked by attempted coups and the collapse of the Republic. The king returned after a dubiously conducted referendum (1935), and a monarch ruled until 1967, up to the **Colonels' Junta.** The Greek monarchy was abolished by referendum in 1974.

Further Reading

Leon, George B. *Greece and the Great Powers, 1914–1917.* Thessalonica: Institute for Balkan Studies, 1974.

Papacosma, S. Victor. *The Military in Greek Politics: The 1909 Coup d'État.* Kent, OH: Kent State University Press, 1977.

Prebelakes, Eleutherios G. *British Policy Towards the Change of Dynasty in Greece, 1862–1863.* Athens: Christou, 1953.

MONEY People say the main thrust of modern Greek literature is the **recording** of village life, or the **language question,**

or the long **Turkokracy.** But the real subject is poverty, ever since the days when **Prodromos** or **Sachlikis** moaned about their lack of funds or profligate spending by their family. Of course, the removal of poverty means money. **Napoleon Lapathiotis** killed himself in January 1944; money was raised by friends to cover his funeral costs. The writer Stratis Doukas died forgotten in an old age home. Konstantinos Pop (1816–1878) died in penury, having invented the writing style known as "current events column" (χρονογράφημα); the state paid for his burial. The story collections of **P. Nirvanas,** *Carefree Days* (1923–1928) mount a parade of jobseekers, travelers, parasites, thieves, moneymakers, and citizens going mildly astray, despite everyday business. P. Axiotis (1840–1918) has a story about a sailor who carried cash across the sea for friends, loses it in a shipwreck, and then blows his brains out "in a single dwelling, in catastrophe, in gloom." In the famous text by **Anonymous Greek,** the *Greek Rule of Law* (1806), the writer rails against the greed and horror of money. Justice is sold and judges are bought because of gold. Gold covers the crimes of the rich, and lack of gold disperses the rights of the poor. Money is what makes ten men run behind one man, like pigs behind a swineherd. Three or four coins are all that prevent an army of slaves from running away from their tormentors, for it cannot be "fear of dishonor." The novel *Honor and Money* (1912) by **K. Theotokis** poses the theme of a girl with meager dowry and a man of "good family" who makes her pregnant. She is left to work at one of the new factories on Kerkyra (at a time when Theotokis, who gave away his inheritance, was finishing his studies).

MONTSELEZE, THEODOROS (mid-seventeenth century). See EFYENA

MORAÏTIDIS, ALEXANDROS (1851–1929) Moraïtidis, cousin of the more celebrated writer **A. Papadiamantis,** was born and died on the isle of Skiathos. He studied literature at the University of Athens and taught at high schools in the city. His sketches and stories, many on themes for religious feasts, first appeared in *Acropolis* and subsequently across a range of many newspapers. Moraïtidis wrote essays, articles, short stories, plays, verse, and some of the best early **travel** pieces in modern Greek. He won the major Literature and Arts Prize (1914) and was elected to the Academy of Athens (1929). He published six volumes of travel impressions, six of short stories. His plays include *Timoleon* and *Fall of Constantinople.* The idiom that he uses is chiefly **Katharevousa;** his fiction is mainly folk realism or recording of **manners** (ἠθογραφία). **Mount Athos** made a lasting impression on Moraïtidis, called "Alexandros the lesser" in relation to Papadiamantis, and at an advanced age he became a monk. He adored the many bells of Mount Athos and their sweet-sounding music. In 1931, when he was walking with an interviewer toward Omonoia Square, in Athens, he stopped near a kiosk and explained that the vendor was a nice man because he let him (Moraïtidis) look at the newspapers each time he passed, without paying: "Unluckily my means are so scanty, that I am not able to be a reader of newspapers."

Further Reading

Néa Estía, no. 559 (1950), and a special number of *Greek Creation,* no. 64 (1 October 1950) concern Moraitidis.

MOUNT ATHOS Many writers have been caught up by the wild allure of Athos, a peninsula that forms the eastern prong of Chalcidice. Xerxes cut a canal 12 to 15 meters wide across this isthmus in 481 B.C. to protect an invasion of Greece by eliminating the journey round the peninsula's stormy tip. The architect Deinokrates planned to carve a statue of **Alexander the Great** out of the mountain at the tip of the peninsula. Called "Holy Mountain," the modern autonomous community of 20 monasteries on Athos retains the Julian calendar and runs 13 days behind the **dating** of the modern world. The day on Mount Athos is divided by **Byzantine** tradition into hours of varying length, ending at 12 o'clock. The monasteries are either coenobite (from the word κοινοβιάτης, "living in common") or idiorhythmic (from the word ιδιόρρυθμος, "idiosyncratic"). The monks attend church for eight or more hours every day. Their principal services are Mass, Vespers, Compline, and Nocturnal Office. This topos of retreat and purity is evoked in writing by **A. Moraïtidis, Papadiamantis,** Adamantiou (see **Schooling**), **P. Soutsos, Z. Papantoniou,** Takis Papatsonis, **Tasos Athanasiadis, K. Ouranis,** Spyros Melás, **Fotis Kontoglou, Kazantzakis,** Nikos Athanasiadis, **Theotakás,** and Th. Athanasiadis-Novas (whose **travel** writing made him, in 1926, the first Greek ever to reach the North Pole). The monasteries possess manuscripts, incunabula, and archives of great value, although fire and depredation have left marks over the millennium up to 1963, since the community's inception.

Further Reading

Armand de Mendieta, Emmanuel. *Mount Athos, the Garden of the Panaghia.* Berlin: Akademie, 1972.

Hellier, Chris. *Monasteries of Greece.* London: Tauris Parke, 1996.

MOURNING FOR DEATH A fine sixteenth-century vernacular poem, *Mourning for Death: Futility of Life and Turning Back to God* (Venice, 1524), could be the work of Yioustos, son of the writer Ioannis Glykýs. It is a robust text in 632 rhyming 15-syllable lines, directed at the "you" and "us" of humanity, highlighting the decrepitude of the human frame and the transience of power. The author laments the silvering hair, wrinkled skin, and dimming eyesight of mortal senescence. He dips frequently into **metaphor** as in "the years drag us with haste towards Hades, and wherever time leads us, there let us follow!" As human bodies turn out to be fraudulent old skinbags, approaching Death removes all consolations, like the rosewater fragrance of breath, the helpful loyalty of a servant, and the beauty of "your abundant wisdom."

MOUTZÁN-MARTINENGOU, ELISÁBET (1801–1832) Moutzán-Martinengou was an **Ionian Islands** woman writer, whose archive of plays, stories, and local sketches was lost during an **earthquake** at Zakynthos (1935). A certain Markos Martinengos was enrolled in the Golden Book (catalogue of Heptanesian aristocrats) in 1572. This woman came from the Moutzán family, which had moved from Italy to Zakynthos. When young, she mastered Greek, Italian, and French. In 1931 she married the Zantiot noble Nikolaos Martinengos. She died on 9 November 1832, after giving birth to a son, later named Elisabetios. She left a large body of work in Greek, including odes, plays, translations from the *Odyssey* and *Prometheus Bound,* as well as essays on economics and poetics. Tragedies drafted by her in Greek include *The Freeing of Thebes, Deception Avenged, Euryma-*

chus, Eurykleia and Theanó, Rodope, and *Celestial Justice.* She wrote plays in Italian, *Numitore, Brutus the First, Henry: or on Innocence, Laodicea: or on Prudence, The Tyrant Punished, Lycurgus: or on Humility, The Virtuous King,* and *Collection of Diverse Verse Compositions.* Passages from these works are quoted in her son's edition of her autobiography: **E. Martinengos,** *My Mother: the Autobiography of Mrs. Elizabeth Martinengos* (Athens, 1881).

Further Reading

Kolias, Helen Dendrinou. "Empowering the Minor: Translating Women's Autobiography." *JMGS* 8, no. 2 (1990): 213–221.

Moutzán-Martinengou, Elisábet. Αυτοβιογραφία [An Autobiography]. Athens: Keimena, 1983. *My Story by Elisavet Moutzan-Martinengou,* trans. by Helen Dendrinou Kolias. Athens: University of Georgia Press, 1989.

MUSES Each of these nine daughters of Zeus and Mnemosyne (Memory) protects one of the arts or sciences: **Calliope,** patron of poetry, **Clio** (history), **Euterpe** (music, lyric verse), **Terpsichore** (dance), **Erató** (love poetry), **Melpomene** (tragedy), **Thalia** (comedy), **Polyhymnia** (religious poetry), and **Urania** (astronomy). "Dear Muse, for whom do you bring this cornucopia of song?" So begins book IV of the *Palatine Anthology.* The composition ends with an assurance: "This sweetly-worded garland of the Muses is for all poetry's initiates." The fifth ode of **Kalvos,** "To the Muses," hails these "voices which enrich the feasts of those who dwell on Olympus," and first placed honey on the lips of **Homer.** Kalvos is composing a legitimizing parable on the continuity of **Hellenism.** The neo-Platonist Proclus exalts the culture of those "who redeem, / By the

blameless, inspiring mysteries of books, / People who have lost their way in the depths of life." The Muses are first referred to by the classical poet Hesiod. Born in Pieria, they are called "dwellers in Pieria." Living on Mount Helicon, they are also known as "Helikoniads." The god Apollo is the "Muse leader." Etymological association gives us the modern term *museum* (μουσεῖον) for **painting** and **sculpture** are stored in the *Muses'* place. So too is music (μουσική) the art where melody is combined with verse.

Various literary periodicals have taken their name from the nine: *Muse* was produced in Athens in 1923–1924 under the editor I. M. Panayotiopoulos. A fortnightly *Muses* ran from September 1892 at Zakynthos, edited by Leonidas Zois. In 1920 its masthead was decorated by a sketch of the nine Muses designed by the cartoonist Dionysios Kapsokefalos. One special number provided a lexicon of Zakynthos's island dialect, compiled by Zois himself. Among distinguished contributors to *Muses* were the brothers **Martzokis.** Up to September 1939 (no. 974) *Muses* was produced at Zakynthos. Until no. 981, it came out at Athens and closed (1941) "on account of the foreign occupation." *Museum* was a fortnightly brought out by Y. Arvanitis in Cairo (1911). *Museum and Library of the Evangelical School* was a Smyrna-based periodical in octavo format with pictures (1873 to 1885) funded by the benefaction of Philhellenes and friends of the Muses.

MUSIC. See GATSOS; HYMN; MANTZAROS; MUSES; OPERA; PALAMÁS; PORIOTIS; REBETIKA; RITSOS; SEFERIS; SIKELIANÓS

MUSLIM also MOSLEM; MOHAMMEDAN. See ISLAM

MYRIVILIS, STRATIS (1892–1969; pseudonym of Evstratios Haralamboús Stamatopoulos) The novelist and short story writer Stratis Myrivilis was born in the village of Skamniá in the north of Lesbos and cut short law studies at the University of Athens to volunteer for service in the **Balkan** and Asia Minor wars of 1912–1922. He was wounded at Kilkís (1913). From 1911 to 1922 he covered war events for Lesbos newspapers, dispatching his copy from the military front. After 1922 he lived for a while in Mytiline, later settling in Athens, where he stayed until his death. His *novella Basil the Albanian* first appeared in an Athens newspaper (1934), followed by a longer version in 1939, and a further augmented version in 1943. The story builds up a male islander hero from the familiar Greek "brave young lad" ($\pi\alpha\lambda\lambda\eta\kappa\dot{\alpha}\rho\iota$) into a drinker, lover, atheist, and brigand. Vasilis Arvanitis becomes a rule unto himself. As a tobacco smuggler, he forces a French officer to hold his wages in his mouth while he smokes a cigarette in front of him. When there is a meat shortage, he forces a butcher to slaughter and skin his animals for public sale. He makes the two 18-year-old daughters of the town harridan into his mistresses. He kills himself with a dagger to avoid capture after falling into a ditch. He is reputed to have fought in Macedonia and, by a nice anachronism, for **Ali Pasha** in Constantinople. The physical setting is Skamniá, Myrivilis's home village on Lesbos, inhabited by mutually suspicious Turks and Greeks. The dramatic date is around 8 November 1912, when four and a half centuries of **Ottoman** rule ended for the island. A new Turkish constitution had been given by the Sultan to the "young Turks" (24 July 1908). Myrivilis wrote an influential antiwar memoir, *Life*

in the Tomb (first ed., 1924). The book is a mixture of narrative fiction and personal journals, revised in various later editions. *Life in the Tomb* purports to narrate the experiences of a sergeant on the war front in Macedonia, in 1917. It adopts a satirical tone toward the officer corps and military brass, while highlighting the drudgery of the man in the trench, who in one symbolic passage exposes himself to snipers in order to admire a single flower peeping out of an emplacement, between its sandbags. The book was considered an implicit attack on Greek militarism and expansion in the Balkans. It came under **censorship** and was banned during the period of the Metaxás dictatorship (1936–1941) and the subsequent **occupation** of Greece by Germany, Bulgaria, and Italy.

Stratis Myrivilis was elected late to the Athenian academy after his seventh application (1958). He gained relatively little literary recognition in his lifetime, earning meager amounts from journalism and teaching. While living in Athens from 1930, he edited liberal newspapers and held a job with Greek National Radio, which he later lost through political disfavor after World War II. Until 1955, he held a job in the library of Parliament. From the 1960s, his reputation grew with the popularity of *The Schoolmistress with the Golden Eyes* (1933) and *The Mermaid Madonna* (1949). L. Politis observed (1973: 249–250) that the aim of every Greek writer in this generation was to produce a novel, and *The Schoolmistress with the Golden Eyes* met the requirements of the pure novel, strengthened by the incidental fact that Myrivilis himself had married a schoolteacher. In the text, the hero, Leonís, battered by fighting, returns from the war to Mytiline. He falls in love with the widow

(Sapphó) of his best friend (Vranás), killed in the Asia Minor campaign. The later book, *The Mermaid Madonna,* examines a group of refugees from the **Asia Minor disaster** who settle in a village by the sea in Mytiline and adopt the life of fishermen in the shadow of an icon that is part divine, part subhuman. For his contributions to the Mytiline newspaper *Clarion,* Myrivilis used the pen name "Little Pencil." While editing the paper *Democracy,* he wrote markedly anti-Communist articles.

Further Reading

Myrivilis, Stratis. *Life in the Tomb,* trans. by Peter A. Bien. Hanover, NH: University Press of New England, 1977.

Myrivilis, Stratis. *Vasilis Arvanitis,* trans. by Pavlos Andronikos. Armidale, New South Wales: The University of New England, 1983.

Myrivilis, Stratis. *The Schoolmistress with the Golden Eyes,* trans. by P. Sherrard. London: Hutchinson, 1964.

Myrivilis, Stratis. *The Mermaid Madonna,* trans. by Abbott Rick. London: Hutchinson, 1959.

MYRTIOTISSA (1883–1973; pseudonym of Theoni Drakopoulou) Myrtiotissa, born in Constantinople, daughter of a Greek diplomat, wrote to and became the friend, lover, or confidant of, **Palamás, Mavilis,** and other men in literary and theater circles. She went to boarding school in Athens, lived two years in Crete, settled in Athens, accepted an arranged marriage with a cousin in Paris, and returned with her young son, who was later well known as the actor George Pappás (1903–1958), who made his debut with Somerset Maugham's *The Swan* (1931). Myrtiotissa was a dreamy, passionate woman, addressing the poem "For My Son" to a growing boy who has the "yearning and craving / To see, to touch and to taste all the honey of life." Her ode "I love you" is a neo-Romantic miniature: "I love you: I cannot / Say anything else / More deep, more simple. / Or more substantial! // Here, before your feet, / With longing, I scatter / The many-leaved flower / Of my life." Her volume *Songs* came out in 1919, followed by *Yellow Flames* (1925, with a preface by Palamás), *The Gifts of Love* (1932), and *Cries* (1939). An *Anthology for Children* came out in 1930 (2 vols.). She translated Euripides's *Medea* and poems by the French woman writer Anne de Noailles (1876–1933). A special issue of the journal *Néa Estía* (no. 990: 1968) was devoted to this writer. Her verse was awarded the State Poetry Prize and the Poetry Prize of the Academy of Athens.

MYTH The classical myth was a compelling, untrue story with supernatural elements. Modern Greek literature has constructed fresh myths from **Achilles** and other stories in **Homer** (see **Seferis**), the **Alexander Romance, Belisarius,** the **Akritic** warriors, **Diyenís Akritas,** the **fall of Constantinople,** the **Uprising, Klephts,** and the **palikari.** Aeschylus's three *Oresteia* plays establish the revenge myth, and the **opera** *Oresteia* (1970) by Yanni Christou (1926–1970) is one of its modern adaptations.

Further Reading

Cahill, Jane. *Her Kind: Stories of Women from Greek Mythology.* Peterborough, Ontario: Broadsview Press, 1995.

Edmunds, Lowell, ed. *Approaches to Greek Myth.* Baltimore: Johns Hopkins University Press, 1990.

N

NAFPLION Dorotheos (or Hierotheos), Metropolitan of Monemvasia, wrote a chronicle of the world. It became popular reading (Venice, 1631) for refugee Greeks and included a section entitled *Siege of Nafplion by the Turks* (in 1538), which exalted the legendary defense of this coastal town, with scenes of the besieged starving for 10 days and then dropping dead or drinking poison and turning black. The Venetian governor of Nafplion, Klouzós, grows jealous of Bozikis, one of the Greek heroes, and has him shot in the back. Nafplion is steeped in these memories and those of early **nineteenth-century theater.** It was the first capital of Greece; its first parliaments were here, and its first high school. **Kolokotronis,** the war hero, was briefly jailed in Nafplion castle, under sentence of death for allegedly betraying the independence cause. Kapodistrias, first President of Greece, was murdered here.

NAKOU, LILIKA (1903–1989) The writer Lilika Nakou was credited with causing the dispatch of International Red Cross aid, including crates of milk, to Greece, after her stories, *The Children's Inferno* (1945) were smuggled to Switzerland during the **occupation** of Athens. She had been working as a nurse, and her reports told stories of tortured, criminal, or starving kids in the occupied city. Nakou was notable in the 1930s for her plain, almost conversational, written Greek. Periklís Rodakis observed that "every woman writing in Greece today is influenced by her style." Nakou's early stories in *The Deflowered One* (1930), and the novel *Those Gone Astray* (1935), dwell on mother–daughter relations and the rigid boarding school that she attended after moving to Geneva with her mother. A shock of surprise greeted *Those Gone Astray* in 1935, because of its unrelieved realism and pessimism. The novel *Towards a New Life* (1956) and the story "Nausicaa" (1954, first publ. in French) altered Nakou's wintry focus to a kind of sisterly understanding of women's place in society. *Ikarian Dreamers* (1963) analyzes a male protagonist, resolving the plot with a not quite conventional marriage. Nakou was capable of light, satirical touches in *Mrs. Do-re-mi* (1958), based on her experiences as a music teacher among the well-off. Promptly translated into French, *Mrs. Do-re-mi* sold 20,000 copies, a huge quantity for a Greek book. Her book *Personalities I Have Known* (1966) presents writers like Gide, Rolland, Colette, Huxley, Unamuno, and Céline.

Further Reading

Stepanchev, Stephen. "Bitter Truth." *New York Herald Tribune Weekly Book Review* 1 (December 1946): 40.

Tannen, Deborah. *Lilika Nakos.* Boston: Twayne Publishers, 1983.

Tannen, Deborah. "Mothers and Daughters in the Modern Greek Novels of Lilika Nakos." *Women's Studies* 6, no. 2 (1979): 205–215.

NARRATIVE ANALYSIS; NARRATOLOGY Greek analysis of narrative is sophisticated and uses clear terminology. Attention is paid to the story or novel's setting, its time, and place. These elements are deemed to control its narrative economy. An exciting tale may use short sentence structure (μικροπερίοδος λόγος) and insert the **historical present.** A gripping narrative gains effect with separate sentences (παράταξη). **Parataxis** is allied to the omission of conjunctions (ασύνδετος λόγος) and a minimum of secondary clauses. A character may control the **plot** in the first person singular; if this character sets events in motion, then s/he is an "actor narrator." Critics note the use of **interior monologue,** which can still relate events in the third person. The real time elapsing in a story differs from its time in the telling (χρόνος αφήγησης). All novels offer some degree of character portrayal. The postmodern novelist Filippos Drakontaeidis

(b. 1940) rejects conventional subtitles for his narrative fiction (*The Message,* 1990; *The Façade,* 1992) and calls it variously a reading-text (ανάγνωσμα), simple tale (αφήγησις αφελής), or "quasi-novel" (σαν μυθιστόρημα).

NATIONALISM Psycharis was a believer in the **Great Idea,** a nationalist who held that Greece's frontiers should be widened to their **Byzantine** dimensions. In the Preface to *My Journey* (1888), he laid down the preconditions for nationhood: "A country needs two things to become a nation: to increase its boundaries and to make a literature of its own." The literary historian D. P. Kostelenos proposed (1977) three underlying ideals of Greek identity: (1) youthful bravery, (2) sacrifice of self for one's comrade, and (3) the aesthetics of landscape. A mix of these elements is found in most Greek writing. Chourmouzios declared (1976): "the Nation's intellectual history is its literature." Christina Koulouri headed a committee that examined contemporary school textbooks in the **Balkans** (Thrace University, 2000). Such history books were found to be permeated with nationalism. They distort **teaching** with ideology, from Turkey to Greece, Macedonia to Albania, and in the divided Cyprus. Nationalist preferences trickle from the formative school years into Greek literature. The Balkan countries have not found it easy to write about the joint Byzantine and **Ottoman** heritage. Interpretations of the **fall of Constantinople** are dogged by contradiction. Did Sultan Mehmet the Conqueror win (1453) a daring victory, marching his troops into the greatest city on earth by outflanking its Christian residents? Or was the fall of Constantinople an onslaught by plundering riffraff from the East? Muslims believe the former, Christians believe the latter.

Charalampos Theodoridis (b. 1883) gained a doctorate in Germany, was appointed professor of philosophy at **Thessaloniki** (1916), was a member of the **Educational Society,** and wrote many primary and middle school textbooks in collaboration with A. Lazaros. In a book that he wrote for the Vth form of state primary school, we read the phrase: "the Greeks were reduced to slavery by a barbarian and uncultured people who came from Asia, namely the Turks." Modern historians accept that both populations butchered each other. Yet Turkish textbooks give plenty of space to centuries of beneficent Ottoman rule. In Greek textbooks this period is dismissed as "the yoke" of Turkish dominion. Turkish schoolbooks hurry across the eighteenth and nineteenth centuries because the Ottomans lost hold of their empire, and so uprisings against Turkey have to be interpreted as the meddling of the European great powers. Greece's **War of Independence** is airbrushed out.

Further Reading

Theodoridis, Ch. Μαθήματα Ἱστορίας· Γιὰ τὴν 5η τοῦ Δημοτικοῦ Σχολείου. Μεσαιωνικὸς Ἑλληνισμός [History Lessons on Medieval Hellenism for the Fifth Form of Primary School]. Athens: Sideris, 1930.

Walbank, F. W. "The Problem of Greek Nationality." *Phoenix,* no. 5 (1951): 41–60.

NATURALISM Naturalism was a philosophical term used to designate the faithful representation of reality, with all its ugliness and evil, and with no hint whatsoever of idealization. The corresponding Greek word (νατουραλισμός) is a transliterated form, used by Greek critics and writers of the turn of the century to designate the French movement associated with Zola, Flaubert, and the Goncourt brothers. The Greek word for *naturalism* is φυσιοκρατία. For Greek intellectuals, naturalism was associated with the scandal surrounding Zola's novel *Nana* (1878) and the frank depiction of erotic material in print. The author Sp. Melás wrote that Mitsakis was "one of the flowers of the slime of Zola." Papadimas called **Karagatsis** "loyal to naturalism, one who does not hesitate to employ expressions which are to be uttered only inside four walls."

See also SEXUAL THEMES

NATURE; NATURE, LOVE OF The worship of nature (φυσιολατρεία) is a thematic obsession that affects the mind and material of many Greek writers. **Solomós** wrote: "Nature is magic, and a dream, in its beauty and grace." **Karyotakis** intoned: "This evening the dusk is like a dream; on this eventide magic abides in the vales." The same ecstatic love of nature is expressed in lines from "Federico Garcia Lorca," by **N. Kavadhias:** "Under the sun the olive trees rejoiced, / And little crosses flourished in the orchards." **Elytis** talked of mankind's inferiority to nature: "We humans are a puff of air, while nature does not even stir." Elytis invites others to join his rapture: "Come, let us gaze together on the tranquillity." **Y. Kotzioulas** has an ode called "Love of Nature": "Under the haze of Nature's mantle / I see the land laugh: / Oh, could I but rise, at such a time / Ever upwards with the smoke."

NÉA ESTÍA In 1933 this literary periodical (*New Hearth*), founded (1927) by **G. Xenopoulos,** came under the direction of Petros Charis, a freelance writer and reviewer (see also **Noumás**). Yannis Chatzinis (b. 1900) reviewed prose writers regularly for *Néa Estía* from 1941. On September 16, 1931, the journal carried an open letter from **Palamás** to **Seferis,** in which he said he needed a cypher to decode texts from Seferis's poems, *Turning-Point.* Palamás found nothing else but amusement in Seferis's "Folksong." He found that most of *Turning-Point* was based on untraditional materials, and he accused the experimental author of being unhelpful to his readers. *Néa Estía* has seen sharper disputes and a more consistent standard of creative writing than any other Greek literary periodical. It is also an on-going tool for **bibliography**; it carries an "analytic bulletin" that glosses articles from more than 130 Greek journals.

Further Reading

Gauntlett, Stathis. "The Monocotyledons of Greek Modernism: Popular Tradition in Twentieth-Century Greek Literature," In *Greek Modernism and Beyond: Essays in Honor of Peter Bien,* edited by D. Tziovas, 49–58. Lanham, MD: Rowman & Littlefield, 1997.

NÉA GRÁMMATA, TÁ The periodical *New Letters* was conceived and bankrolled by **George Katsimbalis,** "modern Maecenas and bibliographer par excellence" (A. Sharon). It ran from 1935 to 1940 and was resuscitated briefly (1944–1945). Edited by Andreas Karantonis, it published prose, verse, and criticism by or about the **Generation of 1930,** as the writers in this group came to be known. The periodical was associated with various novelists who had been involved in the **Asia Minor disaster** or came from Anatolia (**Ilias Venezis,** Stratis Doukas, **Myrivilis**). **Ritsos** published his first free verse in the journal (under a **pseudo-**

nym), as did **O. Elytis.** Many poets (such as **Seferis,** Anastasios Drivas, Yorgos Sarantaris, D. Antoniou) used the periodical to circulate new, experimental verse or to react against the sardonic mode of **Karyotakism.** The journal also produced issues on figures like **Palamás,** or **Periklís Yannopoulos,** the Hellenic zealot.

See also JOURNALISM, TWENTIETH CENTURY

NEKTARIOS OF JERUSALEM (or THE CRETAN) (1605–1680) Nektarios of Jerusalem was a pupil of **Korydalleús.** He first became a monk, then patriarch of Jerusalem, and founder of the School of the Holy Sepulchre, which later had enlightened, pro-**Demotic** patriarchs among its graduates (for example, Chrysanthos, Dositheos). Nektarios compiled an *Epitome of Sacred World History* (Venice, 1677) in **plain Greek.** Many people read this popular account of the sultans up to Selim and of St. Catherine's Monastery at Sinai, which had secured a deed of coexistence *(Ahtimane)* from the Prophet Muhammad himself.

NENEDAKIS, ANDREAS (1918) Born in Rethymno (Crete), Nenedakis was a prolific novelist and critic. He was sentenced to death for involvement in a mutiny against Greek army commanders in the Middle East (1943) and in the post period was shunted round prison camps in the Aegean. When the **Colonels** took power (1967), he left Greece. He supervised a critical edition (Athens, 1979) of Bounialís's classic seventeenth-century text *War of Crete 1645–1669,* which was reviewed by Tomadakis, in *Athens* (vol. 77, 1978–1979: 397–405). Nenedakis edited an anthology of Greek stories (1963). Among his novels are *White*

Fences, Daisies of the Aegean, and *Oranges Are Bitter in October.* He used a first person narrating female voice in *Ten Women,* in which attitudes to prostitution and abortion are questioned, and in *Manuscript from the School of Fine Arts,* which highlights the injustice, for women, of the dowry system.

Further Reading

Herzfeld, M. *Portrait of a Greek Imagination: An Ethnographic Biography of Andreas Nenedakis.* Chicago: University of Chicago Press, 1997.

Nenedakis, A., ed. Ἀνθολογία ἑλληνικοῦ διηγήματος *1900–1963* [Anthology of Greek Short Story: 1900–1963]. Athens: Kouris, 1963.

NEO-HELLENISM Greek nationalism positions itself next to neo-Hellenism, which is a theory of continuity going back to classical Greek culture. Many Greeks see this link as "unmediated," justifying a mystical feeling that their art and letters have been "handed down" from the **Muses. Odysseus Elytis** declared (in an essay, "One-Finger Melodies for Nikos Gatsos"): "A way for you to talk about the past without being suspected of nostalgia has yet to be found." For **Seferis,** the heritage caused nostalgic pain: "Wherever I journey, Greece inflicts wounds on me." Greece never passed through the **Renaissance** or an industrial revolution. The early nineteenth-century revival of **Hellenism** was largely constructed out of nostalgia by foreigners. In 1788 Friedrich Schiller produced *Die Götter Griechenlands* ("The Gods of Greece"), a poem mourning the lost deities of Arcadia, a Greek golden age when mankind could drink at the fount of beauty. Schiller's essay *Über naive und sentimentalische Dichtung* (1800,

On Naive and Sentimental Poetry) posed the duality of nature and culture, offering a Romantic view of **Homer** as an artist in unmediated touch with nature. The poems of André Chenier (publ. 1819) reinforced this view of classical Hellenism as sensuous simplicity.

Hölderlin, Goethe, and Pushkin saw Greece as the space of beauty and passion. Swinburne, Mallarmé, and Frazer's *Golden Bough* (1890) were awash with idealized beauty and divinity. Some critics insist on the renewal of **Hellenism** as the development of an unbroken tradition (παράδοση). Each type of Byzantine literature has been seen as a development from the classical, a precursor of the modern, or as both. Nationalism led to the establishment of a new Greece, but its history was created by foreign ships at the battle of Navarino (1827) and consolidated by a Bavarian monarch (January 1833). Most Western countries have had their Middle Ages. This is what unlocks their modernity (S. Gourgouris), but Greece missed out. In "On Greek Art in Its Time," Karl Marx warned (1859) that the unripe social conditions that gave rise to Hellenism could never occur again. After the Roman conquest, Greece had a dual identity: home of a great civilization but also an insignificant territory protruding into the Mediterranean (Pettifer, 1993: xxv).

Further Reading

Burke, John and Stathis Gauntlet, eds. *Neohellenism.* Canberra: Australian National University, 1992.

Gourgouris, Stathis. *Dream Nation: Enlightenment, Colonization, and the Institution of Modern Greece.* Stanford: Stanford University Press, 1998.

NEREID Dangerous water fairies called Nereids lived by the springs of Arcadia.

These nymphs, seductive and evasive, become a fixed item in **folklore** and literature. Soteris Patatzis, in his story "Nereid of the Deep" (1950), makes a village elder declare that nereids are young, are exquisite (πεντάμορφες), and live in the deep sea with fish for company. When the moon is white, they come up to the surface to comb their hair in its beams. When the moon is red, they bemoan the sufferings of Man. They lurk outside villages, by streams, pools, springs, ravines, bridges, crossroads, or caves. **Palamás** recalls them in the quatrains of "A Mermaid Gave me Birth": "Men call me a ghost, / Tremble, and move away, / Everywhere I'm the stranger, / Like a hermit at bay."

Nereids love dancing to music made by humans, and Charles Stewart (in Alexiou, 1985) noted that a drum or violin tone alerts you that nereids are prowling. Midnight and high noon are likely times for a nereid, dressed in white, to catch a lad and turn his head. They may take your voice or make you a bit crazy, but they are mischievous rather than evil, like the *lamia*. You may be prone to attack by nereids if you are "poorly baptised," "light-shadowed," or "Saturday born." If the nereid puts down her scarf to hear a shepherd's music or leaves behind her robe, a man has a chance of marrying her if he steals the garment. Should she recover it, she will leave that husband and any children they have had. Religious rites may be needed to save a man from a nereid. In Patatzis's story, the local chanter urges the priest to perform Holy Unction in a teacher's room because a fairy had come from the sea and bamboozled a (married) boatman. The poem "Shepherd at Death's Door" by **Krystallis** (1893) closes with the plea "If my poor mother finds out, and comes to the sheep-pen, / Don't tell her that I died [. . .] / Tell her the Nereids envied my manliness, / And stole me away to their deserted places."

See also HOMOSEXUALITY

Further Reading

Alexiou, Margaret, and V. Lambropoulos, eds. *The Text and Its Margins: Post-Structuralist Approaches to Twentieth-Century Greek Literature.* New York: Pella, 1985.

NEW SCHOOL OF ATHENS Also known as The Generation of 1880, the New School of Athens consisted of a group of younger writers who broke with the post-Independence poets of the **Old School of Athens.** Under the wing of **Palamás** at first, writers such as **Nikolaos Kambás** (1857–1932), **Yeoryios Drosinis** (1859–1951), **Ioannis Polemis** (1862–1924), **Yeoryios Stratigis** (1860–1938), **K. Krystallis** (1868–1894), Kostas Chatzopoulos (1868–1920), and **M. Malakasis** (1869–1943) developed differing and, in some cases, prolific careers. Other lyric poets from the 1880s and 1890s in this grouping include **Yeoryios Sourís** (1852–1919), **A. Eftaliotis** (1849–1923), **Dimitrios Kokkos** (1856–1891), **Ioannis Gryparis** (1870–1942), **Lambros Porfyras** (1879–1932). Some of them gathered round the satirical journal *Rabagás,* founded in 1878, which published the work of writers such as Palamás, Drosinis, and Polemis. The year that most closely characterizes this movement was 1880, when Kambás brought out his volume *Verses,* and Drosinis, who had been advised on his postgraduate studies by the great folklore scholar **N. G. Politis,** published his first collection, *The Spider's Web.* In essence, the New School of Athens stood for a rejection of **Katharevousa** and distanced itself from

Romantic form and content. It forged a characteristic medium for poetry writing in the **Demotic.** Much of this work was based on rural life, village sketches, folk material, and everyday events. They were influenced by the French Parnassian poets, especially François Coppée and Sully Prudhomme. Their verse also has echoes from Musset and Heine.

NEWSPAPERS AND MAGAZINES Most Greek newspapers carry a literary column and book reviews. *Macedonia* and *The Greek North* are printed at, and concerned with, **Thessaloniki.** Published in Athens are the following dailies: *The Radical* (organ of the KKE, Greek **Communist Party**), *Daybreak* (a limited-circulation paper, carrying the Communist Party of the Interior line), *The Free Press, The Morning Paper* (a radical Left daily, with a circulation of 20,000), *The News* (a large-circulation afternoon tabloid), *The Tribune* (a long-established, pro-Republican centrist daily), *The Midday News, The Quotidian* (Καθημερινή, conservative, but taking a high stand against the **Colonels**), *The Afternoon Paper, Acropolis, Hearth* (far right, with a steady circulation), and *Free World* (a right-wing paper). Weekly, fortnightly, monthly, or trimonthly papers with book columns include *Sortie, Literary Review* (journal of the Pan-Hellenic Union of Scholars, subtitled *A Tri-Monthly Periodical Devoted to Information and Speculation*), *I Read* (subtitled *A Fortnightly Survey of Books*), *New Hearth* (Greece's main literary journal, fortnightly), *Meeting Place* (a trimonthly journal of literature and the arts), *The Citizen* (a monthly promoting views in the Communist Party of the Interior), *The Word* (a bimonthly on Greek and foreign literature), *The Balance* (a bimonthly art

review), *The Courier* (a weekly with general culture interests), and *Current Events* (founded in 1969 as a news and views organ, published weekly). By 1964 Athens had seven morning newspapers and nine afternoon papers. The Piraeus had six dailies, and Greece as a whole had 108. Nondaily newspapers in the capital area amounted to 484; for the provinces, the figure was 423. The corresponding figures for periodical literature were 350 and 150.

Further Reading

Olson, Kenneth E. "The Newspapers of Greece." In *The History Makers. The Press of Europe from Its Beginnings through 1965,* 253–269. Baton Rouge: Louisiana State University Press, 1966.

NIETZSCHEISM Nietzscheism, in Greek, refers to the Superman (*Übermensch*), classicism, mythography, and Zarathustrianism associated with the great German scholar F. Nietzsche, who thought that the Greeks were "by nature pessimistic." The critic Kleon Paraschos held that all young Greek poets after 1900 were influenced by Nietzsche's *Thus Spake Zarathustra* (and the poems of Walt Whitman and d'Annunzio). For the **Phexi Library,** in 1911 and 1912, **Kazantzakis** translated *The Birth of Tragedy* and *Thus Spake Zarathustra.* Kostas Chatzopoulos (1868–1920), a powerful promoter of the **Demotic,** was enthralled by the haughty megalomania of the Nietzschean hero and wrote his own *Superman* (1915). Antis Pernaris (b. 1904) suggests that the lyre of Orpheus, blind eyes of Homer, and noisy clatter of Nietzsche display better portraits than the deceitful human face in his poem "The Difference": "How delightful for you to pass amid the music of the cries of Nietzsche."

NIHILISM Nihilism (μηδενισμός) is not a movement, but an attitude of obstinate hopelessness about any betterment of the human condition. Greek writers are strongly affected by nihilist postures, and this influence is reflected in twentieth-century poems or novels that harp on the vapid pointlessness of life and a desire for its dissolution (into anarchy, or suicide). Greek writers initially learned this antiphilosophy from the Russian and Western European anarchist movement of the nineteenth century. More than depression, the writer is involved in refusal. R. Apostolidis, in his combative assessment of **Palamás,** sees his poetics as a "pick-and-choose supermarket" of ethnic ideas with a seasoning of fascist authority and nihilist anarchy. He espoused a vague ideal of the proverbial Greece of "five seas and two continents."

The poetry of **K. G. Karyotakis** is the deepest manifestation of this Greek nihilism. Right up to his suicide, his verse is an outpouring of disenrapturement and desire for dissolution. It seems to represent the lowest moment of a moral bankruptcy that prevailed in the Greek soul after the collapse of the Greek settlements in Asia Minor (1922). **Ritsos,** from the committed Left, still takes on this brand of nihilism, yet turns it into a kind of personal melancholy, whereas **Kazantzakis,** a haughtier artist, owing nothing to no one, converts it into a heroic stance of solitariness. **Lapathiotis** (who took his own life) and Mitsos Papanikolaou (1900–1943), who died riddled with narcotics, both display the fatal combination of lyric but existential nihilism. Manolis Kanellis (1900–1980) thickened the dose by fusing a blind death wish and blunt "woman worship" into his own brand of consuming nihilism. Escape and spiritual denial hover strongly in the novels of Panos Karavias (1907–1985), and this mixture lasts through to the end of the century, in the volumes of **Seferis,** the underworld songs known as **Rebetika,** and in the neurotic, defeatist poetry of a writer like Michalis Katsaros (1921–1998). This was the microbe of nihilism, in modern Greek literature, which spread outward from Karyotakis, through Kazantzakis to all the **Surrealists.** After the opening of Greece to tourism and democracy in the 1970s and 1980s, the affliction receded.

NIKODIMOS, THE AGIOREITIS (1749–1805) Nikolaos Kallibourtzis took this name after 1775, when he became "monk of Mount Athos" (Αγιορείτης). He wrote a corpus of learned and mystical **Greek Orthodox** apologetics and was later made a saint (1955). He composed the *Holy Love,* a collection of patristic and devotional texts that enshrine the ideals of monastic withdrawal known as **Hesychasm.** Published at Venice, in 1782, *Holy Love* was soon translated into Russian and became the source of a mystical movement in **Russia,** which was crowned by the "starets" of the nineteenth century and exerted a clear influence on Dostoyevski. The effect of Nikodimos and Hesychasm on Russian culture is misunderstood by those scholars who talk of mysticism as part of the Russian native soul.

NIRVANAS, PAVLOS (1866–1937; pseudonym of Petros Apostolidis) Pavlos Nirvanas, critic, novelist, journalist, and author of four plays (influenced by **Ibsen**) and short stories, was born in Russia. He trained as a doctor, served in the Greek navy (1890–1922), and became a member of the Academy of Athens at its foundation in 1928. His *Literary Memoirs* (1933) contain reminiscences of K. Chatzopoulos, **Christomanos, Palamás,** and **Xenopoulos.** He published an influential essay, *The Philosophy of Nietzsche,* in 1896 and also a study of the poet A. **Valaoritis** in 1916. For 40 years, Nirvanas amused and educated the general reading public with his current events columns, "thousands of them" (Dimarás comments), particularly in the newspaper *Estía.*

Further Reading

Nirvanas, Pavlos. Baletas, Y., ed. Τὰ ᾽Απαντα. Τὰ λογοτεχνικὰ καὶ κριτικὰ μὲ τὰ καλλίτερα χρονογραφήματα [The Works of Nirvanas, Literary and Critical, with a Selection of his Best Journalism]. Athens: Yovanis, 1968.

NOMENCLATURE Whereas an ονοματολόγιον is an indexed dictionary of key terms, or a catalogue of important names, a nomenclature (ονοματολογία) is the classification of terms in a field. An onomasticon (ονομαστικόν) is a lexicon in which terms are arranged by subject, rather than alphabetical order. Sometimes these books set out names only, rather than nouns, as in M. Verettas's *The Great List of Names, or Greek People's Names* (Athens: Verettas, 1997).

See also CHRESTOMATHY; READERS

NOUMÁS The literary periodical *Noumás,* issued in its original format from 1903 to 1924, was edited by Dimitris Tangopoulos. The title recalls Numa Pompilius, second king of Rome (715–672 B.C.), who took advice, in religious matters, from his wife, the nymph Hegeria. The paper's motto was "Deeds rather than words," and it was intended as a "political, scholarly and social paper" in fortnightly, broadsheet form. It was continued, after the death of its founder (1929), by his son P. Tangopoulos, and after his death (1931) by his other son, Yannis, and a committee of assistants. From early on (1906), the journal became the fighting organ for the propagation of the **Demotic** in education, as well as its social and political expansion. The celebrated writer **K. Palamás** was suspended in 1911 from his job at the university for declaring in the columns of *Noumás:* "My hairiness [that is, support for the Demotic] is my greatest virtue!" The journal rallied the partisans of **Psycharis** and promoted his stance on the **language question.** In literature, its leading lights were Palamás, **A. Pallis, A. Eftaliotis,** K. Paroritis, K. Karthaios, I. Vouteriedis, and **Rigas Golfis.** In linguistics, there was M. Fylintas, famed author of *Greek Glossology and Glossography* (3 vols., Athens, 1924–1927). Among educational figures associated with Νουμᾶς were some of the founding members of the **Educational Society,** A. Delmouzos, I. Tsirimokos, Manolis Triantafyllidis (author of the far-reaching *Grammar* of 1941), and **Dimitrios Glinós.** In politics, the journal could count on **Ion Dragoumis** and in sociology, Y. Skliros. Several contributors were female: **Dora Moatsou** (1895–1978) published her first verse there in her 20s. Some budding writers were published even younger. **Kanellopoulos** was 16 when his first poem appeared there, and he went on to adopt the **Demotic** in all his writing, except parliamentary speeches and scientific articles. In 1909–1910, the journal published as a serial the first novel by **Nikos Kazantzakis,** *Broken Souls,* under his pen name Petros Psiloritis.

So Tangopoulos's journal was associated with the most polemical phase of **Vulgarism,** striving to authenticate the Demotic in education as well as literature (1880–1917). It published original writing and criticism, most of it hostile to **Katharevousa** and **purist** diction. Here we find the work of the *Noumás* Group of poets: Leon Koukoulas (1894–1967), **Rigas Golfis** (1886–1958, pseudonym of D. Dimitriadis), Ioannis Zervós (1874–1944), N. Petimezás, and Tsirimokos. **Karyotakis** also contributed, but his attitude to Katharevousa and Demotic is ironically nuanced, so he cannot be counted as a true **Vulgarizer** (or "hairy one"). The first stories of Petros Charis (b. 1902, pseudonym of Yannis Marmariadis) appeared here, and the short story writer Kostas Paroritis (1878–1931) contributed a series of socially committed essays to *Noumás* from the outset. An extended debate in the columns of the journal (1907–1909) about the left-leaning ideology of the language issue was caused by Y. Skliros and his *Our Social Question* (1907). Suspended in 1917, *Noumás* was continued anew in 1919 under a "Communist" program. It closed down again and was reissued 1923–1927 as an academic bimonthly in monograph format. After 1927, it came out irregularly.

See also COMPETITIONS; LANGUAGE QUESTION; PSYCHARIS: VULGARISM

NOUVEAU ROMAN Greeks translate the French term *nouveau roman* (experimental novel) as "antinovel" (αντιμυθιστόρημα). An early exponent of this genre is **K. Mitropoulou** (b. 1927), who blurs actual time and objective events inside her novels, *Boulevard without Horizon* (1961), *Countdown* (1970), *The*

Crime, or 450 Days (1972), *Sunlight 288 Hours* (1974), *Zaar 19* (1978), and *The Enlargement* (1983). A later Greek writer of the "new novel" is Natasha Chatzidaki (b. 1946), who draws on the scorn for capitalism of the "beatniks" and their predilection for filmmaking (zoom, flashback, jump cut), to copy the alienation and reification (πραγματοποίηση), which **Marxist** critics see in the second phase of capitalism (1945–1964). In Chatzidaki's poem "Deep Red," a voice intones "I am the wooden mistress of Charles Manson; tonight I'm inviting you to a blood bath," and in one of her novels we view a sequence of women mistreated, in a randomly alienated London, by casually brutalized men. Several texts by **Gritsi Milliéx** (b. 1920) move toward the *nouveau roman,* for example, her novel *Shall We Change?* (1957), a sequence of six supposedly autonomous stories that can be read as phases in the maturing consciousness of an individual. Other Greek writers who adopted some of the nonlinear, anticharacter tendencies of Gide, Robbe-Grillet, Butor, Sarraute, and Claude Mauriac include **Vasilikós,** with *The Leaf,* and Thalis Dizelos, with his *Deluge.*

Further Reading

Arseniou, Elizabeth. "Between Modernism and the Avant-garde: Alternative Greek Literature in the 1960s." *JMH,* no. 15 (winter 1998): 167–215.

Bosnakis, Panayiotis. "'All Margins, No Page': Unmasking Modernism, Writing the Avant-Garde." *JMH,* no. 15 (winter 1998): 135–149.

NOVEL, GREEK CLASSICAL The historian Xenophon (c. 430–c. 355 B.C.) effectively initiated two genres: biography and the novel. The eight books of Xenophon's *Education of Cyrus the El-*

der amount to the earliest novel. They provide the reader with plot, psychology, and adventure. *Cyropaedia* books V and VI contain the story of Abradatas, King of Susa, and his wife Panthea, a beauty who is captured by the Persian emperor, Cyrus. Abradatas is moved by Cyrus's magnanimity, because Cyrus, despite his power, prevents an associate from exploiting Panthea's captivity. So Abradatas becomes the ally of his former enemy. In general, the classical novel consists of a romantic narrative told in ornate prose. The major **Hellenistic** examples are: *Leucippe and Clitophon* by Achilles Tatius; Chariton's *Chaereas and Kallirrhoe;* the *Aethiopica,* also called *Theagenes and Chariclea,* by Heliodoros; Longus's *Daphnis and Chloe*; and *Habrocomes and Antheia,* by Xenophon of Ephesus. Parthenios, in *On the Mishaps of Love* (first century B.C.), and Antonios Diogenes, in his *For Infidel Legends,* exhibit a treasury of plot situations. Characterization is related to exercises held in schools of **rhetoric.** At a rhetoric lesson, the themes set for extemporization included imaginary situations. Some of these were suitable for elaboration in romances: whether young lovers are destined for misfortune, should a father be tough, is abduction justified, will pirates intervene, is seduction better than shipwreck, can the hero be recognized, is slavery the worst fate, and so on.

See also AKRITIC; ANAGNORISI; EKPHRASIS; HAPPY ENDING

Further Reading

Reardon, B. P. *The Form of Greek Romance.* Princeton, NJ: Princeton University Press, 1991.

NOVEL, GREEK MEDIEVAL Medieval Greek novels are mostly in verse.

The *Story of Rodanthi and Dosiklis,* attributed to **Theodoros Prodromos,** is a twelfth-century work in 4,614 trimeters setting out the mishaps of Dosiklis of Abydus and the girl he loves, Rodanthi. Its model is Heliodoros's *Aethiopica.* The *Drosilla and Charicles* by Nikitas Evgeneianos, in 3,641 trimeter lines, is a late twelfth-century narrative. It draws on *Rodanthi and Dosiklis,* as well as ransacking amorous subplots from the classical novelists (Heliodoros, Achilles Tatius, Longus), Mousaios, and the old anthologies. Nikitas offers sophistic descriptions and weaves in tender love letters. A twelfth-century novel in prose from the Comnenus period, *The Story of Hysmini and Hysminias,* by Efstathios Makremvolitis, has a familiar plot in which Hysminias, a herald, goes to a festival where he falls in love with Hysmini, guest of his host, and runs away with her. A storm arises, and the girl is thrown into the sea as a propitiation. Her lover is captured by pirates and sold as a slave. He meets Hysmini as a slave, after her miraculous escape from the sea. They overcome obstacles, attain freedom, and are finally married. Efstathios, in this composition, tries to avoid **hiatus** and piles up short, antithetically contrasted clauses. It is an imitation of Achilles Tatius's *Leucippe and Clitophon.* The historian Konstantinos Manassís (twelfth century) perhaps wrote what we have of *Aristandros and Kallitheia.* We know that Byzantine novels have been lost, from a passage in **Diyenís Akritas,** where the otherwise unknown story of *Aldelagas and Olopi* is mentioned, at line 2817 of the Sathas and Legrand edition.

Further Reading

Deligiorgis, S. "A Byzantine Romance in International Perspective. The Drosilla and

Charikles of Niketas Eugenianos." *Neo-Hellenika,* no. 2 (1975): 21–32.

Jeffreys, E. and M. Jeffreys *Popular Literature in Late Byzantium.* London: Variorum, 1983.

NOVEL, GREEK MODERN The Greek word for *novel* (μυθιστόρημα) emerged late in nineteenth-century Greek culture. **Koraís** proposed (1804) the use of the term μυθιστορία, to describe the same concept as the French word *roman.* In ancient times, the Greek novel was not a narrative with plot and character development, as understood by modern readers. In European countries its name was "romance" (from Latin), and now the word ρομάντζο refers to a novel with sentimental content. The noun *fable-making* (μυθοπλασία) was invented by academics. It is still occasionally brought out as a generic term for fiction. Publishers and critics prefer to use the term *prose-writing* (πεζογραφία). The term διήγημα, applied now to a short story, was used in the nineteenth century to describe any narrative tale. This concept was also expressed by the noun *narrative* (αφήγημα). Thus a writer's story (διήγημα) could refer to a whole novel, for both were supposed to provide "a helpful and beneficial purpose."

The Greek story starts as a legend and eventually covers an adventure, or "state of affairs" (κατάσταση), that *could well be true* and features major and secondary characters. The characters are shown in one or more "incidents," usually linked by some dialogue. Modern Greek fiction is now divided into genres. Thus the διήγημα may be a historical, didactic, ethnographic, psychoanalytic, educational, edifying, satirical, sentimental, sociological, seafaring, insular (νησιωτικο), rural (αγροτικό), martial, amorous (ερωτικό), or detective (αστυνομικό) story.

The term *genre novel* refers loosely to the fiction of local color and recording of manners known as **ithografía** (ἠθογραφία). The novella (νουβέλλα) is longer than a short story (διήγημα), but shorter than a novel (μυθιστόρημα). It has a more complex plot than the short story, but also contains material "to instruct and entertain." The discussion about what to *call* the Greek novel anticipated by several decades the production of the novel itself. In the late nineteenth century, "story writing" (διηγηματογραφία) referred to all types of prose fiction.

In 1896, Palamás used the phrase "fiction production" (διηγηματογραφικὴ παραγωγή) to define the hybrid narrative that poured out over the last two decades of the century. The critic Papadimas asserts that in the 1920s readers just wanted bandit stories and novels by French hacks. A popular female writer, widely read in the 1970s, Ioanna Boukouvala-Anagnostou (1904–1992) wrote more than 100 long novels. The diffusion of modern Greek novels outside Greece depends on movie versions or the efforts of specialist publishers. Beaton wondered (2001) if occupation and civil war were indispensable to the gestation of Greek novels and proposed the category of "epic magic-realist saga" for Ziranna Zatelli's *And at Twilight They Return* (1993), a book that covers four generations in a late nineteenth-century family in northern Greece.

Yatromanolakis, Rhea Galanaki, Evgenia Fakinou, and Nikos Bakolas contributed to the Greek novel as a sophisticated reinspection of history. A problem with modern Greek fiction is that recent history tends to weigh awkwardly onto its writing (A. Mac-Sweeney), and novelists revert to set pieces like the **Asia Minor disaster, Venizelos,** the **Occupation, Civil War,** or the **Colonels.** For a while, the novels seemed to rattle round inside the corresponding themes of censorship, imprisonment, exile, release, and reaction. Late twentieth-century novels might be avant-garde in form but revisionist in content, like Kotziás's *Usurped Authority* and Michael Faïs's *Autobiography of a Book.*

See also INTERIOR MONOLOGUE; KASDAGLIS; MEDICINE; NARRATIVE ANALYSIS; NOUVEAU ROMAN; ROIDIS; THESSALONIKI

Further Reading

AA.VV. Η μεσοπολεμική πεζογραφία: από τον πρώτο ώς τον δεύτερο παγκόσμιο πόλεμο (1914–1939) [Prose between the Two World Wars: 1914–1939], intro. by P. Moullas. 8 vols. Athens: Sokolis, 1993.

Harvey, Julietta. "'Other Histories': Notes on Modern Greek Fiction, à propos of Recent Translations." *Journal of Mediterranean Studies* 2, no. 2 (1992): 271–279.

MacSweeney, A. "Undiscovered Country? New English Translations of Modern Greek." *TLS,* Oct. 4 1966: 36.

Meraklís, Michalis G. Σύγχρονη Ελληνική Λογοτεχνία *1945–1970:* II. Πεζογραφία [Contemporary Greek Literature 1945–1970. Vol. II. Prose]. Thessaloniki: Constantinidis, 1972.

Mitropoulos, Dimitris. Γιατί δεν εξάγεται η ελληνική λογοτεχνία ["Why Greek Literature Is Not Exported"]. *Tribune,* 2 April 1995: B1–2.

NOVEL, GREEK, NINETEENTH CENTURY Up to the 1820s, Greeks had no narrative prose works of their own. They enjoyed the tales of *Sindibad* and the *Chalimá,* or *The Thousand and One Nights,* whose female narrator was called "Chalimás" in Anatolia, and "Scheherazade" in the West. Greeks liked the *Excellent Wiles of Bertoldo* by Giulio Cesare della Croce (1550–1620), so skillfully translated from the Italian by an (unknown) Venetian subject that many people thought it a **demotic** classic (Venice, 1864). They also read *Paul et Virginie,* by Bernardin de Saint-Pierre (1789), and the Abbé Barthélemy's *Journey of the Young Anacharsis in Greece Towards the Middle of the Fourth Century Before the Modern Era* (1788), a compendium of life in antiquity (translated by no less a figure than **Rigas Velestinlís**). They also liked Ch. M. Wieland (1773–1813), who was the "darling of the reading public all over Europe" (F. Ritter, 1967: 998), especially his *History of Agathon* (*Die Geschichte Agathons,* 1766–1767). The latter book was translated in 1814 by the prolific **Enlightenment** figure **K. Koumas** (1771–1836). Popular, too, was Wieland's *The Republic of Fools* (Τῶν Ἀβδηριτῶν ἡ ἱστορία, or *Die Geschichte der Abderiten,* 1774), also translated by Koumas (1827).

So, at the end of the nineteenth century, Greece still had one of the least-formed traditions of discursive prose writing, compared with European or American literature. **Psycharis** cried out the admonition: "Prose is what we need, prose." Certainly, after Independence the Greeks had some indigenous novelists of their own, among them the influential **Soutsos** brothers. Konstantinos Ramfos's novel *The Last Days of Ali Pasha* (1862) highlights events of December 1821 and January 1822, when Ali Pasha failed in his revolt against the Sublime Porte of Istanbul, but died as the most complex opponent of **Ottoman** absolutism, ambiguously deploying wide-eyed Greek sympathizers. Also by Ramfos is *Halet Effendi* (1867, 3 vols.), in which the intrigues of the Istanbul court clash round the figure of Sultan Mahomet. Greek **nationalism** might just have been accommodated if the Sultan's bureaucracy had thrown off its torpor and became worthy of Turkey's hardworking population. The saga of *Countess Potoski* concerns a French nobleman who goes in disguise to a slave bazaar (1790) and buys a beautiful Circassian girl called Eleni. She is a Christian; he adopts her and gives her an education. Count Potoski sees her in Warsaw, falls in love, and marries her; he is killed within the year, so the woman returns to her adoptive parents. Ramfos brought out most of these books in old age, revisiting episodes from his life as a conspirator, adjutant, magistrate, judge, and civil servant, in which he also ran various consulates. They have been read by Greeks ever since they came out, despite being couched in **Katharevousa** with some concession to **demotic speech** in their dialogue.

A more sober tone runs through *Military Life in Greece* (1870), the "Manuscript of a Greek Non-Commissioned Officer," as Vitti subtitles his modern edition of this fugitive text. It was originally published in Braila (eastern Romania), which had a thriving Greek community. The anonymous writer follows the fortunes of Errikos Skradis, who comes from overseas, at age 18, to volunteer for the 2nd Skirmishers Battalion of the Greek Army and becomes part of a hunt for **brigands** in Lokris, around Atalanti. The autobiographical account shows Skradis putting up with hardship, amid the abuses of the Greek army, but managing to become in turn lance-corporal, corporal, and assistant quartermaster. The novel highlights the scourge of banditry in Greece in the latter days of King Otho's rule, with rugged, ironic dialogue and a winsome female figure in the person of the 45-year-old café-keeper, "Mother-Marje," with two daughters, and her two husbands "in the other world." The narrator eventually arrives in Athens to work in Army accounts and then clear out.

Dimitrios Pantazís of Athens (1813–1884) composed short stories based on classical themes, with a leavening of what Dimarás calls "wisdom" and "refinement." Pantazis's narratives are cold and **Atticizing,** but they look forward to the ironic banter of **Roidis.** Epameinondas Frankoudis's epistolary novel *Thersander* (1847) was popular, with a lush, Romantic plot looking back toward the Uprising. An excess of melodrama pads out the by now *de rigueur* love affair, which ends when the sentimental rival of the hero, Nikolaos, poisons Eleni in her convent, and Thersander kills himself.

Further Reading

[Anonymous]. Ἡ στρατιωτικὴ ζωή ἐν Ἑλλάδι. Χειρόγραφον Ἕλληνος ὑπαξιωματικοῦ [Military Life in Greece: Manuscript of a Greek Non-Commissioned Officer]. Edited by M. Vitti. Athens: Ermis, 1977.

Economopoulou, Marietta. *Parties and Politics in Greece, 1844–1855*. Athens: Economopoulou, 1984.

O

OCCUPATION, GERMAN (1941–1944) The many tales from the German occupation of Greece emphasize pure horror and seem to dispense with exaggeration. The wife of Chrysostomos Yanniaris (1892–1968) lends her name to his 1945 poems, a collection entitled *Efemía*. She was executed by the Germans. One-eighth of the Greek population of 7 million perished because of either hunger or the violence of the Axis forces, in World War II. It is said that, as a very old lady, the children's writer Arsinoe Papadopoulou (1853–1943) committed suicide rather than tolerate the Occupation. So, too, did the poets **N. Lapathiotis** and Penelope Delta. Y. Sarantaris (1908–1941) was the first well-known Greek author to die in the Italo-Greek campaign. Among writers executed by the German troops in this period were Fotis Paschalinos (1913–1943), Yannis Aidonopoulos (1916–1944), and the hero M. Ch. Akulas (1900–1942). The poet Anastasis Drivas died young, in the "black days of the hunger of 1941 to 1942" (Papadimas, 1948: 297). This period of strife and food shortage is written up in **resistance** diaries and fiction. In *This Child Died Tomorrow: An Occupation Diary* (1988), Nestor Matsa documents a Jewish child who toiled in the shadow of death (March-October 1944). The text was praised on its publication by **Ioanna Tsatsou** and Eleni Kazantzaki. The child's neighborhood is obliterated, his family transported, and his father probably perishes at Dachau. Nina Nachmia's *Rena Zilberta: A Child in the Thessaloniki Ghetto* (Athens: Okeanida, 1997) relates how the Jews of Thessaloniki were rounded up. In 1945, a thousand literary figures in Greece failed to wrest, as a war reparation from Fascist Italy, the empty *Casa d'Italia* as a domicile for Greek literary societies. The Italian invasion had destroyed Athens' House of Letters and Arts.

Further Reading

Chourmouzios, Emilios. Ἡ περιπετεία μιᾶς γενεᾶς· κοινωνοπολιτικὰ δοκίμια [The Adventure of a Generation: Sociopolitical Essays]. Athens: Friends Editions, 1976.

Fleischer, H. and S. Bowman. *Greece in the*

1940s: A Bibliographic Companion. Hanover, NH: University Press of New England, 1981.

Papadimas, Adamantios. Νέα Ἑλληνικὴ Γραμματολογία· γενικὰ στοιχεῖα [Modern Greek Literature: General Principles]. Athens: P.A. Feskou, 1948.

OIKONOMOS, KONSTANTINOS (1780–1857)

One of the most celebrated exponents of the oration (λόγος), written and declaimed by a scholar (λόγιος) on a set topic, was the ecclesiastic Konstantinos Oikonomos. Many of his essays were lost in the chaos of Smyrna (December 1818) or in his flights from Turkish authorities. Surviving speeches and commemorations include those for the annual commencement at his school in Smyrna: "On Greek Education," "Admonition to the Young," and "Concerning the Upbringing of Children." He improvised a speech at Odessa, "To the Greeks," and drafted an **address** (Προσφώνημα) to King Otho in 1835, recited on his behalf by the mayor of **Nafplion.** From 1819 is a "Second Kydonian Speech on Love of Our Country." There is a "Commemorative Speech in Memory of the Zosimas Brothers in 1842," a "Funeral Speech for Theodoros Kolokotronis in 1843," and an "Epitaph for the Bishop of Sellasia, Theodoritos" (1843).

See also ADMONITION

OKTOECHOS

A popular **reader** for Greeks in the four centuries of their "enslavement" under the Turks was the *Oktoechos,* a compilation of the eight church services of the day. This **liturgical** book contained the **hymns** and **canons** designated for each day of the week, hence the name "chanting of the eight strains" (popularly called Ὀκτώηχι).

Further Reading

Lowden, John. *The Octateuchs: A Study in Byzantine Manuscript Illustration.* University Park: Pennsylvania State University Press, 1992.

OLD AGE. See SATIRE

OLD SCHOOL OF ATHENS

The "old Athens" or "Athenian School" are conventional names for a loose grouping of poets, based in Athens, with **Romantic** ideals, active from around 1855 to 1880. It includes the brothers **Yeoryios Paraschos** (1822–1886) and **Achilleus** (1838–1895) **Paraschos, Angelos Vlachos** (1838–1920), Alexandros Vyzantios (1841–1898), Dimitrios Paparrigopoulos (1843–1873), Spyridon Vasiliadis (1845–1874), **Aristomenis Provelengios** (1851–1936), and a few others of lesser importance, such as **Dimitrios Vikelas** (1835–1908), D. Kambouroglous (1852–1942), **Timoleon Ambelás** (1850–1926), and Kleon Rangavís (1842–1917). They were well connected to editors, publishers, the poetry prizes, and other academics. They obtained a disproportionate influence on the cultural life of the new Greece. Yeoryios Serovios complained in 1845 that culture was already centralized because only Athens had facilities for publishing. The recurring theme of these Athenian writers was love, death, or the home country. Their guiding spirits were the lays of Ossian, **Byron,** and Lamartine. They opted to write both in **Demotic** and in **Katharevousa,** and the latter, *purifying* form was even preferred. Intellectual circles of the 1860s were beset by "idolatry of the classical." An anthology of 1841 (edited by K. A. Hantserís) gives more space to the Athenian school poets than to **Kalvos** or **Solomós** (see **Roidis**). Most of the poetry prizes endowed by benefactors for this revival of largely nationalist, late Romantic, poetry required that submissions be in the **purist** language.

See also COMPETITIONS; PHILADELPHEIOS; RALLIS; VOUTSYNAS POETRY PRIZE

OLYMPIC GAMES, THE In 1895, the poet **Kostís Palamás** composed a hymn to the Olympic Games, which were held for the first time (in the modern era) at Athens in 1896. The writer **Dimitrios Vikelas,** residing in Paris from 1872, also threw himself into the movement to start the modern Games (1896). Another prominent organizer of the Olympics was the historian Spyridon Lambros (1851–1919), who produced 479 essays and books, wrote a six-volume *History of Greece* (1886–1908), helped found *Parnassós,* and was Prime Minister in 1916. Lambros resigned from the top post in 1917. The new government banished him to the isle of Skopelos. The classical Olympics began in 776 B.C. and were held every four years. They continued until floods and an earthquake ruined the site at Olympia, which was rediscovered in the nineteenth century. Wars were halted so athletes could cross Greece to the five-day festival, and women competitors held a parallel Olympics. Victors received an olive or palm frond.

See also HELLENISM

ONOMATOPOEIA Onomatopoeia (ονοματοποιΐα) is the making of words that imitate noises. Ancient Greeks said "shoo" to scare away birds. Onomatopoeia now refers to the formation of syllables that seem to reproduce a sound. Yannis Skarimbas (1897?/9–1984), in his story "By a Murderer's Hand" (1951), has a man kill his wife's robot, installed while he was absent. This servant is called "Crack-Tock" (Κρὰκ—Τόκ); its gait is rendered as "Taka—Touka" (τάκα—τούκα); its steps go "Tapa" (Τάπα). When the husband knocks the robot's head with a ring, the sound is "Conk" (Κόγκ—κόγκ). When the servant stands to attention, the effect is "Gappa-Goop" (Γκάπα—γκούπ). Its recital of verse starts with "Tsapha"; its squeak before speaking is "Trinx." When the master shoots this valet, the death agony in its guts is rendered by "Bzizzz" (Βζίζζζζζ). Generally, in Greek stories or poems, "ow" (αυ) is for a dog's bark; "kickavow" (κικκαβαύ) for the owl's cry, "cocku" (κόκκυ) for the cuckoo; "bee" (βη) for the lamb, "moo" (μυ) for the cow, "brekekekex" (βρεκεκεκέξ) for the frog; and "mimmy" (μι μυ) for a dolphin. Skarimbas turns the noise of a cuckoo clock into "coo-coo" (Κού-κού).

Translating line 357 of T. S. Eliot's *The Waste Land,* **Seferis** (1936) renders "drip drop" by "brix-brox" (βρὶξ βρὸξ). **K. Asopios** (in 1853) scorns the tragedy *Vlachavas* (1851) by **P. Soutsos,** particularly his verb "they bizz-buzz" (ζιζίζωσι), for the sound made by some bees. Asopios says: "The ζιζί of the bees, mixed with the crickets' γρὺλλ γρὺλλ, and βὲ βὲ from the flocks at pasture, or κωὰ κωά from the frogs, leads to a veritable ecstasy."

OPERA There have been a number of interesting Greek opera composers, some who take their stories from modern Greek literature. A. Katakouzinos (1824–1892) studied music at Vienna and was the first composer to use polyphonic music in the Orthodox **liturgy.** He taught at Odessa and was invited by Queen Olga to set up the Royal Chapel choir at Athens. He composed two operas: *Arethousa* *of Athens* and *The Foscari Brothers*. He wrote a *Methodology of Four-Part Chorus in Church Music* (1843) and several volumes of verse. A language **purist,** but European in formation, Katakouzinos conveys Hellenic elements in his refined opera scores. In Janáček's opera *The Makropoulos Affair* (1925), a girl called Elina obtains the elixir of life. She is 337 years old when she goes to Prague. Centuries of singing practice have made her the best Greek artist ever. A more ethnic heroine is in *Critikopoula* (1916, *The Girl from Crete*), by Spyridon Samarás.

The international repertoire draws on Greek mythology in Strauss's *Elecktra,* Poulenc's *Les Mamelles de Tirésias,* Orff's *Oedipus der Tyrann,* Fauré's *Pénélope,* Rossini's *Ermione,* Monteverdi's *Orfeo,* Gluck's *Iphigénie en Aulide,* Enesco's *Oedipe,* and Stravinsky's *Oedipus Rex.* How do Greeks handle that material? Jani Christou (1926–1970) left unfinished an *Oresteia* (1970). Manolis Kalomiris (1883–1962) leaned toward nationalist music (after teaching in Russia) and championed the **demotic song** and the demotic idiom in Greek music. In his operas, Kalomiris deployed the "endless" melody typical of Wagner.

Kalomiris's *The Master Builder,* which premiered in Athens 1916, was a joint libretto with **Poriotis,** Stefopoulos and **Myrtiotissa,** based on the homonymous **Kazantzakis** play of 1910. *The Mother's Ring,* which had its premiere at Athens in 1917, was based on a **Kambysis** play. Kalomiris's *Konstantinos Palaiologos* (1961) is a musical treatment of the **Byzantine** ruler of that name. His *Sunrise* (1945) and *The Shadowy Waters* (1950) draw on **folklore.** Kazantzakis wrote the libretto for *The Greek Passion* (1957), based on his novel *Christ Re-crucified* (1948). This was set to music by Martinů

(1890–1959), who also wanted to do *Zorba the Greek,* but found it too difficult to shape into a music drama. Maria Callas inspired the *coloratura* passages for the heroine in Martinů's one-act opera *Ariadne* (1958). Samarás (1861/1863?–1917) composed the music for the *Hymn of the Olympic Games* (1896). His teacher, Spyros Xyndas, was the first opera composer to use a Greek libretto. Samarás wrote *Rhea* (1908), which adapts both demotic songs and Byzantine melodies. In 1911, after studying in France with Delibes, Samarás composed operettas in Greek. *The Tigris* was incomplete when he died.

Greece's legend is the opera singer Maria Callas (born Kalogeropoulos; 1923–1977), who grew up in New York and moved to Europe for a short but whirlwind stage career between 1947 and 1961. The only Greek opera she sang in was Kalomiris's *The Master Builder.* Novelists and gossips (Arianna Stassinopoulos, Stelios Galatopoulos, Polyvios Marsan, Terrence McNally and others) used Callas as a subject for narrative invention.

Further Reading

Galatopoulos, Stelios. *Maria Callas: Sacred Monster.* New York: Simon and Schuster, 1998.

Jellinek, George. *Callas: Portrait of a Prima Donna.* New York: Dover, 1986.

Koumandareas, Menis. *I Remember Maria.* Athens, 1994.

Protheroe, Guy. "Greek Music in the Twentieth Century: A European dimension." *Κάμπος: Cambridge Papers in Modern Greek,* no. 4 (1996): 65–79.

Synadinós, Theodoros. *History of Modern Greek Music 1824–1919.* Athens: Typois Typon, 1919.

Zakythinos, Alexis D. *Discography of Greek*

Classical Music. Buenos Aires: Zakythinos, 1988.

ORATORY Nowadays, interest in oratory stems from its link to **poetics.** The techniques of persuasion continue to interest Greek writers, despite the erosion of **Katharevousa.** The oratory of Antiphon, put to death despite a fine speech in his own defense (411 B.C.), created a literary genre. Dionysius of Halicarnassus wrote a treatise analyzing Demosthenes, Isocrates, Lysias, and Isaeus, and soon a prescriptive code of **Atticism** dictated a speaker's choice of nouns. He had to choose dignified forms, but erase any eccentricity that made him appear superior to his audience. Prose was supposed to have rhythm, but not meter. Demosthenes avoids any sequence of short syllables. Poets could write the words πόσις ("husband"), δάμαρ ("wife"), τέκος ("child"), or κασίγνητος ("brother"), but orators had to write ἀνήρ, γυνή, τέκνον, ἀδελφός, respectively. Approved word lists were drawn up. Aelius Dionysius, Moeris, Pausanias, and Phrynichus listed words to avoid and recommended a classical equivalent, especially for the law courts. Until about 1930, men turned to law, when they went to university. Women writers did not expect to write speeches or speak in public one day, so they studied music and modern languages.

ORESTEIAKÁ RIOTS. See LANGUAGE QUESTION

ORFANIDIS, THEODOROS (1817–1886) The writer Orfanidis has an unusual biography. Turkish reprisals against the Greek population of Smyrna after the 1821 **Uprising** uprooted his family, who ventured to Tinos, Syros, and **Nafplion.** He later became an expert on Greek flora and discovered over 50 new types. As well as a botanist, he was a satirist and poet, associated with the **Old School of Athens.** He was sent on a scholarship to Paris by the politician Kolettis, who "was afraid of his tongue and preferred to have him at a distance" (Dimarás). Influenced by the controversy about the impossibility of a modern Greek poetry tradition, launched by **Roidis** (following Hippolyte Taine's notion of the surrounding milieu essential to art and literature), Orfanidis declared that the composition of beautiful poetry required "a profound study of nature." Orfanidis published his satires, *Menippus,* in 1836. When a verse play by **Athanasios Christopoulos,** *Achilles* (1805), was played by amateur actors in Athens on 31 May 1836, the 20-year-old Orfanidis acted in the lead. A traditionalist, Orfanidis aimed, like **Rangavís,** for the revival of ancient **Hellenism** and the use of classical **meter.** He constantly resubmitted his compositions to **poetry competitions** until they won prizes, and he engaged in polemics about the judges' decisions. He won the 1858 Rallis poetry competition with "Chios Enslaved," composed in Homeric hexameters (5 dactyls, $-\smile\smile$, plus a spondee, $\smile-$). The subject was a medieval insurrection on the island, but he also wrote about Turkish atrocities on Chios during the **War of Independence** (1822) in his *Saint Menas.*

ORIGEN (c. 185–?c. 253) Origen, the man who took over Clement of Alexandria's **catachetics** school as an 18-year-old (in the year 202), paved the way for Byzantine theology. In the *Hexapla* (ed. A. Vicenti, Rome, 1840), the original of which is lost, Origen used six columns to set out four translations of the Old Testament, the Hebrew text, and a Greek transcription of the Hebrew.

Further Reading

Scott, Alan. *Origen and the Life of the Stars: A History of an Idea.* New York: Oxford University Press, 1991.

Widdicombe, Peter. *The Fatherhood of God from Origen to Athanasius.* New York: Oxford University Press, 1994.

ORLOFF REBELLION In the late 1760s, the learned **Voulgaris** met Count Theodore Orloff (1741–1796) at Leipzig. Orloff mentioned Voulgaris to Katherine II, and he was invited to **Russia.** Theodore and his brother Alexios (1737–1808) staged a rebellion in Mani (1770–1774). Another Orloff brother, Gregory (1734–1783), the Tsarina's lover, plotted to set up a principality in Greece and harass the **Ottoman** enemy. Alexios was given command of a section of the Russian navy. In April 1770, his fleet appeared off the Laconian coast and called on the Greeks to rebel against the Turks, promising Russian assistance. He failed to back up a Peloponnesian attack on Tripolis, and the Turks made reprisals. Albanian mercenaries were allowed a free hand in the Mani for years. Theodore Orloff, heading a squadron of Russian vessels (1770), sailed to Oitilo, tried to besiege Koroni, fomented an uprising in several Aegean islands, and at Tsesmé pinned down a Turkish fleet, with Alexios Orloff. The rebellion failed, but Orloff's agents initiated the Sphakiot leader Daskaloyannis, who raised the rebellion in Crete at the head of 13,000 Sphakiots (1769–1771). He was skinned alive as punishment. Sphakiá's bishop opposed the insurrection. An illiterate cheesemaker I. Pantzelios dictated the *Song of Daskaloyannis* (1786) to Sifis Skordylis.

Their poetic blend has become famous: "Each Easter Sunday, / Daskaloyannis donned his hat / To go tell the head priest / I'll bring Moscow here, / To crush Sphakiá / And attack the Turks, / And show them the way / To the **Red Apple Tree.**"

ORTHODOX CHURCH, GREEK A subculture of **demotic songs** grew at the edge of Orthodox Church practice. Palm Sunday songs (τὰ Βαΐτικα) were recited by young women before or after church services on the Sunday preceding Easter: "All the laurel fronds are here and all the laurel girls, but the slender new branch isn't here, she's down at the spring for water." Such songs are linked to the **folklore** of spring and prayers for rain: "Palm branches, Palms for Palm Sunday when you eat fish and mackerel; / The following Sunday you eat red eggs." On Naxos, these incantations merge with a call to bless fertility: "Lord, pour down rain, let Thy mercy fall. / Rain, o my God, in abundance that we may have offspring."

Orthodoxy is the pristine doctrine dispensed by Jesus Christ, the Apostles, Scripture, and tradition. After the Western Church split from the Eastern Church (second century A.D.), Clement of Alexandria used the term to distinguish orthodox from "unorthodox thought" (ἑτερο-δοξία). When the Bogomil heresy spread from Bulgaria over the Balkans (eighth to twelfth century), Orthodox Greeks waged war against Bulgarian armies as fraudulent followers of Christ. The Bogomils, in turn, took Orthodox Christians to be mere idolators. The Bogomil heresy was condemned by two synods (Constantinople, 1316 and 1325).

The Church of Hellas was declared independent of Constantinople by a council of 36 bishops at **Nafplion** (June 1833).

A decision of the Synod of Constantinople recognized the Greek Church as autocephalous (July 1850). To Pope Leo XIII's Bull on the Reunion of the Churches (20 June 1894), the Ecumenical Patriarch Anthimus VII answered with a letter listing Catholicism's errors. Historically, the Orthodox Church has seen itself as protecting dogma, which is revealed once and for all. No changes can be made to the Greek church by scholarship or reform. Certain **Catholic** doctrines are held to be mere human invention: (1) the perpetual progression of the Holy Ghost "from the Son as well" (*filioque*), (2) the immaculate conception of the Mother of Christ, (3) the infallibility of the Pope, (4) Papal power over the whole Church, and (5) Purgatory. Orthodoxy encourages reverence for **icons** (προσκύνηση) and relics. The 7th Ecumenical Council ruled that reverence is addressed "not to the wood and the paints, but to the persons represented in them." The Orthodox Church has had an uneasy relationship with alleged heretical writers. After the death of **Yemistos Plethon** (c. 1360–c.1451), his writings were burned by Patriarch Yennadios II, a former pupil and tame head of the reconstituted church after the Turks took Constantinople (1453).

Bible translation has led to Orthodox disapproval. From the sixteenth century, Western missionaries translated books from the New Testament to facilitate pastoral work in poorer parts of Greece. The Orthodox Church viewed all translation as sacrilegious because it widened the gap between religious practice and the origin at Nazareth. **Neophytos Vamvas** (1770–1856) translated the *Gospels* and *Acts* into **plain Greek** and was duly condemned by the Synod. The Church excommunicated **Kazantzakis** (1961) for publishing *The Last Temptation of Christ,* later objecting to Scorsese's film (1988). Finding impious passages in *Freedom and Death* (1950), the Holy Synod accused Kazantzakis of sacrilege. He was symbolically exonerated by the Greek parliament (1955), when it upheld the right of artistic expression.

See also BIBLE; CATECHISM; ICONOSTASIS; LITURGY

Further Reading

Ware, Kallistos. *The Orthodox Church.* London and New York: Penguin, 1993.

Yannaros, Christos. *Elements of Faith: An Introduction to Orthodox Theology.* Edinburgh: Clark, 1991.

OTTOMAN The Turkish conquest of **Byzantium** and Greece (1453–1460) paved the way for Ottoman domination of the mainland and most of the archipelago until 1821. Tinos, an island in the **Cyclades** group, became the Ottomans' last (1715) conquest in Greece. The Ottomans restored Greece's territorial unity, upset 300 years earlier by **Catholic** Crusaders, but divided it into six administrative provinces, called *Sangiaccati.* These provinces correspond to the classical Greek regions: 1. The Morea (that is, Peloponnese); 2. Boeotia and Attica; 3. Thessaly; 4. Aetolia with Akarnania; 5. The Epirus; and 6. Euboea, Greece's largest island after Crete. Each district was divided into feuds, which were left to indigenous overlords or given to Asian Turks who had emigrated to Greece (called *ziamet* and *timarioti*).

Each province was headed by a *Bey,* who could either be a Greek convert to Islam or an Ottoman overlord (less powerful than a Pasha, in his *pashelik*). The Pashas, Beys, and feudal rulers were adept at confiscation and deaf to appeals.

Under them came the Greek clergy, in charge of local justice. Local Greek magistrates or notables were "heads," "leaders," or "gentry" (ἄρχοντες). The Ottomans taxed inheritance, tithes, property assessment, celibacy, betrothals, herds, pasture, and flour mills. They ran a blood levy, called *Devshirmé.* The Greeks saw it as **kidnapping.** Until its abolition in the seventeenth century, this conscription took the best young Greek males every five years and sent them to serve the Sultan or join the **Janissaries.** Until the late nineteenth century, the Turkish word *millet* denoted a religious community inside the Ottoman Empire, like Greece. With the rise of Turkish nationalism in the early 1900s, the term *millet* came to stand for "nation."

Further Reading

Goodwin, Jason. *Lords of the Horizons: A History of the Ottoman Empire.* New York: Holt, 1999.

Sugar, Peter F. *Southeastern Europe under Ottoman Rule, 1354–1804.* Seattle: University of Washington Press, 1977.

OURANIS, KOSTAS (1890–1953; pseudonym of Konstantinos Niarhos)

Kostas Ouranis was an influential writer, elegiac and mournful in much of his poetry. He attended school in Greece and Istanbul and also studied in Paris and Geneva. Ouranis contracted tuberculosis in his early thirties and spent two years in a Swiss clinic. He was a restless character, always on the move, publishing travel essays, working as a Greek consul and also a journalist. His main collection, *Nostalgias,* came out in his lifetime. Another collection, *Journeys,* was posthumous. Typical is "One Day I Shall Die in a Mournful Autumn Twilight." This shows a curious affinity with the Peruvian poet César Vallejo (1892–1938), noted for his melancholy, which made people wonder if Vallejo "died of Spain" or if it was raining when Vallejo died. In Ouranis's poem, the first-person speaker imagines his own forlorn death in Paris. His death will be preceded by the pattern of rain heard in solitary lodgings and lead to missed dates, the shaking of heads, a requiem back home, and even the annoyance of some girl, who thinks he disappeared to give her the slip. Here the nineteenth-century *poète maudit* is merged with Bohemian art-for-art's-sake. Two special issues of *Néa Estía* (no. 632: 1953 and no. 675: 1955) are devoted to Ouranis.

OXYMORON

The figure of contraries, oxymoron (οξύμωρο σχήμα), adds paradox to a phrase by linking words with contradictory meanings, as in line 20 of the "Mad Pomegranate Tree" by **Elytis:** "waving a handkerchief of leaves *made of cool fire.*" Apparently mismatched terms, in oxymoron, hint at a subtler insight, as in *"hasten slowly," "giftless giving* by enemies" (ἐχθρῶν δῶρα ἄδωρα), or, from "The Epilogue" a miniature by **P. Soutsos:** "And only *death* / Was created *deathless;* / Death never ages."

P

PACHYMERIS, GEORGE (c. 1242–c. 1310) Pachymeris was born in Nicaea (Bithynia), during the years of Byzantium's exile from Constantinople. He was remarkably prolific, writing a *Philosophy* based on **Aristotle,** while later following a legal and political career in Constantinople. His *Roman History,* in 13 books covering the period from 1255 to 1308, updates that of **Akropolitis** (1217–1282). It maintains the latter's anti-Western slant, but also puts a theological interpretation on some contemporary events. Pachymeris relates the victory of Osman over a Byzantine army at Baphaeum, in July 1301, part of the steady advance of the Ottomans in that period. In a learned, **Atticizing** style, Pachymeris even writes the names of the months in their older form. A handbook of his teaching texts on the four types of learning (from music to astronomy) uses modern Arabic numerals for the mathematics. This decimal system, based on the signs 1, 2, 3 to 10, had only been introduced in the tenth century. He knew Euclid, but was unusually well versed in the Alexandrian mathematician, Diophantus (fl. 250 A.D.), who wrote the first book of algebra and a text on polygonal numbers that features in the recent proof by Wylie of Fermat's "last theorem."

Further Reading

Constantinides, C. N. *Higher Education in Byzantium in the Thirteenth and Early Fourteenth Centuries, 1204–c. 1310.* Nicosia: Cyprus Research Centre, 1982.

PAINTING. See ART

PALAEOGRAPHY (TEXTUAL CRITICISM) Palaeography is the scientific practice that determines the written words in ancient texts. All classical Greek books were in manuscript form, inscribed on papyrus or vellum (internal pigskin). These had been lost, deteriorated, or destroyed by the time of the middle ages. It is thus essential to establish the original spelling and vocabulary that has been copied, often in an incorrect form, by intermediate scribes *(amanuenses)* or copyists. In a broader sense, palaeography refers to the analytic reading of epigraphs and inscriptions. Any handwritten material can be jumbled up or misunderstood by one who tries to transpose it to a newer form.

Textual critics also had to establish who copied the original (or the *n*th copy of the original), assess how defective his copy was, and then try to repair these defects to make a modern (critical) edition. It also helps to find out the rough date and place of the copy. Much of this work went on in the Renaissance and is actually synonymous with the word *renaissance*. No autograph manuscript of any work by an ancient Greek writer has survived.

The mistakes and variation in transcriptions made by different witnesses of the same classical text are compared in order to sketch a tree diagram of the book's *codices* (manuscript copies). In Plato's *Symposium* 201d, we meet the reading "O beloved Agathon." The Oxyrinchus Papyrus 843 (second century A.D.) gives the alternative reading "O friend." Before Maas, nobody had observed that "beloved one" in the sense "friend" did not occur in any Greek work. The conventions of palaeography dictate that the current reading needs further explanation because of that second-century reading.

In other texts we meet a gap of a complete line, because the eye of the copyist has evidently strayed from the last word of one line to a similar word at the end of the next line, and then recommenced work at the first word of the third line. When a word is repeated consecutively, the palaeographer may often delete it, if the repetition was presumably not intended. Where there is a gap (lacuna), the critic has to make a conjecture (hazard a word similar in shape and meaning). Or he may choose to keep the lacuna and mark the passage as "defective" and even

signify this with a dagger in his footnotes (*apparatus criticus*). Where he has to choose between a harder or an easier word, the palaeographer follows a rule called "more difficult reading," on the grounds that the (ignorant) copyist would be more likely to simplify from the difficult, than to misread a simple word and choose a more abstruse one. The final resort of the palaeographer—which causes scholarly controversy—is "emendation." A portion of Greek text is judged to be unsatisfactory, that is, wrongly copied, and the palaeographer suggests a phrase or word more in harmony with the locus (place in the original text).

Further Reading

Barbour, Ruth. *Greek Literary Hands A.D. 400–1600*. New York: Oxford University Press, 1981.

Maas, Paul. *Critica del testo*. Florence: Le Monnier, 1963.

PALAIOLOGOS, GRIGORIOS (1794–1844)

The versatile, early nineteenth-century Greek intellectual Grigorios Palaiologos was an agronomist in Switzerland, Germany, and France. He was appointed Director of National Estates by the Greek president (1829). *The Artist* (1842) is a sociological novel in two volumes in advance of its time, now "forgotten and unjustly ignored" (Voutieridis, writing in 1930). It rambles over post-Independence Greece, features romantic love interest and a whiff of scandal, despite having "rather more debate than action," as described by "G.X.B.," in *Great Encyclopedia of Greece* (1926–1934). Groundbreaking is *The Polypath* (1839), Greece's first picaresque novel. Palaiologos put out the journal *Triptolemus*, named after the hero in Eleusinian mystery worship who first showed a plough's use. He composed *Letter-Guide, or Examples of Divers Letters* (which went through several editions) and an *Essay on Turkish 19th-Century Customs* (Paris, 1827). He translated the four-act tragedy by Nikolaos Pikkolos, *The Death of Demosthenes* (Cambridge: Harwood and Newby, 1824), which ends with the freedom-loving Athenian orator poisoning himself in a temple besieged by Macedonian troops and is probably the first version of a modern Greek play in English.

Further Reading

Palaiologos, G. Ο πολυπαθής [The Polypath]. Edited by Alkis Angelou. Athens: Ermis, 1989.

Palaiologos, G. Ο ζωγράφος [The Artist]. Edited by Alkis Angelou. Athens: Kostas and Elenis Ourani Foundation, 1989.

PALAMÁS, KOSTÍS (1859–1943) Palamás was at once poet, prose writer, author of a play, translator, and literary critic. Born in Patras to an intellectual family, he was orphaned at seven and brought up by his father's brother, at **Missolonghi.** His uncle's family apparently used **Katharevousa** for private conversation. He found his vocation as a child and was already writing when age nine. Aged 16, he contributed to *The Attic Calendar,* edited by Irinaios Asopios. His verses made use of **hiatus,** which he later condemned, instead of the traditional **synezesis** (eliding of two written vowels). He went to the university (1875) and settled at Athens, hardly moving for the rest of his life. Surrounded by wife and children, he worked first as a journalist and later as registrar of the university (1897–1928). Palamás became the leading intellectual of the so-called **Generation of**

the Eighties and a foremost figure among the **New School of Athens** poets. For half a century he dominated modern Greek literature, operating a gradual shift of content and style, transposing the new language and its literature to Athens from the **Ionian Islands,** where **Solomós** first gave it a national resonance.

Always seeking balance and antithesis, Palamás the lyric poet was a renewer of Greek prose style. He called himself a "thinking poet," a European as well as a Hellene. Voutieridis said: "his poetry can be compared with some large and thick forest, where the twittering of all the birds can be heard" (1976: 318). By 1880, Palamás was breathing life into the declining poetics and genre fiction (the portrayal of homely scenes) associated with the **purist** language. He began producing essays, stories, short poems, satirical pieces, and newspaper articles.

His first book of poetry, *The Songs of My Country* (1886), is a celebration of the beauties of the **demotic song,** an exploration of the common people's language. In summer 1888, he wrote two columns in the paper *Ephemeris* to salute the publication of Psycharis's *My Journey* as a major event, taking the opportunity to query whether stereotyped phrases in Katharevousa can be altered into demotic ones. Palamás's dual program is clear: poetry should seek familiar subjects while exploiting the **Demotic.** With **Aristotelis Valaoritis** as his intermediary, Palamás aligns himself to **Vulgarism,** and to the **Ionian School.** He absorbs the current French and European trends, operating a synthesis, from all that he reads, of the old and the new, the classical and Romantic. There are neoclassical and Parnassian elements in his *Hymn to Athena* (1889), which won the **Philadelpheios Poetry Competition.**

Here, but with more majestic versification than in *The Songs of My Country,* Palamás proclaims **patriotism** and exalts the ancient paganism, which binds modern Greece and trims its existence with a cult of beauty and light. In 1895, he composed a hymn to the **Olympic Games.** The first games of the modern era were to be staged at Athens in 1896. These neoclassical currents recur in *Iambs and Anapests* (1897), which consist of some 42 three-strophe poems. The younger poet **Ioannis Polemis** gave them a stinging notice: "Palamás's verses are unjustifiably obscure either because of an unmethodological abbreviation of many ideas presented simultaneously, or because of inadequacy of expression." Nationalist strains are present in *Iambs and Anapests,* published just before the Turks routed the Greek expedition to Crete in 1897: "I am the Akritas, Death, / I don't pass with the years. / You touched me in the marble threshing-floor. / So didn't you understand me?"

There are strong Symbolist and neo-Romantic strains in *Eyes of My Soul* (1892), which won the **Philadelpheios prize,** and in *The Grave* (1898), a volume of meditations on his five-year-old son Alkis's death. A short novella, *Death of the Brave Young Man,* was published serially in *Estía* (1891) and strengthened Palamás's demotic credentials (see also **Medicine**). Palamás also wrote a verse play, *Royal Blossom or Trisefyeni* (1903).

The Greetings of the Sun-Born (1900) symbolically evokes the catastrophe of 1897, when a Greek naval and military expedition to Crete was routed by the Turks, and the **Great Idea** suffered another cyclical change of fortune. Dimarás relates how, in 1900, an Athenian newspaper conducted a survey among intellectuals to see who they would choose as the contemporary Greek poet laureate. The vote went to Palamás, though Yeoryios Pop came out against him. Up until 1915, Pop's paper *Athens* printed coarse parodies of Palamás's style. A caustic conservative, Yannis Apostolakis (1886–1947), observed that his verses are "fit to wrap round candy for country weddings." In 1901, Palamás published an edition of the complete works of **Solomós.** Three major collections of poetry were produced in the first decade of the new century by Palamás, and they define his position as a master of lyric resource: *Life Immovable* (1904), *The Dodecalogue of the Gypsy* (1907), and *The King's Flute* (1910). In *The Dodecalogue,* Palamás grafts onto the fables of the gypsy people an extended lyric meditation on the negation of all cults, followed by a return of the gods as an effect of the creative power of music. *The King's Flute* evokes the exploits of **Byzantium** as a prolongation of the grandeur of antiquity. This ambitious poem was attacked by Dimitros Zachariadis in the second volume (1914) of the modish Alexandrian periodical *Letters.* Zachariadis, aesthete to the core, accused *The King's Flute* of serving up an incongruous parade of knowledge, lacking real poetic inspiration.

In Palamás's poem, the corpse of the most glorious of Byzantine emperors, the Bulgar-Slayer, is found with a reed-pipe at his mouth, in his tomb. This pipe (usually translated "flute") is a **muse** presiding over the epic of an Emperor, his journey from North to South, and his triumph in the city of Athens, where he kneels to the Virgin Mother in her new temple, the Parthenon. The work is shot through with obeisance to Our Lady, luxuriating in its vocative addresses and resonant compound forms: "O Sweet-Kissing, Unseated, Healer Washer-Away-of-Pains, / Fairy Tale One, Thou art Conspicuous, Immaculate and Leader of wayfarers // O Tower most braided with gold, sun-decorated Throne, // Thou wearest as garment the sun, Thy foot-stool is the moon, / To lean Thy feet, Thy hair spread round, / In a twelve-starred crown, // Thou leader in battle, mediator in peace, / Champion Lady General, to Thee the fruits of Victory."

After these masterpieces, his subsequent work may appear less significant and slighter in volume: *The City and the Solitude* (1912) and *Yearnings of the Lagoon* (1912), *Altars* (1915), *Untimely Poems* (1919) and *Pieces in Fourteen Lines* (1919), *The Pentasyllables and the Pathetic Whispers* (1925), *Timid and Cruel Verses* (1928), *The Cycle of Quatrains* (1929), and *Passings and Greetings* (1931). In 1935, with *The Nights of Phemius,* the poet returns to the simple format of the four-line **strophe** (quatrain). It was his last collection. Palamás's steady, penetrating literary criticism was mixed with autobiographical reflections in *My Years and Papers: My Poetics* (vol. 1, 1933; vol. 2, 1940). He produced monographs on **Krystallis** (1894), **Ioulios Typaldos** (1917), **Vizyinós** and Krystallis (1917), **Aristotelis Valaoritis** (1924), two books on Solomós (1927 and 1933), and *Goethe in Greece* (1932). In 1930, he was elected president of the Athenian Academy.

Romain Rolland considered him the greatest writer of contemporary Europe. In 1934 he was a serious contender for the Nobel Prize for Literature. In 1935, he protested against the sacking of university professors for supporting the Demotic, a measure sponsored by the philistine People's Party of Tsaldaris-Kondylis. Nikos Bees called him "the poetic chronicler of

his race." Six special issues of the literary journal *Néa Estía* were devoted to Palamás in the years following his death (vols. 397, 592, 616, 640, 736 and 928, between 1943 and 1966). Palamás was mistrusted by **Purists** because of his support for the Demotic, and he risked losing his job at the University when the **language question** caused street violence. Some critics considered his work obscure. Kambanis (1971: 250) thought his poetry was "a bit of everything" and summed it up in a metaphor of his own: "Palamás gave all that he had to give. He was a mountain torrent which drags everything along in its course, green branches and dead foliage alike."

Maybe it was lack of self-examination, maybe a father's weakness for his offspring, that made him so uneven, but the reader finds it tough to accept. Each student of Palamás has to stake out his own individual selection from this far-reaching oeuvre. Palamás was above all inclusive: after the military setback of 1897, he said he went from "lyricism of the Ego" to a "lyricism of the We," later reaching "the lyricism of the All." He once declared (1892): "The poet does not work either for the crowd, or for the élite; he works for poetry itself." He said: "I am not merely the poet of myself: I am the poet of my time and of my country" (1906). As a scholar, he united the positivism and mysticism of his age, harmonizing the fashionable cry "art-for-art's-sake" with commitment, linking **Nietzschean idealism** with socialism, melding classical and Byzantine. It was he who rediscovered **Kalvos** (1889) and gave this writer his just estimate. Perhaps his staunch **Vulgarism** led him to shun **Kavafis** and misread the **Generation of 1930.** When Italy invaded Greece on 28 October 1940, Palamás responded in verse: "Only one counsel I have to give you: / Become intoxicated with the deathless wind of the revolution of 1821." His packed funeral on 23 February 1943, which took place in occupied Athens, was transformed into an anti-Nazi expression of **Hellenism.** **Sikelianós** recited a famous poem on the occasion: "On this bier Greece reclines! Let us raise / A mountain with laurels as far as Pelian and Ossa, / And let us tower it as high as the seventh heaven. / My tongue is not worthy of uttering the name of the one who lies within."

Further Reading

Maskaleris, Thanasis. *Kostis Palamas.* New York: Twayne Publishers, 1972.

Palamas, Kostis. *The Twelve Lays of the Gypsy,* trans. with an introduction by George Thomson. London: Lawrence & Wishart, 1969.

Palamas, Kostis. *The Twelve Words of the Gypsy,* trans. by Theodore Ph. Stephanides and George C. Katsimbalis. Memphis: Memphis State University Press, 1975 [bilingual].

PALATINE ANTHOLOGY. See ANTHOLOGY; EPIGRAM

PALIKARI The term *palikari* (πα-λικάρι, also spelled παλληκάρι or παλλικάρι) means "brave young man." He may be a Cretan rebel, the handsome lad from your village, or a warrior from the **Uprising.** In the traditional images he wears a kilt (φουστανέλα), braided cap, tassels, and leather leggings, with pistol or sword in belt, and dashing, twirled moustache. The brave young man is the epitome of romantic **nationalism:** he is not frightened by pain or fights against large odds and likes to live in the mountain, like the bandit **Klephts** or the **armatolí.** The poet **Sourís** applied the term

to volunteers who fought alongside Greeks: "young foreign warriors." In the volume *Islander Tales* (1894) by **Eftaliotis,** the story *Marinos Kontaras* is about an exemplary *palikari* of that name, who sails, parties, robs, and struts with a long sharp knife. Kontaras has specific morals of his own: he would never touch the girl he has kidnapped, and brings her to the altar, agreeing to give up the "the sea and the knife," so they can live together into old age. This hymn to the *palikari* was translated by the French Hellenist Pernot (1901) and made into a **film** in 1948, with M. Katrakis in the lead role.

PALINDROME A palindrome is a phrase that reads the same forward and backward, as in "Evil rats on no star live." **Leo the Wise,** successor of Basil I The Macedonian on the **Byzantine** throne (886–912), wrote palindromes: ῍Ω γένος ἐμόν, ἐν ᾧ μέσον ἐγω ("O my people, among whom I count myself"). The word καρκίνος means the same as palindrome ("running backwards").They were also called "Sotadics," after the scurrilous Greek poet Sotades (third century B.C.), perhaps their inventor. The most memorable, attributed to Gregory of Nazianzus, was inscribed over the wells in medieval monasteries: "Wash my transgressions, not just my face" (Νίψον ἀνονήματα μὴ μόναν ὄψιν). The eighteenth-century monk Ambrosios Pamperis, one-time secretary to Prince Nikolaos Mavrokordatos and later court doctor to his son Konstantinos, published an entire book consisting of palindromes (Vienna, 1802).

PALLADÁS, YERASIMOS THE SECOND (d. 1714) Palladás, a Patriarch of Alexandria (1688–1710), is thought to have studied at the **Greek Col-**

lege at **Rome** and wrote a *Lament on the Fall of Crete* after witnessing the capture of Iraklion (1669). The text has 210 lines, cast in the typical five-line strophe of the dirge: "Don't bother with any frill, / But only think and ponder still / The calamity, / The penalty / Of Crete, and weep your fill." Palladás also wrote hymns, studies on rhetoric, essays on **Aristotle,** and volumes of letters (with correspondents like Peter the Great of Russia and Pope Clement XI). He wrote sermons in a polished but contemporary form of **plain Greek,** suitable to the large Greek community in Alexandria.

PALLI-BARTHOLOMAÉI, ANGE-LIKI (1798–1875)

The woman poet Angeliki Palli-Bartholomaéi came from an aristocratic family once said to have fortified a castle in its historic feud of Belliani, near Paramithiá (40 kilometers south of the Albanian frontier). Her father, Panayotis Pallis, made a fortune in trade at Livorno (Italy), where he was Greek consul. He funneled money, recruits, and solidarity to the **Independence** struggle in Kerkyra and the Epirus. Angeliki learned several languages while at school in Italy and translated sections of Homer into Italian. She later wrote odes on "The Bitterness of Exile," the premature death of Byron, the disaster of Psara, and the accomplishments of Greek generals in the **Uprising.** She produced stories about Souliot and Cretan resistance; wrote a historical novel, *Captain Alexis and The Last Days of Psara,* articles, letters, and translations of two plays by **Shakespeare;** and was a member of the Italian Academy of Livorno and of the local chapter of the Arcadians.

PALLIS, ALEXANDROS (1851–1935)

Pallis, born in Epirus, studied literature and worked as a merchant. He translated widely, especially literary texts, and also Kant, with the special purpose (as L. Politis argues) of showing that **Demotic** was a suitable vehicle for esoteric subjects. Pallis translated Homer's *Iliad* into demotic Greek (Paris, 1903), and this translation had a major influence on Greek twentieth-century poets. Pallis was a poet of the **New School of Athens** and a vigorous fighter for the use of vernacular Greek. D. Ricks notes that **Kavafis** owned a copy of the 1904 edition of Pallis's *Iliad.* Pallis, in turn, admitted in old age that he once hated studying **Homer** at school. His translation of the *New Testament* into the Demotic (published serially in the daily newspaper *Acropolis*) led to riots on the streets of Athens in 1901. Conservative elements that believed in **Katharevousa** as a guarantee of Greek **nationalism** were probably the instigators of this confrontation between reactionary and radical sides of the **language question.** Papadimas (1981: 49), by no means a conservative literary historian, calls Pallis's translation of the *New Testament* "pitiful, to be truthful." Pallis befriended the poet **Eftaliotis** (while trading abroad at Manchester and again at Bombay, in 1888) and converted him into an adherent of the demotic cause. An issue of the journal *Néa Estía* (no. 200: 1935) is devoted to Pallis, as also is a special number of the periodical *Greek Creation* (no. 153: 1 July 1954).

See also EVANGELIKÁ; MISTRIOTIS

Further Reading

Papadimas, Adamantios D. Νέα Ἑλληνικὴ Γραμματολογία· Τὸ γλωσσικὸ πρόβλημα καὶ οἱ ἱστορικὲς ἐξελίξεις του [Modern Greek Literature: The Language Issue and Its Historical Developments], vol. 1. Athens: Dimakarakos, 1981.

Paraschos, Kleon. Κύκλοι [Rings]. Athens, 1940.

PANÁS, PANAYOTIS (1832–1896)
Publisher of the **satirical** journals *Wasp, The Farrago,* and *Gnat* (on Cephalonia), Panayotis Panás was a satirist, poet, and journalist. He took part in the anti-English movement, working for the unification of the **Heptanese** with Greece. He was a pupil and friend of **Laskaratos.** Panás, this "radical romantic" (E. L. Stauropoulou, 1987), took it upon himself to popularize the poems of Ossian, and this is seen as a semirevolutionary as well as Romantic, even Gothic, gesture. He translated the Ossian texts into the **demotic** for various periodicals, using unrhymed **decapentasyllables** collected in his volume *Cephalonia* (1862). He composed light verse subsequently published as *Leisure Tasks* (1883). In the preface he refers to a literary dispute of 1877, "Concerning Contemporary Poetry in Greece," between **Roidis** and **A. Vlachos.** He also indulges in playful sarcasm at the expense of poetry by **A. Paraschos** and **A. Valaoritis.** "His work is 'low' literature of the highest order," said V. Lambropoulos (in Alexiou, 1985: 28). He killed himself in 1896.
See also HOMOSEXUALITY

Further Reading
Alexiou, Margaret, and V. Lambropoulos, eds. *The Text and Its Margins: Post-Structuralist Approaches to Twentieth-Century Greek Literature.* New York: Pella, 1985.

Orkney, G. W. H. F. *Four Years in the Ionian Islands.* 2 vols. London: Chapman and Hall, 1864.

PANAYOTOPOULOS, IOANNIS M. (1901–1982)
Panayotopoulos was a major critic and a writer in all genres. He wrote hundreds of essays for the *Great Encyclopedia of Greece* (1926–1934) on literary topics, the iconography of Christ, painting, and folk art. He was one of the editors of the periodical *Mousa* (1920) and in 1924 produced the first of his five collections of poems, *Miranda's Book,* and a year later, *Hans and Other Prose Pieces* (the first of 10 narrative volumes). He produced six monographs in a series, which he called *Personalities and Texts* (1943–1956), including studies of **Palamás** and **Kavafis,** supplemented by the versatile analyses in *Letters and Art* (1967). There was also a history of Greek literature (1936; 1938), an evocation of literary **café** life at the "Black Cat" and its patrons from the interwar period entitled *Starlight* (1945), and several volumes of **travel** essays, which made him contemporary Greece's leading exponent of this genre.

PAPADIAMANTIS, ALEXANDROS (1851–1911)
Adventure novelist, professional translator, and story writer, Alexandros Papadiamantis was born on the island of Skiathos in the Sporades, son of an impoverished **Orthodox** priest (and schoolmaster). Papadiamantis had a childhood companion in his cousin **A. Moraïtidis** (1850–1929), who later pursued a literary career. As a young boy, Papadiamantis painted icons of saints, scribbled plays or verse, and attended church assiduously. From ages 12 to 16, he wandered around his island, exploring the terrain and rural locations, which later formed the bedrock of his fiction. At age 21, he spent seven months in the monastery of **Mount Athos.** Then he gave up his intention of joining a religious order and devoted himself to what M. Peranthis calls the ideal of being a monk of the world (κοσμοκαλόγερος).

He studied literature for a short while (1874) at the University of Athens. He taught himself English and French and later augmented a wretched allowance from his parents by giving private lessons. In 1879, the newspaper *Neologos* published his first novel, *The Girl Who Emigrated,* as a serial. In 1881 he tried to gain certification as a French teacher and was failed. He made a precarious living as a freelance writer, translating for newspapers, and scraping together money (after the death of his father in 1895) to support three spinster sisters and a mentally ill brother. Papadiamantis began with somewhat pedestrian historical romances, serialized in magazines: *The Girl Who Emigrated, Merchants of the Nations* (1882), and *The Gypsy Girl* (1884).

His *Christos Milionis* (1885) marked a transition to more topical subjects. This was a short historical novel based on a Greek **demotic song** and related the exploits of a group of **Klephts** fighting the Turks a century earlier. In 1893, Papadiamantis's story "Easter Chanter" contained a passionate reaffirmation of his faith in the church, in his adoration of Christ, and the purity of Greek customs. He considered that Greece, whether enslaved or free, would always need her religion. Dozens of his short stories swim delicately in a translucent prism of sea and air. In one text, a student, on an impulse, takes to a boat and brings with him the recent bride of a neglectful, older man. They defy the boatman's dog and row through a moonlit night, between glimmering islets, until she slips off her white gown for him to make a sail to hurry the boat back to harbor. A young priest posts a child in town to make sure his share of the offertory is not spirited away while he is filling in for an unmanned parish in "Country Easter"

(1890). An old widow, in "The Gleaner" (1889), gets a check from her long-lost emigrant son in the Americas, and two merchants dispute its monetary value, which a "good priest" has countersigned on the back. A man comes home early from a storm at sea and is poisoned by the "Christmas bun" that his spiteful mother had baked for his childless wife (1887). None of this prolific writing appeared in book form during his lifetime.

He seems to swim against the current: conservative and pious, when positivism was in the ascendent, holding out for **purism** in language at a time when the **Vulgarizers** were gaining ground. He was a "populist ascetic, a purist user of the demotic for the speech of plebeian characters, but user of an austere **purism** for written description" (Palamás). Papadiamantis chose to lead a withdrawn life, both ascetic and secular, perhaps because his family problems drove him to alcohol. When Princess Marie Bonaparte organized a literary evening in his honor (in 1908), he refused to turn up. Papadiamantis had a detailed knowledge of Byzantine psalms and Orthodox **liturgy.** He was deeply involved with the holy days and traditions, which recur as a fond motif in his writing. He produced more than 180 short stories, from the early 1880s to just after the turn of the century. About 30 of these tales deal with subjects set in Athens; the rest come from Skiathos. At times, he deals with real social problems, such as spinsters lacking a dowry, emigration, and the absence of islander men, who are forced to work for their livelihood on the **sea.** At other times, his mannered and lilting prose tends to draw him away to the escapist idyll of childhood. His writing shows a marked preference for the nostalgia implicit in remote seaside, or rural, locations. Two special issues of the journal *Néa Estía* (no. 355: 1941 and 568: 1951) were later devoted to Papadiamantis.

In *The Gypsy Girl* (which *Acropolis* started to serialize in 1884), Papadiamantis used the technique of first presenting some exciting incident and then explaining its cause by a series of flashbacks. It was the first time this technique had been used by a Greek author, and it had a great impact on readers of the period. Ricks notes parallels between Papadiamantis's Skiathos and the Wessex of Thomas Hardy. Conspicuous in the Greek writer is the introduction of rural events measured by the seasons, the cycle of festivals, based on folk values and distant happenings as though they occurred in the narrator's recent memory. Papadiamantis wrote with a particular appeal to the swelling urban population of Athens in the late nineteenth century. Most of these new city dwellers were just a generation away from being peasants. Indeed, Papadiamantis incorporated into his stories a kind of time of the farmer as opposed to the modern time of the merchant. In 1889 he translated Dostoyevski's *Crime and Punishment.* In 1903, he produced his masterpiece, *The Murderess,* which tells the story of a serial killer of female infants, a woman driven astray by her desire to save little girls from the injustice of unequal dowries and exclusive inheritance by the firstborn.

See also JOURNALISM, NINETEENTH CENTURY

Further Reading

Beaton, Roderick. "Realism and Folklore in Nineteenth-Century Greek Fiction." *BMGS* 8 (1982): 103–122.

Papadiamantis, Alexandros. Η Νοσταλγός και άλλα διηγήματα [The Woman Who Yearned to Go Home, and other Stories]. Athens: Nefeli, 1989.

Papadiamantis, Alexandros. *The Murderess,* trans. by Peter Levi. London: Writers' & Readers' Publishing Co-op, 1980.

Papadiamantis, Alexandros. *Tales from a Greek Island,* trans. by Elizabeth Constantinides. Baltimore: Johns Hopkins University Press, 1987.

Ricks, David. "Aléxandros Papadiamándis and Thomas Hardy." In *The Greek Novel: AD 1–1985,* edited by Roderick Beaton, 23–30. London: Croom Helm, 1988.

PAPADIAMANTOPOULOS, IOANNIS (1856–1910) Born in Patras, to a family descended from **Independence** heroes on both sides, Ioannis Papadiamantopoulos was assigned to a French governess, then studied arts at Athens, law at Paris (where he mixed with avant-garde writers), and set out for Germany and Italy. In 1878 he published a pamphlet concerning the debate between **Roidis** and **Vlachos** on the nonoriginality of current Greek writing. His youthful poems *Vipers and Turtledoves* (1873) attracted attention, partly because it made major concessions to a simple **demotic** idiom that was still unfashionable in Romantic poetry of the time. He wrote angry articles in the *Attic Messenger* attacking the committee of the **Voutsynas Prize** for not giving the award to *Vipers and Turtledoves.* In 1883 he settled in Paris, and was lost to the Greek language, but not to Greek literature, for he was translated by his close friend and pupil **Malakasis** (of whose wife he was first cousin), **Tellos Agras, Karyotakis**, and Kleon Paraschos. In turn, Papadiamantopoulos translated Malakasis and others into French, while gaining a major niche in French literary life as Jean Moréas, the author of two manifestos on **symbolism,** several volumes of poetry, two novels, the play *Iphigénie* (1903), and above all the *Stances,* of which two volumes came out in 1889 and the four others in 1901. *Néa Estía,* no. 707 (1956) is devoted to this writer.

PAPANOUTSOS, EVANGELOS (1900–1982)

Born in Piraeus, Papanoutsos studied at the Theological School of Athens University. After teaching in Greek schools and at Alexandria, Papanoutsos followed graduate courses in philosophy and education (France, Germany), gained a doctorate from Tübingen (1927), held various offices with the Ministry of Education (1944–1952), was Secretary for Education in the Papandreou government (1964–1965), and was the "architect" of the educational reform introduced by that cabinet. He wrote for the newspaper *Tribune,* founded and edited the journal *Education,* which later became *Education and Life* (1945–1961), and published his system of thought in three volumes under the general heading *The World of the Spirit: Aesthetics* (1948), *Ethics* (1949), and *The Foundation of Knowledge* (1954; English translation, 1968). These were foreshadowed in his early, shorter monographs *On Art* (Alexandria, 1930), *On Ethics* (Athens, 1932), and *On Knowledge* (Athens, 1936). He also edited and wrote the critical introduction to *Modern Greek Philosophy* (2 vols., 1953–1956) and many other books: *Freedom of Will, Pragmatism or Humanism* (1924), *Religious Experience in Plato* (1927, in German), *Introduction to the Philosophy of Religion, Trilogy of the Soul, Elements of Psychology* (1940–1947, a primer designed for the fifth form of high school), *Philosophy and Education* (1958), *Philosophical Problems* (1963), *On Palamás, Kavafis and Sikelianós* (1949), and *The Purification of Passions according to Aristotle* (in French). These books make him Greece's most influential modern philosopher. In 1975, he gained a parliamentary seat.

Further Reading

Henderson, G. P. *The Revival of Greek Thought, 1620–1830.* Albany: State University of New York Press, 1970.

Henderson, G. P. *E. P. Papanoutsos.* Boston: Twayne, 1983.

PAPANTONIOU, ZACHARIAS (1877–1940)

Zacharias Papantoniou wrote the well-known **reader** for Greek schoolchildren, *The High Mountains* (1917, see **Educational Society**), and the **prose-poem** *Prose Rhythms* (1923), for which he was later hailed a "prince of Greek style," as a master of this difficult hybrid form. Leandros Palamás called him "an amateur" and said his pretty poems could be counted on the fingers of two hands. He gave up medical school for art studies and in 1911 showed his sketches and cartoons at the Zappeion Art Exhibition. A prolific journalist, at one time editor-in-chief of *Scrip,* he was sent by the newspaper *Forwards* as their correspondent in Paris. This reportage led to his successful volumes *Letter from Paris* (1909–1911). He brought out two collections of lyric poems, *War Songs* (1897) and *Divine Gifts* (1928). He composed poems for children (1920), *The Swallows,* and also a verse play, *The Dead Man's Oath* (1929). Papantoniou was a much-traveled director of the National Art Gallery (appointed 1918). In 1923 he won the national Prize for Arts and Letters. Later he held teaching posts in applied decorative art at the Amalia Orphans' Institute and in aesthetics at the School of Fine Arts. He became a member of the Athenian Academy in 1938.

PAPARRIGOPOULOS, DIMITRIOS (1843–1873) Poet, essayist, theorist of **Romanticism,** and author of prose plays, Dimitrios Paparrigopoulos was the grandson of a major conspirator of the **Uprising** and son of the famous historian Konstantinos. At age 16, while still a schoolboy, he published *Reflections of a Brigand, or The Sentence of Society.* He wrote a doctoral thesis on Plato's theory of punishment and followed it with a study of Christian ethical duty. He worked as a lawyer by day and complained that he had to steal hours for his writing by night. As a neoclassicist of the Old School of **Athens** from its most exuberantly **purist** vintage, he wrote a poem praising the pre-Christian age of **Homer** as a period of Utopian happiness. It suggests that Homer's gods were capable of molding Mount Olympus into a society, and that in Homer's work the "Muse creates the gods anew." Some of Paparrigopoulos's work ("Sighs," "The Swallows," "Orpheus") won awards or favorable mentions at the **Voutsynas Poetry Prize,** but his life was chaotic and bohemian, to the point of romantic self-destruction. Many of his poems were rhapsodies on solitude, futility, or despair. People learned his "Lamp of the Cemetery of Athens" by heart. He collapsed while running an errand and died a few hours later, aged 29. He was idolized by the public of his time. His funeral was attended by a huge crowd, including everyone in contemporary letters. On the same day (20 March 1873), the writer **Ioannis Karasoutsas** committed suicide. Much of Paparrigopoulos's work now seems facile, like the Bacchanalian chant in a poem on drink: "Let's deck our hair with fronds of vine. / Wine, which directs our spirit to the heights, / Cancels out the earth; fill up, let's drink."

Further Reading

Paparrigopoulos, D. Τὰ Ἅπαντα [The Complete Works]. Athens: Phexi Library, 1915.

PAPATSONIS, TAKIS (1895–1976) Papatsonis was a mystical, deeply religious poet. He studied at Athens and Geneva, had a successful career as a civil servant, and represented Greece at several economic conferences. He was unusual as a young poet in attempting to meld the **Orthodox** and the **Catholic,** while merging Western and Anatolian devotional idioms. His first poems came out in 1914–1915. His published volumes were *Selection no. 1* (1934), *Ursa Minor* (1944), and *Selection no. 2* (1962). He was an influential critic, translator, and author of two successful **travel** volumes, the mystical account of a journey to **Mount Athos,** *Training for Athos* (1963), and *Old Romania of Myth* (1968). Months of an idealized travel experience flowed into this latter book, about his meeting and talks with **Seferis** (1939).

Further Reading

Myrsiades, K. *Takis Papatsonis.* New York: Twayne, 1974.

Papatsonis, T. *Ursa Minor and Other Poems,* trans. by Kimon Friar and Kostas Myrsiades. Minneapolis, MN: North Central Publishing Co. [1987].

PARALOGÉS The *paralogés* are a type of folk **ballad,** lyric or narrative in manner, often with supernatural elements. They refer to isolated communities and time long past. Kohler calls them "courts récits dialogués." The *paralogí* has a lively tradition on Crete and Cyprus. It is derived from a Byzantine word for melodramatic utterance (παρακαταλογή) and has many similarities with the ballads of the West (which Greeks called μπαλλάντες). The poems may have amorous subjects, such as, *The Abandoned Girl, The Maid of Honour who Becomes Bride,* or *Chartzianis,* which tells the story of a man who dresses as a woman in order to reach the chamber of the girl he loves. There is the horror story *The Vampire,* which also has the title *The Dead Brother,* or the tale *Prince Mavrianos and His Sister,* also known as *The Wager of Mavrianos.*

Other *paralogés* contain a moral kernel, like *The Two Brothers and the Wife of the First,* also known as *The Wicked Wife.* Widely known and recited was the tale of *The Sun-Born Maiden,* who avoids all but one of the traps set by the mother of a knight who loves her. People knew and recited *The Bridge of Arta* or *The Swimmer.* The *Lay of the Queen and Arodafnousa* is a Cypriot ballad relating the adulterous love of King Peter I (1350–1369) for a local girl called **Arodafnousa,** killed by the queen. Other tragic *paralogés* are popular on the Greek mainland, such as *The Murderous Mother.* Many became popular throughout the Balkans.

See also DRAMATIC PRESENT; POSTPONEMENT

Further Reading

Balaskas, Kostas, ed. Παραλογές: δημοτική ποίηση [The Paralogés: Demotic Poetry]. Athens: Epikairotita, 1996.

Lord, Albert J. "The Heroic Tradition of Greek Epic and Ballad: Continuity and Change." In *Hellenism and the First Greek War of Liberation: Continuity and Change,* edited by Nikiforos P. Diamandouros, 79–96. Thessaloniki: Institute for Balkan Studies, 1976.

PARASCHOS, ACHILLEUS (1838–1895)

Achilleus Paraschos was the much lionized darling of cultural circles in Athens. He was a popular public performer, held various civil service posts, and gave a celebrated recitation on the **Philhellene George Byron,** at **Missolonghi** (1880). He had no formal education and took some lessons with his elder brother **Yeoryios Paraschos.** His brooding glance, deep-set eyes, and straggling moustache were considered the ideal features of the Romantic writer. He was involved with the Golden Youth movement, agitators hostile to King Otho, and in the antimonarchist struggle, which eventually ousted him (10 October 1862, to 1863). He was one of the leaders of the charge against the artillery barracks. On the occasion of his detention in the Mentreses **prison** and subsequent release on compassionate grounds, he composed verse likening himself to a martyr of freedom: "To the Prison Plane-Tree." There is a strong vein of magniloquence, even of turgid romantic outpouring, in Paraschos's patriotic poems. He was heavily influenced, like other nineteenth-century Greek poets, by the French writer Lamartine. His three volumes of *Complete Works* were issued in 1881, followed by two posthumous volumes (1904). Trypanis observes that A. Paraschos was "one of the very few poets who made money out of the sale of his books of verse." His "Elegy on the Death of King Otho" made him well known. His love poems, many written for a shadowy beauty evoked as "Maria," conceal a drama of illness and insanity, in the course of which he used his authority as a provincial governor to have the woman transferred from a convent to an asylum.

Further Reading

Kohler, Denis. *Que sais-je? La littérature grecque moderne.* Paris: P.U.F., 1985.

PARASCHOS, YEORYIOS (1822–1886) Yeoryios Paraschos is the elder brother of Achilleus (see previous entry). His teachers at **Nafplion** (where the family fled from the sack of Chios) were Leontios and **Yennadios.** Two of their sisters were captured by Turks in the sack of Chios, and nothing more was ever heard of them. He was considered a handsome figure, in his Greek national costume, worn as a public statement against the recently introduced Western suits (see **Valavanis**). He won prizes for patriotic compositions (1865), such as "Dawn Chant," "The Sentry," "The National Guard," in a competition sponsored by the Ministry of Defense. They were to be set to music and sung by soldiers on the march. As a young man, he circulated a periodical called *Victory,* in which he inveighed against King Otho and the nation's Bavarian monarch. He was secretary to Prime Minister Kolettis (see **Great Idea**) for a while and held a lifetime post as registrar of the Parliament's proceedings. He composed inspirational patriotic poems on occurrences of national interest. He also wrote *Arkadi* on the siege and fall of the doomed monastery in Crete (1866) and a *Hymn to George I;* translated the *Iliad* of **Homer** into **Katharevousa,** and V. Hugo's *Hernani;* wrote many love lyrics and a play (from which only a few fragments were published in his life).

PARATAXIS Parataxis (παράταξη) is an array of short sentences in direct sequence, with little use of connectives or **conjunctions** and no subordinate clauses. The Greek word means the same as a front line of soldiers, ready for battle. This **figure of speech** is in clear contrast with **hypotaxis.** As a device in expository writing, it conveys immediacy or impas-sioned urgency. The **Anonymous Greek** (1806) employs it in his "Alas! Where are you, hallowed freedom! Where the Laws? Where the lawgivers? You are the mother of great men, you the pillar of justice, you the font of happiness." **Rigas Velestinlís,** in his "Revolutionary Proclamation" (1797), displays heightened conviction by juxtaposing his thoughts: "Our right to assemble in peace. The freedom from all religion, Christianity, Turkism, Judaism, and so on."

PARNASSISM The Greek school of Parnassism revived the **sonnet** and sought gemlike effects inside an overriding perfection of form. Its quintessential representative is **Gryparis,** with **Palamás** and **Mavilis,** followed by **Malakasis,** the early **Varnalis,** and **Drosinis.** These poets caught the imagination of the Greek public for 20 years. Then came the milestone death of the French poet S. Mallarmé (1898), and a different poetics flooded Greek literary life, namely **Symbolism.** The Greek Parnassians fastened on such topics as nature, art objects, wine, the unalloyed Dionysian element in life, and partying. Parnassism also denotes their intense admiration for certain French writers, whose main anthologies appeared between 1866 and 1876: namely Leconte de Lisle, Coppée, Banville, Hérédia, Sully-Prudhomme, and the Verlaine of *Poèmes saturniens* (1866).

Parnassism incarnated the ideal of "art-for-art's-sake," and this lyricism was central to the nineteenth-century **New School of Athens,** mediated by the writer **Papadiamantopoulos,** who went to Paris and turned himself into the French poet Jean Moréas. In an essay on the French writer Paul Fort (1872–1960), Malakasis enumerates the typical Parnassian items in the literary world: "Birds, waters, colors, sensations, the secrets of nature, the open spectacle of creation, good temper of the soul, breath, sea, night, morning, afternoon, the unknown, affection, child, shadows, lights, flower, leaf, October, winter, father, death, melancholy, nostalgia, mother, woods, fire, silence, and destiny, all bound together in lines undying, psychically heightened, original, rich, shiny and victorious."

PARNASSÓS The Parnassós Literary Society is one of the oldest in Greece. It was founded in 1865 at Athens by a group of teenage intellectuals, Spyridón Lambros and his brothers and **Dimitrios Koromilás** (1850–1898), who later became a noted comic playwright. The society espoused high-minded ideals, such as the provision of knowledge, lectures, and exhibitions to the whole community and its moral elevation. It went on to produce a journal, which ran from 30 January 1877 to August 1895, in octavo format, under the name *Parnassós*. In classical art, this was the name of the mountain near Delphi that was the abode of the nine **muses,** sacred to the god Apollo. In 1872, one of its members, **Spyridon Vasiliadis,** proposed that the society should sponsor the foundation of schools for working-class children. Later they promoted a drama prize (see **Roidis**), campaigned for **nationalist** causes, or pushed for the improvement of prison conditions. They produced a *Year-Book* from 1904 to 1907. By 1930, after various changes of address and financial difficulties, successors of the founding members had established their own premises in order to hold "Evening Classes for Needy Children." By 1940, over 40,000 beneficiaries had completed Parnassós courses. Its building, at the crossroads of Themistoklis and Kantakouzenós, also served as a dormitory or sanatorium. A small literary society thus achieved disproportionately large practical results.

PARODY Parody is the comic imitation of a literary model, mentioned in **Aristotle** and present throughout modern Greek. **Seferis** says that *The Mass of the Beardless Man* ridicules the church service "in a rather shocking way. It amuses me especially because I don't see enough light comic texts in our literature" (see **Spanos**). When D. Kambouroglous took first prize in the **poetry competition** of 1873, **Vasiliadis** and **A. Paraschos** were annoyed. They felt they deserved to win, so they parodied his verses. Kambouroglous responded in kind: "Beauty I do not love; / Indeed, I don't love beauty. / However healthy it may be, / Whatever health it has. // Everyone else may love it, / It can be loved by anyone else. / I find it perfectly revolting, / It gives me perfect revulsion." Ten miles from Chios lies the isle of Psara, which the Turks laid waste in the **War of Independence. Solomós** evoked this tragedy (1824–1825) in six lines of scorching fervor: "On island Psara's blackened spine, / Glory paces in a line, / Pondering the glorious dead, / She wears a garland on her head, / Of woven grass, the little left, / Plucked upon a land bereft." This epigram by Solomós, "To Psara," is lampooned by A. Kantounis (1847–1890) in lines of equal pomp but corrosive vocabulary, entitled "Introit:" "On the Kastro's glorious stone, / Madness paces on her own, / Thinks of kings and church and gown, / And wears a garland as her crown, / Made of bundles left around / On land we know as Chasis' ground."

The "Hymn to Glorious France" by **A.**

Martelaos received acid treatment at the hands of the conservative N. Logothetis-Youliaris. The first two quatrains of Martelaos run: "Wherever you are scattered, / Brave bones of old / Hellenic exploits, / Gather now your breath; // At the voice of my trumpet, / Be resurrected from your tombs, / And watch our Race / Rise to its former honor." The parody by Logothetis runs: "Whoever in his life heard / Of bones which start to breathe, / Then understand a trumpet call, / And then climb out of the grave?" V. Lambropoulos observed that parody has been "the most rare and the least appreciated genre in modern Greek literature" and praises the poet **Panás** for the interesting thrust of his "anarchic satires," which mock Athenian or Ionian romantics for getting stuck in the modish formulas that made them so respectable in the critical canon (Alexiou, 1985: 29).

PARRÉN, KALLIRHOE SIGANOU (1861–1940) Most influential of the early Greek feminists; Parrén edited *The Newspaper for Ladies* from 1887 to 1918. Born in Rethymno (Crete), she founded the Athens Lycée for Greek Girls in 1911 and published many politically committed texts, the plays *The New Woman* (1907), *History of Women, History of the Greek Woman, White Rose,* and a **trilogy** of novels, *The Books of Dawn,* that consisted of *The Emancipated* (1900), *The Witch* (1901), and *The New Contract* (1901–1903), which were published in serial form from December 1901 to September 1903, in *The Newspaper for Ladies.*

Further Reading

Anastasopoulou, Maria. "Feminist Awareness and Greek Women Writers: The Case of Kallirrhoe Siganou-Parren and Alexandra Papadopoulou." In *Greek Society in the Making, 1863–1913: Realities, Symbols and Visions,* edited by P. Carabott, 161–175. Aldergate: Ashgate Publishing, 1997.

PASTICHE Pastiche (παστίς) is a genre that constructs one text out of fragments of other books and styles. Though it imitates its sources, it has a mischievous, debunking intent. Apostolos Doxiadis (b. 1953) makes a pastiche of familiar characters from world authors, setting up a satire of modern Greek literature and of scenes from Greek life in his *Meta-Macbeth* (1988). This novel purports to relate the metamorphosis of an exemplary military officer into a tragicomic putsch organizer. Yannis Xenakis (b. 1922) wrote a score for the *Oresteia* (1965–1966) and staged an "opera" called *Polytope* at locations such as Mycenae (1978). Its irreverently assembled cast includes soloists, a choir, electronic music, processions, army platoons, searchlights, fires, cinemascope, and a flock of goats. A comparable example of literary irreverence (1935) is A. Embirikos's *The Kill of High Heat.* These "verses" contain **automatic writing** and chunks of prose. Some of the poetry is recycled **purist** phraseology. Embirikos also imitates scientific formulas or copies gobbets of **newspaper reporting.**

PASTORAL. See VOSKOPOULA

PATRIOT; PATRIOTISM Modern Greek writers regard the patriot as one who *acts* on behalf of his homeland. In the **Uprising of 1821,** the patriots are those who raised the flag, joined the combat, and raised funds. Earlier patriots gave their lives and signally so the writer and "proto-martyr" Velestinlís (1798), but at that stage there was no actual country of Greece to die for. A milder form of patriotism is love of the homeland (πατριδολατρεία). This sentiment drove many authors to a fury of lyricism, even if they were living safely in Paris, like Koraís. **Kalvos,** also living abroad, ends his first Ode, "The Patriot" (1824) with the dictum: "Death is sweet / Only when we repose / In our birthplace." Devotion and irredentism were fused in so many Greek writers that their patriotism teetered on the edge of linguistic violence. **A. Valaoritis,** in "My Love for the Homeland," hints at the unfathomable wrench of love for his country: "For you, my homeland, I sense a tumult in my guts."

Yeoryios Zalokostas joined the Uprising (1822) as a teenager. He fought under the commanders Papastathopoulos, Botzaris, and the **Philhellene,** Richard Church. He took part in the sortie from **Missolonghi** and in later years used these events as literary material. But he felt that his country came before his writing: "The Muse kept silent inside me, since one sole yearning directed the throbbing of Greek hearts: freedom and the rehabilitation of our struggling nation." When he depicts a 20-year-old Greek soldier at Missolonghi, with his flowing hair, tasseled cap, sleeveless greatcoat, silver pistols, and curving sword, Zalokostas incarnates the prototype of youthful bravery, which Greeks call a *palikari*: "The fatherland of such a combatant will not submit to any yoke." When a patriot leads his band of warriors to the mountain pass at Gravia, he yells: "It is our country that calls us here, / Valiant soldiers."

The patriot is exemplified in Spyros Matsoukas (1870–1928), a popular balladist born in Ipati (Thessaly), of Vlachian parents. In 1896, as a law student, Matsoukas joined the student uprising against Professor Galbanis. He caused the siege of the university to be raised, and the most pugnacious hotheads among the students were transferred to the uprising in Crete. He went to America and raised funds from the Greek community to finance a torpedo boat and battery called "Young Generation." In the nationalist struggle, Matsoukas fanned the armed forces' enthusiasm with his songs. He founded the White Cross and from its funds gave dowries to the orphaned daughters of men who fell in combat.

See also BOUBOULIS

Further Reading

Brewer, David. *The Flame of Freedom: The Greek War of Independence, 1821–1833.* London: J. Murray, 2001.

Saïd, Suzanne, ed. *Hellenismos: quelques jalons pour une histoire de l'identité grecque.* Leiden: Brill, 1991.

PEN NAME, LITERARY. See PSEUDONYM

PENGLI, YOLANDA (1934–) Yolanda Pengli produced over 10 volumes of poetry: *February* (1978) constitutes an elegy to the poet Yeoryios Sarantis; *To the Pharisees* (1971) has a preface by **Takis Papatsonis** and illustrations by the painter Alekos Kontopoulos. She translated volume II of Sholokov's *And Quiet Flows the Don* from an English version (with the poet Rita Boumi-Pappá), Jules Verne, Vladimir Majakovsky, and the Romanian novelist Ion Kreanga's *The White Slave,* from a French version.

PERDIKARIS, MIKHAIL (1766–1828; also PREDIKARIS) Born in Kozani (northwestern Greece), Perdikaris studied medicine at Padua and walked (as he was penniless) to Vienna to continue his studies. Later he was personal physician to Mouchtar (son of **Ali Pasha**). His adventures in Moldavia and Wallachia led to a volume of satirical verse in 460 pages, *Hermilos, or Demokritherakleitos* (1817). The compound name is taken from *Logic,* by **Voulgaris**. Almost immediately came an apologia of *Hermilos* (1817), because he feared the church's excommunication. The text is cast as an imitation of Apuleius's *The Golden Ass,* with the hero turned into a donkey because he rejected the advances of an unholy nun called Parthenia. Most of *Hermilos* seems to have been written in 1806. Perdikaris attacks prelates ("janissaries"). He scorns Voltaire, scoffs at **Enlightenment** ideas, but also criticizes established rulers.

PERIODIZATION A key issue in the study of modern Greek literature is the periodization of its chronological boundaries. Modern Greek literature is variously dated from the ninth or the tenth century. Another group of scholars puts the watershed in the early eleventh century, when the first text in **plain Greek,** *Diyenís Akritas,* was thought to emerge. A further school of thought sees 1453 as the dividing date, when Byzantine culture ended with the fall of **Constantinople,** and what follows is the long, sluggish Greek reaction to Turkish rule. An alternative assessment, by the sheer quality of the literary product, dates modern Greek from the flourish of **Cretan** writing, in the seventeenth century. A modern start is placed by some commentators at 1708, the year of publication of the anthology *Flowers of Piety.* The contemporary high school syllabus (see Emmanouilidis, 1999) offers a uniform approved course on modern Greek literature. The

set book for its exams arranges our subject under six headings: (1) ninth century–1453; (2) 1453–1669 (fall of Crete); (3) 1669–1821 (start of the **War of Independence**); (4) 1821–1880 (emergence of **New School of Athens**); (5) 1880–1930 (**Generation of the 1930s** and 1931, publication of first poems by **Seferis**); (6) 1930–the present. There are also good arguments for a division of Greek literature into three historical periods: Antiquity, Byzantium, and Modern. This historical triptych satisfies a need for continuity, and is tailored to patriotic, nationalist, theories of **neo-Hellenism**. M. Katsinis says: "We have ancient Greek literature, Byzantine and neo-Hellenic. Neo-Hellenic literature is found in the space of the last 200 years [he is writing in 1975], and it offers an abundance of worthwhile texts." Knös holds that the notion of the Middle Ages was adopted by Greeks under the influence of the West. Also accepted is the periodization (1) **Hellenistic,** (2) **Byzantine,** (3) **Turkocracy** (1453–1821), and (4) Modern. Another determining date is the fourth Crusade, that is, the fall of Byzantium to Latin invaders in 1204. Many **histories** of modern Greek literature commence at 1000 A.D. They take the epic *Diyenís Akritas* as its first loosely dated text. Emmanuel Kriarás (b. 1906) extended the definition of medieval Greek literature to around 1700, calling 1200 to 1700 "the last medieval period" or "the pro-modern Greek period." A geographical division also helps to define Greek culture up to the twentieth century: (1) Aegean: Rhodes, Cyprus; (2) Crete; (3) Ionian Islands and expatriate **Hellenism;** and (4) Hellenism under the Turkocracy. Ilias Voutieridis (1874–1941) divided Greek literature into ancient and modern. The word *modern* here is used to define differences in exterior shape and "essence" (οὐσία). It is a continuation of ancient literature with an altered linguistic shape. The new form was acquired during the Byzantine empire, which runs, according to Voutieridis, from 330 A.D. (when Byzantium became capital of the eastern Roman empire) to 1453 (fall of Constantinople). Thrakiotis (1965) saw all attempts at periodization, as conventions (συμβατικά). But he accepted the division (1) 1000–1204, (2) 1204–1453, (3) 1453–1821, (4) 1821–1880, (5) 1880–1930, and (6) 1930–1965.

Further Reading

Katsinis, Mitsos. Λογοτεχνία καὶ Βιογραφίες [Literature and Biographies]. Athens: Arkadia, 1975.

Lambropoulos, Vassilis. "Modern Greek Studies at the Crossroads: The Paradigm Shift from Empiricism to Skepticism." *JMGS* 7, no. 1 (1989): 1–39.

PERIPHRASIS Periphrasis (περίφραση) is the **trope** that expresses a concept by using more than a single word. Or it can refer to a sentence that goes a "long way round," instead of using a direct expression. In general, instead of one term, the writer affects a combination of its properties, circumstances or results. Thus the **sun** is "the star of the daytime" or wheat is the "fruit of Demeter." In a poem by **Polemis,** "Hidden Schooling" (1900), about the classes held for Greek children in churches during Turkish rule, the night is called, by periphrasis, "the palpable darkness of bitter enslavement."

PERISSOLOGY. See BABBLING

PERRAIVÓS, CHRISTOFOROS (1773–1863) Perraivós, a soldier from the **Uprising,** became one of the great historians of his period. He was a friend and collaborator of **Rigas,** became Minister of War (1823), and kept high rank and a career in the army after Independence. His *War Memoirs* add to the rich genre of first-person accounts of the Uprising. He wrote *The Story of Rigas* and a *History of Souli and Parga,* in which he used parts of the **Chronicle of Anthimos.**

See also MEMOIRS

PERSONIFICATION Personification (προσωποποίηση) is the presentation, in prose or poetry, of animals or inanimate objects as if they had human emotions. Spyros Melás (1882–1966) composes a newspaper sketch in 1918 about a "baby sparrow" that tries his first flight from the eaves of a farm roof and is nailed by fear to the tiles, before flapping to the ground. A "mother-sparrow" hovers by, scolds the "novice," and then gives him "practical lessons in aviation." This is a "sacred, blessed duality of mother and child," cries Melás, calling it a symbol of the love and the unity of Creation. His piece is a guileless exercise in personification.

PETSALIS-DIOMEDIS, THANASIS (1904–1995) The novelist and playwright Petsalis-Diomedis was very prolific, writing over 10,000 pages and more than one **trilogy** in his career. Beaton considers his early trilogy, *Strong and Weak Generations* (1933–1935), a typical example of the social and urban realism of the decade. Later came another two-volume historical canvas, *The Mavrolykos Family* (1947–1948), which was broadcast on Greek Radio and recommended by the Ministry of Education for school libraries and use in high school history classes. Petsalis developed a vocation for painstaking fictionalized history, especially in *The Bell of St. Trinity* (1949), which relates a life saga of **Hellenism,** five centuries from **Byzantium** to the **War of Independence.** The bell in this book's title was the gift of a Byzantine emperor. It fell silent during the **Turkocracy,** only to ring again at the rebirth of Greek freedom. The saga was followed, among other works, by the 1,200 pages of *Greek Dawn* (3 vols., 1962). Here the story of the Greek revolution is built round the figure of Ioannis Kolettis (1774–1847), physician to **Ali Pasha** and later Prime Minister under King Otho (see also **Great Idea**). The historical canvas of *Greek Dawn* includes writers connected with Hellenic nationalism such as **U. Foscolo, I. Zambelios, Rigas Velestinlís,** and **Kolokotronis.**

Further Reading

"Thanassis Petsalis: Excerpts from Three Novels," trans. by Katherine Hortis, Fotine Nicholas, and Tula Lewnes. *The Charioteer,* no. 6 (spring 1964): 24–70.

PHANARIOT When almost 100,000 inhabitants of **Constantinople** were exempted from the exchange of populations between Greece and Turkey after the **Asia Minor disaster,** they were referred to as Phanariot Greeks. The term comes from the name of the lighthouse ("lantern"), situated in the Gold Horn channel, just northeast of the Patriarchiate. This was the district inhabited by a class of Greeks in the **Ottoman** bureaucracy. Constantinople also had a Genoese, or a Venetian city district. From 1600 onward, the Phanariot upper class developed a minor aristocracy in their enclave of scholars, teachers, lawyers, and civil servants. The term "Phanariot" is also used to denote the cultural or artistic activities of Greeks in Constantinople through the whole period of Turkish rule. Even in their heyday, the eighteenth century, the Phanariots were conservative and conformist. Their Hellenism was introverted, a break with the West. Attached to the past, some Phanariot writers cultivated a frigid **Katharevousa** in a spirit that was archaizing or pious (but see **Tantalidis**). Their educational model was the Great School of the Nation, at Constantinople, founded by the **Orthodox** Church. Other schools on this prototype were set up in the Danube provinces, which had less influential, Greek-speaking populations. From the early 1600s, the Turks employed these nonimmigrant Phanariot Greeks as a permanent administrator class. They were fiscal agents to the Sultan, administrators of the Public Treasure, foreign ambassadors, Dragomans of the Fleet, or rulers of Wallachia or Moldavia (as Hospodars, Voievods, or Beys). The appointment as a Dragoman was a sought-after senior post for an established Greek collaborator with the ruling Ottoman authorities. It meant acting as chief interpreter (and, in practice, naval or foreign policy adviser) to the foreign minister of the Sublime Porte. Phanariot intellectual life eventually looked to the West, and to France in particular. In the later eighteenth and early nineteenth century, Phanariot writers produced erudite works. They founded literary journals (for example, in Vienna, 1790) and contributed to the development of non-Greek theater at Odessa, Bucharest, and Jassy (1810), the Romanian city with its university and two Byzantine churches in pure seventeenth-century style.

Further Reading

Symposium "L'époque phanariote," 21–25 octobre 1970. Thessalonica: Institute for Balkan Studies, 1974.

PHERAIOS. See RIGAS

PHEXI LIBRARY (1909–1917) The Phexi Library was a popular but learned series of modern Greek books, which dates from around 1910. Its owner, Yeoryios Phexis, climbed from backstreet publishing to the democratization of literature. The man who had once hand-printed trashy novellas by Kassiani, Genovesa, and Kakarapis and then hawked them outside the National Bank for a tenth of a drachma, now set about producing Greece's first serious line for the general reading public. He promoted translations of classical texts and world literature for up to 100 drachmas, but enthusiasts could obtain them by paying a subscription of five drachmas per month. The stimulus to launch the series can be traced to the interest aroused by writers who contributed to the journal *Hegeso* and were active in the so-called Generation of 1905. From 1911 to 1915, **Nikos Kazantzakis** worked for Phexi on translations of William James, Nietzsche, Eckermann, Laisant, Maeterlinck, Darwin, Büchner, Bergson, and six **Plato** dialogues. Directed by Ioannis Zervós, G. Phexi Editions published translations of many modern European classics. Zervós himself (1875–1944) was born in Cephalonia, read law at University of Athens, and followed this by studying political science in Paris. He then practiced as a lawyer in Alexandria, but contributed poems and articles to literary periodicals under the pseudonym "Aretas." A collection of his verse, *The Fair Weather Songs,* came out in 1918.

PHILADELPHEIOS POETRY COMPETITION The Philadelpheios was an influential late-nineteenth- and early-twentieth-century competition held at Athens to honor an original volume of poetry. **Ioannis Polemis** (1862–1924) took the prize in 1888 with *Winter Flowers,* whereas the more famous **K. Palamás** won first prize in 1889 with his *Hymn of Athene.* In that same year, **A. Eftaliotis** took the second prize with his *Songs of Exile.* A. **Provelengios** (1851–1936) was another runner-up; in 1890, Provelengios was judge for the competition and awarded the first prize to Palamás for *Eyes of My Soul.* Provelengios used his announcement of the Philadelpheios prizes in the solemnity of the Zappeion Palace (with **Roidis** and **N. Politis** on his committee) to proclaim the end of a linguistic era in poetry. Kostas Krystallis (1868–1894) was one of the laureates in 1890, with his collection *Poems of the Fields,* and in 1892 was cited for *The Singer of the Village and the Pasture.* A citation also went to the 1890 volume *Words of the Heart* by Konstantinos Manos (1869–1913). This was Manos's only volume of verse, published when he was a student. Later he became an organizer of athletics in Greece and a politician. The son of Thrasyboulos Manos, an instigator of the anti-Monarchist uprising of 1862, Konstantinos himself fought in the Cretan uprising of 1896. **Yeoryios Stratigis** (1860–1938) took the prize in 1891 with his poem *Eros and Psyche.* The 1920 laureate was a woman writer from Alexandria (Egypt), Athena Rousaki Germanou, the first **feminist writer** in the history of the prize.

PHILHELLENES;   PHILHELLENISM Travelers, scholars, or revolutionaries who cultivated a special love of Greece were known as Philhellenes. Stilios Seferiades (1873–1951, father of **Seferis**), wrote that his translation of **Byron,** most famous of **Philhellenes,** made him a better **patriot:** "as I hewed out / Each of your lines with Greek words, / It was you who Hellenized / My enslaved Muse." In 1821, the poet Shelley called the contemporary Greek "the descendant of those glorious beings whom the imagination almost refuses to figure to itself as belonging to our kind." Robert Liddell expressed this devotion in its pristine form: "To some of us who most love the Aegean, it is like a type or foretaste of Paradise." Dr. Johnson said, "Greek is like fine lace. A man gets as much of it as he can." In the early nineteenth century, there was a large production of tracts, essays, and poems in Western languages that supported the cause of Greek independence from the Turks and the growth of renascent **Hellenism.** A bibliography of this literature is in L. Droulia (1974). The **Ionian School** poet, **Ioulios Typaldos,** returned the feeling in his "Ode on the Death of the Philhellene Lenormant." Western liberals and intellectuals praised contemporary Greek **patriots,** repaying what they saw as a debt to classical texts and the city–state of Athens, which they revered. Some Philhellenes loved the tradition more than the actual case. Chief among these was Chateaubriand, writing in *L'Itinéraire* (1811) on his travels through Greece in 1806: "I have seen Greece! I visited Sparta, Argos, Mycenae, Corinth, Athens; beautiful names, alas! Nothing more. . . . Never see Greece, Monsieur, except in Homer. It is the best way." Others, like Pierre-Augustin Guys in his *Voyage littéraire de la Grèce* (1783), were able to combine love for two contrasting reference points: classical Attica and the dilapidated cities now ruled by Turks. Leconte de Lisle addressed Greece (1846) as a "sacred mother" and wished he had been born "in the hallowed archipelago / In the glorious

centuries when inspired earth / Saw heaven descend at its first call!" George Byron expounded the dream: "The mountains look on Marathon—/ And Marathon looks on the sea; / And musing there an hour alone, / I dream'd that Greece might still be free." The statesman Metternich failed to discourage waves of Philhellene subscriptions to a cause that, after the fall of **Missolonghi,** was supported by the Crown Prince of Prussia and Ludwig of Bavaria.

The historical record belies the literary romance of the Philhellenes: eight shiploads of volunteers from Marseilles reached Greece at roughly monthly intervals from November 1821. A total of more than 1,000 joined the **War of Independence,** and over a third met their death in Greece. Most of these died of disease. They landed at Navarino, Kalamata, Missolonghi, and Monemvasia. One part of the battalion came ashore at Modon, which was still in Turkish hands. They disliked seeing headless corpses exposed outside town walls, and they were annoyed that they could not use their classical Greek to converse with their hosts. As wandering volunteers, they often found it hard, in 1822, to obtain food and shelter from the Greek peasants whom they were supposedly liberating. Many turned into armed tourists, when they realized that there were no officer commissions to be had in the Greek forces. The *Almanach des grecs pour 1823* is a Philhellene calendar, which lists Saints' Days and anniversaries of battles from the Greek Revolution: "The latter are mostly imaginary" (St. Clair, 1972: 110). D. Howarth calls Frank Hastings, who blew up the magazine of the fort of Vasiladi from his ship *Karteria,* "most useful and faithful of all the Philhellenes." The Irishman William Stevenson was a benefactor of another kind, introducing to Greeks the cultivation of the potato. In 1861, the European colony chose as representative Philhellenes Byron (for England), Fabvier (for France), John J. Meyer (for Switzerland), and Santa Rosa (for Italy). Two editors of newspapers in the infant Greek state were Philhellenes. The Swiss, Meyer, brought out *Hellenic Chronicles,* and the Italian, Joseph N. Chiappe, edited *The Friend of the Law.* Certain foreign language newspapers, such as *Telegrafo Greco* (March–Dec. 1824), and *L'Abeille Grecque* (March 1827–March 1829), were directed primarily at idealist Philhellenes. Meyer's *Hellenic Chronicles* is considered the pick of the many newspapers that were produced during the **War of Independence.** It was issued at Missolonghi, as Meyer and his staff fought alongside the defenders and shared their defense to the death. The paper ran initially from 1 January 1824 to 20 February 1826, with a number of interruptions. Its production coincided with the arrival from Europe of hand-operated printing presses, like those carried by Leicester Stanhope to Athens and **Nafplion,** and those dispatched by Didotos and other Philhellenes. They thought it vital to send descriptions of the siege to Greece and the outside world. The "Ode to the Hellenes" by Iakovos Rizos Neroulos (1778–1850), first published at Leipzig in 1823, appeared in an 1824 issue of *Hellenic Chronicles.* In February 1826, Egyptian bombs hit the building that housed the printing press, destroying its equipment. Copies of the paper have become rare. K. N. Levidis produced a reprint, useful as a source of contemporary information. A continuation of the paper, in a form unrelated to the original, was launched at Missolonghi by the lawyer and writer

Anastasios Yannopoulos (1859). After a patchy run of five years, this new *Hellenic Chronicles* came to a halt in 1864. **Yeoryios Sourís** (1852–1919) has a grandiloquent poem "To the Philhellenes" in which he demands a crown of tear-soaked laurel branches for the "gallant foreign lads" who fought only to gain a funeral shroud of light blue sail cloth. Sourís cries that these European benefactors of Greece found a new homeland, buried in Greek soil. The Philhellenes changed their location, but not their lineage, for "any country can be the grave of superlative men."

Further Reading

Droulia, Loukia. *Philhellénisme: ouvrages inspirés par la guerre de l'indépendence grecque, 1821–1833* [Philhellenism: Works Inspired by the Greek War of Independence]. Athens: Centre de Recherche Scientifique, 1974.

Howarth, David. *The Greek Adventure: Lord Byron and Other Eccentrics in the War of Independence.* London: Collins, 1976.

Spencer, Terence. *Fair Greece! Sad Relic! Literary Philhellenism from Shakespeare to Byron.* London: Weidenfeld & Nicolson, 1954.

St. Clair, W. *That Greece Might Be Free: The Philhellenes in the War of Independence.* Oxford: Oxford University Press, 1972.

PHILIKÍ HETAIRÍA The Friendly Society (that is, Φιλικὶ Ἑταιρία) was the name of a secret group of conspirators that was founded in 1814 and enrolled Greek writers and patriots during the period leading up to the **War of Independence.** It was established at Odessa in southern Russia, the one **Orthodox** country that was not under **Ottoman** rule, and a source of myths about a Balkan uprising against the Turks. The movement was an imitation of Freemasonry, with its rituals, secret passwords, blood bonds, and death as the punishment for betraying its principles. The three founding members were Emmanouil Xanthos, Nikolaos Skoufas, and Athanasios Tsakaloff. Its charter was simple: to promote the cause of liberation for the Motherland, Greece, after the dark centuries of the **Turkocracy.** The Hetairists intended to render peace impossible by baptizing the revolution in blood. General **Makriyannis** became an adherent of the Philikí Hetairía. Makriyannis wrote that he entered the mystery of this society in order to assist "the struggle for our freedom." The Society had four grades in its membership hierarchy: *vlámis* (brother), *systimenós* (recommended), *ieréfs* (priest), and *poimín* (shepherd). It had a ritualistically named Supreme Authority (ἀρχή) and succeeded in gathering about 1,000 adherents by the time of the start of the **War of Independence** in 1821. The initiate swore to tell whether he belonged to any other secret organization. He grasped a candle in his left hand and held his right hand over a sacred icon. When Skoufas enrolled P. Anagnostopoulos (1802–1854), he elaborated a more exotic ceremony. Both held a glass of wine in their left hand and with their right hand over their hearts undertook to devote their mutual efforts to the Society and to shed their blood for it. They poured some wine over a sword, drank the rest of the wine from a shared goblet, and finally kissed each other. Skoufas could not interest merchants in Russia in joining, so he approached young writers like Sekeris, then studying in Paris, enlisting him to enroll **Anthimos Gazís,** who was directing *The Scholar Hermes* in Vienna, and Koraís (who called the city of Vienna "Christ-hating," because of its concentration of

liberal publishers). Both Koraís and Gazís (at first) refused, as they felt that the Greek people needed longer intellectual preparation.

Writers like Kodrikas and Koraís were full of ideological disputes about **neo-Hellenism.** Some expected help for freedom to come from abroad. Originally Tsakaloff was known as initiate "A.B.," Skoufas was "A.Γ.," and Xanthos was "A.Δ." Antonios Komizopoulos was enlisted as the fourth initiate, under the grade "A.E." It was left a mystery who was the prime founder ("A.A."). It was permissible to hint that it was the Emperor of All the Russias. Tsar Alexander I could easily fit the image of a *flavus rex* ("blond king from the North"), who according to legend would come to reinstate Byzantium. Gazís was enrolled as an Authority (ἀρχή), with the grade "A.Z." Skoufas told the Ithacan intellectual, Nikolaos Galatis, that only the top position in the Friendly Society was now left open, and maybe his relative, Kapodistrias, foreign minister in Russia, could fill it. Galatis managed to raise 1,000 roubles in Moscow from A. Mavrokordatos. Galatis worked out the true format of the Friendly Society leadership and was given the initials "A.Δ." (technically already taken). Galatis was something of a hothead, so he was assassinated (by the agreement of his fellows) on a contrived journey out of town. A. Sekeris and P. Anagnostopoulos were enrolled by Skoufas as "A.H." and "A.I." respectively. Others initiated were such "Select Men of the Nation" as Patriarch Gregory, the Ypsilantis brothers, Mavrokordatos, and Mikhail Soutsos, a **Phanariot** intellectual, and Dragoman, familiar to us as the uncle of the writers A. and **P. Soutsos.** Once initiated into the Friendly Society, M. Soutsos adopted their politics. He joined Alexandros Ypsilantis on his unsuccessful incursion into the Danubian principalities, in 1821.

The Hetairists created a cryptic vocabulary for sending lists of names and conspiratorial details. Count Ioannis Kapodistrias, elected first President of Greece in 1827 (and assassinated in 1831) was twice invited to take on the leadership of the Society, in 1817 and 1820. Kapodistrias turned down the conspirators' invitation. He did not consider armed insurrection by the Greek nationalist cause a viable option at the time. **Solomós** wanted nothing to do with it, as a young man on Zakynthos. The poet and jurist **Athanasios Christopoulos** joined the Friendly Society in 1819, but it is not known what part he played in the War of Independence.

Further Reading

Ἄσματα καὶ πονημάτια διαφόρων. *Chansons et opuscules patriotiques publiés à Jassy en 1821 par un hétairiste.* Réédition, avec une étude introductive, par Nestor Camariano. Bucharest, 1966.

Hockecky, Paul L., ed. "Greece." In *Southeastern Europe: A Guide to Basic Publications,* 213–230. Chicago: University of Chicago Press, 1969.

PHILOSOPHY. See **ARISTOTLE; BESSARION; BYZANTIUM; DAMODOS; EPITOME; GERMANY; HELLENISM; HUMANISM; KORYDALLEÚS; MEDICINE; PAPANOUTSOS; PHOTIUS; PLATONISM; PLETHON; TRAPEZUNTIOS**

PHOTIUS (?810–c. 893) "The exceptional Photius" was twice Patriarch of Constantinople, a learned scholar who kept open house for his pupils and was the crucial Byzantine forerunner of the **Renaissance.** As Patriarch, he was dismissed by Emperor Basil I in 867, restored in 878, dismissed in 886, by Emperor **Leo the Wise,** and confined in a monastery till his death. Photius's *The Library* offers excerpts and judgments on 280 authors, many lost. His *Garland of Words* assembles information from various dictionaries, later lost. There are 263 extant letters by Photius, as well as the theological or scholarly *Amphilocheia, Nomocanon, Four Discourses Against the Manichaeans,* and *On Initiation into the Mysteries of the Holy Spirit.*

The Orthodox and Catholic split arises from problems that divided the two churches in 858–880 and again in the eleventh century. When Photius was Patriarch, the dispute between the Orthodox and Latin churches came to a head, with a first schism between Constantinople and Rome (867). Pope Nicholas I, recognizing the Frankish emperor as a Catholic secular monarch, had rejected Photius as Patriarch. Photius then condemned such catholic practices as (1) shaving of priests' beards, (2) use of unleavened bread at Communion, and (3) Lenten eggs. Photius especially rejected (4) the procession of the Holy Spirit from the Father *and* from the Son (*filioque*). This *filioque* had been added to the Nicaean Creed of 381 and designated the Holy Spirit's procession from God the Father, *and* from His Son. These matters, aggravated under Photius, led to a final division (1054) between Orthodox and Catholic, after Patriarch Kiroularios suspended Catholic priests in Constantinople from serving Communion because they used unleavened bread for the Eucharist, and the West still pronounced ". . . and from the Son." Each side excommunicated the other.

Further Reading

White, Despina Stradoudaki. *Patriarch Photios of Constantinople: His Life, Scholarly Contributions, and Correspondence Together with a Translation of Fifty-two of His Letters.* Brookline, MA: Holy Cross Orthodox Press, 1981.

PIGÁS, MELETIOS (c. 1549–1601/02)

Pigás was an enlightened **Orthodox** cleric from Crete. His friend Maximos Margounios (1549–1602) studied at Padua and was known for a reconciliatory stance in the **schism.** Pigás, who also studied at Padua, went on to a career in Crete and Constantinople. He founded the first Greek school in Egypt. He battled against **Catholic** missionaries in Russia. In 1590 he became Patriarch of Alexandria. He initiated the modern tradition of the "literature of Alexandria." He wrote his sermons in the **demotic,** using an impulsive style, without ornaments, which was later followed by Evgenios Yiannoulis (1597–1682; see **Education**). This chatty manner had appeared in Italy after direct communication with the faithful was recommended by the Council of Trent (1545–1563), in an effort to counter the Reformation, modify Catholic discipline, and beat Northern preachers at their own game of appealing to congregations. Pigás was always practical: he criticized Christian mothers who gave their sons earrings so they could pass for girls in the street and avoid the danger of being recruited into a Turkish battalion (see **Kidnapping**). He wrote occasional sonnets in Italian, **epigrams,** a mystery play featuring the virtues and the muses, and some riddles. Aside from his many learned books, *Concerning the Ancient Mysteries, On the Pope,* and *The Orthodox Christian,* what stands out from the work of this imposing Renaissance figure are his sermons in the **plain language,** *Fount of Gold* (1958).

PIKATOROS, IOANNIS (after 1519)

The *Lament on Bitter and Insatiate Hades* by Ioannis Pikatoros tells in 563 rhyming iambic 15-syllable **political** lines how the author went to the Underworld in a dream. It offers a fresco of deceased humanity from the past, groaning, writhing, infested by worms in their joints. The narrator (not unlike Dante in *The Divine Comedy*) observes a large cave. Hell starts from a dark fissure in a sunless gorge. A dragon appears, chasing the hero toward a man in black robes, who emits black smoke. The narrator is swallowed in his mouth and dumped "below the black floor of the world," before locked gates, under flaring pennants. He is inside the domain of Charos, who bears a hawk, has arrow and bow to hand, and "a wild beast's appearance, black and alien, with clothing bronzed and blood-spattered." Pikatoros tells how he rode beside Charos, debating with the king of Hades (see **Folklore**) the justification for such misery after death. People are groaning but speechless. All ranks are there: rulers, aristocrats, young men and women, even little girls riddled with worms. Charos and the traveler discuss the attitude of contemporary religion to mortality. Pikatoros mixes in speculation about the creation of the world, evokes Adam and Eve, explains original sin, and accounts for our expulsion from the earthly paradise. Various explanations of life after death are given, some based on **demotic song,** others drawn from historical chronicles and Scripture. This farrago of superstition and Christian fanaticism breaks off in midnarration, evidently incomplete.

See also APOKOPOS; CRETE; RE-NAISSANCE

Further Reading

Kriarás, Emmanuel, ed. "Ἡ *Ρίμα θρηνητικὴ* τοῦ Ἰωάννου Πικατόρου ["The Lamentation Poem by Ioannis Pikatoros"]. Ἐπετηρὶς τοῦ Μεσαιωνικοῦ Ἀρχείου τῆς Ἀκαδημίας Ἀθηνῶν [Yearbook of the Medieval Archive of the Athenian Academy], vol. 2 (1940): 20–69.

PITSIPIOS, IAKOVOS (1803–1869) Journalist and prose writer Pitsipios was actually a Bey, working for the **Ottoman** administration, despite being Catholic. After the sack of Chios (1822), Pitsipios enrolled in the Great School of the Nation (Constantinople). He was later in dispute with his teaching colleagues and moved to Ermoupolis, in the Northern Cyclades. *The Orphan-Girl of Chios, or the Triumph of Virtue* (1839) is one of the "first novels of modern Greece" (R. Beaton). It shows the effects of the **Independence war** and the subtle imprinting of the **Hellenistic** romance, for Pitsipios probably knew Koraís's recent edition of the *Aethiopica,* by Heliodoros (c. fourth century A.D.). From it, he may have derived the separated lovers plot. The central figures of his novel are a boy and girl in love, Alexandros and Eflalia, at the time of the island's sack, with intrigue, poisoning, duels, and murder between Ottomans and Greeks. **I. M. Panayotopoulos** (1955) dismissed the novel's set piece descriptions of Nature and its "frightful" poetic recitations in their "wearisome" **Katharevousa.** Tsakonas (1999: 184) scoffs at the dose of "jingoism" (πατριδοκαπηλίας) in the book. Pitsipios may not be a natural yarn spinner, but he is of interest in the gradual reassessment of early nineteenth-century Greek fiction. His other prose work is *Xouth the Ape, or the Morals of the Century* (1848). This is a **satire** that, for Voutieridis, makes up Greece's first sociological novel, with its upper-class Greeks and their Western visitors trying to outshine each other like apes in a jungle habitat.

Further Reading

Pitsipios, I. Ἡ ὀρφανὴ τῆς Χίου. Ο Πίθηκος Ξουθ [The Orphan-Girl of Chios; Xouth the Ape], edited by D. Tziovas. Athens: Kostas and Elenis Ourani Foundation, 1995.

Pitsipios, I. Ο Πίθηκος Ξουθ [Xouth the Ape], edited by N. Vayenas. Athens: Nefeli, 1995.

PLAGIARISM Vitruvius reports that Aristophanes of Byzantium, who supposedly studied with Callimachus, Machon, and Zenodotus, spotted and exposed a plagiarized poem during recitation at a poetry festival. The charge of plagiarism (λογοκλοπία), when it arises between modern Greek writers, is treated less seriously than in the West. Some Greeks merely see literary borrowing as evidence of elective affinities between writers.

PLAIN GREEK (SIMPLIFIED GREEK) Plain Greek (ἁπλὴ γλῶσσα) is a simplified, literary language (ἡ ἁπλοελληνική). It was used in many texts from the sixteenth to eighteenth centuries, especially ecclesiastical ones. These were written for a general readership yet contained some learned material. As a form of simplified but not yet **demotic,** plain Greek may be defined as the fusing of the ancient and the vernacular language. A century after **Constantinople's fall,** Nikolaos Sofianós expressed the need for a reform of Greek prose.

Any **enlightenment** of the Greek people struck Sofianós as impossible without revising the **Atticism** and formality of ecclesiastical Greek. He compiled (1550), but could not publish, his *Grammar of Plain Greek.* It was eventually issued by E. Legrand in 1874. In this text, Sofianós gives a working definition of correct expression (ὀρθοέπεια): a person writes correctly when he follows the grammar and syntax of the spoken language. Sofianós translated into plain Greek the classical treatise *The Education of Children, by the Philosopher Plutarch,* which was influential in the Italian **Renaissance.** This *De Liberis Educandis* is a "moral" work incorrectly attributed to Plutarch (c. 50–c. 125), but published in 1544 (at Venice) by Sofianós as such. This choice of text announces an implicit program of enlightenment for Sofianós's educationally deprived contemporaries. His promotion of plain Greek, though he did not always write **Demotic** forms himself, aimed to bring literature to the semi-literate.

Further Reading

Horrocks, Geoffrey. *Greek: A History of the Language and Its Speakers.* London: Longman, 1997.

Legrand, E., ed. *Collection des monuments pour servir à l'étude de la langue néoellénique* (Nouvelle Série, no. 2). Paris: Maisonneuve, 1874.

PLAKOTARI, ALEXANDRA (1907–)

Plakotari was born at Constantinople and studied in Berlin and Paris. In 1927 she married the painter Kostas Plakotaris. She published several volumes of verse between the 1940s and 1980s, including *Missolonghi* (1958), *Penelope* (1962), and critical works on Dylan Thomas, **Byron,** Emily Dickinson, **Shakespeare,** Yeats, Sophocles, and Ionesco. She was a professor of English and of modern Greek literature. She translated widely: Scott's *Kenilworth,* Kakridis's *Homer,* essays by **A. Terzakis**, and poems by **Angelos Sikelianós,** who became a close friend and collaborator of hers (from 1947).

PLANOUDIS, MAXIMOS (c. 1260–c. 1305)

Planoudis was a **Byzantine** writer, born in Nicomedia, who worked at Constantinople as director of a public school attached to a monastery with its own library. He was also a copyist in the Emperor's court (from 1283). He was sent on an imperial mission to Venice (1296). The intellectual temptation to produce a theory of everything drives Planoudis, whether as scholar, monk, diplomat, annotator, editor, or rhetorician. He was the last Byzantine forerunner of the Renaissance tendency to edit the classics and also probe into phenomena that call for reinvestigation. Thus he drafted a *Life of Aesop,* an essay *On Grammar,* a select anthology of *Proverbs of the People,* a treatise *On Truth,* a volume of *Annotations on Theocritus and Hermogenes,* some 121 letters, a *Gathering of Choice Passages from Divers Works,* a collection of Plutarch's complete works, an *Anthology of Divers Inscriptions,* an essay *On Composition,* and an edition (1301) of the *Palatine Anthology* (from a tenth-century manuscript) with its 6,000 short poems and epigrams, for which he managed to rediscover and add some 400 more.

Planoudis, in his *Arithmetic after the Indian Method* (c. 1300), is the first Greek writer to use the numeral as a digit rather than an "exponent." He reconstructed the lost maps in Ptolemy, a dazzling task of itself, yet perhaps the most important facet of his versatility was his drive to translate Latin works (that is, knowledge from the West) into Greek: hence his version of the *Consolation of Philosophy,* by the sixth-century scholar and diplomat Boethius.

Further Reading

Wilson, N. G. "Books and Readers in Byzantium." In *Byzantine Books and Bookmen,* 1–15. Washington, DC: Dumbarton Arts Colloquium, 1975.

PLASKOVITIS, SPYROS (1917–) Plaskovitis, from Kerkyra, became a member of the State Council and made **Demotic** the normal idiom for its proceedings. Plaskovitis was condemned to exile and **prison** under the **Colonels.** After his release (1972), he returned to his post as a judge when democracy returned. He then resigned, as a gesture of protest, when the Colonels were acquitted on the charge of having ordered the Polytechnic massacre. Plaskovitis contributed the story "Radar" to *Eighteen Texts* (1970, a famous volume that passed **censorship** under the Colonels), where it professes to offer a straight account of what happens to a group of intellectuals in detention. Plaskovitis has extended his repertoire as a writer of short stories, novels, and after the 1960s, verse. Best known to this day is his novel *The Dam* (1960), an **allegory** with a wide canvas, ostensibly featuring a righteous hydrologist who is appointed by the authorities to investigate a barrage dam that may or may not crack and flood a certain town. But dam, authorities, and engineer *also* suggest a critique of the first Eight Year Plan of Karamanlis, with an aura of projects, contracts, rigged auctions, and instant wealth. It was made into a film (1982, *The Dam*) by Dimitris Makris.

Further Reading

Veremis, Thanos. *The Military in Greek Politics: From Independence to Democracy.* Buffalo, NY: Black Rose, 1998.

PLATONISM Platonism is the legacy of ideas and influences from the philosopher of ancient Athens called Plato (c. 428–348 B.C.). It fosters various key themes of all European literature, such as the theory of ideas, the eternity of the soul, the hope for a political Utopia, the potential harm caused by literature (seen as a "lie," whereas the real world is the "truth"), the splitting of man into two sexes, the theory of recovered knowledge from a previous existence, and the intellectual love of men for youths (*epheboi*). Plato had been tutor to autocratic rulers, so could princes be taught good behavior? Plato had worked in Sicily in a political context, so could literature and politics be combined?

Platonism influenced modern Greek literature in the writing of **Psellus** (eleventh century) and in many other philosophers up to Yemistos Plethon (fifteenth century). Many Byzantine scholars knew of Plato through the mediation of Plotinus (205–270), Porphyry (232–304), Origen (185–253), pseudo-Dionysius the Areopagite, Iamblichus (c. 270–330), and Proclus (411–485). In these early sources on Platonism, which make up the so-called school of neo-Platonism founded by Plotinus, the accuracy of the legacy is wrapped in mysticism.

Platonism is later seen as a champion of Greek freedom. Markos Mousouros (1470–1516), a colleague of the printer Aldus Manutius, issued an appeal to Pope Leo X in the preamble to his edition of Plato (Venice, September 1513). It was the first **printing** of Plato in the world and caused intense excitement among scholars. Mousouros speaks through the mouth of Plato in its opening ode, begging the Pope to come to the aid of Greece. At this point Platonism dwindled from modern Greek literature and gave way in the seventeenth century to a revival of **Aristotle.**

Further Reading

Allen, M.J.B. "Ficino, Hermes and the corpus Hermeticum." In *New Perspectives on Renaissance Thought: Essays in the History of Science, Education and Philosophy in Memory of Charles B. Schmitt,* edited by John Henry and Sarah Hutton. London: Duckworth, 1990.

Walker, D. P. *The Ancient Theology: Studies in Christian Platonism from the Fifteenth to the Eighteenth Century.* London: Duckworth, 1972.

PLEONASM The figure of speech called "pleonasm" (πλεονασμός) involves the use of surplus words. In a literary passage, pleonasm is a device for making one term very clear by adding excess or redundant material, as in W. B. Yeats's "When you are old and grey and full of sleep." Zacharias Papantoniou's "The Old Shepherd" (1931) begins with the same idea and the same pleonasm: "*How many years* I have passed / And become *white-haired,* and become *old,* / Up on the peaks / Tending the sheep." In "Unquenched Hope" (1899), a story by **Christos Christovasilis,** an aged widow refuses to consider that her son, who emigrated years before, may never return. Using a simple pleonasm, the narrator observes: "*The whole world, all the men and women,* commiserated with poor Mitraina."

Further Reading

Johnstone, C. L., ed. *Theory, Text, Context: Issues in Greek Rhetoric and Oratory.* Albany: State University of New York Press, 1996.

PLETHON, YEORYIOS YEMISTOS (c. 1360–c. 1451) While on a legation with the Byzantine emperor John VIII to Italy (1439), Yemistos Plethon regaled Cosimó de' Medici with the philosophy of **Plato,** leading Florence's first citizen to found a kind of Platonic Academy. This influenced the course of the **Renaissance.** Plethon became famous as a legal and theological thinker throughout Europe. He gathered at Mistra a select group of pupils and acolytes, just as the fourth-century neo-Platonist philosopher Iamblichus (one of Plethon's admired sources) founded a school in Syria. Plethon conceived the project of reconstructing, under Theodore II Palaeologus, despot of Morea (Peloponnese), an ideal state that would dispense with Christianity. This *polis* was based on three categories of people: farmers, merchants, and craftsmen, and the rulers, from whom magistrates and soldiers would be drawn. Plethon proposed a civil hierarchy matching Plato's *Republic,* with a polytheist state religion, reflecting the works of Iamblichus (c. 270–330) and Proclus (411–485). In his "Hymn to the Cultural Muses," Proclus had written: "Initiate me into the orgiac mysteries. / Reveal them by the hallowed ceremony of words." Plethon argues that all land "perhaps in accord with its natural state, should be owned by nobody and used by all. Plethon's program, in fragments preserved from his *Book of Laws,* foreshadows communal ownership, rational taxation, currency reform, import tariffs, blocks on the export of commodities, and a supervised morality.

Further Reading

Masai, François. *Pléthon et le Platonisme de Mistra.* Paris: Les Belles Lettres, 1956.

Moreau, J. "Concordance d'Aristote et de Platon." *XVIe Colloque International de Tours, Platon et Aristote á La Renaissance.* Paris: Librairie Philosophique, J. Vrin, 1976.

Plethon, Y. Νόμων συγγραφή [Book on Laws]. In *Patrologiae Cursus Completus . . . Series Graeca in qua prodeunt patres, doctores scriptoresque Ecclesiae Graecae a S. Barnaba ad Photium,* vol. 160, edited by J. P. Migne, 881–932. Paris: Migne, 1857–1866.

Plethon, Y. *Traité des lois.* Edited by C. Alexandre and translated by A. Pellissier. Paris: Firmin Didot, 1858, reprint Amsterdam [1966].

Plethon, Y. Περὶ ων Ἀριστοτέλης πρὸς Πλάτωνα διαφέρεται [Concerning Matters in Which Aristotle Differs from Plato], edited by B. Lagarde. *Byzantium* 43 (1973): 312–343.

PLOT Plot (πλοκή) is the arrangement of step-by-step episodes and the development of a coherent set of actions in a play or novel. Structure (δομή) is the synthesis of the main elements in a plot. When Greek critics analyze a book's plot, they tend to concentrate on the latter term. Does the novel have a clear beginning, middle, and end? Is one sequence speeded up by ellipsis? Are there omissions in the plot, which make for excess voids in the narrative (αφηγηματικά κενά)? Has the author been tempted to insert a digression (παρέκβάση)? To bring the reader into the thick of a plot, *in medias res,* the writer may dispense with a prologue and go straight into the events he or she narrates (εις μέσα τα πράγματα). To spin out suspense near the conclusion of the narrative, the writer may use **postponement** (επιβράδυνση).

According to **Aristotle,** in his *Poetics*, a dramatic plot is an imitation (μίμηση).

Imitation on stage concerns an action "that is serious, complete and of a certain magnitude." Plot is the soul of a drama, so the plot should "imitate one action, and a whole one. It should be a structural union of parts, such that if any one part is removed, the whole structure will be disturbed and become disjointed." Each act of the drama must follow or precede other acts in a plausible sequence. This is the unity of action stressed in the 1576 version of Aristotle's *Poetics* by Lodovico Castelvetro (1505–1571). A plot's resolution ("unravelling") must flow from the plot and not be provided by surprise, or by a "god on a platform" (Θεὸς ἀπὸ μηχανῆς). Plots often have a **recognition** scene and generally involve a "change of fortune" (περιπέτεια).

POETICS In *The Poetics,* Aristotle discussed the ingredients of tragic drama: **plot,** character, diction, subject, thought, and spectacle. His book explains how a certain kind of person will act on certain occasions, according to probability, driven by fate. A play is *made* (this is what "poetics" means) in a certain way. It is presented in language, embellished by various, different ornaments. What is represented is action, rather than narrative. By way of pity and fear, this action causes a "purging of the emotions" (κάθαρσις). There are also rules of time and place. In order to make what is happening on the stage plausible, the audience must believe the events before their eyes are realistic. So the time duration of the play should be "one revolution of the sun or a little more." Its location should not change during the action. This leads to what the **Renaissance** knew as the unity of time and place. The drama should contain a startling discovery. Tragic or violent events are to be kept invisible and may be narrated on stage by a messenger. The character of a tragic protagonist is not necessarily good. His misfortune is caused not by depravity or arrogance (ὕβρις), but by frailty (ἀμαρτία). Character reveals προαίρεσις ("moral choice") and shows what kind of things a person ought to choose or avoid.

POETRY, MODERN GREEK David Connolly, in the journal *Agenda* (vol. 36, no. 3–4, 1999) assembles English translations of texts by 26 Greek poets born in the period 1943–1963. A useful label for the first wave of these writers has been "Generation of the 70s." They were also dubbed the "Generation of contention." Poets who first appeared in the 1980s attracted the characteristic label "Generation of the private vision" (I. Kefalas, 1987). N. Vayenás warns (in *Diavazo,* January 1987): "a generation does not comprise the total number of versifiers who appeared in the chronological limits set, but rather a number of poets (perhaps very few) who modify to a greater or lesser extent the traditional form of expression."

Further Reading

Crist, Robert, ed. *Grind the Big Tooth: A Collection of Greek Poetry.* Pittsburgh, PA: Sterling House, 1998.

Houzouri, Elena. "The Multifarious Collection of Poets During the '80s." *Hellenic Quarterly,* no. 9 (June–August 2001): 33–34.

POLEMIS, IOANNIS (1862–1924) After law studies at Athens, Polemis received a city scholarship to study aesthetics at Paris (1888–1890). He later held various posts in Greece, at the Ministry of Education, the University regis-

try, and as secretary of the School of Fine Arts (1915). In 1918 he was awarded the national prize for letters. From the age of 13, he published a variety of poems in **albums,** periodicals, calendars, and newspapers. As an adult, he published nine collections: *Poems* (1883), *Winter Flowers* (1888), *Alabasters* (1900), *Heirlooms* (1904), *The Old Violin* (1909), *Broken Marbles* (1918), *Words of Peace* (1919), *Exotic Poems* (1921), and *Evening Star* (1922). In 1910, Polemis edited an *Anthology of Modern Greek Poetry* (Athens: Association of Greek Publishers). He was close in age to **Palamás**, and they shared in the **Philadelpheios Prize** awards (1888, 1889, respectively). Polemis wrote educational material for children: the poetry **reader** *First Steps* (1909), the school reader *Youthful Lyre* (1914, with a preface by **Drosinis**), and many educational stories in the magazine *The Moulding of the Young* (founded in 1879 by Nikos P. Papadopoulos). Polemis became popular, and many of his poems were set to music or made into songs. The critic Dimarás calls his verse "flabby with hiatus and padding, matched by its disregard for the austere morphology of the Demotic." The poet **Rigas Golfis** (1886–1958) once opined that "Polemis writes journalism in his poems while Stratigis writes poems in his journalism." Palamás sketched an amiable model of Polemis's output: "A shady, flowering garden in which the cricket sings, the owl laments, the daisies, the roses and the acacias are fragrant. There, under the April stars, shy maidens promise eternal love." Voutieridis is more dismissive: "Often he produced facile verse." Polemis won prizes repeatedly in the Averoff drama competition: for his one-act play *Once Upon a Time* (1924) and for his three-act play *King Sunless* (1910). Altogether he wrote 17 plays. He translated Theocritus, Euripides, Molière, and the bestseller *Under the Linden Trees* (1832) by the French writer Alphonse Karr (1808–1890).

POLITICAL VERSE The term *political,* to describe the Byzantine and later Cretan 15-syllable nonrhyming line in poetry, is derived from the medieval meaning of *politikos* ("common"). Political verse is a kind of Alexandrine line, unrhymed, formed by joining eight- and seven-syllable segments, separated by a **caesura** (breath pause; break in grammar). This new prosody is based on the sequence of **accent** because all sense of vowel quantity had been lost at the end of the classical period. Evstathios Katafloros, archbishop of Thessaloniki in the twelfth century, wrote commentaries, one on the differences between the *Iliad* and *Odyssey* of **Homer.** Evstathios observes that "political" verse had already acquired its modern meaning by the eleventh century. It easily replaced the classical hexameter (five dactyls and a spondee). The phrase political line even came to signify unrhymed prose (πεζός λόγος) in the midst of poetry in formal **meter.** "Political" verse was first used in Byzantine religious and didactic poetry, as in the epitaphs for Leo VI the Wise (who reigned 886–912) and in penitential alphabets supposedly by Symeon Metaphrastes in the tenth century. Later it became familiar in chivalric and **epic** romances, such as *Erotokritos*. Among earlier Byzantine poems, only the epitaphs for the death of Christopher (in 959) are written wholly in political verse, without the seven- or eight-syllable refrains that make the other ceremonial laments resemble songs for recitation (Trypanis: 1981).

Further Reading

Alexiou, Margaret and David Holton. "The Origins and Development of 'Politikos Stichos': A Select Critical Bibliography." *Mantatoforos* 9 (November 1976): 22–34.

Jeffreys, M. "The Nature and Origins of the Political Verse." *Dumbarton Oaks Papers* 28 (1974): 141–193.

POLITICIANS The first Greek **constitution** (December 1821) declared that (1) the ruling religion of Greece was the Eastern Orthodox Church of Christ, (2) individual freedoms of all Greeks were guaranteed, and (3) there was separation of powers between the deliberative and executive arms of government. The third assembly (1827) assigned legislative power "to one individual." The constitution of May 1827 was the most democratic in the world, for example, "Power is held by the nation itself." Kapodistrias delayed its implementation, considering it too liberal. After his assassination, a fifth assembly assigned authority to Agostino Kapodistrias and voted for the Royal Constitution of 1832. In June 1832, a continuation of the fourth assembly met and approved the European powers' nomination of King Otho.

Serious unrest came in 1862, and King Otho was replaced by a provisional government. The Second Athens National Assembly of Greeks (10 December 1862) invited the young prince Alfred to assume the Greek monarchy, and he declined. On 18 March 1863, it invited Prince George of Denmark, and on 15 July 1863 declared him of age, though not yet 18. Under the constitution of

1864, the highest entity of Greece was not the king, but the wish of the people.

King George II was ousted in 1923. In 1924, Greece became a republic. From 1932 to 1935, the Royalists regained influence. King George II returned to the throne in 1935. General **Metaxas** took dictatorial powers in August 1936. Political parties were again suspended by the **Colonels** in 1967. King Constantine II left for exile in Italy (December 1967), and on 15 March 1968 Colonel Papadopoulos drafted a fresh constitution. In 1973, the monarchy was abolished again, and Greece declared a republic. The 1975 constitution of the Hellenic Republic (Ελληνική Δημοκρατία) at last affirmed the right to political parties.

This is not an edifying story, and the politicians' handling of the **Civil War** made it worse. All modern Greek writers deplore it, and many have lampooned it savagely. **Kazantzakis** wrote novels containing violent allegories of Crete's fight for freedom. **Myrivilis** and others score their pages with the bloodshed caused by the politicians' handling of the **Asia Minor disaster** (1922). Hardly a nineteenth-century writer (**Soutsos, Paraschos, Valaoritis, Sourís**) can be found with a good word to say of the King. More than one writer has been Prime Minister (such as, **Venizelos**), a minister (Trikoupis), or even President (Tsatsos). However, just as most Greek writers had studied law, so most writers were among the few people qualified to hold high office anyway. **Kolokotronis** and **Makriyannis** are among the many memoirists who describe the way the ideals of the **War of Independence** were subsequently betrayed by the politicians. "Traitor," "Bavarian," "Turk," "torturer," and "hangman" are among the hundreds of pejorative terms for politicians in modern Greek literary works.

Further Reading

Legg, Keith R. *Politics in Modern Greece.* Stanford: Stanford University Press, 1969.

Sarafis, Marion and Martin Eve. *Background to Contemporary Greece.* 2 vols. Savage, MD: Barnes and Noble, 1990.

POLITIS, KOSMÁS (1887–1974; pseudonym of Paris Taveloudis) Novelist, translator, and political activist, Kosmás Politis added to the genre of the "novel of adolescence" with *Eroica* (1938) and the introverted, springtime atmosphere of his *Lemon Grove* (1930), set in the meadows of Poros. He also published *Hecate* (1933), *Three Women* (1943), short stories based on three romantic figures (Marina, Julia, Eleonora), *Gyri* (1946), and a last, major novel, *At Hadjifrangou's* (1963), which returns to the idealized dimension of a district in Smyrna before the **Asia Minor disaster.** His family had moved to Smyrna after a financial blow, and the young Politis worked in banks at Smyrna (1905–1922). After 1923, he traveled in France and England, later returning to Athens and a job at the Ionian Bank. Politis was one of the first Greek writers to develop an interest in the psychological analysis of human characters, which he considered the main purpose of fiction, and he became a skilled practitioner of **interior monologue.** His plots turn on confrontations due to some morbid or obsessive condition, such as unrequited passion, or the pursuit of an ideal. Politis lost his job in 1942 and after World War II made a precarious living by translations.

Further Reading

Mackridge, Peter. "The Two-Fold Nostalgia: Lost Homeland and Lost Time in the Work of G. Theotokas, E. Venezis and K. Politis." *JMGS* 4, no. 2 (October 1986): 75–83.

Politis, Kosmás. *Eroica*. Edited and intro. by Peter Mackridge. Athens: Ermis, 1982 [first publ. 1938].

POLITIS, NIKOLAOS G. (1852–1921)

The founding father of Greek folklore studies was N. G. Politis. He tried to collect a disparate, coacerval mass of popular material on a scientific basis, under the heading folklore (λαογαφία, "study of the common people"). He assembled a large corpus of folk poems and ballads on the **Akritic** theme, concerning the guards that formed a military bulwark, fostering a code of perseverance and chivalry, along the Anatolian borders of the Byzantine Empire. In 1907 he applied the term national **epic** to modern Greek literature's first great **demotic** poem, *Diyenís Akritas*, now seen as epic-romance. Politis's *Neo-Hellenic Mythology* came out in 1871. **Drosinis** commented: "He led us to the still unexplored treasure of traditions, legends, perceptions, customs of the Greek people, and incited us to study our national heirlooms and to use them each one of us according to his art." Politis proposed (before its Western model was discovered) that **Erotokritos** was an original Greek work, and that it was futile to hunt down Western sources for it. He also collected and classified many thousand Greek **proverbs,** publishing this work in four volumes, between 1899 and 1902. Two special issues of the literary journal *Néa Estía* (no. 458: 1946 and 643: 1954) were devoted to N. G. Politis. His work was followed in part by Agis Theros, who produced *Songs of the Greeks* (2 vols., 1952) by recording his samples exactly as he heard them from the mouth of people who sang folk motifs. Theros did not use the method of

Politis in *The Selections of the Songs of the Greek People* (1914). Politis had taken the best or representative lines of all the known variations of demotic songs and formed his version of each song by combining the lines thus assembled without editorial revision. Apostolakis later criticized Politis for this procedure, though it produced the now classic anthology of love and wedding songs, lullabies, workers' songs, **Klephtic** ballads, shepherds' songs, carols, satires, teasing ditties, rhymed couplets, wise saws, comic skits, and prison songs, which Greeks know by heart.

POLYDOURI, MARIA (1902–1930)

Born in Kalamata, translator and poet, Maria Polydouri died of consumption, after final stays at clinics in Sotiria and Patissia, suburbs of Athens. Her father was principal of a high school and introduced her to French Symbolist poetry. She published a slim volume of poems entitled *Daisies* when aged just 15. She was a tempestuous, gifted girl who ran away from home and was dismissed for irregular attendance at her civil servant's job (1922). Writers of religious magazines found her life an example of the kind of love that should never be imitated. She threw herself into an affair with the equally ill-starred poet **Karyotakis,** who had worked in the same office as Polydouri and cited problems of his own for declining to marry her. She was engaged for a while to another man, but eventually broke this off, never resolving her love for Karyotakis (R. Dalven, 1994: 32). She later went away to a Bohemian and impoverished sojourn of two years in Paris (1927–1928). Her verse, collected in *The Trills That Fade* (1928) and *Sound in Chaos* (1929), is often erotic, always sentimental. In 1928 she was admitted to the Charité hospital in Paris and soon obliged to return for treatment in Greece. She drew a considerable amount of poetic material from the relationship with Karyotakis, which remained violent and vivid in her mind after he left her, and later after his suicide (21 July 1928). She translated poems by the Greek-French writer **Papadiamantopoulos,** Leconte de Lisle, and Henri Bataille. Her complete works were published, with a preface by **L. Zografou,** in 1961. The lyricism of her manner commemorates Karyotakis in a walnut casket with the fatal mark on his temple: "He was oddly beautiful, like those / Whom death has set apart. / He gave himself up to the direst hazards, / As though something had made him immune." The poignancy of her own approaching death is echoed in the restrained gloom of "Sotiria," where she murmurs: "They will dim the lights of the chambers; / Sleep will come like a fainting fit. / One empty bed, here, makes no / Particular impression."

Further Reading

Anagnostopoulos, Athan, ed. "The Poetry of Maria Polydouri: A Selection." *JHD* 5 (spring 1978): 41–67.

POLYHYMNIA Karyotakis (in *Nepenthe,* 1921) and **Varnalis** (in *Honeycombs,* 1905) address poems to the Muse Polyhymnia, mother of Orpheus, inventor of the lyre, patron of sacred poetry, and protector of dancing. In art she is depicted pausing in thought, her chin resting on her knuckles, or a finger on her lips. **Palamás** also has an ode to Polyhymnia.

POLYLÁS, IAKOVOS (1826–1898)

The scholar and future politician from Kerkyra Iakovos Polylás was tutored as a child by his mother, who had aristocratic connections. In 1847, Polylás himself married the daughter of a count. He spent the years 1852–1854 in Naples for his wife's health and studied aesthetics and literature at the university while there. He subsequently worked as a librarian on Kerkyra and for the island's union with Greece, assisting the *Rebirth* movement and its magazine. In 1871, he founded the nationalist society *Rigas Pheraios,* which issued a journal in that name. To us, the crucial point is that Polylás edited (1859) the *Complete Found Works of Solomós* (1798–1857). He also corrected some of his verse, for example, "The Shade of Homer."

In 1881 Polylás completed a translation of Homer's *Odyssey* into the **Demotic** preferred by his revered mentor, Solomós. He was an instinctive comparativist: he wrote an essay on the controversial compilation (1850) of demotic songs by **A. Manousis** and a version of Book VII of the *Iliad* for the **Parnassós** society (1890); versions of the remaining books of the *Iliad* were among his papers at his death. Polylás shows his hand as a literary critic *ante diem* in the *Critical Preface,* written to accompany his edition of Solomós (1859), assessing the relevance of the national poet three years after his death. One twentieth-century commentator, P. Mastrodimitris, considers the *Critical Preface* by itself enough to rank Polylás among the supreme theoreticians of Greek literature, and the single best exegesis of **Solomós** (see **Varnalis**). In his *Hamlet,* Polylás taught a generation of Greek poets a newly flexible 13-syllable line (**Kogebinas, Kalosgouros, Poriotis, Melachrinós, Gryparis**). Multifaceted, Polylás represented Kerkyra at the Greek parliament for five sessions. He responded polemically to an essay by

Spyridon Zambelios with his own *Whence Is Derived Mr Zambelios's Fear of Mystery: Some Reflections* (Kerkyra 1860). Here he rejects Zambelios's arguments about poetic style and the suggestion that in his Kerkyra period Solomós deviated from his natural manner. Polylás dismisses Zambelios as a late arrival imitating a classic master. In 1892 he produced another major critical work, *On Our Literary Language,* in which he balanced the elevated style of Solomós with an eclectic appreciation of more recent language developments.

See also KALOSGOUROS; KOGEBINAS

Further Reading

Mastrodomitris, P. D. Εἰσαγωγὴ στὴ Νεοελληνικὴ Φιλολογία [An Introduction to Modern Greek Literature]. Athens: Domos, 1990.

Polylás, I. "The Error." Translated by Theodore Sampson. In *Modern Greek Short Stories,* vol. 1, edited by K. Delopoulos, 11–28. Athens: Kathimerini, 1980.

A special number of the periodical *Greek Creation* (no. 57: 1 June 1950) concerns Polylás.

POLYZOIDIS, ATHANASIOS (1802–1873) Athanasios Polyzoidis, who had been sent by his widowed mother to study in Vienna and Germany, became a powerful opponent of Greece's first president, **Kapodistrias** (see **Politicians**). Kapodistrias, a nepotist who appointed two incompetent brothers to senior posts, thought he could gain more authority (1830) if the powers could be made to delay sending their agreed monarch to Greece. At the Pronoia assembly, on 26 August 1823, Polyzoidis risked murder at the hands of the opposition. In 1827, he was elected plenipotentiary at the na-

tional assembly in Troizene. The text of the original Greek **constitution** (1821) allowed freedom of the press. So, on 10 March 1828, Polyzoidis started the revolutionary newspaper *Apollo,* with its office at **Nafplion,** right under the eyes of the administration.

He was the judge who, with **Tertsetis,** refused to sign the death penalty for **Kolokotronis** and Dimitrios Plapoutas (7 September 1834), though they were prodded to do so by the royal guard's spears. Plapoutas (born 1786) was married to the niece of Kolokotronis (1803). A rendering of this standoff is in Panos Glikofridis's film *The Trial of the Judges.* Later, King Otho made Polyzoidis minister of education (1837) and of foreign affairs. He published, at **Missolonghi** (1824, during the siege), *Proclamation of 1822 Appended to the Provisional Constitution of Epidavros: A Comparison with the Constitutions of England and America.* At Alexandros Mavrokordatos's request, it was added to the constitution.

Further Reading

Horton, Andrew. "The New Greek Cinema." *The Athenian* 1, no. 4 (1974): 40–41.

Kaldis, William P. *John Capodistrias and the Modern Greek State.* Madison: State Historical Society of Wisconsin, 1973.

Woodhouse, C. M. *Capodistria: The Founder of Greek Independence.* London: Oxford University Press.

PORFYRAS, LAMBROS (1879–1932; pseudonym of Dimitrios Sypsomos) Lambros Porfyras is the witty and allusive **pseudonym** for Dimitrios Sypsomos, a shy, reserved, and sickly poet from Chios. His name combines the title of two **Solomós** poems and also the words for *radiant* and *purple,* respectively. He completed high school in the Piraeus, an area that he deeply loved. He went on to live near Pashalimani, the old harbor of Zea, becoming a night owl and haunter of the **taverns.** Everyone in Freathys knew Mr. "Dimitrakis" Sypsomos. A Prime Minister, **E. Venizelos,** came to appreciate him, and the municipality of Piraeus eventually placed his bust in Freathys. He wrote verse as a schoolboy and had his first poem, "The Grief of Marble," published in *Stadium* (1894) and in *Town* (18 September 1894), which was run as a weekly newspaper from 1885 to 1889 by Babis Anninos, then as a daily by Themos Anninos (1889–1907). Porfyras traveled in Italy, France, and England, failing to finish Law at Athens University. He contributed to periodicals in Alexandria, as well as the Athenian *Techni*, Mousa, Artist, *Panathinaia,* and *Dionysos* (1901–1902). He collected his poems from the new century in *Shadows* (1920). This volume subtly influenced a stunted, rather choked manner of verse, which became prevalent in the 1920–1930 period. There was a further (posthumous) volume with the title *Musical Voices* (1934). He translated poems by Shelley, Coleridge, and V. Hugo.

In his poem "The Outing," he and a girl called Annoula go boating on a "sunjoyous day," which is a "dream beyond belief," for in the "intoxicated peace" of their craft they are sailing for the "isle of Joy," next to snowy female forms and the "sweet company" of old friends. The poem (in three quatrains) tells that it matters not if they arrive at the isle of Joy, for they are "undulating in the infinite." Annoula sings that the island will appear, however far away it may be. This poem is a cameo of ardent affection for the ideal of a fraternity of pals, a threnody to

vanishing youth. Porfyras received permanent financial help from his brother, Theodoros, who had a job with the Rallis merchant house in India. It was a position the poet's father had hoped he might fill. Porfyras refers to the crushing loss of his sister and their emptied house in the poem "Lacrimae rerum." His verse is mainly about landscapes, the **sea,** simple port workers, or fishermen, in the gentle chromatic tints of a largely derivative **symbolism.** See also *Néa Estía,* no. 155: 1933 and no. 682: 1955, monographic issues on L. Porfyras, and *Greek Creation,* no. 98: 1 March 1952.

Further Reading

Anagnostopoulos, Athan, ed. "The Poetry of Lambros Porphyras: A Selection." *JHD,* no. 3–4 (1980): 47–71.

Katsimbalis, Y. K. Βιβλιογραφία Λάμπρου Πορφύρα [A Bibliography of Lambros Porfyras]. Athens: Sergiadis, 1956.

Porfyras, L. Άπανα [The Complete Works]. Edited by Y. Valetas. Athens: Pighis, 1956 [3rd revised ed.]. Athens: Vasileiou, 1982.

PORIOTIS, NIKOLAOS (1870–1945)

The multitalented translator and writer Nikolaos Poriotis was also a passionate exponent of the **Demotic.** He contributed his first poems to *Noumás* (1913); he translated Molière, Goldoni, Giacosa, Grazia Deledda, Sam Benelli, Lipperini, Wilde, Maeterlink, Gorky, Traversi, and Rispen; he wrote for *The Moulding of the Young*; and he produced stories and opinion pieces for *Estía.* He composed a tragedy, *Rodope,* in 1913 and a novel, *The Stranger* (1910). He produced play versions (not for written publication) of **Shakespeare,** *Taming of the Shrew* (in 1906, for the Royal Theater), and *The Merry Wives of Windsor* (1906, for the

Pantopoulos troupe). Poriotis was a skilled translator of words already set to music: he rendered Mendelssohn's oratorio, *Paul* (1926) and could catch the underlying rhythm in songs, such as Schumann's *Dichterliebe* and airs from Beethoven, Wagner, and Rouget de L'Isle (1760–1836), composer of the French national anthem "La Marseillaise." In his *Lyrics from Overseas* (1925), Poriotis attempted an anthology of foreign songs translated with Greek words, adapted to musical rhythm. He also revised the use of classical prosody (Alcaic, Sapphic, dactylic, choral) by determining a tonic line and devising a mathematical tabulation of a particular time rhythm for each tonic accent. For example, in the 15-syllable line he made dissonance familiar by introducing anapests in the second hemistych (half line). With the 13-syllable line, Poriotis developed a tripartite division, not yet adopted by **Polylás** or **Palamás,** using an extra final syllable, on the model of the French Alexandrine verse.

POSTPONEMENT "Retardation" (επιβράδυνση) creates **suspense** by postponing the solution of a **plot** and thus slightly frustrating the reader's desire for the conclusion, or **happy ending.** In a narrative **ballad** called *The Suffering Bride,* Rini comes home after years of impoverished marriage. First we read through a series of retarding episodes: Rini prays God that her mother's slaves will not recognize her. Then she talks to the servants at a spring where they are doing the laundry. Then she asks them for a job. She tells them they are pretty. She asks them for water. They say that there is no job, but they go and ask their mistress anyway. Finally, after all these narrative checks, she may be recognized.

She is revealed as Rini to the household after she is told to weave her own half-finished loom.

PREVELAKIS, PANDELÍS (1909–1986) Prevelakis was a novelist, essayist, dramatist, and art critic born at Rethymno (Crete). He composed the saga, *Chronicle of a Town* (1938), about the period when a Cretan town saw the exchange of its Greek-speaking Muslim population for Greeks from Anatolia, after the **Asia Minor disaster** of 1922. In the 1940s, he produced a **trilogy** thick with local color, in the format of a family saga: *The Tree* (1948), *First Freedom* (1949), and *City* (1950). This trilogy of titles offers a fictional history of Crete's struggle for freedom, spanning the period 1866 to 1910. Prevelakis's novel *The Sun of Death* (1959) is the story of a Cretan vendetta that hangs over a boy as he grows up and is diverted from falling on him by the self-sacrifice of his finely drawn aunt, Rousakí. This novel of development (*Bildungsroman*) forms the first part of a **trilogy,** followed by *Head of the Medusa* (1964) and *Bread of the Angels* (1966). Prevelakis called this, his second trilogy of novels, *Roads to Creativity.* The title of its centerpiece uses the **image** of the Medusa's head to represent the attraction exerted by **Marxism** on the intellectuals of his time. Here the character Yeorgakis reappears, a mask for the identity of the author himself, and next to him stands the friend and older figure of Loisos, in whose features many readers see a portrait of **Kazantzakis,** himself a friend and mentor to Prevelakis. The third novel in *Roads to Creativity* brings Prevelakis's hero along a spiritual journey in 16 episodes to a closing resolution in solitude, until the "bread of the angels" can be seen as a symbol of artistic creativity. In the years before his death, he labored on *The New Erotokritos* in three editions (1973, 1978 and 1985), a modern version of the seventeenth-century poem named after its enamored hero. The author Papathanasopoulos considers that Prevelakis's epic rewrite converts the episodes of the original into feelings, whereas idiomatic or insular words are used sparingly, and the adventure, prison and exile of the source are brought to a **happy ending.**

Further Reading

Decavalles, Andonis. *Pandelis Prevelakis and the Value of a Heritage: A Talk.* Edited by Stavrou Theophanis. St. Paul, MN: North Central 1981.

Prevelakis, Pandelis. *The Tale of a Town.* Translated by Kenneth Johnstone. London/ Athens: Doric Publications, 1976.

Prevelakis, Pandelis. *The Sun of Death,* Translated by P. Sherrard. London: John Murray, 1965.

PRINTING Printing of Greek books during Turkish rule (1453–1821) went on mainly outside Greece, and copying from manuscripts remained the sole way of **publishing** in cities where the ruling Turks forbad books and printeries. The *Epitome of the Eight Parts of Speech* by **Konstantinos Laskaris** came out in Milan, in January 1476. For a while, this was thought to be the first Greek book ever printed. It is a fine volume of 72 leaves, 22 x 16 cm., with the first letter, Γ (*G*), hand-painted. A. Pertusi posited (1962) an even earlier date for the **grammar** by another **humanist** from Constantinople, namely the *Questions* by **M. Chrysoloras** (1471), printed by Adam von Amlergau. This soon went to a second printing, by Giovanni Remo. In 1627 a wealthy monk and patriot called Niko-

demos Metaxás (1585–1646) carried his printing press on a British merchant vessel from London to **Kyrillos Loukaris,** in Constantinople. Under a surety provided by the British Ambassador to the Turkish authorities, Nikodemos reprinted an essay by Patriarch Loukaris against Jewish dogma. One of the first books printed by a Greek in Greece, it included sermons by Maximos Margounios. The second book from his printery contained a series of anti-Papist tracts, which gave rise to a Jesuit plot that nearly cost his life. Between 1489 and 1499, major classics were printed: Homer, Callimachus, Lucian, Apollonius Rhodius, and the *Suda*. Arsenios of Monemvasia printed (1532) the first medieval Greek, a *quadrivium* (see **Humanism**) and *Solution to Methods Derived from Philosophy,* by **Psellus.** From the invention of printing until 1790, about 5,000 Greek books were printed. Between 1790 and 1821, the number jumped to 1,800 texts. When Florence fell to the French at the end of the fifteenth century, various Greek scholars fled to Venice, where Aldus Manutius was realizing his ambitious printing project. Markos Mousouros (1470–1516) advised Manutius on the printing of classical tragedians and lyric poets, intervening on the text of some manuscripts to make textual emendations.
See also PALAEOGRAPHY

Further Reading

Layton, E. "Nikodemos Metaxas, the First Greek Printer in the Eastern World." *Harvard Library Bulletin* 15, no. 2 (April 1967): 140–168.

Roberts, R. J. "The Greek Press at Constantinople and Its Antecedents." *The Library* 22, no. 1 (March 1967): 13–43.

PRISON Many Greek writers, Byzantine and modern, describe a period of imprisonment. Some, like Ilias Petropoulos (see **Rebetika**) were imprisoned as a result of what they wrote (see **Censorship; Kairis**). Ioannikios Kartanos of Kerkyra (c. 1500–c. 1550) was involved in a controversy about the apostasy of the Metropolitan Arsenios Monemvasia (Venice, early 1530s). Arrested and held in jail, Kartanos wrote an encyclopedic work in four volumes on the doctrinal, historical, ethical, and ceremonial aspects of Scripture: *Flower and Essence of the Old and New Testament* (1536). So influential was this prison work, that Kartanos was held to be an archheretic. Panayís Skouzés (1776–1847), in *A Chronicle of Athens Enslaved* (1841), recalls the mass detention of citizens ordered by the administration of Hatzí Alís (1772–1796): there were 150–250 inmates in the men's prison and 25–80 in the women's section. Many of the women were widows or arrested because their husbands were in hiding, and they were whipped by Turkish soldiers against a marble column fixed in their yard. In the men's prison hung the "rack" (φάλαγγας), made of a plank, with two holes and rope. This bastinado was strapped on and tightened, while the soles of the feet were battered. Prisoners who did not pay their jailers after a week were given this torture. The men could not sit in their confined spaces, so they passed fellow prisoners over their heads, if they had to go to speak at the window. Food was lifted in from hand to hand, till it reached the back of the cell. Skouzés, at the age of 11, spent a week in this place, as a pledge (ἀμανέτι) during his father's release to find money for the fine imposed by Hatzí Alís. All the boy says to his father is, "Just get me released!"

The journalist and poet Sofoklis Karoudis ran a satirical journal *The Light* (1860–1878). His pen more than once landed him in court or prison (see **Journalism, Nineteenth Century**). Jailed in 1857, Karoudis wrote a sarcastic poem, "Tears from the Heart," about the dark of the cell, with a lyre hanging on the dry branches of himself as a willow tree: "I'm not crying because Fate sent me to prison, / And all my friends and acquaintances / Abandoned me like birds / Leaving their nest in the winter." An unknown writer from **Thessaloniki,** Yorgos Iordanou, published *From the Tomb of the Living* (1921) to document conditions in the Yedi Koulé prison, part of a fortress with seven towers at the summit of Thessaloniki's Acropolis. This keep, clustered round an imposing central tower, was built by Sungur Çauş Bey in 1431. Iordanou describes the damp cells and grim correction in this prison, in which he was detained for insolvency. He announced a second volume, which did not appear, and we hear nothing more of him. The poet T. Leivaditis (1921–1988) was exiled to various islands during the **Civil War.** His tone of disenchantment is typical of the **defeatist** poetry of the 1950s, which followed the postwar disillusionment of young Left writers: "I too was ingenuous, an ideologue without a ticket; / Like all of you, I dreamt of a better world." Menelaos Loudemis (1912–1977, pseudonym of Yannis Valasiadis), whose books include *Awaiting the Bow of Heaven* (1940), *A Child Measures the Stars* (1956), and *The Clock of the World Strikes Midnight* (1961, in Romanian; 1963, Greek version), joined the Communist Party when young, fought in the **resistance,** and at the end of the **Civil War** was exiled to island prison camps.

The island of Makronisos, 5 kilometers off shore from Thorikos, was known to the ancients as "Helena" after the Helen of classical myth, who supposedly paused there when she eloped with Paris. Makronisos, the one-time deportation center, is now only used by a few shepherds in summer (see **Ritsos**). The isle of Ayios Evstratios is situated 32 kilometers south of Lemnos, and with a size of just 17 sq. miles, has one village on the northwest coast, scarce food, rocky beaches, and little water.

See also ANAGNOSTAKIS; DELLAPORTAS; DOUKA; GLYKÁS; KAMBANELLIS; MAKRIYANNIS; PARASCHOS, A.; RITSOS; SACHLIKIS

PRODROMIC POEMS; **PRODROMOS (twelfth century)** Among early Greek vernacular compositions are the four *Prodromic Poems.* The author of this mix of satirical, personal, and didactic themes is probably the Byzantine scholar Theodoros Prodromos. He may have been a teacher in the Patriarchal School of Constantinople. He perhaps became a monk when advanced in age, taking the name Hilarion. He died around 1166 (see **Animal Stories**). The *Prodromic Poems,* and a mass of other semilearned, popular texts of the mid-twelfth century and the Comnenian age, are associated with a supposed **Ptochoprodromos.** The four poems have a mendicant subject matter and a beggarly tone. The author poses as an itinerant courtier, pleading for financial assistance from princes and emperors. He curses the insecure profession of the secretary, who strives to live off documents, rather than a trade. Two of the four poems come down in variant versions, so we have six in all. The cumulative length of the *Prodromic Poems* is about 2,259 unrhymed **decapentasyllables.** They exhibit a few cases of **rhyme,** almost certainly accidental. In the first text, the author makes many references to his demanding, scolding wife, supposedly of high birth. There is always nagging in his house. He has to steal his own food, while his wife and kids dine well. He needs help: "I live in fear and trembling of being killed at any moment, / And then you, Sir, would lose Prodromos, your worthy suppliant." The second poem renews the request to the Emperor for assistance in the suppliant's household. Here there is no mention of his whining wife. The third poem is a satire against life in monasteries and a poisonous accusation of their abbots. The author now poses as a monk. He seeks the Emperor's protection, because the monks around him eat, and grow fat. In the fourth poem, he returns to the theme of poverty and the uselessness of literature, which can never provide a man with food. The classical editor **Koraís** was one of the first Greeks to draw people's attention to these poems when he published two of them in volume 1 of his *Irregular Texts* (Paris: Everard, 1828).

PROGONOPLIXÍA Ancestor obsession (προγονοπληξία) goes hand in hand with insisting that only the classical inheritance is of value. **Pachomios Rousanos,** who criticized Kartanos's language in *Flower and Essence of the Old and New Testament* (1536), says: "It is impossible to write differently from the ancient tradition, otherwise it would be futile that the Ancients composed such an admirable work for their descendants as grammar." The obsession still resounds in recent Greek writing, as when Nikos Karouzos (1926–1990), in "Triplets for Beautiful Mistra," evokes the ruined palace of the place where **Plethon** once strolled, now a weedy slope gazing over past Byzantine glory: "Mistra like some innocent passion / Rests its illustrious dead in the sun."

See also ARKHAIOFILIA

Further Reading

Vryonis, Speros, ed. *The "Past"' in Medieval and Modern Greek Culture.* Malibu, CA: Undena Publications, 1978.

Zafiropoulos, Simoni, ed. *Greece in Poetry: With Paintings, Drawings, Photographs, and Other Works of Art.* New York: Harry Abrams, 1993.

PRONUNCIATION In the sixteenth century, conservative publishers and scholars of Greek, among them Aldus Manutius, Hieronymos Aleander, Antonios Lebrissensis, and Erasmus, considered the sounding aloud of Greek words in the European Renaissance depraved. A conservative way of keeping to the presumed length of classical Greek vowels was suggested by Erasmus (1467–1536), the peripatetic Dutch-born scholar, and his followers. These Erasmians were called "etacists" (ἠτακισταί), because they pronounced Greek *eta* (-η-) long, so that it sounded like -έε- (*ehe*). The Erasmian pronunciation of Greek was gradually introduced in the West. It contrasts with modern Greek's universal iotacism, which alters -η-, -υ-, and the diphthongs -ει-; -οι-; -υι-; and -η- into the sound -ι- (*iota*). In his essay on Greek phonetics (Switzerland, 1528), Erasmus discussed lisping, wrong production of *lambda,* inability to pronounce R (ρωτακισμός), and slurring (μογιλαλία).

Further Reading

Erasmus, D. "De Recta latini graecique sermonis pronuntiatione dialogus" ["A Dialogue on the Right Way to Pronounce Latin and Greek"]. In *Collected Works of Erasmus,* edited by J. K. Sowards, 347–475. Toronto: University of Toronto Press, 1985.

PROPEMPTIKON The "farewell" (προπεμπτικόν) is written to send off a friend on a safe journey. Third-century treatises give rules and *topoi* to be used in this form, traces of which are left in the modern verb "to see off" (προπέμπω).

PROSE POEM The prose poem (πεζοτράγουδο) is a highly lyrical, descriptive composition. Often it consists of several, loosely connected prose passages. It sounds like poetry, but is set out in what looks like prose. Or it may be a poem with a sequence of very extended verse lines, which might as well be sentences in prose. It is called by Nasos Vayenás a "hermaphrodite" or "crossbreed" genre. Mastrodimitris takes the view that it belongs to poetry, not prose. In *Prose Rhythms* (1923), **Papantoniou** tried to make each single word count, as in the French genre of *poème en prose.* It was **Psycharis** (1854–1929), the language reformer, who first launched this genre, with compositions such as "The Songs of Marianna" or "Margarita's Garland." The first composition of **Maria Polydouri,** at age 14, was a prose poem called "Mother," printed in the *Family Star.* The form was used by N. Nikolaïdis (early twentieth century), in *Lives of Men and Flowers* and *Golden Myth,* by **Stratis Myrivilis,** in *The Song of the Earth,* and by Apostolos Mammelis (1876–1935) in *Stop-Overs* (1928).

Further Reading

Vayenás, N. Γιὰ ἕναν ὁρισμὸ τοῦ μοντέρνου στὴν ποίηση ["Towards a Definition of the Modern in Poetry"], in Ὁ Πολίτης, no. 57–58 (January-February 1983): 108.

PROTEST POETRY Protest poetry is a modernist, left-wing cry from the dissident intellectual, often in free verse. It is characterized by political rebelliousness and angry commitment to a Utopia, or better future. Its main writers, in Greek, were young, postwar Marxists, or ex-**Resistance** fighters. During the **Colonels' Junta,** the detained intellectual Alekos Panagulis smuggled lines of furious incitement out of prison. In his underground cage, Panagulis bellowed out the prison director's perversions. Scraps of his writing and a biography of mythic dimensions can be found in *Un uomo* (by Oriana Fallaci). The 1960s and 1970s witnessed a swing to radical, left-wing dissent in other new or established poets. Collections of verse by **Y. Ritsos, N. Vrettakos,** Y. Yeralís, L. Kasdagli, **N. Valaoritis,** P. Trogadis, K. Steryiopoulos, A. Lentakis, M. Kanellis, and Th. Papadopoulos rail against the political crisis of that generation. A more generalized protest against the Greece of their time is raised in the verse of **K. Varnalis,** K. Kulufakos, N. Phocas, M. Anagnostakis, T. Patrikios, A. Doriadis, Y. Negrepontis, and A. Phocas, as well as a number of **feminist** authors.

Further Reading

Panagulis, Alekos. *Altri seguiranno (Poesie e documenti dal carcere di Boiati).* Edited by Kris Mancuso, presented by Ferruccio Parri, and intro. by P. P. Pasolini. Palermo: Flaccovio, 1974.

Panagulis, Alexandros. *Vi scrivo da un carcere in Grecia.* Edited by F. M. Pontani, Oriana Fallaci, and Pier Paolo Pasolini and preface by Pier Paolo Pasolini. Milano: Rizzoli, 1974.

Rotolo, V. "La protesta di Niceforo Vrettakos." *Problemi,* no. 43 (1975): 245–249.

Sangiglio, C.G., ed. and trans. *Album di poesia greca d'oggi.* Milano: Ceschina, 1971.

Sangiglio, C. "Poesia greca d'oggi. Gli anni del dissenso." *Ausonia* 30, no. 1–2 (1975): 31–39.

PROTOPORIA Taking the lead (πρωτοπορία) is the Greek equivalent of "avant-garde" and has been used as a label for certain 1930s writers who rejected the prevailing pessimism of **Karyotakis,** grew tired of neo-**Parnassian** or **Symbolist** mannerism, and offered a new, positive vision of Greek literature beyond that date. By extension, the term is now used for innovators such as the poets Tasos Denegris, Alexander Pop and **Nanos Valaoritis.** The term for "modernism" (μοντερνισμός) is of English derivation, but the trend is debated by Hellenists, who link urban literature to items such as multifaceted narration, **interior monologue,** cinematographic technique, and even sexual freedom.

See also NOUVEAU ROMAN

Further Reading

Barbayiannes, N. and Nousia Dimos, eds. *Anthology of Contemporary Poets and Writers.* Athens: Iolkos, 1985.

Faubion, James D. *Modern Greek Lessons: A Primer in Historical Constructivism.* Princeton, NJ: Princeton University Press, 1993.

Layou, Mary N., ed. *Modernism in Greece? Essays on the Critical and Literary Margins of a Movement.* New York: Pella, 1990.

PROVELENGIOS, ARISTOMENIS (1850–1936) Born on the isle of Sifnos (**Cyclades**), educated in Germany, Aristomenis Provelengios was a Romantic, close in manner to the **Old School of Athens.** The committee of the **Voutsynas** competition (1870) praised his *Theseus,* inspired by Plutarch's *Parallel Lives.* He was one of the first members of the Academy of Athens (1926). He represented the constituency of Milos in the Greek Parliament from 1899 to 1905. He wrote many plays, including three historical tragedies. *Return of the Prodigal,* with its sociological content, was the only one written in prose. It was performed at the Royal Theater in 1907. His verse recalls the "haunted lyre" of **Homer,** which he compares to "the whisper of the infinite." In 1890 he was judge of the **Philadelpheios Poetry Competition** and awarded the prize to **Palamás.** His early verse, collected in *Poems Old and New* (1896), was described by Palamás as "exuding a Lamartinean aroma." They were followed by *Poems* (1916), *In Front of the Infinite* (1925), *Font of Gold* (1930), and *Aegean* (1934). An issue of *Néa Estía* (no. 623: 1953) is devoted to him, as is a monographic number of *Greek Creation* (no. 80: 1 June 1951).

PROVERBS A proverb is a brief saying, usually with a metaphorical meaning, that expresses a truth or an amusing opinion (see also **Gnomic**). The truth of the proverb is self-evident from the experience of the common people, so its wording suggests the practical. In modern Greek literature, the proverb was always popular, and it had an educational purpose when collected in books, as well being a dilettante form of readable verse, easily memorized. A *Rose Garden* was compiled in mid-fourteenth century by Makarios Chrysopefalos, metropolitan bishop of Philadelphia. It is a collection of wise sayings from **Aesop,** Plutarch, Dio Chrysostom, Synesius, Procopius of Gazi, the ecclesiastical historians Eusebius (c. 260–339), Theodoret (c. 393–c. 466), Nikiforos Choumnos, and others. Many proverbs refer to literature itself:

"Letters require wetter eyes," "Work is a strain, letters a pain," "The sea can be emptied, but letters never run dry." When Moisiodax explains in "Rebirth of Greece" how Peter the Great saved Russia from ignorance, he quotes "Producers of gold, receivers of brass."

Nirvanas recalls how his father said it was time to learn to write. When he asked his mother about writing, she offered four words: "Unlettered man, unchopped wood." Nirvanas starts a short story (1923) with "Where there's a poor man, there stands his Fate" and coins his own proverb in the second sentence: "show me a refugee and I'll show you suffering." Petros Charis (1902–1998) told Bastiás in an interview (1932) about the intellectual life of the early 1930s. To say a few new books are insignificant, he uses the proverb "One cuckoo doesn't make spring." A poem by **Markorás,** "Work," is an expansion of the saying "Idleness is the mother of all evil." The fugitive in Doukas's *Prisoner of War's Story* (1929) says: "A starving dog can split an oven." **Karkavitsas,** in his novella *The Slender Maid* (1896), passes on village wisdom in a proverb: "Two things can't be concealed in this world: a cough and a love affair."

Further Reading

Constantinidou-Partheniadou, Sofia. *A Travelogue in Greece and a Folklore Calendar.* Athens [privately publ.], 1992.

PSATHAS, DIMITRIS (1907–1989)

Psathas was a humorous, worldly feature writer. He was also a popular journalist, author of theater comedies and writer of ironic travel impressions: about Britain, *In the Land of M'Lud,* and about America, *Under the Skyscrapers.* On France, Turkey, and Egypt, Psathas composed

Paris, Stambul and Further Jolly Travels (1951). Psathas had the typical literary career of an early-twentieth-century freelance writer. For the popular papers of the day, he composed affectionately followed current event columns. He constructed his books out of humorous pieces, and his plays were skits on issues of the day, with a vaudeville touch: *The Old Curmudgeon* (1941), *Looking After Number One* (1941), *Little Pharisees* (1954), *Von Dimitrakis* (1947), *Looking for a Liar* (1953), *A Blockhead and a Half* (1955), *The Brigand Summons* (1958), *Let's Get Undressed* (1962), *Cardgames* (1963), and *Wake up Vasilis* (1965). Among his other plays are *The Wild Ones, Scatter-Brained People, The Ingénu,* and *Club for Miracles.* His best prose work, *Madam Shou-shou* (1940), studies a heroine who lives in a neurotic world and battles gray reality. It was adapted successfully both for stage and **television.**

PSELLUS, MIKHAIL KONSTANTINOS (1018–?1081)

The consummate scholar and aesthete Mikhail Psellus tells us that Symeon Metaphrastes (mid-tenth century) adapted old lives as a modern *menologion* for a silenced sorority of the **saints** and brought them to a level worthy of contemporary needs. It was the dynamism of Psellus under the Comneni emperors that set in motion a renaissance of art and letters. He wrote a prose translation of Homer's *Iliad, A Topography of Attica, On the Agreement of the Parts of Speech, On Rhetoric, An Explanation of the Chaldaean Utterances, The Birth of the Soul According to Plato, The "On Interpretation" of Aristotle, Concerning the Five Voices, Praises Concerning the Soul, A Synopsis of Rhetorical Notions,* a historical **digest,** and studies in **medicine, grammar,** law, physics, and mathematics. There is conflicting evidence on his birth and death dates, but all witnesses accept the importance to literature of this teacher, historian, philosopher, poet, courtier, and politician. He taught in **Constantinople,** was the first historian and philosopher of **Byzantium** with a background that was not royal or ecclesiastical, became a monk in 1054, returned to court, and under Emperor Isaac I Comnenus was chief minister.

Further Reading

Karahalios, G. "Michael Psellos on Man and His Beginnings." *Greek Orthodox Theological Review* 18 (1973): 79–96.

Sewter, E. R. A. *Fourteen Byzantine Rulers: The "Chronogaphia" of Michael Pseullus, translated with an introduction.* Harmondsworth: Penguin Books, 1966.

PSEUDONYM Antonis Kuriazis, Greece's first political martyr and writer, *needed* a pseudonym like **Rigas** Velestinlís Pheraios (1757?–1798) because he was a covert conspirator. Pen names became a common feature of Greek literary life between 1880 and the 1960s. They were adopted not just by women concealing their surname or writers eluding **censorship.** As a Bohemian or stylistic stance, they were used by aspiring authors for newspaper columns. Some have an enigmatic cachet, such as "Ana Zan," or "Phaedo," or "Ariel." Some selected a pseudonym that stayed with them through their career and was better known than their real name: **Elytis, Myrivilis, Seferis.** Others took a pseudonym that was outlandish: thus Petros Pikrós was Seat no. 13, Yorgos Kotzioulas took the biblical moniker Sem, Ham and Japheth (three tribes descended from Noah's sons in *Genesis,* 32). Euridice Dimitrakopoulou (b. 1890) was Irene the

Athenian, which can also mean "Athenian Peace." **Angelos Vlachos** signed himself Gnat. Helen Ourani (Negreponti by birth, married to K. Ouranis) took a masculine name, Alkis Thrulos (that is, "legend"). "Kostas Ouranis" itself is the pseudonym of Konstantinos Niarhos (1890–1953). Both **Kazantzakis** and his wife, **Galateia Alexiou,** used "Psiloritis" at one time. Thus he was "Petros" and she was "Petroula" (before Psiloriti). **E. Roidis** used the names "Dionysios Sourlis," "Agrafiotis," or the rubric "Gnats," "Gusts of Wind," "Hornet," "Theotoubis," and "Mr. Mosquito." Takis Papatsonis (b. 1895) used the sobriquet "Nobilissimus." "Aris Diktaios" is the pen name of Konstantinos Konstantourakis (born 1919); "Angelos Doxas" stood for N. N. Drakoulidis; "Tasos Galatis" for Tasos Papadopoulos (born 1937); Kostas Varnalis occasionally used the pen name "Kostas Yiabis." Milanos Parthenis (d. 1943) signed his humorous articles "The Utmost." Dimitrios Sypsomos (1879–1932) took the name "Lambros Porfyras," conflating the title of an unfinished poem ("Lambros") by **Solomós** with a fragmentary one "Porfyras" (1847, "The Shark"). **Lambros Porfyras** did not intend this name to be taken as "shining purple"! **Andreas Martzokis** called himself "Hyacinth." Dimitri Tangopoulos took the name of the devil Belfagor (Μπελφεγκόρ).

PSYCHARIS, YANNIS (1854–1929)

The potent modernist Yannis Psycharis was a poet, scholar, linguist, and leading theoretician of the **demotic** cause in the **language question.** Born at Odessa, Psycharis went to school in Constantinople until he was 15. Later he studied in Paris and Germany. He eventually became Director of Studies at the École Pratique des Hautes Études and a professor in the School of Oriental Languages. He married the daughter of a French writer, Ernest Renan (1823–1892). He worked with fierce concentration, perhaps to make up for his physical handicap, a gangrene that caused the amputation of first one foot, then the other just before he died. Psycharis (as he liked to be called) built up a formidable position as a Greek linguistic scholar writing in French intellectual circles. His was the strongest voice in a movement that sought, toward the end of the nineteenth century, to have demotic language adopted as the sole vehicle of expression. His position was scientific, rather than creative. He examined the historical roots of popular language to determine its natural laws, especially in pronunciation. He tried to show how the demotic idiom had developed, what its rules were, and how this knowledge could be used to justify the demotic and present it as the sole vehicle for modern writing and speech. Psycharis condemned **purism** as artificial, lacking in homogeneity, and contrary to the natural rules of Greek. His *Essays in Neo-Hellenic Grammar* (1884) and *Studies in Modern Greek Philology* (1892) propose that demotic Greek is the end product of the evolution of the language since classical times, and that history bears this out.

Psycharis held that the language question could only be solved by achieving a linguistic unification based on the sole premise of what was commonly accepted Greek parlance. From this base in speech, a standard form for written Greek could be evolved. Its users had to draw on the store of the popular idiom and enrich it by borrowing from dialects, ancient sources, and other language blocks and adapt these borrowings into the structure of living Greek. Psycharis's own literary production in the Greek language bears out his aspirations. His book *My Journey,* published in 1888, was a major literary event. It amounted to a formal manifesto of **Vulgarism,** giving a seal of consecration to the demotic idiom. Contemporary and subsequent Greek prose production now had to come to terms with a benchmark. Two issues of the journal *Néa Estía* (no. 534: 1949 and no. 544: 1954) are devoted to Psycharis. *My Journey* presents the author's impressions of a trip to Constantinople, the island of Chios, and Athens. Its style is richly textured, yet rigorous. As a polemical choice, it confirmed Psycharis's standing in Greek culture and also established the future direction of its literature. His other fiction, *The Dream of Giranniris* (1897), *Life and Love in Solitude* (1904), *Agní* (1913), and *In the Shade of the Plane Tree* (1911, short stories) was written in Greek or French and never enjoyed the reputation of *My Journey.* Psycharis was given to argument with other celebrities and jeers at the cute, chatty style of Palamás: "He gathers all sorts of quotations from here and there and goes on saying: Goethe says this, Voltaire says that, Carducci says the other, and so forth."

Further Reading

Psycharis, Y. "The Earrings." Translated by Alice-Mary Maffry. *The Charioteer,* no. 4 (1962): 93–100.

Thrilos, A. Μορφὲς τῆς ἑλληνικῆς πεζο-γραφίας καὶ μερικὲς ἄλλες μορφές, II [Figures of Greek Prose with Various Others]. Athens: Difros, 1963.

PTOCHOLEON (twelfth century) *The Tale of Ptocholeon, or of the Wise Old Man in Tatters* is a very early, pre-Frank-ish, story about a rich man, Leon, who became poor *(ptochos)* after an Arab invasion, when he asked his sons to sell him as a slave. They sell their father to the treasurer of the king (of Constanti-nople), claiming that he knows the value of precious stones, horses, and men. Pto-choleon gains the king's favor, finding opportunities to display his cleverness, showing, for example, that a worm is hidden in a gem. At this he is treated better and given two loaves of bread instead of one. He tells the king his intended bride is of low origin and the daughter of a Muslim. The king inquires about his *own* parentage, and Ptocholeon reveals the king was not the son of his father, Petros, but of some humble slave. The king checks with his mother, then asks Pto-choleon not to reveal the truth, and re-wards him. Honored by a king, he ends his life in comfort, illustrating the moral (perhaps originally from India) that God rewards the wise. The same story is re-lated in the twelfth-century French epic *Erakles* (referring to the Byzantine em-peror Herakleios), in the Russian poem *Ivan,* and in the Turkish tale "The Wise Traveler and the Illegitimate Sultan." The Greek version is thought to be a late branch of the source used by Gautier d'Arras for *Erakles.* The three versions of the Greek tale, all in trochaic eight-syllable meter, were published by E. Le-grand and W. Wagner in the 1870s.

Further Reading

Megas, G. "Η περὶ Πτωχολέοντος διήγη-σις καὶ τὰ σχετικὰ πρὸς αὐτὴν παραμύθια"["The Tale of Ptocholoeon and Other Folk Stories Related to it"]. Λαογραφία [*Folklore*], no. 16 (1956): 3–20.

PTOCHOPRODROMOS   (twelfth century, died c. 1166) Several semilear-ned, popular texts are associated with the author called "The Poor Forerunner." He seems to be the first writer capable of breaking through centuries of **Atticism** and learned **Hellenism** to address a common audience, using everyday vocabulary. This writer appears to be the Theodoros Prodromos, identified with the authorship of the four ***Prodromic Poems***. **Koraís** first suggested that the author of all the *Ptochoprodromic Poems* was this one person. Subsequent scholarship decided that two or more authors may have produced the poems, or that some were youthful works by Theodoros. They include epitaph dialogues (discussion between a tomb and a passerby), **satire,** two verse calendars, rhetorical exercises, the "beggar verse" in *Prodromic Poems,* panegyrics on imperial engagement or marriage, encomiastic poems (written to praise an individual), and a **romance,** *Rodanthi and Dosiklis,* in 4,614 iambic trimeters. This is an imitation of the separated lovers in the **Hellenistic** novel *Theagenes and Charicleia,* known as *Aethiopica,* by Heliodorus (Emesa, Syria; c. fourth century A.D.). Ptochoprodromos imitates the pseudo-Homeric *War of Frogs and Mice* (? fifth century B.C.) with his own *War of the Cat and Mice,* a playlet in 12-syllable lines. He writes an astrological poem (in 593 **decapentasyllables**), a poem on the 12 months of the year with advice on food for each season, **epigrams** (some **bawdy**), riddles, a lament in hexameters (*Verses of Indignant Complaint at the Lack of Honor Shown to Reason*), a scientific poem *On Equivalents,* and lively samples of letter-writing.

Further Reading

Browning, R. "Literacy in the Byzantine World." *BMGS* 4 (1978): 39–57.

Trypanis, C. "Byzantine Oral Poetry." *Byzantinische Zeitschrift* 56 (1963): 1–3.

PUBLISHING   Until the fifteenth-century invention of **printing,** publishing was a matter of scribes and handwritten copying in workshops (εργαστήρια), many located in monasteries. Some Byzantine copyists recorded their name, place of origin, a maxim, or a prayer in the leaves of the manuscript: "I am the scribe of this book, / My name is Dimitrios, Lerni my home; / I shall die and turn into dust, / Yet a book survives the circuit of years." Probably K. Laskaris's *Corona preciosa* (Venice, 1527) was the first published work to contain vernacular Greek vocabulary. Certainly he was a less-eminent classical scholar than his brother (see **Janos Laskaris**). **Koraís,** in his 1805 *Dialogue of Two Greeks Resident in Venice: What the Greeks Ought to Do in the Present Circumstances,* points out that in the last decade of the eighteenth century, France's period of revolution, more schools were introduced in Greece and more foreign books printed there than in the whole period since 1453.

Vasos Varikas and Yannis Chatzinis have calculated that, since the 1950s, at least one new volume of poetry is published in Greece every day. Valetas notes the fervor of publishing initiatives in the period 1950–1960, when thousands of volumes in free verse came out "and critics were incapable of distinguishing the poetry from the gas." Fiction is currently the most popular branch of Greek publishing: between 1990 and 1998, novel and short story production increased by 45 percent, whereas in 1996–1997 one publishing house in five, in Greece, issued at least one book of poetry. Total Greek poetry published in those years was around 600 new titles. A. Christakis has edited the seventh annual catalog of Greek books in print: *General Catalog of Books 1997: Wholesale and Retail,* a paperback (Athens: Greek Book Agency,

1977, 380 pp.). It is not as weighty as *Bowkers* (UK), or *Libri in commercio* (Italy). There are 316 active Greek publishing houses. Seventy-one publishers specialize in books for children.

In April 1996, the Greek Ministry of Culture invited a group of novelists, translators, and publishers to Delphi for a conference about the reception of modern Greek literature in France, Germany, UK, Italy, and Spain. In June 1966 Velissaris convened delegates from literary translation centers outside Greece. A symposium of 55 publishers from France, Germany, Italy, and UK met in September 1997 at Villa Bosi and at the University of Athens to promote links between writers, publishers, and state agencies as part of an effort by the National Book Center to promote Greek literature, particularly modern fiction, in countries with a stronger reading tradition than Greece's.

Further Reading

Layton, E. "Notes on Some Printers and Publishers of 16th Century Books in Venice." Θησαυρίσματα, no. 18 (1981): 119–144.

Pertusi, A. *Storiografia umanistica e mondo bizantino.* Palermo: Istituto Siciliano di Studi Bizantini e Neoellenici, 1967.

Proctor, Robert. *The Printing of Greek in the Fifteenth Century.* Oxford: Bibliographical Society, 1900.

PUN A pun is a play on words, in which one meaning is offered, by an association of sound or spelling, together with another. It is frequently tedious and forced, as when we write "I fought in the fort." Greek writers do not like puns as a **figure of speech.** Classical Greek stylists taught orators to avoid puns like the scabies. So **Babis Anninos,** a humor columnist (εὐθυμογράφος), wrote an essay "On Puns" to defend their good name. He admits that word play (λογοπαικτειν) is a bad habit, but says he is not the sole offender, for puns are no worse than nettle, funeral speeches, paté, or gnats. There may be verbal laxity in puns, but they are justified by their occasional use in good books. Thus the Gospel says "You are *Peter* and on this *rock.*" One martyrologist says "You lost the D when you lost your head, Danax, / And became lord [anax] of Heaven."

PUPPETS; PUPPET THEATER Fasoulis was the main comic figure among the wooden puppets of Greek popular theater. The characteristics of Fasoulis are energy, quick-wittedness, sharp anticipation, and service in a good cause. He has a shapeless face, single eye, large, and knotty nose and wears a high fez with a big tassel, which he swings round energetically by movements of his head in order to hint at gratitude, daring thoughts, or the launching of an attack. Fasoulis is a cunning servant, full of peasant wit, and usually gets the upper hand by the end of the show. He was renamed Paschalis, by the puppeteer Christos Konitsiotis, but the name Fasoulis has remained dominant in the wooden puppet theater. Next came the complementary off-sider figure of Perikletos, who quarrels constantly with Fasoulis and then gets a merciless beating at the end of the piece, because of his illogical answers and antics. In the early twentieth century, the puppet Perikletos began to disappear, giving way to the character Pericles, a valiant lover who ventures all for the sake of a pretty girl puppet called Kleonike.
See also COMEDY; SOURÍS

PURISM; PURISTS, THE In the **language question,** the purist stance has evolved through three different positions. First there was **Atticism.** Writers of the **Hellenistic** age endeavored to reproduce the language of Attic (= Athenian) writers of the Periclean and Peripatetic periods. It was crucial for an Atticizing Hellenist to adopt the style of Demosthenes or Isocrates. Any cacology or inopportune metaphor was considered "Asian." "Wine-dark sea," "rosy-fingered dawn," or "far-shadowing spear" were approved for use, because they were found in **Homer.** Atticism disappeared in the course of the nineteenth century. A second purist attitude was to preserve **Byzantine** idiom, like St. Basil's epistolary "Your Honorableness" or "Your Worthiness" rather than "you," which revels in the prestige nouns. In the 1800s, the main thrust of purism was toward "learnedness" (λογιοτατισμός). This term was coined by N. Dragoumis (1865) to refer to the selection of learned forms in written Greek and their recycling in speech. A third purist tendency, in the modern period, has been to neutralize the development of **demotic** usage and replace popular words with a learned equivalent. This was rebutted by **Vulgarizers,** who isolated manifestations of purism, such as the genitive singular ending -*eos,* or the word-final -*n* of the classical neuter singular, as in κρεοπωλεῖο(ν), for "butcher's shop" and ἀρτοπωλεῖο(ν) for "bakery." The old genitive plural ending -τῶν (-*tón*) now seems unmanageable to most Greeks. In the 1970s, they fumbled for others ways to express it, except in the phrase τῶν ψαράδων ("of the fishermen"), which seemed the only viable genitive plural in spoken Greek. Purists who spurned the **Demotic** stuck to the polytonic system (despite the **accent** reform of the early 1980s), or retained breathings; a few tried to hold on to iota subscripts: ᾳ, ᾴ, ᾱ, ῃ, ῄ, η, ῳ, ῴ, ῷ. These were already considered wasteful of typesetting. One problem of purism is that it allows language to be used as an oppressive tool because Greek has a high incidence of instability of spelling, even with common words. By adhering to classical orthography, there could be, strictly speaking, no less than 24 different ways to print the letter alpha.

Modern newspapers use a **mixed language** form, to ensure egalitarian access for all. **Koraís** (1748–1833) was one of the earliest and most influential purists. His faith in the classical tradition caused him to associate a classicizing form of language with Hellenic freedom. Despite his call for a new dictionary of Greek to record current usage and his rejection of Atticism and outmoded forms, Koraís is the one nineteenth-century intellectual most responsible for Katharevousa. Until late in his career, the writer **Kondylakis** (1862–1920) was an opponent of demoticism and laughed at the Vulgarizers as "hairy." Not all expressions of purist concern are examples of the reactionary stuffiness that **Solomós** once called "being chained by the circumflex." In March 1982, the newly formed Greek Linguistic Society expressed fears about **Vulgarism** at home, in Greece, and its misunderstandings abroad. In 1985, 28 writers (the figure later grew to 48) signed a statement rejecting further spelling changes and the single accent sponsored by the PASOK (Panhellenic Socialist Movement) government. This was the monotone reform, passed by presidential decree in 1982. Is the purist position a reactionary lament about declining standards? Savvopoulos and others argued that because Greek is the only language that is essentially sung, it should retain its historical accent system. Some academics supported Katharevousa and the reading of classical Greek in schools on the grounds that without the classics, the Greeks "would have been Balkanized!" The newspaper *Estía* still printed Katharevousa in 1989. The *Modern Greek Grammar* by M. Triantafyllidis (revised edition, Thessaloniki, 1978) was incorrectly thought by many to express an approved national language. The fear driving the purists' campaign against what they called the "idioms" or "extremities" (ἀκρότοτητες) of demotic reform was that it might lead to the adoption of the Roman alphabet in Greece. For purists, this would be the worst possible hemorrhage of Greek.

See also VULGARISM

Further Reading

Foris, V. D. "Ελληνικά παρατράγουδα" ["Greek Improprieties"]. Η Λέξη 47 (1986): 728–736.

Mackridge, P. A. "Greek as She Is Spoke." *Aegean Review* 1 (1986): 6–7.

Savvopoulos, D. "Τα Ελληνικά ως Τραγούδι" ["Greek as Song"]. Η Λέξη 45 (1985): 423.

R

RABAGÁS The periodical *Rabagás* was intended as a political and satirical newspaper. It was founded by two journalists who fled, or were expelled, from Constantinople, Kleanthis Triantafyllos and Vlasis Gavriilidis (see **Aodo; Don't Get Lost**). It ran from August 1878 to May 1889 and became the virtual mouthpiece of the **Generation of the Eighties** and **New School of Athens.** One issue was suspended because of public scandal over the periodical's installments from E. Zola's novel *Nana* (1878), the story of an actress who humiliates her suitors, loves only her little son, milks her noble benefactor of his money, and dies to the sound of street demonstrations against the king of Prussia. This translation (by Dimitrios Kambouroglous made a strong impression on other Greek novelists. Most of the writers in the group round *Rabagás* read or spoke French. The title of the periodical came from a play by the prolific French dramatist Victorien Sardou (1831–1908). In Sardou's *Rabagás* (which Kambouroglous also translated), the protagonist is a colorless republican who worms his way to power and then turns into a court-flatterer. The government of Koumoundouros forbade production of the Greek version, on the grounds that it constituted libel at the expense of Léon Gambetta, the politician who ushered in the French Republic (1875). The Greek journal's political ideas were "so bold" that Triantafyllos, the editor, later said *Rabagás* "served as an entry ticket to the country's prisons." Its leading figures were the radical lawyer Rokkos Hoïdas (later a parliamentarian), **Nikos Kambás, K. Palamás, Ioannis Polemis** (1862–1924), **Yeoryios Sourís** (1852–1919), and **Yeoryios Drosinis** (who published *The Spider's Web* in 1880, after contributing his first verses to *Rabagás*). They admired the French Parnassian poets, whom they viewed as opponents of the moribund **Romanticism.** Prudhomme's *Reliquaire* and Coppée's *Stances et poèmes* became, as Trypanis puts it, their Gospel. They imitated the Parnassians' abandonment of loftiness and their acceptance of homely, day-to-day themes in poetry. **Achilleus Paraschos** derided them as "silly youngsters."

Gavriilidis, coeditor of *Rabagás,* edited the other main satirical journal of this period, *Don't Get Lost.* Aggravated by his troubles as sole editor of *Rabagás,* Kleanthis Triantafyllos committed suicide (25 May 1889), a few days after being forced to close the journal (because of Gavriilidis's withdrawal, lack of financial support by friends, and a **prison** sentence).

RAIAS. See JANISSARIES

RALLIS POETRY COMPETITION

The Rallis was an important poetry prize of the Othonian (immediate post-Independence) period, awarded annually from 1850 to 1861. It was founded by a prosperous immigrant, Ambrosios Rallis. Its judges, drawn from the University of Athens faculty, followed conservative, **Katharevousa** values and were opposed to the style of **Romantic** poetry. Some, like the University rector Spiros Pilikas (1805–1891), pronounced against the linguistic conservatism of Rallis's intentions, holding that "the wind from the cemeteries desiccates the delicacy of sentiment." In assessing the entries for 1857, they criticized the use of Homeric vocabulary and the aspiration "to resurrect the old Achaeans of the Trojan age to read and enjoy them" (translation by D. Ricks). Nonetheless, a poem in Homeric hexameters by **Th. Orfanidis,** "Chios Enslaved," won the 1858 poetry competition. There was considerable public and academic enthusiasm for Rallis's initiative, which the writer S. Karydis hailed in nationalist tones: "Our liberated youth / Will soon act with courage, / Will become involved in new battles / And chase the Turks away." In 1876, **Palamás** entered his "Epics of Love Affairs" in the University poetry competition, and Orfanidis, then chairman of the judges, dis-

missed them as "cold exercises in verse of a pedantic grammarian."

See also COMPETITIONS; PHILA-DELPHEIOS

RANGAVÍS, ALEXANDROS RIZOS (1809–1892)

Archaeologist, intellectual, short story writer, and novelist, Alexandros Rangavís was born in Constantinople to a noble **Phanariot** family. Rangavís was also a cousin of the **Soutsos** brothers. He went to the Bavarian military academy in Munich. Subsequently he was an officer, professor, and foreign secretary and held senior ambassadorial posts. He was the first Greek intellectual to attempt a short history of modern Greek literature (1877). Rangavís published *The Lord of Morea* (1850), a long **historical novel** (Greece's first), which was based on the medieval **chronicle of Morea.** It deals with the aftermath of the thirteenth-century **crusades** and the Frankish adoption of a slice of disputed Greek territory, which became a principate with courtly, European manners and was then plundered in over 130 years of high-handed administration by Italian and Catalan warlords (*condottieri*). Rangavís's long romantic poem of 1837, *Dimos and Elena,* and the collection *Various Poems* (1837) show an early tendency to join the **Vulgarizers** and promote the use of **demotic** vocabulary, though not its grammar. The complete works of Rangavís, published in his lifetime, run to 19 volumes. For his many plays, see also **Dramatists** (nineteenth century) and **Voutsynas.**

Further Reading

Lurier, Harold E., trans. and ed. *Crusaders as Conquerors: The Chronicle of Morea.* New York: Columbia University Press, 1964.

Ricks, D. B. "A. R. Rangavis, 'The Voyage

of Dionysus.'" *Greek* 38, no. 1 (1987): 89–97.

READERS The school reader (ἀναγν-ωστικόν) was a nineteenth- or early twentieth-century school primer containing literary, historical, and philosophical selections from Greek authors, for the moral development of pupils who did not read them in the original (see **Papantoniou**). Members of the **educational society,** including **Nikos** and **Galateia Kazantzakis,** set themselves to writing readers in the reforming period after World War I. Between 1918 and 1920, **Andreas Karkavitsas** produced various readers: *In the Time of Alexander the Great,* for the third form of elementary school; *Our Homeland,* for Form 4; and *Diyenís Akritas*, for form 5.

A typical reader is Petros Papadeas, *Modern Greek Readings* (6th ed., Piraeus: I. Liontis Brothers, c. 1925, no date given). This is a book for grades 1 and 2 of technical and trade school. It starts with the **Provelengios** poem "To Young People": "O golden youth of a glorious race! / Perceive in your bodies, perceive in your soul / The impulse and the pride, / Which in war and in peace / Elevate men and glorify nations." Next comes a passage entitled "A Book Is Our Best Friend," at the foot of which the pupils are invited to learn the spelling of 15 difficult words in the passage, such as, ἡ μόρφωσις, which equals modern μόρφωση ("education"). This is followed by "True Treasures" (that is, learning and virtue, which are useful to other people). Next, in the Papadeas reader, are stories about "Poor Kleanthis," "Demosthenes the Orator," "The Path of Good and the Path of Evil," a graphic sketch by Metropolitan All-Beneficent Faustinis about the "Prodigal Son," a passage from

the novelist **I. Kondylakis** (1861–1920) on the desire for wealth, the **Mavilis** poem "To the Fatherland," **Nikiforos Theotokis** on Love, and the unsigned (by Papadeas) "Ali Pasha and the Souliots." **Solomós** is represented by the first 16 quatrains of the "Hymn to Liberty." There follows a **Vlachoyannis** story on rural life and his "Sortie" from Missolonghi, **Sourís** "To the Philhellenes," a letter from **Koraís** to Odysseus Androutsos, a speech by **Kolokotronis**, the "Chronicle of 1940" by **Ilias Venezis, Ilias Miniatis,** "On the Crucifixion of the Saviour," a passage from Hesiod's *Works and Days* translated by **S. Skipis,** a poem by **Polemís,** followed by an interpretation of that poem by **G. Xenopoulos,** and other, less literary items, such as "the Corinth Canal," "artificial lakes," "water transport," lignite deposits, Edison, Bell, Marconi, lead, steel, bronze, Samuel Morse, Philo of Byzantium (250 B.C.) discovering "Steam as a Source of Energy," "Electrification in our Country," tombs, churches, Acropolis, **Hagia Sophia,** wood, vase, mosaic, Minoan palace, Gutenberg, and papyri.

This kind of book puts together wisdom and homespun practicality. Readers used from before **Independence** up to the present day are reprinted in Evgenia Kefalinaiou's *Modern Greek Primers 1771–1981* (Athens: Paraskinio, 1996). Kefalinaiou edited *The Noumás Primer of 1906: Greek Readers* (1996). The latter is a reprint of the first Greek school reader in **Demotic,** which caused positive and negative comment when it came out in 1906. I. Gianneli has edited a reprint of a reader that was used in schools in the first half of the twentieth century, namely *Spelling Primer* (Athens: Didymoi, 1995).

REBETIKA The *Rebetika* (Ρεμπέτικα) are traditional underworld songs of the urban tough guy, the *mangas* or *rebetis* ("outcast," "misfit"). Played on the *baglama,* or bouzouki, these songs recreate the low life of hash dens and have Byzantine or **Islamic** undertones. The fiction of Petros Pikrós (1896–1957) charts the wandering of lost, lower-caste people between **prison,** brothel, and drug dealing. His 1922 volume of short stories, *Lost Bodies,* is a precursor of the music subculture of *rebetika.* The poet **Nikos Gatsos** wrote the lyrics for a setting called *Rebetiko,* which has music by Stavros Xarhakos. The genre expresses the distinctive melancholy of Greek poetry and the expatriation theme (see *xenitiá*), as in a *rebetiko* by Yannis Papaioannou (1913–1972): "To give you another embrace, / So my sadness can be lifted. // But you are in a foreign place, / Who knows where you have drifted?" (from "Nights I Stay Awake without Hope").

Markos Vamvakaris (1905–1972) made 20 recordings of his own *Rebetika* and was a master of the bouzouki. A bust of Vamvakaris faces the sea from the small town square, named after him, on Syros. Ilias Petropoulos (b. 1928), who left Thessaloniki in 1973 to live in Paris, was sentenced to prison four times for his writings, in 1969, twice in 1972, and in 1979. His *Rebetic Songs* (1968) are a mélange of folk essay, photographic documentary, and personal anthology. They deal with a taboo theme for the 1960s, the subculture of the outcasts, and Petropoulos was jailed. He got a prison sentence again in 1972, after the publication of his innovative lexicon of gay Greek (1971). Petropoulos (and his publisher) also got 18-month sentences for his *Manual of the Good Robber* (1979), a novel that combines shocking details about prison with a racy lampoon on some ideal country (clearly Greece) that sanctions

them. He wrote a history of the Greek brothel (1980), as well as *Little Holy Hash* (1987) and *Rebetika Culture* (1990), which contains sociological and folk material on the outcasts.

Further Reading

Butterworth, Katherine and Sara Schneider, eds. *Rebetika: Songs from the Greek Underworld.* Athens: Komboloi, 1975.

RECOGNITION. See ANAGNÓRISI

RECORDING OF MANNERS. See ITHOGRAFÍA

RED APPLE TREE. See KING TURNED TO MARBLE

RELIGIOUS INSTRUCTION. See CATECHISM

RENAISSANCE Greece, a much-defeated territory (in 1204, 1453, 1552, 1571, and 1669) had no Renaissance to speak of. It did not import scholars, and Greek is the only European literature not influenced by Latin. Among Greece's own scholars are **Chrysoloras, Bessarion, Y. Trapezuntios,** Theodoros Gazís, Ioannis Argyropoulos, Mikhail Apostolis, Andronikos Kallistos, **Konstantinos Laskaris, Leon Allatios, Dimitrios Chalkokondylis,** Yeoryios Hermonymos, **Janos Laskaris,** and Markos Mousouros (Boerner, *De doctis hominibus Graecis Litterarum Graecarum in Italia instrautoribus,* 1750). As these men worked in Italy, we have to ask if Greece had a Renaissance. Spandonidis declares (1962) that **Hellenism** is either "absolute" or "transitional." Goethe warned that "Whoever does not die, cannot be reborn." Montaigne remarked of the period: "Tout fourmille de commentaires" ("Everything swarmed with commentaries"). It was not so in Greece. During Turkish rule, there were no aristocratic Greek courts. There were no princes to subsidize **translation,** and no foundation of libraries, no recovery of archaeology, music, or **palaeography.** After the **fall of Constantinople,** Greek culture disappeared, except in a few monastic libraries or among the **Phanariots.** After studies at Constantinople, Theodoros Gazís (1400–1475/?78) went to Italy to attend the Council of Florence (1438) and later lived there. He was the first professor of Greek at the University of Ferrara (1447–1449). Gazís worked in Rome, Naples, and southern Italy. He compiled a Greek grammar and translated the zoological books of **Aristotle** and Theophrastus on botany. Yeoryios Trapezuntios (George of Trebizond) taught at Vicenza and Rome. He was interpreter with the papal court at Bologna, Florence, and Ferrara (1437–1443). In the early 1450s, he was secretary to the patron and antiquarian Pope Nicholas V. George of Trebizond allied himself with the **Catholic** curia in the dispute over the possible unification of the Roman and **Orthodox** churches (1438–1443). He wrote both in Greek and Latin on philosophy and **rhetoric.** He produced a commentary on Ptolemy and translations of Aristotle, **Plato,** Demosthenes, Ptolemy, Eusebius, and the Cappadocian fathers. He was an advocate of Aristotle, like his friend Francesco Barbaro, and disapproved of Plato. He attacked Yeoryios Yemistos Plethon (who lived at the Peloponnesian court of Mistra and visited Italy. This supposed heretic and **neo-Platonist** (c. 1360–c. 1451) spans the **Hellenistic** and the Byzantine.

Plethon appeared to reconcile the Christian and the pagan in a way that at-tracted great attention in the West. He sparked the wider debate between Platonists and Aristotelians, with his essay on their supposed incompatibility: *Concerning Matters in Which Aristotle Differs from Plato* (1449). Ioannis Argyropoulos (c. 1410–c. 1491) was another Greek who remained in Italy after traveling as a delegate to the Council of Florence. In his lectures at the University of Florence, Argyropoulos aimed to reconcile Plato and Aristotle. He influenced many Italian Renaissance luminaries who heard his classes: Cristoforo Landino, Marsilio Ficino, Angelo Poliziano. Ghirlandaio painted Argyropoulos as the apostle St. Peter, in the Sistine Chapel. So Greece lost out: its classical heritage gathered dust or was transferred to the West. Greeks were forced back on devotional texts, **readers,** saints' lives, histories of the world since the creation, **hagiography,** and the **demotic song.** Their leader was the Patriarch of Constantinople, permitted by the Turks to act for Greeks. Culture evaporated toward Rhodes, **Crete, Cyprus,** and the **Heptanese,** variously held by Franks, Knights Templar, or the maritime republic of **Venice.** Venetian influence led to a tradition of love poetry on Rhodes and narrative poems by **Emmanuel Georgillás** like *The Plague of Rhodes* (1498) or *The Tale of Belisarius* (whose attribution to Georgillás is disputed). Literary activity was intense on Cyprus: a translation of Petrarch's *Rime* (*Poems*) shows that Italian was known, and its influence may be deduced from written and oral love poems in the Cypriot vernacular. After the fall of Rhodes (1522) and of Cyprus (1571) to the Turks, the sole center of literary activity was Crete, under Venetian administration until its fall to the Turks (1669). This Cretan period boasts books that stand almost on a par with the Italian Renaissance. At their head are **Erotokritos,** by Kornaros, and **Voskopoula** (*The Pretty Shepherdess*). This pastoral idyll by an as yet unidentified author was published by Nikolaos Drimytinós at Venice (1627). Drimytinós was at first wrongly believed to be its author. Well-known was Bergadis's *Apokopos,* story of a journey through the nether world and the first book composed in demotic Greek to be published at Venice (1519). From the early sixteenth century comes the *Lament on Bitter and Insatiate Hades,* by **Ioannis Pikatoros.** Also from the sixteenth century comes the anonymous Cretan *Story of a Girl and a Young Man,* as well as an *Exile,* discussing the suffering of one who lives far from his native country, a contribution to the evergreen theme of **diaspora** and *xenitiá.* Achelis, in his *Siege of Malta,* adapted to verse form (20 chapters; 2,500 lines) a story in prose by P. Gentil de Vendôme about the attack on Malta by Turks (1565). Malta was defended by the Knights of St. John, who had been driven out of Rhodes in 1522. This *Siege of Malta* was published at Venice, in 1571. Conspicuous is the poetry of **Stefanos Sachlikis,** who writes on the verge of Rabelaisian **bawdy** about the perils of an ill-spent youth.

From around 1635 comes the masterpiece of Cretan theater, *The Sacrifice of Abraham.* The five-act play by **George Chortatsis,** *Erofili* (first publ. 1637), can stand alongside the best of Italian Renaissance drama. There is a convincing *Zeno* by an unknown hand, an imitation of the tragedy in Latin by the Jesuit Joseph Simons (publ. Rome, 1648). This Greek *Zeno* was written and performed at Zakynthos in 1682 or 1683. For noncomic Renaissance theater, a first tentative modern interpretation is offered by the Italian scholar M. Vitti in his introduction to the tragedy *Efyena* (which he discovered) by the **Heptanesian** writer Montseleze (mid-seventeenth century). The comedy *Stathis* (perhaps by Chortatsis) shows traces of Italian models, like Pasqualigo's *Fedele.* Chortatsis's pastoral tragicomedy, *Gyparis,* includes translated verses from Tasso, Guarini, and Ongaro. This Cretan literature shows the effect of the Renaissance (1490–1560), yet is written in a dialect that achieves dignity as an idiom.

See also ARISTOTLE; PHOTIUS; SEVENTEENTH-CENTURY ERUDITION; THEATER

Further Reading

Geanakoplos, D. J. *Interaction of the "Sibling" Byzantine and Western Cultures in the Middle Ages and Italian Renaissance, 330–1600.* New Haven, CT: Yale University Press, 1976.

Georgopoulou, M. "Late Medieval Crete and Venice: An Appropriation of Byzantine Heritage." *Art Bulletin* 77 (1995): 479–496.

RESISTANCE, THE Fiction and song are entwined with the national resistance (Αντίσταση), which opposed Germany and the Greek government during the **occupation** (1941–1944) and **Civil War.** In 1945 the humorous writer Dimitris Psathas (1907–1989) published the novel *Resistance,* in which events and extensive dialogue serve to vilify collaborators. Dido Soteriou's novel *Electra* (1961) highlights Electra Apostolou, a pro-Communist in EAM, the abbreviation for Ἐθνικὸν Ἀπελευθερωτικὸν Μέτωπον ("National Liberation Front"; see **Glinós**). A romantic phraseology develops in such books: the wise and provident Stalin is "Big Moustache"; students daub "Stalingrad" round the town; an intellectual is called a "cadre" (κα-θοδηγτής). You join the resistance by "going to the mountain"; you fight for the "Democratic Army"; you hide your instructions (επιταγές); you can be arrested for spying (κατασκοπεία); as a person, you must do nothing "anti-conspiratorial" (αντισυνωμοτικό). Activists block the road with a barricade (οδόφραγμα). Party meetings debate a member's expulsion (διγραφή). Members of the Central Committee wear double-breasted jackets and wide trousers; if you take food to a partisan, you are a "brigand-feeder" (ληστοτρόφος), and the punishment is death; a partisan may be from the EAM (εαμίτης), or he may be from the EPON (ΕΠΟΝίτης). For the Fascists he is merely a "bandit." The acronym EPON stands for United Panhellenic Youth Organization, whose members spread slogans, ran messages, or acted as partisans in the mountains. Rebels sing "EAM is the people's voice" (*EAM, EAM, EAM, EAM,* φωνή λαού). KKE is the **Communist Party** of Greece (Κομμουνιστικὸν Κόμμα Ἑλλάδος), born in 1924 from the Socialist Labour Party (founded 1918).

The KKE lurked, in the early occupation, behind EAM, whose military wing Greek National Liberation Army (Ἐθνικὸς Λαϊκὸς Ἀπελευθερωτικὸς Στρατός), had the acronym ELAS (which resembled Ἕλλας, "Greece"). Its commander (καπετάνιος) was Aris Velouchiotis. All three organizations aimed at converting Greece into a people's democracy, affiliated to the Soviet Union. Resistance paperwork was drafted in the **Demotic,** never in **Katharevousa.** Against them stood the royalist Greek National Democratic Union (Ἐθνικὸς Δημωκρατικὸς Ἑλληνικὸς Σύνδεσμος, or EDES) led by Napoleon Zer-

vas. There was a republican EKKA, Movement for National and Social Liberation, led by Col. Psaros (the 5/42 Regiment). The One Republic movement, known by the acronym AAA and led by General Serafis, was broken up in March 1943. EKKA was liquidated by ELAS (April 1944). PEAN was the acronym of the Panhellenic Union of Fighting Youth, a rightist student group. The so-called "X Organization" was led by General Grivas, future leader of EOKA against the British in Cyprus. "X" was a pro-Nazi commando of nationalists, supplied with German weapons, who apparently used police cars to spread propaganda and attack reds at night, as part of a "white terror." PAO, or Pan-Hellenic Resistance Organization, was a residue of 3,000 collaborators (left behind by the Germans), who took over the city of Kilkis, about 60 kilometers from **Thessaloniki** (E. Ioannou, in Scarfe 1994).

Further Reading

Alexiou, Elli. Ἀνθολογία Ἑλληνικῆς ἀντιστασιακῆς λογοτεχνίας, *1941–1944* [Anthology of Greek Resistance Writing: 1941–1944], 2 vols. [1. Prose; 2. Poetry]. Berlin: Akademie-Verlag, 1965–1971.

Eudes, Dominique. *The Kapetanios: Partisans and Civil War in Greece, 1943–1949.* London: Monthly Review Press, 1972.

Sarafis, Stefanos. *ELAS: The Greek Resistance Army.* London: Merlin, 1980.

RESULTS OF LOVE, THE (Vienna, 1792)

The Results of Love is a series of three licentious short stories. They follow the narrative experiment set in *The School for Delicate Lovers* by **Rigas.** Of uncertain authorship, the stories Hellenize the penchant for Parisian adaptation made popular by Rigas Velestinlís. They are no longer attributed to Velestinlís, but to Karatzas (see P. M. Kitromilidis, *Rigas Velestinlís: Theory and Practice* [in Greek], Athens: Greek Parliament Publications, 1998: 32–33). Hellenization is provided in *The Results of Love* by introducing Dragoman and Corfiot characters, by the inclusion of songs and poems in the vernacular, and by using a plausible mixture of narrative and dialogue, together with sophisticated speech credits and the omniscient, authorial point of view.

REVIEW. See COMEDY

RHETORIC Gibbon said of Byzantine rhetoric that "our taste and reason are wounded by the choice of gigantic and obsolete words." But from the seventeenth century, rhetoric taught Greeks how to compose speeches and succeed as lawyers. It provided the tools of **oratory** and political debate. It codified techniques useful in writing, as well as forensic eloquence: the ordering of material, choice of vocabulary, length of **sentence,** allusions, arrangement of words, avoidance of **meter,** apt quotation, persuasiveness, **tropes,** ornaments, use of **figures,** and proverbs.

RHETORICAL QUESTION The rhetorical question is one that the writer puts to the reader, when both know the answer. It often lurks in **patriotic** or didactic texts. **Rigas** (1757–1798) asks in the "Revolutionary Proclamation" from his *The New Political Dispensation:* "Is there any man who will tell me the opposite, namely that these things do not happen? Does anyone exist with the soul of a tiger to agree with such lawless acts?"

RHYME; RHYMING The effect of rhyme (ομοιοκαταληξία) is crucial to

Greek poetry from the fourteenth century onward. A poem or song has rhymed or unrhymed lines. This is the primary feature that defines verse by genre and type up to our own day, when some Greek songs still exhibit rhyme. **Koraís** (1748–1833), who disliked the early vernacular masterpiece *Erotokritos*, castigated end-line rhyme in poetry as "the wrath of the Muses." **Kalvos** (1792–1869) censured rhyme at the end of lines as a barbarism that "stuck to the Greeks like scabies." The conservative critic Y. Apostolakis (1886–1947) remarked, in an essay on **Solomós,** that the highest moments of his fragmentary epic sketches in *The Free Besieged* dispense with rhyme, for rhyme is "the ultimate sign of foreign enslavement." The writer **Kalosgouros** (Kerkyra, 1849–1902) observed that Greek is actually poor in rhymes. Its polysyllabic vocabulary makes it hard to form a **strophe** of 4 hendecasyllabic lines (11-syllable verse).

The way modern Greek rhyme works is that the last one, or two, syllables of certain paired lines have similar endings. Clearly the stress must fall on the same syllable in rhyme words that are paired: a line whose stress falls on the final syllable is called oxytone, that is, "accented on the last" (οξύτονος). When the stress falls on the penultimate syllable, the line is accented on the last-but-one (παροξύτονος). If the stress falls on the antepenultimate, the line is called "accented on the last-but-two" (προπαροξύτονος). Now rhyme requires variety to arrest the reader's attention. For this reason, Greek poets try to choose pairs of rhyme words with differing grammatical value. A pronoun should not be rhymed with another pronoun or an adverb with an adverb. When successive lines are rhymed, as in two couplets that end " . . . the reed-*pipe;* / the *snipe;*

/ the *dusk;* / the *flocks,*" we have the rhyme scheme AABB, which in Greek is called "spliced."

A different rhyme scheme, ABAB, is seen in this quatrain from *The Free Besieged*: "Day marches *forth;* / Scatters the cloud; / While night steals *off,* / One star still *proud.*" This frequently used rhyme in lyric verse is called "woven." A less common rhyme is ABBA (formed like a chiasmus), as in the quatrain from Dimitrios Vyzantios (1834–1854), "Yearning": "I bound in a ribbon of flowers this impoverished *verse* / Which I produced on the instant in the springtime of *life*; / But that season has fled swift as the wind's *knife,* / Now these lines resemble echoes of the *hearse.*" The preceding rhyme is called "crossed." The rhyme pattern AABCCB is called "spliced-cum-woven" (ζευγαροπλεχτή). An example of this pattern can be seen in a six-line brevity that runs: "The carriage stands *apart,* / An hour in the *shower;* / And does not *care:* / It seems left *oppressed* / By the neighbouring *address* / Which does not want it *there.*" A rhyme scheme that is "mixed" may combine elements of all the different types enumerated earlier.

Kavafis says: "Many people have remarked 'Why don't you use rhyme, Cavafy?' But they are wrong to ask *me.* They should address the question to poets from before my time. Those good souls didn't use it either, though rhyme was the established thing in their day!"

Further Reading

Mitsakis, K. Τὸ σονέτο στὴν ἑλληνικὴ ποίηση [The Sonnet in Greek Poetry]. Athens: Phexi, 1962.

RIGAS VELESTINLÍS [PHERAIOS] (1757?–1798; pseudonym of Antonis Kuriazis) Born at Velestinlo (Thessaly)

and educated in Constantinople, Rigas Velestinlís occupied administrative posts in the Balkans. His name is a conspirator's mask. He was in the service of **Phanariot** *hospodars,* dependent princes under the **Ottoman** hegemony. The poet **A. Soutsos** sings of "Rigas, martyr and forerunner of our sacred struggle." According to legend, Velestinlís was forced to emigrate because he killed a Turkish citizen. During a visit to Vienna in 1796, he may have formed a secret revolutionary society. He met with Lavrentios Aléandros of Préveza, who had contacts among revolutionaries in Greece. He wrote letters to Napoleon Bonaparte from Vienna and was invited to meet him at Venice (his last journey). In 1797, he produced a *Map of Greece* in 12 sheets. He also published *A New Map of Wallachia* and a *General Map of Moldavia.* Around this time (1797) he wrote an outline for the new state that could be brought into being, modeled on the French constitution of the 1790s, to take the place of the Ottoman Empire: *New Political Constitution of the Inhabitants of Roumeli, Asia Minor, the Islands of the Aegean and the Principalities of Moldavia and Wallachia.* This inflammatory document, which we know indirectly, contained a manifesto starting with the phrase "Liberty, Equality, Fraternity," a dissertation on the flag of the proposed Republic, a hortatory poem, a manual of military tactics, a democratic catechism, and two marching songs. Greek was to be the language of Velestinlís's envisaged state, which was based on the French republic. Within this framework, the Greeks were to enjoy certain privileges. Considered the first historical martyr of the Greek nationalist cause, Velestinlís printed nationalist pamphlets (*Declaration of the Rights of Man*) and revolutionary songs bound up with the independence movement, such as the *War March* with its furious simplicity: "How long are we to lose brothers, fatherland, parents, / Our friends, our children, and relatives? / Better would be one of hour in life as free men / Than forty years of slavery and imprisonment. / What does it profit you, that you should live but be in slávery?" The satirist Mikhail Perdikaris (1766–1828) composed a tract attacking Velestinlís, entitled *Rigas, or Against Pseudo-Hellenes.*

Velestinlís translated the French *Declaration of the Rights of Man* into Greek. **Byron** translated his version of the Marseillaise back into English, as "Sons of the Greeks Arise." From Vienna, Velestinlís dispatched 3,000 copies of his *New Political Constitution* to Trieste. Before arriving there, he was (late 1797) betrayed by the Austrians to the Pasha of Belgrade. In the fortress, he was executed with certain fellow conspirators who were Ottoman citizens. Their bodies were thrown into the Sava River. Velestinlís also published the *School for Delicate Lovers* (Vienna, 1790). This was a translation from Restif de la Bretonne (1734–1806), French author of some 190 stories or novels, many licentious. Velestinlís offers a Greek version of six stories from Restif's *Les Contemporaines* (1780–1783). It is a free adaptation that retains Parisian elements, such as authentic French names, adding Greek items, with the **Katharevousa** of Constantinople as a linguistic vehicle. He incorporated vernacular songs into his text. In 1790, Velestinlís published an *Anthology of Physics,* drawn from Western manuals and learned papers. Later (1797), our versatile nationalist produced translations of Pietro Metastasio and J. -F. Marmontel, as well as selected chapters from Abbé Jean-Jacques Barthélemy's *Jour-*

ney of the Young Anacharsis in Greece Towards the Middle of the Fourth Century Before the Modern Era (1788), a compendium of everyday life in antiquity. **Ioulios Typaldos** wrote a poem, "Rigas," which typecast Velestinlís as a romantic bard who incited the Greeks into their **War of Independence** with his songs.

"Just as the Prophet Moses changed a dry rock into a cool-flowing spring, so Rigas transformed his naked, sterile, firstborn verse into a chant of resurrection," Palamás once wrote, with an ecstatic flourish (1897).

Further Reading

Frazee, Charles. *Catholics and Sultans: The Church and the Ottoman Empire, 1453–1923.* Cambridge and New York: Cambridge University Press, 1983.

Vitti, Mario. "The Inadequate Tradition: Prose Narrative During the First Half of the Nineteenth Century." In *The Greek Novel: A.D. 1–1985,* edited by Roderick Beaton, 3–10. London: Croom Helm, 1988.

RITSOS, YANNIS (1909–1990) The socially committed poet Yannis Ritsos published more than 100 volumes in his life, and around 5,000 pages came out between 1930 and 1988. In 1975 he was nominated for the Nobel Prize for the seventh time. Ritsos fought in the EAM (National Liberation Front) during the German **occupation** (1941–1944). He supported the Communist side during the **Civil War,** which broke out after Greece's indecisive parliamentary elections in March 1946 and the plebiscite in September of that year, which led to the second recall of the monarch, George II. Ritsos was born in Monemvasia (southern Peloponnese). He was the youngest child of a landowning family that had once been prosperous and was now in difficulties. His eldest brother and mother died of tuberculosis (1921). He himself contracted tuberculosis in 1925 and was in and out of sanatoriums. He worked at various stages as an actor and a dancer. He was detained in **prison** or in camps on Greek islands (Lemnos, Makronisos, and Ayios Evstratios) during the post–Civil War period (1948–1952). He was arrested after the establishment of the **Colonels' Junta** (1967), held in various camps, and then exiled to the isle of Samos. M. Savvas points out how the poems in the collection *Time of Stones* (written 1949, publ. 1957) "give us a good look at the poet-as-exile on the island of Makronisos, a concentration camp filled with rocks, lizards, thornbushes, barbed wire and sadistic guards." During these periods of internment, his books were banned. His recognition as a major writer came late in his homeland. After 1957, his work was honored in Greece, Bulgaria, Belgium, Italy, and France. In the Soviet Union, he was awarded the Lenin Peace Prize (1976) and the Order of the October Revolution (1977) a few years after it had again become legal to join the Communist Party, which was banned between 1944 and 1974.

Ritsos's initial collections of poems were published in the mid-1930s (*Tractors; Pyramids*). At first he seemed unable to expunge the characteristic manner of **Karyotakism,** a kind of enduring pessimism related to the memory of the suicide–poet **Kostas Karyotakis** (1896–1928). Later came Ritsos's shocking lament *Funereal* (namely **Epitaphios,** 1936), a politically committed effusion of tears for a killed striking tobacco worker. Ritsos's best lyric verse, such as "The Moonlight Sonata" (1956), captivates by its mixture of elements from a poignant story with the beauty of landscape, and rough, populist items from the poet's left-wing ideology. The musical refrain of the opening voice in several reprises ("Let me come with you [. . .] / Let me come with you"), and the moonlight turning an observer's hair white and gold, modulate into statements of despair that choke the poem in **parataxis.** In all his verse, there is a reconciliation of mundane objects with cosmic ideas. He draws our eyes to a clock or a cup, while just off the stage we hear the cannons of war (see **Diminutive**). Raw left-wing hagiography is transfused into Ritsos's emblematic text, *Romishness* (see **Romiosini**) (1945–1947). The title means a "Greekness" encrusted in the values of **Byzantium.** Ritsos links martyrs and survivors of the Communist fight of the 1940s to this Romish, Hellenic, antiquity: "From now on each door will have a name chipped on it from somewhere in our three millennia." Half of the true believers will be dead, the other half in prison. They await their resurrection, in a new political order. Some of this hymn to the **resistance** was set to music by Mikis Theodorakis and became the anthem of the left.

Further Reading

Beaton, Roderick. "Lyricist of the Left." *TLS* 14–20 Dec. 1990: 1358.

Hadas, Rachel. "Two Worlds According to Ritsos." *Parnassus: Poetry in Review* 9, no. 1 (spring-summer 1981): 342–355.

Makrynikola, Ninetta. "Yanni Ritsos: Bibliography." *Mantatoforos* 12 (May 1978): 12–87.

Ritsos, Yannis. *Gestures and Other Poems.* Translated by Nikos Stangos. London: Cape Goliard Press, 1971.

Ritsos, Yannis. *Eighteen Short Songs of the Bitter Motherland.* Translated by Amy

Mims; with illustrations by the poet; edited and with an introduction by Theophanis G. Stavrou. St. Paul, MN: North Central Publishing Company, 1974.

Ritsos, Yannis. *The Fourth Dimension: Selected Poems of Jannis Ritsos.* Translated by Rae Dalven. Boston: David R. Godine, 1977.

Ritsos, Yannis. *Exile and Return: Selected Poems, 1967–1974.* Translated by Edmund Keeley. London: Anvil, 1990.

Ritsos, Yannis. *Selected Poems, 1938–1988.* Translated and edited by Kimon Friar and Kostas Myrsiades. Brockport, NY: BOA, 1990.

Ritsos, Yannis. *Scripture of the Blind.* Translated and edited by Kimon Friar and Kostas Myrsiades. Columbus: Ohio State University Press, 1979.

Ritsos, Yannis. *The Lady of the Vineyards.* Translated by Apostolos N. Athanasakis. New York: Pella, 1981.

Ritsos, Yannis. *Erotica.* Translated by Kimon Friar. Old Chatham, NY: Sachem Press, 1982.

Ritsos, Yannis. *Iconostasis of Anonymous Saints: Ariostos the Observant Recounts Moments of His Life and Sleep. Such Strange Things. With a Nudge of the Elbow.* Translated by Amy Mims. Athens: Kedros, 1996.

Ritsos in Parentheses. Translations and introduction by Edmund Keeley. Princeton, NJ: Princeton University Press, 1979.

Robinson, Christopher. "A Greek Baudelaire." *TLS,* 25 Oct. 1996: 26.

Savvas, M. *Books Abroad* 50, no. 3 (summer 1976).

RODOKANAKIS, PLATON (1883–1919)

This writer from Smyrna was also known as Rodokanakis-Souliotis, after his mother and his father's surnames. But he chose to use the former surname. He studied for the priesthood at Chalkis, but did not take orders. He journeyed across the Aegean (1916) and then devoted himself to Byzantine studies. In 1917 he became director of the Byzantine section at the Ministry of Education. His articles, essays, and **prose-poems,** much influenced by **Christomanos,** were collected in *De Profundis* (1908), *The Blazing Habit* (1911), *The Triumph* (1912), and *The Crimson Rose* (1912). In 1917 his Byzantine enthusiasms inspired the play *Saint Dimitrios, A Mystery in Three Acts,* staged by Marika Kotopoulis's **theater** group. It was published, like *The Queen and the Noblewomen of Byzantium* (1920), posthumously.

ROIDIS, EMMANUEL (1836–1904)

Novelist, essayist, **satirist,** and critic Emmanuel Roidis was born at Syros, in the Cyclades, and taken to live at Genova, where his father was Greek consul. In 1817 Stamathis Rodocanakis, known for his satirical poetry, married Catherine Roidis. As a girl, Emmanuel Roidis's mother was ransomed from Turkish merchants, who kidnapped her until the family paid $6,000 to get her back. Her son, our writer, moved from Genova to France, then Berlin, traveled for a while in the East, and eventually settled at Athens in 1863. For 20 years he was director of the National Library of Greece, a post to which he was appointed by Prime Minister Trikoupis in 1880. From time to time Roidis had to resign this post as a consequence of his political pamphlets, during the intervals when the butt of his satire, Deliyannis, was Prime Minister. Roidis inherited a fortune of 500,000 gold drachmas, three-fifths of which he lost in a stock market crash of 1873. He became deaf, was abandoned by his friends, and died in solitude. In his last few years he pioneered a short story manner based on psychological observation and personal memories of his childhood on the isle of Syros. A typical period piece is "Dog's Story" (1893), in which a political refugee smashes his leg doing a stunt for money and undergoes amputation without anesthetic, attended by the faithful Pluto; this dog is caught for vivisection, saved by the kindly surgeon, follows his master's scent toward a cemetery, and runs into stone-throwing boys. Though Roidis was a defender of the **Demotic,** his works were written in **Katharevousa.** A. Saris, in an analysis of 1956, calls him "participle lover" (φιλομέτοχος). As a scholar and translator into Greek, Roidis was indefatigable. He translated Chateaubriand's *L'Itinéraire* (1811), with its rapid, bird's-eye view of the Mediterranean including visits to Kerkyra, Sparta, Argos, Athens, Chios, Smyrna, Constantinople, Rhodes, and Cyprus. Roidis also translated T. B. Macaulay's *History of England from the Accession of James II* (written 1848–1861) and Edgar Allan Poe's "The Gold Bug" (which had won an 1843 literary prize).

Roidis wrote literary and historical articles (collected in *Parerga,* 1885). He published an important volume of essays, *Idols,* which promoted liberal causes, with a study on the **language question** (1893) and a surprising piece on Vyzantios's comedy of linguistic errors, *Babylon:* "The value of the play lies not so much in its frankly defective imitation of speech modes from different Greek provinces as in its felicitous representation of the character of each—the day-to-day wisdom of the Anatolian, the fierceness of the Albanian, the slyness of the Moriot, the pseudo-refinement of the Heptanesian, the Chiot's conviction that money is all-powerful, and so forth." In 1896, Roidis's article, "Greek Women Writers," concerning the author Arsinoé Papadopoulou, stirred controversy among literary men by posing the possibility of women in literature. Roidis's political pamphlet *Let There Be Light* attacked Theodoros Deliyannis, then Greek foreign minister, for his poor handling of the country's interests at the Congress of Berlin (1878). The book for which Roidis is particularly remembered is *Pope Joan* (1866), based on the spurious medieval story of a female Pontiff. Although there is no dialogue in the book, and it is written in **Katharevousa,** it is far from conservative in values, being a scorching satire on church life in the mock-historical manner. When the book was anathematized by the Holy Synod of Greece, Roidis composed four letters of rebuttal to the bishops and a further letter for the Synod. These were published in a contemporary newspaper under the pseudonym "Agrafiotis." The excommunication helped launch *Pope Joan* to a wider public. On the strength of its success, Roidis was invited to be the judge of a drama competition for 1877, instituted by the literary society **Parnassós** (founded 1865). He rejected all the submissions to that competition and wrote an interesting essay to accompany his verdict: *On the Present State of Poetry in Greece.* Here Roidis undervalues his contemporaries, argues that the time was not yet ripe for a renascence of Greek culture, and debunks the notion of neo-Hellenic literature: "Greece cannot hope for poetry at the present time, since she has denied her ancestral customs, and since she has yet to participate in the intellectual life of other peoples."

In the same year (1877), the intellectual **A. Vlachos** (1838–1920) wrote a response to Roidis. Vlachos admitted that the ambiance for literary creation was lacking in Greece, but he stressed the counterargument that writers needed an inner gift of inspiration. Roidis returned to the assault with negative comments on all contemporary writers, except **A. Valaoritis** and **A. Paraschos,** and some positive comments on the pioneers of the last 80 years, notably **A. Christopoulos, I. Vilarás,** and **D. Solomós** (see also **Asopios**). Of Paraschos, Roidis declared, with real insight: "In all his poems, we can admire cries that rise to his lips from the recesses of a genuinely sorrowing heart, as well as eloquently turned abhorrence, intensity of passion, and highly poetic metaphor, coexisting with repetitions and yawning gaps." In 1883, the newspaper *Estía* instituted a short story competition. Roidis was invited to sit on the jury, with S. Lambros and **N. G. Politis.** Many of his satires were published in the journal that he helped Themos Anninos found, *Asmodaeos,* and Roidis was for a while editor-in-chief of the magazine *Greece.* A witticism by Roidis has it that "each place suffers from something, England from fog, Romania from locusts, Egypt from eye diseases, and Greece from the Greeks."

See also CHRISTIAN; FEMINISM AND GREEK WRITERS

Further Reading

Macrides, Ruth. "'As Byzantine Then as It Is Today': Pope Joan and Roidis's Greece." In *Byzantium and the Modern Greek Identity,* edited by David Ricks and Paul Magdalino. Aldershot, Hampshire: Ashgate, 1998.

Roidis, Emmanuel. *Pope Joan: A Romantic Biography.* Translated by Lawrence Durrell. London: André Deutsch, 1960.

ROMAIC The influential linguist **Yannis Psycharis** composed a three-volume *Romaic Grammar* (1929–1937) and *Towards a Romaic Theater* (1901). For **pa**triots, "Romaic" is an accepted, technical term. It acts as the guarantee of a medieval tradition. Indeed, some argue that Greeks can be subdivided into an educated class, who identify with classical antiquity, and a subordinate class, whose memory turns toward Byzantium before the Turkocracy, that is, a second "Rome" (W. Spanos); the first group are Hellenes, the second group are Romish (ρωμιόι). After the nineteenth century, the adjectives meaning "Romaic" (ρωμιός or ρωμαίικος) could still mean "Greek." **Byron** knew the demotic pedigree of the adjective when he penned his "Translation of a Romaic Love Song," with couplets like "A bird of free and careless wing / Was I through many a smiling spring." Byron's translation of "I enter thy garden of roses, / Beloved and fair Haidée" has the singsong vigor of the Romaic, and his "Maid of Athens, ere we Part" (1810) imitates another Romaic song, with its iambic lilt "My life, I love you." It was translated in mock-popular vein by **Kambouroglous**: "Maid of Athens, ere we part / Give, oh, give me back my heart!"

Further Reading

Spanos, William V. "Yannis Ritsos' 'Romiosini': Style as Historical Memory." *The American Poetry Review* (Sept.-Oct. 1973): 18–22.

ROMANCE, BYZANTINE The romance is an adventure saga with alternating fortunes, starring a young couple who are separated and tested by events before being reunited: "Like ivy clinging to a tree, so the girl entwined herself with the young man, / And she was scarce to be untangled from him." Vitti comments that the romances are "vacuous and abstract like the shadow of a shadow."

Alexiou calls them "a bloodless, unheroic literature of escape." Greek romance takes up (in the thirteenth century) where the Greek **novel** left off (fifth century). The classical novel was replaced by "Lives of Saints," or biographies of emperors. Romance was brought to Greece in large part by the **crusaders,** when they overran **Byzantium** in the early thirteenth century. The chivalry of the Byzantine romance is Frankish and Western, with such elements as infatuation, falconry, equestrianism, tournaments, gallantry to women, and the clemency of rulers. The plot ingredients of romance include enchanted palaces, monsters, devices that render the wearer invisible (and confer supernatural powers), escape, shipwreck, disguise, and **recognition.** As a rule, the more manuscripts of a romance are preserved, the more popular it must have been. Some romances retell Trojan War material, like the fourteenth-century *Achilleid.* Longest and seemingly most popular of the medieval romances was *Livistros and Rodamni,* written by a demotic writer in Crete or Cyprus (where Frankish influence was strongest). The poem tells the twinned stories of Livistros and his ally Klitovós, who together rescue the royal wife of the former, Rodamni, from an Egyptian king who was assisted by a witch in abducting her. The beardless, short-haired aspect of the hero, and the fact that he carries a hawk, suggests a Frankish background. The romance *Kallimachos and Chrysorrhoe* may have been composed between 1310 and 1340 by the nephew of an emperor (Michael VIII was uncle to its putative author, Andronikos Palaeologus). Surviving, perhaps from the early fifteenth century, by way of a sixteenth-century manuscript, is *Velthandros and Chrysantza,* a work of 1,348 political lines.

The verse romance *Imperios and Margarona* is a popular Greek version of a French twelfth-century story, *Pierre de Provence et la Belle Maguelone,* which may have gone through a period of oral transmission before being recast in late fifteenth- and sixteenth-century Greek versions of around 1,000 lines. Some quatrains by **Palamás,** "From Far-Away Realms," repeat the motif in the modern era: "From far-away realms, / From the Middle Ages, / Imperios came by, / And Margarona came too. / This wild young knight, / And his beauteous princess, / They knocked at my door. / I invited them in. / And I taught them to tell / In my language, / With fiery words, / The travails of love." Derivative, to modern taste, are two surviving versions of *Florios and Platzia-Flora,* an early fifteenth-century Greek remake of the French twelfth-century romance, *Floire et Blanchefleur.* The basic plot concerns boy and girl. They are brought up together and fall in love. Change of fortune in this romance is effected by devices, like the magic ring that loses its shine when its wearer is in danger or the magic fountain that betrays the young lovers' tryst.

See also NOVEL

Further Reading

Beaton, Roderick. *The Medieval Greek Romance.* Cambridge: Cambridge University Press, 1989.

Fouriotis, A. Tὸ Μυθιστόρημα. Ἀπὸ τοῦ 2000 π. X. ἕως τὸ 1700 μ. X [The Novel from 2000 B.C. to 1700 A.D.]. Athens: Difros, 1959.

Meunier, Florence. "Le voyage imaginaire dans le roman byzantin du XIIème siècle." *Byzantion* 68, no. 1 (1998): 72–90.

ROMANTICISM; ROMANTIC Romanticism is an intellectual and artistic movement that spread all over Europe in the first half of the nineteenth century. It sprang from a new distrust in hard reality, and in literature it replaced the crude fact of living with a morbid sensitivity or with illogical flights of the imagination. Romantic poetry and fiction involved an attitude of escape, flight, and pessimism. Romanticism had two crucial strands. One, a combative Romanticism, produced the rebel stance of **Byron,** Shelley, Hugo, or Pushkin. The other, a resigned Romanticism, was more the fashion in Greece and France. Most Romantic writers were committed, however, to the ideal of patriotism, and to ethnic, national storytelling. Greek literature developed these aspirations, and a keen interest in Greek **folklore,** under **K. Palamás,** and in the verse outpouring of his so-called **New School of Athens.** Also the poets of the **Ionian Islands,** in the mid- or late-nineteenth century, followed one or the other strand of Romanticism: be it a Byronic melancholy, pride in the homeland, or the rediscovery of the love of nature.

Palamás himself dated the inception of Greek Romanticism to 1831, the year in which **P. Soutsos**'s *The Traveler* came out. Both Panayotis and Alexandros Soutsos revered the French Romantic poet Lamartine. They read other Romantic works from the West, and the *mal de siècle* entranced their imagination. Greek Romantic poets then released this creativity into the theme of cemeteries, tombstones, and dissolution. Several writers from this period succumbed to their "struggle to make a living." They died too young or committed suicide, like **Karyotakis, Karasoutsas, D. Paparrigopoulos, Vasiliadis, Panás, Krystallis, Vyzantios,** or the journalist Triantafyllos.

The encompassing dates of the Greek Romantic movement are 1830 to 1890.

These dates enclose a poetry of pale corpses, thwarted love, shrouds, lamentation, the slab above a tomb, twilight, and cold weather. In novel or theater, the hallmark of the Greek Romantic plot is a ghastly death. A performance of Victor Hugo's *Hernani* in Paris on 25 February 1890 is the swan song of Romanticism. Before this date, French and Greek Romantics had already begun to turn to **Parnassism,** that is, to a cult of formal perfection. Mirasgezi (1982: 116) notes the Greek Romantic writers' penchant for exclamation marks, rows of dots, and "prolonged ohs and ahs, and woe is me, and alas and alack."

For thirty years, **A. Paraschos** wove his repertoire out of "laurels," "myrtles," "willows," "grass," and "bay leaves," transcribing his tears for a Theresia, Catherine, Angelika, Lydia, Eleni, Henrietta, or Maria of the moment. Tsokopoulos once commented (in a 1925 lecture), that every girl from the *Arsakeion* (the Apostolos Arsakis foundation high school) copied a couplet by P. Soutsos into her **album**: "The leaf must dry, the flower must wilt, the world pass by, / For death alone, made ageless here, must never die."

ROMAS, DIONYSIOS (1906–1981)

D. Romas came from an aristocratic family, studied in Germany, and was later appointed secretary of the National **Theater** (1938–1952). After the discovery of the play *Efyena,* by Montseleze, Romas argued that Heptanesian theater could be redated to an earlier period and one less dependent on the arrival of writers, or actors, from Crete after that island's fall to the Turks (1669). He saw the **Ionian Islands** as "the most easterly boundary of the Western world and the most westerly boundary of the Eastern." He wrote a trilogy of novels about sixteenth-century Zakynthos mariners, naval battles, and the feuding of noble and popular factions on the island, *The Circumnavigation, 1570–1870* (1968). This work of historical fiction eventually won an Academy of Athens prize (1981). A further title in its containing nine-volume saga, *The Captain Count* (1968), was *The Affairs of Zakynthos.*

Further Reading

Romas, D. Τὸ ἐπτανησιακὸ θέατρο [Heptanesian Theater]. *Néa Estía,* (Christmas 1964): 97ff.

ROMAS, KANDIANOS YEORYIOS (1796–1867) The **Ionian Islands** poet Kandianos Romas published (1853) a collection entitled *Flowers,* with a dedication to his friend **D. Solomós,** and in 1856 another volume, entitled *Odes.* He was a leading light among the Zakynthos reform group. He became president of the Ionian Islands Assembly. He wrote patriotic articles and sketches in **Heptanese** newspapers.

ROME, GREEK COLLEGE AT The Greek College of St. Athanasios at Rome was planned by M. Mousouros (1470–1516), the famed editor of **Plato.** The Ginnasio Greco had been instituted on the Quirinal Hill by Pope Leo X, following a suggestion by the **humanist** scholar **Janos Laskaris,** who became its first director. The Ginnasio Greco was short-lived (1516–1521). Among its pupils were Nikolaos Sofianós and Matteo Devario. Sofianós was the first theoretician and grammarian of the Greek vernacular (see **Plain Greek; Demotic**). He produced a study of the ringed astrolobe, which he dedicated to the Pope (c. 1542). More influential was the Greek College

in Rome's Via del Babuino, founded by Pope Gregory XIII in accordance with a Bill of 13 January 1577. Among the pupils of the Greek College was the bibliophile **Leon Allatios** of Chios (1588–1669). Allatios wrote the long iambic song *Hellas* to the Dauphin of France, later King Louis XIV, for his birthday in 1638, hoping the future king might resolve to liberate Greece (see **Turkocracy**). A printery was set up at the Ginnasio Greco. A stream of Greek scholarship students worked at St. Athanasios in the sixteenth and seventeenth centuries, often coming via Padua or bound for Venice, which hosted other Greek schools and intellectuals. Iason Sozomenos, a seventeenth-century Cypriot writer, taught rhetoric at Rome and wrote a commentary on Aristotle's *Poetics.* Ioannis Sozomenos, also from Cyprus (d. about 1626), studied philosophy and Greek at Rome and went on to teach at the College. Later he became superintendent of the Marciana library at Venice and drew up a **catalogue** of its manuscript and printed holdings. He annotated Plato's *Republic* and Longinus's *On the Sublime.*

ROMIOSINI *Romiosini,* the Greek word for "Greekness," comes from the notion that **Byzantium,** and hence modern Greece, is a "new Rome." Thus a word that seems to mean "Romishness" (ρωμιοσύνη), refers to contemporary Greek culture as a continuation of world dominance under the Western Empire (Rome), which Byzantium supposedly annexed. As for "sorrow at being Greek," **Seferis** thought this phrase so deeply Hellenic that any translation should be regarded as a distortion.

Sultan Mehmet started his final assault on Constantinople on Monday 28 May

1453. The date of the fall of Roman Byzantium was Tuesday 29 May, so for Greeks Tuesday is a day of evil omen. When the Sultan went to conquer the residual Comnenus empire at Trebizond, the ballad makers mourned: "Romania has passed away; Romania is conquered." **Palamás** has a poem that starts "O Roman spirit, o my true mother!" Mirasgezi notes that **Eftaliotis** was attacked for calling his work a history "of Romiosini" rather than "of Hellenism." Soteriadis argued that the word "Romish" (that is, "Greek," in the sense of Ρωμιός) means "a base and vulgar man, and so should not be employed." In October 1901, Palamás published an article "Romish and Romiosini" in which he stressed that the terms were honorable and historically sanctioned. He observed that, in **demotic songs,** the term *Romios* was preferred to *Hellene,* and *romiopoula* was preferred to Hellenopoula ("Greek kids"). Palamás was then attacked for "denying the name *Hellenes* to the Hellenes."

N. G. Politis wrote an article, "Hellenes or Romans," pointing out that in demotic songs both words are found. In the *Song of Vlachavas,* the terminology for **patriotism** is quite clear: "*Romios* I was born, and I shall die a *Romios.*" To denote a modern Greek citizen, Romios might be written instead of Hellene, to convey a notion of cultural superiority and historical evolution. **Makriyannis, Kolokotronis,** and Miaoulis fought (as P. Green notes) for this new Rome, as well as for independence. It is "the Byzantine traditionalism that fused medieval Orthodoxy with populist balladry and stubborn klephtic resistance under the centuries-long Turkish occupation."

It has been suggested that debate and representation are the characteristics of Greekness (ελληνικότητα). Although the quintessential Greek feeling in literature is *romiosyni,* certain parasites crept into this spirit during Turkish rule and could not be flushed out. According to Spandonidis (1962), these parasites are the overvaluation of "smartness" (ἐξυπνάδα), a lack of simplicity, and suspiciousness (κακυποψία).

"Blindly given over to the honey of our sun," cries Seferis about the Greeks. This metaphor from his poetry is one of many representations of the ambiguously ardent star that hangs over Greekness. **Ritsos** cries out in the poem *Romiosini* (1945–1947): "All have been petrified, trees, rivers and voices, in the whitewash of the sun."

Further Reading

Green, Peter. "Inventing Greece: Nationalism and the Hellenist Dream." *TLS* 12 (April 1996): 4–6.

Runciman, Stephen. *The Fall of Constantinople: 1453.* Cambridge: Cambridge University Press, 1965.

ROTACISM. See PRONUNCIATION

ROUFOS, RODIS (1924–1972) Career diplomat and novelist Rodis Roufos produced (1972) a **trilogy** entitled *Chronicle of a Crusade,* consisting of three novels originally published in the 1950s under the pseudonym Rodis Provelengios. Like his colleague, the writer **Th. Frangopoulos,** Roufos based one of his fictional protagonists on the historical figure Kitsos Maltezos, a friend of theirs who was murdered by Communist partisans in February 1944 (Mackridge 1988: 96). There is a sequel by Roufos to the *Chronicle of a Crusade,* entitled *The Age of Bronze.* This latter diary-journal (1960), picks up the story of the character, Dion, based loosely on the author's own self and values, to dramatize the struggle for independence in Cyprus.

Further Reading

"Athenian" [pseudonym of Roufos]. *Inside the Colonel's Greece.* Translated and intro. by Richard Clogg. London: Chatto & Windus, 1972.

Mackridge, Peter. "Testimony and Fiction in Greek Narrative Prose, 1944–1967." In *The Greek Novel: A.D. 1–1985,* edited by Roderick Beaton, 90–102. London: Croom Helm, 1988.

Roufos, Rodis. *The Age of Bronze.* London: Heinemann, 1960.

ROUSANOS, PACHOMIOS (1509–1553) The theologian and scholar Rousanos, born at Zakynthos, became a monk when young, but expanded his zeal beyond the anchorite's cell, founding schools at Chios and Lesbos and traveling in Epirus, Thessaly, Macedonia, and Smyrna. He was one of Greece's first transcribers of dialect and **folklore.** In 1564 he observed: "It is possible for distant inhabitants of the fields to speak Greek in a more skilful way than town dwellers, for in town people try to alter their words into something stylish, out of snobbishness. This just makes things worse, and unreasonably they scoff and jeer at farmers and villagers." He visited Venice, but always argued for Orthodoxy against **Catholicism.** He wrote various interesting letters; his manuscripts were published in 1734.

RULE OF THREE Readers soon detect a rule of three (νόμος των τριών), a pattern of tripling, in the **demotic song.** In *The Suffering Bride,* lines 4–8 make a list and create a climax: "Her father gives her a fitted ship; / Her brothers give her a loaded wagon; / Her mamma gives her a goblet of pearls, / And a gold throne to sit on, a gold apple to play with, / A gold-rumped mule to ride on." Here there are three sets of gifts; the third is finest. Also there are three gifts made of gold; the third is the most ostentatious. Some exploits in *Diyenís Akritas,* the first great narrative in modern Greek, trace thematic patterns, like a list of sins of the hero, or a set of *three* tests, or marriage by abduction. A set of *three* challenges occurs when the hero meets, first, a three-headed dragon (followed by a lion), second, a challenge from a cohort of warriors, and third, a challenge from the allies of an Amazon, and the Amazon (Maximó) herself. This leads to a fight scene in *Diyenís Akritas,* a Byzantine version of Hector versus Achilles, in **Homer.**

RUSSIA A **demotic song** from the period of Turkish domination evokes Greece's simple faith in a saving army from the Russian north: "Just one more spring, / Bondsmen, o bondsmen, / One summer more, / O sorrowing Roumeli, / Until the Muscovite comes, / Bondsmen, o bondsmen, / To bring the campaign / To Morea and Roumeli." Greece and Russia are linked by their shared religion, conspiratorial distrust of Turkey, shipping, commerce, and exchanges between merchants, officers, and writers. Some Greeks were tutors to the Tsar's family. Constantine VII Porphyrogennetos describes, in one of the encyclopedic works attributed to him, the tenth-century trade highway from the Baltic Sea that passed along various rivers of Russia, up the Neva and Volkhov, and down the Dnieper, to reach the Black Sea, and Constantinople. Greek writing cultivates a myth of salvation from the North (see **King Turned to Marble; Philikí Etairía; Vizyinós**). **K. Dapontis** (c. 1713–1784) attributes to the seventeenth-century divine **Y. Vlachos** a *Triumph against the Reign of the Turks,* subtitled *Hortatory Address to the Ruler of Moscow Alexis Mikhailovich.* Vlachos encourages Peter the Great's father to save Greece from Turkish rule.

In 1859 **Spyridon Zambelios** published *On the Establishment of the Patriarchate in Russia.* Zambelios here writes an introduction to a reprint of a poem, in 1620 **political lines,** by Arsenios (c. 1548–1601), archbishop of Elassona, who made a journey in 1588 to escort Patriarch Jeremias II Tranos as he went about establishing the Muscovite **Orthodox Church.** Dimarás notes the charm of the eyewitness narrative by Arsenios. Trypanis finds its merits very limited: "When the Tsar saw us, he stood up from his throne / And down he came with a scepter in his hand." In Russia, the Christian religion was first spread by missionaries from **Byzantium.** It was the religion of the Kievian state by the year 988. From 1037 to 1448, the Russian church was run by a Metropolitan elected by Constantinople. The Russian church acquired its autonomy after the Metropolitan of Kiev became a signatory of the Union of Florence. In 1589, the Metropolitan of Moscow, Job, was appointed Patriarch. He became fifth in seniority, ranking after the patriarchs of Constantinople, Alexandria, Antioch, and Jerusalem.

See also THEOTOKIS, NIKIFOROS; VOULGARIS

Further Reading

Constantine VIII. *De Administrando Imperio,* vol. 1. Edited by G. Moravcsik and translated by R.J.H. Jenkins. Washington: Dumbarton Oaks, 1967.

Meyendorff, John. *Byzantium and the Rise of Russia: A Study of Byzanto-Russian Relations in the Fourteenth Century.* Cambridge and New York: Cambridge University Press, 1981.

Obolensky, Dimitri. *Byzantium and the Slavs.* Crestwood, NY: St. Vladimir's Seminary Press, 1994.

S

SACHLIKIS, STEFANOS (before 1332–c. 1403) Sachlikis was a Cretan from a wealthy family in Candia (Iraklion) who, during Venetian rule, fell foul of the court and was sent to **prison** for obscure offenses. He drew on the Duke of Crete's influence to gain release and subsequently work as a lawyer. Sachlikis wrote an amusing autobiographical tirade in 908 **political verses,** with scattered use of end-line rhyming. It is the first example of this format in modern Greek poetry (see **Rhyme**). Sachlikis strikes the pose of eyewitness, to convey the unhappy lot of the convict: "Those lice, in prison, are just like gnawing bugs, / And those prison fleas seem to me a crowd of fat ants," and "As souls are punished down there in the nether world, / So too prison punishes human beings in life." *Strange Narrative* relates Sachlikis's release and return among the vicious lawyers of the town of Candia. There are warnings, in the poems of Sachlikis's apparent old age, against dice, low living, and women of pleasure to a youth called Frantzeskis. These are collected in the so-called *Verses, and Interpretations.*

See also ADYNATON

SACHTOURIS, MILTOS (1919–) Sachtouris was born in Athens to a well-known Hydra family, and like other writers, he studied law but did not practice. He published volumes of verse (1945, 1948, 1952, 1956, 1958, 1960, 1962, 1964, 1971, 1977, 1980, 1986), which familiarized educated readers with his compassionate, macabre, and terrified poetics. The critic Yiorgos Themelis saw Sachtouris's product as "bloodshed made myth, death-in-life, a message among the most lethal and bitter ever uttered in Greek verse." He won the State Poetry second prize (1964) and a First Prize, shared with N. Karouzos and Takis Varvitsiotis (1972). He glosses his work in "The Poet Militant": "Poems, no, poems are not / What I have written; / I merely nail Crosses / On tombs."

Further Reading

Dallas, Yannis. Εισαγωγή στην ποιητική του Μίλτου Σαχτούρη [Introduction to the Poetics of Miltos Sachtouris]. Athens: Keimena, 1979.

Sachtouris, Miltos. *Selected Poems.* Translated with intro. by Kimon Friar. Old Chatham, NY: Sachem Press, 1982.

Sachtouris, Miltos. *Strange Sunday: Selected Poems, 1952–1971.* Translated by John Stathatos. Frome, Somerset: Bran's Head: 1984.

SACRIFICE OF ABRAHAM The 1,144 rhyming lines of the *Sacrifice of Abraham* constitute the masterpiece of postclassical Greek theater. Composed some time between 1586 and 1635, it may come from the youthful hand of V. Kornaros, author of *Erotokritos*. This attribution is partly based on the presence of telltale phrases in both works. Y. Mavrogordatos (in an article of 1928) identified the prototype for *Sacrifice of Abraham* in a religious play, *Lo Isach* (publ. 1586), by the Italian writer Luigi Groto. The Greek author eliminates the prologue and choruses in his Italian source, discarding its division into separate scenes. He uses the characteristic 15-syllable rhymed couplets of the Greek popular tradition. The treatment is down-to-earth and full of homespun psychology. Sarah says she knows Abraham cannot sleep, and Abraham grumbles that he cannot reveal why. Abraham talks plaintively about God's command, while loyal slaves go round trying to look on the good side of things. Both the Angel and Sarah refer to young Isaac as "little pet." Sarah's cries against his fate have the exemplary vigor of popular *mirologia* (lamentations): "Bewail the command, the Voice, the agony in my heart, / Bewail the light that has scorched me, and the trembling in my body!" Our author uses folk elements from **Cretan** writing: aphorisms, blessings, parables, **metaphors,**

and **rhetorical questions,** such as "Who sent the light of my eyes into exile?" or "How are my eyes to see it, how is my hand to manage it, / How is my body to go along with it, trembling like a reed?" The many early editions of the *Sacrifice of Abraham* printed at Venice (1668, 1694, 1709, 1719, 1746, 1755, 1760, 1777, 1798) attest the popularity and diffusion of this retelling of the Bible story (*Genesis* 22), in which Jehovah tells Abraham to slay his son, and at the last moment an Angel stays his knife.

See also THEATER, SEVENTEENTH CENTURY

SAINTLINESS, FEMALE. See FOLK-LORE

SAKELLARIOS, YEORYIOS (1765– 1838) A learned doctor, like his friend and fellow Macedonian M. Perdikaris, Yeoryios Sakellarios wrote a *Summary of Greek Archaeology* (Vienna, 1796), translated Barthélemy's *Young Anacharsis* (a version finished by **Rigas**), owned a collection of classical coins, and may have written a play after **Shakespeare** (1789). He collected his poems in *Lyric Poems* (Vienna, 1817), some gloomy on the death of his wife, some tingling on the foreshores of **Romanticism,** some reproving **Christopoulos** for his hedonism, but clearly influenced by this "second Anacreon." More than once he makes mistakes in the spelling of Homeric epigraphs over his compositions (D. Ricks).

SAMARAKIS, ANTONIS (1919–) After law studies, Samarakis worked for the Greek Ministry of Labor. He later traveled extensively in Europe, Africa, and America to represent the Ministry and as a delegate of the International Labour Organization. Samarakis is a novelist, story writer, and poet, who fought in the **resistance** against the German **occupation** and took a strong stance against the **Colonels' Junta.** He went on two UNICEF missions to Ethiopia (1980s), in response to world concern over famine in northeast Africa. His short stories are characterized by a terse manner, in the tradition of the Mitteleuropean figure acting on his own, aware of his inadequacy inside some reactionary apparatus. Spare and ironic prose dominates in *Wanted: Hope* (1954), with its sketches on the twilight of ideology. An ex-resistance fighter, now a disenchanted Communist, sits and smokes in a café, reading in his newspaper about Korea and Indochina. After scanning headlines like "Massacre on Both Sides," he spots the "wanted" and "for sale" column. He walks to the newspaper's office, to insert an ad requesting "hope." Equally terse are the stories of *Danger Signal* (1959). Samarakis progresses toward longer narrative structures in *I Refuse* (1961), *The Jungle* (1966), and the novel *The Flaw* (1965), which E. Jahiel ranked with the works of Kafka, Koestler, or Orwell. Six stories from *The Jungle* and three other stories written for periodicals between 1971 and 1973 were collected in *The Passport.* In the eponymous story, we have an inept poet whose travel abroad is blocked by an allegorical system resembling the Junta (which confiscated Samarakis's own passport). The censors here rule that a harmless poem is dangerous, but then allow a subversive text to be broadcast. Preoccupied with a police state, the author warns that there can be no such thing as neutrality. In *I Refuse,* an ex-resistance fighter goes to a riverbank opposite his childhood home (blown up as a reprisal by the Germans). Our hero skipped stones across the water more neatly "in

the old days," but he is now there to finalize "the other matter." He repeats this phrase in order to avoid the bourgeois sentimentality of the term *suicide.* In 1992, Samarakis published *The Close Shave,* eight stories about a garrulous barber or a cop who hides his whisky in a jar of correcting fluid.

Further Reading

Jahiel, Edwin. "Antonis Samarakis: Fiction as Scenario." *Books Abroad* 42, no. 4 (autumn 1968): 531–534.

Samarakis, Antonis. *The Flaw.* Translated by Peter Mansfield and Richard Burns. London: Hutchinson, 1969.

Samarakis, Antonis. *The Passport and Other Stories.* Translated with an introduction by Gavin Betts. Melbourne: Longman Cheshire, 1980.

SARCASM Sarcasm is bitter or brutal **irony,** turned with animosity against the author himself, the forensic speaker's adversary, or some other entity. The classical rhetoricians tended to classify sarcasm as a figure of thought, rather than **figure of speech.** Etymologically the gibe or taunt, in sarcasm, tears "flesh" (σάρκα) off its target.

SATIRE Literary satire involves the use of sarcasm or gross language to comment on a fact of society. In modern Greek examples of the genre, the author shows disgust for the things he writes about, and his satire becomes a grid of loose and coarse references to those things. Whatever situation is posed, it is then wrapped up and delivered in a mocking style. Often the target is the church or oppressive churchmen. In the medieval period, the target may have been the rich, who never seemed to help the poor. The Royal Family in the nineteenth century was another target of this genre.

The late-Byzantine *Mass of the Beardless Man* (or *Spanós*) refers with obscenity to a priest offering his daughter to a eunuch, and the target is the castrating pomp of the Orthodox liturgy. *The Mass of the Beardless Man* is a parody of the divine offices, in a 1553 codex of a fourteenth-century (or earlier) work. We read such caustic gems as "Blessed are the wicked beardless ones, for they shall be called sons of goats" (at line 1220). "On Old Men and Why They Should Not Marry a Young Girl" is a fifteenth- or sixteenth-century poem in 199 rhymed **decapentasyllables,** possibly by a writer from Zakynthos or Crete. It contains satirical motifs from classical times, such as "an oldster is all silvered like a goat in its fold," and "you need to marry a youth of your own age." It shares some lines with the Indian didactic narrative *Hitopaedesa,* and Boccaccio's *Ameto.*

Early manuscripts (from 1824) of the national poet **Solomós** contain similar attacks on personalities. The "Dream" resurrects the figure of the satirical poet Koutouzis (d. 1813), who was a fanatical opponent of the democratic party on Zakynthos (see **Painting**). Koutouzis lashes the character of Ioannis Martinenkos, who once led a faction strongly opposed by the poet's own father, Nikolaos Solomós. The unfinished "Woman of Zakynthos" (1826–1833) by Solomós, narrated by a lofty monk, features a decaying, whorish, ultimately unidentifiable local woman who represents all that is ungenerous and antinationalist in relation to ladies from **Missolonghi,** who used to beg on behalf of the besieged. The satire "The Hair" attacks Napoleon Zambelis, a lawyer who appeared for Solomós's probable half-brother in their family dispute. A dwarfish Catholic priest, later seen to be a disguise for the Devil, appears in the poet's dream and places the hair of a whore (or Zambelis's mother) on a pair of weighing scales. Whatever men are placed on the other side of the scales, the one with the hair is always heavier.

In the notes for a satire called "The Hanged Man," a knight–lawyer condemns a **Klephtic** robber to the noose. He sees the corpse of the man, once a cosoldier of Botzaris, jerk its head toward Greece, facing it as he drops. The knight is homosexual. His father is a moneylender, who betrays his friends as willingly as his country. Later, on Zakynthos, there were two short-lived satirical periodicals called *Snake* (founded 1873; 1880).

Minos Lagoudakis published (1922) a satirical record of manners, *Mr. Parlayvous Francais and Mrs. It's-a-Long-Way.* The author was a nephew of the Lagoudakis who issued broadsheets of the poems of **Kavafis.** Lagoudakis's text traces the disappointments and reverses of two likable, morally unimpeachable, young lovers. The heroes provide a contrast to Thessaloniki's turn-of-the-century, multiethnic, opportunistic, moneygrubbing society. Lagoudakis uses irony, derision, sarcasm, and even fury to pillory the ways of his age. There is influence from the translations of contemporary French popular prose and an analogy with the political commitment of **Kondylakis.**

See also TSAKASIANOS

Further Reading

Solomós, Dionysios. "The Woman of Zakynthos." Translated and introduction by Peter Colaclides and Michael Green. *Modern Greek Studies Yearbook* 1 (1985): 153–171.

Tsantsanoglou, E. [with 10 others]. Σάτιρα και πολιτική στη νεώτερη Ελλάδα

[Satire and Politics in Modern Greece]. Athens: Society for Studies in Modern Greek Civilization & General Education, 1979.

SATIRICAL DRAMA At Zakynthos, in 1745, a play by Savoyias Soumerlís, *Comedy of the Quack Doctors,* or *Those of Ioannina,* was put on and caused an uproar. In five acts, like the Cretan plays, it pillories the activity of four quack doctors from the Epirus and their behavior on Zakynthos, laced with digs at the ruling nobility on the island. We know of a play by Soumerlís entitled *Those of the Morea,* which apparently contained social content, and a play called *Fiorenza,* based on items from *Erotokritos.* Another surviving Soumerlís play is a compact dialogue in short five-line strophes called *Mistress Elia,* in which a procuress, Lia, urges a young girl called Miliá to take a lover, but the corrupter is tied up and handed to a judge.

SCHISM. See PHOTIUS

SCHOOL; SCHOOLING Evyenios Yiannoulis (1597–1682) was among the first writers to call for free schooling. His letters exhorted Greeks of all ages to turn to education and training. He founded the schools of Agrafa, was educated in a monastery, and while on a pilgrimage to the Holy Land met Patriarch **Loukaris,** who ordained him (1619). He took classes with **Korydalleús** at Zakynthos and then (1636–1639) in Constantinople with Meletios Syrigos. He ran a school at Arta, others in Aetolia, and one at **Missolonghi.** He established a school for advanced studies at Karpenisi. At times, his educational impulse went as far as providing board and lodging for poor pupils, anticipating today's scholarships.

Later came the primary, or "start-up school" (σχολαρχείο), which refers to a school of three grades, for children aged 10 to 13. **Kondylakis,** in a novel of 1916, has a boy at primary school who can only learn the phrase "O Cross, help us," which in those days was uttered before reciting the alphabet. Nowadays, primary school is followed by high school (γυμνάσιο). From early in Turkish rule come rumors of a Greek secret school (κρυφό Σχολείο). Supposedly these were reading and writing classes for the children of Greeks, to whom education had been forbidden. Secret classes were taught by altruistic priests at night, outside towns, in a church or a cellar. A **demotic song** fosters this romantic image: "Shining little moon of mine, / Shine for me so I may pass, / So I may go to school, / To learn my letters, / Letters for study, / The business of God."

Adamantios Adamantiou (1875–1937) exemplifies the link between Greek schooling and literary careers. He studied Literature at the University of Athens and was then appointed a primary school headmaster at Ermoupolis, chief town on Syros (in the **Cyclades**). From this remote job (on an island that **Homer** called rich in flocks), Adamantiou progressed to a professorship at Taïyani (Russia) and later made a contribution to the provision of better textbooks and readers in the school system.

SCIENCE FICTION The science fiction genre is called, in Greece, ε.φ. (from the initials of the two Greek words for science fiction, επιστημονική φαντασία). It is well entrenched, in Greece, with its own fanzines (fan magazines), clubs, periodicals, **literary competitions,** and an astral UFO-contact research series. Historically, Greek science fiction began with journeys to the moon, in the prototypes *True History* and *Icaromenippus* by Lucian of Samosata (c. 115–c. 180 A.D.). Lucian was followed, 16 centuries later, by E. Dimitriadis (1760–1827). His *Selections* (1797) deal with a future society (μελλοντική κοινωνία) in the year 2100. These stories challenged Greeks, long before the French science fantasy writer Jules Verne (1828–1905), with futuristic motifs. The hero falls into a centuries-long sleep and wakes to a world of inventions, such as the telephone, control of epidemics, traffic policemen, skyscrapers, and synthetic food. In 1924, Petros Charis published his first book *The Last Night of the Earth,* which contains his eponymous story about world panic after the news that a comet will destroy planet Earth (in 1910). Here the maid is told which lights to leave on in the house, while Greek families slip away to the hills. Yet the stars come out, the moon sets, and a scent of pine blows by. In 1930, Yeoryios Tsoukalás wrote *The Invisible Man,* about a pirate with the magic power to disappear from his enemy's sight. Tsoukalás is one of the first to exploit the theme of the invisible man (αόρατος άνθρωπος), used by H. G. Wells (1866–1946), and already present in **romance.** In later novels of the 1930s, P. Pikrós (*The Man Who Lost Himself; From the By-Gone World to the Future*) adapted Fritz Lang's 1929 film *Woman on the Moon,* or placed three Greek kids in a time warp (χρονοστρέβλωση). He used standard gadgets of the modern genre like robots, flying saucers (ιπτάμενοι δίσκοι), and rockets that propel ships.

From 1929 is a text by the mainstream writer, **D. Voutyrás,** *From the Earth to Mars,* applying the science fiction formula of a discovered Utopia. Five Greeks visit the planet Mars. They stumble across a perfectly regulated community. Creatures of all sizes speak **demotic** Greek and live in harmony, but they tear each other to bits when brought to Earth. Voutyrás tried science fiction again with *Counterfeit Civilizations* (1934), in which five Greeks stumble on an underground society at the South Pole. The inhabitants have devised artificial suns and rainfall, making giant seas and lakes. One of the Pole-dwellers returns with the travelers to Europe, where he experiences the "false" cultures of the title. In some Greek science fiction novels, like Angelos Doxas, *The Planet Grows Dark* (1946), the solution is interstellar flight. In Athanasios Tsonkas's *Pirates of the Planets* (1948) a team of Greek experts needs the help of a mechanical man. In 1952, Virginia Zanna became the first Greek woman to compose a volume of science fiction stories, in *Journey to the Moon and Other Matters.* Zanna was followed by many other women into this genre, such as Calliope Venizelou, who used (1957) the idea of an electric submarine-airship, or Francesca Stellakatou, *Travelling to the Moon and Mars* (1963), who used the hypermodern "hard" (σκληρή) science fiction fantasy style, or Maria Labouraka whose *The Planet with Life* (1967) won a gold medal of the International Academy of Letters, Arts and Sciences (Paris, December 1972). Alki Youlimi is a woman writer who adapts science fiction material for children, as in *The Destruction of Antaios* (1974), a story about a prototype magnetic car called "Antaios." Anna Safiliou, in *Simon's Secret* (1977), writes science fiction for smaller kids. Nitsa Jortjoglou arouses the reader's affection, in *My Visitor Totó* (1977), for a tiny extraterrestrial (εξωγήινο). Jolanda Pateraki, in *Moon-*

men on the Earth (1978), uses the well-worn theme of men from the moon. A staple interest is UFOs ("Unidentified Flying Objects"). This acronym is adapted to ATIA, to stand for άγνωστα ιπτάμενα αντικείμενα ("unknown flying objects"). In the 1990s came the themes of acid rain, the black hole, and cloning (κλωνοποίηση).

Further Reading

Panorios, Makis. "Greek Fictitious Literature and Science Fiction: The Decades of 1970 and 1980." *Hellenic Quarterly,* no. 9 (June–August 2001): 43–46.

Theodhorou, Nikos and Christos D. Lazos. Βιβλιογραφία Ελληνικής Επιστημονικής Φαντασίας (από το Λουκιανό μέχρι σήμερα) [A Bibliography of Greek Science Fiction, from Lucian to the Present Day]. Ioannina: Zosimas Central Public Library, 1998.

SCRIPTS When the Venetian occupation of Crete became stable, in the sixteenth century, its cultured class chose to write Greek in Latin script. This was in line with their acceptance of Greek popular traditions, but their maintenance of Catholicism. **Frangochiotika** was a Latin phonetic spelling of Greek, used in **Catholic** propaganda sent from Rome to Greek Catholics in the **Heptanese** during the seventeenth and eighteenth centuries. The priest and travel writer Ignatios of Nazianzou (1739–1820) used the Greek alphabet for his Turkish translation of Jeremias Sinaite. In the late nineteenth century, the Constantinople newspaper *The East* ran an edition in Turkish, using Greek characters. A learned monk of the eighteenth century, Germanos (1775–1805), founded a school for Greek children in Asia Minor who only spoke Turkish and translated books from the Old Testament into Turkish for them, while writing improved texts in Turkish, with Greek characters.

Further Reading

Zakhos-Papazahariou, E. "Babel balkanique: histoire politique des alphabets utilisés dans les Balkans" [The Babel in the Balkans: Political History of Alphabets Utilized in the Area.] *Cahiers du Monde Russe et Soviétique* 13, no. 2 (April 1972): 145–179.

SEA The Mediterranean is traversed by a family of winds, each with a name of its own, filling the sails in many Greek books inspired by the sea (North Wind, from-the-mountain-wind, N.-Easter, N.-Northeaster, E. Wind, the S.-E. Wind, S.-Easterly, the South Wind, Southerly, Sou'wester, Nor'wester, the North-West Wind, annual N.-Easter, W. Wind, west breeze of spring). A poem by Sarantaris (1908–1941) cries "O dove of the soul, farewell, / I bid you adieu with the *Meltemi,* / Kiss any pearls which you see, from me." Tasos Leivaditis (1921–1988) calls on the prevailing breeze in "Our Lady of the South Wind": "Young sailors of the east wind greet you from the sky." The sea is at the heartbeat of Greek writing. **Seferis** muses: "The sea swells indolently, the rigging shows its pride, and day proceeds to sweetness."

This Romantic stance toward the sea is partly because there are no rivers that can be navigated in Greece. The Corinth Canal (1839), by cutting the Isthmus, turned the Peloponnese into an island. The classical geographer Strabo said of Greece "the sea presses in upon the country with a thousand arms." The large islands (Euboea, **Crete,** Heptanese, Dodecanese, Rhodes) make a kind of sea kingdom, matching the mainland in extent. The country's only good harbors are Piraeus, Patrai, and Kerkyra. Xenophon describes, in *Anabasis* (c. 370 B.C.), the cry of his advance guard, "At last, the sea!" when they glimpse the coast.

The word *sea* subsequently spawns a prodigious repertoire in modern Greek literature. Writers use it to form compound words, like "Aegeanish," "a swarm of men," "seafarer," "in sun-kissed Cyprus." Kazhdan observes that the image of a ship on a stormy sea is common in Byzantine literature (1984: 263). Among the many hundreds of modern Greek writers on the sea, **Elytis** writes one line that is a whole allegory of Greek waters: "Fishing, the sea arrives." In 520 A.D., Mousaios Grammatikos refers to a storm with graphic verve: "Then the water leapt up, wave rolled onto wave / And the heavens and sea were made one." Later, in medieval times, the romance of the sea was blunted by piracy, whereas in the **demotic song,** there is an explosion of reflection about sea, storm, shore, net, boat, fish, gull, rock, wave, tears, drowning, and grief.

There is a tart vignette on sea commerce in "Ship comes from Chios, / Moors on the sand, / Bears ladies from Chios, / And from Vlachobouchtania. / They came to the mole, / And parceled them out, / Pricing by kisses, / The value of each one." Another demotic song tells the sea that if it drinks the poet's tears, as well as estuaries and rivers, it will become ever wider. The novelist Emmanuel Lykoudis (1849–1925), familiar under the journalistic pseudonym Fajax, winner of the Literature Prize for 1923, published several sea stories in the 1920s. "The Withering" is about a dog that gets rowed to shore from a lugger because it fails to bark at thieves; it never moves from the spot where it is dropped on land. Nikos Veliotis (b. ?1905), from Ios in the Cyclades, worked as deckhand, captain, and customs broker, bringing his experiences to life in *Sea Birds* (1955) and other books.

Yannis Manglis (b. 1909) wrote about drunken sailors killing for a woman, or about a tailor, needing to earn a dowry for his daughter, who loses his life in a helmet and diving suit as he tries to prospect underwater for the first time. Yorgos Thrabalos (b. 1926), in a story from *The Lost Tomorrow* (1956) manages to portray a lighthouse-keeper who shoots his wife in an act of jealousy because she talks too long with one of their boatmen suppliers. The writing of Kostas Faltaïts (1891–1944) looks back at a sailor's experience in the **Balkan Wars,** from which he sent regular features to the paper *Acropolis.* Faltaïts wrote several works based on the life of the simple deckhand and naval combatants, like *The Wreck of the Helle* (1919), and was wounded while covering the Asia Minor expedition (1921–1922) as a correspondent for the paper *Forwards.*

The sea also represents the verdant paradise of youthful love: "My early years, those unforgettable years, I lived them! / Down by the shore, / The sea that lay there, shallow and calm" (**Palamás,** from *Yearnings of the Lagoon*). A noted war novel is *The Broad River* (1946), by **Yannis Beratis.** The last sentence of this book foretells absorption into the sea, as an assessment of postwar peace: "Sea, ancestral memory; the path is clear!" Kambanis (1971: 271) calls the **Sikelianos** poem "Beach with Cattle" an "exceptional seascape" (θαλασσογραφία). This critical phrase shows how writing about the sea is on a par with landscape painting for Greeks. The written "seascape" becomes a genre of its own. In her "Thanksgiving," writer and painter **Athena Tarsouli** (1884–1975) declares

"In blue-white foam, / In sweet-scented flowers, / With light, I grow drunk." The tesselated haze of **blue and white,** in the Aegean, becomes an invitation for synesthesia (when different senses perceive the same object): "You succumb, sweetly dizzy, you are tipsy, and you declaim sounds without meaning over its rhythm" (**S. Myrivilis**). For other writers, sea is a **metaphor** of work, or poignant longing (πόθος), or the **diaspora,** or **xenitiá:** "We, the men, soar upwards to the sky / To glut ourselves on the distant glimmer" (Y. Sarantaris). **Seferis** calls it a reality that is never consumed: "However, I do not think people have exhausted the sea." The poet **Varnalis** writes: "Would that I could scan you, Sea, and never have enough of you." Y. Molfetas (b. 1871) evokes St. Yerasimos of Cephalonia, who protects the population of his island and grants benediction to "each honorable sailor / Who battles day and night with the wild beast of the sea wave, / So his mother, alone in her village home, may suffer less hunger."

The sea is a temple priestess, in a text by **I. M. Panayotopoulos**: "The mystical hour is ready for descent into the depths. / I bend to utter words in your ear, / So I may sense your swirling like ringlets of hair on my skin." In his *Novel,* Seferis hints that Greeks inclined toward the sea because their land was dry. They observed a marine adventure because the harbor and the shore were ambiguous: "We don't have rivers, we have no wells, no fresh springs. / Only a few empty cisterns, which echo as we bow down to them." In a **sonnet** by **Drosinis,** "Our Town," a setting has white, miniature houses that set sail, "spread in single clumps across the opposite sea, / Scattered, companionless, thinly woven / Chunks of stone." **Sikelianós** states the exaltation of sea odors for the man-goat, in the last two lines of his "Pan": "smelling the froth-foamed marine until dusk." Drosinis says: "When sweet on the sea blows the North-West wind, my mind is exalted." **N. Lapathiotis** (1888–1944), in "Musings and Queries," launches a simile posing as a definition: "The sea is like an everlasting poem, or like a limitless melody, which has the waves as its lines and the foam as its rhyme."

Further Reading

Constantinides, Elizabeth. "Love and Death: The Sea in the Work of Alexandros Papadiamantis." *Modern Greek Studies Yearbook* 4 (1988): 99–110.

Higgins, M. D. and Reynold Higgins. *A Geological Companion to Greece and the Aegean.* Ithaca, NY: Cornell University Press, 1996.

Panayiotounis, Panos N., ed. Θαλασσινὴ ποιητικὴ ἀνθολογία [An Anthology of Sea Poems], 21–203. Athens: Dodekati Ora, 1968.

Papadiamantis, Alexandros. Θαλασσινὰ εἰδύλλια [Sea Idylls]. Athens: Mari, 1961.

Warmington, Eric Herbert. *Greek Geography.* New York: AMS Press, 1973 [first ed. 1934].

Warn, Faith. *Bitter Sea: The Real Story of Greek Sponge Diving.* South Woodham Ferrers, UK: Guardian Angel, 2000.

SEFERIS, YORGOS (1900–1971; pseudonym of Yorgos Stylianou Seferiades) Some commentators (for example, N. Pappás) have been dismissive, claiming that the towering poet Seferis really wrote weak poetry, angled for privilege, cultivated acolytes, absorbed too much T. S. Eliot, was prone to plagiarism, and shilly-shallied over political commitment. Yet if the true sign of genius is a posthumous productivity (Goethe's phrase), then Seferis is a signal example. His novel *Six Nights on the Acropolis* and most of his prodigious correspondence have come since he died. The seven volumes of Seferis's personal diaries, *Days,* quarried so far from the archive of his unpublished work at the Gennadius Library (Athens), cover the years 1925 to 1960. Two volumes of his *Political Diary* have been published posthumously, covering the years 1935 to 1952; one is still to come. He was the first Greek writer to win the Nobel Prize for Literature (1963). Born in Smyrna, he moved with his family from Asia Minor to avoid disturbances leading up to the outbreak of World War I. He thus became another in a long line of Greek writers to represent the **diaspora.** Seferis was at high school in Athens during the period 1914–1918. He later went to Paris (where he is said to have experienced great loneliness) to study law. Returning to Greece, he entered government service (1926–1964) and subsequently took diplomatic posts overseas (1931 to 1962). His first slim volume, *Turning-Point,* was published in Athens (1931). It represented innovation and an exercise in renewing the versified stanza (στροφή). His **pseudonym** is derived both from his patronymic (his father was a professor and accomplished writer) and from the Arabic word for "journey," *sefer,* which also has this meaning in Turkish. Seferis once wrote that "the first thing God made is the long journey" (in "Stratis Thalassinos Among the Agapanthi," written in Transvaal, South Africa, in 1942).

The destruction of the Asia Minor outposts of **Hellenism,** such as his birthplace, Smyrna, in the Greco-Turkish War of 1922 gave Seferis a sense of loss and nostalgia. **Images** of marine animals, of **sea** travel and drifting uncertainty char-

acterize many parts of his large output in verse. He was influenced by Rimbaud (1854–1891), Mallarmé (1842–1898), and *The Waste Land* (1922). Seferis published a modern Greek translation of *The Waste Land* in 1949. It is packed with news about Eliot, with letters to and from the American poet, visits to his broomcupboard office in London, and their walks. Later, he added a translation of three other Eliot texts (1936): "Difficulties of a Statesman," "Marina," "The Hollow Men." Seferis's glosses and annotations, both on Eliot and his Greek translation, are candid and informative. The last edition of his book of Eliot translations represents a wrestling, by Seferis, to match the range and quaint allusiveness of T. S. Eliot's critical pieces (on **Dante,** or the metaphysical poets). Seferis stresses the determining influence of the French poet Jules Laforgue (1860–1887) on Eliot. This is obvious, but prompts a feeling that Seferis was preoccupied by the youthful cessation of writing in any author. Laforgue's premature silence (when aged 27) was perhaps more interesting to Eliot and Seferis than Rimbaud's similar defection at 18. Laforgue: "Ce soir un soleil fichu gît au haut du coteau" reminds Seferis of Eliot's "Come let us go, you and I." Seferis wrote criticism, for example, *On the Greek Style: Selected Essays in Poetry and Hellenism.* He translated T. S. Eliot's play *Murder in the Cathedral* (1965).

From his earliest poems, Seferis sought an arcane but chatty tone, inserting images that possess enormous evocative power. He addresses Jerusalem as "drifting city," or he compares 1938 with its imminent threat of Nazism to "a thousand scythe-bearing chariots," or watches "how the water blossoms at the rudder." Seferis moves us by his meditation on collective experience: "in the light that other people see things, / The world is spoiled." He notices that "the poem is everywhere / Like the wings of the wind." He strives to renew both the manner of expression and the writer's way of seeing objects in nature. He writes "our life shrinks every day." He asks, ironically, "[H]as anyone considered the suffering of a sensitive pharmacist on night duty?" His starting-point is the status of men in a world that is basically alienating. Dreams are "a school of forgetfulness," and "Each person dreams separately without having anyone else's nightmares" (from *Three Secret Poems*). The isolation of the individual leads to a colloquium of suffering. In Seferis's verse, the simplest phrase can acquire a violent force, as in "the inexplicable hurricane" or "a rotund stone," or a mouse "who is gnawing the floor" (πού ροκανίζει τό πάτωμα). Single nouns acquire a strange and turgid menace, like "loophole" (πολεμίστρα), "horse dung" (καβαλινά), "candelabra" (πολυέλαιος), "coffin shop" (φερετροποιεῖα), "shutters" (παραθυρόφυλλα), and "mosquito net" (κουνουπιέρα). Seferis's reader is arrested by the panoply of nouns that denote weather conditions: "frost," "fog," "mud," "damp," "stench," "sulphur," "wind," "storm," and so forth. In his glancing manner, Seferis mentions a "here" that is an island place of muddled weather realities: "At this place where the passing of the rain and the wind and destruction meet, / Here exist faces, emotions, a pattern of love" (from "The King of Asine"). Climatic phenomena swirl above a population that includes (in different poems) a ghost, sea-monster, cow, buffalo, ewe, slave, she-wolf, camel, kingfisher, wagtail, peacock, eagle, hangman, refugee, sea-urchin, defrocked nun,

anaesthetist, introverted snob, farmer, merchant, slanderer, cook, archer, counselor, disembarked sailor, money changer, suitor, or go-between. Keeping an odd balance, there are unnamed women, with soft skin and full breasts, sometimes addressed as "you."

In the mid-1930s, Seferis began to overcome his metaphysical anguish and achieve a kind of reconciliation with the contemporary world. He discovered the scenario of Hellenism with its cultural baggage and mythical symbols: war, the **Asia Minor disaster,** national frontiers. He established a relationship between the epic of a wandering Odysseus and the drama of modern Greece, balanced uneasily between Anatolia and Europe. The fatalism of his early poetry gave way to a notion of the saving cosmos of Hellenism. This is enshrined in the country's luminous landscape and warm, voluptuous sea, which promote images of justice and harmony. He plays with ambiguous, opulent verbs, like "lie in warmth" (λουφάζω), "be filled with tears" (βουρκώνω), σκοντάπτω ("stumble"), "grope" (ψηλαφῶ—his favorite verb), "squirm" (σφαδάζω), "promenade" (σεργιάνω), "crackle" (πλαταγίζω), "dazzle" (θαμπώνω), and "get tuberculosis" (χτικιάζω). His enigmatic title Μυθιστόρημα (1935) is translated by Roderick Beaton as *Novel.* Keeley and Sherrard prefer to retain the Greek noun, *Mythistorema.* Rex Warner translates it as "Myth of Our History." A French translation (Lacarrière) opts for *Légendaire.* Seferis used the title in the sense of "fictional process." It is a long prose sequence, where the poet asks: What can our soul seek from the timbers and stones of sea travel? Sherrard suggests that Seferis answered this by apprenticeship to the complexity of language, writing far more rejected poems than those eventually published.

Seferis adopted a policy of political noncommitment, which he only broke twice. In 1955 he published a volume of poems dedicated to the people of Cyprus, apparently espousing a nationalist stance and proposing that the position of the intellectual should be to support ENOSIS (Union of Cyprus with Greece). In March 1969 he made a statement about the **Colonels' Junta** (1967–1974): "Now for some months I have felt, within me and around me, that more and more it is becoming imperative for me to speak out on our present situation." The 18 members of the Royal Swedish Literary Academy awarded the Nobel Prize to Seferis "for his eminent lyrical writing, inspired by a deep feeling for the Hellenic world of culture." In his acceptance speech, Seferis hinted that the award was for modern Greek, rather than for his own writing. He explained that the language he championed was one that had been spoken for centuries but had not received honor in its present form: "I belong to a small country, a rocky cape in the Mediterranean Sea, which possesses nothing of any value other than the struggle of its people, the sea, and the light of its sun. Our place of origin may be a small one, but its tradition is colossal and its most characterizing element is the way it has been handed down to contemporary Greeks without interruption; for Greek never ceased being a spoken language." In *Logbook I,* Seferis pays attention to a paramount topic in the poem "Return of the Exile." Here he describes the delusions of the man living in expatriation: "In your nostalgia you have formed / The image of a non-existent land, / Alien to the real earth and its inhabitants." Seferis asked who could tell the truth about the catastrophes of his century. Who was to choose between the Greeks and the Turks, when each claimed that the other side burned down Smyrna?

He expressed the misery of lost love in the poem "Word of Love." The humanity of Seferis's verse, and its acceptance across cultures, comes from the consolation of Nature. Sea, sky, pasture, and mountain are shown in fine-veined consciousness. His poetry leads us to acceptance, even a mystic return to a mother and rebirth. His late translation of *The Revelations of St. John* shows that the struggle to convey the mystery of life stayed with him to the end. To other Greek poets, Seferis once gave a reminder that poetry is the only job in which you cannot lie. To **Theotokás,** in a letter of 1931, Seferis quoted Mallarmé on "the unfilled sheet of paper protected by whiteness," and also the mysterious program involved in "giving a purer sense to the words of the tribe." When Seferis wrote the phrase "twisting spindles," he was reviving the dying island culture that provided him with such words as *yardarm, bowstring, loom, ploughman's rod,* and the *bowsprits* that lunge out in front of the *caique,* as it traverses the *glare* of his Mediterranean. Melancholy was always close to exaltation for Seferis: "there is an absolute blackness behind the golden web of the Attic summer." Lawrence Durrell commented that Seferis's observations on poetry and life "tumbled into the mind like pebbles down an empty well and echoed on for years."

Adamantios Diamantis dedicated his music "The World of Cyprus" to Seferis. It was played at an international conference on the occasion of Seferis's centenary (29 February 2000); Diamantis also composed songs based on the poet's "Cypriot Poems."

Further Reading

Beaton, Roderick. *Seferis.* Bristol: Bristol Classical Press, 1991.

Keeley, Edmund. *Six Poets of Modern Greece.* Chosen, Translated and Introduced by Edmund Keeley and Philip Sherrard. New York: Knopf, 1961.

Krikos-Davis, Katerina. "At the Smyrna Merchant's: Aspects of George Seferis as Revealed in his Personal Diaries." *TLS,* 20 Oct., 2000: 13–14.

Levi, Peter. "George Seferis." In *The Art of Poetry: The Oxford Lectures, 1984–1989.* New Haven: Yale University Press, 1991: 209–233.

Politis, Linos. *A History of Modern Greek Literature.* Oxford: Clarendon Press, 1973: 230–238.

Seferis. *The King of Asine and Other Poems.* Translated by Bernard Spencer, Nanos Valaoritis, and Lawrence Durrell. London: John Lehman, 1948.

Seferis. *Poems.* Translated by Rex Warner. London: The Bodley Head, 1960.

Seferis. *On the Greek Style: Selected Essays in Poetry and Hellenism.* Translated by Rex Warner and Th. D. Frangopoulos and introduction by R. Warner. Boston: Atlantic-Little Brown, 1966.

Seferis. *Collected Poems 1924–1955.* Translated and edited by Edmund Keeley and Philip Sherrard. Princeton, NJ: Princeton University Press, 1967.

Seferis. *Three Secret Poems.* Translated by Walter Kaiser. Cambridge, MA: Harvard University Press, 1969.

Seferis. *Days of 1945–1951: A Poet's Journal.* Translated by Athan Anagnostopoulos. Cambridge, MA: Belknap Press of Harvard University Press, 1974.

Seferis. *Mythistorima and Gymnopaidia.* Translated by Mary C. Walton. Athens: Lycabettus Press, 1977 [bilingual].

Sherrard, Philip. *The Wound of Greece: Studies in Neo-Hellenism.* London: Rex Collings, 1978, 94–107.

Vayenás, Nasos. "Seferis' Six Nights on the Acropolis: The Diary as Novel." In *The Greek Novel: A.D. 1–1985,* edited by Roderick Beaton, 54–62 London: Croom Helm, 1988.

SÉGUR, NICOLAS (1874–1944). See EPISKOPOPOULOS

SELF. See INTROSPECTION

SENTENCE STYLE Lengthy sentences in Greek prose gradually went out of fashion. The desirable sentence now consists of a main clause with few, or no, clauses in modification. In contemporary Greek style, the main verb is no longer accompanied by a set of dependent verbs in the same sentence. **Parataxis** is seen as a sign of clarity, even a guarantee of sincerity (ειλικρίνεια), a Greek preoccupation reminiscent of Walt Whitman's championing of "perfect candor" as a feature of poetry. Twentieth-century Greek critics urged a writer not to be long-winded (which is also called perissology) and to avoid **babbling.**

SEPTUAGINT The **Greek Orthodox Church** regards the *Septuagint* as the standard text of the Old Testament" (Waskey, in *FD:* 1519). According to **legend,** it was a team translation of the Old Testament into **Greek.** It was ordered by Ptolemy II Philadelphus (285–246 B.C.) and done by "the 70 scribes." This special muster of translators (perhaps 72 in number) was dispatched from Jerusalem to Alexandria and worked on an island in the Nile. Their work set a historical standard for Scripture. It absorbed non-Greek (that is, Semitic) words into a learned vocabulary and molded anthropomorphic Hebrew expressions into the imaginative flights of the **Hellenistic.** It initially consisted of the *Pentateuch,* namely *Genesis, Exodus, Numbers, Leviticus,* and *Deuteronomy.* By 130 B.C., the other Old Testament books had been translated and added to the *Septuagint* by different contributors. Further mystical books written by Jews in Greek also made their way into this omnibus Scripture. They are now retained, or rejected, as the *Apocrypha.*

Further Reading

Dogniez, Cecile. *Bibliography of the Septuagint, 1970–1993.* Leiden and New York: Brill, 1995.

SEVEN WISE MASTERS. See SINDIBAB

SEVENTEENTH-CENTURY ERUDITION The seventeenth century is a season of Greek scholarship, much of it done far away from Greece. Literature was silent at Athens. From the mainland came some works of **liturgy**: *Pentekostarion, Canons and Prayers, Horologion, Anthologies of Canons,* and *Paschal Canons.* A book on Aristotle's logic by **Sougdouris** was published (1792) by Ioannis Karatzás at his own expense. Karatzás (1767–1798) was a conspirator with **Rigas,** murdered by the Pasha of Belgrade (with Rigas and five others) in the first, abortive uprising. The Chiot monk Grigorios Chrysovelonis (1604–1679) trained teachers who founded colleges at Constantinople, Patmos, and Smyrna: he composed a *Convention on the Seven Mysteries.* From Epirus came Nikolaos Kerameús, who studied in Italy and then went to Constantinople as a teacher. From 1663 to his death (1672), Kerameús taught at Jassy. He composed theological and philosophical essays, among them "On Friendship and Love."

Nathanael Xykas, an intellectual from Athens, was priest of the Greek parish in Venice and taught from 1614 to 1617 at the Greek college there. He composed a *Manual Concerning the Primacy of the Pope* (Leipzig, 1869; also translated into Arabic), and two dissenting works on the Latin church. Grigorios Murmekousianos, a pupil of Yeoryios Koresios, became abbot of the New Monastery of Chios and senior archimandrite of the Great Church (at Constantinople). Murmekousianos composed a *Synopsis of Sacred and Religious Doctrines of the Eastern Church* (Venice, 1635). Another Chiot scholar, Zakras Libios, taught in the Greek school at Venice from 1602 and was later professor at Ferrara University.

Emmanuel Timonis, from Chios, studied medicine at Padua (and later Oxford); an expert on smallpox, he was appointed professor at Padua (1691) and published "Methods of Propagation of Smallpox by Insect or Vaccination, as Practised at Constantinople" (1713). N. Comnenus Papadopoulos (1661–1740) was sent from Crete, aged 12, to the Greek college of Rome (St. Athanasios). He embraced the Catholic faith, became a Jesuit, and rose to prominence as a canon lawyer. He held that the differences between the Orthodox and **Catholic** churches were insubstantial. In the volume *Praenotiones Mystagogicae ex jure canonico* (1697, *Guiding Principles from Canon Law*), Papadopoulos attacked the views of Margounios, Bishop of Cythera, and Yeoryios Koresios. His *History of the University of Padua* (Venice, 1726), though written in Latin, includes valuable information about sixteenth- and seventeenth-century Greek writers. Ioannis Abramios, son of Cretan parents in Venice, was ordained by the Archbishop of Philadelphia (formal title for the Orthodox primate of Greeks in Venice), became priest of the parish of St. George's, and taught in the community school (1694). In 1691 he edited a reprint of *Convention on the Saintly and Holy Mysteries,* first published in 1600 by Gabriel, "Bishop of Philadelphia." Abramios issued the *Edifying Book of Psalms* by Bishop Theodoritos of Cyprus, translated by Brother Agapios of Cyprus (Venice, 1692), and *The Twenty-Four Houses of Our Most Holy Everlasting Virgin Mary Mother of Christ* (Venice, 1695), a paraphrase in **plain Greek** by Brother Kallonás, from the Ankaranthos Monastery of Kithuria. Meletios Kallonás, abbot of the celebrated Ankaranthos (in Crete), won fame as a **hymn** writer. Kallonás translated the *Acathistus* into plain Greek (Venice, 1695) and collected sung canons for the service "Miracles of the Virgin Girt with Myrtle" (published 1744). In 1709 Abramios issued an anthology of poems to honor the degree conferral of Yeoryios Hypomanís, "noble and most learned doctor from Trebizond." Abramios's anthology was dedicated to Hypomanís's patron, Ioannis K. Bassarabas, Prince of Wallachia. Bassarabas's chief doctor was Ioannis Comnenus (last surviving member of the old imperial family), another cleric educated in Italy. From 1680 to 1700, Comnenus taught physics at Bucharest and took the style Hierotheos when appointed Bishop of Silistria. He wrote a *Devotional Book of Mount Athos.*

Ioannis Makolas translated Ovid's *Metamorphoses* (Venice, 1680) into plain Greek. Another priest, Ioannikios Markorás (from Kerkyra), wrote the scientific treatises *On Meteors* (1642) and *On Metals* alongside religious tracts; it was a familiar curriculum for an intellectual of this period. Andreas Marmarás, descen-

dant of a marriage into the imperial Comnenus family, wrote a history of Kerkyra in eight volumes (Venice, 1672). This was translated from Italian into Greek by Andreas's descendant Ioannis Marmarás (1902). A protonotary of the Great Church, Philip the Cypriot, composed a *Chronicle of the Church* (published by Nikolaos Blankardos, 1679), which was translated into Latin and printed in Leipzig as *Chronicon Ecclesiae Graecae* (1681), with a commentary by Errikos Hilarios. The monk Petros Moyilas, who came from an old Moldavian family, rose to be Metropolitan of Kiev. Moyilas wrote several learned works, partly to blunt Protestant and Catholic propaganda, including *Liturgical Offices* (1629) and *Orthodox Confession* (1642). The latter was adapted by the Cretan theologian Meletios Syrigos (d. 1664). Bearing the Patriarch's *imprimatur,* it later became a key work of Orthodox doctrine. The monk Athanasios Gordios (c. 1650–1729) came from Braniana in the Agrafa area (Thessaly) and studied in Athens and Italy. He trained other educators (Theofanis of Agrafa, Mikhail Mavrommatis) and composed an array of learned works: *On the Nature of the Kingship of Mohammed and Concerning the Antichrist, On Syllabic Quantities in Individual Words, On Noun Terminals and Methods of Spelling,* together with a catalogue of fauna and flora: *A Nomenclature of Four-Footed Livestock, Birds, Fish, Trees, Fruit, and Plants.*

Further Reading

Henderson, G. P. *The Revival of Greek Thought, 1620–1830.* Albany: State University of New York Press, 1970.

Makrides, Vasilios. "Science and the Orthodox Church in Eighteenth and Early Nineteenth Century Greece: Sociological Considerations." *Balkan Studies* 29, no. 2 (1988): 265–282.

SEXUAL THEMES Kordatos (a **Marxist** critic) comments loftily that the poet **Napoleon Lapathiotis** (1888–1944) took narcotics, was sexually deviant, joined the *Hegeso* group, stayed at home all day, and went out at night to satisfy his amorous desires. **Romos Filyras,** a contemporary (1889–1942), is said to have devoted his energies to women, caught syphilis, and died of it. The cult of the flesh (σαρκολατρεία) is at the heart of the four volumes of *The Common Man* by **G. Xenopoulos,** a novel all about an individual who falls in love with every woman he meets. There is a scene with mirrors, which infinitely multiply the embrace of an ardent couple in the fitting room of a dressmaker's. Xenopoulos's novel *Teresa Varma Dakosta* contains passages like "With me, at least, albeit unwillingly, she actually enjoyed moments of pleasure that made her quiver and faint." Papadimas, a near-contemporary of Xenopoulos, blames these flights of the pen on the "obvious sexual thirst" of an age when love affairs were not permitted.

Closer to our time, V. Raftopoulos published *Loula: A Novel* (Athens: Kedros, 1997), 450 pages on a heroine whose inability to reach orgasm takes her on a certain quest. Katerina Tsemperlidou has *No More Sex, Let's Just Be Friends: Short Stories* (Athens: Modern Times, 1997), analyzing physical relationships from a humorous viewpoint. In **V. Vasilikós,** *Brushwood of Love: a Novel* (Athens: Nea Synora, 1997), a sophisticated plot is flooded with sexual themes. A collection of short stories by Sotiris Dimitriou (b. 1955), *My Little Child, My Little Christ* (1987), explores deviant characters, a woman who turns her young son into a transvestite whore or another woman whose grief at her son's death is converted into a violent passion for his best friend. Andreas Stafylidis says, in an encyclopedia of Greek literature from 1000 to 2000 A.D. (1996: 259): "Sexual stories, which concern base instincts and passions, are designed to stimulate the imagination of the reader towards the improbable cosmos of sex. They are usually linked to crime. This is not literature, but a coarsening of art to its lowest level."

See also FEMINIST POETRY; HOMOSEXUALITY

Further Reading

Dubisch, J. "Greek Women: Sacred or Profane?" *JMGS,* no. 1, 1983: 185–202.

Loizos, P. and Evthymios Papataxiarchis, eds. *Contested Identities: Gender and Kinship in Modern Greece.* Princeton, NJ: Princeton University Press, 1991.

SHAKESPEARE, WILLIAM (1564–1616) There is a tradition that the doctor–poet **Sakellarios** wrote a five-act *Romeo and Juliet* in prose (1789). The first Greek Shakespeare translation was by Andreas Theotokis: *Macbeth* (1819). The influence of Shakespeare on Greek literature came later, after the 1850s, when the English dramatist was repeatedly translated. **Iakovos Polylás** published a translation of Shakespeare's *Tempest* (1855), followed by his translation and an influential commentary on *Hamlet* (1889). The playwright Dimitrios Vernardakis, in a preface to a German edition of his work (1858), praised Shakespeare as a people's poet. The writer **Angelos Vlachos** (1838–1920) translated *King Lear, Macbeth, Othello,* and *Hamlet.* The poet **Stratigis** translated *A Midsummer Night's Dream.* The writer and philanthropist **D. Vikelas,** with his versions of *Romeo and Juliet, Othello, King Lear* (1876), *Macbeth, Hamlet* (1882), and *The Merchant of Venice* (1884), made Shakespeare accessible to the man in the street. Vasilis Rotas (1889–1977) in 1930 founded the People's Theater and wrote dramas based on patriotic topics like **Missolonghi, Rigas,** and **Kolokotronis.** Rotas translated all 35 Shakespeare plays, helped (according to N. Pappás) by his partner Voula Damianakou (b. 1914). The novelist **Konstantinos Theotokis** (1872–1923) did *Tempest, Macbeth, King Lear, Othello,* and *Hamlet.* K. Karthaios (1878–1955: pseudonym of Kleandros Lakon), a leading radical in the **language question,** translated *Richard III* and *Macbeth.* These versions were both played in the Kotopoulis Theatre. **Anghelaki-Rooke** more recently rendered *The Taming of the Shrew* (1989).

Further Reading

Karagiorgos, Panos. "The First Greek Translation of Shakespeare." *Shakespeare Translation* 2 (1975): 65–73.

SHEPHERDESS. See VOSKOPOULA

SIEGE OF MALTA Written by Antonios Achelis of Rethymno (fl. c. 1560), the *Siege of Malta* (1571), like most early modern Greek classics, was published in **Venice.** A chronicle in verse consisting of 20 sections running to 2,500 lines, it brings to life an assault on Malta (1565) by Turkish forces and the defense of the island by the Knights of St. John, who a generation earlier had been driven off the island of Rhodes (1522).

SIGOUROS, MARINOS (1885–1961) Sigouros, a diplomat, historian, and biographer of the **Heptanese** poets, believed in the splendor and primacy of **Solomós.** He translated the *Sonnets* of Petrarch (1304–1374) and asserted the tight kinship of Italian and Greek culture. **K. Theotokis, S. Martzokis, Tsakasianos,** and Sigouros are the last guardians of the flame that shone for a while from *The Free Besieged.*

SIKELIANÓS, ANGELOS (1884–1951) Born on the Heptanesian island of Levcas, Sikelianós became a neo-Hellenist visionary. He spent his childhood in a cultivated, Greek-speaking environment. He went on to study law at Athens for a short while, before turning to full-time writing. His first important work, *The Light-Shadowed,* was written in early 1907 and privately published in 1909. Its title picks up two lines from Solomós's enigmatic masterpiece *The Free Besieged:* "Light-shadowed seer, what did you see last night? / Miraculous night, night sown with magic!" Both the Solomós and Sikelianós texts announce the confidence of the two poets and their fidelity to plebeian images and the **demotic song.** Sikelianós's *The Light-Shadowed* has over 2,000 lines, in a mixture of free and metrical verse, with unexpected **rhyme** choices. Between 1913 and 1915, he published some **sonnets** and assorted poems in *Aphrodite Urania,* "The Song of Calypso," "Pan," "John Keats," "Thaleró," "The Mother of Dante," "By the Cold Waters, by Pentavlí," as well as victory songs based on incidents from the **Balkan Wars,** historical landscapes, or pieces dedicated to other Greek writers, like the Corfiot **Lorentsos Mavilis** (b. 1860), who fought on Crete in 1896, at Epirus in 1897, and then died in battle at Ioannina (1912), or Alkiviadis Yannopoulos (1896–1981), who returned from Italy to Greece for World War I.

Sikelianós traveled all over Greece, absorbing its monuments and art; studying classical literature by himself; devouring Orphic writing, Aeschylus, and Pindar; and preparing the ambitious synthesis of Hellenist and personal spiritualism that spilled forth in his *Prologue to Life* (1915–1917). This work was published privately in four parts, each consisting of a "Consciousness": namely "The Consciousness of My Earth," "The Consciousness of My Race," "The Consciousness of Woman," "The Consciousness of Faith," characterized by **free verse,** rapid digressions, and the incorporation of pre-Christian, pantheist sources. This *Prologue to Life* was complemented three decades later by *The Consciousness of Personal Creation* (1943–1947). Sikelianós was fascinated by the Greek religious mysteries of Eleusis, Delphi, and Olympia and by what he knew of matriarchal cults. The mystery and Orphism of Sikelianós's early writing blossomed in his *Mother of God* (1917–1919), an attempted configuration of a new collective **myth** in a new musical **structure.** Here the primary unit is the rhymed couplet (**distich**), in a traditional 15-syllable line. It looks back to the Aeolian elegiac couplet and to classical Greek **epigram.** The Madonna's lament over Christ's death may have absorbed some of Sikelianós's mourning for his sister Penelope (who had married the brother of the American dancer Isadora Duncan). Some cantos of *Easter of the Greeks* were published in 1918 and later revised for the 1947 edition of Sikelianós's complete works, *Lyric Life.*

Easter of the Greeks (unfinished) was a bold attempt to reinterpret the **myth** of Christianity in narrative verse. Sikelianós directed his poetry increasingly toward the lofty ideal of religious syncretism.

His *Sacred Way* (1935) evokes the road to the primitive shrine of the mother–goddess Eleusis, and several poems of the 1940s, such as "Lilith," "Doves," "Study of Death," and "Jesus at the Gates of Zion," foreground sacred elements inside the familiar lush texture of his lyric. He was forging ahead with his Delphic project, fueled by the enthusiasm (and funds) of Eva Palmer, an American graduate student in Paris. He met Eva in Athens and married her in Bar Harbor (near New York) in 1907. He made other trips: to Italy, France, Libya, and Palestine. Like **Palamás,** he wrote a youthful Delphic hymn. From 1921, he started giving talks and speeches on his Delphic ideal. His dream was to establish an international center of peace and goodwill at Delphi, where the Amphictyonic Council, a first League of Nations, once held assemblies. In 1927 and 1930, he and his wife, with hundreds of volunteers, organized the Delphic festival. Their plan was to link mankind to the wellsprings of the classical past and achieve cosmic fraternity after the most frightful war in human history. There was talk of founding an international university at Delphi. Sikelianós put on Aeschylus's *Prometheus Bound* and then *The Suppliants* at the two Delphic festivals, in a format as close as possible to antiquity, using danced choruses, costumes copied from folklore, Byzantine music, and authentic outdoor settings. His Delphic festivals were supposed to conjure up the Pythian Games, which welcomed ancient Greeks to athletic contests on the southwest slopes of Mount Parnassus and were held, like the **Olympic Games,** every four years. Here at Delphi, in Phocis, the god Apollo once had his shrine and delivered his prophecies through the mouth of the Pythian priestess.

Sikelianós's festivals thus took place in a highly charged symbolic setting, the center of ancient Greek religion. They featured a public fair, dancing, the recital of Greek **demotic songs,** naked wrestling, and exhibitions of folk art. In 1933 Eva and Angelos staged his neoclassical play *The Dithyramb of the Rose* in a theater on the hill of Philopappos, opposite the Acropolis of Athens. It was the first of his tragedies and such was his creative enthusiasm that it was written in a week (published 1932). Eva Sikelianós then went back to America to raise more money for the Delphic festival and continued preaching its related ideals. She was cut off in America by World War II and even accepted (1939) Sikelianós's relationship with another woman, Anna Karamani, whom he married in 1940. Eva Sikelianós and her daughter-in-law, Frances, translated Angelos's *Dithyramb of the Rose* into English (1939). Eva returned to Greece in 1952, died, and was interred at Delphi. Sikelianós gave a public reading of his tragedy *The Sybil,* just after Greece and Italy went to war (1940). In this play, a Roman emperor journeys to Delphi to consult the oracle. Next came the tragedies *Daedalus in Crete* (1943) and *Christ in Rome* (1946). *Sybil* was published in 1944 and *The Death of Diyenis* in 1947. The play *Asclepios* (unfinished) came out posthumously in 1954. The first of the three volumes of Sikelianós's collected verse, *Lyric Life* (1946–1947), reprinted the author's presentation of his poetry, vigorous and unorthodox to a degree. This prologue sparked fiery debate when it appeared in *Néa Estía* (1942). Two special issues of *Néa Estía* (no. 611: 1952 and no. 936: 1966) were later devoted to him.

Further Reading

Sherrard, Philip. "Anghelos Sikelianós and His Vision of Greece." In *The Wound of Greece: Studies in Neo-Hellenism,* 72–93. London: Rex Collings, 1978.

Sikelianós, Angelos. *Six Poems from the Greek of Sikelianós and Seferis.* Translated by Lawrence Durrell. Rhodes, 1946.

Sikelianós, Angelos. *Akritan Songs.* Translated by Paul Nord. New York: The Spap Company, 1944 [bilingual].

Sikelianós, Angelos. *The Dithyramb of the Rose.* Translated by Frances Sikelianos, privately printed by Ted Shawn [U.S.A.], 1959.

Sikelianós, Angelos. *Selected Poems.* Translated by Edmund Keeley and Philip Sherrard. Princeton, NJ: Princeton University Press, 1979.

SIMILE Simile, or comparison (πα-ρομοίωση) is the most recognized device in modern Greek poetry. It occurs with conspicuous frequency and variety, from Byzantine to modern times. The simile is generally accompanied by ως ("as, thus"), or σαν ("as, like"), or "equally," or "it resembles" (μοιάζει). In the poem "Helen" by **Seferis,** we read (at lines 17–18) a simile that reminds us of Cyprus, the foam, the moon, and the divine all at once: "The moon / Came up out of the sea *like Aphrodite.*" From the time of **Aristotle,** simile has been considered a means for creating the **figure** of **icon,** or **imagery.**

SIMPLIFIED GREEK. See PLAIN GREEK

SINDIBAD Known in the West as *The Tale of the Seven Wise Masters* (drawing on a treasury of probably Indian stories dating to c. 100 B.C.), popularized by the fourteenth-century French verse romance *Roman des Sept Sages* and a prose variation *Dolopathos* (c. 1225), the Greek version of *Syntipas* (or *Sandibar*) has the title *The Wonderful Story of Syntipas the Philosopher.* In the standard version, a king has a wise son, brought up by a wise teacher. When the time of his instruction is over, the teacher reads in the stars that a great danger threatens his pupil, so he vows him to silence for 7 (or 10, or 40) days. The boy's stepmother makes advances to him, is rejected, and so accuses him. The king condemns him to death. The 7 (or 10, or 40) wise men tell daily tales about the cunning ways of women or the injustice of the boy's accusation, and the wicked stepmother tells opposing stories each day, to hasten his execution. When the days of the son's silence are terminated, he can declare the truth, and the queen is punished. *Syntipas* is prefaced by an iambic poem in which one Mikhail Andropolos tells that he translated the book, written in the Syrian language, by order of Prince Gabriel of the "honeyed city," perhaps the Byzantine satrap of Melitini (modern Malatia), in Cappadocia (Armenia). The Greek *Syntipas,* with its many pro-Christian elements, is extant in three different versions: the Moscow codex is the only one containing the Andropolos verse. It is couched in learned Byzantine forms and seems to have an eleventh-century source. A third version (Codex Dresden D. 33) is a translation into vernacular Greek, dated 1626.

SINOPOULOS, TAKIS (1917–1981)

Takis Sinopoulos, a doctor with the Greek army, witnessed the savagery of the **Civil War.** His first poems came out in 1951. His later, famed piece "Death-feast" is a poetic requiem, orchestrating an exorcism of the fateful dead on both sides of the 1945–1949 conflict, slain travelers who leave behind "a stream of light, the fruitful sun a monument to the darkened dead." Sinopoulos offers a modern version of the old "Ulysses theme" (W. B. Stanford's phrase). He poses a kind of second Odyssey (like those of **Kavafis,** Tennyson, **Seferis,** and **Kazantzakis**). The wanderer returns from war so scarred that he is not recognized by his dog, contrary to an iconic motif in **Homer** (M. Pieris). Sinopoulos depicts a hero who is unable to adapt to his old environment. He cannot incarnate the self that preceded the wanderer, who is transposed into a survivor of World War II: "One afternoon, hearing some shouts, he was subjected to / A stream of hideous memories." Under the **Colonels,** in the 1970s, Sinopoulos worked on the cycle "Chronicle," expressing the anguish and **defeatism** of 1973–1974, the confluence of Cyprus, the Athens Polytechnic massacre, and the clamped fist of the Colonels: "Do you cooperate? Conform? Show me your identity card. The real one. Excellent. Stoop now. Stoop. Sign."

Further Reading

Pieris, Michalis. Ο χώρος και τα χρόνια του Τάκη Σινόπουλου [Place and Times of Takis Sinopoulos]. Athens: Ermis, 1988.

Sinopoulos, Takis. Συλλογή *1, 1951–1964* [Collection no. 1: 1951–1964]. Athens: Ermis, 1976.

Sinopoulos, Takis. Νυχτολόγιο [Night Speech]. Athens: Kedros, 1982.

Sinopoulos, Takis. *Landscape of Death. The Selected Poems of Takis Sinopoulos.* Edited and translated by Kimon Friar. Columbus: Ohio State University Press, 1979 [bilingual].

Sinopoulos, Takis. *Selected Poems.* Introduction and translation by John Stathatos. San Francisco: Wire Press, 1981.

SKIPIS, SOTERIS (1881–1951) Skipis

was a prolific writer, who brought religious and sentimental verse to a nonintellectual audience but never joined the contemporary trend toward the use of the **Demotic.** He lived in Provence with a French wife, was a pupil of Moreás, and was elected to the Academy of Athens with 11 votes (against four for Sikelianós, and three for Kazantzakis, according to the ever-vigilant Nikos Pappás). From 1900 to 1945, Skipis published 24 volumes, winning prizes from the French Academy (1919) and the Athenian Academy (1930); see *Néa Estía,* no. 634: 1953. Pappás commented on *Circuit of the Hours* (1905): "Our poet has acquired an insurmountable need to dish out poems and prose pieces at every jump of a flea, and most of the time these works lack any real artistry" (in the journal *New Life,* Alexandria, May 1912).

Further Reading

Skipis, Soteris. *Patterns from a Grecian Loom: Selections from the Works of Sotiris Skipis.* Translated [from a French version] by J. Harwood Bacon, with introduction by Sir Edmund Gosse. London: Unwin Bros., 1928.

SKOUFOS, FRANKISKOS (1644–1697)

Skoufos, originally from Crete, was another **seventeenth-century** scholar who taught at Flanginianon College, in **Venice** (from 1669). Skoufos began studies, aged 13, at the Greek college in **Rome.** He gained a doctorate in theology and philosophy (1666). He composed a rhetorical digest, *Words of Comfort and Blessing on the Nativity of the Baptist* (1670) and an *Art of Rhetoric,* published in Venice (1681). Here examples of rhetorical devices are described individually, usually drawn from Skoufos's own writing. The work was composed in a flowery **Demotic,** a first-time

creation that Politis described as modern Greek baroque. It draws instances from Christian writing, devising some episodes with a narrative touch, as in "City Raided by a Barbarian Foe," or "How St. Nicholas Caused the Cessation of a Storm."

SOCIALIST REALISM

Socialist realism is used by Greek critics to denote the choice of specific left-wing topics, such as a police charge on picket lines. Greeks embrace the abolition of property, the dictatorship of the proletariat, and the dictates of the Third International (May 1919) less rigidly than in the USSR or Western Europe. The Communist Party of Greece was formed (1924) out of the Socialist Labour Party (founded 1918). Partial, aspiring adherents to socialist realism are the novelists Kostas Paroritis (1878–1931), Kostas Chatzopoulos (1868–1920), and **Konstantinos Theotokis** (1872–1923).

In Paroritis's novel *Grown-up Kid* (1916), workers are seen freezing on a cold night outside the factory, where the poor neighborhood labors under belching black smoke by day. Beneath the high chimneys there is a tiny chapel tucked away like a leeward harbor. Here the antithesis between capitalist and spiritual values could hardly be blunter. Other journeymen writers in socialist realism were **Varnalis** and Petros Pikrós (1896–1957), who also wrote **science fiction.** Manolis Kanellís (1900–1980) wrote for the paper *Chania Herald* at age 17 and produced naturalist stories based on the life and unlovely passions of marginalized people, *The Dregs* (1924), *The Flesh* (1930), and the pessimistic poems of *The Shudders of the Earth* (1928). In 1932 he declared: "This problem, this tragedy of the enslaved who are marching towards a heroic rising . . . is not some trifling historical phenomenon, or an image which can pass before the poet's sight without shocking him into tears. Once an intellectual has faced the spectacle offered by today's human society, there is no question what his intellectual or ethical duty must be. *Today one thing alone is urgent: the ending of injustice,"* from an interview in Bastiás 1999: 285–290).

SOLOMÓS, DIONYSIOS (1798–1857)

The great intellectual and poet Dionysios Solomós, born on Zakynthos, was the (illegitimate) son of a Hellenized Venetian aristocrat. His father, Count Nikolaos Solomós, had been assigned the tobacco monopoly of the island by Venice. Solomós was probably named after the local Zantiot saint, Dionysios, whose church in the town is decorated with paintings by the Zantiot artist Koutouzis (1741–1813), who was himself a caustic satirist of Zantiot customs in his poems (which passed in manuscript from hand to hand) and was once a pupil of Tiepolo. Solomós had an aristocrat's childhood, tutored by the Abbot Santo Rossi. He went to the Italian school on Zakynthos till he was 10. His father was a widower who, 11 years before the birth of Dionysios, took up with the teenage daughter of his servant, Dimitrios Nikly. On his deathbed (in February 1807), Count Nikolaos married this girl, Angelica. The formality made Dionysios and his brother Dimitrios legitimate heirs (and rich). The young Dionysios was accompanied to Italy by his tutor and studied there till the age of 20. First he was enrolled at the Seminary of St. Catherine, in Venice. Later, because of poor discipline, he was transferred to high school in Cremona. After matriculation, he went to University of Padua, where he turned from his prescribed law studies to follow lecture courses on literature and philosophy. In 1818, he was able to graduate in Law, "by the favor," as he put it, "of the university authorities." While in Italy, Solomós began to compose conventional **sonnets,** some chivalric tales, and an "Ode for a First Mass." He met the poet Vincenzo Monti and the writer Alessandro Manzoni, soon to publish the first edition (1827) of his great historical novel about seventeenth-century factionalism, *The Betrothed.* Solomós returned to Zakynthos and began to write, for the first time, in **demotic** Greek. This was an anticonformist step. Italian, especially on the main islands of the **Heptanese,** was the prestige idiom. Demotic Greek was not yet a vehicle for any kind of thought or verse.

Solomós was influenced in his move to forge a national language by his meeting with **Spyridon Trikoupis** (1822). The latter, a diplomat and historian, urged him to write in the language that he had imbibed "with his mother's milk." Solomós and his circle were brought up on **Dante,** Petrarch, and Tasso. Striving to match Dante's handling of Florence's educated idiom, Solomós converted common Greek into a potential national language. At last, the Demotic could be made into a prestige vehicle for literature. The English poet Shelley dedicated his dramatic poem *Hellas* to Alexandros Mavrokordatos, whose family sought asylum on Zakynthos after the massacre at Chios. Solomós's first poem in Greek was "The Blonde Girl" (1822), directly inspired by their daughter, Catherine Mavrokordatos. In May 1823, Solomós composed the 158 quatrains of his "Hymn to Liberty." King George I later proclaimed its first two strophes the Greek national anthem (1865) after they were set to music by **Nikolaos Mantza-ros** (1864). Also in 1823, he composed the poem "Marcos Botzaris," inspired by the heroic death of a Greek defender, in the **War of Independence.** In 1824, came Solomós's ode "On the Death of Lord Byron" in 166 quatrains, and the same year (1824) saw his prose manifesto on the demotic language, *The Dialogue.* He wrote "The Dream" (1826), a **satire,** and in the same year "The Poisoned Girl," responding in a lyric composition to gossip on the island after the suicide of his friend Maria Paraskevopoulos, desperate over a love affair with an Italian music teacher. In 1826, Solomós began a fragmentary **epic,** allusively entitled *The Free Besieged,* about the defenders of **Missolonghi** during its final encirclement, which lasted from 1825 to the eve of Palm Sunday in 1826. The poet **Sikelianós** was entranced by the lines in which spring stirs hope in the defenders' hearts: "Light-shadowed seer, what did you see last night? / Miraculous night, night sown with magic! / With neither earth nor sea nor sky breathing." Longinus says: "Greatness appears suddenly; like a thunderbolt, it carries all before it and reveals the writer's full power in a flash." The reader is made giddy by this intuition in *The Free Besieged.*

In 1828, Solomós moved to Kerkyra. The cultivated circle in which he moved on the capital of the Heptanese fostered the conception of *Lambros,* a fragment of romantic epic, which investigates a gloomy conscience and celebrates the innocent beauty of womanhood. In 1833, he produced a fragment of a projected epic poem: *The Cretan.* Despite the provisional nature of this work and the restless abortion of his projects, Solomós was a profound observer of nature. There are passages in which a breath of air

seems to skim across the paper. A mother is seen mourning her dead children in a graveyard, when the text makes a graceful change of topic: "a cool breeze stirs. It comes whispering to her, and it is heavy with the scents of the dawn" (Bradford, 1964: 62). Solomós evokes a "Cretan nightingale beside his nest, high on the mountain rocks, showering over the distant plain and sea his music all night long. The stars fade and the breaking dawn, in wonder, lets fall the roses from her hand." Goethe called him "the Byron of the East." Solomós was a British subject, since Zakynthos was under British administration at his birth. The Greek Parliament was adjourned, when the news of his death reached Athens (21 February 1857). The day of his death was proclaimed a public holiday. A special issue of *Néa Estía* (no. 731: 1957) is devoted to this writer.

See also STAIS

Further Reading

Bradford, Ernle. *The Companion Guide to the Greek Islands.* London: Collins, 1964.

Jenkins, Romailly. *Dionysios Solomos.* Cambridge: Cambridge University Press, 1940.

Pagoulatos, Andréas. "Solomos, Notre Contemporain." *Temps Modernes,* no. 473 (December 1985): 1003–1008.

Raizis, M. B. *Dionysios Solomos.* New York: Twayne Publishers, 1972.

Solomos, Dionysios. *The Free Besieged and Other Poems* (bilingual edition). Edited by Peter Mackridge and translated by Peter Thompson, Roderick Beaton, Peter Colaclides, Michael Green, and David Ricks. Nottingham: Shoestring Press, 2000.

Solomós, D. *The Greek National Anthem. Rendered into English by Rudyard Kipling.* Garden City, NY: Doubleday Page, 1918.

SONNET This 14-line lyric form has a ten-syllable iambic line and final **couplet**

in English verse and 11-syllable lines, set in two quatrains and two tercets, in the hundreds of Italian poets who made the *sonetto* ("little sound") popular in Europe. In Greek, the sonnet is an outsider form, for special, elegiac use. There is little enough Greek lyric poetry in the eighteenth century, but in 1708 four sonnets were included in the Phlanginian miscellany, *Flowers of Piety.* In 1834, two sonnets appeared in the Kerkyra journal *Ionian Anthology.* Solomós wrote many sonnets in Italian, but none (unless they are lost) in Greek. In the nineteenth century, more sonnets appeared, by **A. Rangavís, Koumanoudis, Manousos, Mavilis, Drosinis,** and the short-lived **D. Vyzantios** (1834–1854; see under **Rhyme**). The first sonnet in *Flowers of Piety* is by Frankiskos Kolombís, a deacon from Cephalonia. The second is by Antonios Stratigós, a student from Kerkyra (he later translated the pseudo-Homeric *War of Frogs and Mice* into Cretan dialect). The third, entitled "To Greece," is by Andreas Muaris (from Athens), a hymn to Hellenic renascence under **Turkocracy** and an appeal for the freedom of Athens. The fourth sonnet is by Laurentios Venerios, a Cretan. He flays a vain poetaster, telling him that he is a swan only fit for a few fishermen to hear. He should recall the saying that someone drops dead when a neighborhood raven sings by night: "But when you chant, the crow itself expires."

Further Reading

Leontis, Artemis. "The 'Lost Center' and the Promised Land of Greek Criticism." *JMGS* 5, no. 2 (1987): 175–190.

SOTERIADIS, YEORYIOS (1852–1941) The noted scholar and archaeologist Yeoryios Soteriadis excavated at Chaironea, Dodoni, and Thebes; was professor at Athens University from 1912; and made a translation of the Orestes plays in **mixed Greek** (a hybrid of **Demotic** and learned vocabulary). This caused the Oresteiaka riots of 8 November 1903. Soteriadis wrote *History of the Oriental Nations and Greece* and *The Acropolis and Its Museum.* He translated Krumbacher's *History of Byzantine Literature* (1900).

SOUGDOURIS, YEORYIOS (flourished end seventeenth century) The printer Nikolaos Glykis married a sister of the philosopher Yeoryios Sougdouris, who edited or prefaced several Glykis editions (from c. 1670). Moving from Venice to Ioannina, Sougdouris conducted a dispute with Bessarion Makris and the city's bishop, Klimis, about the distinction between the Divine essence and effect. Sougdouris followed Korydalleús's teaching method in continuing to introduce philosophy to Greeks of his time. He wrote an introduction to **Aristotle,** *Complete Logical Method,* and drafted a *Synopsis of Grammar* (published in Venice, 1752, with many later reprints).

Further Reading

Pelikan, Jaroslav. *The Spirit of Eastern Christendom, 600–1700.* Chicago: University of Chicago Press, 1974.

SOURÍS, YEORYIOS (1852–1919) Sourís, a prolific humorist, writer of **satirical** verse, and magazine editor, attended high school in his birthplace Ermoupolis, on the isle of Syros (Northern Cyclades). He went to seek his fortune in **Russia** because he lacked funds for higher studies. He later recalled this period in *My Journey to Russia.* Back in Athens, he took up classics at the University of Athens, but was failed in Latin by the "beardless" professor Semtelos and later parodied this setback in his verse. He did not complete undergraduate studies. **Roidis** encouraged Sourís and ran some pieces by him in the journal *Asmodaeos.* Sourís worked on several of the newspapers of his time, among them *Rabagás, Don't Get Lost,* and Piyadiotis's *Aristophanes.*

For many years (from 2 April 1883 to 17 November 1918) he brought out the weekly journal *The Greek,* crammed with his verse commentary on any topic that might conceivably interest the general reader. Sourís mirrored the political and social life of his country in a running dialogue between two imaginary characters like the British Punch and Judy, namely the puppets **Fasoulis** and Perikletos. The critic D. Zachariades (1879–1922), who praised the *Satirical Exercises* of **Palamás** as a kind of model for the evaluation of satirical verse, said: "They save us from the duty of swallowing weekly national pills of Perikletophasouliads." This is a snide reference to the running commentary between Perikletos and Fasoulis by Sourís.

Sourís once said about himself: "He mocks everything, and he parodies everything." In his *Eastern Question,* a satirical trilogy, he scorned Deliyannis's 1878 representation of Greece at the Congress of Berlin and his own part as an infantryman at war with "blank bullets" in the subsequent military operations in Thessaly. His "Cornflower-Blue Book" satirizes the correspondence between Koumoundouros and **Xenos** on the Eastern question. In his comedy *Don Juan* (1884), he transported Byron's hero from London to Athens and used him as a vehicle to mock Athenian customs.

He offered populist comment on the **Balkan Wars** of the period 1912 to 1913 and was honored by a state funeral with full military honors. Sourís became the most popular of all Greek poets and was the first to receive the state literary prize after its inception. He had a house bought for him at Phaleron by friends and admirers, where he subsequently held a literary salon. An idea can be formed of his influence and popularity by the list of his regular visitors. Palamás, **Malakasis, Drosinis, Provelengios, Babis Anninos, Z. Papantoniou, Polemis,** and other such figures were habitués of his salon from 1877. He was nominated for the Nobel Prize and awarded the Order of the Saviour after his death. Later he was discussed in a special issue of the literary journal *Néa Estía* (no. 634: 1953).

Among his many light verse comedies, Trypanis (1981: 783) picks out *Eastern Question, The Periphery* (1886), *He Does Not Qualify* (1885), and *The Penniless* (1884). His verse is by turns affectionate and viciously sarcastic. It is full of rough diamond connotations: monks who count their rosary beads and dream of plump nuns or adulterous deacons who end up with the priest's wife, to the ultimate boredom of both, a cuckolded school teacher with his neglected, wriggling wife, boys who pluck kisses from a woman's lips when her priestly husband is in the vineyard gathering grapes. There are **epigrams** to suggest that all Greeks claim just two rights: namely, to urinate or to assemble where they wish. There are ferocious attacks on Athens as the capital of vote-rigging, flighty women, jackass singing, mugging, knife attacks, and starvation suppers, in short, "an immense latrine in a thicket of latrines."

Further Reading

Phoutrides, Aristides. "Soures and His World." *The Classical Journal* 15, no. 8 (May 1920): 494–498.

SOUTSOS, ALEXANDROS (1803–1863) The poet and novelist A. Soutsos, from a patrician **Phanariot** family, was three years older than his equally famous brother, **Panayotis Soutsos.** In 1820 he was sent by his uncle, Mikhail Soutsos, to study in Paris. He became gravely ill when he learned of the death of his brother Dimitrios (June 1821, as a centurion in the sacred battalion at Dragatsani, in the **War of Independence**). So A. Soutsos was sent to convalesce in Italy. On returning to Greece, he published some **satirical** sketches, *A View of Greece* (1827). Angry reactions to this book obliged him to take refuge outside Greece, so he went again to Paris. Here he wrote (in French) a *History of the Greek Uprising,* which contributed notably to the development of French **Philhellenism.** Ioannis Kapodistrias, first President of Greece (1827–1831), had attempted to muzzle the freedom of the Greek press, and this subject is aired in Alexandros Soutsos's tragicomic novel, *The Banished One of 1831* (1835). **Angelos Vlachos** judged this book "full of tearful pomp and interjection." In 1836, A. Soutsos issued a satirical prose and verse newspaper called *The Greek Scales.* This was an imitation of Auguste Barthélemy's versified weekly *La Némésis* (France, March 1831–April 1832), which crowned Barthélemy's excoriating attacks (1825–1828) on the French Restoration government and his ambivalence over the 1830 Restoration. Soutsos was again obliged to go abroad. Until 1839, he was in Anatolia and the West.

On his return to Athens, he published the opening sections of *The Wanderer,* a rather flat imitation of Byron's *Childe Harold.* A. Soutsos was later influential in causing the end of the Othonian **monarchy.** He was referred to, in **Romantic** style, as "the untamed and fearless poet." He opposed all the political arrangements set up for Greece after 1830. Using his satire to flail the autocratic tendencies that had followed success in the **War of Independence,** A. Soutsos helped form public opinion. Vikelas said that the verse of Soutsos had a greater effect on public attitudes than any journalism. He wrote convivial drinking songs and several comedies: *The Prodigal, The Premier, The Constitutional School, The Untamed Poet.* He published a series of satires (1827, 1839) and several odes. He praised the Mani landowners, Yeoryios and Konstantinos Mavromichalis, who killed Kapodistrias (October 1831) as tyrannicides, like the assassins of Peisistratus in ancient history: "O Mavromichalis, imitator of Harmodios, and latterday Aristogeiton, / Wreathe your sword with myrtle, / Strike down the betrayer of our country, / Strike him and strike again; / Prepare to die nobly as they did!" With Romantic dash, Soutsos left numerous works unfinished. In his poem "The Ruins of Troy" (1836), he evokes with contemporary *arkhaiolatría* "The memory of the great Hellenic past. / The comparison with our humble wretched present." After his death (in a hospital at Smyrna), the National Assembly passed a decree that his complete works be published at state expense, but the project was not realized. The Greek writer Jean Moreás offered (1874) to edit Soutsos, whom he called "the father of neo-Hellenic poetry and reformer of the language."

Further Reading

Soutsos, A. Ἅπαντα [The Complete Works]. Edited by Y. Zervós. Athens: Phexi, 1916.

SOUTSOS, PANAYOTIS (1806–1868)

The poet, novelist, and Romantic theorist Panayotis Soutsos was born in Constantinople to an aristocratic **Phanariot** family. In 1835 he suggested a revival of the **Olympics.** He was educated at the Chios School. Among his teachers were **Neophytos Vamvas** and Konstantinos Vardalachos (1755–1830), who had published a *Physics* (1812) and *Rhetoric* (1815). P. Soutsos subsequently studied in Paris, where he printed (1828) his *Odes d'un jeune grec,* and Padua (Italy). In 1823 he passed through Transylvania on his way back to Greece. His eldest brother was killed at the battle of Dragatsani, having been excommunicated by the **Orthodox Church** (to mollify the Sultan) alongside Prince Alexandros Ypsilantis, who was offered the leadership of the secret society *Philikí Etairía,* and for whose family the Greek political martyr, **Rigas,** had worked in the 1780s. P. Soutsos used **Katharevousa** and justified it in his conservative linguistic pamphlet *New School of the Written Language.* This manifesto declares that "our language and that of the ancients will be one and the same; our grammar and theirs will also be one and the same. Only words and phrases of theirs will be accepted; every word or phrase that is alien will be eliminated." *The Soutsos Question* was dispatched by **K. Asopios** (1853) as a fitting response.

The works of Soutsos are passionate Romantic outpourings that match the Italian fashion of the time, particularly the literary production of **U. Foscolo** (1778–1827). With *Leander* (1834), P.

Soutsos is considered to have produced the earliest of the first wave of modern Greek novels. His debt to Foscolo lies in the tangle of nationalism and amorous turmoil in the plot. Soutsos's verse drama in five acts, *The Traveler* (1831), modeled on Byron's *Manfred,* marks the outset of **Romanticism** in Greece. It was so popular that it was reprinted and hawked in the streets until the 1930s by ambulant vendors together with pamphlets and lives of the **saints.** He also composed a five-act verse play, *The Passion of the Messiah, Jesus Christ.* The prose letters of *Leander* bring the effulgence and broken hearts of the German and Italian Romantic novel to Greece approximately a generation late, but in time to tell a story set against the **War of Independence.** *Leander* is a first-person narrative in which the storyteller comments, with "highly-charged emotive terms" (M. Vitti), in the fabric of a fictional autobiography. The most important poems by Panayotis Soutsos are to be found in the collection *The Guitar* (1835).

See also ASOPIOS

Further Reading

Mackridge, Peter. "Testimony and Fiction in Greek Narrative Prose 1944–1967." In *The Greek Novel: A.D. 1–1985,* edited by Roderick Beaton, 90–102. London: Croom Helm, 1988.

Soutsos, P. Ποιήματα [Lyric Verse]. Introduction by Y. Zervós. Athens: Phexi, 1915.

SPANEAS (twelfth or thirteenth century)

The *Spaneas* is a medieval poem extant in many different manuscripts, whose length varies from 148 to 674 unrhyming **decapentasyllables.** It is hard to determine a date of composition. The title of the work, as first published in mid-sixteenth century by the Venetian printer

Cristoforo Zanetos, is *Admonitory Teaching of Lord Alexios Comnenus, Known as the Beardless One.* The title suggests that it was written for or by Alexius, son of John II Comnenus (1118–1143), or addressed to a nephew, son of his twin sister Mary. She had married the Sicilian ruler John Roger II, a Norman adventurer who invaded Greece in 1146, installing himself at **Corinth** and perhaps reaching **Athens.** These identifications are now generally doubted. *Spaneas* is thought to be a late Byzantine work, written well before the **fall of Constantinople** (1453). It is a collection of advice on how to behave in the community, relayed by an experienced courtier to a young prince, a "beardless one" (Σπανέας). The text is modeled on the ever-popular *Admonitions to Demonikos,* fancifully attributed to Isocrates. The young man is advised to revere his God, report slander to the Emperor, and adopt reciprocal behavior: "As you observe, young lad, your friend behave to you, / You should behave in like manner with him." The lad is to listen carefully and to sift out any excessive words addressed to him. He should not let his voice reveal his inner thoughts, for "many people are carried away by their tongue, and it betrays them." He should hold fast to virtue, for nothing is more honorable than virtue. Although beauty is withered by disease and age, virtue shines brighter as its owner grows old. The courtier also insists that a good man never accepts bawdy language.

Further Reading

Schmitt, John. "Über den Verfasser des Spaneas." *Byzantinische Zeitschrift* 1 (1892): 316–332.

Spadaro, Giuseppe. "Spaneas e Glikas: note filologiche." Δίπτυχα 1 (1979): 282–290.

Spadaro, Giuseppe. "Il Πρὸς Δημόνικον pseudoisocrateo e Spaneas." Δίπτυχα 3 (1982–83): 143–159.

SPANÓS, that is, THE MASS OF THE BEARDLESS MAN. See SATIRE

STAIS, EMMANOUIL (1817–1895)

Born on the southerly isle of Kythira, Emmanouil Stais became a lawyer in the **Ionian Islands** and a senator in the Ionian Parliament. He was rediscovered with the reprint of his 1853 essay on Solomós's *Lampros*, in Voutieridis's bulletin *Library of Neo-Hellenic Literature* (nos. 2, 3, and 4, 1927). In *Solomós and the Greeks* (Athens, 1937), Voutieridis again points out that Stais was one of the first articulate **demoticists,** and the one who fully developed the implications of Solomós for the **language question.** Stais's work on Solomós (together with the famous dispute between **Spyridon Zambelios** and Polylás on the national poet) can be read in Kitsos-Mulonás, 1980.

Further Reading

Kitsos-Mulonás, A. Th., ed. Σολωμός. Προλεγόμενα κριτικὰ Στάη—Πολυλα—Ζαμπελίου [Solomós. Prolegomena by Stais, Polylás and Zambelios]. Athens: E.L.I.A., 1980.

STEFANOU, LYDIA (1927–)

Lydia Stefanou published several volumes of verse and also articles on modern literature (for example, on Greek literary magazines 1944–1954) and a book on critical method (1981). Stefanou translated a selection of poems by Dylan Thomas (1982), Maurice Bowra's *Poetry and Politics* (1982), and Apollinaire's *La femme assise* (1983).

STEPHANITIS AND ICHNELATIS

The Story of Stephanitis and Ichnelatis

was a popular **Byzantine** saga, with origins in the Buddhist *Pantchatantra.* Two jackals, with Hellenized names, give a royal pupil an outline of correct behavior. The narrative is translated from the Arabic *Kalilah-va-Dimna,* also called *Mirror of the Prince,* and is fused with the *Pantchatantra.* In the sixth century it had been translated by a doctor (Varzois) into Persian (Pehlevi). In the eighth century, 100 years after the Mohammedan conquest of Persia, it was translated into Arabic, taking its authorial name from the philosopher Βιδπάϊ, one of the characters we meet in the text, as is the case with the *Sindibab* (Συντίπας), an alternative title for *The Seven Wise Masters.* There was an inferior Latin translation of *Stephanitis and Ichnelatis* by John of Capua, made between 1267 and 1278. A Greek version in verse was commissioned by Emperor Alexius Comnenus (1080) from one of his court bureaucrats, Symeon Syth, and later refashioned in the Greek vernacular (sixteenth century). Syth, in his first section, deals with the Persian doctor's acquisition and treatment of the Indian book. In his second section, he considers the Indian story, followed by the doings of Stefanitis and Ichnelatis and then the story of a wood pigeon.

STICHOMYTHY Stichomythy (στιχομυθία) is dialogue between two characters in alternating lines of a poem. It is common in verse drama, or **epic,** whereas αντιλαβή, in drama, is the division of a line between two speakers.

STRATIGIS, YEORYIOS (1860–1938) The poet Yeoryios Stratigis, born on the isle of Spetsai (off southern Argolis), studied law at Athens, Berlin, and Paris. He followed a legal career in Al-exandria and then Piraeus. His first poems came out in *Don't Get Lost.* Stratigis later collected them in *Oleanders* (1880). He translated Goethe's *Faust,* Rostand's *Cyrano de Bergerac,* Schiller's *Intrigue and Love,* and other German and French poetry. His composition *Eros and Psyche* won the Philadelpheios Poetry Competition (1892). Over the years came two other collections, *Songs from Home* (1889) and *What the Waves Say* (1919), in which he moved gradually, but not yet decisively compared with other poets of the 1880s (see **New School Of Athens**), from **Purist** language toward **demotic** diction. He wrote the plays *Basil the Bulgar-Slayer* and *Archilochus,* a study of Dante's *Divine Comedy,* and a volume of short stories with the title *Book of the Soul.*

STREAM OF CONSCIOUSNESS Some recent Greek novelists seem to bathe their characters in a "stream of consciousness," a notion familiar from William James's definition (1890) of the continuous, random activity of the human mind. The effect is created by the drift of apparently rambling, associative but disconnected thoughts and perceptions in the characters of Laurence Sterne, James Joyce, Virginia Woolf, Dorothy Richardson, Arnold Bennett, and Katherine Mansfield. Greek novelists have tended to revivify it with multiple narrators and layers of emotional investment in the **plot,** as in Nikos Bakolás's *The Great Square* (1987), which focuses on **Thessaloniki** in the 1940s.

STROPHE Lines of poetry in traditional Greek **meter** are arranged in a verse or stanza, called "strophe" (στροφή). The commonest strophe is the four-line "quatrain" (τετράστιχο). A strophe of two lines is a couplet (δίστιχο, see **Dís-tichon**). Strophes of three lines were used in the modern *villanelle* and also the Greek popular song, in which the three lines may share just one rhyme. Italian *terza rima,* a series of interlinked three-line strophes, gave rise to the Greek tercet. Greek lyric poetry also exhibits 5-, 6-, and 7-line strophes and a single poem formed of a 10-line strophe with **rhyme.**

STRUCTURE Greek literary criticism had emphasized a poem's framework, or structure (διάρθρωσις, drawing on German *Struktur*), before the advent of structuralism. Literature students in Greece are taught to identify the main structure (δομή) of a text. Then they observe how it subdivides into units (ενότητες). This reveals the artistic construction (τεχνική κατασκευή) of the literary object and shows how its content is forged into a sequence, that is, "the opening unit," "second unit," "third unit," and so on, through the text's complexity. Poems, in particular, are scanned for their introduction, and one introductory format is the vocative address, as at the beginning of this 1919 poem by **Soteris Skipis** (1881–1951): "O Salamis, island of glory, / The loveliest of bays cajoles / Your white beaches, till they flush pink / Like a maiden's cheeks." Another format is dialogue, as in the opening of the **Mavilis** sonnet, "Kallipateira," about a woman who journeys to watch her menfolk in the **Olympic Games:** "'Noble lady from Rhodes, why are you at the Games? / Long-standing custom bans women / From here.' 'I have a nephew, Euklis, / Three brothers, a son, and father among the Olympians: // You should let me enter, Umpires, / So I may take pride in the fine / Bodies that strive for the wild olive

crown of Herakles.'" Critics comment on inserted dialogues, as in the narrative "The Kiss," by **M. Mitsakis,** which describes the solemn scene on 20 May 1825, when Papaphlessas and his "gallant young men" lie dead on a hill, and General Ibrahim gazes on the carnage, saying, "What a pity, so many fine men wasted!" and then, "Which corpse is Papaphlessas?" and, "Lift him up; wash him," and then, "Lean him against that tree."

When a text is built to a climax, Greek critics refer to steplike ascent. We see a linear structure in the demotic song "About Dhespo" (published 1914, by **Politis**). This has three segments: an introduction, in which the anonymous poet hears rifles, so asks if there is a marriage, and answers that a hero's wife, Dhespo, is besieged with other women, all fighting against Albanians. This sets up a segment that could be called "culmination of the action." Dhespo is called on to surrender, refuses, declares that women do not accept such masters, and tells her defenders to grab torches. Then comes the third segment, a resolution. Her women ignite gunpowder, and they blow themselves up.

STYLE; STYLISTICS Greeks have adopted a saying from the **Hellenistic** writer Dionysius of Halicarnassus that says "the style is the man." The Hellenistic writer Demetrius, in a first-century B.C. work, *On Interpretation,* describes four different sorts of style: "plain," "powerful," "grandiose," and "elegant." In modern verse, style is often assessed in terms of "lyricism" and "impulsiveness." Care is given to assessing description, for modern style censures use of "ornamental adjectives" and comes down hard on long-windedness, which is variously called "verbiage," "the prolix," or "surplus writing" (perissology).

See also FIGURES OF SPEECH; ORATORY; SENTENCE STYLE; TROPE

SUDA (SUIDAS) In the late tenth century, an unknown **Byzantine** author, wrongly thought to be a man called Suidas, compiled *The Suda* (that is, *Palisade*). This text is an **encyclopedia** with some 30,000 thematic or lexical entries, of different lengths, arranged in a special alphabetical series. Items beginning with the diphthong αι- are located not after α- but after δ-, because that diphthong is the equivalent of ε-; words beginning with ει- are placed after ζ-, because that diphthong is the equivalent of η-; words beginning with ω- are located after those starting with o-. The *Suda* was in use at the time of Efstathios Katafloros (born c. 1125), author of the *Digressions,* concerning the differences between Homer's *Iliad* and *Odyssey.* Efstathios is the first author to mention the *Suda.* It constitutes a digest of other dictionaries and of various biographies and historical works: Eudemos, Helladius, Zosimos Gazaios, Caecilius, Longinus, and (lost) **epitomes,** such as the **nomenclature** of Hesychius. It provides information on many classical and some medieval Greek authors, using glossaries of Herodotus, Euripides, and Menander, or George the Monk, chief source for information on **Christian** authors. It copies out annotations on manuscripts that might otherwise be unknown and elucidates **proverbs,** etymologies, personalities, grammatical types, scientific points, concepts, and difficult terms. Thus the *Suda* tells us that Menander wrote 100 comedies, and 8 of them won the Athenian prize. Its longest articles are

those on **Origen,** Jesus, **Homer,** Pythagoras, Dionysius Areopagite, and Demosthenes. Passages from some 400 writers are included, often quoted by name, for example, Diogenes Laertius, Artemidorus, Herodianus (the historian), and the traveler Pausanias. From the twelfth century, the title *Suda* was taken to mean that it had a compiler called Suidas. The **Renaissance** poet Angelo Poliziano (1454–1494) ridiculed this notion. The scholar Lepsius (1547–1606) said: "Suidas is a sheep, but a sheep with a golden fleece."

Further Reading

Lemerle, P. *Le premier humanisme byzantin* [Early Byzantine Humanism]. Paris: Bernard Flusin, 1971.

Wilson, N. G. *Scholars of Byzantium.* Cambridge, MA: Medieval Academy of America, 1996.

SUN. See ROMIOSINI

SURREALISM; SURREALIST   In Greek literature, the surrealist movement was designated both by the word *hyperrealism* and the Western term *surrealism.* It was a manner of writing verse or prose-poems full of psychic spontaneity, lacking logical boundaries or respect for grammar rules. The material of Greek surrealist writing also disregards social and ethical models. Greek surrealism, in literature as well as art, affects a total lack of interest in its own aesthetic quality. Its lack of respect for any difference between the actual and the fantastic, between true and false, life and death, allows the writer to create a product in which confusion and darkness are uppermost, as in **Pantelis Prevelakis,** *Bread of the Angels,* his last novel (1966).

The poet **Elytis** was interested in French surrealist writers, particularly André Breton and Paul Eluard. In spring 1935, he was assisted in an intellectual conversion to dream images and **automatic writing** by his friendship with the iconoclastic **Andreas Embirikos,** who was bringing out his surrealist pamphlet *The Kill of High Heat.* In 1935, Elytis showed a series of **collages** at the First International Surrealist Exhibition in Athens. Elytis declared that in this period he became the amazed spectator of an unbidden world rising up inside him. Surrealist items that coalesce in Greek twentieth-century poetry are dream settings, visionary landscapes, absurdist elements, and illogical speech, typically deployed in the work of **N. Gatsos, M. Sachtouris, I. Kambanellis,** and their imitators. The poet (and medical doctor) **Takis Sinopoulos** accused the Greek surrealists of being unable to transplant the socialist, revolutionary aspect of French surrealism to Greece, because they were from upper-middle-class families, or their conscience was stunted by the **Metaxás** dictatorship. Elytis and Embirikos moved to a socially committed stance in the 1940s, but **Engonopoulos** continued to conduct a monologue with himself in the 1970s, because "nothing disturbs his conscience."

Further Reading

Robinson, C. "The Greekness of Modern Greek Surrealism." *BMGS* 7 (1981): 119–137.

SUSPENSE Suspense (αβεβαιότητα) is the response aroused in the reader when there is protracted uncertainty as to how the plot of a story, or crime novel, can be solved or reach its denouement (λύσις).

See also PLOT; POSTPONEMENT; THRILLER

SYKOUTRIS, IOANNIS (1901–1937) The distinguished classicist Ioannis Sykoutris studied four years in Germany and later argued that the term *Hellene* had been forged during a **nationalist** period and could not mean "classical Greek." For centuries the term *Hellene* was a way of making a pagan allusion. Byzantine tradition had created this Greek nationality by making from the "Roman" (ρωμιός) an identity that was felt as "Hellenic" (Ἑλληνικὸς). In his note "Literature" for the *Great Encyclopedia of Greece* (1926–1934), Sykoutris points out that literary interpretations, at the time of the thirteenth century Provençal poets, were "feebler" than in medieval times. He weighs up romantic thought, assesses German classicists, is unsurprised by their poor reception of Nietzsche's *The Birth of Tragedy,* and approves the triple formula "the inherited, the learnt, the lived" (*das Ererbtes, das Erlerntes, das Erlebtes*) as a critical method to deal with modern writers. He cites "nation description" (φυλογραφική, from German *Stammesgeschichtich*) and suggests applying it to Greece: the characteristic music and soft poetics, in Heptanesian writers could be used to distinguish them from the robust, combative idiosyncrasy of the Roumeliot poets (Palamás, Malakasis, Valaoritis) and from the aesthetic, aristocratic, anemic literature of the "diaspora" poets (**Nirvanas, Gryparis, Kavafis**). A special issue of the literary journal *Néa Estía* (no. 738: 1958) covers Sykoutris.

SYMBOLISM; SYMBOL Symbolism is a nineteenth-century movement that devised entirely new expressive forms in comparison with the **Romantic** one. The symbolist writer expresses his or her interior world in an exotic correspondence with the reality outside. Neither the outside world nor inner sensations are described exactly as such. What is catalogued are the sensations and reflections that they create in their subconscious. Standard metrical forms are abolished and the new **free verse** is introduced everywhere. Symbolists unite their reader with them in the unexplained exploration of Nature and its myriad symbols, yet their intuitions are kept fugitive and highly musical.

The French Symbolists influenced Greek writing strongly after 1898. Greek Symbolist writing cultivated a certain nostalgia for the past, a melancholy, pessimistic disposition, and the vague exaltation of ethnic values. Most of the early **Sikelianós,** as well as **Elytis, Vrettakos,** Tasos Livaditis, and **Seferis** are affected by Symbolist values. They refashion in a Greek mold the fleeting evocation and musical disconnectedness of French symbolism. Vrettakos's *Mt. Taugetos and Silence* (1949) shows many such points and becomes practically a poetic symphony in music. He says: "And so the Taugetos took for me the place of my mother's bosom / It served me milk, tart blood, sun and greenery / As if to give me a soul like the rock."

SYNAXARION The synaxarion (συναξάριον) is the tale of a saintly person, with a moral message, written by a sympathizer or contemporary, who infuses his work with popular language and tone. These lives of monks, priests, saints, anchorites, or ascetics constitute the *Acta Sanctorum,* or martyrology, of the **Orthodox Church.** The account of a religious life is thus the dominant narrative form of **Byzantium literature.** The first writer of synaxaria is supposed to be Timothy of Alexandria (fourth century), who circulated a series of lives of the **saints.** Athanasios of Alexandria composed a life of St. Antony, which describes how this ascetic resisted assault in the desert from his senses and temptation from demons and gained felicity among "blessed endowments" granted by the Almighty. This devotional prose was followed by authors like Cyril of Scythopolis (*St. Sabas; St. Euthymius*), and Ioannis Moschos (c. 550–619), who went around monasteries in Syria, Egypt, Palestine, the Aegean Islands, and Alexandria to write down what he saw and heard, seeking ascetic goals. Moschos flourished under Tiberius (578–602) and called the book of his memoirs *The Spiritual Meadow* because of many carefully arranged flowers in it. Sophronios of Damascus composed *Lives of John and Cyrus* and *Mary the Egyptian.*

Leontios of Neapolis in Cyprus (c. 590–668) composed a life of John the Almsgiver and a story of Symeon Salos, earliest of the blessed "fools for the sake of Christ." Leontios wrote a third biography on Spyridon, bishop of Trimithountos (Cyprus), and a treatise in five books against the Jews. Epifanios (fl. c. 780) wrote a life of the apostle Andrew, with a treatment on the life of the Virgin Mary and passages on the first period of **iconoclasm.** In his introduction, Epifanios complains about the lack of historical biographies of the Apostles. Symeon Metaphrastes (mid-tenth century) wrote a life of Sampson, and the second part contains a list of the saint's miracles up until the writer's time, referring to emperors Romanos II (959–963) and John I Tzimiskis (969–976). The text of many of Symeon's 136 biographies of saints was printed in a plain Greek adaptation by **Agapios Landos** in the books *New Paradise* (Venice, 1641) and *New Treasury* (1679).

Other synaxaria were composed by Nikitas Stathatos, Gregory of Cyprus, Konstantinos Akropolitis, Nikiforos Grigorás, and Philotheos of Constantinople. In the eighth to eleventh centuries, the genre grew into a prose literature for uneducated Christians. From the fourteenth and fifteenth centuries come the last writers in this genre: **Planoudis,** Grigorios Palamás, Kallistos Xanthopoulos Patriarch of Constantinople, Ioannis of Nicomedeia, Neïlos Metropolitan of Rhodes, who around 1366 wrote a panegyric of St. Matrona of Chios, and Filotheos Archbishop of Sylumbria in Thrace, who wrote (c. 1365) lives of bishop Agathonikos and the monk Makarios of Constant. Beaton notes (1994: 179) how the synaxarion's typical subtitle, "The Life and Times of . . . ," influenced **Kazantzakis** to call his novel *The Life and Manners of Alexis Zorba* rather than "The Synaxarion of Zorbas." In early vernacular literature, the term can be used satirically, as in the fifteenth-century *Legend of the Estimable Donkey,* where three animals (wolf, fox, and donkey) travel together, but the **donkey** outwits the other two, who want to eat him. The novelist and scriptwriter, Thanasis Valtinos (b. 1932), parodies the saint's life in his *Legend of Andreas Kordopatis: Part 1, America* (1972). Here an old man from the Peloponnese recounts his attempts to migrate and his troubles as an illegal immigrant in early twentieth-century America. Female saints are often recorded in medieval lives (Talbot, 1996) celebrating the cenobite, the pious housewife, the female hermit, the nun disguised as a monk, or the holy Empress.

Further Reading

Chrysostom, John. *On Virginity: Against Remarriage.* Translated by Sally Rieger Shore. Lewiston, NY: Mellen Press, 1983.

Talbot, Alice-Mary, ed. *Holy Women of Byzantium: Ten Saints' Lives in English Translation.* Washington, DC: Dumbarton Oaks, 1996.

SYNECHDOCHE Synechdoche (συνεκδοχή) is a **metaphor** based on altered proportion and a frequent **trope** in Greek writing. One name replaces the species, the part may stand for the whole, or an attribute represents its owner. Writing about the beauty of Greece for the magazine *The Moulding of the Young* (established 1879), **G. Xenopoulos** declares that there are summits from which the sightseer can revolve his gaze through 360 degrees and perceive "just about the entire country of Greece." By the rhetorical device of synechdoche, here Xenopoulos says "almost all" to signify "a big part."

SYNEZESIS The important term *synezesis,* from Greek verse prosody, approximates to the English noun *elision.* It refers to Greek poetry's tendency to collapse into a single vowel sound a group of two vowels or syllables within a word. A word-final diphthong or word-final long vowel can be merged by synezesis (also called synecphonesis) with the initial vowel of a following word. If the following word begins with -ε, we have the common phenomenon of prodelision. When the merging of vowels is shown in writing, the resultant compound form is called crasis. If it is not shown in writing, we have synezesis. For example, ἢ οὔ ("or not") may be written as two syllables but pronounced as a monosyllable.

SYNONYM Because of its huge, extended vocabulary, Greek is rich in synonyms. When Yeoryios Patousas composed his formal dedication of the first demotic verse anthology *Flowers of Piety* to the Virgin Mary (Venice, 1708), he deployed several variant terms for Our Lady. All these words have the same meaning, but their differences in etymology and reference show devotion and learning all at once. The synonyms are an extended rhetorical **trope.** It combines **Orthodox** devotion with outspoken **patriotism** on behalf of an unliberated Greece, which the Mother of Christ will intervene to save. She comes over, in these 23 short paragraphs, as "Virgin," "Mother," "Mother of God," "Mother of God as Ruler," "the Sun-born," "Mary the Eternally Virgin," "undefeated General," "the Genitrix of God as Overlord," "Virgin Mother," "Mistress of the Universe," "Immaculate one as Queen," and "unvanquished Maiden." So too Greek poets called Cyprus "Snake-Filled, Kypris, Blessed, Simple, Hidden Isle," and so on.

***SYNOPSIS (OF SATHAS,* "Σύνοψις"** Σάθα**). See CHRONICLE, HISTORY**

SYNTIPAS. See SINDIBAD

T

TACHTSÍS, KOSTAS (1927–1988)

The verse plaquettes of Kostas Tachtsís from the 1950s had little success, but his campy, bitchy novel, *The Third Wedding,* in 1963 was admired as far away as Japan. It relays the nattering of Nina, a rough, working-class woman who gets married for the third time. She is the center of a chorus of chatter that hints at a marginal Greek history from the **Balkan Wars** to the **Resistance,** spiced by the slang and values of the underworld. They talk about Oedipus complexes, marital strife, infidelity, tarts, tricksters, addicts, and pimps. The reader senses the loathing of daughter for mother, or wife for mistress, with verbal shocks like "There exists no object so tasteless as the low-arsed woman wearing trousers." It was followed by *Small Change* (1972). According to Faubion (1993: 268), Tachtsís lived in the '80s as a recluse in a rundown part of Athens. He was apparently murdered in the summer of 1988. He was buried at state expense.

Further Reading

Kazazis, Kostas. "Learnedisms in Costas Taktsis's Third Wedding." *BMGS* 5 (1979): 17–28.

Taktsis, Costas. *The Third Wedding.* Translated by Leslie Finer. London: Alan Ross, 1967.

TAMBURLAINE *Lament concerning Timur i Leng* is a poem in 96 unrhymed **political verses,** found in a Paris codex of 1403, written around the time when Persia was invaded by the so-called Timur the Lame (1336–1405), great-great-grandson of Genghis Khan (1162–1227). The Greek text starts with the siege of Constantinople by Bajiazit, caused by the lightning appearance of the Mongol conqueror. It then tells by **ekphrasis** the horrors visited on Asia Minor by Tamburlaine's troops after the defeat of the Turkish army at Ankara (1402). The unknown author of this *Lament* is an eyewitness to atrocities suffered by Greeks and by the family, wives, and sons of Bajiazit, at the hands of a tyrant who died on the point of marching against China after wasting the cities of Ephesus and Smyrna, killing 100,000 citizens of Delhi, and making pyramids out of his vanquished enemies' skulls.

TANTALIDIS, ILIAS (1818–1876) Ilias Tantalidis was a well-known **Phanariot** writer in his day. He spent his whole life at Constantinople, personally removed from the climate of Greek **independence.** There are lively touches in his verse, which moves between the learned and **demotic** idiom. Some of his writing seems to continue the hedonistic realism of **Athanasios Christopoulos** (1772–1847). He can write fierce **satire** against his own background, as in "Mme Crystal": "Little Madame Crystal has the wits of a pip / And the tongue of a boot, / So when she puts on her Phanariot airs, / Wow! see what a nerve and the lash of her verve, / Pitter patter pun! / Tons of words on the run. // With the crew of her kids and her bleary-eyed spouse, / With mussels in the lunch-tin, / She's off to the country, where she natters and fusses, / With shrieks and with curses, burdening the nurses, / Pun pitter patter, / Chubby madame chatter!"

Further Reading

Kalodikis, Periklis N. Ἡ Ἑλληνικὴ Λογοτεχνία [Greek Literature]. Athens: Gutenberg, 1984, vol. II: 11–12.

TARSOULI, ATHENA (1884–1975) Athena Tarsouli studied European languages at a school in Athens and went on to art studies in Paris (at the Susanne Hurel College). This was not an uncharacteristic upbringing for an upper-class Greek girl. Her published work is extensive and varied. She illustrated many of her own volumes of verse and folklore studies, had 15 national or international exhibitions of her painting, and won various prizes for her contribution to Greek literature and local history. She added original photographs to her own illustrations for her two-volume *Cyprus,* which came out in 1955 and 1964. She is among a number of Greek critics to have written a study of the **sea** theme (1969) in Greek **demotic song** and poetry. Her short stories and prose range from *ithografía* ("recording of manners") and historical biography to the generalized psychological introspection that came later to Greek than to Western novelists and was much in the air at Athens and **Thessaloniki,** during the 1920s and 1930s.

TAUTOLOGY Tautology (ταυτολογία) is the repetition of the same meaning by using the same or other words. This superfluous repetition of a word or a phrase, or a repetition of the same concept by different words, is thus close to **pleonasm.** Tautology is used in philosophy and **oratory** to mark a circular definition, but in other Greek prose it merely serves to give great emphasis by seeming to say the obvious. Thus Ilias Voutieridis (1874–1941) wrote: "Like birds who *take wing and fly away* one by one / Are the fragrant dreams of my youth."

TAVERN The wine-bar or tavern (καπηλειό) was the haunt of many Greek writers and the undoing of some with a *penchant* for alcohol, such as **A. Papadiamantis.** Among these was the nineteenth-century **satirist** Angelos Kantounis (1847–1890), who drank himself to an early grave, but in his short career founded four satirical papers (sniping at church, business, and politics on Zakynthos). Kantounis wrote a whole poem with words rhyming in "M-OUTO" (μοῦ-το -) to celebrate a patrician winebar owner named Komouto (Κομουτο). The poet **Lambros Porfyras** was a quiet, shy trawler of the taverns, where he met up with the likes of **Voutyrás, Varnalis,** Spatalás, and Sp. Pasayiannis. Porfyras drained his wine at the Pasalimani bar, as a regular, or at Phreatys, where he rubbed elbows with fishermen. Uncle Kostas's Bar, in Deinokratos Street, was a writers' retreat, in the first 15 years of the twentieth century, counting **Vlachoyannis, Karbounis, Varnalis, Avgeris,** and Papadiamantis among its regulars.

TEACHER The word *educator* (διδάσκαλος) evolves into the modern teacher (δάσκαλος). "Educator," in **Byzantine** times, designated a trained cleric from the Patriarchal School at Constantinople, entitled to preach on behalf of bishops. Emperor Alexius Comnenus set up (1107) this pool of preachers, and later we meet I. Bryennius as "teacher of the preachers" (fifteenth century). The monk Daniel Kerameús (d. 1801/?1804) is characteristic of eighteenth-century teachers. He wrote a panegyric on Katherine, Empress of **Russia** (1762–1796), who constituted an icon for ethnic Greeks as their imagined liberator from the Turks. Kerameús wrote an explanation of *A Grammar in Four Parts* (Venice, 1870) by Theodoros Gazís (1400–1475/?78), compiled a **grammar** of his own, and wrote textbooks that circulated in manuscript among a variety of schools in the late eighteenth century. Some copies survive, at **Mount Athos,** or in Aegean libraries, whereas others were lost when the Evangelical School of Smyrna was torched in the **Asia Minor disaster.**

Further Reading

Constantinides, C. N. *Higher Education in Byzantium in the Thirteenth and Early Fourteenth Centuries, 1204–c. 1310.* Nicosia: Cyprus Research Centre, 1982.

Davidson, Thomas. *The Education of the Greek People and Its Influence on Civilization.* New York: AMS Press, 1971 [first publ. 1894].

Kitromilides, Paschalis. *Tradition, Enlightenment, and Revolution: Ideological Change in Eighteenth and Nineteenth Century Greece.* Cambridge, MA: Harvard University, 1978,

TECHNI *Techni* was an influential literary periodical (1898–1899), issued monthly and edited by Konstantinos Chatzopoulos (brother of the editor of *Dionysos*), written entirely in the **simplified** idiom (see **Language Question**). *Techni* cultivated French, German, and English literary values, as well as publicizing the Parnassian and Symbolist French poets, including Laforgue, Maeterlinck, and decadent writing (Verlaine, Baudelaire). K. Chatzopoulos (born in Agrinion) was adopted as a child by a wealthy man, whose fortune he duly inherited. This money enabled him to travel widely, give up his work as a lawyer, and contribute to the publishing ventures of the journal. The journal's circle included the writers **Mavilis, Palamás, A. Papadiamantis, Gryparis, K. Theotokis,** and **Lambros Porfyras** (1879–1932, pseudonym of Dimitrios Sypsomos). The long poem in **decapentasyllables** by Spilios Pasayannis (1874–1909), *Echoes,* was published by *Techni* in 1899 (see also *Greek Creation,* no. 86: 1 Sept. 1951). It also published *Fragments,* by M. Malakasis (1869–1943; see issues no. 384: 1943, 615: 1953, and 803: 1960 of *Néa Estía,* which refer to Malakasis, as also does a special no. of *Greek Creation,* no. 95: 15 Jan. 1952). *Techni* sponsored the naturalist currents in **theater,** influenced from abroad by Ibsen and Strindberg. In criticism, it adopted a position opposed to the progressives and **Vulgarizers.** These latter were greatly reinforced after 1903 by the periodical *Noumás.*

TELEVISION In the 1980s and 1990s, a successful novel was often made into a miniseries for Greek TV. The writer Maria Iordanidou (1897–1989), who was trapped in Batoum (Caucasus) in 1914, and so lived through the Russian revolution there, wove echoes of her youth into a novel published when she was 66, *Loxandra* (1963), which was turned into a TV series. The short novel *The Notary* by **Rangavís** (1855) was a surprising choice for a Greek television series (1971). It has a gloomy, romantic plot about a forged will and a man who stops at nothing for the love of his daughter. He dies melodramatically, stepping into the sea that separates him from Cephalonia.

In the 1980s, the novel *Chatzi Manuel* (1956), by **Th. Kastanakis,** was another runaway TV success. The hero's part was acted by Yannis Mortzos. A television version of *Mrs. Do-re-mi* (1955) by **Lilika Nakou** was popular in the oppressive period of the **Colonels.** Dora Yiannakopoulou's *The Wedding Dress Fitting* also became popular on the small screen.

TERPSICHORE One of the nine **Muses,** Terpsichore was the patron of choral music. She is depicted dancing or holding a lyre.

TERTSETIS, YEORYIOS (1800–1873) One of the first judges of the new Greek state, Yeoryios Tertsetis studied law (and Italian literature) at Bologna and Padua. He was from Zakynthos, joined the **Friendly Society,** and crossed into the Morea at the start of the **Uprising** (1821). He became ill and returned to Zakynthos, becoming a close friend of **Solomós.** He helped **Kolokotronis** draft his *Memoirs,* and it was his refusal in 1833 to sign the warrior's death certificate that led to his own trial, and a period of wandering, which included Paris and London. He wrote down the *Memoirs* of Nikitarás and of other **Independence** rebels. Tertsetis also published eulogies, essays, journalism, plays, and lyric verse.

TERZAKIS, ANGELOS (1907–1979) Angelos Terzakis, novelist, short story writer, dramatist, and director of the scholarly journal *Periods* (Athens, 1963–1967), was born in **Nafplion,** where he also spent his early childhood. Terzakis moved with his family to Athens in 1915, attended high school, and took a law degree. In 1932 he was appointed General Secretary to the State **Theater.** A year later he was Artistic Director, and in 1944 he was Director of Repertory. In the 1950s he contributed regularly as a cultural commentator and theater critic to the daily newspaper *The Tribune.* He continued to produce articles and essays until the year of his death. When still a student, in 1925, he published a collection of short stories, *The Forgotten One.* Terzakis later brought out a striking novel of adolescence in the quest form, *Voyage with the Evening Star* (1946), where growing into maturity has tragic repercussions because of the disillusionment of the young male in an ambiance of sexual rivalry. There had been other short stories, and then a series of three novels in the 1930s. *The Violet City* (1937) was his most advanced work to date and looked forward to the experimental effects of his **historical novel,** *Princess Ysabeau* (1946), with its strong female protagonist.

Terzakis also wrote novels with a marked contemporary interest. *Without God* (1951) deals with Greek national events from the defeats of 1897 to the **Asia Minor disaster** of 1922. *Secret Life*

(1957) posits an individual's choice of solitude and his persistent self-disclosure. It is an autobiographical narrative: for the woman met by the first-person narrator, the solution is escape by sacrifice; for the hero, the solution is the bitterness of memory or death. In both these books, L. Politis picks out a dominant confessional tone and the combination of pessimism with doubt that shapes Terzakis's approach to the grayness of a common, bourgeois life. From 1964 came *Greek Heroic Exploits,* which portrayed events of the **Resistance,** particularly during the winter of 1940–1941, and included maps of the campaign.

Further Reading

"Anghelos Terzakis: Excerpts from Two Novels and a Play" [by various translators]. *The Charioteer,* no. 4 (1962): 15–49.

Chatzinis, Y. Προτιμήσεις [Preferences]. Athens: Phexi, 1963.

Terzakis, Angelos. *Homage to the Tragic Muse.* Translated by Thanasis Anagnostopoulos, with a preface by Cedric Whitman. Boston: Houghton Mifflin, 1978.

TEXTUAL ANALYSIS. See LITERARY ANALYSIS

TEXTUAL CRITICISM. See PALAEOGRAPHY

THALIA Thalia is the classical Muse who protected comic poetry and the pastoral idyll. She rejoices in banquets and is shown in Greek art with a shepherd's crook or holding a comic mask.

THEATER, SEVENTEENTH CENTURY One of the "three Fathers of the Church," Dio Chrysostom in the fourth century made drama anathema for Christians, calling it the work of the devil. By the end of the tenth century, Greek theater was forgotten. The terms *Tragedy* and *Comedy* were wrongly related to lyric poetry, and people imagined that a single reader had recited those parts in plays, accompanying the action with mime or gestures, an opinion that resulted from a faulty reading of **Aristotle.** For seven more centuries, Greek drama was dormant, but in the seventeenth century a small revival appeared, although there was still not much outside Crete that amounted to a play.

When Sathas edited a group of **Renaissance** Greek plays (Venice, 1879), this eminent nineteenth-century scholar chose the title *Cretan Theater.* That term is now used to refer to the genre that includes *Zeno, Stathis, Katzourbos,* ***Fortounatos,*** *Erofili, Gyparis* (or *Panoria*). L. Politis, who edited the play *Katzourbos,* accepts a generative Italian background to Cretan theater, but rejects the notion that *commedia erudita* ("learned comedy") was its source. The historical tragedy *Zeno,* by an unknown Cretan author, stages intrigue devised by the Byzantine emperor Zeno (474–491) and his cousin Longinus to secure a dynasty. They receive dire punishment: Zeno is buried alive, Longinus is executed. The script is modeled on a Latin drama, *Zeno* (1648), composed by the Jesuit monk Joseph Simons (1595–1671). The Cretan play starts with a prologue addressed to Ares, god of war. The action is packed with killings. It ends with the ghosts of the murdered principals assembled on stage. *Zeno* was written and performed at Zakynthos (1682–1683). The comedy *Stathis* (dated 1604 or later) consists of a prologue, three acts, and two *intermezzi,* that is, separate interval playlets. Written perhaps by **Chortatsis,** possibly by the actor Folas named in the text, it concerns the return of the prodigal son to his father's house and ends in a double marriage.

Among the stock characters present in the three Cretan comedies are the wealthy old reprobate, young son, girl in love, braggart warrior (ψευτοπαλληκαράς), or thug, together with his cunning servant (πονηρὸς ὑπηρέτης), the boaster (παινεψάρης), the schoolteacher (or pedant), the procures (προξενήτρα), the hungry slave (δοῦλος φαγᾶς), and the quack (ψευτογιατρός). Other stock characters are the flatterer (κόλακας), the fawning toady (συκοφάντης), the madam (ξεμαυλίστρα), and the mother-in-law (πεθερά).

The *Fortounatos* by Markos Antonios Foskolos, written between 1655 and 1662, may be Cretan, despite the author's Latin name. Is there any seventeenth-century Greek drama from elsewhere? Only a curiosity entitled *The Stable* by Neophytos, a cleric in Bucharest. The plot, in 394 rhyming decapentasyllables, tells how the Rev. Cyril beats up the Rev. Neophytos, then steals his clothes. Cyril calls doctors to attend the victim, just in case he dies. He beats him up again. Neophytos takes him to court. Cyril is arrested and held prisoner in a stable. He addresses the stable, then the Devil, in the opening dialogues. To dramatize the punishment, Neophytos introduces 13 separate characters, including the miscreant's deceased father from the Underworld, and the Patriarch.

THEATER COMPANIES, TWENTIETH CENTURY In 1900, the Athens Municipal Theater (founded 1888) gave a performance of Aristophanes's *Clouds,* which counted an audience of 1,500 at a single sitting. **Konstantinos Christomanos** (1867–1911) helped to found a

progressive theater group called New Stage in 1901. New Stage was aimed at a younger audience and featured the soon-to-be legendary actresses Kyverli Adrianou and Marika Kotopouli (longtime girl friend of the wild **nationalist** writer **I. Dragoumis**). An actor named Karolos Koun (b. 1908) founded the Arts Theater. This developed into a performance center after World War II. Helen Sikelianós, sister of the poet **Angelos Sikelianós,** was formed as an actress in the Christomanos school. She was married to the Greek poet Spilios Pasayannis, but gave him a hard time. The poet returned to Greece and died after she left him. New Stage followed ideas made current by nineteenth-century French naturalism. It promoted use of the common spoken language (see **Demotic**) and overtook the fossilizing form *komeidyllio*, comic idyll with songs. Christomanos put on Euripides's *Alcestis,* Tolstoy's *Power of Darkness* (1886), Goldoni's *La locandiera,* and Ibsen's *The Wild Duck.* Melpomeni Constantinopoulou (born in Athens, 1865) was the leading female figure in early Greek **theater.** Her parents were both actors, and she joined the Tavoularis brothers' repertory company. She appeared in many European roles while starring in Greek *komeidyllio* plays, most of which she launched herself.

New Stage was in competition with the Royal National Theater, founded in 1901. Royal Theater was built with the patronage and contributions of the conservative King George, after a sustained campaign of some 20 years. Its first influential stage director was Thomas Oikonomos. It presented Aeschylus's *Oresteia* plays in a demotic translation by **Soteriadis** (1903). This led to language riots (see **Evangelika; Language Question; Mistriotis; Oresteiaká**). Venue for

this *Oresteia* was the Herod Atticus Theater, on the Acropolis. The Herod Atticus
was traditionally employed for academic
productions, those designed to highlight
the classical language. Athens could
hardly support two theaters. The Royal
closed down in 1908, and New Stage lost
its initial impetus with the withdrawal
(1906) of its founder Christomanos.
Ioannis Polemis (1862–1924) was
founder and first President of the Association of Greek playwrights. In 1932 the
Royal Theater was resuscitated by Fotos
Politis, under the name National Theater.
Nikolaos Paraskevás (d. 1959) played the
male lead for the National Theater from
its new inception under Politis; among
his roles were Shylock and the Pedant in
Babylon (by **Vyzantios**). Thanks to the
National Theater, there were many reviv-
als of the classical repertoire after 1938.
Some productions centered around the
prestige of National Theater's leading actors, Alexis Minotis and Katina Paxinou.
An annual festival was staged from 1954,
giving performances before audiences of
thousands in the ancient stone theater at
Epidavros. An avant-garde group chaired
by Karolos Koln formed the so-called Art
Theater (1942), which performed at Epidavros, Athens, and foreign locations,
specializing in Aristophanes, absurdist
drama, and English playwrights such as
Shaffer and Pinter. By the 1980s, there
were about 40 winter theaters in Athens.
The popular theater of Katrakis was established in 1955 and had many stage
successes, especially with open-air productions in the summer months. The
summer theaters offered mostly open-air
performances, consisting of revues,
farces, and musicals. The Spyros Evan-
gelatos Theater revolved round its creative director more than its leading actors.
  See also GERMANY; KARAGH-
IOZIS; OPERA; PUPPETS; ROMAS;
SHAKESPEARE; TERZAKIS

Further Reading

A special number of the literary periodical
Greek Creation (no. 83: 15 July 1951) deals
with K. Christomanos.

(See also special issue of *Néa Estía,* no. 826:
1961)

**THEATER; DRAMATISTS, NINE-
TEENTH CENTURY** Alexandros
Rangavís (1809–1892), a **Phanariot**
from Constantinople, lists 90 dramatists
in an essay of 1877, but says the list is
incomplete. A prototype of nineteenth-
century drama is *The Death of Demosthenes* (1818), by **N. Pikkolos** (1792–
1866), the first modern Greek play
translated into English (see *Néa Estía,* 1
October 1942). It was played, in Odessa,
by the star of an earlier *Philoctetes* in a
modern adaptation, Y. Abramiotis, some
traders, and an English Philhellene, F.
Wilkinson. Aside from **Antonios Matesis** (1794–1875), with his trailblazing
vernacular play *The Basil Plant* (written
c. 1830), the main authors writing drama
after the **War of Independence** adopted
a learned, neoclassical tone, and their
characters' idiom on stage is **Katharevousa,** usually in unrhyming 12-syllable
iambics (the stressed iambic trimeter).
Chief among these is Dimitrios Vernardakis (1833–1907), who began with
Shakespeare as a model but turned to Euripides. His commentaries on Euripides
have considerable exegetical insight.
Much admired was Vernardakis's *Maria,
Daughter of Doxapater* (1858), a Byzantine historical drama based on the sacrifice of a Greek girl under Frankish rule.
His *Merope* came out in book form, in
1865, but his great stage success (Athens,
1893) was *Fausta,* based on Flavia Max-

ima Fausta, the second wife of Constantine the Great (293–326). The imperial plot fanned the flames of the **Great Idea,** evoking feelings of Byzantine expansionism. In provincial towns and parts of Greece not yet redeemed from the **Ottomans,** *Fausta* was the favorite bill of fare. Crispus is Constantine's son by his first wife, Minervina, and at age 17 he wins glory in a campaign that ends with the crushing of Licinius's fleet (323). Back at the royal court, he unwittingly tempts his stepmother Fausta (in a plot analogous to Euripides's *Hippolytus*). Her advances are rebuffed; she makes false reports on Crispus to his father, who orders his execution. When she repents, it is too late; she herself dies in a boiling bath prepared for her by order of Constantine.

The Athenian public so relished this drama that it was staged simultaneously in separate productions for the two great tragic actresses of the time, Katherine Veroni-Yennadi and Evangelia Paraskevopoulou. The play *Galateia* was read aloud to a meeting of the **Parnassós** in 1871 and first performed in 1872. This work by Spyridon Vasiliadis (1845–1874) became the other great stage favorite of the late nineteenth century. Drawing on a **demotic song,** "The Unfaithful Wife," and based on the myth of Pygmalion, *Galateia* is set in four acts that revolve around a man's infatuation with his sculpted bust of Galateia. His ardor and Aphrodite's influence bring her to life, but the miraculously created wife falls for his brother, the Argonaut Renos, urging him, in turn, to murder Pygmalion. Renos is tempted, but comes to his senses and slays Galateia. The writer, A. Vlachos (1838–1920), became the recognized father of the Greek one-act play and adapted European drama in Greek.

The best of his one-act plays is *The Grocer's Daughter* (1866), which was so popular that it reached 28 performances, an unheard-of figure for the time. Much loved was his prize-winning three-act play of 1870, *Siege of the Bridegroom.* **Babis Anninos** (1852–1934, from Cephalonia) composed comedies in **mixed** Katharevousa and Demotic: his *Wanted, One Servant* (1898) and *Leonidas the Conqueror* (1895) are saturated with comic turns. **Nirvanas** later said that for half a century Anninos's services to the state had been directed at "public health . . . and the rejoicing of the soul." Rangavís published plays at regular intervals in the course of his glittering political career. Best known are his tragedy *Frosyne* (1837), the historical tragedy *The Thirty Tyrants* (1866), and the popular comedy *Koutroulis's Wedding* (1845). The latter title has become a proverb indicating a state of general confusion. Alexandros's son, Kleon Rizos Rangavís (1842–1917), appointed first secretary when his father was American ambassador (1867), was an ambitious playwright: he wrote *Julian the Apostate, Theodora, The Isaurians, Herakleitos,* and *The Duchess of Athens,* plays mostly set in archaic, **purist** Greek. Plays full of satirical wit were produced by Dimitrios Byzantios-Aslanis (1770–1853). Iakovos Rizos Neroulos (1778–1849), cousin of the A. Rangavís mentioned earlier, wrote the tragedies *Aspasia* (1813) and *Polyxena* (1814).

See also CHOURMOUZIS; KARAGHIOZIS; THEATER COMPANIES; THEATER PERFORMANCES

Further Reading

Laskaris, N. Ἱστορία τοῦ νεοελληνικοῦ θεάτρου [A History of Modern Greek Theater]. 2 vols. Athens: Vasiliou, 1938–1939.

Lighizos, M. Τὸ νεοελληνικὸ πλάϊ στὸ παγκόσμιο θεάτρο [Modern Greek Theater in the Context of World Drama]. Athens: Saliveru, 1958.

Muzenidis, T. Τὸ Ποντιακὸ θεάτρο [Theater from Pontis]. Athens: Phexi, 1959.

Rangabé, Aléxandre Rizos. *Précis de la littérature néo-hellénique* [A Summary of Modern Greek Literature]. 2 vols. Berlin S. Calvary, 1877.

Sideris, Y. Ἱστορία τοῦ νέου ἑλληνικοῦ θεάτρου *1794–1944.* Τόμος πρῶτος *(1794–1908).* [A History of Neo-Hellenic Theater: Vol. 1 1794–1908] Athens: Ikaros, 1951.

Valsa, M. *Le Théâtre Grec Moderne de 1453 à 1900* [Modern Greek Theatre from 1453 to 1900]. Berlin: Akademie Verlag, 1960.

THEATER; DRAMATISTS, TWENTIETH CENTURY

With the foundation of the Royal Theater and New Scene in 1901, the Athens public began to go out for the evening. The Royal staged plays with indigenous, homegrown sources: by Y. Tsokopoulos, Y. Pop, **Koromilás,** Laskaris, **Anninos, Polemis,** and M. Lidorikis. Much admired from this first crop was Tsokopoulos's *The Child.* K. Chatzopoulos and Thomas Oikonomou were among a group of energetic translators, directors, organizers, stage designers, and adaptors into **Demotic.** The **actress** Marika Kotopouli triumphed in Goethe's *Iphigeneia.* Classical tragedy came back in vogue with an *Antigone* produced by K. Manos, and much dispute was generated around the ***Oresteiaká.*** Christomanos used New Scene to promote texts written in contemporary spoken language, sponsoring work like Ilias Kouloubatos's *Merrymaking* (1906) or M. Avgeris's *In Amongst the Humans* and such authors as **Sikelianós,** Sp. Pasayannis, and **Skipis.** D. Tangopoulos's *Chains* (1907) and **Rigas Golfis** with

Monster from the Deep (1908) wrote Greece's first socialist drama, in a productive two-year period. Indeed, Golfis was involved in the translation of early twentieth-century workers' songs. Spyros Melás (1882–1966) also sprang to notice in 1907 with the play *Son of the Shadow* and subsequently seems to sketch a Greek response to the First and Second International (1864; 1889), and the Comintern (1919) with such plays as *The Red Shirt, White and Black,* and *The Ruined House.* Later came fully rounded plays: *Judas* (1935), *Papaphlessas, Rigas Velestinlís,* and *One Night, One Life.*

Melás wrote two witty comedies: *Dad's Getting Educated* and *The King and the Hound.* Pantelis Horn (1881–1941) was one of a select few who devoted themselves solely to theater. He had a considerable hit with *The Sapling,* which was set in working-class Athens and featured a girl of humble family who faces up to moral collapse. Horn published *The Outsider* (1906) in ***Noumás*** and had his performance debut (1908) with *Stone-Cutters.* Later Horn wrote a series of pieces with local color, in the modish recording of manners, set in the Greek communities of Asia Minor. **Pavlos Nirvanas** (1866–1937) poured out four socialist dramas: *Maria Pentayiotissa,* with its authentic working-class setting, and a beautiful doomed heroine of the people, a play now highly regarded, but judged a failure by **Kazantzakis** (1909); *Architect Marthas; Swallow;* and *When He Breaks His Bonds.* **Zacharias Papantoniou** followed in the steps of **Eftaliotis,** composing *Oath of the Dead Man,* based on the noted folk ballad (***paralogé***) "The Dead Brother." **Galateia Kazantzakis** composed some 20 plays and one-acts, collected in *The Curtain.* Her characterization and dialogue achieve sharp effects in *The Darkness Grows Thicker, The Russian Woman, Light Blue Bird, The Monastery at Arkadi,* and *Wounded Birds.* Theodoros Synadinós (1880–1959) devoted himself solely to drama, with comedies and pieces on local custom like *Miss Lawyer* and *Bluffs.* Dimitris Bogris (1890–1964) took the recording of local custom further. His first play was *Doctor Mavridis* (in three acts), put on by the National Theater (1921), with sets by the renowned stage designer Oikonomou. Bogris also wrote *The Squall* (1934), *In Front of the Abyss* (1926), *The Shrew* (1928), *Broken Wings* (1931), *Life Anew* (1936), *Sea Swell* (1937), *The Girl from the Harbor* (1947), *Waves of Hydra* (1951), *Darkness at Nafpaktos,* and *The Betrothals* (1925), which won the Kotopoulis and Averoff prizes. It was staged by the theater group The Moderns, directed by Kostís Belmyras.

Angelos Simiriotis (1873–1944) wrote tragedies that enjoyed productions at Constantinople, Smyrna, or Athens and were based on **Byzantine** topics: *Froso Notará* (1926), *Astraea* (1929), *The Respondent Spoke, or Zoë Born to the Purple* (1931), which won the Stathás Prize. He also translated Aeschylus's *Agamemnon* (1931). With Dimitrios Tangopoulos (1867–1926), **Kambysis, Xenopoulos, Sikelianós, Theotokás, Golfis, Psathas, Terzakis,** K. Bastiás (1901–1972), and T. Moraïtinis (1876–1952), their activity hints at the panoply of twentieth-century Greek stagecraft. The bimonthly journal *Theater* (founded in 1962), edited by Kostas Nitsos, printed primary material, essays, research, and criticism on twentieth-century Greek drama. An annual review, also called *Theater* (started in 1957), was edited by the experienced critic Marios Ploritis. This periodical printed key works performed in Athens during preceding seasons.

See also KAMBANELLIS; KAZANTZAKIS; SHAKESPEARE

Further Reading

Athanasiadis Novas, Th. Ἀθηναϊκὴ Δραματουργία [Athenian Play-Writing]. Athens: privately printed, 1956.

Athanasiadis Novas, Th. Θεατρικὰ μελετήματα [Theater Studies]. Athens: privately printed, 1963.

Glinós, Y. Ὧρες σκηνῆς [Hours On-Scene]. 2 vols. Athens [privately publ.], 1953–1961.

Politis, F. Θεατρικὲς Ἐπιφυλλίδες, κείμενα ἀφορῶντα εἰς τὸ Ἑλλ. Θεάτρο δημοσιευθέντα κατὰ τὰ ἔτη *1915–1934* [Theater Serials: Texts Referring to the Greek Theater Published in the Period 1915–1934]. Athens: Galaxia, 1964.

Thrilos, Alkis. Μορφὲς καὶ θέματα τοῦ θεάτρου [Figures and Themes from the Theater]. 2 vols. Athens: Difros, 1961–1962.

THEATER PERFORMANCES, NINETEENTH AND TWENTIETH CENTURIES Memorials of classical performance are the open-air theaters at Delphi, Epidavros, Messini, Dodoni (Epirus), Argos (Argolis), Amfiario (Oropos), Megalopoli (Arkadia), Lavrion (Attica), Festos (Crete), and the islands of Delos and Thassos. In 1818, Nikolaos Pikkolos (1792–1865) produced his play *The Death of Demosthenes* at Odessa. A work by the Italian writer Metastasio, *Olimpia,* was one of the first plays performed at Athens (1836) since antiquity. It was translated by the Greek political martyr **Rigas Velestinlís.** The pro-Independence conspirator, **Lassanis** (1793–1870), composed a patriotic drama, *Greece and the Outsider* (1819), and the tragedy *Harmodios and Aristogeiton. The Basil Plant,* by **A. Matesis** (produced at Zakynthos in 1832, publ. 1855), is the first bourgeois play with a modern plot set in demotic prose. Matesis called it "a historical novel presented under dramatic form." Set in Zakynthos (1712), *The Basil Plant* tells of an aristocratic family, whose daughter insists on arranging her own marriage with a commoner. It was not followed by other drama in the demotic idiom.

From 1927, in the classical theater at Delphi, **Sikelianós** and his wife mounted choreographed and sung productions of Aeschylus's *Prometheus Bound* and *Suppliants.* Theodoros Synadinós (1880–1959) wrote successful and popular plays with contemporary plots or clear sociological relevance, like *The Buffoon Karaghiozis* (a Hamletian arrangement with aspirations toward theater of ideas and a box-office hit), *Man of Hades, Bluffs, The Dexterous Man, Patron of the Arts, The Wild One, The Red Mask, George's Honor, The Duellist, Feathers, Social Mobility,* and *It's Your Fault.* He made a theater adaptation of the ***Erotokritos,*** which was praised by the eccentric, influential critic Fotos Politis. Synadinós adapted Cervantes's *Don Quixote* for the stage and the Homeric *Odyssey.* Vangelis Kadzanis (b. 1935) caused public uproar with an anti-Monarchist tragedy, ostensibly concerned with the mythological curse on the royal house of Atreus. Another successful playwright of the post–World War II period, Fofi Tresou (born 1929), produced a tragedy exploring this theme for its contemporary repercussions.

See also THEATER COMPANIES

Further Reading

Pontani, F. M. *Teatro neoellenico* [Modern Greek Theater]. Milan: La Nuova Accademia, 1962.

Wiles, David. *Greek Theatre Performance: An Introduction.* Cambridge: Cambridge University Press, 2000.

THEMELIS, YORGOS (1900–1976)
Yorgos Themelis, born in Samos, taught in **Thessaloniki** from 1930. He studied literature at Athens, did further work at the University of Thessaloniki, and then taught in its Experimental School (1934–1949). As an associate (1933–1938) of the important journal *Macedonian Days* and from 1945 to 1947 coeditor of the avant-garde poetry journal *The Snail,* Themelis influenced fellow writers with his essays, criticism, and the verse of *Bare Window* (1945), *Men and Birds* (1947), *The Return* (1948), *Accompaniment* (1950), *The Face and the Idol* (1959), *The Sortie* (1968), and other volumes. He wrote books on **Solomós, Kavafis, Papadiamantis,** modernism, and theory of interpretation and translated Aeschylus's *Prometheus Bound* and Sophocles's *Oedipus Tyrannus.*

THEODOROU, VICTORIA (1926–)
Victoria Theodorou is a poet, translator, and prose writer. She was born in Khania (Crete) and became active as a runner of messages in the Cretan **resistance.** In 1947 she went to study at Athens; in 1949 she was arrested for illegal activities during the **Civil War** and banished to a small, uninhabited island called Trikeri, where she spent four years, living in a tent. Her collection of poetry, *The Ex-*

cursion (1973), is dedicated to women who were fellow-exiles on the island, one of whom dug up in 1973 a set of Theodorou's notebooks buried under the soil. These concealed memoirs described the conditions endured by internal exiles on the postwar losing side. They appear in Theodorou's book *Women's Concentration Camps.* Twenty years after her detention, she made a journey of return (described in *Picnic*) to the place of exile where she had been locked up with women aged 17 to 70. They had all refused to sign a document of repentance after supporting the armed struggle of the Left. She has produced 10 books of verse, edited *Demotic Songs of Yugoslav Macedonia and Folk Fairy Poetry* (1979), and translated texts by Mateja Matefski, Boris Vichinski, and Kosta Ratsin.

Further Reading

Fourtouni, Eleni, ed. *Contemporary Greek Women Poets.* New Haven: Thelpini Press, 1978.

THEOTOKÁ, KORALIA (1926–1976)

Born Koralia Andreadi, this existentialist poet married the writer **Yorgos Theotokás** just a few months before he died (1966); she had already published *Attempts* (1963). After his death she was shattered. She made this bereavement the central act of her remaining years, until she committed suicide by throwing herself from the roof of a condominium. Her husband Yorgos was the nucleus of her poetry in that last decade: *In Another Light* (1967), *The Identity* (1971), and *The Poem: The Major Proceedings* (1975). Meraklís said of her that "she jumped to death from the rope-ladder of love." She was shocked by the **Colonels' Junta** and on top of her domestic misfortune found it too hard to bear, judging

herself ill-adapted, impractical, and unable to match the positive attitude of the young people all around her. She ended her life as a writer by scribbling a simple message that the world should become a better place to live. Her poems circle around the doom of grief: "Flowers arise and down comes the beloved / In the mud of sleep; / The days disperse us, / Like salt on snow," and around the short ecstasy of their shared past: "In one night you made the addition of my life, / You filled the empty bed with spasms / And lit the deserted chamber with torches."

Further Reading

Theotoka, Koralia. "Two Poems." Translated by Theodore Vasils. *The Charioteer,* no. 14 (1972): 29–31.

THEOTOKÁS, YORGOS (1906–1966)

Essayist, novelist, dramatist, and travel writer, Yorgos Theotokás was born in Constantinople, to a family of Chiot origin, and he attended school there. After the **Asia Minor disaster** (1922), his family went to Athens. He returned once to Constantinople (1962); he enrolled in the Athens Law School and graduated in 1926. For the next two years, he studied philosophy, sociology, and aesthetics in Paris. He went on to London for a year of further studies. He became proficient at languages, especially French and English. When Theotokás returned to Greece (1929), he carried not a first volume of poems or novel, but a manifesto for Greek culture entitled *Free Spirit* (1929), published under the pseudonym Orestes Digenes, which suggested East–West diversity. This essay was widely interpreted (Beaton: 1994) as the real entrance to the "rich period of the 1930s and 1940s" (P. Bien's phrase). It is so opinionated that it undermines its real conviction. It exalts the fiction of **Ion Dragoumis** and trumpets that a single peasant from the Greek mountains is more interesting than the "poet of Alexandria" (**Kavafis**). Theotokás adds that the Criminal Court can often produce, in a simple divorce case, "much more soul and much humanity than in the collected works of Kavafis." Indeed, *Free Spirit* was a challenge by the **Generation of the Thirties** to an exhausted society and its ruling class. It also attempted to reform the prevailing, listless attitude to prose fiction. Tziovas points out (1988) how Theotokás considered the touchstone of creative prose to be "the creation of living people." If a writer could not invest his characters with individuality on the page, then Theotokás saw them as a failure.

His own novel *Argo* (1933–1935), set in Istanbul and Athens, tells a story of the turbulent period between the World Wars. The title is taken from the quest of the golden fleece. In the novel, it is applied to a disaffected student group that seeks linguistic and social reform. Its pages are suffused with nostalgia for the old Greek presence in the Ottoman capital. The later novel *Leonís* (1940) shows what it was like to grow up as a Greek in Constantinople. Both books concern the struggle of young people trying to find their way in life, as P. Mackridge expresses it, "against a background of politics (including war), love and art." Theotokás became a respected figure in Greek society, almost a face of the Establishment. Twice he was appointed General Director of the Ethnic Theater (in the periods 1945–1946 and 1950–1952). He was Chairman of the Organizing Committee of the State Theater of Northern Greece from 1961 to 1964. He received three major state prizes for his work; he published an *Essay on America* (1954) and *Travel in the Middle East and the Holy Mountain* (1961). All through his career, Theotokás was interested in the theoretical aspects of narrative prose. In a 1934 article entitled "The New Literature," he suggested that the modern novel could take the place of the classical **epic.** D. Tziovas quotes a striking metaphor by Theotokás to express how "the winds of Greek literature will blow towards the direction of the novel," and also underlines this Greek novelist's rejection of *ithografía,* the portrayal of homely scenes, with the recording of manners and moral sketch. In an essay of 1964, Theotokás rejected the idea of the "death of the character," though he noted how advances in technology and psychology seemed to underpin the work of the *nouveau roman* group and Nathalie Sarraute. Theotokás prepared accounts of his travels in Persia, the Soviet Union, and Romania, which were published posthumously. His correspondence with **Seferis** (1930–1960) also came out after his death.

See also THEOTOKÁ, KORALIA

Further Reading

Bien, Peter. "Victory of Demotic." *TLS,* 11 Nov. 1994: 25.

Doulis, Thomas. *George Theotokas.* Boston: Twayne Publishers, 1975.

Theotocas, George. *Leonis.* Translated by Donald E. Martin. Minneapolis, MN: North Central Publishing Co., 1985.

Theotokás, Yorgos. Ἐλεύθερο πνεῦμα [Free Spirit]. Edited by K. Th. Dimarás. Athens: Ermis, 1973 [first publ. 1929].

Theotokás, Yorgos. "I néa logotehnía" [The New Literature]. *Idea* 3, no. 13 (1934): 11–17.

Theotokás, Yorgos. "To mithistórima ston kéro mas: i parádosi ke i ananéosi tou ídous" [The Novel in Our Time: Tradition and Renewal of a Genre]. *The Tribune* (Athens), 3 May 1964.

Theotokas, George. *Argo: A Novel.* Translated by E. Margaret Brooke and Ares Tsatsopoulos. London: Methuen, 1951.

Theotokás, Giorgos. Σημαίες στον ήλιον [*o 'Leonís' tou 1940 me to imerolóyio ergasías tou 'Leoní' ke ta diíymata tis 'Pedikís Ilikías'*]. Edited by G. P. Savidis and M. Pierís. Athens: Ermis, 1985.

Tziovas, Dimitris. "George Theotokás and the Art of Fiction." In *The Greek Novel: A.D. 1–1985,* edited by Roderick Beaton, 70–80. London: Croom Helm, 1988.

THEOTOKIS, KONSTANTINOS (1872–1923) An aristocrat of the **Ionian Islands,** Konstantinos Theotokis married Baroness Ernestine von Mallowitz when aged 19 and took her to live at his family castle. He studied in Germany, fought in the Cretan uprising (1896), and embraced socialism so staunchly (in the early 1900s) that he declined to accept his inheritance. He and his friend **Mavilis** organized a brigade of military volunteers to join insurrectionists in Crete. Theotokis wrote a series of four novels concerned with social realism, the modes of production, and the class struggle, using Greek settings that were free of folkloric realism (recording of manners, but see under **Honor**). In *Honor and Money* (1912), *Condemned* (1919), *Slaves in their Chains* (1922), and *The Life and Death of the "Hangman"* (1920), he renews the descriptive canvas of writers like **Karkavitsas,** but moves to the political commitment of the generation that came after the **Asia Minor disaster.** *Honor and Money* was made into a color film entitled *The Price of Love* (1984) by Tonia Marketaki. He gives a fresh impulse to village themes, while devising a palette for urban realism. The decline of

an island aristocracy dominates in Theotokis's last, ambitious work, *Slaves in their Chains* (1922). In this novel, Beaton detects the first use in Greek fiction of the *leitmotiv* ("repeated phrase"), elaborate sentences of Proustian length, and a precocious handling of time settings. A special issue of the journal *Néa Estía* (no. 624: 1953) concerns Theotokis, as does a monographic number of the periodical *Greek Creation* (no. 92: 1 Dec. 1951).

Further Reading

Eklund, Bo-Lennart. "The Socialism of Constantinos Theotokis: An Analysis Based on the Concepts 'TIMH' and 'XPHMA' in Two of his Works." *Scandinavian Studies in Modern Greek* / Νεοελληνικά Μελετήματα 3 (1979): 3–27.

Katsimbalis, Yeoryios. Βιβλιογραφία Κωνστ. Θεοτόκη [A Bibliography of Konstantinos Theotokis]. Athens: Sergiade, 1952.

Theotokis, K. Ἡ τιμὴ καί τὸ χρῆμα [Honor and Money]. Athens, [in the periodical Νουμάς], 1912; also Athens: Keimena, 1978.

Theotokis, K. Κατάδικος [Condemned]. Athens, 1919; also edited by G. Dallas, Athens: Keimena, 1979.

Theotokis, K. Οἱ σκλάβοι στὰ δεσμὰ τους [Slaves in their Chains]. Athens, 1922; also intro. by G. Dallas, Athens: Keimena, 1981.

Theotokis, K. Ἡ ζωὴ καὶ ὁ θάνατος τοῦ Καραβέλα [The Life and Death of the 'Hangman']. Athens, 1920; reprinted Athens: Vasiliou, 1961; also Athens: Nefeli, 1990.

Theotokis, K. "Face Down!" Translated by Theodore Sampson. In *Modern Greek Short Stories,* vol. 1. Edited by K. Delopoulos, 267–271. Athens: Kathimerini, 1980.

THEOTOKIS, NIKIFOROS (1731–1800) The scientist and theologian Ni-

kiforos Theotokis grew up and studied at Kerkyra. One of his teachers was the ecclesiastic Jeremias Kavvadias, who taught **Voulgaris.** In 1762, Theotokis took orders as a monk. Patriarch Samuel Chantzeris invited him to Constantinople. In Italy, he studied under Giovanni Poleni, who also taught Moisiodax, **Zarzoulis,** and Voulgaris. He went to Lepizig for further study in physics (1765). His *Elements of Physics* became a basic Greek science text. He taught physics at Jassy and was the first to introduce modern scientific analysis to Moldavia. Conservative elements drove him away, and he succeeded Voulgaris as archbishop of Kherson and Slaviansk (the frontier diocese of Novorossia). In 1786, he became archbishop of Astrachanios and Stavropol (a see of the Caspian and N. Caucasus). After he resigned, he lived out his years in a monastery (Moscow). His early sermons and religious writing were in **plain Greek.** For his later scientific work, he adopted a simplified archaic, finally reaching a classical style, by the same route as Voulgaris. This constitutes him as the forerunner, if not the actual founder, of **Katharevousa.**

THESAURUS The noun *treasure* denoted a repository in a building (οἰκοδόμημα) set aside for votive offerings at a center of worship, like Olympia, Delos, or Delphi. The **Renaissance** made the word, by **metonymy,** into a title for the first historical **dictionaries.** *Treasure of the Greek Language,* edited by a French scholar (1572) in five volumes, was reissued (Paris: Firmin-Didot 1831–1865) in nine volumes. From 1955, a German dictionary called *Thesaurus of Greek* was issued from Hamburg under the direction of Bruno Snell, subdividing the vocabulary into the literary genres where it was found. In modern times, Berkowitz and Squitier produced *Thesaurus Linguae Graecae: Canon of Greek Authors and Their Works* (New York: Oxford University Press, 1990). The CD-ROM of this work, *TLG CD-ROM 'C,'* is available from the *Thesaurus Linguae Graecae* Project, in the United States. The book is a database registering 61 million words, from Homer to 400 A.D., found in some 700 classical and early Byzantine texts. Now there is some doubt over a phrase in **Bessarion,** "in a specifically characteristic way" (κατ᾽ ἐξιδίωσιν). The single word ἐξιδίωσις ("peculiar characteristic") is used once, attributed in a *String* (bunch of excerpts from Bible commentators), to the learned Arethas, Archbishop of Caesarea. Arethas (850–932) was a scholiast on classical texts and the patristic writers: he uses the verb "be peculiar to" (ἐξιδιοῦσθαι) in his commentary on *Revelation,* where he assesses distinguishing elements of the Trinity and its member Persons. "If the *Thesaurus Linguae Graecae* (CD-ROM D) can be trusted" (P. Lautner, 1995), the phrase κατ᾽ ἐξιδίωσιν and the noun ἐξιδίωσις are absent from **Aristotle, Hellenistic,** and **Neoplatonic** texts. Damascenus Stouditis (d. ?1577) compiled a work on ecclesiastical authorities, with 42 religious addresses of his own, entitled *Book Known as the Thesaurus.*

Further Reading

Lautner, P. "Theoprastus in Bessarion." *Journal of Hellenic Studies,* no. 115 (1995): 155–60.

THESIS The terms *thesis* and *arsis* (θέσις, ἄρσις) indicate which parts in oral poetry are accompanied by the measured beat of the performers on the floor, by the *thesis* ("strong down beat") and *arsis* ("light raising") of their foot. These tapping movements correspond to the down- and upbeat of a poem's rhythm. After classical Greek, the terms were reversed by the Latins. In modern Greek metrics, ἄρσις ("raising") denotes a strong (ισχυρή) syllable. Consequently, θέσις ("downbeat") now denotes a "weak" (ἄτονη) syllable. Music has preserved the classical Greek distinction, *up* for light and *down* for strong beat. W. Meyer, in an 1891 study, showed that euphony in Byzantine prose, at the end of sentences, did not take into account the length or shortness of syllables, but only the tone of the words, placing at least two cases of *thesis* before the closing *arsis.*

THESSALONIKI (Salonika) Greece's second city is named after a daughter of Philip of Macedon, Thessaloniki, who was married to Kassandros. This short-lived monarch was without descendants, so he gave Thessaloniki's name to the capital (founded 315 B.C.) to remind posterity of his family's royal descent. The Byzantine monk Ioannis Kameniatis, in *On the Fall of Thessaloniki,* gives an account of the city's capture by Saracen pirates under captain Leon Tripolitis (3 June 904). The Arabs sacked the city and carried off 22,000 prisoners. In later centuries, Thessaloniki became a target for plunder and invasions: it fell into Norman hands in 1185. Its cultural fortunes have fluctuated over three main periods: 1204–1430, post-Byzantine control, under Bonifazio of Monferrato and Th. Comnenus; 1430–1912, Turkish control; and 1912 to the present day, Greek centralism. The first printery of the East was founded in Thessaloniki (1506). A rare *Talmud* (1521) was produced in this Jewish firm. Other Jewish printeries were founded in 1532, 1554, 1578, 1592, and

1695. The first Greek printery at Thessaloniki was founded in 1850 by Miltiadis Garbolás and produced six books in its single year of operation. By 1912, some 250 titles had been published by Greek printeries in Thessaloniki.

In the first **Balkan War,** the Greek Army marched into the city on 8 November 1912 (New Style date). Thessaloniki was ceded to Greece by the Treaty of Bucharest in 1913. In March 1913, King George I was assassinated here. In World War II, the Western powers established their bridgehead here (12 October 1915). The politician **Elevtherios Venizelos,** pushing for Greece to ally with the Entente, set up his government of National Defence at Thessaloniki, in opposition to the government at Athens. In 1917 a fire destroyed most of the commercial center of the city, including bookshops, publishers, and newspaper offices. This loss of several newspaper and municipal archives made the later history of Thessaloniki harder to compile. By 1932, 20 years after its liberation from the Turks, there were 43 printeries in the city, of which 36 were Greek and 7 Jewish. From 1920 (1930, according to others), an intellectual circle developed and generated what is now called the "Macedonian School" of writers. This circle includes Alkiviadis Yannopoulos (1896–1981), who has been called the narrator of the "closed space," because of his attention to the house, the office, and so on. Other productive writers under this Macedonian heading are Y. Delios (born 1897), **Stelios Xefloudas** (1901–1984), Y. Vafopoulos (1903–1996) and N. G. Pentzikis (1908–1992, with **Yorgos Ioannou** (1927–1985), and poets like Varvitsiotis, Th. Fotiadis (b. 1921), Kleitos Kyrou (b. 1921), and **Manolis Anagnostakis** (b. 1925). Vafopoulos has a haunting poem addressed to "Thessaloniki! Thessaloniki!," which he calls "Monologue at Very Grievous Moments." The journal *Macedonian Days,* founded at Thessaloniki, ran from 1932 to 1939. It pursued Modernist and Symbolist goals, while exhibiting less social commitment than the **Generation of the Thirties** and the writers associated with the journal *Ta Néa Grámmata.* The first Greek translations of Franz Kafka appeared in *Macedonian Days.* The journal *Macedonian Letters* was founded in 1942. The poet Zoe Karelli, sister of local author Pentzikis, was born here in 1901. The writer Yeoryios Vafopoulos was appointed Secretary to the City Council (1931), and in 1939 he set up the Municipal Library. Vafopoulos was its Director up to his retirement (1963). He was awarded the Medal of the Municipality of Thessaloniki. In 1963, the poet Stefanos Tilikidis (born 1923) was a prize winner in the Municipality literary competition.

The poet Yeoryios X. Stoyannidis (b. 1910), who owned or managed various sweet shops between Kavala and Thessaloniki, settled in the city in 1970. The second university of Greece was founded at Thessaloniki in 1926, at first with a small Arts faculty. Another university at Thessaloniki started in 1957. From 1936 to 1940, the journal *Olympos,* jointly published in Greek and Italian, was produced at Thessaloniki. In World War II, German motorized columns thrust south along the river Vardar, to enter Thessaloniki on 9 April 1941. In the **occupation,** most of the Jewish population of 60,000 was deported to Poland. The high number of Jewish residents in Thessaloniki was due to the ancestral eviction of Jews from late-fifteenth-century Spain, when, in accordance with the Edict of Alhambra (1492), 20,000 Jews were driven

to the East. Most settled in Thessaloniki, where they merged with a contingent of Jews expatriated from Bavaria 20 years before. The Jews brought with them to Thessaloniki a form of Castilian speech. They developed it into the idiosyncratic Greek-Jewish creole known as Ladino, sometimes written with Hebrew characters. The year 1961 saw the foundation of the first state theater outside Athens, the so-called National Theater of Northern Greece at Thessaloniki; its first director was Sokratis Karantinos (b. 1906). The city now has a song festival. A Greek Film Festival was established in 1960. The International Film Festival of Thessaloniki followed (1972).

Further Reading

Kazantzis, Tolis. Ἡ Πεζογραφία τῆς Θεσσαλονίκης (1912–1983). Μελετήματα 1966–1991 [Thessaloniki Prose Writing from 1912 to 1983. Essays 1966–1991]. Thessaloniki: Vania, 1991.

Thaniel, George. *Homage to Byzantium: The Life and Work of Nikos Gabriel Pentzikis.* St. Paul, MN: North Central, 1983.

Vafopoulos, Y. Σελίδες αὐτοβιογραφίας τοῦ Γ. Θ. Βαφοπούλου [Autobiographical Pages by G. T. Vafopoulos]. Athens: Estía Bookshop Editions, 1970.

Vafopoulos, George. *The Complete Poems.* Translated by Thom Nairn and D. Zervanou. Edinburgh: Dionysia, 2000.

THRILLER The thriller or detective plot, in twentieth-century Greek publishing, often has a serious sociopolitical purpose (see **Vasilikós; Yatromanolakis**), but in the popular writer Neni Efthumiadi (b. 1946) it showcases the **suspense** and intrigue associated with Western whodunits or espionage fiction. Thus in Efthumiadis's *Quiet Days* (1983), a Greek couple's household in

Germany is upset by the arrival of the husband's half-brother, who has weapons and appears to be in a terrorist **plot,** when events take an unexpected course. In *Color of the Future* (1988), a complex, indifferent hero takes on a job for a terrorist outfit, whereas in *Sensitive Death* (1990) an individual confesses to a murder he did not commit, so his friends try to save him from arrest.

Further Reading

Maglinis, Elias, ed. "Interviews: The Detective Story, Andreas Apostolidis, Athina Cacouri, Petros Markaris, Petros Martinidis, Philippos Philippou." *Ithaca: Books from Greece,* no. 6 (November-December 2000): 20–29.

THUNDER. See MEDICAL TRACT

TOCCO. See *CHRONICLE OF THE TOCCO FAMILY OF CEPHALONIA*

TORTURE After the coup by the **Colonels,** a so-called National Government ran Greece (1967–1974). Its opponents were subject to prison, deportation, or exile. But was there systematic torture? P. Korovesis (from Cephalonia), in his *The Method* (1969), gives a cold, first-person account of the arrest, interrogation, torture, solitary confinement, and conditional discharge of a theater worker suspected of Communist conspiracy. He is picked up by Security Police. In detention, he is beaten and kicked. The soles of his feet are swollen by repeated applications of the old Turkish bastinado. He is addressed as "poofter" (πούστης) and "wanker" (μαλάκας). A silent 18-year-old girl is held on the prison roof, left for a night stark naked, hanging from manacles, with wood poked up her rectum and genitals (πρωκτός, αἰδοῖο), tricky

words to bring into written Greek. Each camp had its own torture. At Thessaloniki, they beat your feet with guns and hanged you upside down; at Piraeus, they used a braided rope; at Dionysos, they buried you in the ground; each prison used electric shocks (with the help of trained doctors) and staged sham executions.

Further Reading

Amnesty International. *Torture in Greece: The First Torturers' Trial, 1975.* London: Amnesty International Publications, 1977.

Becket, James. *Barbarism in Greece.* New York: Walker, 1970.

Korobesis, Periklís. ᾽Ανθρωποφύλακες [The Method]. Lund: Tryckeri, 1970.

TRADITION; TRADITIONAL The Greek term *tradition* usually requires decoding. Tradition (παράδοση) can refer, depending on the occasion, to what is conservative and neoclassical or to verse that has **rhyme** and **meter** or to prose that relays the **recording** of manners or to "our glorious Byzantinism." Beaton (1998) notes the complexity of this allusion to a difficult verse in **Kavafis.** "Our glorious Byzantinism" was used by **T. Papatsonis** as the title for a 1948 essay (in *Nea Estia,* vol. 43), which offered a provocative redefinition of certain heroes in the Greek literary pantheon: **Seferis, Elytis,** and **Gatsos** are seen as foreign-inspired underminers of the Greek tradition. The "brave" who sustained it are **Kalvos, Papadiamantis,** Kavafis, **Embirikos,** Matsas, and **Engonopoulos.** Papatsonis ponders including **Rodokanakis** and **Christomanos** in the latter group. In general, the adjective *traditional,* in critical code, tends to mean "old-fashioned."

Further Reading

Beaton, R. "Our Glorious Byzantinism." In *Byzantium and the Modern Greek Identity,* eds. David Ricks and Paul Magdalino. Aldershot: Ashgate, 1998.

TRAGIC IRONY. See IRONY

TRANSLATION INTO GREEK

Translation into modern Greek goes back five centuries. The initial need in the sixteenth and seventeenth century was for translations of the Bible. Soon readers required versions of **Aristotle** and material on **rhetoric.** The **Enlightenment** needed translations of the classics, especially ethics and history. In the last century, the force behind translation into Greek was the leisure market and the need for foreign scientific material. Among modern translations into Greek, 50 percent consists of literature, and another 25 percent comes from science. **Seferis** translates a limerick by Lear ("There was an old man of Thermopylae, / Who never did anything properly"), with the rhyming couplet Ἥτανε ἕνας γέρος ἀπ᾽ τὶς Θερμοπῦλες / ποὺ ὅλο πάθαινε νίλες).

In the sixteenth century, only one book translation was published in Greece. In the seventeenth century, the figure rose to five. In the eighteenth century, there were 57 translations (see Kassinis, 1995). In the nineteenth century, there were 3,000. In 1878, Stamatios Valvis (c. 1850–1916), a relative but eventual enemy of **Palamás,** published *On the Translation of Poets.* Valvis himself had translated Pindar's *Triumphal Odes* and now raised the issue of ethnocentric vocabulary. In 1936, Ioannis Kakridis (colleague of **Kazantzakis** in translating **Homer**), published *The Translation Problem.* Now the real explosion was in the twentieth century, with 2,500 trans-

lations published to 1950, and 13,000 more to 1990. After 1990, some 4,000 books per annum, on average, were published in Greece. Of these, up to a third have been translations (see Connolly and Bacopoulou-Halls 1998: 431). In 1978, a conference was organized by the Classics Department at the University of Athens. Convened under the heading Original and Translation, this was the first step to establishing the academic study of translation in modern Greece.

See also KALOSGOUROS; KOGEBINAS; PALLIS; POLYLÁS; SHAKESPEARE

Further Reading

Connolly, David and Aliki Bacopoulou-Halls. "Greek Tradition." In *Routledge Encyclopedia of Translation Studies,* 428–438. London: Routledge, 1998.

Kassinis, K. "Literary Translation: A Mapping of the Currents and Trends in the Nineteenth and Twentieth Centuries." Paper presented at Goulandris-Horn Foundation, Athens, 5 May 1995.

TRANSLATIONS FROM MODERN GREEK

Foster's 1918 bibliography lists classical and Byzantine authors translated between 1476 and 1917 by English or American hands. Layton lists Canadian and American translations of modern Greek writers produced between 1945 and 1981. Mackridge lists translations by English and Irish hands for the same period. Stavropoulou (1986) provides a bibliography of 1,895 translations from modern Greek literature, into over 30 languages. Dionysia Press (Edinburgh) was one of a few publishers in the late 1990s involved in the piecemeal, unprofitable task of bringing out English translations of modern Greek authors: *The Collected Poems of George Vafopoulos* (1998); Klitos Kirou, *Poems* (1999);

A. Mitsou, *The Feeble Lies of Orestes Halkiopoulos* (a novel, 1999). These publications, translated by D. Zervanou and Thom Nairn, were cofunded by the Greek Arts Council, or the E.E.C. Meanwhile, French translations of Greek are more numerous than into any other language, and French translation of Greek novels was promoted by Actes Sud (after 1980), sponsored by the French Institute at Athens. The director of its Center of Literary Translations, Catherine Velissaris, told D. Mitropoulos (1995) that print runs of Actes Sud went up to 3,000 copies. University of Minnesota sponsored the Nostos Book Series, edited by Theofanis Stavrou and members of the Modern Greek department. The publisher Niki Eideneier (Hamburg) carried a series called Romiosini, which had a list of serious Greek prose writers. In the late 1990s, Birmingham University (UK) started a Modern Greek Translations series, which produced the **Chatzís** novel *The Double Book* (1999), Haris Vlavianos's poems *Adieu* (1998), and *Prisoner of War's Story* by Doukas (1999). In the United States, Northwestern Press (see V. Calotychos, under **Kedros**), published Valtinos's *Deep Blue, Almost Black*. In 1999, Northwestern Press produced Valtinos's **collage** of news snippets, bureaucratic letters, and appeals to an agony aunt, *Evidence for the Sixties*. Other such sponsors are Shoestring Press, Kedros, University of Birmingham, and Pella.

Further Reading

Foster, F. M. K. *English Translations from the Greek: A Bibliographical Survey.* New York: Columbia University Press, 1918.

Layton, Evro. "Ἐπισκόπηση μεταφράσεων καί μεταφραστῶν: Ἡνωμένες Πολιτεῖες (καί Καναδᾶς) 1945–1981" ["A Survey of Translations and Translators: USA and Canada, 1945–1981"]. *Mantatofóros* 20 (1982): 30–48.

Mackridge, Peter. "Ἐπισκόπηση μεταφράσεων καί μεταφραστῶν: Μεγάλη Βρεττανία καί Ἰρλανδία 1945–1981" ["A Survey of Translations and Translators: U.K. and Ireland, 1945–1981"]. *Mantatofóros* 20 (1982): 49–61.

Stavropoulou, Erasmia-Louiza. Βιβλιογραφία Μεταφράσεων Νεοελληνικῆς Λογοτεχνίας [Bibliography of Translations of Modern Greek Literature]. Athens: Ἑταιρεία Ἑλληνικοῦ Λογοτεχνικοῦ καί Ἱστορικοῦ Ἀρχείου [Society of the Greek Literary and Historical Archive], 1986.

TRAPEZUNTIOS, YEORYIOS (1395–1472/3?1484), Around the year 1416, Yeoryios Trapezuntios (= George of Trebizond) migrated and taught Greek philosophy in Italy. He gained a post in the Vatican and became a leading classical scholar, debating **humanist** issues in the circle of intellectuals that convened at the house of **Bassarion** in Rome. He was allied with the Vatican on the unification of the Western and Eastern churches, in the debate of 1438–1443. He was an advocate of **Aristotle** and disapproved of **Plato.** Consequently he attacked **Yemistos Plethon** (c. 1360–c. 1451), who aspired to a new social order (in his *Book of Laws*) and queried Aristotle's formulations. Plethon had fomented debate with his treatise *Concerning Matters in Which Aristotle Differs from Plato* (1449). George denounced this book in his *Comparisons of Aristotle and Plato* (1458), but was then counterblasted by Bessarion's *Against the Calumniator of Plato* (1469). Trepezuntios's *Rhetoric* (1434) was a large-scale work that succeeded in spreading knowledge of Hellenistic or Byzantine rhetoricians (Dionysius Halicarnassus,

Hermogenes, Maximus) and combining them with the better-known authorities Livy and Cicero.

TRAVEL LITERATURE Herodotus first made the distinction between traveling "for trade" (πρὸς ἐμπορίαν) and travel "to see things" (πρὸς θεωρίαν). The grand tour made by artists or **Philhellenes** from the West has a large bibliography of its own. Greek writers give personal accounts of journeys abroad and (in a hackneyed genre) of their trips around Greece. This travel writing (ταξιδιωτική) involves a set of "travel impressions" as the writer circles round the Balkans and makes the obligatory call at **Mount Athos.** Some late nineteenth- and twentieth-century Greek writers were obsessed with their country's backwaters. Writers like Kostas Pasayannis (1872–1933) would trawl rural areas like the Mani to collect folk material. Petros Charis (1902–1998) was much admired for his complete travels, collected in 1970 as *From Antiquity to the New World.* Perhaps the best of Greek travel writing is represented by three twentieth-century writers: **Kostas Ouranis,** with his *Sol y sombra* (1934) and *Sea-Green Pathways* (1947); **Kazantzakis,** with *Travels in Greece: Journey to the Morea* (1927, trans. by F. A. Reed, Oxford: Cassirer, 1966), *What I Saw in Russia* (1928), and *Spain* (1937). Preeminent was **I. M. Panayotopoulos,** whom the critic Hourmouzios called (1953) "the most pleasant and instructive person to travel with; he makes you become a poet, without having the gift, and a voracious learner." Travel titles by Panayotopoulos include *Shapes of the Greek Land* (1937), *Greek Horizons* (1940), *Positions and Counter-Positions of the Greek Landscape* (1953), *A Journey to Cyprus* (1962), *Scarab the*

Holy: Egypt (1950), *Africa Is Awakening* (1963), and *The World of China* (1961). A different kind of travel commentary was put together by Charis in his anthology for the publisher Phexi, *Greeks and the World: Impressions from Greece.*

Ilias Venezis, famous as a novelist, brought out *The Land of America* (1955), *Tours: In Russia, Dalmatia, Switzerland and England* (1973), and *Spring in Italy* (1949), an earlier "travelogue" that included short visits to Livorno, Rome, Florence, Venice, and the Greek areas of southern Italy and Sicily known as Magna Graecia. **Myrivilis,** who published the volume *From Greece* (1954), opined that "travel impressions, whenever they are sincere, do not describe things objectively. They only describe ourselves, and our stance in relation to those things. What we have is simply the writer inside his journey." Maria Ralli (1905–1976) was a widely traveled writer: her *Time-Tables and Delays* (1956) cover America, Egypt, Monet's use of water-lilies in the celebrated paintings of his old age, and a Poetry Congress of Europe (Belgium, 1952). Her two-volume *Geography as a Dream* (1956–1964) presents a "stroll" across Germany and Romania/Moscow, respectively. She says: "I shall not be concerned with objective illustration, but will convey my tour impressions as a traveler returns with a mass of reminiscences, bearing this cargo of unsorted gifts, made up of emotions that may refer to works of art, governments, characters or circumstances that he chanced on." Another woman writer, Alkis Thrulos (that is, Eleni Ourani), brought out *Journeys and Excursions* in three volumes (1962, 1963, 1968) and reminded her readers, in the first, that when a travel narrative aspires to be literature, it should avoid recording every detail or following the tour step by step and discard purely informative items, for these cannot reveal a personal point of view. Y. Suriotis (1892–1962), in *America without Fantasies* (1954), gives a practical account of a visit to 14 states of the USA. In *I Remember America* (1963), Andreas Karantonis (1910–1982), critic and "king-maker" of the Nobel prizes for **Seferis** and **Elytis,** drafts a sympathetic essay on the continent and its citizens. He matches this with a national portrait, *Greek Places: Travel Pictures and Reflections* (1979).

Yannis Sfakianakis (1903/7?–1987) formulates another national perspective in his *Land of Greece: A Travelogue* (1977) and in *On the Aegean Seas* (1962), where he says he was "possessed by the flaming passion to know what was his own and to live it with all his existential identity, and to express it with the cry of pure facts when they are interwoven with the first guileless gaze of our soul." *Land of the Blue Lakes* (1949), by M. D. Stasinopoulos, is an account of Switzerland seen through practical, businesslike eyes. The well-known novelist **Theotokás** produced a *Journey to the Middle East and Mount Athos* (1961), which proposes a mystical release from the distresses of normal life by dwelling on the significance of religious houses and holy sites. In 1971 came another, more secular, volume from Theotokás, *Travels: Persia, Romania, Soviet Union, and Bulgaria.* Petros Glezos (1902–1996) links famous Greek writers to their personal locations, in *Journey to the Past: Travel Essays* (1977). He covers the period 1946–1974 and visits the isle of Madouri (for **A. Valaoritis**), the island of Levkas (for **Sikelianós**), Sifnos (for **Provelengios**), and Artemona, on Sifnos (for **Gryparis**). Asimakis Panselinos (1903–

1984), a heretic of the extreme Left whose poems include openly erotic elements from his early years on Lesbos, composed *To Moscow with the Youth of the World* (1962) and *Journeys with Many Winds* (1964).

See also KAVVADIAS; KOKKOS; MELISSANTHI, MITSAKIS; PSYCHARIS; XEFLOUDAS

Further Reading

Bouboulidis, Faidon and Glykeria. Ἔδη Νεοελληνικῆς Λογοτεχνιάς τῆς "Μεσοπολεμικῆς" περιόδου [Types of Neo-Hellenic Literature in the Inter-War Years], vol. III, part 3. Athens [no publ. listed], 1997.

Dodwell, Edward. *Classical and Topographical Tour Through Greece.* London: Rodwell & Martin, 1819.

Galt, John. *Letters from the Levant.* London: T. Cadell & W. Davies, Strand, 1813.

Panaretou, Annita P. Ἑλληνική Ταξιδιωτική Λογοτεχνία. Η μακριά πορεία των απαρχών ως τον 19° αιώνα [Greek Travel Literature: The Long Journey from the Origins to the Nineteenth Century]. 5 vols. Athens: Epikairoteta, 1995.

Paton, James Morton. *Medieval and Renaissance Visitors to Greek Lands.* Princeton: The American School of Classical Studies at Athens, 1951.

Stoneman, R., ed. *A Literary Companion to Travel in Greece.* Malibu, CA: J. Paul Getty Museum, 1994.

TRAVLANTONIS, ANTONIS (1867–1943) The journalist, novelist, and educationist Antonis Travlantonis was born at **Missolonghi.** He published stories and serialized novels in newspapers and periodicals: *Girl Cousin* (1892), *Two Years' Military Service* (1892), *Crystalline* (1922), *The Traitor's Daughter,* and his most broadly plotted novel, *Squandering* *of a Life* (1936). In his distinguished teaching career, Travlantonis was appointed an inspector of schools, headmaster, lecturer, and government education adviser.

TRIKOUPIS, SPYRIDON (1788–1873) Spyrison Trikoupis was related to a leading nationalist, Alex. Mavrokordatos (1791–1865), who presided over the first Greek national assembly, at Epidavros (January 1822), composed a history of the **War of Independence,** and was descended from a leading **Phanariot,** Nikolaos Mavrokordatos (1670–1730), the first Greek ruler in the Danubian principalities. Catherine, Alexandros's sister, was an orphan in Constantinople at the outbreak of the **Uprising.** After the hanging of Patriarch Grigorios, an event that shocked the world, she saw her house invaded and the brother of her father impaled. She escaped by jumping from a window with her sister Eufrosyne, joined her brother in Greece, and married Trikoupis. Their son, Charilaos, became a key Prime Minister of the late nineteenth century. Trikoupis himself was a member of the provisional revolutionary government of Greece (1826). He fled to Hydra with the anti-Kapodistrias faction. He wrote his *History of the Greek Uprising* while Ambassador to Britain. He composed war hymns, like "Brothers, the time for freedom has come." His songs "Demos" and "The Lake of Missolonghi" mark him as one of the first to give value to the plain **Demotic.** He was the public orator of Independence, composing eulogies on Karaïskakis and on the popular **Philhellene,** marquis Frank Abney Hastings (1794–1828), who was appointed admiral in 1827, and died, mourned by Kapodistrias, a year later. Trikoupis celebrated Andreas Zaïmis, Pe-

trobey, Byron, and Ioannis Notarás (1805–1827), who was a lieutenant-general at age 18 and in 1824 was appointed a general. Despite dissuasion from Cochrane and Church, Notarás led a doomed relief of the Acropolis and met a hero's death at age 22. Trikoupis also wrote speeches about the victories of Navarino, Kafireos, and the recovery of Missolonghi.

Further Reading

Trikoupis, Sp. "Translation of the Funeral Oration of the late Lord Byron." In *Selections from Modern Greek Writers in Prose and Poetry,* edited by C. Felton. Cambridge, MA: 1856.

TRILOGY For a conspicuous group of twentieth-century Greek writers, there was a vogue for writing a set of three novels (that is, "trilogy"), on a broad theme or canvas. A woman author, Kallirrhoe Parrén, produced a trilogy of novels entitled *The Books of Dawn* (1900–1903). Others who produced sets of three novels are **Athanasiadis, Roufos, Tsirkas, Vasilikos, Xenopoulos,** and **Petsalis.** M. Karagatsis (1909–1960, pseudonym of Dimitrios Rodopoulos), published a series of three novels in the 1930s, each with a tragic protagonist from a non-Greek environment: *Colonel Lyapkin* (1933), *Chimaera* (1936), and *Jungermann* (1938). Th. Petsalis wrote more than one group of three fictional works, notably *The Strong and Weak Generations* (1933–1935). **Pandelís Prevelakis** composed a set of three works entitled *The Cretan* (1948–1950) and a second trilogy called *Roads to Creativity* (1959–1966).

Further Reading

Vasilikos, V. *The Plant, The Well, The Angel: A Trilogy.* Translated by Edmund and Mary Keeley. New York: Knopf, 1964.

TRIOLET The "triolet" (τριολέτο) is a light verse form consisting of eight lines. Its main **rhyme** scheme is aba/aa/b/ab. Line 1 returns twice more in the course of the poem, hence the *tri-* of its name.

TRÍTO MÁTI, TÒ *The Third Eye* was a literary periodical, more radical than Τὰ Νέα Γράμματα (NÉA GRÁMMATA), which ran from 1935 to 1937. It made the eclectic decision to boost the *Memoirs* of **General Makriyannis**. One of its editors was Stratis Doukas (1895–1983), author of a documentary novel of escape, disguise, ethnic denial, and shifting identities, *Prisoner of War's Story* (1929).

See also JOURNALISM

TROILOS, IOANNIS-ANDREAS (mid-seventeenth century), Archival documents from **Venice** (1618–1639) tell us something of Troilos, a Cretan writer from Rethymno, who composed the second great **tragedy** of Cretan **seventeenth-century theater,** *King Rhodolinos*. The play was printed just once, in 1647 at Venice, by the author himself. This exemplar is in the Gennadius Library (catalogued as MGL 72, B). The origin of Troilos's plot is to be found in the verse tragedy *Il re Torrismondo* (1587), by the Italian poet T. Tasso. *King Rhodolinos* features a sophisticated Prologue, spoken by a mystical character "What is to Come" (Fortune, the future). The text consists of 3,128 lines, divided into the five acts and five separating choral odes familiar from **Chortatsis.** The scholar M. I. Manousakas, who supplemented the critical edition left unfinished by Stefanos Xanthoudidis (1864–1928), points out that three of these choruses (nos 1, 3, and 5) are among the earliest examples of the **sonnet** in modern Greek literature. Troilos freely alters the structure of his source, *King Torrismondo,*

by adding, eliminating, or modifying episodes in the story.

Further Reading

Aposkitis, Martha, ed., Alexiou, Stylianos, pref. *Ροδολίνος. Τραγωδία Ἰωάννη Ἀνδρέα Τρωίλου* (17 αἰωνα) [The Seventeenth Century *Rhodolinos* by Ioannis-Andreas Troilos]. Athens: Stigmi, 1987 [reviewed by G. P. Savidis in the newspaper *The Tribune,* Sunday ed., 27 March 1988: 55].

Lowe, C. G. "The *Rhodolinos* of Joannes Andreas Troilos." In Εἰς μνήμην Σπυρίδωνος Λάμπρου [A Memorial Volume for Spyridon Lambros], 190–198. Athens: Estía, 1935.

TROJAN WAR, THE **(mid-thirteenth century)** An unknown Greek poet adapts Benoît de Sainte-Maure's *Le Roman de Troie* (twelfth century) in the 11,074 unrhymed **decapentasyllables** of his *Trojan War.* Here a **Byzantine** writer seems to be using a Western source to reawaken Greeks to an awareness of their own heroes, showing the effects of Frankish rule and the relative ignorance of contemporary Greeks. The treatment contains some medieval anachronism, matches the French source closely, and has bursts of plebeian vigor: "Along came dukes, princes, rulers, and notables, / Elect in beauty and wisdom, vessels of valor, / Embarking, under review, setting sail."

See also BOOK OF TROY; HOMER

Further Reading

Mavrofrudis, Dimitrios, ed. Ἐκλογὴ μνημείων τῆς νεωτέρας ἑλληνικῆς γλώσσης [Selected Monuments of Modern Greek Writing], vol. 1. Athens: X. N. Philadelpheus, 1866 [ed. contains also *Spaneas, Prodromika,* **Romances**].

TROPARION The troparion (τροπάριον) began as a short ecclesiastical chant. Most **hymns** composed before John Damascenus are called troparia, possibly on account of the different manner (τρόπος) in which they were sung or because they seemed like "trophies" (τρόπαια) of martyrs. After the time of John Damascenus, a collection of troparia with corresponding odes made up the Canon.

Further Reading

Conomos, D., ed. *Studies in Eastern Chant.* Crestwood, NY: St. Vladimir's Seminary Press, 1990.

TROPE A trope is a turn of words or a verbal trick to make a phrase more surprising. Whole phrases can also be rendered more stylish by a "turn" (τροπή). The trope alters the sense of a word. The altered sense causes a "change of direction," and this new direction constitutes a new thought (διάνοια). Thus Papadiamantis writes in a two-line poem: "Loves that are travelers on the dim wave. / And the boat capsized and they fell on the beach." Here several tropes are employed to make love a *traveler,* a traveler on a *sea* which is dim, and become a *boat* which sinks, so the love is wrecked, but it falls on the *shore.*

Further Reading

Schiappa, Edward, ed. *Landmark Essays on Classical Greek Rhetoric.* Davis, CA: Hermagoras, 1994.

TSAKASIANOS, IOANNIS (1854–1908)

Ioannis Tsakasianos, from Zakynthos, was a self-taught man. Orphaned early, he supported his family by working as a hairdresser, or face-powder salesman. He issued a self-financed journal, *Bloom of Zante* (1874–1878). Later (from 1886), he edited 52 issues of the journal *Poetic Bloom.* He was called the "poet of sparrows," and, with the **pseudonym** "Sparrow," he mocked the customs of his island. He is one of a whole line of Heptanese **satirists** from the **Ionian Islands: Solomós, Laskaratos,** Michelis Ablichos (1844–1917), Antonis Fatseas (1823–1879) from Cythera, and Yeoryios Molfetas (1876–1916), from Cephalonia, who put out the satirical periodical *Mischief* (1892–1916).

TSALOUMAS, DIMITRIS (born 1921)

The best-known twentieth-century Greek-Australian poet, Tsaloumas grew up on Leros and later emigrated for political reasons. At first he published a number of volumes in Greek. Gradually, like many Hellenic Americans at the antipodes, Tsaloumas turned to his second language. In *The Harbour* (fourth of his English volumes) he celebrated an obvious symbol of arrival and departure for the *xenitiá* experience. The act of slipping anchor and taking to the waves, personal and political in Greek authors, is full of nostalgia for this Greek intellectual, who casts off from coastlines that are ". . . loud with the colour / Of fretting boats and Sunday bells."

Further Reading

Perkins, Elizabeth. "Dimitris Tsaloumas: Interview." *Literature in North Queensland* 15, no. 1 (1987): 96–103.

Rodriguez, Judith. "Dimitris Tsaloumas Observed." *Meanjin* 42, no. 1 (March 1983): 104–109.

Tsaloumas, Dimitris. *The Observatory.* Translated by Philip Grundy. St. Lucia: University of Queensland Press, 1983 [bilingual].

Tsaloumas, Dimitris. *The Book of Epigrams.* Translated by Philip Grundy. St. Lucia: University of Queensland Press, 1985 [bilingual].

Tsaloumas, Dimitris. *The Harbour.* St. Lucia: University of Queensland Press, 1999.

TSATSOU, IOANNA (1909–2000)

Ioanna Tsatsou published an impressive stream of verse collections, such as *Debt* (1979), and many works in prose, notable among which are *The Executed of the Occupation* (1947), *The Sword's Fierce Edge: A Journal of the Occupation of Greece, 1941–1944* (1965; trans. by Jean Demos, Nashville: Vanderbilt, 1969), *Hours of Sinai* (1981), *Pierre Emmanuel and Greece* (1987). Her monograph *My Brother George Seferis* (1973, trans. by J. Demos, Minneapolis: North Central Publishing Co., 1982), won a first State Prize for Biography. She translated several of her volumes into French. She was married to Constantine Tsatsos, a philosophy professor who was first President of the new Greek republic (1975–1980).

Further Reading

Schwab, Peter and George D. Frangos, eds. *Greece under the Junta.* New York: Facts on File, 1973.

TSIRKAS, STRATIS (1911–1980; pseudonym of Yannis Chatziandreas)

The novelist and scholar Stratis Tsirkas, born in Egypt, lived his first 50 years between Cairo and Alexandria, which had significant **diaspora** communities. The writer's early fiction was based on Egypt, at the crossroads, poised between two world wars and two domestic revolutions, the first in 1919 and the second in Nasser's coup d'état of 1952. *The Green Paradise* relates memories of a childhood spent in the traditional Greek quarter of an oriental city. *Noureddine Bomba: The Man of the Nile* draws the reader's interest to the peasants of middle Egypt during the decline of Farouk's enfeebled kingship. In the late 1940s, Tsirkas started on a series of three novels, with the collective title *Drifting Cities* (the title borrowed from a line of poetry by **Seferis**). This powerful **trilogy** was published later (1960–1965), around the time that Tsirkas settled in Athens (1963). He deals, in a narrative fresco, with the three "ungovernable" cities: Jerusalem, Cairo, and Alexandria. The dramatic setting is from 1942 to 1944, when Rommel's army controls Egypt and the Soviets are trapped in the Caucasus. Tsirkas conjures up the insignificant populations on the sideline of the Soviet, German, British, and Italian war machines. Egyptians and Palestinians were cramped in the Middle East bottleneck created by the belligerent powers. Tsirkas assembles a cast of Greek refugees of every stripe: liberals, Communists, ex-ministers, secret agents, heroines, widows, freedom fighters, and diehard conservatives, variously involved in the upheavals at Jerusalem, Alexandria, or Cairo. The plot weaves in the attempted British normalization of elements in the Greek expeditionary force. The work was turned into a **television** film, running in episodes through the 1980s. Tsirkas was nominated as a candidate for the Nobel Prize for Literature. He published a book on **Kavafis** and the Greek presence in Egypt up to the late nineteenth century, *Cavafy and His Age* (1958). Here Tsirkas spells out the disruptive effect of the British occupation on the Hellenic community. He delineates the difference between the "first class Greeks," who settled in Egypt up to 1863, when Ismail was appointed Khedive, and a later group of bankers and merchants who constituted "second class Greeks." The latter, more dependent on British interests, arrived in the following decades and tended to support the anglophile politician Trikoupis.

Further Reading

Karampetsos, E. D. "Stratis Tsirkas and the Arabs." *JMGS* 2, no. 1 (May 1984): 39–51.

Kitroeff, Alexander. *The Greeks in Egypt, 1919–1937: Ethnicity and Class.* London: Ithaca, 1989

Mackridge, Peter. "Testimony and Fiction in Greek Narrative Prose, 1944–1967." In *The Greek Novel: A.D. 1–1985,* edited by Roderick Beaton, Roderick, 90–102. London: Croom Helm, 1988.

MacSweeney, Alix. "Letter from Alexandria." *TLS,* 12 Oct. 2001: 15.

Tsirkas, Stratis. Ἀκυβέρνητες πολιτείες [Drifting Cities]. Vol. I: Ἡ Λέσχη [The Club], Athens, 1961; Vol. II: Ἀριάγνη [Ariagni], Athens, 1962; Vol. III: Ἡ Νυχτερίδα [The Bat], Athens, 1965.

Tsirkas, Stratis. *Drifting Cities: A Trilogy.* Translated by Kay Cicellis. New York: Alfred A. Knopf, 1974.

TSOKOPOULOS, YEORYIOS (1871–1923)

Yeoryios Tsokopoulos was a prolific journalist of the turn of the century period. He wrote a preface to the important novel by **P. Kalligás,** *Thanos Vlekas* (1923). He began journalism with *Regeneration* and was a correspondent of *Lightning, New Town,* and *New Day.* He contributed to *Athens, Times,* and *Hearth.* He became director of *Estía* (1920–1922). He used amusing **pseudonyms,** such as Falstaff, Phineas Fogg, and Rip. He wrote many theatrical works, among them a **komeidyllio,** *Main Gate Street.*

TURKEY

Printing came very late in Turkey's history (1850). Thus a relatively late modernism, its reaction to the *Divan* ("anthology of classical Turkish"), was spearheaded by the *Tanzimat* (1859–1891). Just like Greece, Turkey rediscovered its **demotic song,** *kochma* (a metrical form with 11-syllable lines, set in an 11-line strophe). **Thessaloniki,** known as "Selaïnik" to the Turks, fomented intrigue against the rule of Sultan Abdul Hamid, and a Turkish Committee of Union and Progress was formed there in 1906. Several currents merged: the Turkish insurrection of 1908, the Jewish "Federation" movement under Abraham Benaroja, and the *Young Turks.* Till 1870, the Young Turks were a group of artistic liberals. As a reformist league, polarized by Sinazí Effendis, they aimed to release Turkey from Persian and Arab influences and modify its Islamic base. In 1908, the New Turks forced the granting of a constitution. This was followed by the abdication of Abdul Hamid (1909). The military successes of Mustafa Kemal (born and educated in Thessaloniki) and his manipulation of Young Turk ideology led to the establishment of the Republic (1923). He was President of Turkey (1923–1938) and in 1935 adopted the style Atatürk, "Father of the Turks."

S. Xenos, in his historical novel *The Devil in Turkey,* evokes the Ottoman court of the early-nineteenth-century Greek. Writing about the Turks is habitually derisive: they oppressed a civilized land for centuries and stole back a slice of **Cyprus** in 1974 (north of the Attila and Green Line). Papathanasopoulos calls it "the enslavement of half of Cyprus to the hordes of Attila" (1992: 176). Slavery, kidnapping, and treachery (απιστία) are the stock vocabulary of anti-Turkish prose. Christos Samouilidis (b. 1927), in his first novel, *People of Karaman* (1965), evokes the Turkish-speaking Greeks of the Pontus, who dominated the main urban centres in Turkey as traders and awed the Turks into a kind of inferiority complex. In *Black Sea* (1970), Samouilidis turns to the tragedy of Pontus under the New Turks and the effects of Kemalism and foreign intrigue.

Further Reading

Aydin, Kamil. *Images of Turkey in Western Literature.* Huntingdon: Eothen, 2001.

Fleming, Katherine. *The Muslim Bonaparte: Diplomacy and Orientalism in Ali Pasha's Greece.* Princeton, NJ: Princeton University Press, 1999.

TURKISH, LITERARY USE OF Eighteenth- and nineteenth-century **Phanariot** poets, such as A. Kalfoglou (b. 1725), Yakoumakis Protopsaltes, Petros Lampadarios, or Ioannis Karatzas (1760–1845), some of them princelings in the Danubian provinces, and well-born women writers from **Constantinople,** such as Doudou Ypsilantis or Domna Katingko, added Turkish words to their Greek poems, rehashing the hybrid language of the capital city. Some adopted a verse form that used one line in Turkish and an alternating line in Greek.

TURKOCRACY The period in which Greece was ruled by Turks, from 1453 to around 1828, was called by Greek writers the Turkocracy (τουρκοκρατία). In this time, the subjugated Greeks produced a limited literature. The *Thesauros* of Damascenus the Stoudite (1528) is a farrago of minor prophecies. So, too, are the *Predictions* of A. Rartouros (1560), from Kerkyra, who offers written preaching for the laity. "Turkocracy" is the title of a text by **A. Valaoritis:** "You never ate dry bread, made moldy / And damp by your sweat, your tears and your blood. / You never woke at night to see your spouse / Dragged naked from your side." John Gemistus, a sixteenth-century Greek intellectual harassed by the Turks, went

to Italy, where he published *Protrepticon et Pronosticon* (Ancona, 1516), advising Pope Leo X to sponsor the redemption of Greece. Leonardos Filaras (1595–1673) devoted much of his career to coaxing Western European intellectuals to support Greek liberation. Two letters from Milton (1608–1674) attest Filaras's patriotic crusade. In 1675, **Kontaris** drafted a history of Athens. He called contemporary Greeks "descendants of men both great and wise" (see **Seventeenth Century**). The polarization is total: Kontaris considers the Turks an "impious and barbarous people." The Sublime Porte was despised for its abolition of all culture but religion and hated for the conscription of Christian boys (see **Janissaries**) and judicial murder. **Patriarch Kyrillos Loukaris,** who approved a translation of Scripture into the **Demotic,** was betrayed to the Turks by a **Catholic** faction and strangled. His successor was also executed (1639). **Orthodox** patriarchs were allowed to administer their dioceses on condition they quashed rebellion. Gregory V was executed on Easter Sunday 1822.

The main difference in treatment for Muslims and Christians was the payment of a capitation tax, called *haratch,* by every male unbeliever over the age of 10. During the Turkocracy, the study of classical Greek shifted from Greece to Italy. Some Greek clergy maintained a bookish tradition, particularly at the Great School of the Nation, the Patriarchal seminary at **Constantinople.** Schools were modeled on it all over the Balkans: at Arta, Smyrna, Ioannina, Chios, Athens, Patmos, and Adrianople. From the cliffs of Zalongo, in Epirus, came an anti-Turk fable from before the **Uprising.** The women of a town called Souli jumped to their death with their children clasped in their arms, avoiding surrender to the

Turks. The poem, "Souliótisses," by **Myrtiotissa** gives these women a symbolic altar: "on the peak, a lily flowers, / Where she spent her final hours." It is said that **Ali Pasha** ordered a nationalist in Epirus skinned and roasted alive on a spit when Byron was visiting his autocratic court. An epic tale in six cantos by A. Valaoritis, *Athanasios Diakos* (1867), devotes its final canto to the fate of the **Klepht** roasted alive by his captors.

TYPALDOS, IOULIOS (1814–1883)

Ioulios Typaldos (see special issue of *Greek Creation,* no. 49: 15 Feb. 1950) was a successful lawyer and writer of jurisprudence, as well as an Ionian patriot and poet committed to the demotic tradition of his personal friend (and teacher) **Dionysios Solomós.** His mother was a well-born noble from Verona (Italy), Countess Teresa Ringhelli, and Typaldos went to Italy with her for further studies. His output is slight, but it channels a mixture of romantic and patriotic exaltation. There is the ode to the martyr **Rigas Velestinlís,** the truncated translation of Tasso's pointedly anti-Islamic **epic** *Gerusalemme Liberata* (1565–1575), a single volume of 14 "diverse poems" dedicated to Solomós (1856), and the funeral oration to Solomós (Zakynthos, 1857). In 1881, he wrote an "Ode on the Union of the New Greek Provinces with Greece." The *Great Encyclopedia of Greece* (1926–1934) dismisses Typaldos as a shallow sentimentalist. Others call attention to the modish despair of his poem "Creature of the Imagination," with its evocation of a love-object, always courted, never obtained, conveying the quintessence of the late Romantics, equipped with tripping, seductive end-line rhymes, and a simplicity not far from the **demotic song:** "Oh how often, my love, / I have sought you in alien places,

/ Lifting my enamored eyes / With yearning all around, / Where the beauties of nature shone forth / From amidst the flowers, the blossoms, / Where dancing and song / Enchant the human heart." Several Typaldos manuscripts were found in private libraries on Zakynthos by his twentieth-century editor, Konomos.

Further Reading

Bouboulidis, Faidon. Ἰούλιος Τυπάλδος, 1814–1883 [Ioulios Typaldos]. Athens: Heptanisia, 1953.

Konomos, D., ed. Typaldos, I. Ἅπαντα. Ποιήματα, πεζά, γράμματα, μεταφράσματα, ἰταλικά [The Complete Works: Verse, Prose, Letters, Translations, Italian Texts]. Athens: Pighi, 1953.

TZIGALAS, HILARION (1624–1682)

Son of the Cypriot ecclesiastical writer Mattheos (see following), Hilarion Tzigalas studied at the Greek college of St. Athanasios in Rome, which had been founded by Pope Gregory XIII in 1581. Also a priest, he directed the Kottounianon college at Padua (from 1657). After 1660, he traveled in Greece and the islands, where he founded several schools. He swapped religious allegiance (**Orthodox, Catholic,** Orthodox) a number of times. He visited Jerusalem, Cyprus, Bucharest, and Constantinople. He wrote Latin essays and composed an elegy *To the Illustrious Martyr St. Gobdelás,* and a *Grammatical Science.* He was archbishop of Cyprus from 1674 to 1678.

TZIGALAS, MATTHEOS (early seventeenth century)

From Cyprus, Mattheos Tzigalas became a rector, in the 1630s, of St. George of the Greeks (Venice) and translated classical texts into the **demotic.** He composed *A New Digest of Sundry Histories* (1637), an *Easter Perpetual* (1677), and *Exposition of the Divine Office* (1690).

U

UNIVERSITY; UNIVERSITIES French occupation forces sponsored a tertiary college at the island of Kerkyra, and this operated from 1807 to 1814. It was called "Ionic Academy" and offered arts, letters, math, physics, political science, and ethics. This college then opened Greece's first School of Fine Arts (1810). Young painters, architects, and sculptors from all the **Ionian Islands** came there. The **Philhellene** Lord Guildford opened the "Ionian Academy" in 1824. This was the single university in Greece until the National and Capodistrian University of Athens was founded in 1837. The country's next university was inaugurated in 1925 and called Aristotle University of **Thessaloniki,** 13 years after the incorporation of this territory into an expanded Greece. The new University at Thessaloniki chose a radical stance in the **language question** by using the demotic language as its medium of instruction. In 1925, this was a revolutionary gesture. The National Technical University of Athens, and Higher School of Fine Arts (also Athens), were inaugurated in 1936. The Graduate School of Industrial Studies at Thessaloniki opened in 1957. There followed University of Ioannina, and University of Patrai (1964), Demokritos University of Thrace, at Komotiní (1973), Technical University of Crete (1977), and the University of the Aegean (1984), with campuses at Athens, Rhodes, Samos, Mytiline, and Chios.

UPRISING. See WAR OF INDEPENDENCE

URANIA One of the nine **Muses,** Urania was patron of astronomy and didactic poetry. She is depicted holding a globe.

V

VAKALÓ, ELENI (1921–2001) The family of Eleni Vakaló, from Constantinople, settled in Athens after the **Asia Minor disaster,** and she did postgraduate work in art studies at the Sorbonne (Paris). She married the painter Yioryos Vakaló, and in 1958 they founded the School of Decorative Arts (where she taught). She did a regular art column for the Athens newspaper *The News.* She published 15 well-received verse collections between 1945 and 1984. An edition of her *Genealogy* (1972) came out in England, translated by Paul Merchant (Exeter: Rougemont Press, 1971). She translated Marianne Moore and built up a portfolio of art criticism, from *Physiognomy of Post-War Art in Greece,* which consisted of the volumes *Abstraction* (1981), *Expressionism and Surrealism* (1982), *The Myth of Greekness* (1983), and *After Abstraction* (1984).

Further Reading

Friar, Kimon. "Eleni Vakalo: Beyond Lyricism." *JHD* 9, no. 4 (1982): 21–27.

VALAORITIS, ARISTOTELIS (1824–1879) Poet, aristocrat, and politician, Aristotelis Valaoritis regarded the warriors in **Homer** as early **Klephts,** fortunate to be immortalized in a classic. Greece's new freedom fighters had different names, but deserved grand, new verses. Panás, his contemporary, penned a recipe for the Valaoritis style: "Take two clouds, a litre of air, / Two grains of dew and a flute; / Three tons of Pindar, four of snow; / A liter of breath, and a nightingale, / Four sprigs of laurel, of myrtle; / Cassocks; rags; gypsies; dawns. // Two drams of wild, durable worms; / Rumbling of thunder, wind from the North, roses and seaweeds. // Countless oaths, some flesh and a clump of flowers from the cemetery. // Toss these in a large pot, / Add ice-cold water, // Bring to a boil just three times." Valaoritis studied law at Pisa and Paris before returning to his native isle of Levcas. He left the island for political duties, to sit in the Ionian Assembly or attend Parliament at Athens. He welcomed the fall of King Otho and till 1867, after the unification of the Ionian Islands with Greece, was a friend and supporter of King George I.

When George succumbed to foreign pressure and agreed to "close the Cretan question" by leaving the island with Turkey, Valaoritis was shocked and retired to his estate on Madouris. As a poet, he cultivated an epic rather than lyric manner. It was said of him that he was the first to put "the poetry into patriotism and the patriotism into poetry." He was strongly influenced by Victor Hugo, and this influence shows in his love of romantic contrasts. Early in his career, he grasped the importance of the **demotic** for the emancipation of post-Independence Greece. He derived his themes from the struggle of the generation before his. He exalted clashes between *armatoli* and Klephts, turning the messy battles for independence into grandiose encounters. **Nationalism** reaches such a pinnacle of romantic yearning in Valaoritis, that his work seems to rest on one motif, the "death of the hero." As heroism is the supreme virtue, so the task of a poet is to place the hero's acts on record, marking out the conflict between imagination and reality and the struggle beneath the Romantic countenance. In his patriotic verse, Valaoritis liked to use a plebeian-sounding 11-syllable line, with the **accent** on the fourth syllable and the **caesura** after the sixth. Typical is the escape speech, sung by **Ali Pasha** in "The horse, the horse, Omer Vrionis." Valaoritis's first collection was *Verse Pieces* (1847), followed, among major works, by *Commemorative Requiem* (1857), *Kyra Frosyne* (1859), and *Athanasios Diakos* (1867). His life was as eventful as his verse: roaming the Bois de Boulogne (Paris) one night in 1848, he was nearly killed when two thugs tried to rob him. In 1868, he punched and slightly wounded a reactionary opponent, in the Greek parliament (one Jakovatos).

Valaoritis said of **Solomós** that for someone to last so long in Greek poetry and die at 70, his work should not have been limited to a single hymn and a handful of disconnected strophes. A fervent supporter of Solomós, Apostolakis, fired back that the **Uprising** was "defunct in the soul of Valaoritis," and that Valaoritis turned its living forms into marble and rocks. A century later, those poems were recited in schools, on the anniversary of the Uprising (March 25). **Roidis** remarked that his descriptions do not resemble paintings or sculpture, but the branches of a virgin forest.

See also DIASPORA

Further Reading

Rennell, Rodd. "The Poet of the Klephts: Aristoteles Valaoritis." *The Nineteenth Century,* no. 173 (July 1891): 130–144.

Santas, Constantine. *Aristotle Valaoritis.* Boston: Twayne Publishers, 1976.

VALAORITIS, NANOS Great-grandson of the writer Aristotelis Valaoritis, Nanos is innovative in the manner of **Andreas Embirikos** and given to experimental compositions in the mixture of prose and verse, which the Greek **surrealist** group characteristically copied from the early manner of André Breton (1896–1966) and Tristan Tzara. The critic Nikos Stangos calls Valaoritis's narrative texts open-ended, "manic parables," lacking an answer or a solution; although one of his characters, a writer-within-the-text decides to possess all other contemporary writers by telepathy. The narrator's ironic purpose here is for the production of books to be slowed down, so that he can be the author of all texts in the universe.

Further Reading

Levi, Peter. "The Last Greek Surrealist." *The Spectator,* 23 Feb. 1991: 31.

Ollier, Nicole. "Nanos Valaoritis: Métamorphose et surréalisme." In *Multilinguisme et multiculturalisme en Amérique du Nord: Survivances, transfert, métamorphose,* edited by Jean Beranger, 151–161. Bordeaux: Presses Universitaires de Bordeaux (Annales du Centre de Recherches sur l'Amér. Anglophone, no. 13), 1988.

Stangos, Nikos. "Poems by Proxy." *TLS,* 26 April 1991: 24.

Valaoritis, Nanos. *My Afterlife Guaranteed and Other Narratives.* Translated by Mary Kitroeff and others. San Francisco: City Lights, 1991.

Voulgari, Sophia. "Playing with Genre(s): The 'Prose Poems' of Nanos Valaoritis." In *Greek Modernism and Beyond: Essays in Honor of Peter Bien,* edited by D. Tziovas, 229–242. Lanham, MD: Rowman & Littlefield, 1997.

VALAVANIS, DEMOSTHENES (?1828–1854),

Losing both parents as a child of 10, dying of consumption at age 26 (though his date of birth could be 1824, 1829, or even 1830), Demosthenes Valavanis had a romantic, brief existence. Born in the medieval town of Karitaina (a single hill over the river Alpheios, in the northwest corner of the plain of Megalopolis, Peloponnese), he was helped through school by an uncle. He enrolled (1842) to study medicine, at Athens. Not much is known of his life. He died of galloping consumption on May 11, 1854, just after he had qualified as a doctor. His illness must have discouraged anyone from sorting through his papers. There was no close relative at his deathbed. Possibly his manuscripts were hastily disposed of to curtail infection. Valavanis's production is minuscule, but steeped in demotic and populist attitudes in advance of their time. His three or four poems in **Katharevousa** and a handful of texts in the **Demotic** are forerunners of **Palamás, Noumás, Eftaliotis** and the **nationalist,** late-Romantic values of the **New School of Athens.** Dimarás calls his linguistic intuition "unique for Athens, at this period." Valavanis composed "My Dream," "That Woman" (1852), and the justly famous 27 quatrains of "Burial of the Klepht," in anapestic **decapentasyllables.** Fellow-poet **Y. Paraschos** (1820–1886) is said to have spoken at Valavanis's funeral, with a black band on his waistcoat and black crepe on his tarboosh. His eulogy has not survived.

Further Reading

Gounelas, C. D. "Neither Katharevousa nor Demotic: The Language of Greek Poetry in the Nineteenth Century." *BMGS,* no. 6 (1980): 81–107.

VAMVAS, NEOPHYTOS (1770–1856)

The educator and **Enlightenment** figure Neophytos Vamvas was born on Chios and brought up in schools on Chios, Sifnos, Patmos, and Simi. Among his teachers were M. Patmios, D. Kerameús, Athanasios Parios, and Dorotheos Proïos, who had recently returned from Europe. Vamvas was ordained deacon and in 1791 accompanied Proïos to Constantinople. Here he helped to edit entries up to the letter epsilon (ε) for the lexicon *Ark of the Greek Language.* He intended to further his studies in Italy, but money problems forced him to abandon the project. He started to make a living as interpreter to the Ottoman navy and by tutoring in Constantinople and Bucharest, to the families of K. Hadzeris, Y. Mavrokordatos, and the latter's sister, Eufrosyne. The proceeds (2,000 piastres) got him to Paris in 1807, where he met **Ko-**

raís and became his close collaborator. Vamvas found a livelihood for seven years in the French capital by teaching Greek and helping Koraís edit volumes of the *Hellenic Library* for a modest payment of 50 francs per month. In 1813, he published his treatise *On Rhetoric*. After eight years in the West, he returned to Chios, where he became principal of his old school, which he reorganized to conform with the pedagogic principles of Koraís. Vamvas established a printing press to provide textbooks for his pupils and a lending library on the island (1817), which he enriched by purchases to the value of 3,000 francs a year from community funds. Committed to the **Uprising,** Vamvas dashed from Chios to the island of Hydra, where his speeches helped recruit allies and fan the revolt, while he took monastic orders. **Dimitrios Ypsilantis** met with Vamvas and made him his secretary. From Paris, Koraís rued the Turks' sack of Chios, but rejoiced that Vamvas had been saved.

Koraís expressed the hope that Vamvas would found a "national school" in the Peloponnese, but he was forced on to Cephalonia, where he taught Greek letters to Italophone islanders and to refugees from the Uprising. He was appointed a professor in the Ionian Academy on Kerkyra (1828), the equivalent of a university chair, which he held for six years. He continued to revise and publish philosophical texts. Next he directed a school at Hermoupolis, along the lines of his Chiot model, but he was suspected of pro-Protestant conspiracy, even of spying, and forced to move on to Athens. Here, in 1837, he was involved with the founding of modern Greece's first university. He acted as Vice-Rector and delivered the inaugural address, "On True Fame," to an audience that included the King. In 1845 he was appointed Rector. Voutyrás (in his *Dictionary of History and Geography*) called Vamvas "a polymath who found time, in his new Chair, to pass on the intellectual gifts of his writing, thought, work, and energy until the end of his life." He taught 18 more years at the University, retiring on grounds of age in 1853. His *Elements of Moral Philosophy* went through two editions (1818, 1845). His *Theoretics* (Chios, 1820), which analyzed the theories of Koraís and other modern writers, went through three editions (1820, 1825, 1846). At Syros, in 1834, he published inaugural speeches given at Chios school exam sittings and his *Inner Clarifications of the Inspiration of Holy Scripture,* while from Kerkyra (1828) came his *Syntax of the Classical Language, with Introductory Notions on Poetics* (revised ed., Athens, 1848). Vamvas produced a primer, *The Elements of Philosophy* (1838, 1856), a *Commentary on the Speeches of Demosthenes* (1849), a *Manual of Rhetoric from the Holy Altar* (1851), a *Manual of Ethics* (1853, all published at Athens), works of devotion, and translations from the Bible.

Further Reading

Argenti, Philip. *Bibliography of Chios, from Classical Times to 1936.* Oxford: Clarendon Press, 1940.

VARIKAS, VASOS (1913–1971) Vasos Varikas, critic, journalist, and social commentator, wrote (after 1953) regular columns for the leading Athenian daily newspapers. Born at Karpathos in the **Dodecanese,** he studied literature at the University of Athens and, later, art history at university in Paris. From 1945 to 1971 he wrote for the daily afternoon paper *The News,* first as a leader-writer and theater correspondent, eventually as an editor. From 1951, he was chief executive of the *News Bulletin* and a contributor of literary and political programs to Greek National Radio. From 1953 he was a general contributor and book critic for the morning newspaper *The Tribune*. In 1955, he was appointed General Secretary to the Commission for the Award of State Prizes and became a member of the Society of Greek Authors and also of the Union of Athenian Daily Newspaper Editors. In 1935 he published an essay *The Poet Kostas Varnalis;* in 1937 this was followed by a monograph, *K. G. Karyotakis: The Drama of a Generation,* and in 1939 by the essay *Our Post-War Literature.* A posthumous selection of Varikas's articles and criticism came out in 1972.

VARNALIS, KOSTAS (1884–1974)

Varnalis, critic, poet, prose writer, and essayist, was born in Bulgaria and sent at age 14 to high school in Philippopolis. When he completed school, the community of Varna sent him to study literature at the University of Athens (1902). Some of his verse appeared in the periodical *Noumás* in 1904. He took a degree in classics and literature (1908) and the following year was appointed a primary school master. From 1917 to 1925, he was a teacher in the secondary school system. In 1919 he went to Paris with a scholarship to study at the Sorbonne and came under the influence of the Greek scholar who lived in France, **Psycharis** (1854–1929), and the French novelist Henri Barbusse (1873–1935). In 1904, Varnalis published a first volume of verse under the title *Honeycombs* with a preface by the distinguished Ionian poet **S. Martzokis.** In 1910, he brought out a translation of Euripides' play *Bacchae.*

In 1910, too, his controversial poem "Sacrifice" caused a split in the membership of the journal *Modern Life.* The conservative faction of *Modern Life* disapproved of Varnalis's poem after it was already set on the first page of the 16-page issue of the journal. The conservatives overruled its then-editors P. Petridis, I. Kasimatis, and S. Pargas, after a special meeting was called. As a result, the plates were destroyed, and Varnalis's contribution was replaced by another poem.

He fought as a soldier in the **Balkan Wars** (1912–1913), but his motivation for joining in the struggle was no longer the old patriotic dream of restoring the frontiers represented in the irredentist vision of the **Great Idea,** for Varnalis was moving to the political left. During his later stays in Paris, he exchanged his early allegiance to the **Parnassian** poets for a commitment to postwar **Marxist** ideology. He was impressed by the revolutionary socialist movement, with its call for an end to wars, violence, and human exploitation. Out of this Paris period in Varnalis's life sprang two long poetic compositions, the first containing prose and satire. *The Light That Burns* may be considered the first Marxist work in Greek literature. It was published in 1922 by the Alexandrian journal *Literature* under the pseudonym Dimos Tanalias. Here, in the cerebral debate between Varnalis's alter ego, Momos, and the martyrs Prometheus and Jesus, a philosophy of **nihilism** and self-sufficiency is thrown in Christ's face by his Greek predecessor in charity: "Power is taken by force from the powerful. That is not a law made by the gods. It exists prior to us. It is Necessity."

In 1927 came *Slaves Besieged,* a book of proletarian verse. These early poems present Christ as one of the revolutionary heroes of world history. In 1925, Varnalis brought out his first collection of short stories, *The Eunuch People,* full of pungent satire against the middle class. In the same year he lost his teaching job: from then until 1938, he made a living as a journalist, while producing a flow of criticism and prose. *Solomós Without Metaphysics* (1923) was an attack, on Marxist lines, against the sociopolitical consecration of the poet **Solomós.** Varnalis's *The True Apology of Socrates* (1933) and *The Journal of Penelope* (1946) are his longest prose works, firing satire at icons from the past. In the former, Socrates presents his speech for the defense in Marxist, not Platonist, terms. He expounds the bourgeois motivation behind the accusations of Anytus, Lykon, and Meletus. He attacks the state religion of ancient Athens, its suppression of free speech, its middle-class work ethic, the disenfranchisement of manual laborers, and its lawmakers, who are fellow travelers. His lesser works, like *Living Men* (1938), and his *Literary Memoirs* (posthumous, 1980) are now widely quoted. Greek authorities considered Varnalis a Communist Party hack. He was arrested more than once and his writing condemned as subversive. With his support for the **demotic language** and his vigorous populism, Varnalis became well known in the Soviet Union, which awarded him the International Lenin Peace Prize (1959).

Further Reading

Friar, Kimon, transl. and ed. "Introduction: The Social Poets." In *Modern Greek Poetry,* 88–97. New York: Simon & Schuster, 1973.

Varnalis, Kostas. *The True Apology of Socrates: A Satire.* Translated by Stephen Yaloussis. London: Zeno, 1955.

VASILIADIS, SPYRIDON (1845–1874) Vasiliadis's first collection of poetry, *Images and Waves* (1866), won the **Voutsynas poetry prize** for 1865. In his second volume, *Winged Words* (1872), Vasiliadis inveighs against the poverty of contemporary inspiration: "Homer's word no longer pours forth, / But the string groans out of tune" (trans. D. Ricks). He disliked the medieval tradition, thought Byzantium "rotten and degenerate," and believed that a new Greek literature could only come from its **demotic songs.** Vasiliadis seems to be the last of the Greek **Romantics:** he revels in archaic forms like "ragged," "bough." Yet he looks towards **Parnassism,** and he worked with the youthful society **Parnassós.** Several of his theater works, which were a hit with the Athenian public, were collected in the four volumes of *Attic Nights* (1873–1874), including his four-act *Galatea,* whose lead role caught the interest of the great French actress Sarah Bernhardt.

VASILIKÓS, VASILIS (1935–) The poet, novelist, screenwriter, and playwright Vasilis Vasilikós was born in Kavala and lived in Thessaloniki, Athens, New York, Rome, and Paris. He had 80 books to his credit by the year 1995. Vasilikós produced a major work in his **trilogy** of novels (1961), *The Leaf, The Well,* and *The Angel.* This won the Group of Twelve Award and teased out a manner that displaced the *angst* of the student generation into situations on a borderland between the erotic and the impossible. He spent the years of the **Colonels' Junta** (1967–1974) in self-imposed exile as a consequence of his novel *Z* (1966), made into a classic film by Kostas Gavrás in 1968. *Z* (English trans., 1968) is a paranoid **thriller** about the police state, set in Necropolis, a city of the dead where justice has been put to sleep, among shady bodyguards, conspirators, and corrupt police. These figures surround a charismatic politician who cannot be dissuaded from addressing a compromised political rally. The story is based on the assassination of the Greek Socialist deputy, Grigoris Lambrakis, who was an **Olympic** athlete before the War. When he was run down by right-wing hooligans with a motorcycle at a peace rally in May 1963, Lambrakis was professor of medicine at Thessaloniki University and a United Democratic Left parliamentarian. The killing seemed to stem from the far-right underworld of the Parastate and led (as R. Clogg observes) to a feeling that the Karamanlis government of the early 1960s had "lost its way" and also that the Parastate had links to senior figures in the police. Vasilikós left Greece (1967) to live in Western Europe. His experience of self-imposed exile was transmuted into novels like *Coffeehouse Émigrés* (1968), *The Tape-Recorder* (1970), and a collage of 19 prose pieces in *The Harpoon Gun and Other Stories.* In a number of these pieces, a book salesman travels among Greeks living outside the homeland, a device that knits together the conflicting thematic strands of Vasilikós's composition. *The Photographs* (1964) and *The Monarch* were translated into English in the early 1970s. The seven stories of . . . *And Dreams Are Dreams* (English trans., 1996) show a sharp modernization of the author's prose manner, as though he had absorbed and expropriated the lesson of the *nouveau roman.* Here narrative boundaries are fluid, and characters pass over into each other's tales, while the reader is invited to explore the

fantasy life of Athenian taxi drivers, or the penetration of Greece by the energy of randy tourists.

Further Reading

Georgakas, Dan and Peter Pappas. "To Be a Writer in Greece: A Discussion with Vasilis Vasilikos." *JHD* 7, no. 3–4 (fall-winter 1980): 7–26.

Jahiel, Edwin. In *Books Abroad,* 48, no. 2 (spring 1974): 409.

Peckham, R. S. "In the Front of the Cab." *TLS,* 4 Oct. 1996: 36.

Vasilikos, Vasilis. *The Harpoon Gun.* Translated by Barbara Bray. New York: Harcourt Brace Jovanovich, 1973.

Vasilikos, V. Z. Translated by Marilyn Calmann. New York: Farrar, Straus, and Giroux, 1968.

VAUDEVILLE. See COMEDY

VELESTINLÍS. See RIGAS VELESTINLÍS

VELMOS, NIKOS (1892–1930; pseudonym of Nikos Boyatzakis) Nikos Velmos was an impoverished, Bohemian figure of the new century. He was an anarchist, founder of a satirical journal *The Scourge,* where he published (1927) his *Story of a Kid,* written while he was detained, for leftist sympathies, at Averoff Prison (November 1916). Velmos organized an Art Shelter at his house in Nikodimos Street. Young and established artists started their careers or exhibited there. Velmos also adopted a pose of hectoring rebellion: "Hate your fatherland, hate the rich. That way, you will love all the poor of the world. Love deserters from your fatherland. Those who desert from the ranks of its army are deserting from among traitors to a truth, for one who betrays a truth hands life over to death."

VELTHANDROS AND CHRYSANTZA

(thirteenth century) Probably an adaptation of a lost earlier work, *The Excellent Story of Velthandros the Greek* consists of 1,348 unrhymed **decapentasyllables,** preserved in one manuscript (sixteenth or seventeenth century). The subject matter seems to come from the age of the Comnenus dynasty. The magnanimous Velthandros is one of two sons of King Rodofilos. Rodofilos protects his favorite son, Filarmos, while despising Velthandros. The latter leaves home, travels through Turkey and Asia Minor, and vanquishes a larger group of bandits in a defile. In a magic, Eastern motif, the hero comes across a star, reflected in a stream, moving along its water. He follows these portents to a palace made of porphyrean rock, out of which flows a river of fire. Golden heads of lions look out at him from the turrets of the Castle of Love. An inscription set in diamond says that he will pine for Chrysantza, daughter of the King of Antioch. There is a visionary panel of 40 princesses: he must select the most beautiful, whom he is destined to marry.

Velthandros presently travels to Antioch and serves the king of the city, recognizing in his daughter the Chrysantza whom he had met symbolically at the beauty contest in the Castle of Love. Velthandros is arrested for meeting Chrysantza in the palace gardens by night, but her chambermaid Faidrokaza takes the blame by declaring Velthandros had visited her. He is now forced into an (apparent) marriage with the maid, but they make an escape with Chrysantza. His escort (including Faidrokaza) is drowned. The couple flees in a small boat. He returns

to rule his country, with Chrysantza as his queen (their wedding is blessed by a Patriarch). This occurs after they have survived challenges and attacks by monsters.

See also HAPPY ENDING

Further Reading

Hunger, H. "Die Schönheitskonkurrenz in 'Velthandros und Chrysantza' und die Brautschau am byzantinischen Kaiserhof." *Byzantion* 35 (1965): 150–158.

Kahane, H. and R. Kahane. "The Hidden Narcissus in the Byzantine Romance of Belthandros and Chrysantza." *Jahrbuch der Österreichischen Byzantinistik* 33 (1983): 199–219.

Papayeoryios, Alekos and Eleni, eds. Βελθάνδρος καὶ Χρυσάντζα. Μεσαιωνικὸ ἐρωτικὸ μυθιστόρημα [*The Excellent Story of Velthandros the Greek: A Medieval Romance of Love*]. Athens: Gregory Editions, 1968.

VENEZIS, ILIAS (1904–1973; pseudonym of Ilias Mellos) The novelist and short story writer Ilias Venezis, later a member of the Athenian Academy, was born at Ayvalik (Asia Minor). In 1914 his family took refuge across the water in Mytiline, to avoid Turkish harassment during World War I. Thus Venezis grew up on the island of Mytiline and attended secondary school there. After the Armistice, he returned with his family to Turkey and completed his schooling at Ayvalik. During the Asia Minor expedition of 1920–1922, Venezis was captured by the Turks and conscripted into a work corps of Greeks and sent inland on forced labor. His first novel, *The Number 31328,* is a graphic evocation of this experience. Parts of the text were published in 1924 in the paper *The Bell,* run by **Myrivilis,** and it came out in book form at Mytiline (1931). It was made into a color film, en-

titled *1922,* by the director Nikos Koundouros (1978), dwelling in a pointedly anti-Turkish way on Venezis's passages about rape, arbitrary killing, and deprivation of water imposed on a forced march of Greeks. On his return from the labor camps, Venezis settled first at Mytiline (1925) as an employee of the National Bank. His volume *Manolis Lekas and Other Stories* (1928) was praised, and promoted, by **Varnalis.** Later Venezis moved to Athens, where he worked at the Bank of Greece (1930–1957). In 1957 he became a member of the Athenian Academy. In 1962, he was appointed President of the Order of Writers, within the Academy. In the 1930s, Venezis embarked on writing the collective story of the **Asia Minor disaster.** How a band of refugees make their way to settle at Anabyssos is related in *Tranquillity* (1939), a novel permeated with nostalgia for his childhood years. The feel of his early, lost homeland returns in the novel *Aeolian Earth* (1943). A play, *Block C* (1945), and the later novel *Exodus* (1950) try to forge analogous tensions in response to the **Occupation.**

See also DIALOGUE

Further Reading

Cadbury, Alison. "Against Return: Genre and Politics in Elias Venezis' *Aeolian Earth.*" *JHD* 18, no. 1 (1992): 27–39.

Karanikas, Alexander and Helen Karanikas. *Elias Venezis.* New York: Twayne Publishers, 1969.

Venezis, Ilias. *Aeolia.* Translated by E. D. Scott-Kilvert, with a preface by Lawrence Durrell. New York: Vanguard Press, 1957.

VENICE Bessarion called Venice *alterum Byzantium* ("a second Byzantium"). K. Paparrigopoulos observed that the rebirth of Hellenic civilization is owed to the Greek community at Venice. Greek printing was at the heart of this development. In the sixteenth century there was Andreas Kounadis of Patras, and the printery of Glykis from Ioannina (founded 1670) and of Saros (from Epirus, founded 1681). The house of Glykis had printed some 250 Greek books by the end of the seventeenth century. The later decline of Greek printers at Venice was offset by the rise of Greek publishing at Bucharest, Vienna, and Jassy. In a fifteenth-century poem conventionally called "To Venice," or *Narrative about Misty Venice,* an unknown writer expresses his admiration for the Palace of the Doges, the watery streets of the city, and the cathedral. This text, in 84 unrhymed **political lines,** was published by Wagner in his *Carmina graeca medii aevi* (Leipzig, 1874). The classic *Mourning for Death* went through five editions at Venice between 1524 and 1600. The *Theseid* was published there in 1529. The *Alexander Romance* was printed there in 1529, 1553, and 1600. The romance *Imperios and Margarona* appeared at Venice in 1543, the romance *Apollonios* in 1534.

Further Reading

Geanakoplos, Deno John. *Greek Scholars in Venice: Studies in the Dissemination of Greek Learning from Byzantium to Western Europe.* Cambridge, MA: Harvard University Press, 1962.

Thiriet, Freddy. *La Romanie vénitienne au Moyen Age.* Paris: Boccard, 1975.

VENIZELOS, ELEVTHERIOS (1864–1936),

Venizelos was the leading twentieth-century Cretan nationalist and Greek politician, more than once Prime Minister. Although Greece was defeated in the war with Turkey over the Cretan insurrection of 1896–1897 and lost territory in Thessaly, the European powers applied pressure for Crete to be independent and then (1908) entrusted it to Greece, later confirming sovereignty (Treaty of Bucharest, 1913). As head of Enosis ("union"), Venizelos proclaimed the island's annexation in 1905. In the **Balkan Wars,** Greece gained western Thrace, southeast Macedonia, and a large slice of Epirus, at the expense of the new Albania. While King Constantine promoted Greek neutrality in World War I, Venizelos, as head of the Liberal Party, forged a pro-Allied policy and created a rump government at **Thessaloniki** (1916), after allowing the Allies to land in his northern city (1915). Constantine abdicated in favor of his son Alexander (June 1917), Venizelos took over as Prime Minister from Zaïmis (June 12, 1917), and Greece entered the war on the side of the Allies (27 June 1917). Thanks to Venizelos's policies, Greece was rewarded in postwar treaties with further territorial expansion. Greece gained the European parts of Turkey and the Bulgarian coastline on the Aegean Sea (Thrace, 1919; Smyrna, 1920). The Allied Supreme Command gave Venizelos, as Prime Minister, a mandate to restore order in Anatolia. Greek forces occupied Bursa and Adrianople (1920), advancing as far as the river Sakarya. In 1921, the Greek offensive collapsed on the Sakarya and at Inönü. General Mustapha Kemal (1881–1938; from 1935 Atatürk, "Father of the Turks") counterattacked, pushing the Greeks back on Smyrna. Venizelos's policies thus led, ultimately, to the **Asia Minor disaster,** as it is called. In 1924–1935, Greece became a Republic, and there was strife between pro-Monarchists and Venizelists, until Venizelos returned to power in 1928–1932 and effected rec-

onciliation with Turkey (Treaty of Ankara, 1930). After an unsuccessful Venizelos coup, the monarchy (1935) was restored, and King George II returned to power (1922–1924; 1935–1947). In the year of Venizelos's death (1936), General **Metaxás** became Prime Minister. Later he suspended Parliament. Metaxás liquidated the agrarian reforms and dismantled the heritage of Venizelos.

See also GREAT IDEA

Further Reading

Alastos, Doros. *Venizelos: Patriot, Statesman, Revolutionary.* Gulf Breeze, FL: Academic International, 1978.

VERBOSE; VERBIAGE. See BAB-BLING

VIKELAS, DIMITRIOS (1835–1909)
Dimitrios Vikelas was a novelist, short story writer, poet, and philanthropist. As a boy aged 17, he went to London to work in his uncle's company, which traded in corn. He stayed in England, became a partner, and eventually amassed a fortune of his own (1855–1872). As a retired merchant, Vikelas founded an Association for the Distribution of Useful Books. He was involved in the planning and establishment of the modern **Olympic Games.** His historical novel, *Loukís Laras* (1879), brought events from the **War of Independence** into powerful focus and was considered by Palamás to mark the starting point of the new prose of the last two decades of the Greek nineteenth century.

Further Reading

Bikelas, D. *Loukis Laras: Reminiscences of a Chiote Merchant During the War of Independence.* Translated by J. Gennadius. London: Macmillan, 1881; revised by D.

Trollope, London: Doric Publications, 1972.

Bikelas, Demetrios. "The Priest's Tale." In *Great Short Stories of the World,* edited by B. H. Clark and M. Lieber, 861–868. London: Spring Books, 1965.

Vikelas, Dimitrios. "Why I Remained a Lawyer." Translated by Alice-Mary Maffry. *The Charioteer,* no. 4 (1962): 82–93.

VILARÁS, IOANNIS (1771–1823) The patriot, conspirator, and **Enlightenment** thinker Ioannis Vilarás was a private doctor to Veli, son of the tyrant **Ali Pasha.** Vilarás wrote lyric poetry and fables. He proposed an unusual solution to the **language question** in his *The Romaic Language,* the only book by Vilarás to come out in his lifetime (1814). It avoided the **purist** orthography and proposed a new, Latin spelling system adapted to the sounds of Greek. Vilarás's closely argued support of the **demotic language** anticipates Psycharis's *My Journey* by 74 years. It opens with a prologue and a formal dedication to Athanasios Psalidas (1764–1829), whose works posited the impossibility of certain knowledge. The main text contains guidance on the letters and spelling of modern Greek, with a set of examples showing Vilarás's literary and linguistic principles taken from his own love poetry (quoted) and two model translations, one from Plato's *Crito,* the other from Thucydides's funeral speech for Pericles. These two translations judiciously include Epirot idioms to show that demotic Greek, with its natural sprinkling of regional forms, can constitute a prestige variety and be used for the translation of the classics. Elsewhere, he asks in what language Xenophon spoke to the officers and soldiers of his 10,000 troops. Did he use the syntax and vocabulary of the *Anabasis,* in which he described their expedition? In that case, did Xenophon march with a platoon of interpreters, in order to be understood by fellow Greeks? Vilarás refutes the argument that, without purist Greek, scientific and philosophical notions cannot be expressed: "What splendid reasoning! So all the other nations in the world, insofar as they have never learnt Greek, or don't know it, must have no science or art, and are unable to philosophize?" Vilarás was born in Cythera; his father had gone to that island to practice medicine. When the boy was six, his father removed the family to Ioannina, where there was an intellectual court, and set about teaching his son Latin, Italian, and French. By 1794, Vilarás was in Italy, studying medicine at the University of Padua. He read widely and wrote a number of poems during his stay abroad, including a lament on expatriation, *xenitiá:* "Little foreign bird, / Bird gone abroad, / Lost bird, as I am, / Where shall I come to rest?" This was written in Venice, where Vilarás went from Padua to collect money for a cadre of revolutionary plotters. Another man from the **Ionian Islands,** Ioannis Krassas, headed the conspirators and for a while met them at the Greek-owned café, Florian's, on St. Mark's Square. Later, to avoid attention, they moved on to Emperor's, near the Greek church of St. George's. Vilarás was arrested on a charge of pro-French espionage. A Greek merchant testified that Vilarás lived near his house, and the court case lapsed when Venice was overrun by Napoleonic troops, in 1797. In 1800, married to that merchant's daughter, Vilarás returned to Ioannina and became Veli Pasha's doctor. This gave him the opportunity to travel to his master's pasheliks all over Greece. He became the foremost botanist in the country. He treated many poor patients free of charge. He compiled lexical lists for the conversion of foreign pharmaceutical terms into demotic Greek.

His knowledge of chemistry went as far as the discovery of the metal base of alkalines. He was on close terms with writers and "teachers of the nation" such as Psalidas, Kolettis, **Sakellarios,** and Tagapieras (1777–1842), for whom he wrote a comic "Pancakes of Tagapieras." It is not documented when Vilarás became a member of the *Philikí Etairía* ("Friendly Society"), but by 1820 or 1821 he was in charge of the considerable Ioannina war chest (to finance local actions in the cause of independence). He moved it, along with the Ioannina exiles, to the Zagora district of Thessaly. His own son went to fight with the defenders of **Missolonghi,** and Vilarás wrote him a kind of valedictory letter (a year before his own death at the age of 52) advising that "pretence is a vice, but it may become a virtue when it does not contribute to the injury of others. Socrates drank the hemlock so as not to betray his usefulness to his country and to virtue itself." A translation of *Frog and Mouse War* was included in a posthumous volume of his complete poems (Kerkyra, 1827). This subject typifies Vilarás's publicizing, Enlightenment attitude because the *Frog and Mouse War* was a pseudoheroic text that had been very popular in the **Byzantine** period. It was written some time after Aesop's *Fables* (?fifth century B.C.): in 303 dactylic lines, the characters of the *Iliad* are replaced by mice and frogs, with names like "Lick-Platter," "Mud-Coucher," "Lick-Meal."

Further Reading

Pontani, F. M. "Αἱ σπουδαὶ τοῦ Βιλαρᾶ εἰς τὸ Πανεπιστήμιο τῆς Παδούης" [The Studies of Vilarás at Padua University]. Παρνασσός 3, no. 2 (1961): 281–287.

Vilarás, I. Ἅπαντα. Ἔμμετρα καὶ πεζά [The Complete Works in Prose and Verse]. Athens: Panekdotikí, 1962.

VILLANELLE The villanelle was a poetic form elaborated in the late **Renaissance** and popular in France. The lines are arranged with a **rhyme** scheme aba/aba, in three-line **strophes.** The first, or last, of the characteristic four strophes may be a quatrain (consist of four lines). The last line of the poem is repeated. Line 1 returns at lines 6, 12, 18; line 3 at lines 9, 15, 19. A variation is to compose the poem in quatrains, with a rhyme scheme abab/abba/abab, and to make a reprise of line 4 at lines 7, 12, 15, 20, and a reprise of line 3 at lines 8, 11, 16 and 19.

VISION OF AGATHANGELOS Agathangelos (Ἀγαθάγγελος) is the name of a supposed compiler of oracles that refer to Byzantium's liberation. This text was called *Vision of Agathangelos,* or *Prophecies Concerning the Future of Nations, and Especially of Greece.* It refers (as though verifying them in advance) to real events of the seventeenth and eighteenth centuries. These fantastic pamphlets helped Greeks, during the years of Turkish rule, to believe in a coming freedom and return to the old order. Supposedly first written down in Messina (Sicily), in 1279, an Italian version was produced in 1555. A learned monk who traveled in Germany, Sweden, and Italy, Theoklitos Polyidis, did a Latin translation, which led to a **plain Greek** version (c. 1751), which went, in turn, through several editions (Venice, Vienna) and awoke uneducated Greeks to the notion of an uprising. It seems likely that **Rigas Velestinlís** adapted Agathangelos to his own revolutionary purpose at the end of the eighteenth century. He took the "blond race," which Agathangelos foresees coming from **Russia** to save the Greeks, and turned them into saviors from France (the French Revolution).

VIZYINÓS, YEORYIOS (1849–1896)

The poet, scholar, and short story writer Yeóryios Vizyinós was born in the Thracian village of Vizyi to a poor family. He was enabled by a benefaction from the philanthropist Y. Zarifis to study in Athens and later Germany. In 1873, he won first prize in the **Voutsynas literary competition** with an **epic** poem about Kodros, a king of prehistoric Athens, while Rangavís and Vlachos secured honorable mentions. Some newspapers ridiculed the university professors for awarding the prize to a mere student. In 1876, Vizyinós won second prize for the poems of *Stuff and Nonsense,* later published as *Breezes from the Bosphorus.* Between 1883 and 1895, Vizyinós published six short stories (in *Estía*), not well received at the time, but now regarded as the essential stepping-stones into modern Greek prose. The stories ran serially, as was the custom, over successive editions of the paper. They were a remarkable innovation for the time. The story "My Mother's Sin," which first appeared in a French version for the *Nouvelle Revue* of Juliette Lambert-Adam, has a jealous son rehearse the guilt felt by a morbidly sensitive mother over the death of her baby daughter, due to an ironically inflated act of negligence after an evening dance. Other persistently ironic studies are sketched in the stories "Who Was the Killer of My Brother?" (1883), "Between Piraeus and Naples" (1883), "The Consequences of an Old Story" (1884), "The Only Journey of His Life" (1884), "Mos-kov-Selim" (1895), "A Sad Festival," and the tales of "The Arab and His Camel."

The device of first-person narrator in Vizyinós's narrative relates to his interest in mental processes, but is not an autobiographical event. His stories can hardly be related to the heading of *ithografía.* They show sympathy for Turks, even some identification with Russian claims on the **Balkans.** They broach the topic of insanity as social stigma, while shifting geographical background and narrative point of view in a precocious manner, characteristic of modern stories. This author's mind was eventually clouded by a belief that there was gold on a family property in Thrace and by his secret, desperate love for a girl called Bettina Fravasili. In 1892, he was tricked, or obliged, to go into an insane asylum. A special number of *Greek Creation* (no. 40: 1 Oct. 1949) is devoted to Vizyinós.

Further Reading

Alexiou, Margaret. "Writing against Silence: Antithesis and Ekphrasis in the Prose Fiction of Vizyinos." *Dumbarton Oaks Papers,* no. 47 (1993): 263–286.

Chryssanthopoulos, Michalis. "Reality and Imagination: The Use of History in the Short Stories of Yeóryios Viziinós." In *The Greek Novel: A.D. 1–1985,* edited by Roderick Beaton, 11–22. London: Croom Helm, 1988.

Mamoni, K. Βιβλιογραφία Γ. Βιζυηνοῦ (1873–1962)— Ἀνέκδοτα ποιήματα ἀπὸ τὸ Χειρόγραφο. "Λυρικά" [Bibliography of G. Vizyinós from 1873 to 1962: New Poems from the Manuscript "Lyric Pieces"]. Athens: Association for Thracian Studies, 1963.

Vizyenos, Georgios. *My Mother's Sin and Other Stories.* Edited by Roderick Beaton and translated by W. F. Wyatt, Jr. Hanover, NH: University Press of New England, 1988.

Vizyinós, Y. M. Ἅπαντα [The Complete Works]. Edited by K. Mamoni. Athens: Biblos, 1955.

VLACHOS, ANGELOS (1838–1920)

The versatile figure Angelos Vlachos was an ambassador, Foreign Minister, Minister of Education, editor, and publisher (see special issue of *Néa Estía,* no. 539: 1949). Vlachos commented, in the journal *Estía,* on the controversial suspension in 1879 of the Greek translation of Zola's novel *Nana* (see under **Rabagás**). He polemicized bitterly against **Roidis,** mustering arguments against Roidis's insistence on the unavoidable emptiness of contemporary Greek culture. Vlachos produced many collections of lyric verse, *Dawn* (1857), *Hours* (1860), and *Lyric Poems* (1875), as well as translations of poetry and drama, including Lamartine, Goethe, Heine, and **Shakespeare.** These helped introduce the late-nineteenth-century reading public to the novelty of reading foreign literature. Most popular of his many hit comedies was *The Grocer's Daughter* (1866), which had an opening run of 28 performances.

Further Reading

Mitsakis, K. Ο Ἄγγελος Βλάχος καὶ τὸ ἱστορικό μυθιστόρημα [Angelos Vlachos and the Historical Novel]. Athens: Kardamitsas, 1988.

Vlachos, A. Κωμωδίαι. Athens, 1871.

Vlachos, A. Λυρικὰ ποιήματα [Lyric Verse]. Athens: Perri Brothers, 1875.

Vlachos, A. Ὁ νέος κριτικός [The Young Critic]. Athens: n.p., 1877.

VLACHOS, YERASIMOS (1607–1684)

The *Sermons* of Yerasimos Vlachos (from Crete) are among early works written in a popular idiom (see **Demotic**). Their devotional content leans toward rhetoric; their style follows the **tropes** of persuasive composition. Vlachos was a popular Archbishop to the Greek community of **Venice** (that is, Philadelphia), succeeding Methodios (1679), and followed in turn by Mattheos Typaldos (1685). He wrote a *Four-Language Thesaurus of Encyclopedic Knowledge* (Venice: Pinelos, 1659), which circulated widely and was reprinted in the eighteenth century, making Vlachos the first modern Greek lexicographer. Seven poems by Vlachos are placed at the front of his lexicon, with a Latin translation.

See also RUSSIA

VLACHOYANNIS, YANNIS (1867–1945)

Yannis Vlachoyannis was born to poor Roumeliot parents, steeped in family memories of the **Uprising.** He listened to Souliot women, among them a great-grandmother and an aunt, who told him stories from the **War of Independence,** around the fireplace in his childhood Nafpaktos. Driven by curiosity and **patriotism,** he collected documents of the Uprising, issued *The Athenian Archive,* and in 1915 was invited by **Venizelos** to run the General National Archive. By this time, he owned about 300,000 items from the war, subdivided into folders, in a private archive. He was a prolific writer of stories, novels, and poems, all in pure **demotic.** Typical is the sketch of Chaido, a Souliot girl who routed the Turks like a phantom "sent from God," or "The Vow," in which a red-eyed partridge perches on the shoulder of Karaiskakis just before his assault on the Acropolis (1827). Karaiskakis takes the partridge as a good omen and vows that they will attend mass and dine at Daphní (a monastery near Eleusis), if they free Athens. He dies, and his lieutenant, Kallergis, recalls the vow as *he* lies dying.

Vlachoyannis's lasting work is the bibliography, reconstruction, and editing of **memoirs** from the Uprising, using personal documents of military heroes who were also writers: **Nikolaos Kasomoulis** (1795–1872), Yeoryios Karaiskakis (1780–1827), Spyromilios (1800–1880), and **Makriyannis.** The complete works of Vlachoyannis were edited and published by his colleague Papakostas, in seven volumes (1965–1967).

Further Reading

Papakostas, A. N. Βιβλιογραφία Γιάννη Βλαχογιάννη ["A Bibliography of Yannis Vlachoyannis"]. *Néa Estía* 44, no. 515, (Christmas 1948): Ἀφιέρωμα στὸν Βλαχογιάννη [A Tribute to Vlachoyannis].

Petropulos, John Anthony. *Politics and State-craft in the Kingdom of Greece, 1833–1843.* Princeton, NJ: Princeton University Press, 1968.

VLAMI, EVA (1910–1974)

Eva Vlami was born in the Piraeus, but grew up in Galaxidi, an old, picturesque seafaring town on the northern side of the Gulf of **Corinth,** southwest of Delphi. This place, with its striking view of Mount Parnassós and the nineteenth-century mansions along its waterfront, is steeped in memories of the wealth once gathered by the its shipbuilding industry. A dreamy nostalgia seeps into Vlami's 1947 literary debut *Galaxidi: The Destiny of a Sailing Township.* As a child, she drank in the sea tales of her father, a well-known captain, and drew on this store of narrative treasure to relate, in *Galaxidi,* the tales of passing refugee fishermen from Smyrna, of stolen bait, and snagged trawling lines. She sets up an epic conflict between sail and steam in the romanticized canvas of her second novel *The Man Skeletonrock* (1950). Here the eponymous hero is the sole survivor of a collision between "The Great Eastern" steamer and the tiny boat "Galaxidi 1856." On his return, paralyzed, he is cursed for the loss of his crew and dies asking their pardon. The lexical palette is colored by dialect spellings, sailors' shouted orders, and the technical vocabulary of jib, sail, gaffs, boom, jigger, luff, and top-gallant.

Further Reading

Doulis, Thomas. "Eva Vlami and the Imprisonment of the Past." *Balkan Studies* 10, no. 1 (1969): 95–104.

VOCABULARY In the wake of the 1985 Greek school leaving exam, there was discontent at the poor vocabulary displayed by candidates. People expressed anxiety that few high school students understood the meaning of the words ευδοκίμηση ("success") and αρωγή ("assistance"). Kavafis once joked that Mistriotis wanted half the language thrown in the sea, and Psycharis wanted the other half thrown in the river. Kavafis realized most Greeks do not know their language: "What treasures are hidden within! Our thoughts ought to be on how we can enrich it and bring to light what is hidden in it!" In 1976, the Minister of Education, Rallis, in a parliamentary speech, objected to the sentence "*Alcohol* was the cause of death" because the noun οἰνόπνευμα ("alcoholic spirits") was available. Minister Rallis deplored the writing of σοκ ("shock") instead of κλονισμός. Analogously, the Academie Française (1998) tried to ban French forms like "le cash-flow" or "overbooké."

Further Reading

Landsman, D. M. "The Greeks' Sense of Language and the 1976 Linguistic Reforms: Illusions and Disappointments." *BMGS* 13 (1989): 159–182.

VOSKOPOULA (early seventeenth century)

Voskopoula is the conventional way of referring to the Cretan poem of 476 11-syllable lines, *The Pretty Shepherdess*. It is a pastoral idyll dating from around 1600, first published by Nikolaos Drimytinós at Venice, in 1627. He was wrongly believed to be its author. The actual author and its likely Italian source are still unidentified. The narrative is unaffected and economical: a young male rustic meets a shepherdess in a mountain valley. He is struck (like Guido Cavalcanti and other contemporaries of Dante) by her beauty and by Cupid. She returns his affection. He accompanies her to the cave that she uses for a home. As her father is absent, they spend days of passion, an unusual element in Cretan writing of this time. They make rings out of bay leaves for each other's fingers, and are thus betrothed. The shepherd is obliged to return to his valley, and the girl awaits her father. The boy promises to come back to the cave in a month, but does not do so, because he falls ill. The girl wastes to death, believing her betrothed has forgotten her. On his return, three months later, the boy finds only the old man, lamenting the decease of his daughter. The poem closes with a picture of the boy's cosmic mourning, ranging across the mountains, carrying the lamb that was her present to him: "This creature alone I'll take with me, / So the two of us may roam as one" (vv. 451–452).

The text is in rhyming couplets, incorporating Cretan idiom and some naive, popular formulae, like love's double-edged knife: "It's hard for some to believe how / A knife that wounds can cure"

(vv. 103–104). The idyll was transmitted like a demotic song over Crete and the islands of Naxos, Melos, and Chios, where extracts were chanted at festive occasions. In the seventeenth century, it was cast in vernacular 15-syllable lines and translated into Latin by the French bishop, P. Daniel Huet, who called its verses so many "roses in the garden of the muses." **Solomós,** in his dialogue on the demotic language, calls *Voskopoula* a "poem with a universal heroine despite its venerable 200 years."

Further Reading

Alexiou, Stylianos. Ἡ βοσκοπούλα· Κρητικὸ εἰδύλλιο τοῦ 1600. Κριτικὴ ἔκδοση Στηλιανοῦ Ἀλεξίου [The Shepherdess: A Sixteenth Century Idyll from Crete. Critical Edition by Stylianos Alexios]. Iraklion: Association for Cretan Historical Studies, 1963.

VOTSI, OLGA (1922–) Olga Votsi produced 14 volumes of poetry and essays on St. Francis's *Fioretti,* Baudelaire, **Sikelianós** and **Papadiamantis** (1980), **Kavafis** (1983), **Kalvos** and **Solomós** (1986), and T. S. Eliot (1988). Votsi translated texts by Kafka, Georg Trakl, Rilke, Thomas Mann, Paul Celan, Patrice de la Tour du Pin, Claudel, Pierre Emmanuel, W. H. Auden, Emily Dickinson, and Kathleen Raine.

Further Reading

Capri, Karka C. and I. Karka. "Poems by Olga Votsi." *The Charioteer,* no. 31–32 (1989–1990): 85–130.

VOULGARIS, EVYENIOS (1716–1806) The "educator of the nation," Evyenios Voulgaris, was born on Kerkyra and died in **Russia.** The name Elevtherios ("free") was given to him because on the day of his birth, 11 August 1716, a

Turkish fleet raised the blockade of Kerkyra. As a deacon, he later took the name Evyenios. After schooling at Arta and Ioannina, sponsors aided his studies at Padua (Italy) in theology, philosophy, Greek and Hebrew literature, maths, physics, Italian, French, and German. Voulgaris returned in 1742 and taught at the Maroutsaia School (Ioannina). His Western, liberal philosophy created hostility. So began an itinerary of flight or exile: from Kozani to the Athonias Academy (the school founded at Mount Athos in 1749 by Patriarch Kyrillos V), then on to Thessaloniki, the Patriarchal School (Constantinople), Romania, Leipzig, and Halle.

Voulgaris later went to Russia, as librarian at St. Petersburg (1771) in the court of the Empress Katherine II (see **Orloff**). Voulgaris taught that tolerance was the golden mean between brute force and indifference; he opposed any notion that the church was permitted to fight or pursue an enemy. Such means were permitted to an Orthodox prince, so it could be hoped that the Russian emperor would expel the **Ottoman** from Greece. Ordained in 1775, Voulgaris became archbishop of Kherson and Slaviansk, a see created for him in 1776 (see **N. Theotokis**). His anti-Turk sentiments were not needed at court, when the Russo-Ottoman war of 1768–1774 ended in a treaty. In 1779, he resigned as archbishop and lived on in Russia as an academician, editing his manuscripts (some published at the expense of the Zosimades). His list of books includes *Logic* (1766), *Essays on Religious Tolerance* (1768), *On Death without Pain* (1804), *Elements of Metaphysics* (1805), *A Theology, Antiquities in Homer* (4 vols., 1808), translations of Virgil's *Georgics* and *Aenaid* (Moscow, 1791), a *Treatise on Music,* and the *Battle*

of the Bosphorus. When Katherine II repudiated the French revolution (1789), she aimed at a conciliatory peace with the Ottomans (1790). Voulgaris accordingly became conservative, rejecting the liberalism of Voltaire, the Empress's former tutor. The Orthodox patriarchate followed suit, officially condemning Voltaire in 1793.

Further Reading

Batalden, Stephen K. *Catherine II's Greek Prelate: Eugenios Voulgaris in Russia, 1771–1806.* New York: Columbia University Press, 1982.

VOUTSYNAS POETRY PRIZE The annual Voutsynas Poetry Prize, also known as the University Prize, was founded and endowed by a writer from Odessa with a background in banking, Ioannis Voutsynas. He had launched similar initiatives in Odessa and Constantinople, but the present proposal was taken up by the Senate of the University of Athens. A committee of four was appointed by the Senate to determine the prize winners and to issue honorable mentions among the works submitted, which could be in the **epic,** lyric, or dramatic genres. The report on the contestants, together with the conferral of a 1,000 drachma first prize and a crown of laurels, was made at an annual ceremony in the Great Hall of the University, in the presence of the royal family and government dignitaries. The first committee met on 28 April 1862, with **Alexandros Rizos Rangavís** as spokesman. **K. Asopios,** Konstantinos Paparrigopoulos, and **Stefanos Koumanoudis** were the other three judges. In his presentation, Rangavís argued that the only appropriate language for lyric poetry was **Demotic.** Nonetheless, the 1862 prize went to the poet Alexandros Vyzantios for his epico-lyric composition *Socrates and Aristophanes.*

Winners in subsequent years, listed by Exarchakis (*MENL,* vol. IV: 326), include three honorable mentions in 1863: **Achilleus Paraschos, Angelos Vlachos,** and Sofoklis Karoudis. In 1864, the competition was not held. In 1865, a headmaster, **Antonios Antoniadis** (1836–1905), took the prize with his play *Philip of Macedon.* **Timoleon Ambelás** (1850–1926) became a frequent applicant and in 1869 submitted two plays, *King Nisus* and *The Simpleton,* with its trial based on a donkey's shadow, which the judges disregarded. Next Ambelás sent in a five-act drama, *Peter Kantanoleus,* dealing with an uprising on Crete, from medieval times. The Voutsynas jury praised the work and suggested he redraft several scenes to improve the text. Ambelás resubmitted it under the new title, *Men of Crete and Venice.* It gained the special mention for a historical play and was often performed. In 1870, he submitted three plays: *Nero, Virginia of Rome,* and *Hebros of Thrace.* None took the prize, but *Nero* was singled out for mention, and he gained another mention, in one of the last rounds of the competition (1875), with his tragedy *Cleopatra,* which was performed at Syros by the Soutsa company, with Soutsa scoring considerable success in the role of Mark Anthony.

In 1866, two poets came equal first, **Dimitrios Paparrigopoulos** (1843–1873, son of the historian mentioned previously), for his volume *Sighs,* and Angelos Vlachos. In 1867, the prize went to an epic poem on the Cretan insurrection by A. Antoniadis, *The Creteid;* a mention went to D. Paparrigopoulos for his *Swallows.* In 1868, the prize went to a three-

act comedy by Vlachos, *Captain of the National Guard.* Mentions went to a play by S. Karoudis, *The Children of Doxapatris,* and to an epico-lyric poem by D. Paparrigopoulos, *Orpheus.* In 1869, the prize went to a tragedy, *Krispos,* by Antoniadis; mention to the lyric poem "Pygmalion" by D. Paparrigopoulos. In 1870, a satirical play by Konstantinos Versis took the prize; Spyridón Lambros, A. Antoniadis, Panayotis Zanos, and **Aristomenis Provelengios** gained mentions. In 1871, mentions went to Antoniadis for an epic poem, *Katsantonis,* and to A. Provelengios for an epico-lyric poem, *The Apple of Discord.* Also in 1871, Antonis Fatseas (1821–1872) entered a comedy entitled *Bertoldos,* which was written in Demotic and gained a mention. Prefacing a published edition of that year, Fatseas argued the vital importance to Greece of demotic idiom: "What profit to the nation if the idea of free development of the language expressed by **Vilarás** had prevailed! The nation would be wise and enriched, consequently, strong" (transl. by M. Gianos).

In 1872, the prize was divided between an Antoniadis play and a comedy called *The Lover of His Belly.* In 1874, the prize went to **Vizyinós** for his epico-lyric poem *Codrus.* The year 1875 saw the prize shared between the play *Sampson and Delilah,* by K. Versis, and Antoniadis's comedy *Faithless Woman.* In 1876, the prize was again won by Vizyinós, for the poems *Stuff and Nonsense,* later expanded as *Breezes from the Bosphorus;* a mention was gained by K. Skokos for *Light Beams and Fragrances.* The competition was then halted, because nonwinners argued too fiercely with the committee.

See also COMPETITIONS; KAMBOUROGLOUS; LASSANEIOS; OLD SCHOOL OF ATHENS

Further Reading

Bien, Peter. "The Predominance of Poetry in Greek Literature." *WLT* 59, no. 2 (spring 1985): 197–200.

Zoras, Yeoryios Th. and Ioannis M. Chatzifotis, eds. Μεγάλη Ἐγκυκλοπαίδεια Τῆς Νεοελληνικῆς Λογοτεχνίας (ἀπὸ τὸν 10° αἰῶνα μ.Χ. μέχρι σήμερα) [Great Encyclopedia of Modern Greek Literature from the 10th Century A.D. to the Present]. 12 vols. Athens: Chari Patsi, 1969–1971.

VOUTYRÁS, DEMOSTHENES (1872?–1958)

Demosthenes Voutyrás was a novelist and short story writer, born in Constantinople. His date of birth is uncertain: the Piraeus deme gives it as 1872; reference works say 1879, or 1888; L. Politis hazards 1871. In his old age, the writer said that the actual date was known to nobody (but his birth occurred some miles out from the harbor), and he would reveal his birthdate when the time was right (the time never came). At age three, his family took him to Athens. He grew up around the harbor, lazy at school, except in history and geography. He began writing sketches for the Piraeus paper *The Chronicle*. His first fiction followed the contemporary sketch of regional customs and came out in a slim volume entitled *Langás and Other Stories* (1902), which had two editions in Greece and two in Alexandria. Voutyrás focuses on gritty items from everyday life, portraits of the poor as victims of society or industry, and hints at the battle cries of early socialism. The narrative is loose, not tied to beginning, middle, and end. The **imagery** is dreamy and evasive. This man published more than 30 volumes in 50 years (1901–1950), more than 400 short stories, and yet was afflicted by epilepsy. He died alone and in grinding poverty. His narrative epicenter moves away from the village to the suburbs, the city, and even space! He influenced upcoming authors, with volumes that include *Twenty Stories* (1920), *In Hell* (1927), *With the Man-Eaters* (1928), *Counterfeit Civilizations* (1934), *Nights of Enchantment* (1938), and *Storms* (1946). A special number of *Néa Estía*, no. 755 (1958), was devoted to him.

See also SCIENCE FICTION

Further Reading

Levandas, Chr. Δύο μορφές [Two Figures]. Piraeus: Chronicles of Piraeus Editions, 1952.

Perlorentzu, Maria. "Terra Marte Terra: Satira, fantastico e utopia in Vutiras." *Il lettore di provincia* 15, no. 56 (March 1984): 63–76.

Voutyrás, D. Ἅπαντα [The Complete Works]. 2 vols. Athens: Difros, 1958; 1960.

VRETTAKOS, NIKIFOROS (1912–1991)

Nikiforos Vrettakos's poetry is sustained by the metaphysics of injustice. He is stunned by the multitude killed by American bombs at Nagasaki, on 5 August 1945. From that date, Vrettakos was opposed to nuclear armament, and he campaigned among the intelligentsia, seeking a total ban. When 11 citizens were executed in Prague (1952) for "anti-Communist" activities, he wrote in verse that his face was filled with wrinkles: "full of horizontal and vertical sword cuts." His mother might see his face, but "she would not know that above it / Can be distinguished eleven gallows from Prague." Vrettakos carries the **protest** by running his **metaphor** to its full extent: "how they are the trajectories from the bullets that furrowed / The light of my own country; how they are the patterns / Of the hurricane that is our age." He was appointed to the Academy in 1987.

Further Reading

Doulis, Thomas. "Nikiphoros Vrettakos." *The Texas Quarterly* 10, no. 2 (summer 1967): 95–96.

Vrettakos N. "14 Poems for the Same Mountain." Translated by M. B. Raizis. *Greek Letters* 4 (1986–1989): 13–40.

VULGARISM; VULGARIZERS, THE

The word *Vulgarizers* is the name for certain opponents of the **purist** language (**Katharevousa**), who were vigorous partisans of the **Demotic** at various stages of the **language question. Solomós** refutes a pedant, who claims the Demotic suffers from lexical poverty, by reversing the claim in favor of the vernacular (vulgar) language: "The poverty of the language is not a sufficient justification to have important people change it. Secondly, who decided that it is poor? **Dante** also was accused of using a corrupt, humble, and poor language. But today everyone studies Dante." The **Ionian** poet **Lorentsos Mavilis** composed a celebrated **sonnet,** "To the Demotic," evoking the vernacular language as a village maiden, to whom he declares his love. Let others flock to court the raddled hag in cosmetics. The latter figure, occupying the first tercet of Mavilis's sonnet, is a symbol of Katharevousa.

Another convinced "vulgarizer" was the twentieth-century poet and novelist **Kazantzakis.** As a young man, Kazantzakis journeyed to remote locations to collect words and expressions that might be lost unless he recorded them in his writing. P. Bien (1989: 90) records how Kazantzakis, as a "fanatical demoticist,"

recovered the otherwise unknown verb "act like a hare" (λαγάζω, from λαγός), to use in place of verbs meaning "cower" or "hide oneself." Kazantzakis registered the word "lamp-extinguisher" to denote a moth, and the **compound adjective** "incomplete + unswollen by yeast" to denote a man looking like rag and bones (λυχνοσβήστης, λιψανάβατος, respectively). Kazantzakis chose to publish his *Odusseia* in a simplified syntax and spelling. He also removed accents from the text, keeping acute accents only for certain syllables, to indicate stress. He felt obliged to attach a special lexicon of almost 2,000 words to his *Odusseia* to explain rare terms. K. Friar believed that many of these were in daily use by fishermen and shepherds.

Kazantzakis finds words known among the peasantry but not to educated Greeks: λιόκρουσι ("the moment when the full moon is struck by the rays of the setting sun") and γιορτόπλασμα ("child lazily conceived during a fiesta"). As for entirely new words invented by Kazantzakis, Friar counts five or six in the translations, but the diction is always original. Kazantzakis gathered notes for a dictionary of demotic Greek, which no publisher put on the market. The writer **Kondylakis** referred to the vulgariser Pasayannis, who used a vigorous **demotic,** as "hairy" (μαλλιαρός) just because he happened to affect long hair. The epithet has survived to denote any Vulgarizer who employs markedly plebeian language.

In 1917, 1920, 1923, 1927, 1932, and 1933 there were changes in the law, or reversals of policy, on the imposition of the Demotic in primary school teaching. The educationist Ch. Lefas complained that therefore ". . . every two years the language of their books changed." The demotic fanaticism of Th. Nikoloudis went as far as adapting terms like τὶς ἀπόλαψες, for "treats," σκεφτικισμός, for "scepticism," and τὸ θεϊκὸ πιοτί, for "heavenly booze."

See also ATTICISM; DEMOTIC LANGUAGE; LANGUAGE QUESTION; PURISM

Further Reading

Householder, Fred et al. *Reference Grammar of Literary Dhimotiki* (Indiana University Research Center in Anthropology, Folklore, and Linguistics, publication no. 31; *International Journal of American Linguistics,* 30: 2, part 2). Bloomington: Indiana University, 1964.

Meillet, Antoine. *Aperçu d'une histoire de la langue grecque* [Sketch for a History of the Greek Language] [1920]. 2nd ed. Paris: Hachette, 1965.

Prevelakis, Pandelis. *Nikos Kazantzakis and His "Odyssey": A Study of the Poet and His Poem.* New York: Simon and Schuster, 1961.

VYZANTIOS, DIMITRIOS (1790–1853)

Dimitrios Vyzantios wrote four further works for theater, apart from his *Babel, or the Regional Corruption of the Greek Language,* which was published at Nafplion, 1836. This slapstick piece of linguistic miscomprehension and *double entendre,* the first Greek play from newly independent Greece, shows a group of Greeks speaking different dialects. They are in a tap-room on the night in 1827 when the naval victory of Navarino is announced. They cannot agree on a common vocabulary to order food, and simple remarks are converted into references to bowel functions. Seven different regional variations of everyday words and phrases are aired in the play, while the pedant has to cobble together an eighth **dialect** in order to replace words that are too "common" with illustrious ones, a procedure that makes it difficult to order in a restaurant, one of the basic functions (as the author has determined) of a new culture or a national language.

VYZANTIOS, DIMITRIOS (1834–1854)

This Dimitrios Vyzantios is another **Romantic** poet who disappeared prematurely. Vyzantios was dead by the age of 20, before finishing his studies. Many poems of his had already come out in the journal *Pandora* or in anthologies. He made a verse translation of a pastoral idyll in prose and verse, *Galatée* (1783), by the French writer J.-P. Claris de Florian (1755–1794).

W

WAR OF INDEPENDENCE, THE
Referred to by Greek writers as the
Struggle, struggle for freedom, "Uprising," "revolt," or Rebellion of the Nation
(Ἐθνεγερσία), this war, waged with unequal energy from 1821 to 1829 by the
Greek people against the **Turkocracy,**
has been told in many books, surveys,
and memoirs. **Byron** (1818) cries out in
Childe Harolde the thoughts of Europe:
"Greece, change thy lords, thy state is
still the same; / Thy glorious day is o'er,
but not thine years of shame." Panayotis
Andronikos, when he died in 1820, was
hailed by the words: "Thus is lost one of
the golden hopes of the Motherland." A
famous poem by Andronikos, which
fanned flames across the country, imagines Greece crying out: "Wake up, children! / Now the hour comes by. / Wake
up all, / Rush here. / The Last Supper is
nigh!"

The date 1821 is sacred. It marks the
year when liberation sputtered into action
and is traditionally called "the Twenty-
One" (ὁ Εἰκοσιένα). **K. Palamás** sings
out this date in lines from "To Our

Youth" (November 1940): "Lightly he
carries amid the windstorm, / That head
aged by the commotion of the world; /
This message I shall give you, I have
none other to give: / Become intoxicated
with the deathless wine of '21." This
consecration does not dwell on the Greek
fighters' preference for sniping from behind cover, or the fact that the **Klephts**
liked to point their bare buttocks at the
Turks, while the latter were loading their
rifles.

Some fighters in the War of Independence became legendary, and their names
soared in later verse. Nikitaras and Plapoutas appear as walk-on celebrities in
"Death and the Knight" by **Gatsos:** "I
could place meadows, / Waters that once
irrigated the lilies of Germany, / And
these arms that you wear, I could deco-
rate them for you / With a sprig of basil
and a spray of mint, / With the weapons
of Plapoutas and Nikitaras' trophies."

The role of Greece's men of letters in
this revolutionary period is told in Angelou's *The Savants and the Struggle.* Essays and biographies, collected in *Mem-*

oirs of the Fighters of '21, were brought out by E. Protopsaltes, in 20 volumes. They include a Greek translation of Henri Fornézy's *Le monument des Philhellènes.* Wagner, the German composer, was an ardent sympathizer. The date 25 March (1821), now a national holiday, marks the moment when the Archbishop of Patras, Germanos, raised a red cloth with a black cross as a standard of revolt, calling the Greek people to arms after he had been summoned by the Turks to answer for his congregation (the *millet*), with other Greek archbishops, at Tripolis. The hallowed date is recalled in the poem "25th March" by Eleni Gousiou (born 1840), a (blind) Greek-Egyptian poetess: "Germanos the Bishop / Took up the banner, / Raised it proudly on high / And declared to the people: //—Unsheath your swords—." Tradition turns the letter written by Germanos to foreign consuls at Patras into a heroic text: "We, the Hellenic race of Christians, noting that the Ottoman race scorns us and seeks our ruin, have firmly decided to perish or be free, and with this purpose we now take up arms." Peter Mavromichalis, Bey of Maina, took the field, and the Klephts of the Morea, under **Kolokotronis** and other warlords, followed his example. Tripolis fell in October 1821. In 1822, Kolokotronis defeated Dramali in the defile of Dervenaki and went on to capture **Corinth.** In 1823, **Nafplion** fell. Greek fortunes were reversed in 1825, when Ibrahim Pasha invaded the Morea with an Egyptian force.

There was a long siege of **Missolonghi** (1825–1826), immortalized in memoirs, verse, and painting, like *Greece on the Ruins of Missolonghi* (1826), by Eugène Delacroix. The massacre inflicted by the Turks on the isle of Chios (1822) led to French intervention (1827) in the struggle. A few months after the Great Powers' naval victory at Navarino (1827), the French, under General Maison, established a beachhead in the Gulf of Koroni. Ibrahim took flight. Turkish forces evacuated the Greek mainland in October 1828. The French withdrew soon afterwards. In 1831, an insurrection of the Mani, an area where local factions resented yielding their autonomy, was suppressed by Bavarian troops. The kings of Europe, whose protection Germanos invoked, were aware of atrocities by the freedom fighters against the Turks. Acts of plunder by both sides are recorded in *History of the Greek Revolution,* by the Scottish **Philhellene** Thomas Gordon (1788–1841).

Some 57 Turkish prisoners captured from a corvette were roasted to death one by one over fires lit on a beach at the island of Hydra. In spring 1821, the Turks, who had lived for centuries in Greece, virtually disappeared. More than 20,000 Turks were murdered by their Greek neighbors in a few weeks of slaughter. Greek islanders put to death the crews of Muslim ships, as well as their passengers sailing to Mecca. On 15 June 1821, the Ottoman government hanged five archbishops and three bishops. On Cyprus, the archbishop, five bishops, and 36 priests were executed. In Khormovo, Ottoman soldiers roasted the son of the priest alive. Military actions during the war were ragged and usually disorganized. A corps of Philhellene volunteers was destroyed at the battle of Peta, in western Greece (1822). People were led to give a religious significance to the War and interpreted it as a sacred struggle (Ἱερὸς Ἀγών). Admiral Miaoulis, General **Makriyannis,** and other writers thought that its ideals were betrayed in the aftermath.

Further Reading

Angelou, Alkes. Οἱ λόγιοι καὶ ὁ Ἀγώνας [Scholars and the Struggle]. Athens: Ermis, 1971.

Clogg, Richard. *The Struggle for Greek Independence*. London: MacMillan, 1973.

Lord, A. B. *The Heroic Tradition of Greek Epic and Ballad. Hellenism and the First Greek War of Liberation*. Thessaloniki, 1976.

Protopsaltes, Emmanuel. Ἀπομνημονεύματα ἀγωνιστῶν του '21 [Memoirs of the Fighters of '21]. 20 vols. Athens: The National Printery, 1956–1959.

WEDDING. See MARRIAGE

WINE Wine is entangled with Greek **myth:** Nemean wine is called "Herakles' blood," and retsina is the teardrop of a wood nymph. In Greek literature, wine is both exalted and condemned. A late **Byzantine** attack on the grape in a story on **fruit** (in the twelfth- or thirteenth-century humorous prose work Πωρικολόγος) is reversed in a similar medieval work (wrongly attributed to the Prodromic poet). The latter work, entitled *Naturalist's Tale of the Greatly Esteemed Wine-Father Peter the Ferment Juice,* has 118 **decapentasyllables.** It is generally referred to as *Philosophy of the Wine-Father,* a title applied by its first editor, E. Legrand. It was a popular work. Its archetype may date to the twelfth century, and it features a rascal who irreverently praises wine: "This alone is what grieves me about you, that you can't raise your vines / To spread above the highest peaks of Mt. Ararat." He wishes that wine might flow along the four rivers of Paradise, supplying each of our four meals of the day. When the author himself fell sick through lack of wine, his only salvation was for Christ to send a keg, or Holy Communion (!), to wet his lips. The Jews under Moses were saved by 12 springs of living water. They would be better served if the springs in the desert spouted wine. The whole text contributes to the literary pose known as "eat, drink and be merry" (φάγε-πίε-εὐ φραίνου).

See also TAVERN

Further Reading

Lambros, Sp. Φυσιολογικὴ διήγησις τοῦ ὑπερτίμου Κρασοπατέρος Πέτρου τοῦ Ζυφομούστου [*Naturalist's Tale of the Greatly Esteemed Wine-Father Peter the Ferment Juice*]. Νέος Ἑλληνομνήμων [The New Greek Memorialist] 1 (1904): 433–449.

WORLD HISTORY. See CHRONICLE, HISTORY

WORLD WAR II Greek authors replicate every phase of the War: the Italian invasion (1940), the German **occupation,** famine, the campaign for Crete, government in exile, deportation, **holocaust, resistance, prison, civil war,** and reprisal. **P. Kanellopoulos,** later a prime minister, fought on the Albanian front (1940–1941) in Greece's repulse of Italian troops. In the occupation, he organized anti-German operations. He published (1964) a memoir entitled *The Great War Years, 1939–1944*. A trilogy of novels by **Roufos** describes the **occupation,** War, and **Civil War,** from an anti-Communist viewpoint. A book by **Xefloudas,** *Men of Fable* (1944), is a robust essay in realism from the Greco-Albanian front.

Further Reading

Papastratis, Procopios. *British Policy towards Greece during the Second World War*. Cambridge: Cambridge University Press, 1984.

X

XEFLOUDAS, STELIOS (1902–1984)
One of the first revisions of the traditional notion of character, in the Greek
novel, is in the work of the **Thessaloniki**
writer Stelios Xefloudas. He used the
narrative device of **interior monologue**
in *The Copybooks of Paul Photinus*
(1930) and *Inner Symphony* (1932). He
published several more narrative works
geared to the analysis of the mind and
emotions of single characters: *Eve, Odysseus without Ithaca,* travel impressions
and a study of early-twentieth-century
Greek fiction, *The Modern Greek Novel:
Nirvanas, Christomanos and Others.*

Further Reading

Paraschos, Kleon. Προβλήματα Λογοτεχνίας [Problems in Literature]. Athens:
Zarbanos, 1964.

XENITIÁ *Xenitiá* is a Greek word
meaning "foreign lands." A character in
Galaxidi (by **Eleni Vlami,** 1947) imagines that once upon a time a hundred-
weight scale was used to compare the
relative weight of *xenitiá,* orphanhood,
sorrow, and love: "of all of them, the tear
shed by *xenitiá* was far the heaviest." The
word refers to any expatriate status or sojourn in foreign parts. An anonymous lament, probably belonging to the fifteenth
century, is entitled *Life Abroad.* It has
survived in two different versions, one of
548 lines. It typifies a popular subgenre,
made up of short segments of sorrow
concerning existence abroad, the lost
home, and people cut asunder. In a
seventeenth-century poem by **Bounialís,**
based on the war that ended with Crete
annexed by Turks, there are lines about
Cretans who had to seek exile on other
shores: "When they meet, they do not
know each other, they are content to ask:
'From where do you come, stranger?'
They can say nothing more. 'From
Crete,' they say, and one grasps the hand
of the other while bursting into tears."
Interest in foreign sojourn is a characteristic obsession of migrants. It is also the
collective destiny of Greeks forced elsewhere by the alteration of boundaries. **G.
Drosinis** has a poem, "The Soil of
Greece," in which he pleads only to be
allowed an amulet from his country to

wear in all his travels, to give him certainty that he will return to Greece: "My last plea for forgiveness, / My last kiss will be for you / If I should die on foreign soil, / The foreign tomb will be sweeter, / If you, soil of Greece, are placed upon my heart, / Beloved earth of Greece."

A common type of **demotic song** centers on departure. The speaker predicts the sorrow of living overseas, torn from their native soil and the family's embrace. **Nikos Gatsos** adapts it in the closing lines of his poem "Elegy," altering it again for the poem "Take Your Ring": "With your own heart warm, and facing foreign parts, / Towards the crumbling teeth of another shore, / And towards the fragmented islands of the wild cherry tree, of the sea lion." In another poem, "Song of Kalymnos," the speaker promises to accompany the expatriate as a magic bird, with reminders of his homeland: "Now as you journey to foreign parts, / I shall turn into a little bird, / And meet you soon. / My husband and my lord, I bid you well, / And may the Virgin Mother keep you company."

Further Reading

Kulukundis, Elias. *The Feasts of Memory: A Journey to a Greek Island.* New York: Holt, Rinehart & Winston, 1967.

Saunier, Guy, ed. Το δημοτικό τραγούδι της ξενιτιάς [The Demotic Song concerning Exile]. Athens: Ermis, 1983.

Sultan, Nancy. *Exile and the Poetics of Loss in the Greek Tradition.* Lanham, MD: Rowman & Littlefield, 1999.

XENOPOULOS, GRIGORIOS (1867–1951)

The novelist, short story writer, journalist, and playwright Grigorios Xenopoulos was elected a member of the Academy in 1931. He was born on Zakynthos, where he experienced, like many Ionian intellectuals, the liberalizing influence of ancestral Venetian, and later British, administration. Xenopoulos claimed to be the first Greek writer from the interwar period to live entirely by his own pen. He developed a fluent, professional touch that made him the author of more than 20 novels, 20 collections of stories, and 38 plays. He began his career very young, as runner-up in the 1884 *Estía* short story competition. Rather than going on to compose a systematic fresco of contemporary social life (like the realist novelists Balzac and Zola, his declared inspiration), Xenopoulos allowed two preferred locations, Zakynthos and Athens, to map out a local **naturalism** for his readers. As a socially committed writer, he conceived a **trilogy** of novels to chart the fortunes of the haves and have-nots (*Rich and Poor; Honest and Dishonest; Fortunate and Unfortunate*). In 1903, he wrote an article that is said to be responsible for the discovery of **Kavafis**. At a certain point (1905), Xenopoulos began to move to a controlled, rather somber version of the demotic language. He relates the trials and tribulations of a seducer in *The Common Man* (1930), gradually adopting an internal, psychoanalytic stance in his later fiction. His plays are the first to put middle-class, city families on the stage. Particularly memorable is their depiction of female characters, as in *The Secret of Countess Valeraina* (based on a story of 1897, and turned into a **television** film with Anna Synodinós in the title role of an aristocrat who pretends to invent a miraculous cure for the eyes), *Fotino Santri,* and *Stella Violanti* (1909).

Stella Violanti was staged more than 500 times, beginning with the great actress Marika Kotopouli, who mastered the heroine's role and performed it throughout her career (1909–1937). Aspiring Greek tragic actresses have always tended to aim at this part. The comedy *Divine Dream* presents an Athenian banker called Morsimos, who thinks the god Dionysus wants him to become a dramatist. Because Sophocles would be his rival, Morsimos refuses to allow his daughter to marry Sophocles's son. In another divine dream, Morsimos sees himself in the Athens of 2,400 years later. The citizens are different, but they still go to see the plays of Aeschylus, so Morsimos decides that Dionysus wants him to have a good life rather than write rival tragedies. In 1927, Xenopoulos founded *Néa Estía,* and it has consistently been the leading Greek literary periodical. Two commemorative issues of *Néa Estía* (no. 587: 1951 and no. 805: 1961) were devoted to him, as founder and editor; also a special issue of *Greek Creation* (no. 72: 1 Feb. 1951).

Further Reading

Constantinidis, Stratos E. "Greek Theater: An Annotated Bibliography of Plays Translated and Essays Written from 1824 to 1994." *JMGS* 14, no. 1 (1996): 123–176.

Farmakis, F. Τὸ νεοελληνικὸ διήγημα καὶ ἄλλες μελέτες [The Modern Greek Story and Other Studies]. Athens: n.p., 1962.

Xenopoulos, Grigorios. *Red Rock: From Ecstasy to Tragedy.* Translated by William Spanos. New York: Pageant Press, 1955.

Xenopoulos, Grigorios. "Divine Dream." Translated by Mary Gianos. In *Introduction to Modern Greek Literature: An Anthology of Fiction, Drama and Poetry,* edited by Mary Gianos, 289–318. New York: Twayne, 1969.

XENOS, STEFANOS (1821–1894) Stefanos Xenos wrote the novels *The Devil in Turkey or Scenes in Constantinople (*1851) and *Andronike: The Heroine of the Greek Revolution* (London, 1861). Coming from parents with social pretensions in Smyrna, Xenos liked to cut a dash. He fought a duel with an army colleague when young and was seriously wounded. After sundry travels, he settled down as a merchant-trader in London for 30 years (from 1847). He gave his fleet of 25 ships (1856, "Greco-Anatolian Sailing Line") the names of heroes from the **War of Independence.** He endowed the Athens Municipal Gallery with a nucleus of **paintings,** including Correggio's "The Upbringing of Love." He ran for Mayor of Athens in the late 1870s, proposing to erect a beacon on the Acropolis and to open a cave in its rock so that breezes from Phaleron Bay could cool the city. He lived an old age of extreme poverty: three neighbors attended his funeral in July 1894.

See also NOVEL, GREEK, NINETEENTH CENTURY

Y

YANNOPOULOS, PERIKLÍS (1869–1910) Periklís Yannopoulos was a well-known nationalist and art critic. He had a strong influence on the poet **Sikelianós** when the latter was young. In his *Contemporary Painting* (1902), he declared "the purpose of each work of art should be to express Hellenism's geoclimatic particularity. This is essential work in building a homeland." He was a stubborn classicist, with a romantic pre-Raphaelite streak smacking of Wilde and d'Annunzio. He went down in the annals for the opulent manner of his suicide: he anointed himself with perfume, crowned his head with wild flowers, and rode a horse into deep sea waters off Skaramanga. Carrying an elegantly packed ballast of weights, he shot himself while on horseback and disappeared into the waves. In *Appeal to the Greek Nation* (1907), Yannopoulos says: "When Greece is silent, all humanity ceases; and when the Greek falls silent, the Human is suppressed; and when the Greek imitates barbarians, he commits suicide and no Greek is left on Earth; because the European is by nature barbarian, and consequently all his manifestations are savage."

YATROMANOLAKIS, YORYIS (1940–) Born at the village Zaros, near Iráklion, Yoryis Yatromanolakis, after studying classics at Athens, completed postgraduate studies at King's College London (1973) and was later professor of classics at University of Athens. His debut novel, *Biographical Treasury* (1974), analyzes the first 24 hours of a prospective high school teacher on an imaginary Greek island. This was followed by *The Fiancée* (1979), and the highly successful *History of a Vendetta* (1982), which traced the illogical, atavistic tensions of a prewar Cretan feud, with its prejudices and false glories (and Yatromanolakis's faint sociological overview). Then came an analogous rural perspective in *A Useless Story* (1993), which tells a tragic, recent event, the killing of two Crete University professors by a deranged student and his flight to the mountains and suicide. He has also produced a monograph on **Embirikos.**

Further Reading

Yatromanolakis, Yorgi. *History of a Vendetta.* Translated by Helen Cavanagh. Sawtry: Dedalus, 1992 (reviewed in *TLS,* 6 March 1992: 22 [first publ. 1982]).

YENNADIOS, YEORYIOS (1786–1854) Yeoryios Yennadios, erstwhile pupil of Lambros Fotiadis (1752–1805) in Bucharest, is renowned as writer, translator, teacher, and "Savior of the Nation." His legacy was visionary and practical. He founded the first Greek school with desks, and his *Grammar* (Aegina, 1832) was used in elementary classrooms for the following 100 years. One of his pupils was **A. Rangavís.** In 1824, Yennadios left the Danubian principalities and his studies in Germany to act as an organizer in Greece during and after the Uprising, founding schools, teaching, donating cash, and using his powers as an orator to serve the people's cause. At one point, **Kolokotronis** called him "Father of the Nation." Greece's Yennadios Library, the first public such institution, has carried his name since his son Ioannis (1844–1932) gave 24,000 volumes to the American School of Archaeology and organized (1921) American funds for a building that now houses, among many treasures, the archive on Greek history assembled by the prominent nineteenth-century British **Philhellene** George Finlay.

Further Reading

Finlay, George. *History of the Greek Revolution.* 2 vols. Edinburgh: Blackwood, 1861.

Z

ZALIKOGLOU, GRIGORIOS (1776–1827) Born at Thessaloniki, Grigorios Zalikoglou died in Paris after the typical life of a roving **Enlightenment** intellectual. He was the author of a French-Greek dictionary and left a dialogue, *The Greek Revolution.*

ZALOKOSTAS, YEORYIOS (1805–1858) Yeoryios Zalakostas was born in the remote village of Syrrakhion, in Epirus. His whole family fled to Italy, expropriated by an edict issued by **Ali Pasha.** After schooling in Livorno, which had been a temporary home to some of the associates of **Rigas Velestinlís,** Zalokostas came back to Greece (1822) and threw himself into the **Uprising.** His parents died, and his elder brother was killed during the struggle. He is remembered as **patriot,** painter, and author of popular verse like *The Hostel at Gravia* (1852). His style and thought are saturated with the **War of Independence,** for Zalokostas actually took part in the siege of **Missolonghi** and the famed sortie of April 1826. His epico-lyric poem on the subject, *Missolonghi,* won the 1851 poetry competition endowed by Ambrosios Rallis. Zalokostas was handed his prize by King Otho in person. He contributed to the journals *Euterpe* and *Mnemosyne.* He witnessed the death of seven of his nine children, and the critic **Panayotopoulos** makes much of Zalokostas as "the poet of paternal grief." A short poem inspired by one of the deceased has been frequently anthologized, namely his "North Wind That Freezes the Little Lamb."

Further Reading

Zalokostas, Yeoryios. *Rupel.* Introduction by A. Papagos. Athens: Stef. N. Taraossopoulos, 1945.

ZAMBELIOS, IOANNIS (1787–1856) Born to nobility, a family inscribed in the "Golden Book" of Levkas (in the **Heptanese**), Ioannis Zambelios mingled with the major Italian writers of the period (Monti, Vittorio Alfieri, **Foscolo**) and with Greek intellectuals in Italy, such as Th. Kairis (see **Kairi**), **Solomós,** Metzofantis, Kolettis. In Paris, Zambelios had a letter of recommendation to **Koraís**

from the merchant and patron Michael Zosimas. He composed a tragedy, *Timoleon* (Vienna, 1818), and sent Koraís a copy. There followed a correspondence between the two, which was lost in the Levkas earthquake (1825). In 1817, Zambelios was initiated into the Friendly Society (see **Philikí**). He enrolled other Levkas citizens in the conspiracy (1820) and set up a bank to help fund the **Uprising.** The following year he crossed into Akarnania and helped to start the revolt in Aetolia. He established a corps of 853 Levkas volunteers, who crossed to Akarnania and took part in the sortie from **Missolonghi,** the battles of Salona, Brachorion, Arta, and the siege of the Acropolis (see **War of Independence**). He was offered inducements by the British administration of the Heptanese to hand over any written documentation that would incriminate Kapodistrias (1776–1831), later first president of Greece (1828 to 1831). Zambelios eluded the British and helped provision the brigade of Karaiskakis. He retired to Italy after a legal career of 17 years. Inspired by Alfieri, the Italian neoclassical tragedian, Zambelios devoted himself to forging a genre of modern tragedy in Greek. He used nonrhyming 12-syllable lines, with iambic trimeters (alternating short/long syllables: ˘ — ˘ — ˘ —). This **meter,** followed by Iakovos Rizos Rangavís and Antoniadis, dominated Greek theater for several decades after Zambelios. He was the major force in reviving a dormant Greek **theater.** He took his subjects from Byzantine tradition (as in *Constantine Palaeologus*) and from the contemporary war (*Markos Botzaris*). He composed a *Medea* and wrote *Rigas from Thessaly* (see **Rigas**) and a play, *Ioannis Kapodistrias.*

ZAMBELIOS, SPYRIDON (1815–1881) Son of the renowned patriot and playwright (see **Zambelios, Ioannis**), Spyridon Zambelios followed law studies in Italy. He toured European libraries to examine manuscripts and glossological documents. He published (anonymously) in Kerkyra the poem "The Last Night of the Condemned Prisoner," erroneously attributed to **Solomós.** In 1852, he brought out *Folk Songs of Greece,* with an introduction that tried to trace the origin and tradition of Greek **demotic song** in parallel with the nation's history. Zambelios published an important essay (Athens, 1859) entitled *Whence Is Derived the Common Word "Sing,"* in which he tries to explain why the verb "I sing," derived from the word *tragedy,* can be applied to the laments in demotic song and criticizes the edition of the complete works of **Solomós** (1859) by the scholar and frank devotee of Solomós, **Iakovos Polylás.** Polylás refuted this essay in a pamphlet printed under the ironic title *Whence Is Derived Mr. Zambelios's Fear of Mystery: Some Reflections* (Kerkyra, 1860). Zambelios was a considerable historian. His main work in this area was *Byzantine Studies: On the Sources of Modern Greek Ethnicity* (Athens, 1857). In 1879, a Greek etymological lexicon was published in Paris, *Parlers grecs et romains* (one volume of a projected longer work), and Spyridon Zambelios's contributions were criticized by experts in linguistics for trying to relate certain Celtic and Latin words to ancient Greek roots. He was elected deputy for Levkas in the ninth Assembly and later retired to his villa in Livorno (Italy).

Further Reading

Kofos, Evangelos. *Greece and the Eastern Crisis, 1875–1878.* Thessalonica: Institute for Balkan Studies, 1975.

ZARZOULIS, NIKOLAOS (c. 1710–1766; Zertzoulis, Zartoulis) The **Enlightenment** scholar Nikolaos Zarzoulis studied at the Balanaia School (Ioannina) and taught 12 years at Trikke. He went to Italy for further studies (1754) and later worked at Metsovo, **Mount Athos,** and Jassy. His only extant work is *Theater of Politics* (1749), which contains rules for civic behavior, examples of good or bad rulers, and philosophical maxims.

Further Reading

Dimaras, K. T. *A History of Modern Greek Literature.* Albany: State University of New York Press, 1972.

ZEI, ALKI (1925–) Alki Zei describes the compulsory Youth Movement promulgated by **Metaxás** in a novel (probably based on her own experiences) written for **children,** *Wildcat under Glass.* Zei had a respected name as a children's writer when she published *Achilles' Fiancée* (Athens: Kedros, 1987). This was a runaway success and sold 100,000 copies in three years. Moving on a vast canvas (Athens, Rome, Paris, Tashkent, Moscow), the novel traces the lives of Greek refugees from December 1944, through the Civil War, the **Colonels' Junta,** and the thaw in the Soviet Union, set inside a recent movie script about the aging **Resistance** activists on a train journey.

Further Reading

Zei, Alki. *Wildcat under Glass.* Translated by Edward Fenton. New York: Holt, Rinehart and Winston, 1968.

Zei, Alki. *Petros' War.* Translated by Edward Fenton. New York: Dutton, 1972.

Zei, Alki. *The Sound of the Dragon's Feet.* Translated by Edward Fenton. New York: Dutton, 1979.

Zei, Alki. *Achilles' Fiancée.* Translated by Gail Holst-Warhaft. Athens: Kedros, 1991.

ZERVOU, IOANNA (1943–) Ioanna Zervou has written verse and an essay on the Greek composer Xenakis. She contributes to contemporary journals and publishes on children's education. She translated (1976) Gombin's *The Origin of Leftism* and Marguerite Dumas's *Capital Letter,* as well as "Le Ravissement de Lol V. Stein," in the journal *Film* (vol. 17, 1979).

ZEUGMA Zeugma (ζεύγμα) is a grammatical **figure** (see also **Trope**) in which one verb governs different propositions, or phrases, which should technically be governed by a separate verb. Zeugma involves a logical discord that is modified by a construction according to sense.

ZEVGOLI-GLEZOU, DIALECHTI (1907–) Zevgoli-Glezou was born in the picturesque, rural community of Apeiranthos of Naxos. She recorded its **folklore** and collected local sayings in her *Proverbs of Apeiranthos of Naxos* (1963). She studied at Athens and (1944) married the short story writer Petros Glezos. Her first poems, *Songs of Loneliness* (1931), appeared with a flattering introduction by **K. Palamás.** Other distinguished poets (**Drosinis, Gryparis, Sikelianós**) added their praise. Two larger volumes followed in 1964, *Cycle of Love* and *Cycle of Bitter Hours;* the latter deals in part with the bitterness of the German **occupation.** All her poetry is interwoven with visceral nostalgia for her childhood in Naxos. For her it was "the complete source" of her poetic achievement.

Further Reading

Papazoglou-Margaris, Theano. *Poetess Dialechti Zevgoli-Glezou and Her Poetry.* Chicago: Modern Greek Studies Series (University of Illinois at Chicago), 1986.

ZITSAIA, CHRYSANTHE (1902–1995; pseudonym of Chrysanthe N. Oikonomidou) Born at Zitsa (Epirus), Chrysanthe Zitsaia moved with her family in 1930 to live permanently at **Thessaloniki,** where she was a founding member of the Association of Thessaloniki Writers and wrote for the journal *Forms.* Spandonidis dismisses her "tasteless poetic stereotypes," which stem from the **album** and the romantic farrago of the interwar years. Tsakonas says she rejected the fragmented dazzle of the modern age, steeped in nostalgia for the Epirus, her rehashed "Palamism" (see **Palamás**), and her irredentist patriotism. Zitsaia was admired in her time and published many volumes of stories and verse between 1929 and the 1960s; also an essay, *Women Writers of Cyprus* (1963).

ZOGRAFOU, LILÍ (1922–1998) Journalist, essayist, and novelist, the prolific woman writer Lili Zografou (from Iraklion, Crete) published an influential biography: *Nikos Kazantzakis: A Tragic Figure* (1960), about her famed compatriot, the novelist of *Zorba the Greek.* In this generally negative assessment of **Kazantzakis,** Zografou attempts to adjust the literary perspective forged in their own respective memoirs by his two wives, **Galateia Alexiou** and Eleni Kazantzakis, that is, Eleni Samiou, who wrote about him retrospectively as monster or saint. Zografou's first literary effort came in 1949, with the short story collection *Love Affairs.* Later she edited the complete literary works of **Maria Polydouri** and wrote a harrowing novel about the Nazi extermination camps: *Michael: Like as to God.*

Select General Bibliography

AA.VV. Η μεταπολεμική πεζογραφία· Από τον πόλεμο του '40 ως την δικτατορία του '67 [Post-War Prose: From the War of 1940 to the Dictatorship of 1967]. 8 vols. Athens: Sokolis, 1988–1990.

AA.VV. Η παλαιότερη πεζογραφία μας. Από τις αρχές ως τον πρώτο παγκόσμιο πόλεμο [Our Older Prose-Writing: From the Origins to the First World War]. 8 vols. Athens: Sokolis, 1996–1997.

Abatzoglou, Petros. *What Does Mrs. Freeman Want?* Translated by Kay Cicellis. Athens: Kedros, 1991.

Alexiou, Margaret. *The Ritual Lament in Greek Tradition.* Cambridge: Cambridge University Press, 1974.

Alison Phillips, W. *The War of Greek Independence: 1821–1833.* London: Smith, Elder & Co., 1897.

Alithersis, Glavkos. Ἱστορία τῆς Νέας Ἑλληνικῆς Λογοτεχνίας [A History of Modern Greek Literature]. Alexandria: Kasimatis and Ion, 1938.

Anagnostaki, Loula. "The Overnight Visitor," "The City," "The Parade." Translated by G. Valamvanos and K. MacKinnon. *The Charioteer,* no. 26 (1984): 37–54; 55–72; 73–88.

Anagnostaki, Loula. "The Town" [= "The City" above]. Translated by Aliki Halls. *Chicago Review* 21, no. 2 (1969): 88–105.

Anagnostakis, Manolis. *Poems.* Translated by Philip Ramp. Nottingham: Shoestring Press, 1998.

Anagnostakis, Manolis, ed. Η χαμηλή φωνή· Τα λυρικά μιας περασμένης εποχής στους παλιούς ρυθμούς [The Lowered Voice: Lyric Poems of a Past Age in Ancient Rhythm]. Athens: Nefeli, 1990.

Anghelaki-Rooke, Katerina. *Beings and Things on Their Own.* Translated by K. Anghelaki-Rooke and Jackie Willcox. Brockport, NY: BOA Editions, 1986.

Anghelaki-Rooke, Katerina. Ποιήματα [Lyric Poems]. Athens: Ermeias, 1971.

Anghelaki Rooke, [Katerina]. "A Note on Greek Poetry in the 1970s." *Modern Poetry in Translation* [Greek], no. 34 (summer 1978): 3–4.

Anthias, Tefkros. *Cyprus Village Tales.* Translated by Antoinette Diamantis. Nicosia, 1942.

Anthias, Tefkros. *Greece, I Keep my Vigil over You.* Translated by Jack Lindsay. London: Anthias, 1968.

Anton, John P. *The Poetry and Poetics of Constantine P. Cavafy: Aesthetic Visions of Sensual Reality.* Chur, Switzerland: Harwood Academic, 1995 [reviewed by Minas Savvas in *WLT,* 70, no. 4 (autumn 1996): 1003].

Antonakes, Michael. "Christ, Kazantzakis, and Controversy in Greece." *Modern Greek Studies Yearbook,* no. 6 (1990): 331–343.

Arseniou, Elizabeth. "The Emergence of a Hybrid Avant-Garde: The Response of the Magazine *Pali* to Greek Modernism." In *Greek Modernism and Beyond: Essays in Honor of Peter Bien,* edited by D. Tziovas, 217–227. Lanham, MD: Rowman & Littlefield, 1997.

Augustinos, Olga. *French Odysseys: Greece in French Travel Literature from the Renaissance to the Romantic Era.* Baltimore: Johns Hopkins University Press, 1994.

Avgeris, M. "I Proclaim Good News." Translated by M. Byron Raizis. *Journal of the Hellenic American Society* 1, no. 3 (1974): 12–13.

Bacopoulou-Halls, Aliki. *Modern Greek Theater: Roots and Blossoms.* Athens: Diogenis, 1982.

Baggally, John W. *The Klephtic Ballads in Relation to Greek History (1715–1821).* Oxford: Blackwell, 1936.

Baldick, Julian. *Homer and the Indo-Europeans.* London/New York: I. B. Tauris, 1994.

Bancroft-Marcus, Rosemary. "Georgios Chortatsis and His Works: A Critical Review." *Mandatoforos* 6 (1980): 13–46.

Barnstone, Willis, ed. *Eighteen Texts: Writings by Contemporary Greek Authors.* Cambridge: Harvard University Press, 1972.

[Bart-Hirst] Μπὰρτ—Χίρστ. Ἐγκυκλοπαιδικὸν Λεξικόν [The Encyclopedic Dictionary]. 6 vols., with suppl., illustrated. Athens: Bart kai Chirst, 1889–1898.

Basch, Sophie. *Le Mirage grec: La Grèce moderne devant l'opinion française depuis la création de l'Ecole d'Athènes jusqu'à la guerre civile grecque (1846–1946).* Paris: Hatier, 1995.

Bastiás, Kostís. Φιλολογικοί περίπατοι· συνομιλίες μέ 38 συγγραφεῖς τοῦ 20οῦ αἰώνα [Literary Perambulations: Interviews with Thirty-Three Writers of the 20th Century]. Athens: Kastaniotis, 1999.

Baud-Bovy, Samuel, ed. *Chansons du Dodecanèse.* Athens: J. N. Sideris, 1935.

Baud-Bovy, Samuel, ed. *La chanson populaire grecque du Dodecanèse.* Paris: Société d'édition "Les Belles Lettres," 1936 [Collection de l'Institut néohellénique de l'université de Paris. 2 sér. vol. III].

Beaton, Roderick. "Cavafy and Proust." *Grand Street* 6, no. 2 (winter 1987): 127–141.

Beaton, Roderick. *Folk Poetry of Modern Greece.* Cambridge, UK/New York: Cambridge University Press, 1980.

Beaton, Roderick, ed. *The Greek Novel: A.D. 1–1985.* London: Croom Helm, 1988.

Beaton, Roderick. *An Introduction to Modern Greek Literature.* Oxford: Clarendon Press, 1994.

Beaton, Roderick. "Land without Novels? Occupation and Civil War: The Midwives of Greek Fiction." *TLS,* 12 Oct. 2001: 14.

Beaton, Roderick and David Ricks, eds. *"Digenes Akrites": New Approaches to Byzantine Heroic Poetry.* Aldershot: Variorum, 1995.

Bien, Peter. "Cavafy's Homosexuality and His Reputation Outside Greece." *JMGS* 8, no. 2 (October 1990): 197–211.

Bien, Peter. *Constantine Cavafy.* New York/London: Columbia University Press, 1964.

Bien, Peter. *Kazantzakis and the Linguistic Revolution in Greek Literature.* Princeton, NJ: Princeton University Press, 1972.

Bien, Peter. "Nikos Kazantzakis: A Check List of Primary and Secondary Works Supplementing the Katsimbalis Bibliography." *Mandatoforos,* no. 5 (November 1974): 7–53.

Bien, Peter. *Nikos Kazantzakis: Novelist.* Bristol: Bristol Classical Press, 1989.

Biris, K. Ὁ Καραγκιόζης ἑλληνικὸ λαϊκὸ θεάτρο [Karaghiozis as Greek Popular Theater]. Reprint. Athens: New Estía, 1952.

Bolgar, R. R. "The Greek Legacy." In *The Legacy of Greece: A New Appraisal,* edited by M. I. Finley, 429–472. Oxford: Clarendon Press, 1988.

Bouboulidis, Faidon. Βιβλιογραφία νεοελληνικῆς φιλολογίας τοῦ ἔτους *1973* [A Bibliography of Modern Greek Literature for the Year 1973]. Athens: Gregory, 1977.

Bouboulidis, Faidon and Glykeria Bouboulidis. Βιβλιογραφία νεοελληνικῆς φιλολογίας τῶν ἐτῶν *1977–1978* [A Bibliography of Modern Greek Literature for the Years 1977–1978]. Athens: Gregory, 1981.

Bougas, Nikos. Ἱστορία τῆς Νεολληνικῆς Λογοτεχνίας, *1000–1977* [A History of Modern Greek Literature from 1000 to 1977]. Athens: Stafylidi, 1977.

Brooten, Bernadette J. *Love between Women: Early Christian Responses to Female Homoeroticism.* Chicago: University of Chicago Press, 1996.

Brown, Duncan, Anne and Helen Dudenbostel Jones. *Greece: A Selected List of References.* Washington, DC: Library of Congress. Division of Bibliography, 1943.

Browning, Robert. *History, Language and Literacy in the Byzantine World.* Northampton: Variorum Reprints, 1989.

Campbell, John K. *Honour, Family and Patronage; A Study of Institutions and Moral Values in a Greek Mountain Community.* Oxford: Clarendon Press, 1964.

Campbell, J. and P. Sherrard. "Modern Greek Literature." In *Modern Greece,* 214–244. London: Ernest Benn, 1968.

Chaconas, Stephen George. *Adamantios Korais: A Study in Greek Nationalism.* New York: Columbia University Press, 1942.

Chaïchalis, Stamatis. Βιογραφίες Ἑλλήνων λογοτεχνῶν [Biographies of Greek Writers]. 2 vols. Athens: Institute for the Promulgation of the Greek Book, 1980.

Chalkiopoulou, Maria D. Βιβλιογραφία νεοελληνικῶν ποιητικῶν ἀνθολογιῶν *1834—1978* [A Bibliography of Modern Greek Poetry Anthologies from 1834 to 1978]. Athens: Minyma [Μήνυμα], 1978.

Charis, P. Ἕλληνες Πεζογράφοι [Greek Prose-Writers], I. 2nd ed. Athens: Kollaros, 1963.

Charis, P. Ἕλληνες Πεζογράφοι [Greek Prose-Writers], II. Athens: Kollaros, 1963.

Chatziyakoumis, M. K. Τὰ μεσαιωνικὰ δημώδη κείμενα. Συμβολὴ στὴ μελέτη καὶ στὴν ἔκδοσή τους [A Contribution to the Study and Editing of Medieval Popular Texts]. Athens, 1977.

Clay, Diskin. "C. P. Cavafy: The Poet in the Reader." *JMGS* 5, no. 1 (May 1987): 65–83.

Clogg, Mary Jo and Richard Clogg. *Greece.* Oxford and Santa Barbara: Clio, 1980.

Clogg, Richard. *A Concise History of*

Greece. Cambridge: Cambridge University Press, 1992.

Constantinidis, Stratos E. "Greek Theater: An Annotated Bibliography of Plays Translated and Essays Written from 1824 to 1994." *JMGS* 14, no. 1 (May 1996): 123–176.

Costas, Procope S. *An Outline of the History of the Greek Language, with Particular Emphasis on the Koiné and the Subsequent Periods.* Chicago: Ukrainian Academy of Sciences of America, 1936 (reprinted, Chicago: Ares, 1979).

Craik, Elizabeth, "The Library of Mirivílis." In *The Greek Novel: A.D. 1–1985,* edited by Roderick Beaton, 63–69. London: Croom Helm, 1988.

Dalven, Rae, ed. and trans. *Daughters of Sappho: Contemporary Greek Women Poets.* London/Toronto: Associated University Presses, 1994.

Danforth, Loring. "Humour and Status Reversal in Greek Shadow Theater." *BMGS* 2, (1976): 99–111.

Darakis, L. "Interview with Kazantzakis." Ἠχὼ τῆς Ἑλλάδος [*The Echo of Greece*], no. 16 (March 1935): 3.

Dawkins, Richard M. *Modern Greek Folktales.* Oxford: Clarendon Press, 1953.

Decavalles, Andonis. "Pandelis Prevelakis: An Introduction." *The Charioteer,* no. 16 and 17 (1974–1975): 10–40.

Decavalles, Andonis. *Ransoms to Time: Selected Poems.* Translated with an introduction and notes by Kimon Friar. Rutherford, NJ: Fairleigh Dickinson University Press, 1984.

Dicks, Brian. *Greece: The Traveller's Guide to History and Mythology.* Newton Abbott: David & Charles, 1980.

Dieterich, Karl. *Geschichte der byzantinischen und neugriechischen Litteratur.* Leipzig: C. F. Amelang Verlag, 1902.

Dimaras, C. Th. *A History of Modern Greek Literature.* Albany: State University of New York Press, 1972.

Dimaras, C. Th., C. Koumou, and L. Droulia. *Modern Greek Culture: A Selected Bibliography (in English, French, German, Italian),* 3rd ed. revised. Thessaloniki: Institute for Balkan Studies, 1970.

Dimitrakopoulos, F. D. Ο Νεοελληνισμός στη λογοτεχνία 19ος—20ός αι. [Neo-Hellenism in the Literature of the 19th and 20th Centuries]. Athens: Epikairotita, 1990.

Dio Chrysostom. *Orations VII, XII and XXXVI.* Edited by D. A. Russell. Cambridge: Cambridge University Press, 1992.

Dölger, Franz. "Die Byzantinische Literatur." In *Kindlers Neues Literatur Lexikon,* vol. 19, Munich: Kindler, 1988, pp. 961–965.

Dölger, Franz. "Die Griechische Patrologie." *Kindlers Neues Literatur Lexikon* vol. 19, Munich: Kindler, 1988, pp. 966–971.

Doulis, Thomas. *Disaster and Fiction: Modern Greek Fiction and the Asia Minor Disaster of 1922.* Berkeley: University of California Press, 1977.

Drandakis, Pavlos, ed. Μεγάλη Ἑλληνικὴ Ἐγκυκλοπαίδεια [The Great Greek Encyclopedia]. 24 vols. Athens: Pyrsos, 1926–1934; Supplement, 4 vols., 1957.

Durant, Will. *The Life of Greece.* New York: Simon and Schuster, 1939.

Eisner, Robert. *Travelers to an Antique Land: The History and Literature of Travel to Greece.* Ann Arbor: University of Michigan Press, 1993.

Emmanouilidis, P. and E. Petridou-Emmanouilidou. Νεοελληνική Λογοτεχνία· Τα 14 Κείμενα της εξεταστέας Ὕλης [Modern Greek

Literature: The Fourteen Set Books for School Examination]. Athens: Metaichmio, 1999.

Encyclopedia of Greece and the Hellenic Tradition. Edited by Graham Speake. 2 vols. London: Fitzroy Dearborn, 2000.

Faubion, James D. *Modern Greek Lessons: A Primer in Historical Constructivism.* Princeton, NJ: Princeton University Press, 1993.

Finley, M. I. *The Ancient Greeks.* Harmondsworth: Penguin, 1971.

Finley, M. I., ed. *The Legacy of Greece: A New Appraisal.* Oxford: Clarendon Press, 1988.

Fleming, K. E. *The Muslim Bonaparte: Diplomacy and Orientalism in Ali Pasha's Greece.* Princeton, NJ: Princeton University Press, 1999.

Four Greek Poets: C. P. Cavafy, George Seferis, Odysseus Elytis, Nikos Gatsos. Edited and translated by Edmund Keeley and Philip Sherrard. Harmondsworth: Penguin, 1966.

Freri, Marika. Η Ἑλλη Αλεξίου σαν γυναίκα [The Woman Elli Alexiou]. Athens: Vasileiou, 1988.

Galanaki, Rhea. *The Life of Ismail Ferik Pasha: "Spina nel Cuore."* Translated by Kay Cicellis. London: Peter Owen, Paris: UNESCO, 1996 [reviewed in *TLS,* 5 July 1996: 23].

Gatsos, Nikos. *Amorgos.* Translated by Sally Purcell. London: Anvil Press Poetry, 1999 [reviewed by David Constantine in *TLS,* 24 Sept. 1999: 25].

Geddes & Grosset. *Classical Mythology.* New Lanark: Geddes & Grosset Ltd., 1995.

Gkinis, Dimitrios. Κατάλογος ἑλληνικῶν ἐφημερίδων καὶ περιοδικῶν *1811–1863* [A Catalogue of Greek Newspapers and Periodicals]. 2nd ed. Athens: Academy of Athens, 1967.

Gkinis, Dimitrios. Κατάλογοι ἑλληνικῶν κωδίκων ἐν Ἑλλάδι καὶ Ἀνατολῆ [Catalogues of Greek Manuscripts in Greece and the East]. Athens: Academy of Athens, 1935.

Gkinis, D. S. (in collaboration with V. Mexis). Ἑλληνικὴ Βιβλιογραφία *1800–1863* [A Greek Bibliography for the Years 1800 to 1863]. Athens: Academy of Athens Editions, vol. I, *1800–1839,* 1939; vol. II, *1840–1855,* 1941; vol. III, *1856–1863,* with an Index, 1957.

Greece in Modern Times: An Annotated Bibliography of Works Published in English in Twenty-Two Academic Disciplines During the Twentieth Century. Edited by Stratos E. Constantinidis. vol. 1. Lanham, MD: Scarecrow, 2000.

Gritsopoulos, Tasos A. Εἰσαγωγὴ εἰς τὴν Νέαν Ἑλληνικὴν Λογοτεχνίαν [An Introduction to Modern Greek Literature]. vol. 1. Athens: Books of Neo-Hellenism, no. 1, 1969.

Gryparis, I. Ἅπαντα [The Complete Works]. Athens: Pigi, 1952 [398 pp.].

Gudas, Rom. *The Bitter-Sweet Art: Karaghiozis, the Greek Shadow Theater.* Athens: Gnosis, 1986.

Hadas, Rachel. "Spleen à la Grecque: Karyotakis and Baudelaire." *JMGS* 3, no. 1 (May 1985): 21–27.

Halim, Hala Y. "Cavafy's Alexandrian Ideology: From the Dionysian to the Apollinean." In *Images of Egypt in Twentieth Century Literature,* edited by Hoda Gindi, 245–256. Cairo: Faculty of Arts, University of Cairo, 1991.

Haviaras, Stratis. *When the Tree Sings,* drawings by Fred Marcellino. New York: Simon and Schuster, 1979.

Herzfeld, Michael. *Ours Once More: Folklore, Ideology, and the Making of Modern Greece.* New York: Pella, 1986.

Hesseling, D. C. *Histoire de la littérature grecque moderne.* Translated by N. Pernot. Paris: [Collection de l'Institut Néo-Hellénique de l'Université de Paris, no. 1], 1924.

Horrocks, Geoffrey. *Greek: A History of the Language and Its Speakers.* London: Longman, 1997.

Howatson, M. C., and Ian Chilvers, eds. *The Concise Oxford Companion to Classical Literature.* Oxford: Oxford University Press, 1995: 369.

Jeffreys, Elizabeth M. "The Popular Byzantine Verse Romances of Chivalry." *Mandatoforos* 14 (November 1979): 20–34.

Joseph, Brian D., and Irene Philippaki-Warburton. *Modern Greek.* London: Croom Helm, 1986.

Kalamatianós, Yeoryios N. Σύντομη Ἱστορία τῆς Νεοελληνικῆς Λογοτεχνίας [A Short History of Modern Greek Literature]. Athens: Kollaros, 1951.

Kalligás, Pavlos. Θάνος Βλέκας. Μυθιστορία. Πρόλογος Γεωργίου Τσοκοπούλου [*Thanos Vlekas:* The Novel, with a Preface by George Tsokopoulos]. Athens: Elevtheroudakis, 1923.

Kalodikis, Periklis N. Ἡ νεοελληνικὴ λογοτεχνία. (Κοινωνικοὶ προβληματισμοί) [Modern Greek Literature: Social Issues]. 4 vols. Athens: Gutenberg, 1978–1979.

Kalodikis, Periklis N. Ἡ Ἑλληνικὲ Λογοτεχνία. Athens: Gutenberg, 1984.

Kambanis, Aristos. Ἱστορία τῆς νέας ἑλληνικῆς λογοτεχνίας [A History of Modern Greek Literature]. Athens: A. Karabias, 1971.

Kambysis, Y. Ἅπαντα [The Complete Works], restored by Valetas, Y. Athens: Pigis, 1972.

Karandonis, A. Εἰσαγωγὴ στὴ νεώτερη ποίηση [An Introduction to Modern Greek Poetry]. Athens: Difros, 1958.

Karandonis, A. Πεζογράφοι καὶ πεζογραφήματα τῆς γενιᾶς τοῦ '30 [Prose-Writers and Prose Works of the Generation of 1930]. Athens: Phexi, 1962.

Karapanou, Margarita. Ἡ Κασσάνδρα καὶ ο λύκος [Kassandra and the Wolf]. Athens: Ermis, 1977.

Karapanou, Margarita. Ο υπνοβάτης [The Sleepwalker]. Athens: Ermis, 1985.

Karapanou, Margarita. Λούκα [Luke]. *The Word [ἡ λέξη]*, no. 153 (September-October 1999): 550–551.

Karkavitsas, A. Ἅπαντα [The Complete Works]. Introduction and edited by Niki Sideridou, preface by I. M. Panayotopoulos, illus. by P. Balasakis. 4 vols. Athens: Zacharapoulos, 1973.

Karkavitsas, A. *The Beggar.* Translated by W. F. Wyatt, Jr. New Rochelle, NY: Caratzas Bros., 1982.

Katsimbalis, Y. K. Βιβλιογραφία Γιάννη Καμπύση [A Bibliography of Yannis Kambysis]. *Néa Estía* [*Νέα Ἑστία*], no. 50 (1954): 1487–1494.

Kazantzakis, Helen. *Nikos Kazantzakis: A Biography Based on His Letters.* Translated by Amy Mims. New York: Simon & Schuster, 1968.

Kazantzakis, Nikos. *The Odyssey: A Modern Sequel.* Translated by Kimon Friar. New York: Simon & Schuster, 1958.

Kazantzakis, Nikos. *Freedom or Death: A Novel.* Translated by Jonathan Griffin, preface by A. Doolaard. New York: Simon & Schuster, 1956.

Kazantzakis, Nikos. *The Last Temptation of Christ.* Edited and translated by P. A. Bien. New York: Simon & Schuster, 1961.

Kazantzakis, Nikos. *Zorba the Greek.* Translated by Carl Wildman. London: John Lehmann, 1952.

Kazdhan, Alexander. *Studies on Byzantine Literature of the Eleventh and Twelfth Centuries.* Cambridge: Cambridge University Press, 1984.

Keeley, Edmund. *Modern Greek Poetry: Voice and Myth.* Princeton, NJ: Princeton University Press, 1983.

Keeley, E. and P. Bien, eds. *Modern Greek Writers: Solomos, Calvos, Matesis, Palamas, Cavafy, Kazantzakis, Seferis, Elytis.* Princeton, NJ: Princeton University Press, 1972.

Kehayioglos, Yiorgos. Οἱ ἱστορίες τῆς νεοελληνικῆς λογοτεχνίας. Ἐπιλογὴ καὶ παρουσίαση—Ἐρευνητικὴ ἀναφορά [An Investigative Report, Selecting and Presenting Histories of Modern Greek Literature]. *Mandatoforos,* no. 15 (March 1980): 5–66.

Kirchner, Walther. *Western Civilization to 1500.* New York: HarperCollins, 1991.

Knös, Börje. *L'Histoire de la Littérature Néo-grecque: La période jusqu'en 1821.* Stockholm: Almqvist & Wiksell, 1962.

Kordatos, Yannis. Ἱστορία τῆς Νεοελληνικῆς Λογοτεχνίας (Ἀπὸ τὸ 1453 ὡς τὸ 1961) [A History of Modern Greek Literature from 1453 to 1961]. Preface by K. Varnalis. 2 vols. Athens: Academy Book Editions, 1962.

Kostadinka, Paskaleva. *Icons from Bulgaria.* London: Fine Arts, 1991.

Kostelenos, D. P. Σύγχρονη Ἱστορία Νεοελληνικῆς Λογοτεχνίας ἀπό τήν ἄλωση ὥς τίς μέρες μας [accents *sic*] [A History of Modern Greek Literature from the Fall of Constantinople to Our Times]. Athens: Pagoulatos, 1977.

Kotziás, Alexandros. Πολιορκία [Siege]. Athens: Kedros, 1961 (first publ. 1953).

Kotziás, Alexandros. In *I Read* [Διαβάζω], no. 28 (1980): 42–54 [Interview].

Kourtovik, Dimosthenis. Ἕλληνες Μεταπολεμικοί Συγγραφείς, ἕνας κριτικός ὁδηγός [Greek Post-War Writers: A Critical Guide]. Athens: Patakis, 1995.

Kretzmann, Norman and Anthony Kenny, eds. *The Cambridge History of Later Medieval Philosophy: From the Rediscovery of Aristotle to the Disintegration of Scholasticism 1100–1600.* Cambridge: Cambridge University Press, 1982.

Kriarás, Emmanuel, ed. Βυζαντινὰ ἱπποτικὰ μυθιστορήματα [The Byzantine Courtly Romances]. Athens: Aetós (The Basic Library, no. 2), 1955.

Krumbacher, Karl. *Geschichte der byzantinischen Literatur.* Munich: 1891; 1897 [with A. Erhard and H. Gelzer]; Greek trans. Ἱστορία τῆς Βυζαντινῆς Λογοτεχνίας [A History of Byzantine Literature], 3 vols., by Yeoryios Soteriadis. Athens: Maraslis, 1897–1900; 1964, intro. N. Tomadakis.

Krumbacher, Karl, ed. *Das mittelgriechische Fishbuch.* Munich: Akademie der Wissenschaften, 1903.

Laskaratos, A. Ἄπαντα [The Complete Works], intro. and ed. by Alekos Papayeoryiou and Antonios Moschobakis. 3 vols. Athens: Atlas, 1959.

Lavagnini, Bruno. *La letteratura neoellenica.* Florence: Sansoni-Accademia, 1969.

Layoun, Mary, ed. *Modernism in Greece? Essays on the Critical and Literary Margins of a Movement.* New York: Pella, 1990.

Legrand, Émile Louis Jean. *Bibliographie ionienne; description raisonnée des ouvrages publiés par les Grecs des Sept-Îles ou concernant ces îles du 15. siècle à l'année 1900. Oeuvre posthume complétée et publiée par Hubert Pernot.* Paris: Leroux, 1910 [contents: vol. I, 1494–1854; vol. II, 1855–1900].

Legrand, E., ed. Ἰλιάδος Ραψῳδίαι Κδ΄. *La guerre de Troie.* Vol. 5. Paris: Bibliothèque Grecque Vulgaire, 1890.

Legrand, Émile Louis Jean. *Bibliographie hellénique, ou, Description raisonnée des ouvrages publiés en grec par des Grecs aux Xve et XVIe siècles.* Paris: Leroux, 1885–1906, 4 vols. Repr. Paris: Maisonneuve, 1963, 4 vols. [contents: vols. I-II: works published in Greek by the Greeks, 1476–1599; vol. III: works published in Latin by the Greeks, 1469–1550; vol. IV: works published in Greek and other languages, 1551–1600].

Legrand, Émile Louis Jean. *Bibliographie hellénique, ou, Description raisonnée des ouvrages publiés par des Grecs au dix-huitième siècle: oeuvre posthume, complétée et publiée par Louis Petit et Hubert Pernot.* 2 vols. Paris: Garnier, 1918, 1928.

Leontis, Artemis. *Topographies of Hellenism: Mapping the Homeland.* Ithaca, NY: Cornell University Press, 1996.

Litsas, Fotios K., ed. Ἑλληνικά Γράμματα (Essays in) *Tribute to Hellenic Letters.* Modern Greek Studies Series. Chicago: University of Chicago at Illinois, 1985.

Livas, H. P. "Modern Greek Writers Series published by Kedros." *P.E.N. International Bulletin of Selected Books* 47, no. 2 (1997): 26–27.

Lorenzatos, Zissimos. *"The Lost Center"*

and Other Essays on Greek Poetry. Translated by Kay Cicellis. Princeton, NJ: Princeton University Press, 1980.

Mackridge, Peter, ed. *Ancient Greek Myth in Modern Greek Poetry: Essays in Memory of C.A. Trypanis.* London: Cass, 1996.

Mackridge, Peter. *The Modern Greek Language.* Oxford: Oxford University Press, 1985.

Makriyánni, Strategoú. Ἀπομνημονεύματα [The Memoirs]. 2nd ed. Athens: Bayonakis, 1947.

The Memoirs of General Makriyannis, 1797–1864. Edited and translated by H. A. Lidderdale. London: Oxford University Press, 1966.

Malclès, L. -N. *Les sources du travail bibliographique,* Tome II, *Bibliographies specialisées (Sciences Humaines).* Genève: Droz, 1965: "Grèce Moderne," pp. 795–799.

Mascaro, Vincenzo. *Narrativa Neogreca (Νεοελληνική πεζογραφία).* Athens: Difros, 1973.

Mastrodimitris, P. D. Εἰσαγωγή στή Νεοελληνική Φιλολογία [An Introduction to Modern Greek Literature]. Athens: Domos, 1990.

McDonald, Robert. "The Greek Press Under the Colonels." *Index on Censorship* 3, no. 4 (winter 1974): 27–41.

Μεγάλη Ἐγκυκλοπαίδεια τῆς Νεοελληνικῆς Λογοτεχνίας (ἀπὸ τὸν 10° αἰώνα μ.Χ. μέχρι σήμερα) [Great Encyclopedia of Modern Greek Literature from the 10th Century A.D. to the Present]. Edited by Y. Th. Zoras and I. M. Chatzifotis, 12 vols. Athens: Charis Patsis, 1969–1971.

Meraklís, Michalis G. Σύγχρονη Ἑλληνική Λογοτεχνία *1945–1980:* Μέρος πρώτο: Ποίηση [Contemporary Greek Literature from 1945 to 1980: First Part: Poetry]. Athens: Patakis, 1987.

Meraklís, Michalis G. Η σύγχρονη Ελληνική Λογοτεχνία 1945–1970: II. Πεζογραφία [Contemporary Greek Literature from 1945 to 1970: Second Part: Prose]. Thessaloniki: Konstantinidis, 1972.

Milas, Spyros. Ανθολογία Ελλήνων ποιητών [An Anthology of Greek Poets]. Athens: Karanasis, 1987.

Mirambel, André. La langue grecque moderne: Description et analyse. Paris: Klincksieck, 1959.

Mirasgezi, Maria D. Νεοελληνική Λογοτεχνία [Modern Greek Literature], 2 vols. Athens: privately published, 1978, 1982.

Mitsakis, K. Εἰσαγωγὴ στὴ Νέα Ἑλληνικὴ Λογοτεχνία. Πρωτονεοελληνικοὶ χρόνοι. Part I: Ἀπὸ τὰ τραγούδια τοῦ Ἀκριτικοῦ κύκλου ἕως τοὺς θρήνους γιὰ τὸ πάρσιμο τῆς Πόλης [An Introduction to Modern Greek Literature: Early Modern Greek Period. 1: From the Songs of the Akritic Cycle to Laments for the Loss of Constantinople]. Thessaloniki: n.p., 1973.

Moennig, Ulrich. "Die Neugriechische Literatur." Kindlers Neues Literatur Lexikon 19. Munich: Kindler, 1988, pp. 972–979.

Motsios, Yannis, ed. Ελληνική πεζογραφία 1600–1821 [Greek Prose-Writing from 1600 to 1821]. Athens: Grigoris, 1990.

Myrsiades, Kostas. "Odysseus Elytis and the Thirties Generation in Modern Greek Poetry." JHD 22, 1 (1996): 105–121.

Myrsiades, Kostas and Linda S. Myrsiades. The Karagiozis Heroic Performance in Greek Shadow Theatre. Hanover, NH: University of New England Press, 1988.

Myrsiades, Linda. "Adaptation and Change: The Origins of Karaghiozis in Greece." Turcica, no. 18 (1986): 119–136.

Nicolai, Rudolf. Geschichte der Neugriechischen Litteratur. Leipzig: F. A. Brockhaus, 1876.

Paganós, Yiorgos. Η νεοελληνική πεζογραφία· θεωρία και πράξη [Modern Greek Prose: Theory and Practice], vol. 2. Athens: Kodikas, 1993.

Panayotopoulos, Ioannis M. Στοιχεῖα Ἱστορίας τῆς Νεοελληνικῆς Λογοτεχνίας [Elements for a History of Modern Greek Literature]. Athens: Kyklos, 1936; 2nd ed., Athens: Promulgation of Intellectual Services, 1938.

Panayotounes, Panos N. Ἐπίτομη Ἱστορία τῆς Ἑλληνικῆς Λογοτεχνίας (1000 π.Χ.—1991 μ.χ.) [A Short History of Greek Literature from 1000 A.D. to 1991 A.D.]. Athens: Gkouzon, 1991.

Papadimas, Adamantios D. Νέα Ἑλληνικὴ γραμματολογία· γενικὰ στοιχεῖα [Modern Greek Writing: General Elements]. Athens: Feskos, 1948.

Papathanasopoulos, Thanasis. Επισημάνσεις στο χώρο της λογοτεχνίας. Μελετήματα. [Investigations in the Area of Literature: A Series of Studies]. Athens: Friends' Editions, 1992.

Pappageotes, George C. The Story of Modern Greek Literature from the 10th Century to the Present. Preface by Rae Dalven. New York: Athens Printing, 1972.

Pappás, Nikos. Ἡ ἀληθινὴ ἱστορία τῆς νεοελληνικῆς λογοτεχνίας (ἀπό 1100 ὡς 1973). [The True Story of Modern Greek Literature from 1100 to the year 1973]. Athens: Tymphae, 1973.

Paraschos, Kleon. Εἰσαγωγὴ στὴ σύγχρονη ἑλληνικὴ ποίηση [An Introduction to Contemporary Greek Poetry]. Athens: n.p., 1940.

Paraschos, Kleon. Ἕλληνες Λυρικοί [Greek Lyric Poets]. Athens: Spiropoulos, 1953.

Paraschos, Kleon. Δέκα Ἕλληνες Λυρικοί [Ten Greek Lyric Poets]. Athens: Phexi, 1962.

Passow, Arnold, ed. Carmina popularia graeciae recentioris. Leipzig: n.p., 1860.

Peranthis, Mikhail. Κεφάλαια νεοελληνικῆς λογοτεχνίας [Chapters on Modern Greek Literature]. Athens: Chiotelis, Figures and Texts of Our Literature, vol. 1, 1976.

Pettifer, James. The Greeks: The Land and People since the War. London: Viking, 1993.

Pfeiffer, Rudolf. "The Future of Studies in the field of Hellenistic Poetry." Journal of Hellenic Studies 75 (1955): pp. 69f.

Philippides, D. M. L. Census of Modern Greek Literature: Checklist of English-Language Sources Useful in the Study of Modern Greek Literature (1824–1987). New Haven, CT: Modern Greek Studies Association, 1990.

Pierris, Nakis. Bibliographie Ionienne. Suppléments à la Description raisonnée des ouvrages publiés par les Grecs des Sept-Iles ou concernant ces Iles du quinzième siècle à l'année 1900 par Emile Legrand. Athens: Klisiounis Brothers, 1966.

Politis, Linos. A History of Modern Greek Literature. Oxford: Clarendon, 1975.

Rangabé, Alexandros Rizos. Histoire littéraire de la Grèce moderne. 2 vols. Paris: C. Lévy, 1877.

[Rangavís]. Geschichte der neugriechischen Litteratur ... von A. R. Rangabé und Daniel Sanders. Leipzig: W. Friedrich, n.d.

Ricks, David. Byzantine Heroic Poetry. Bristol: Bristol Classical Press, 1990.

Ricks, David. The Shade of Homer: A Study in Modern Greek Poetry. Cambridge: Cambridge University Press, 1989: 19–35.

Ritter, F. European Authors. New York: H. W. Wilson, 1967: 998.

Rizo-Néroulos, Jacovacy. Cours de littérature grecque moderne. Genève: Jean Humbert, 1827.

Roussel, L. Karagheuz ou la comédie grecque dans l'âme du théâtre d'ombres. Athens: A. Raftanis, 1921.

Sachinis, Ap. Ἀναζητήσεις τῆς νεοελληνικῆς πεζογραφίας στὴ μεσοπολεμικὴ εἰκοσαετία [Searches in Modern Greek Prose-Writing from the Inter-War Years]. Athens: Ikaros, 1945.

Sachinis, Ap. Νέοι πεζογράφοι, εἴκοσι χρόνια νεοελληνικῆς πεζογραφίας, 1945–1965 [The New Prose-Writers: Twenty Years of Modern Greek Prose from 1945 to 1965]. Athens: Kollaros, 1965.

Sachinis, Ap. Ἡ πεζογραφία τῆς κατοχῆς [Prose-Writing from the German Occupation]. Athens: Ikaros, 1948.

Sachinis, Ap. Ἡ σύγχρονη πεζογραφία μας [Our Contemporary Prose]. Athens: Ikaros, 1951.

Sachinis, Ap. Τὸ Νεοελληνικὸ Μυθιστόρημα. Ἱστορία καὶ κριτικὴ [The Modern Greek Novel: History and Criticism]. 5th ed. Athens: Estía Bookshop Editions, 1980.

Scarfe, Allan and Wendy. All That Grief: Migrant Recollections of Greek Resistance to Fascism, 1941–1949. Sydney: Hale & Iremonger, 1994.

Scherer, Margaret R. *The Legends of Troy in Art and Literature.* New York: Phaidon, 1963.

Seremetakis, C. Nadia. *The Last Word: Women, Death and Divination in Inner Mani.* Chicago: Chicago University Press, 1991.

Seremetakis, C. Nadia, ed. *Ritual, Power, and the Body: Historical Perspectives on the Representation of Greek Women.* New York: Pella, 1993.

Shaw, Stanford J. and Ezel Kural Shaw. *History of the Ottoman Empire and Modern Turkey. Vol. II: Reform, Revolution, and Republic: The Rise of Modern Turkey, 1808–1975.* Cambridge: Cambridge University Press, 1977.

Sherrard, Philip. "Andreas Kalvos and the Eighteenth-Century Ethos." In *The Wound of Greece: Studies in Neo-Hellenism.* London: Rex Collings, 1978: 17–50.

Sherrard, Philip. "Epilogue; The Figure of Aretousa." In *The Wound of Greece: Studies in Neo-Hellenism.* London: Rex Collings, 1978: 118–124.

Sideris, Yannis. Ἱστορία τοῦ νέου ἑλληνικοῦ θεάτρου *1794–1944.* Τόμος δεύτερος *(1794–1908)* [A History of Modern Greek Theater from 1794 to 1944: 2nd Vol.]. Athens: Kastaniotis, 1999.

Siotis, D. and J. Chioles, eds. *Twenty Contemporary Greek Poets.* San Francisco: Wire Press, 1979; consists of contents of *The Coffeehouse,* vols. 11–12 (1982): 96 pp.

Skoubarás, Vangelis A. Τὰ νεοελληνικὰ γράμματα. Σύντομο διάγραμμα ἱστορίας τῆς νέας ἑλληνικῆς λογοτεχνίας [An Epitome of the History of Neo-Hellenic Literature from Its Outset until the 18th Century]. Athens: The Scholar's Bookshop, 1976.

Spandonidis, P. Ἡ σύγχρονη ποιητικὴ γενεά *(1930–1960)* [The Contemporary Generation of Poets: 1930 to 1960]. Athens: Difros, 1962.

Spandonidis, Petros. Ἡ ἑλληνικότητα [The Concept of Greekness]. Athens: Astrolabos-Euthuni, 1994 [first published 1962].

Spatharis, S. Ἀπομνημονεύματα Σ. Σπαθάρη καὶ ἡ τέχνη τοῦ Καραγκιόζη [Memoirs of S. Spatharis and the Art of Karaghiozis]. Athens: Pergamos, 1960 [illustrated].

Stafylidis, Andreas. Εγκυκλοπαίδεια τῆς Νεοελληνικῆς Λογοτεχνίας *1.000 μ.Χ.—2.000 μ.Χ.* [An Encyclopedia of Modern Greek Literature from 1000 A.D. to 2000 A.D.]. Athens: Stafylidis Editions, n.d. [but c. 2001].

Stanford, W. B. *The Ulysses Theme: A Study in the Adaptability of a Traditional Hero.* Oxford: Blackwell, 1954.

Steryopoulos, K. Ἀπὸ τὸν συμβολισμὸ στὴν νέα ποίηση [From Symbolism to the New Poetry]. Athens: Bacon, 1967.

Swanson, D. C. E. *Modern Greek Studies in the West. A Critical Bibliography of Studies on Modern Greek Linguistics, Philology, and Folklore in Languages Other than Greek.* New York: New York Public Libraries, 1960.

Tarn, W. W. *Hellenistic Civilization.* New York: New American Library, 1974.

Tarsoulis, A. Ἑλληνίδες ποιήτριες, *1857–1940* [Greek Women Poets from 1857 to 1940]. Athens: Greek Society of Editors, 1951.

Taylor, John. *Icon Painting.* London: Phaidon, 1979.

Thasitis, Panos L. Γύρος στὴν ποίηση [All About Poetry]. Thessaloniki: n.p., 1966.

Thorlby, A., ed. *The Penguin Companion to Literature: Classical and Byzantine,*

Oriental and African. London: Allen Lane, 1969.

Thrakiotis, Kostas. Σύντομη Ἰστορία τῆς Νεοελληνικῆς Λογοτεχνίας [A Short History of Modern Greek Literature]. Athens: Difros, 1965.

Thrasyboulos, Stavros. Στοιχεῖα Ἰστορίας τῆς Νεοελληνικῆς Λογοτεχνίας [Elements for a History of Modern Greek Literature] (place and year of publication omitted from the text).

Tofallis, D. K. Ἰστορία τῆς Νεοελληνικῆς Λογοτεχνίας ἀπὸ τὸν 11° αἰώνα μέχρι τὴν ἐποχή μας [A History of Modern Greek Literature from the 11th Century to Our Own Times]. London: Greek Institute, 1976.

Trikoupis, Spyridon. Ἰστορία τῆς ἑλληνικῆς ἐπαναστάσεως. *[1853–1857]* [A History of the Greek Revolution, 1853 to 1857]. 2nd ed. London: Red Lion Yard, Taylor and Francis Printers, 1861.

Trypanis, C. A. *Greek Poetry from Homer to Seferis.* Chicago: University of Chicago Press, 1981.

Trypanis, C. A. *The Penguin Book of Greek Verse.* Harmondsworth: Penguin Books, 1971.

Tsakiridou, Cornelia. "Hellenism in C. P. Cavafy." *JHD* 21, no. 2 (1995): 115–129.

Tsakonas, Dimitrios. Επίτομη ιστορία της νεοελληνικής λογοτεχνίας. Από την Κρητική Σχολή του ΙΔ΄ αιώνα μέχρι σήμερα [A Concise History of Modern Greek Literature from the Cretan School of the 14th Century to the Present Time]. Athens: Kaktos, 1999.

"Twelve Poems by Younger Greek Poets." Translated by John Chioles, in *Translation: The Journal of Literary Translation* [Greek Issue], no. 14 (spring 1985): 86–97.

Tziovas, Dimitris. "Mapping out Greek Literary Modernism." In *Greek Modernism and Beyond: Essays in Honor of Peter Bien,* edited by D. Tziovas, 25–39. Lanham, MD: Rowman & Littlefield, 1997.

Usher, Stephen. *Greek Oratory: Tradition and Originality.* Oxford: Oxford University Press, 1999.

Vacalopoulos, Apostolos E. *The Greek Nation, 1453–1669: The Cultural and Economic Background of Modern Greek Society.* Translated by Ian and Phania Moles. New Brunswick, NJ: Rutgers University Press, 1976.

Valetas, Y. Λεξικὸ νεοελληνικὸ φιλολογικό. Βιογραφίες ποιητῶν καὶ συγγραφέων. Στοιχεῖα γραμματολογίας καὶ μετρικῆς—Ἀναλύσεις καὶ ἑρμηνεῖες—Βιογραφικὰ σημειώματα [A Modern Greek Literary Dictionary: Biographies of Poets and Writers. Elements of Philology and Prosody, with Analysis, Interpretation, and Biographical Annotations]. Athens: Parnassós, 1964.

Valetas, Yeoryios. Ἐπίτομη Ἰστορία τῆς Νεοελληνικῆς Λογοτεχνίας [A Concise History of Modern Greek Literature]. Athens: Petros K. Ranos, 1966.

Van Dyck, Karen, ed. and trans. *The Rehearsal of Misunderstanding: Three Collections by Contemporary Greek Women Poets: The Cake, by Rhea Galanaki; Tales of the Deep, by Jenny Mastoraki; Hers, by Maria Laina.* Hanover, NH: University Press of New England, 1998 [bilingual].

Vitti, Mario. Ιδεολογική λειτουργία της ελληνικής ηθογραφίας [The Ideological Function of Greek Ethnography (i.e., Recording of Manners)]. Athens: Kedros, 1980.

Vitti, Mario. Ιστορία της νεοελληνικής λογοτεχνίας [A History of Modern Greek Literature]. Athens: Odysseas, 1987.

Voutieridis, Ilias P. Σύντομη ιστορία τῆς νεοελληνικῆς λογοτεχνίας *(1000– 1930).* Τρίτη ἔκδοση. Μὲ συμπλήρωμα τοῦ Δημήτρη Γιάκου *(1931–1976)* [A Short History of Modern Greek Literature from 1000 to 1930: 3rd Ed., with a Supplement Covering 1931 to 1976 by Dimitris Yiakos]. Athens: D. N. Papadimas, 1976.

Wagner, G., ed. *Carmina Graeca Medii Aevi.* Leipzig: B. G. Teubner, 1874.

Wagner, Wilhelm, ed. *Medieval Greek Texts: Being a Collection of the Earliest Compositions in Vulgar Greek, Prior to the Year 1500. Edited, with Prolegomena and Critical Notes.* London: Asher and Co, 1870 [reprint, Amsterdam, 1970]: 63–90.

Walton, F. R. *The Greek Book, 1476– 1825.* Athens: Dixième Congrès International des Bibliophiles, 1977.

Wilson, N. G. *From Byzantium to Italy: Greek Studies in the Italian Renaissance.* London: Duckworth, 1992.

Winterer-Papatassos, Mary. *Doorway to Greece: An Introduction, Not in the Guidebooks, to Life in Greece.* Athens: Lycabettus, 1984.

Woodhouse, C. M. *Modern Greece: A Short History.* London: Faber and Faber, 1991.

Woodhouse, C. M. *George Gemistos Plethon: The Last of the Hellenes.* Oxford: Clarendon Press, 1986.

Xanthos, Markos. "The Seven Beasts and Karaghiozis." Translated by K. and L. Myrsiades. *The Charioteer,* no. 19 (1977): 20–49.

Yanni, Mara. "Kostis Ghimosoulis. *Mia níhta me tin kókkini.*" *WLT* 70, no. 4 (autumn 1996): 1002.

Zoras, G. Th. *Lineamenti storici della letteratura neoellenica.* 2nd ed. Rome: Studium, 1939.

Index

Bold page numbers indicate main discussion of an entry.

About the Author

BRUCE MERRY is Associate Professor of English at Kuwait University. His previous books include *Women in Italian Literature* (1990).